# PROPORTIONALITY IN /

*Proportionality in Action* presents an empirical and comparative exploration of the proportionality doctrine, based on detailed accounts of the application of the framework by apex courts in six jurisdictions: Germany, Canada, South Africa, Israel, Poland, and India. The analysis of each country is written and contextualized by a constitutional scholar from the relevant jurisdiction. Each country analysis draws upon a large sample of case law and employs a mixed methodological approach: an expansive coding scheme allows for quantitative analysis providing comparable and quantifiable measurements, which is enriched by qualitative analysis that engages with the substance of the decisions and captures nuance, contextualizing the data and providing it with meaning. The book concludes with a comparative chapter that synthesizes some of the most interesting findings. Focusing on deviations of the practice of proportionality from theory, the authors conclude their argument in support of an integrated approach to the application of proportionality.

MORDECHAI KREMNITZER is Professor Emeritus of the Faculty of Law at the Hebrew University of Jerusalem and senior fellow at the Israel Democracy Institute. He was formerly Dean of the Law School, Vice President for Research at the Israel Democracy Institute and President of the Israeli Press Council. He is a leading Israeli expert on criminal and constitutional law, having headed several governmental committees, including examination of the use of force by the police, civic education, and reform of the Israeli Criminal Code.

TALYA STEINER is a PhD candidate at the Hebrew University Law School. She holds an LLM from Harvard Law School and an LLB from the Hebrew University of Jerusalem and is admitted to the Israeli Bar. She clerked at the Israeli Supreme Court, and has managed the 'Proportionality in Public Policy Project' at the Israel Democracy Institute, a six-year ERC-funded project focusing on the balancing between rights and public interests in the policy process from a comparative and empirical perspective. She has previously published on the topic of non-discrimination in employment and equality commissions.

ANDREJ LANG is a Senior Researcher at the Chair for Public Law, European Law and International Economic Law of the Martin-Luther-University Halle-Wittenberg, Germany, and former research fellow at the Israel Democracy Institute. He holds a PhD from Freie Universität Berlin, an LLM from New York University School of Law, and is admitted to the Bar in Berlin and in New York. He was a visiting scholar at Yale Law School and at Harvard Law School and has authored a number of articles on constitutional law.

CAMBRIDGE STUDIES IN CONSTITUTIONAL LAW

The aim of this series is to produce leading monographs in constitutional law. All areas of constitutional law and public law fall within the ambit of the series, including human rights and civil liberties law, administrative law, as well as constitutional theory and the history of constitutional law. A wide variety of scholarly approaches is encouraged, with the governing criterion being simply that the work is of interest to an international audience. Thus, works concerned with only one jurisdiction will be included in the series as appropriate, while, at the same time, the series will include works which are explicitly comparative or theoretical – or both. The series editor likewise welcomes proposals that work at the intersection of constitutional and international law, or that seek to bridge the gaps between civil law systems, the US, and the common law jurisdictions of the Commonwealth.



*Books in the Series*

*Proportionality in Action: Comparative and Empirical Perspectives on the Judicial Practice* Edited by Mordechai Kremnitzer, Talya Steiner and Andrej Lang

*Constitutional Dialogue: Democracy, Rights, Institutions* Edited by Geoffrey Sigalet, Grégoire Webber and Rosalind Dixon

*The Veiled Sceptre: Reserve Powers of Heads of State in Westminster Systems* Anne Twomey

*Vigilance and Restraint in the Common Law of Judicial Review* Dean Knight

*The Alchemists: Questioning Our Faith in Courts as Democracy-Builders* Tom Gerald Daly

*Australia's Constitution after Whitlam* Brendan Lim

*Building the Constitution: The Practice of Constitutional Interpretation in post-apartheid South Africa* James Fowkes

*Dimensions of Dignity: The Theory and Practice of Modern Constitutional Law* Jacob Weinrib

*Reason of State: Law, Prerogative, Empire* Thomas Poole

*Bills of Rights in the Common Law* Robert Leckey

*The Guardian of the Constitution: Hans Kelsen and Carl Schmitt on the Limits of Constitutional Law* Translated by Lars Vinx, with an introduction and notes by Lars Vinx

*Parliamentary Bills of Rights: The Experiences of New Zealand and the United Kingdom Experiences* Janet L. Hiebert and James B. Kelly

*Lawyering for the Rule of Law: Government Lawyers and the Rise of Judicial Power in Israel* Yoav Dotan

*Balancing Constitutional Rights: The Origins and Meanings of Postwar Legal Discourse* Jacco Bomhoff

*Judges on Trial: The Independence and Accountability of the English Judiciary* Shimon Shetreet and Sophie Turenne

*Proportionality and Constitutional Culture* Moshe Cohen-Eliya and Iddo Porat

*The Politics of Principle: The First South African Constitutional Court, 1995–2005* Theunis Roux

*The New Commonwealth Model of Constitutionalism: Theory and Practice* Stephen Gardbaum

*Searching for the State in British Legal Thought: Competing Conceptions of the Public Sphere* Janet McLean

*Judging Social Rights* Jeff King

*Proportionality: Constitutional Rights and their Limitations* Aharon Barak

*Parliamentary Sovereignty: Contemporary Debates* Jeffrey Goldsworthy

# PROPORTIONALITY IN ACTION

## Comparative and Empirical Perspectives on the Judicial Practice

Edited by

MORDECHAI KREMNITZER
*The Israel Democracy Institute*

TALYA STEINER
*Hebrew University of Jerusalem and The Israel Democracy Institute*

ANDREJ LANG
*Martin-Luther-University Halle-Wittenberg and The Israel Democracy Institute*

**CAMBRIDGE**
**UNIVERSITY PRESS**

University Printing House, Cambridge CB2 8BS, United Kingdom

One Liberty Plaza, 20th Floor, New York, NY 10006, USA

477 Williamstown Road, Port Melbourne, VIC 3207, Australia

314-321, 3rd Floor, Plot 3, Splendor Forum, Jasola District Centre, New Delhi - 110025, India

103 Penang Road, #05-06/07, Visioncrest Commercial, Singapore 238467

Cambridge University Press is part of the University of Cambridge.

It furthers the University's mission by disseminating knowledge in the pursuit of education, learning and research at the highest international levels of excellence.

www.cambridge.org
Information on this title: www.cambridge.org/9781108740166
DOI: 10.1017/9781108596268



First published 2020
First paperback edition 2022

*A catalogue record for this publication is available from the British Library*

*Library of Congress Cataloging in Publication data*
Names: Kremnitzer, M., editor. | Steiner, Talya, editor. | Lang, Andrej, editor.
Title: Proportionality in action : comparative and empirical perspectives on the judicial practice / [edited by] Mordechai Kremnitzer, Talya Steiner, Andrej Lang.
Description: 1. | New York : Cambridge University Press, 2020. | Includes bibliographical references and index.
Identifiers: LCCN 2019038868 (print) | LCCN 2019038869 (ebook) | ISBN 9781108497589 (hardback) | ISBN 9781108740166 (paperback) | ISBN 9781108596268 (epub)
Subjects: LCSH: Proportionality in law.
Classification: LCC K247 .P7625 2020 (print) | LCC K247 (ebook) | DDC 342/.0011–dc23
LC record available at https://lccn.loc.gov/2019038868
LC ebook record available at https://lccn.loc.gov/2019038869

ISBN 978-1-108-49758-9 Hardback
ISBN 978-1-108-74016-6 Paperback

CONTENTS

# FIGURES

# TABLES

# CONTRIBUTORS

APARNA CHANDRA, Assistant Professor of Law and Director, Centre for Constitutional Law, Policy, and Governance, National Law University, Delhi, India

LORIAN HARDCASTLE, Assistant Professor, Faculty of Law, University of Calgary, Canada

MORDECHAI KREMNITZER, Senior Fellow, The Israel Democracy Institute, Israel

ANDREJ LANG, Senior Researcher, Chair for Public Law, European Law and International Economic Law, Martin-Luther-University Halle-Wittenberg, Germany; Research Fellow, The Israel Democracy Institute

ANNA ŚLEDZIŃSKA-SIMON, Professor, Faculty of Law, Administration, and Economics, University of Wroclaw, Poland

RICHARD STACEY, Associate Professor, Faculty of Law, University of Toronto, Canada

TALYA STEINER, PHD candidate, Hebrew University Law School, Israel; Manager, 'Proportionality in Public Policy' project, The Israel Democracy Institute

# PREFACE

This book is the result of six years of research. The research, conducted as part of the 'Proportionality in Public Policy' project from 2013 to 2019, was funded by the European Research Council under the European Union's Seventh Framework Programme (FP7/2007–2013), grant no. 324182. The project was based at the Israel Democracy Institute and was headed by Professor Mordechai Kremnitzer.

The project focused on the frameworks used by policy-makers and judges for resolving conflicts between the promotion of public interests and the protection of human rights. It explored these frameworks from the comparative and interdisciplinary perspectives by utilizing a range of empirical methodologies and was organized around three central strands of research, each emphasizing specific research questions and using distinct methods.

The research presented in this book was part of the first strand: a comparative study of the judicial application of proportionality. A second strand involved detailed case studies tracking specific legislative processes, in an effort to deepen our understanding of the dynamic through which rights-restrictive policies are initiated, shaped, and approved. The case studies explored how rights considerations and the logic of proportionality are expressed outside the judicial arena and mapped the actors who play a role in bringing up the effect on rights and framing the debates on this matter. A third strand of research adopted a behavioural perspective to examine decisions made in the face of conflict between rights and competing interests. An experimental methodology was used to study how experts apply the proportionality doctrine, as well as to determine the effects of context and psychological biases on the outcomes of balancing decisions.

We would not have been able to complete this book without the invaluable and generous support of many persons to whom we are greatly indebted. The astute advice of Professor Raanan Sulitzeanu-Kenan contributed to the empirical underpinning of the book. Viki

Auslender, Amit Haim, Laura Plodek, and Lisa Marie Dammann provided excellent and meticulous research assistance. Aharon Barak, Liora Lazarus, Barak Medina, and Niels Petersen patiently read drafts of the book and offered valuable comments. Deborah Stern provided excellent language editing.

The unequivocal support of the Israel Democracy Institute throughout the proportionality project was instrumental to its success. In particular, we wish to recognize the contributions of Dr Jesse Ferris, Deena Pulitzer, Avigail Yohanan, Shirli Ben-Tolila, Amarilli Narkis, Maayan Ravitz-Shalom, Anat Bernstein, Nirit Ben Bassat, and Dorit Shoval, each of whom provided guidance and support at the highest professional level and enabled us to successfully overcome numerous challenges.

Finally, Finola O'Sullivan of Cambridge University Press provided support for the book from the very outset and demonstrated kind patience throughout the process.

We sincerely thank them all.

# CASES

## Germany

## Canada

## South Africa

*S v Makwanyane & Another*, 1995 (3) SA 391 (CC) 194, 196, 206–7, 209–10, 236–39, 249, 258–60, 262, 272, 282, 570

*S v Williams*, 1995 (3) SA 632 (CC) 237, 239, 250

*Coetzee v Government of the Republic of South Africa, Matiso & Others v Commanding Officer Port Elizabeth Prison & Others*, 1995 (4) SA 631 (CC) 196, 214, 217, 232, 235, 263, 269, 280, 593

*Transkei Public Servants Association v Government of the Republic of South Africa*, 1995 (9) BCLR 1235 (Tk) 211

*S v Mbatha*, 1996 (2) SA 464 (CC) 222, 270

*Bernstein v Bester NO*, 1996 (2) SA 751 (CC) 214, 229, 233

*Nel v Le Roux No & Others*, 1996 (3) SA 562 (CC) 264

*Case & Another v Minister of Safety and Security; Curtis v Minister of Safety and Security & Others*, 1996 (3) SA 617 (CC) 229, 253, 262

*Du Plessis & Others v De Klerk & Another*, 1996 (3) SA 850 (CC) 226

*Azanian Peoples Organisation (AZAPO) & Others v President of the Republic of South Africa & Others*, 1996 (4) SA 671 (CC) 233, 248

*S v Bhulwana, S v Gwadiso*, 1996 (1) SA 388 (CC) 214–16, 249, 260, 548

*Shabalala & Others v Attorney-General of the Transvaal & Another*, 1996 (1) SA 725 (CC) 226

*Ferreira v Levin NO & Others; Vryenhoek & Others v Powell NO & Others*, 1996 (1) SA 984 (CC) 206–7, 232–33, 237–38, 250, 283, 589

*S v Ntuli*, 1996 (1) SA 1207 (CC) 272

*Brink v Kitshoff* ,1996 (4) SA 197 (CC) 272

*President of the Republic of South Africa and Another v Hugo*, 1997 (4) SA 1 (CC) 210, 226, 228–29

*Prinsloo v Van der Linde and Another*, 1997 (3) SA 1012 (CC) 210

*Scagell v Attorney General, Western Cape*, 1997 (2) SA 368 (CC) 207

*Mohlomi v Minister of Defence*, 1997 (1) SA 124 (CC) 214, 245–47, 251

*S v Lawrence; S v Negal; S v Solberg*, 1997 (4) SA 1176 (CC) 243–44

*S v Ntsele*, 1997 (11) BCLR 1543 (CC) 240, 275–76

*Transvaal Agricultural Union v Minister of Land Affairs and Another*, 1997 (2) SA 621 (CC) 209, 212, 231

*Larbi-Odam and Others v MEC for Education (North-West Province) and Others*, 1998 (1) SA 745 (CC) 202, 226, 241, 255, 572

*City Council of Pretoria v Walker*, 1998 (2) SA 363 (CC) 226–27, 245

*Bruce & Another v Fleecytex Johannesburg CC & Others*, 1998 (2) SA 1143 (CC) 200

*De Lange v Smuts NO*, 1998 (3) SA 785 (CC) 234, 258, 570

*Mistry v Interim Medical and Dental Council of South Africa & Others*, 1998 (4) SA 1127 (CC) 265

*De Lille & Another v Speaker of the National Assembly*, 1998 (3) SA 430 (C) 195, 226

*Lawyers for Human Rights & Another v Minister of Home Affairs*, 2004 (4) SA 125 (CC) 255–56

*Bato Star Fishing (Pty) Ltd v Minister of Environmental Affairs and Tourism & Others*, 2004 (4) SA 490 (CC) 205

*Bhe and Others v Khayelitsha Magistrate and Others*, 2005 (1) SA 580 (CC) 218, 226, 237, 239, 249, 253, 274, 559

*Taylor v Kurtstag NO & Others*, 2005 (1) SA 362 (W) 226

*Minister of Home Affairs v National Institute for Crime Prevention and the Re-Integration of Offenders (NICRO) and Others*, 2005 (3) SA 280 (CC) 219, 220, 240, 244–47, 251, 274, 279

*President of the Republic of South Africa v Modderklip Boerdery*, 2005 (5) SA 3 (CC) 227

*De Vos N.O and Others v Minister of Justice and Constitutional Development and Others*, 2015 (9) BCLR 1026 (CC) 218, 253, 261, 271–72

*Jaftha v Schoemann & Others; Van Rooyen v Stoltz & Others*, 2005 (2) SA 140 (CC) 240, 250, 280

*Du Toit v Minister of Transport*, 2006 (1) SA 297 (CC) 226

*Minister of Home Affairs & Another v Fourie & Another*, 2006 (1) SA 524 (CC) 205, 230, 240, 256, 274, 571–72

*Magajane v Chairperson, North West Gambling Board*, 2006 (5) SA 250 (CC) 200, 241, 265

*South African Broadcasting Corp Ltd v National Director of Public Prosecutions*, 2007 (1) SA 523 (CC) 230–31, 237

*Union of Refugee Women and Others v Director: Private Security Industry Regulatory Authority and Others*, 2007 (4) SA 395 (CC) 210, 253, 266

*MEC for Education: KwaZulu-Natal v Pillay*, 2008 (1) SA 747 (CC) 202, 210

*Independent Newspapers (Pty) Ltd v Minister for Intelligence Services In Re Masetlha v President of the Republic of South Africa & Another*, 2008 (5) SA 31 (CC) 200

*Nyathi v Member of the Executive Council for the Department of Health Gauteng and Another*, 2008 (5) SA 94 (CC) 272

*Glenister v President of the Republic of South Africa & Others*, 2009 (1) SA 287 (CC) 242, 563

*Richter v Minister of Home Affairs & Others*, 2009 (3) SA 615 (CC) 200, 274

*Johncom Media Investments v Minister for Justice and Constitutional Development*, 2009 (4) SA 7 (CC) 214

*Center for Child Law v Minister for Justice and Constitutional Development*, 2009 (6) SA 632 (CC) 244

*Reflect-All 1025 CC v MEC for Public Transport, Roads and Works, Gauteng*, 2009 (6) SA 391 (CC) 210–22

*Mazibuko & Others v City of Johannesburg & Others*, 2010 (4) SA 1 (CC) 201

*Poverty Alleviation Network & Others v President of the Republic of South Africa & Others*, 2010 (6) BCLR 520 (CC) 242

## Israel

## Poland

Judgment of 28 October 2015, Case No. K 21/14 OTK-A 2015, No. 9, Item 152, *tax-free amount* 387, 436

Judgment of 28 October 2015, Case No. SK 59/13 OTK-A 2015, No. 10, Item 162, *forfeiture of crime commitment assets* 437, 449

Judgment of 4 November 2015, Case No. K 1/14 OTK-A 2015, No. 10, Item 163, *Open Pension Funds* 389, 446

Judgment of 3 December 2015, Case No. K 34/15 OTK-A 2015, No. 11, Item 185, *Constitutional Tribunal Act* 391

Judgment of 9 December 2015, Case No. K 35/15 OTK-A 2015, No. 11, Item 186, *Constitutional Tribunal Act* 391

Decision of 9 March 2016, Case No. K 47/15 OTK-A 2018, Item 31, *Constitutional Tribunal Act* 391

Decision of 11 August 2016, Case No. K 39/16 OTK-A 2018, Item 32, *Constitutional Tribunal Act* 391

Judgment of 22 November 2016, Case No. K 13/15 OTK-A 2016, Item 88, *marriage for persons with intellectual disabilities* 389

Judgment of 16 March 2017, Case No. Kp 1/17 OTK-A 2017, Item 28, *assembly law* 391

## India

*Romesh Thapar v State of Madras* AIR 1950 SC 124 506

*State of Madras v Champakam Dorairajan* AIR 1951 SC 226 469

*Chintaman Rao v State of MP* AIR 1951 SC 118 459, 477–78, 571

*State of West Bengal v Anwar Ali Sarkar* AIR 1952 SC 75 469, 494, 526

*Kathi Raning Rawat v State of Saurashtra* AIR 1952 SC 123 527

*R M Seshadri v District Magistrate, Tanjore* AIR 1954 SC 747 526

*Kedar Nath Bajoria v State of West Bengal* AIR 1954 SC 660 527

*Ebrahim Vazir Mavat v State of Bombay* AIR 1954 SC 229 535

*V. G. Row v State of Madras* AIR 1952 SC 196 459, 478

*Saghir Ahmad v State of UP* AIR 1954 SC 728 492

*Thangal Kunju Musaliar v M. Venkitachalam Potti* [1955] 2 SCR 1196 517

*State of Bombay v R M D Chamarbaugwala* AIR 1957 SC 699 504

*Virendra v State of Punjab* AIR 1957 SC 896 528

*Pannalal Binjraj v Union of India* [1957] SCR 233 517

*Ram Krishna Dalmia v Justice S. R. Tendolkar* AIR 1958 SC 538 492, 516–17

*Mohd. Hanif Quareshi v State of Bihar* AIR 1958 SC 731 492

*Superintendent, Central Prison v Ram Manohar Lohia* AIR 1960 SC 633 520, 575

*Sakal Newspapers v Union of India* AIR 1962 SC 305 496

*Jyoti Pershad v Administrator, Union Territory of Delhi* [1962] 2 SCR 125 527

*Kedar Nath Singh v State of Bihar* AIR 1962 SC 955 536

*Parmanand Katara v Union of India* AIR 1989 SC 2039 498, 501
*Synthetics and Chemicals Ltd. v State of U.P.* (1990) 1 SCC 109 513
*M/s. Shantistar Builders v Narayan Khimalal Totame* AIR 1990 SC 630 498
*Sashikant Laxman Kale v Union of India* (1990) 4 SCC 366 517
*Shrilekha Vidyarthi v State of UP* (1991) 1 SCC 212 481, 510, 529
*Regina v Secretary of State for the Home Department ex parte Brind* [1991] UKHL 4 458
*Mohini Jain v State of Karnataka* (1992) 3 SCC 666 497
*C.E.S.C. Ltd. v Subhash Chandra Bose* (1992) 1 SCC 441 500
*Peerless General Finance and Investment Co. Ltd. v Reserve Bank of India* (1992) 2 SCC 343 497
*All India Imam Organisation v Union of India* AIR 1993 SC 2086 513–14
*Supreme Court Advocates on Record Association v Union of India* (1993) 4 SCC 441 466
*Unni Krishnan v State of AP* AIR 1993 SC 2178 498
*P. Rathinam v Union of India* AIR 1994 SC 1844 497, 500
*Secretary, Ministry of Information and Broadcasting, Govt of India v Cricket Association of Bengal* (1995) 2 SCC 161 499, 511
*Kartar Singh v State of Punjab* (1994) 3 SCC 569 526–27, 537–38
*Premium Granites v State of Tamil Nadu* AIR 1994 SC 2233 529
*Tata Cellular v Union of India* (1994) 6 SCC 651 459, 473, 481
*M. J. Sivani v State of Karnataka* AIR 1995 SC 1770 521
*Sushila Saw Mills v State of Orissa* AIR 1995 SC 2484 528
*Centre for Public Interest Litigation v Union of India*, 1995 Supp. (3) SCC 382 538
*Chameli Singh v State of UP* (1996) 2 SCC 549 508
*State of Andhra Pradesh v McDowell & Co* (1996) 3 SCC 709 459, 473–74
*Vineet Narain v Union of India* (1996) 2 SCC 199 467
*Bodhisattwa Gautam v Subhra Chakraborty* AIR 1996 SC 922 483
*Vellore Citizens Welfare Forum v Union of India* AIR 1996 SC 2715 498
*Paschim Banga Khet Mazdoor Samity v State of West Bengal* (1996) 4 SCC 37 513–14
*D. K. Basu v State of West Bengal* AIR 1997 SC 610 537–38
*M.P. Oil Extraction v State of M.P.* (1997) 7 SCC 592 494–508
*Union of India v G. Ganayutham* (1997) 7 SCC 463 459
*PUCL v Union of India* (1997) 1 SCC 301 499, 537
*Vishaka v State of Rajasthan* (1997) 6 SCC 241 467, 471
*State of Punjab v Ram Lubhaya Bagga* (1998) 4 SCC 117 514
*Malpe Vishwanath Acharya v State of Maharashtra* (1998) 2 SCC 1 512, 560
In Re *Special Reference 1 of 1998* (1998) 7 SCC 739 466
*Communist Party of India (M) v Bharat Kumar* (1998) 1 SCC 201 503
*Union of India v Motion Pictures Association* (1999) 6 SCC 150 503
*Consumer Education & Research Centre v Union of India* (2000) (2) SCC 599 498
*Om Kumar v Union of India* (2001) 2 SCC 386 459, 473, 576

# Introduction

## Analysing Proportionality Comparatively and Empirically

TALYA STEINER, ANDREJ LANG, AND MORDECHAI KREMNITZER

Proportionality is widely accepted as one of the most important constitutional principles of our time, and the current constitutional era has been termed the 'age of proportionality'.[1] In many jurisdictions around the world, the proportionality doctrine serves as the definitive reasoning framework for cases in which human rights conflict with other public interests, to the point where it has been said that 'to speak of rights is to speak of proportionality'.[2] Due to its 'viral quality',[3] proportionality is often cited as a leading example of the migration of constitutional ideas across the globe.[4] Originating in German jurisprudence,[5] it has been incorporated as a central constitutional feature in Canada,[6] South Africa,[7] and Israel,[8] and has been adopted or referenced in countries across Europe,[9]

[1] Vicki C Jackson, 'Constitutional Law in the Age of Proportionality' (2015) 124 Yale Law Journal 3094.

[2] Grant Huscroft, Bradley W Miller and Grégoire Webber (eds), *Proportionality and the Rule of Law: Rights, Justification, Reasoning* (CUP 2014) 2.

[3] Alec Stone Sweet and Jud Matthews, 'Proportionality, Balancing and Global Constitutionalism' (2008) 47 Columbia Journal of Transnational Law 72, 113.

[4] Lorrain Weinrib, 'The Post-War Paradigm and American Exceptionalism' in Sujit Choudhry (ed), *The Migration of Constitutional Ideas* (CUP 2007) 84; Vicki C Jackson, *Constitutional Engagement in a Transnational Era* (OUP 2010) 60; Stone Sweet and Matthews (n 3) 72, 113.

[5] See Chapter 1.

[6] See Chapter 2.

[7] See Chapter 3.

[8] See Chapter 4.

[9] For an overview, see Carlos Bernal Pulido, 'The Migration of Proportionality across Europe' (2003) 11 New Zealand Journal of Public and International Law 483. For an analysis of the case law of the Polish Constitutional Tribunal on proportionality, see Chapter 5.

Asia,[10] and Latin America,[11] with yet more countries joining in every year.[12] It is also a staple of jurisprudence in international and supranational courts.[13] Accordingly, proportionality has been described as 'a universal criterion of constitutionality'.[14]

While no single common formulation of proportionality exists, its basic structure is shared across countries. Proportionality comprises a series of subtests, typically including four elements: the worthy purpose requirement, according to which the rights limitation must be for the sake of promoting a legitimate public interest; the suitability test (also called the 'rational connection' or 'rational nexus' test), establishing a rational connection between the means and the public goal pursued; the necessity (or less-restrictive-means) test, inquiring whether the goal can be attained by some other means that would not restrict rights as much;

10 Proportionality-based fundamental rights review appears to assume a significant role in South Korea and in Hong Kong. On South Korea, Kyung Park, 'Korean Principle of Proportionality, American Multileveled Scrutiny, and Empiricist Elements in U.S.-Korean Constitutional Jurisprudence' (2001) 1 Journal of Korean Law 105, and, more recently, in the context of constitutional review of adultery laws, Seokmin Lee, 'Adultery and the Constitution: A Review on the Recent Decision of the Korean Constitutional Court on "Criminal Adultery"' (2016) 15 Journal of Korean Law 325; and on Hong Kong, see Lo Pui Yin, *The Judicial Construction of Hong Kong's Basic Law: Courts, Politics, and Society after 1997* (Hong Kong University Press 2014) 281–312. On India, see Chapter 6.

11 See for Brazil: João Andrade Neto, *Borrowing Justification for Proportionality: On the Influence of the Principles Theory in Brazil* (Springer 2018); for Mexico and Colombia: Luisa Conesa, 'The Tropicalization of Proportionality Balancing: The Colombian and Mexican Examples' (Cornell Law School Inter-University Graduate Student Conference Papers. 13, 2008) <https://scholarship.law.cornell.edu/lps_clacp/13> accessed 16 December 2019; for Peru: Marcial Antonio Rubio Correa, *El Test de Proporcionalidad en la Jurisprudencia del Tribunal Constitucional Peruano* (Fondo Editorial de la Pontificia Universidad Católica del Perú 2011); for Chile: Dante Figueroa, 'Constitutional Review in Chile Revisited: A Revolution in the Making' (2013) 51 Duquesne Law Review 387, 411–13.

12 One of the most recent countries to have adopted the proportionality framework is Australia. See: Anne Carter, 'Proportionality in Australian Constitutional Law: Towards Transnationalism' (2016) 76 ZaöRV 951.

13 Including the ECJ, ECHR, WTO DSU and IACHR. See, e.g., Marc-André Eissen, 'The Principle of Proportionality in the Case-Law of the European Court of Human Rights' in Ronald StJ Macdonald, Franz Matscher, and Herbert Petzold (eds), *The European System for the Protection of Human Rights* (Nijhoff 1993) 125, 146; Mads Andenas and Stefan Zleptnig, 'Proportionality and Balancing in WTO Law: A Comparative Perspective' (2007) 20 Cambridge Review of International Affairs 71; Jonas Christoffersen, *Fair Balance: Proportionality, Subsidiarity and Primarity in the European Convention on Human Rights* (Nijhoff 2009) 37; Tor-Inge Harbo, 'The Function of the Proportionality Principle in EU Law' (2010) 16 European Law Journal 158.

14 David M Beatty, *The Ultimate Rule of Law* (OUP 2004) 162.

and the strict proportionality (or balancing) test, weighing the benefit of the public policy relative to the harm caused to the right.[15]

The proportionality framework has been employed in endless individual cases for nearly half a century. This widespread use of its subtests has given rise to multiple interpretations of how they are to be understood and used that have not been systematically mapped out or compared. In fact, there has been nearly no comprehensive empirical analysis of its application. Although the normative literature is often speckled with assumptions about how proportionality functions, these are not empirically grounded and little is actually known about how proportionality is used in judicial practice across jurisdictions. The result is that 'despite the abundant literature, a multitude of enigmas seem to remain unsolved when it comes to defining the common language called proportionality'.[16]

This book presents one of the first empirical and comparative explorations of the proportionality principle in constitutional adjudication in several jurisdictions and across contexts. It provides a detailed account of proportionality in action in six jurisdictions – Germany, Canada, South Africa, Israel, Poland, and India – written and contextualized by constitutional scholars from each of the relevant jurisdictions. Based on large samples of constitutional court and supreme court case law, the analysis set forth in the book uses a combination of common legal hermeneutics and empirical legal research methods to assess what these courts actually do when they apply the proportionality framework. We believe that the combination of in-depth qualitative analysis and robust quantitative analysis provides a fresh, evidence-based prism through which the application of the proportionality framework by courts throughout the democratic world can be re-evaluated and debated. After presenting an overview of strands and developments in the scholarship on proportionality to date (Section I), we will set out the book's main goals (Section II) and describe its research design and methodology (Section III).

[15] Robert Alexy, *A Theory of Constitutional Rights* (Julian Rivers tr, OUP 2002); Matthias Klatt and Moritz Meister, *The Constitutional Structure of Proportionality* (OUP 2012) 7–10; Stone Sweet and Matthews (n 3) 72, 76. In some systems, there is a preliminary requirement that precedes the proportionality tests, regarding the format in which a limitation shall be enacted. It requires, for example, that a limitation be based on a parliamentary statue. See elaboration on the specific requirements in Chapters 1–6.

[16] Sofia Ranchordas and Boudewijn de Waard (eds), *The Judge and the Proportionate Use of Discretion: A Comparative Administrative Law Study* (Routledge 2016) 3.

## I Scholarship on Proportionality: Strands and Developments

Considering the central role played by proportionality across the globe, it is only natural that it has been the subject of an ever-growing corpus of academic research and debate. The research angle of most publications on proportionality is normative in nature, evaluating the virtues and vices of the framework for purposes of judicial review (Section A). Some writing on proportionality undertakes a historical inquiry, attempting to document and explain the global diffusion of the principle of proportionality, as well as to explore the philosophical origins of the concepts of balancing and proportionality and their evolutionary development across legal traditions.[17] In contrast, our research on proportionality focuses on analysing actual judicial practice. It builds on two other strands of constitutional scholarship, both of which place descriptive findings front and centre: comparative constitutional law (Section B) and empirical constitutional law (Section C). By infusing the debate on proportionality with empirically grounded and detailed comparative descriptive findings, we hope to invigorate the discussion with fresh perspectives.

### *A The Predominance of Normative Approaches to Proportionality*

The most dominant strand in the literature is the ongoing normative debate over proportionality. This normative literature is, roughly speaking, either critical or supportive of the proportionality principle, and revolves primarily around two central themes: the relationship between proportionality and theories of rights, and the institutional justifications and ramifications of proportionality as the standard for judicial review.

Within the theme of proportionality and theories of rights, critics view proportionality as the antithesis of the liberal tradition of rights, essentially robbing rights of their privileged status relative to other

[17] Two leading books in the historical genre are Jacco Bomhoff, *Balancing Constitutional Rights* (CUP 2013), and Moshe Cohen-Eliya and Iddo Porat, *Proportionality and Constitutional Culture* (CUP 2013). Also see, Martin Luteran, 'The Lost Meaning of Proportionality' in Grant Huscroft, Bradley Miller, and Grégoire Webber (eds), *Proportionality and the Rule of Law: Rights, Justification, Reasoning* (CUP 2014); Stone Sweet and Mathews (n 3) 74. A seminal book in support of the principle of proportionality is Aharon Barak's book on proportionality. Aharon Barak, *Proportionality: Constitutional Rights and their Limitations* (CUP 2012). While including historical elements on the origins of proportionality, Barak presents a theory of and a justification for proportionality, devoting specific sections to his own position on the proper interpretation of each of the stages of PA.

considerations.[18] Supporters, on the other hand, have either interpreted proportionality in a way that is still compatible with the 'rights priority' approach,[19] or developed alternative theories of rights that place rights more broadly into a culture of justification.[20] Within the institutional theme, critics view proportionality, and specifically the practice of balancing, as licence for unconstrained moral reasoning left to the discretion of judges.[21] Some supporters have attempted to frame proportionality-based judicial review as an objective process of turning questions of value into questions of fact.[22] Others have openly accepted that proportionality-based judicial review entails judicial moral reasoning,

18 Stravos Tsakyrakis, 'Proportionality: An Assault on Human Rights?' (2009) 7 International Journal of Constitutional Law 468; Gregoire Webber, 'The Loss of Rights' in Grant Huscroft, Bradley Miller, and Grégoire Webber (eds), *Proportionality and the Rule of Law: Rights, Justification, Reasoning* (CUP 2014) 123; Francisco J Urbina, *A Critique of Proportionality and Balancing* (CUP 2017).

19 For example, Klatt and Meister have advocated for what they call a 'soft trumping' approach to balancing, in which rights are assigned with a higher abstract weight than other considerations, achieving a trumping effect, without assigning rights categorical priority. See: Matthias Klatt and Moritz Meister, 'Proportionality – a Benefit to Human Rights? Remarks on the ICON Controversy' (2012) 10 International Journal of Constitutional Law 687. Fredrick Schauer has held that although rights under proportionality are not absolute, the very language of the strict proportionality test recognizes that they carry special weight in relation to other interests. He declares proportionality a special form of balancing that differs from regular cost-benefit analysis, since proportionality includes a presumption on behalf of the right. See Fredrick Schauer, 'A Comment on the Structure of Rights' (1993) 27 Georgia Law Review 415; Fredrick Schauer, 'Proportionality and the Question of Weight' in Grant Huscroft, Bradley Miller and Grégoire Webber (eds), *Proportionality and the Rule of Law: Rights, Justification, Reasoning* (CUP 2014) 173, 175–81. Aharon Barak is also in line with this type of interpretation of the strict proportionality stage. In his view it is only the strict proportionality stage that tackles, head on, the question of the weight afforded to rights in relation to the competing interest. See Barak (n 17) 344. In his view, any principled approach to the status of rights can be integrated into this stage, including approaches that provide rights with special status and therefore a high level of protection. ibid 367.

20 Mattias Kumm, 'The Idea of Socratic Contestation and the Right to Justification: The Point of Rights-Based Proportionality Review' (2010) 4 Law and Ethics of Human Rights 141; Moshe Cohen-Eliya and Iddo Porat, 'Proportionality and the Culture of Justification' (2011) 59 The American Journal of Comparative Law 463; Kai Möller, *The Global Model of Constitutional Rights* (OUP 2012); Mattias Kumm, 'Is the Structure of Human Rights Defensible? Three Puzzles and Their Resolution' in Vicki C Jackson and Mark Tushnet (eds), *Proportionality: New Frontiers, New Challenges* (CUP 2017) 30.

21 See Fredrick Schauer, 'Balancing, Subsumption and the Constraining Role of the Legal Text' in Mattias Klatt (ed), *Institutionalized Reason: The Jurisprudence of Robert Alexy* (OUP 2012) 307; Grant Huscroft, 'Proportionality and Pretense' (2014) 29 Constitutional Commentary 229; Urbina (n 18) 150–212.

22 Beatty (n 14).

while pointing out that the proportionality framework requires courts to be more transparent about the fact that this is what they are doing.[23] Finally, some have developed the idea that proportionality-based judicial review is not an act of independent value balancing but rather a tool or mechanism for challenging and assessing the decision-maker's justification for impairing constitutional rights.[24]

Since the normative literature is geared towards making general claims in support of or against proportionality, it tends to place at its centre either an idealized or deprecated – in any case, abstract – version of the doctrine, rather than any specific application of it.[25] When such writing does make reference to case law it is highly selective, using it specifically to demonstrate and support the positions asserted.[26]

Beyond the central normative debate for or against proportionality, an emerging yet still underdeveloped strand of literature has more recently begun to emerge: research that adopts a pragmatic approach, accepting the proportionality framework as a given in our judicial landscape and focusing on how it operates and ought to operate in practice. Unlike much of the more theoretical literature on proportionality, its focus is not the abstract concept or principle of proportionality, but rather the concrete formula of the proportionality test.[27] The goal of this type of scholarly effort is to characterize a version of the test that best

[23] Barak (n 17) 462–63; Wojciech Sadurski, 'Reasonableness and Value Pluralism in Law and Politics' in Giorgio Bongiovanni, Sartor Giovanni and Chiara Valentini (eds), *Reasonableness and Law* (Springer 2009) 129, 139. Also see Stone Sweet and Matthews (n 3) 72, 78: 'PA does not camouflage judicial law making. Properly employed, it requires courts to acknowledge and defend – honestly and openly – the policy choices that they make when they make constitutional choices.'

[24] Mattias Kumm, 'Political Liberalism and the Structure of Rights: On the Place and Limits of the Proportionality Requirement' in George Pavlakos (ed), *Law, Rights and Discourse: The Legal Philosophy of Robert Alexy* (Hart Publishing 2007); Kumm, 'The Idea of Socratic Contestation and the Right to Justification' (n 20) 142; David Dyzenhaus, 'Proportionality and Deference in a Culture of Justification' in Grant Huscroft, Bradley Miller and Grégoire Webber (eds), *Proportionality and the Rule of Law: Rights, Justification, Reasoning* (CUP 2014) 234; Kumm, 'Is the Structure of Human Rights Defensible?' (n 20) 30.

[25] Urbina (n 18) 3.

[26] See, e.g., Tsakyrakis (n 18) 468; Beatty (n 14); Kumm, 'The Idea of Socratic Contestation and the Right to Justification' (n 20) 141.

[27] Möller has pointed out that 'the question of which specific conception of the test is preferable is underexplored and only rarely even identified as a problem'. Kai Möller, 'Constructing the Proportionality Test: An Emerging Global Conversation' in Liora Lazarus, Christopher McCrudden and Niels Bowels (eds), *Reasoning Rights: Comparative Judicial Engagement* (Hart Publishing 2014) 31. See also Margit Cohen, 'Proportionality

operationalizes the normative goals underlying the proportionality principle.[28] Some of the work that has been done along these lines has focused on the relationship between the necessity and strict proportionality tests, pointing to advantages and disadvantages of different formulations of each of these tests, and ultimately advocating for a specific version.[29]

### B *The Appeal of Comparative Constitutional Inquiries into Proportionality*

Despite the fact that the proportionality framework is applied across the globe, very little comparative analysis has been done regarding the differences and similarities in when and how the doctrine is applied in different countries, and the ramifications of the differences. In the vast majority of the writing on proportionality the very existence of variance is ignored or glossed over, and when it is mentioned anecdotally it is treated as 'a mystery worth exploring'.[30] We believe, however, that exposure to a fuller spectrum of proportionality models will provide a rich basis for comparative insights, expanding our understanding of proportionality and its manifestations in the context of different jurisdictions.

One of the goals of the practice of comparative law that is particularly relevant for our undertaking is to deepen the understanding of a legal phenomenon by comparing and contrasting jurisdictions. The differences identified through the juxtaposition of two seemingly similar doctrines can lead to a deeper understanding of each system in practice: characteristics that weren't even considered 'characteristics' emerge once

in Israel and Beyond: Four Aspects' in Gideon Sapir, Daphne Barak-Erez and Aharon Barak (eds), *Israeli Constitutional Law in the Making* (Hart Publishing 2013) 189.

28 Möller, 'Constructing the Proportionality Test' (n 27).

29 David Bilchitz 'Necessity and Proportionality: Towards a Balanced Approach' in Liora Lazarus, Christopher McCrudden and Niels Bowels (eds), *Reasoning Rights: Comparative Judicial Engagement* (Hart Publishing 2014) 41; Jochen von Bernstorff, 'Proportionality without Balancing: why Judicial Ad Hoc Balancing in Unnecessary and Potentially Detrimental to the Realization of Individual and Collective Self Determination', in Liora Lazarus, Christopher McCrudden and Niels Bowels (eds), *Reasoning Rights: Comparative Judicial Engagement* (Hart Publishing 2014) 31; Brems and Laverysen, 'Don't Use a Sledgehammer to Crack a Nut: Less Restrictive Means in the Case Law of the European Court of Human Rights' (2015) 15 Human Rights Law Review 139, 146.

30 Stone Sweet and Matthews (n 3) 72, 164.

they are highlighted through contrast.[31] A second prevalent goal of comparative law is to identify the scope of possible solutions to a common problem, as a basis for an informed normative discussion of the ideal approach.[32]

The field of comparative constitutional law has flourished in recent years. Self-reflective efforts have been made to classify the varied goals of different endeavours and match them with the appropriate methodologies and research designs. More critical analyses have been done of the limitations or flaws of such research, and attempts have been made to point such efforts in new directions.[33] As part of an emerging debate on how the comparative study of constitutional law should be done, a distinction has been drawn between comparative constitutional *law* and comparative constitutional *studies*.[34] Traditionally, comparative work on constitutional law has taken an internal, legal perspective, focusing on the application and interpretation of legal doctrine. In contrast, comparative constitutional studies adopt a social science perspective on the law, treating constitution-making and jurisprudence as products of various external factors that themselves become the focus of research. These differences in approach dictate the goal of the comparative endeavour, the types of research questions posed and the research design and methodology. Despite this conceptual distinction, there does seem to be agreement that rather than an either-or approach, a plurality of methods

[31] According to Liora Lazarus, *Contrasting Prisoners' Rights: A Comparative Examination of England and Germany* (OUP 2004) 19–20, this practice allows uncovering the 'strangeness in the familiar'.

[32] Vicky C Jackson, 'Comparative Constitutional Law: Methodologies' in Michel Rosenfeld and András Sajó (eds), *The Oxford Handbook of Comparative Constitutional Law* (OUP 2012) 54, 60–66. Jackson classifies five main goals of comparative approach: classificatory, historical, normative, functional, and contextual. Also see Christopher McCrudden, 'Introduction' in Liora Lazarus, Christopher McCrudden and Niels Bowels (eds), *Reasoning Rights: Comparative Judicial Engagement* (Hart Publishing, 2014) 3, 5.

[33] Mark Tushnet, 'The Possibilities of Comparative Constitutional Law' (1999) 108 Yale Law Journal 1225; Ran Hirschl, 'The Question of Case Selection in Comparative Constitutional Law' (2005) 53 American Journal of Comparative Law 125; Vicki C Jackson, 'Methodological Challenges in Comparative Constitutional Law' (2010) 28 Penn State International Law Review 319; Tom Ginsburg and Rosalind Dixon (eds), *Comparative Constitutional Law* (Edward Elgar 2011); Ran Hirschl, *Comparative Matters: The Renaissance of Comparative Constitutional Law* (OUP 2014) 10; Stephen Gardbaum, 'How Do and Should We Compare Constitutional Law?' in Samantha Besson, Lukas Heckendorn and Samuel Jube (eds), *Comparing Comparative Law* (Swiss Institute of Comparative Law 2016) 10.

[34] Hirschl, *Comparative Matters* (n 33) 151–91.

in research should be encouraged,[35] along with a more developed self-awareness regarding choice of goals and methodology.

Although systematic (rather than anecdotal) comparative constitutional research on proportionality is still in its infancy, some important comparative work has been conducted that serves as a foundation for our current research efforts. The comparative lens first drew attention to the global nature of the proportionality, and to some of the causes for its global success.[36] Comparative undertakings have also pointed out variance between jurisdictions in applying the proportionality doctrine, while offering some reasoning and initial normative judgment of these differences. One of the first to address this issue was Julian Rivers, who argued that there were two competing conceptions of proportionality.[37] These conceptions differ with regard to the role played by the courts when applying proportionality, the overall function of the doctrine, and the emphasis on particular subtests. According to his argument, the German model of proportionality presents an optimization conception of proportionality, in which the overarching goal is the optimization of the common good, and the court uses proportionality to ensure that rights and public interests are balanced in the best possible way. In contrast, the Commonwealth model of proportionality presents a state-restricting conception, in which the court protects individuals from other branches of government by placing limits on their actions. It therefore uses proportionality to scrutinize the importance of the public objective and to ensure that no excessive and unnecessary restrictions are imposed on rights.

A seminal comparative article by Grimm distinguishes between the Canadian and German models of proportionality, pointing out in detail the differences between the models and attempting to explain their causes.[38] In particular, Grimm addresses the most striking differences: the strong emphasis on the balancing test in Germany and its more residual function in Canada, and the Canadian court's more value-laden approach to the less-restrictive-means test. A comparative study by

35 Gardbaum (n 33).

36 Weinrib (n 4) 84; Stone Sweet and Matthews (n 3) 72, 113.

37 Julian Rivers, 'Proportionality and Variable Intensity of Review' (2006) 65 Cambridge Law Journal 174.

38 Dieter Grimm, 'Proportionality in Canadian and German Constitutional Jurisprudence' (2007) 57 University of Toronto Law Journal 383. Similarly, see Guy Davidov, 'Separating Minimal Impairment from Balancing: A Comment on R. v. Sharpe' (2000) 5 Review of Constitutional Studies 195.

Goold, Lazarus, and Swiney analysed the application of proportionality by courts in the United Kingdom, France, Germany, and Spain and by the European Court of Human Rights, in the specific context of conflicts between rights and national security. Among other findings, the study found that British courts were less consistent than the other courts examined in their application of proportionality, and tied this to the fact that the British courts rely solely on the European Convention of Human Rights, rather than on constitutional protection of rights.[39]

Recently, a rather strongly stated claim was put forward by David Kenny regarding the global nature of the proportionality framework.[40] Based on a comparative analysis of the application of proportionality in Canada and Ireland and the differences found, including in the formulation of the subtests, the allocation of the burden of proof and introduction of evidence, he concludes that there is actually no common global doctrine, and that proportionality is merely rhetoric linking drastically divergent local and contextual practices.[41] While Kenny's observation that legal variance in fundamental rights jurisprudence between different jurisdictions can express itself within the overarching proportionality doctrine is an important one, our research indicates that the applications of proportionality across most of the countries analysed in this book are more similar than Kenny's argument suggests.

## C *The Value of the Empirical Turn in Proportionality Scholarship*

Legal scholarship has undergone an empirical turn over the past century,[42] and as part of this trend, empirical methods are increasing in comparative constitutional scholarship. Some significant milestones in empirical work in the field of comparative constitutional law include research on trends in global constitutionalism based on a coding of all

39 Benjamin Goold, Liora Lazarus, and Gabriel Swiney, 'Public Protection, Proportionality and the Search for Balance' (2017) Ministry of Justice Research Series 10/07 <https://papers.ssrn.com/sol3/papers.cfm?abstract_id=2022365> accessed 16 December 2019.

40 David Kenny, 'Proportionality and the Inevitability of the Local: A Comparative Localist Analysis of Canada and Ireland' (2018) 66 American Journal of Comparative Law 537.

41 ibid 571–78.

42 See, e.g., Michael Heise, 'The Past, Present and Future of Empirical Legal Scholarship: Judicial Decision Making and the New Empiricism' (2002) University of Illinois Law Review 819; Daniel E Ho and Larry Kramer, 'Introduction: The Empirical Revolution in Law' (2013) 65 Stanford Law Review 1195.

rights-related content of all national constitutions since World War II;[43] a study of transnational communication between courts based on references to foreign case law in court decisions;[44] and a qualitative and quantitative comparative analysis of constitutional reasoning in terms of form, style, and language.[45]

Each of these groundbreaking works has demonstrated that although empirical methodology cannot replace normative discussion, it can significantly enrich normative debate. By sharpening our understanding of how constitutional law actually operates, the normative debate can evolve in new directions. The aforementioned studies also demonstrate the value of methodological approaches that combine quantitative and qualitative elements: while qualitative analysis remains essential for providing background needed to understand and interpret quantitative indicators, quantitative measures can enhance comparability.

Specifically, Hall and Wright have pointed to systematic content analysis of legal opinions as an empirical methodology that can be uniquely utilized by legal scholars.[46] Such content analysis allows the development of a more scientific understanding of the law itself. It has previously been recognized that such systematic content analyses have the power to discover 'anomalies which may escape the naked eye',[47] 'set our mind going along new paths and yield unexpected insights,[48] and help uncover areas for future research.[49]

Besides a handful of country-specific empirical analyses of proportionality (or elements thereof),[50] only one major effort has been made to date to conduct a comparative analysis of proportionality in an empirically

[43] David Law and Mila Versteeg, 'The Evolution and Ideology of Global Constitutionalism' (2011) 99 California Law Review 1163.

[44] Tania Groppi and Marie-Claire Ponthoreau (eds), *The Use of Foreign Precedents by Constitutional Judges* (Hart Publishing 2013).

[45] András Jakab, Arthur Dyevre and Giulio Itzcovich, *Comparative Constitutional Reasoning* (CUP 2017).

[46] Mark A Hall and Ronald F Wright, 'Systemic Content Analysis of Judicial Opinions' (2008) 96 California Law Review 63.

[47] Alan L Tyree, 'Fact Content Analysis of Case Law: Methods and Limitations' (1981) 22 Jurimetrics 1, 23.

[48] Lon F Fuller, 'An Afterword: Science and the Judicial Process' (1996) 79 Harvard Law Review 1604, 1622.

[49] Karen A Jordan, 'Empirical Studies of Judicial Decisions Serve an Important Role in the Cumulative Process of Policy Making' (1998) 31 Indiana Law Review 81, 88.

[50] For an empirical analysis of proportionality in a single jurisdiction (Canada), see Leon E Trakman, William Cole-Hamilton and Sean Gatien, 'R v. Oakes 1986–1998: Back to the Drawing Board' (1998) 36 Osgoode Hall Law Journal 83; Christoph Engel, 'Das legitime

grounded manner: Niels Peterson's excellent book on proportionality and judicial activism includes an empirical analysis of judicial overturning of legislation by constitutional courts in Germany, Canada, and South Africa. In it, he systematically records the argumentation patterns used in such cases, including those represented by subtests of proportionality.[51] The main conclusion of his book is that courts' justifications for striking down legislation are rarely based on balancing; instead they make use of a variety of additional forms of argumentation and considerations. The focus of Petersen's research, however, is not on a comprehensive analysis of the proportionality doctrine per se but rather on the narrower issue of whether proportionality serves courts as a means of judicial activism. In our research we build on his important work and extend it by focusing on a differently formulated research question, while also providing an opportunity for partial assessment of his findings.

## II The Goals of This Book

More than a hundred years ago, Roscoe Pound famously distinguished between 'law in books and law in action'.[52] He defined the former as 'the rules that purport to govern the relations of man' and the latter as 'those that in fact govern them'.[53] Although shelves have been filled with books and articles about the doctrine and theory of the proportionality principle, we know relatively little about how proportionality is actually applied in judicial practice across jurisdictions or, to put it more sharply: what the 'law in action' of proportionality is. What is missing in the existing literature on proportionality is a comprehensive, empirically informed analysis of its application *in practice*, in different jurisdictions and in different contexts.

This book contributes to the understanding of the global constitutional phenomenon of proportionality by taking an empirical and comparative approach. The book provides an empirically grounded, doctrinally thorough, descriptive account of the diverse practices of proportionality in action by six apex courts. The detailed, complex picture that emerges

Ziel in der Praxis des Bundesverfassungsgerichts' in Matthias Jestaedt and Oliver Lepsius (eds), *Verhältnismäßigkeit* (Mohr Siebeck 2015) 97.

51 Niels Petersen, *Proportionality and Judicial Activism: Fundamental Rights Adjudication in Canada, Germany and South Africa* (CUP 2017).

52 Roscoe Pound, 'Law in Books and Law in Action' (1910) 44 The American Law Review 12.

53 ibid 15.

provides an opportunity to challenge some of the prevalent assumptions about proportionality, enrich the normative debate over proportionality and provide a basis for argument regarding the optimal model of applying the doctrine.

One of the goals of the comparative element of the study is to sharpen our understanding of the scope of possible applications of the proportionality doctrine. By mapping the nuances within each context and between contexts, we expand the range of possibilities to be considered. Since courts often consciously imitate others when adopting this globally spreading doctrine,[54] we believe it is important that they be aware that adopting the proportionality framework does not dictate how it should be applied, and thus that a critical approach should be taken towards the diverse possibilities. An illuminating example is the recent Indian Supreme Court decision in *Puttaswamy v Union of India*,[55] viewed as the first explicit attempt to apply the proportionality framework to limitation review in Indian case law. In this decision concerning the right to privacy, the court explicitly recognized the existence of scholarly debate over the proper application of the proportionality doctrine, referencing the Canadian as opposed to the German approach while attempting to reach a compromise between the two that deals with some of the difficulties raised by each.[56]

A second goal of the comparative undertaking is normative. We believe that the gaps uncovered by the comparative analysis between doctrinal theory and practice should evoke a re-evaluation of the theory, and the range of existing practices should serve as the basis for a normative evaluation of the advantages and disadvantages of different approaches, with the goal of achieving optimal operationalization of the doctrine.

We recognize that reservations have been raised regarding the comparability of a similar concept across jurisdictions, where the concept

[54] See, e.g., the Israeli Supreme Courts references to the Canadian and German Practice of Proportionality in CA 6821/93 *United Mizrahi Bank Ltd v Migdal Cooperative Village* [1995], IsrSC 49(4) 221, 436–37, available in English at: <https://supremedecisions.court.gov.il/Home/Download?path=EnglishVerdicts%5C93%5C210%5C068%5Cz01&fileName=93068210_z01.txt&type=4> accessed December 16 2019. Regarding German and European influences on the Canadian Oakes test see Robert J Sharpe and Kent Roach, *Brian Dickson: A Judge's Journey* (University of Toronto Press 2004) 334; Aharon Barak, 'Proportional Effect: The Israeli Experience' (2007) 57 University of Toronto Law Journal 369, 370.

[55] *Puttaswamy v Union of India* Writ Petition (Civil) No. 494 of 2012, decided on 26 September 2018.

[56] ibid 211–15.

does not necessarily have the same meaning. The result may be comparing the incomparable.[57] Nevertheless, we believe that our comparative analysis is based on a sufficient degree of comparability, considering that we are comparing the application of the multi-stage proportionality framework rather than a more abstract concept, such as balancing. In addition, we place great importance on the local contextualization of our findings, which we believe is achieved by having the individual country analyses conducted by local authors who are sensitive to local nuances.

## III Methodology and Research Design

The book comprises six country-based chapters, each analysing the application of proportionality in one of six apex courts: the Federal Constitutional Court of Germany, the Supreme Court of Canada, the Constitutional Court of South Africa, the Supreme Court of Israel, the Constitutional Tribunal of Poland, and the Supreme Court of India. Although proportionality serves as a dominant constitutional principle for the first five of these, the countries are diverse in terms of geography, political background, democratic history, and legal culture, and they include both relatively mature democracies and a new post-Communist democracy, as well as Western and non-Western countries. The countries also reflect diversity in terms of whether they established or later joined the global trend of proportionality: Germany is the place of origin of the proportionality doctrine in the modern age, while Canada is considered to have made a major contribution to the spread of proportionality across the globe after adopting the doctrine in the mid-1980s, and serves as an inspiration for other countries. Israel, Poland, and South Africa represent 'second-generation' countries that adopted proportionality in the mid-1990s, consciously mirroring Germany and Canada.

We have also chosen to include a chapter on the limitation analysis of the Supreme Court of India, which appears to be in the process of adopting the proportionality framework. Although the Indian Supreme Court has only recently and very tentatively embraced proportionality as a general doctrine for adjudicating cases of rights limitation, it previously recognized that its method of analysis mirrored that of proportionality

[57] Jacco Bomhoff, 'Balancing the Global and the Local: Judicial Balancing as a Problematic Topic in Comparative Constitutional Law' (2008) 31 Hastings International and Comparative Law Review 555.

analysis (PA), and recently explicitly adopted the proportionality framework in the specific context of the right to privacy.[58] We believe that the chapter on India is invaluable, both on its own and from a comparative perspective. It provides unique access to an unprecedented, systematic deconstruction of Indian limitation analysis, based on a large set of Supreme Court decisions, making order in an otherwise dizzying body of case law. The analysis in the book takes a comparative look at the various elements that make up PA, evaluating their individual contributions to the overall analysis, as well as the similarities and differences in how they are formulated and applied. The Indian chapter demonstrates how these elements are utilized in Indian limitation analysis outside the official proportionality framework. Thus the inclusion of a chapter on India provides an illuminating reference point for contrast and comparison.

In terms of the jurisdictional selection, we are sensitive to the critique that our comparison is weighted in favour of certain jurisdictions that typically tend to be included in comparative constitutional studies. According to this critique, claims made regarding global phenomena based on the experience of these few states are problematic.[59] Although we generally agree with this criticism, in the context of this particular topic – application of the proportionality doctrine – we believe it poses less of a challenge. Considering that this is a first systematic effort at comparative empirical research on this topic, it was important to include the two dominant 'trend-setters' of the proportionality doctrine, namely Germany and Canada. Because the South African court has uniquely chosen to explicitly reject the traditional sequential structure of proportionality, it was particularly intriguing to include it in our investigation, in order to test the extent to which this conceptual proclamation plays out in practice. In choosing additional countries, we tried to diversify and include less-studied countries such as Israel and Poland, as well as India for the aforementioned reasons. The constraints dictated that we could not further increase the number of countries included, although we recognize the potential contribution of including Latin American

[58] See *Puttaswamy v Union of India* (2017) 10 SCC 1. Generally, see Ashish Chugh, 'Is the Supreme Court Disproportionately Applying the Proportionality Principle?' (2004) 8 SCC (J) 33; Abhinav Chandrachud, 'Wednesbury Reformulated: Proportionality and the Supreme Court of India' (2013) 13 Oxford University Commonwealth Law Journal 191.

[59] Tom Ginsburg and Rosalind Dixon (eds), *Comparative Constitutional Law* (Edward Elgar 2011); Ran Hirschl, *Comparative Matters* (n 33) 205–24.

countries such as Mexico, Peru, Colombia, and Brazil in such a study; we hope they will be the focus of future research efforts.

The courts analysed vary in terms of the institutional model of constitutional review, the scope of their jurisdiction and the areas of law to which proportionality has been applied. Three courts (Germany, South Africa, and Poland) are specialized constitutional courts that are – at least to some extent – separate from ordinary courts and are only entitled to adjudicate constitutional issues, while the other three (Canada, India, and Israel) are generalized supreme courts that serve as courts of last instance for all legal issues, including non-constitutional matters.[60] In addition, three of the country-based chapters (South Africa, Canada, and Poland) deal solely with reviews of legislation, while the other three (Israel, India, and Germany) deal both with reviews of legislation and reviews of other forms of governmental and administrative action. Despite the problems that such a difference may create, we preferred not to limit our analysis to reviews of legislation only, and to include administrative reviews in the analysis where relevant.[61]

Because little systematic comparative work has been conducted on proportionality and considering the uncharted nature of the field, we adopted an exploratory research design involving a broad investigation of the characteristics of proportionality as applied rather than focusing on one particular research question or hypothesis. The advantages of such an exploratory approach are its ability to uncover unexpected findings by allowing them to surface organically and its creation of a primary level of knowledge from which research questions and hypotheses can be generated, thus laying the groundwork for future research and development. On the flip side, such an approach is generally not able to provide definitive answers to specific research questions.

The study combines both quantitative and qualitative comparative analysis. This mixed methodological approach was chosen in order to accommodate both the need for meaningful engagement with the substance of the decisions so as to capture the rich context of the application

[60] For more detail on this distinction, see Lech Garlicki, 'Constitutional courts versus supreme courts' (2007) 5 International Journal of Constitutional Law 44. See also Favoreu's distinction between the centralized European and the decentralized American model of constitutional review: Louis Favoreu, 'Constitutional Review in Europe' in Louis Henkin and Albert Rosenthal (eds), *Constitutionalism and Rights* (Columbia University Press 1989) 38.

[61] Contributors were instructed to pay attention to possible differences stemming from the nature of the reviewed measure, and this was mentioned where found relevant.

of proportionality, and the benefits of quantifiable, comparable measures as a basis for systematic comparative analysis. The result is a combination of quantitative measures, contextualized and nuanced with qualitative insights, producing a comparable, contextualized description of judicial practice.

The quantitative analysis was based on a systematic coding of a large sample of proportionality-based decisions. In each country, a case law database was created by the authors of the country chapters, each of whom is intimately acquainted with constitutional law in his or her home country. In Germany, Israel, and India the cases were selected in a two-stage process: first a textual search was conducted on the relevant case law database within a limited time frame. In Israel and Germany the search was for the term 'proportionality' and other forms of the word; in India the search was for constitutional articles on specific rights. The resulting cases were then read and screened to ensure that they fulfilled the criteria of application of the proportionality framework, or limitation analysis more broadly in India.[62] In Canada, Poland, and South Africa the cases were selected based on a case-by-case evaluation of all cases

[62] The **German** sample began with a search of FCC First or Second Senate decisions (eight judges as opposed to Chamber decisions with only three judges) within the 2000–17 time frame that contain a variation of the term 'proportionality' in German, as well as the German terms *Übermaß* and *Untermaß*, which are sometimes used synonymously with proportionality. The 368 results of the search were then read to locate those which applied the proportionality doctrine. FCC chamber decisions were excluded, due to the combination of their vast quantity and their limited decision-making authority. For more detail on the sample, see Chapter 1.

The **Israeli** sample began with a search of the 'Nevo' database for the term 'proportional' (מידתי), including morphological forms, within the 2006–15 time frame. The 2,698 results were reviewed to locate those in which the outcome was based upon multi-stage PA. For more data on the sample, see Chapter 4.

Since Indian case law has not officially adopted the proportionality doctrine, the **Indian** sample comprises all cases where the Supreme Court analysed whether there had been a limitation of one of the three most important fundamental rights: the right to equality (Article 14), fundamental freedoms (Article 19) or life and personal liberty (Article 21). The cases were selected using a combination of two complementary selection methods, meant to create an overall representative portrait of Indian Supreme Court limitation analysis. The database includes all Constitution Bench (five or more judges) decisions regarding these rights from the years 2004–13 (21 out of 89 Constitution Bench decisions in this time period), and all decisions regarding these rights regardless of bench size from the years 2014–16 (77 decisions out of the 506 cases tagged as relating to these rights in the case reporter Supreme Court Cases). For more detail on the sample, see Chapter 6.

handed down in the relevant time frame to locate those that fulfil the criteria of applying the proportionality framework.[63]

The specific time frame sampled was tailored to the individual country, contingent upon the overall volume of court decisions. Courts with a low annual volume (the apex courts in Canada and South Africa) required the coding of a longer time frame to reach a large sample and could encompass all cases in which the principle of proportionality was applied since the adoption of the proportionality framework in 1986 and 1995, respectively. Apex courts with a high annual volume, namely, those in Israel, India, Germany, and Poland, needed a shorter time span (between 4 and 18 years), leading to a focus on the more recent period. Table 0.1 shows the number of cases and time frame per jurisdiction.

We recognize that the different time spans analysed may have ramifications for the comparability of the findings. In countries in which longer time spans are analysed, there may have been shifts over time that our analysis does not address, and in countries in which shorter time spans are analysed earlier periods may have exhibited different trends.[64] In order to generate a large enough sample (a minimum of 100 cases per country), and due to the differences in annual volume between countries,

[63] The **Canadian** sample includes all Supreme Court cases involving a PA from *R v Oakes* in 1986 until the end of 2017. The dataset was arrived at by reading the headnotes of all Supreme Court of Canada cases (2,688) from the Court's official website during this 31-year period to determine which involved the adjudication of a charter right and the application of the *Oakes* test. For more detail, see Chapter 2.

The **Polish** sample includes all judgments rendered in the time period of 2010–15 in which the Constitutional Tribunal applied the proportionality test as part of its decision, either using the word 'proportionality' (or its modalities) or explicitly referring to the general limitation clause (Article 31(3) of the Constitution). The selection of cases was based on a case-by-case study of all judgments in the defined time frame (329 cases). For more detail, see Chapter 5.

The **South African** sample includes all Supreme Court cases in which the court both found that some government conduct limited constitutional rights and went on to consider whether the limitation was justifiable in terms of section 33 of the interim Constitution or section 36 of the 1996 Constitution, beginning with *S v Makwanyane & Another* 1995 (3) SA 391 (CC). The sample was reached based on an initial reading of all decisions (703) handed down by the Constitutional Court in the relevant time period. For more detail, see Chapter 3.

[64] The fact that our study only goes up to a certain point of time is a further limitation: In Poland, for example, the case law sample only includes cases until 17 November 2015, i.e., shortly before the governing PiS party had completed its political assault on the Constitutional tribunal, effectively ending its independence and impartiality. It is therefore possible, if not probable, that the application of the proportionality doctrine has since changed.

Table 0.1 *Number of cases and time frame of the case sample in each jurisdiction*

| Court | Number of cases | Years |
|---|---|---|
| Federal Constitutional Court of Germany | 114 | 2000–17 (18 years) |
| Supreme Court of Canada | 120 | 1986–17 (31 years) |
| Constitutional Court of South Africa | 101 | 1995–17 (22 years) |
| Supreme Court of Israel | 161 | 2006–15 (10 years) |
| Constitutional Tribunal of Poland | 100 | 2010–15 (4.5 years) |
| Supreme Court of India | 98 | 2004–16 (13 years) |

we chose not to prioritize a uniform time span for all countries. However, being cognizant of the limitations this may raise, we offer the issue of time as a potential perspective for future research designs.

The cases in each country database were coded according to several variables, including the contexts in which PA is applied; the rights limited in the proportionality cases; the contested measures to which proportionality is applied; the final outcomes of the analysis at each stage and of the PA overall; the frequency of termination of the analysis after failure as opposed to continuation of the analysis; the use of negative signalling at the different stages of the analysis; and the frequency of skipping stages. The main focus of the quantitative comparative analysis was on the function of the internal multi-stage mechanism of the doctrine, i.e., the relationship and division of labour between the subtests. Since our main research question concerns how courts utilize the multi-stage doctrine in practice, our coding follows the courts' self-definition of the structure of their analysis.[65]

[65] Put differently, we categorized the different stages based on the court's proclamation of the stage it was applying, rather than on a critical interpretation of the reasoning applied at each stage. Thus, even if reasoning at what the court described as the strict proportionality stage included arguments pertaining to the worthiness of the purpose as the basis for failure, the quantitative coding considered this failure to have been at the strict proportionality stage. Similarly, even if the discussion of alternatives at the least restrictive means test included balancing language, this was coded as the necessity stage, if that was how the court structured it.

This coding method has several advantages: from a methodological point of view it increases the reliability of the coding since it is based to a larger extent on objective cues provided in the text of the judgment than on the coder's substantive interpretation of the content. Furthermore, it provides an unobstructed reflection of the way the decision is structured by the court itself, which is better suited to our research question pertaining to the courts' application of the multi-stage doctrine.[66]

In order to simplify the data and to achieve the highest level of comparability across countries, we applied two types of aggregation to the data: the first was an aggregation of different justices' opinions, so that the coding was based on the majority opinion.[67] The second concerned cases where a single court decision included multiple applications of proportionality. In such cases the decisions were aggregated into a single coding.[68]

Based on the quantitative findings, the qualitative research dimension involved a detailed doctrinal and hermeneutical analysis of the selected proportionality case law.[69] The qualitative analysis followed a detailed questionnaire, resulting in a common structure for all the country chapters, constructed for maximum comparability on main issues across the six countries included in this book. Each of the country-based chapters opens with a brief introduction of the legal and institutional context, and continues with an overview of the structure of PA in that jurisdiction, the

[66] While we recognize the legitimacy of alternate approaches to coding, such as Petersen's approach based on the content of the arguments regardless of the labels and divisions created by the court, considering the focus of our research question on the relationship between the doctrine's theory and utilization in practice, we attributed importance to the labels provided by the court itself.

[67] While in some countries coding minority justices separately would have provided additional data on the application of proportionality by the majority as opposed to the minority, the added complexity involved, as well as the differences between the countries in terms of the centrality and meaningfulness of minority opinions dissuaded us from choosing this path.

[68] When all applications of proportionality within a single court decision ended in passing the stages of analysis, the coding simply reflects the aggregated outcome of the entire decision. When some of the applications of proportionality within the decision ended up passing and others failed, the coding reflects the outcome of the failure decisions, considering our focus on the division of labour between the stages, which is reflected most clearly in failure decisions. For more detail on the aggregation method, see detail in the individual country-based chapters.

[69] The qualitative analyses were based on the same sample of cases used for the quantitative database. However, these were enriched by additional cases selected based on their centrality and importance, as inferred primarily by references in secondary literature.

sequential or non-sequential character of the tests, the roles of the different subtests, and the interplay among them. The chapters then go through each of the stages of limitation analysis, beginning with establishing an infringement of a constitutional right, proceeding through requirements prior to PA, and finally addressing the four stages of proportionality – worthy purpose, suitability, necessity, and strict proportionality.

The qualitative analysis looks beyond the formal definition of the stages of proportionality to observe to what extent the court actually applies them. The analysis includes the ways in which courts establish the purpose of the policy, how they deal with multiple purposes and what purposes they consider to be worthy, the extent to which the courts evaluate alternatives and their methods of conducting such evaluations, the level of incorporation of fact-finding and evidence into the framework, the allocation of the burden of proof at each stage, and how the courts act when the factual circumstances are unclear. The country chapters conclude with an overview of measures found to be disproportional and a discussion of what can be learnt from them about disproportional policy-making. In summary, each individual country chapter presents one of the most thorough and empirically grounded analyses of the constitutional practice of proportionality in that jurisdiction, at times exposing gaps between the accepted scholarly view and the actual practice of proportionality in that country.

The book concludes with a comparative chapter that brings together some of the most interesting findings that emerge from the chapters overall, addressing both recurring themes and patterns and points of difference and also assessing some of these differences and their possible ramifications. In particular, the final chapter confronts two central attributes of the proportionality doctrine in the theoretical literature – the sequential structure of the analysis and the conception of a single dominant element – with the empirical and comparative findings. Taking a normative perspective, and inspired by the divergences uncovered between theory and practice, we propose an integrative approach to the application of proportionality and find that several courts already exhibit such tendencies in practice.

1

# Proportionality Analysis by the German Federal Constitutional Court

ANDREJ LANG

## I Introduction

Proportionality is the foundational principle of German law. The notion that governmental measures must be proportional – and thus comply with the requirements of the legal proportionality test – is deeply engrained in German legal and political culture.[1] For the Federal Constitutional Court (hereinafter 'FCC'), it is the central framework to decide fundamental rights cases. There are over two thousand decisions of the FCC alone that explicitly refer to the proportionality principle ranging from the 1950s to today and countless cases by ordinary and specialized courts.[2] Proportionality analysis ('PA') as a decisional framework has been the subject of dozens of books in German legal scholarship.[3] It is

[1] Moshe Cohen-Eliya and Iddo Porat, *Proportionality and Constitutional Culture* (CUP 2013) 156.

[2] In the period between the founding of the Federal Republic of Germany on 23 May 1949 and 31 December 2017, a search with the search engine 'juris' for the term 'proportionality' (in German: 'Verhältnismäßigeit') returns 2,341 decisions of the Federal Constitutional Court and 54,124 decisions of all German courts.

[3] See in particular Ruprecht von Krauss, *Der Grundsatz der Verhältnismässigkeit in seiner Bedeutung für die Notwendigkeit des Mittels im Verwaltungsrecht* (Appel 1955); Peter Lerche, *Übermass und Verfassungsrecht* (Carl Heymanns 1961); Bernhard Schlink, *Abwägung im Verfassungsrecht* (Mohr Siebeck 1976); Lothar Hirschberg, *Der Grundsatz der Verhältnismäßigkeit* (Otto Schwartz and Co 1981); Michael Jakobs, *Der Grundsatz der Verhältnismäßigkeit* (Carl Heymanns 1985); Rainer Dechsling, *Das Verhältnismäßigkeitsgebot* (Franz Vahlen 1989); Walter Leisner, *Der Abwägungsstaat* (Duncker and Humblot 1997); Laura Clerico, *Die Struktur der Verhältnismäßigkeit* (Nomos 2001); Renata Camilo de Oliveira, *Zur Kritik der Abwägung in der Grundrechtsdogmatik* (Duncker and Humblot 2013); Mathias Dumbs, *Die Entwicklung des Verhältnismäßigkeitsgrundsatzes in der Rechtsprechung des Bundesverfassungsgerichts* (Verlag Wissenschaft and Öffentlichkeit 2015); Niels Petersen, *Verhältnismäßigkeit als Rationalitätskontrolle* (Mohr Siebeck 2015); Matthias Jestaedt and Oliver Lepsius (eds), *Verhältnismäßigkeit* (Mohr Siebeck 2015); Alexander Tischbirek, *Die Verhältnismäßigkeitsprüfung* (Mohr Siebeck 2017).

laid down in government handbooks about the legality review of legislative proposals and is taught in law schools across the country. Even in the political arena, references to the proportionality principle are common: Popular German chancellor Angela Merkel regularly references the principle in her public statements.[4]

Germany is also the birthplace of the proportionality principle. It is here where administrative courts in nineteenth-century Prussia first engaged in a primal form of PA and where it was – in collaboration with legal scholars – fully developed to a refined judicial decision-making procedure before it migrated to different legal orders around the world to become 'a foundational element of global constitutionalism'.[5] As a judicial check on state measures, the Prussian administrative courts developed two key doctrines: the formal reservation of law that requires that police measures are explicitly authorized by law, and the substantive proportionality principle that further constrained police measures by subjecting them to a judicially reviewable means-ends analysis.[6] PA hence served as a judicial vehicle to protect the individual sphere from excessive police measures, although a positivist rights conception did not exist at the time.

Notwithstanding this historical precedent, the Basic Law does not contain any textual reference to the proportionality principle. Instead, it is the remarkable product of judicial lawmaking by the FCC who seized the concept of proportionality from Prussian administrative law and introduced it into Germany's post–World War II constitutional realm

[4] Here is a small sample: In several public statements concerning US surveillance by the National Security Agency (NSA) on German soil, Merkel cautioned that in balancing freedom and security, particularly when it comes to data surveillance, 'not everything that is technically feasible should be done'. Summer Press Conference, 19 July 2013, available <www.bundesregierung.de/ContentArchiv/DE/Archiv17/Mitschrift/Pressekonferenzen/2013/07/2013-07-19-merkel-bpk.html>. She stressed that '[t]he end does not justify the means' and that '[t]he principle of proportionality must always be respected'. ibid. In her view, the debate in the United States after the events of 9/11 'had lost sight of the proportionality principle'. ibid. It was 'too much focused on "what is technically feasible" and not on whether "this is still proportionate or not"'. ibid. She argued that 'everything must obey the principle of proportionality'. Giovanni di Lorenzo and Tina Hildebrandt, 'Ich bin mit mir zufrieden' *Die Zeit* (Hamburg, 18 July 2013) <www.zeit.de/2013/29/angela-merkel-interview> accessed 16 December 2019.

[5] Alec Stone Sweet and Jud Matthews, 'Proportionality, Balancing and Global Constitutionalism' (2008) 47 Columbia Journal of Transnational Law 72, 160–61.

[6] For a detailed analysis, see Barbara Remmert, *Verfassungs- und verwaltungsrechtsgeschichtliche Grundlagen des Ubermaßverbotes* (C. F. Müller 1995) 109–66.

'as if it could be taken for granted',[7] in other words: without any detailed elaboration as to its origin. From the establishment of the FCC in 1951 to the 1960s, it is illuminating to observe how the Court proceeded to establish the proportionality principle into German constitutional law. In fact, the three foundational constitutional decisions for the construction of the German constitutional order were all decided at the end of the 1950s. They give a better sense of the different steps that the FCC took to establish PA as the primary mode of constitutional adjudication. They are – in chronological order – *Elfes*, *Lüth*, and *Pharmacy*[8]: *Elfes* stands for an extremely broad conception of the scope of protection of fundamental rights that is conducive to PA because it necessitates a decision on whether the infringement of the protected scope constitutes a fundamental rights violation;[9] *Lüth* conceptualizes fundamental rights as objective principles the harmonization of which necessarily requires some form of balancing;[10] and *Pharmacy* introduces PA as a decisional framework designed to cope with the balancing of competing interests required by the fundamental right of occupational freedom.[11] In combination, these decisions provided the foundation for the thorough constitutionalization of the entire German legal order and for the rise of the proportionality principle.

The aim of this chapter is to analyse the judicial practice of PA in the context of fundamental rights by the FCC today. It does not discuss the normative question of the merits and demerits of PA as a judicial methodology but it seeks to understand how the Court applies PA and, in particular, to identify specific patterns in the judicial practice. Methodologically, this chapter combines qualitative and quantitative elements. It conducts a hermeneutic analysis of the case law that is enriched by a systematically coded quantitative analysis of a robust sample of FCC cases. The sample includes decisions from 1 January 2000 until 31 December 2017 in which the FCC was sitting as (either the First or the

[7] Dieter Grimm, 'Proportionality in Canadian and German Constitutional Jurisprudence' (2007) 57 University of Toronto Law Journal 383, 385.

[8] Before those decisions, the Court had already made sporadic references to the proportionality principle in several cases but without engaging in any systematic analysis that would resemble PA. See for a brief recapitulation of those cases: Eberhardt Grabitz, 'Der Grundsatz der Verhältnismäßigkeit in der Rechtsprechung des Bundesverfassungsgerichts' (1973) 98 Archiv des Öffentlichen Rechts 568, 569 n 1.

[9] Entscheidungen des Bundesverfassungsgerichts BVerfGE 6, 32.

[10] BVerfGE 7, 198.

[11] BVerfGE 7, 377.

Second) Senate with eight judges (as opposed to sitting as Chamber with only three judges) and that contain a variation of the term 'proportionality' in German.[12] Overall, 368 decisions fit these criteria and search terms but most of those decisions were discarded from the quantitative analysis after a careful review because they only use the term 'proportionality' incidentally and do not actually apply the proportionality framework in a fundamental rights context. The ultimate dataset contains 114 FCC cases. Those 114 decisions were coded in multiple dimensions, including subject matter, adjudicated right, contested measure, procedure, final outcome, and the outcome in the various subtests of PA.[13] To put the final dataset into a broader perspective, the FCC published 5,890 decisions during the investigation period from 2000 to 2017,[14] most of them holding constitutional complaints inadmissible, of which 558, or 9.5 per cent, were decisions of the Court sitting as Senate. Decisions rendered by either one of the two Senates should generally be considered to constitute 'hard cases', in which the result is not dictated by constitutional text or precedent.[15] The fact that 368 of 558 of all Senate decisions, or 66 per cent, contain a variation of the term 'proportionality'

[12] The search included the alternative search terms: 'proportionality principle', 'proportionality', 'proportionate', 'disproportionate' as well as the German terms 'Übermaß' and 'Untermaß', which are sometimes used synonymously with proportionality. In other words, a FCC Senate decision was included in the analysis if it contained one of those terms. On the other side, FCC chamber decisions were excluded even if they applied the proportionality framework. Although an analysis of the practice of the three-judge chambers of the Constitutional Court would have been instructive for this analysis of the Court's PA jurisprudence, the combination of the vast amount of chamber cases and the limited decision-making authority of chambers spoke against including chamber decisions in the analysis. The main function of FCC chambers is to handle inadmissible constitutional complaints, which are irrelevant for proportionality because PA presupposes an admissible complaint. While a chamber is also entitled to grant a constitutional complaint and to find a public act unconstitutional, it may only do so if the complaint is patently well founded and the point of law has already been decided by a Senate. Moreover, Section 93c(1) s. 3 provides that a decision that declares a law to be incompatible with the Basic Law shall be reserved to the Senate. See for an analysis of the FCC's chamber-system Georg Hermes, 'Senat und Kammern' in Peter Badura and Horst Dreier (eds), *Festschrift 50 Jahre Bundesverfassungsgericht* (Mohr Siebeck 2001) vol 1, 725–49.

[13] It is important to note that FCC Senate decisions are occasionally not neatly structured into the different subtests of PA, requiring interpretation to determine whether certain passages in the judgment constitute a PA subtest.

[14] Compare homepage of the Federal Constitutional Court at <www.bundesverfassungsgericht.de/SiteGlobals/Forms/Suche/Entscheidungensuche_Formular.html> accessed 16 December 2019.

[15] See for an analysis of this category of cases: Ronald Dworkin, 'Hard Cases' (1975) 88 Harvard Law Review 1057.

but that only 114 of those 368, or 31 per cent, actually apply the proportionality framework is indicative of a widespread use of the term in all fields of constitutional law, beyond fundamental rights.

## II Legal and Institutional Context

If we want to understand the rise of the proportionality principle to the German legal order's foundational principle on a deeper level, it is important to first consider the historical and institutional context of the foundational period of post–World War II Germany. In reaction to the catastrophe of World War II, the establishment of the German constitution, the Basic Law ('BL'), constitutes a 'constitutional moment' that thoroughly transformed Germany's political and legal system.[16] The founding mothers and fathers agreed during their deliberations in the Parliamentary Council in 1948/49 that the legal and institutional arrangements of the Weimar Republic had failed to prevent the Nazis' rise to power. As a consequence, the Basic Law had to be drafted in a way that avoided the institutional pitfalls of the Weimar Republic. Above all, the guiding objective in drafting the Basic Law was to find a new constitutional order in which the disaster of World War II could never be repeated.

In response to that challenge, the drafters grounded the Basic Law in a firm commitment to human rights and established a constitutional court as the guardian of the constitution ('Hüter der Verfassung'[17]). In German legal scholarship, this has been described as the rebirth of the German legal order from the spirit of fundamental rights.[18] Emphasizing this choice, the fundamental rights catalogue constitutes the first part of the Basic Law (Articles 1–19). The first provision, Article 1(1) BL, provides

[16] See for the notion of 'constitutional moment' Bruce Ackerman, *We the People*, vol 1: *Foundations* (Harvard University Press 1991) 273. Of course, this categorization may not be without dispute as the foundation of the Basic Law occurred without any revolutionary spirit, which is a critical element in Ackerman's constitutional theory.

[17] This term commonly used to describe a central function of the Federal Constitutional Court took centre stage in the famous scholarly dispute between Hans Kelsen and Carl Schmitt about which institution would be better suited to act as guardian of the constitution: a constitutional court or the President of the Weimar Republic. Carl Schmitt, *Der Hüter der Verfassung* (Duncker and Humblot 1931); Hans Kelsen, 'Wer soll der Hüter der Verfassung sein?' (1930/31) 6 Die Justiz 576.

[18] Rainer Wahl, 'Die objektiv-rechtliche Dimension der Grundrechte im internationalen Vergleich' in Detlef Merten and Hans-Jürgen Papier (eds), *Handbuch der Grundrechte in Deutschland und Europa*, vol 1: *Entwicklung und Grundlagen* (C. F. Müller 2004) 745.

emphatically that '[h]uman dignity shall be inviolable'. In stark contrast to the constitution of the Weimar Republic, in which the legal status of fundamental rights was limited to non-enforceable guidelines, Article 1(3) BL states expressly that the 'fundamental rights shall bind the legislature, the executive and the judiciary as directly applicable law' and thus establishes a new hierarchy between fundamental rights and legislation.[19] The so-called eternity clause of Article 79(3) BL deems the principles laid down in Article 1 BL unamendable and hence entirely removes them from the disposition of the political process.[20]

The framers of the Basic Law made the conscious choice to assign to the FCC the task to protect fundamental rights. While judicial review was not without precedent in pre–World War II Germany,[21] the establishment of the FCC in the Basic Law and its endowment with sweeping powers of review is unprecedented. In contrast to the United States and Israel, there was a broad consensus at the constitutional convention at Herrenchiemsee and in the Parliamentary Council that a powerful constitutional court was needed for the new constitutional order to enforce the Basic Law.[22] The constitution is the supreme law of the land and the FCC is provided with a clear mandate to declare laws that violate the Basic Law unconstitutional and void.

### *A The Expansion of the Court's Powers*

Although the FCC's extensive jurisdiction indicates that the Basic Law vested the Court with remarkable powers, the Court itself played a vital role in expanding its powers from the moment of its establishment by giving meaning to the constitutional order established by the Basic Law and putting fundamental rights at centre stage. The outstanding status

19 Article 20(3) BL establishes the hierarchical supremacy of the constitution over legislation in general by binding the 'legislature' to the 'constitutional order'.

20 For an analysis of the intricacies of the eternity clause in German constitutional law, see Ulrich Preuss, 'The Implications of Eternity Clauses: The German Experience' (2001) 44 Israel Law Review 429.

21 For an overview of nascent forms of judicial review in German history before 1949, see Claus Bönnemann, *Die Beilegung von Verfassungskonflikten vor der Zeit des Grundgesetzes* (Frank and Timme 2007).

22 For an analysis of the genesis of the Federal Constitutional Court, see Heinz Laufer, *Verfassungsgerichtsbarkeit und politischer Prozeß* (Mohr Siebeck 1968) 35–93; Karlheinz Niclauß, 'Der Parlamentarische Rat und das Bundesverfassungsgericht' in Robert van Ooyen and Martin Möllers (eds), *Handbuch Bundesverfassungsgericht im politischen System* (2nd ed., Springer 2015) 191–204.

that the Court enjoys in the German legal order today was by no means predetermined by the provisions of the Basic Law, nor does it signify the crowning of the 'Rechtsstaat', as is sometimes suggested.[23] Instead, the FCC's remarkable institutional success story was the historically contingent result of the particular circumstances that the Court encountered and used to its own advantage in post-war Germany.[24]

The common narrative that successful newly established constitutional courts first slowly and carefully build up their institutional authority before they render politically consequential judgments only holds true in part with respect to the FCC.[25] While the Court has been careful in the first years of its existence not to declare important federal statutes unconstitutional, it positioned itself in a self-confident and status-conscious manner as a key institution in Germany's new political system already soon after starting its operations in 1951.[26] Before the end of the 1950s, the Court had rendered the arguably three most important constitutional decisions from the point of view of constitutionalist construction, the aforementioned *Elfes*, *Lüth*, and *Pharmacy* decisions. In driving the process of constitutionalization of the German legal order, the Court exploited a significant moral gap. The old institutions and traditions of the Nazi regime, but also of the German empire and the authoritarian Prussian State, were largely weakened and discredited.[27] In contrast, the Court appeared as a new and modern institution that contributed to liberalizing German society and to reconciling the German people with the concept of democracy – albeit by benefiting from those very predemocratic attitudes and the deep-seated trust in authority and

[23] Karl Schachtschneider, *Res publica res populi* (Duncker and Humblot 1994) 932.

[24] Christoph Schönberger, 'Anmerkungen zu Karlsruhe' in Matthias Jestaedt and others (eds), *Das entgrenzte Gericht* (Suhrkamp 2011) 9, 40–48.

[25] See for this narrative Tom Ginsburg, *Judicial Review in New Democracies* (CUP 2003) 65–89.

[26] In a famous dispute with the federal government in 1952 concerning the FCC's status and organizational autonomy, the Court challenged the supervision of the Ministry of Justice regarding the Court's budget and staff arguing in a memorandum that '[t]he Federal Constitutional Court in its capacity as the guardian of the Constitution is a supreme constitutional organ, equipped with the highest authority, on par with the Bundestag, the Federal Council, the Federal Chancellor, and the Federal president'. See Gerhard Leibholz, 'Status-Bericht vom 21.3.1952' (1957) 6 JöR 120. The Court's request was granted and Chancellor Adenauer, who had been a member of the Parliamentary Council himself, meekly admitted that 'this is not what we had in mind' (with the establishment of the Court). See Uwe Wesel, *Der Gang nach Karlsruhe* (Karl Blessing 2004) 76.

[27] Schönberger (n 24) 9, 43–44.

expertise.[28] The role of PA in the expansion of the Court's powers should also not be underestimated: it provides the Court, as we will see in more detail, with a high degree of flexibility to make the best possible decision under the particular circumstances of a case, considering the political and institutional context, largely uninhibited by the constraints of legal methodology and past decisions.

### *B A Powerful Court and Its Limits*

Today, the FCC is undoubtedly one of the most powerful constitutional courts in the world. In a legalistic political culture, the FCC is 'at the epicenter of the Federal Republic's political system'.[29] Unlike the US and the Israeli Supreme Court, which claimed the power of judicial review without express constitutional authorization, the FCC's power of constitutional review is firmly embedded in the text of the Basic Law as the framers of the Basic Law decided, following the catastrophe of World War II, to vest the Court with truly remarkable competencies. Over the course of its existence from 1951, the Court had until the end of 2017 found 748 statutes and administrative regulations unconstitutional.[30] On the basis of the eternity clause of the Basic Law, the Court confidently assumed the power to even subject constitutional amendments to judicial review.[31] In addition, the FCC has creatively extended its conception of fundamental rights beyond defensive or negative rights against the state and derived positive state duties from the fundamental rights.[32] All this has not hurt the popularity of the Court that has consistently been confirmed in opinion polls as the most popular governmental institution in Germany.[33]

[28] ibid.

[29] Donald Kommers, 'The Federal Constitutional Court in the German Political System' (1994) 26 Comp Polit Stud 470, 471.

[30] Federal Constitutional Court, *Jahresstatistik 2017* (February 2018) 31 <www.bundesverfassungsgericht.de/SharedDocs/Downloads/DE/Statistik/statistik_2017.pdf> accessed 16 December 2019.

[31] BVerfGE 109, 279 [309]–[26].

[32] As a result, the state's refusal to perform certain actions or to grant certain benefits was deemed a fundamental rights infringement. In its first Abortion decision, the Court derived from the state's positive duty to protect the life of the unborn the legislative obligation to make abortion – apart from certain exceptions – a crime. BVerfGE 39, 1.

[33] Georg Vanberg, *The Politics of Constitutional Review in Germany* (CUP 2005) 97–99. In an extensive public opinion poll concerning the perception of the Federal Constitutional Court among the population in Germany, the Allensbach Institute found in 2012 that the

At the same time, the popular strand of legal scholarship that criticizes the 'global expansion of judicial power'[34] tends to overlook the inherent structural limitations of courts. Possessing neither sword nor purse,[35] they are comparatively still the 'least dangerous branch' of government[36] as they are thoroughly dependent on others to activate their jurisdiction to decide a case and to implement their decisions. If German legal scholars call the FCC the 'delimited court'[37] or suggest that the proper name for the German Federal Republic would be – based on the location of the FCC – the 'Karlsruhe Republic',[38] they give the impression of a political system dominated by its constitutional court. This is not the case. The Court is embedded within a larger political-institutional context that limits its powers and which the Court must consider if it does not want to jeopardize its continued impact on the political process.[39] And today, the role of the Court is noticeably more controversial in German legal academia than it was in the 1980s and 1990s when the Court was largely admired by legal scholars and defended against criticism.[40] At its core, however, the legitimacy of constitutional review

Court is the governmental institution in which the population has the most trust (75 per cent), followed by the Federal President (63 per cent), the Bundesrat (41 per cent), the Bundestag (39 per cent), and the Federal Government (38 per cent). See Renate Köcher, 'Institut für Demoskopie Allensbach' Frankfurter Allgemeinen Zeitung (Frankfurt, 22 August 2012) 30 <www.ifd-allensbach.de/fileadmin/kurzberichte_dokumentationen/August12_Bundesverfassungsgericht_01.pdf> accessed 16 December 2019.

34 See, e.g., Neal Tate and Torbjörn Vallinder (eds), *The Global Expansion of Judicial Power* (New York University Press 1995).

35 Alexander Hamilton, 'Federalist Paper No. 78' in David Wootton (ed), *The Essential Federalist and Anti-Federalist Papers* (Hackett Publishing Company 2003) 283, 284.

36 Alexander Bickel, *The Least Dangerous Branch* (2nd ed., Yale University Press 1986).

37 Matthias Jestaedt and others (eds), *Das entgrenzte Gericht* (Suhrkamp 2011).

38 Gerhard Casper, 'The "Karlsruhe Republic"' (2001) 2 German Law <germanlawjournal.com/wp-content/uploads/GLJ_Vol_02_No_18_Casper.pdf> accessed 16 December 2019.

39 For example, in the 1970s when the Court declared several important legislative projects of the ruling social-liberal coalition unconstitutional, a vivid discussion about the limits of constitutional review arose that arguably led the Court to turn down its level of judicial activism. Similarly, the Court's famous *Crucifix* decision (BVerfGE 93, 1) provoked a wave of protests that prompted Judge *Dieter Grimm*, one of the five justices in the majority, to respond to the criticism with a public letter titled 'Why a Judicial Ruling Merits Respect' printed in a major newspaper. Dieter Grimm, 'Unter dem Gesetz - Warum ein Richterspruch Respekt verdient' *Frankfurter Allgemeine Zeitung* (18 August 1995) 29. Translation from Donald Kommers and Russell Miller, *The Constitutional Jurisprudence of the Federal Republic of Germany* (3rd ed., Duke University Press 2012) 584.

40 In a surprising move that speaks volumes about the recent criticism against the Court, the Minister of Interior, Thomas de Maizière, recently met with several law professors for

remains unquestioned. Notwithstanding the confidence of the judges, their holistic style of reasoning and their occasional lack of political sensibilities, their decisions are generally characterized by a judicial ethos of restraint and they are determined to stay within the realm of the law (as opposed to politics) whatever that may be.

### C *The Ways in Which Cases Are Brought before the FCC*

The German system of constitutional review is representative of the centralized continental European model of judicial review: The specialized constitutional court's jurisdiction is limited to deciding constitutional issues and it alone has the power to set aside legislation.[41] In addition, the Court is to a certain extent separated from the ordinary judiciary and its decisions have *erga omnes*-effect. This institutional design choice can be explained by two factors: first, against the backdrop of the implication of the judiciary in the crimes of the Nazi regime, it ensured that a new, unencumbered institution carried out the delicate task of constitutional review; second, this choice seemed prudent in order to ensure the uniform interpretation of constitutional law when considering that Germany has five separate judicial branches, each with a supreme court at the top of the judicial hierarchy.[42]

The FCC's character as a specialized constitutional court is reflected in the various proceedings that establish the Court's jurisdiction. Arguably, the four most significant proceedings provided for in the Basic Law today are the constitutional complaint procedure in Article 93(1) No. 4a of the Basic Law, the concrete judicial review procedure in Article 100(1), the abstract judicial review procedure in Article 93(1) No. 2, and the Organstreit proceedings in Article 93 I Nr. 1 BL.[43]

dinner to discuss ways to limit the Court's power. It is unlikely, however, that a major backlash will ensue from these controversies. See Reinhard Müller, 'Berliner Gedankenspiele zur dritten Gewalt' *FAZ* (3 April 2014) 4.

41 Louis Favoreu, 'Constitutional Review in Europe' in Louis Henkin and Albert Rosenthal (eds), *Constitutionalism and Rights* (Columbia University Press 1990) 38, 41.

42 These are the administrative, social, fiscal, labour, and ordinary courts, the latter of which are divided into civil and criminal courts.

43 The Basic Law provides for many more procedures that can establish the jurisdiction of the FCC, including controversies between the federal government and states, Article 93(1) No. 3 BL, or between different states, Article 93(1) No. 4 BL, constitutional complaints of municipalities against legislative acts, Article 93(1) No. 4b BL, and temporary injunctions. Moreover, the FCC has exclusive jurisdiction for prohibiting political parties, Article 21(2) BL, and for impeachment of the Federal President, Article 61 BL.

The constitutional complaint is the most important constitutional procedure. During the investigation period from 2000–2017, on average 5,827 constitutional proceedings overall were initiated before the Court each year, 5,664, or 97.2 per cent, of which were constitutional complaints.[44] A constitutional complaint entitles any person to access the constitutional court alleging that one of his or her fundamental rights or equivalent rights has been infringed by a public authority. Although only 2 per cent of all constitutional complaints succeed,[45] no other constitutional procedure similarly provides redress against fundamental rights violations. In my dataset that contains all Senate decisions in a fundamental rights context from 2000 until 2017 that apply PA in a systematic manner, 94 out of 114 cases, or 82 per cent, were initiated with the constitutional complaint procedure.

The constitutional complaint procedure is both a blessing and a curse for the Court. It is a blessing because it is a significant factor for the popularity of the Court: every individual whose fundamental rights have been infringed can go to the Court and receive individual justice. Although the great majority of constitutional complaints are deemed inadmissible, they provide the Court with an extensive repository of cases from which it can choose and serve, to some extent, as a functional equivalent to the US Supreme Court's writ of certiorari-procedure. It is a curse because it generates a substantial case overload and ties up significant resources to dispose of all those cases. Several reforms, such as the introduction of an inter-chamber system,[46] were enacted to address this issue but more far-reaching reforms were not taken out of fear of adversely impacting the popularity of the Court.[47]

The abstract judicial review procedure, which may only occur after the completion of the legislative process and the promulgation of the law under review, is particularly paradigmatic for a centralized system of

[44] See Federal Constitutional Court, *Jahresstatistik 2017* (n 30) 9, for data between 2017 and 2008; and Federal Constitutional Court, *Jahresstatistik 2009* (February 2010), 9. <www.bundesverfassungsgericht.de/SharedDocs/Downloads/DE/Statistik/statistik_2009.pdf> accessed 16 December 2019. for data between 2008 and 2000.

[45] See Federal Constitutional Court, *Jahresstatistik 2017* (n 30) 20–21.

[46] The great majority of constitutional complaints are disposed off by chambers of three justices. See above for more details on the FCC's chamber-system at Section II, n 12.

[47] In 1998, a Commission on Relief for the Federal Constitutional Court, set up by the Federal Ministry of Justice, issued a report that contained numerous proposals to ease the Court's case-load. See Federal Ministry of Justice (ed), *Bericht der Kommission zur Entlastung des Bundesverfassungsgerichts* (1998). However, most of the reform proposals were never enacted.

judicial review. In this procedure, the Federal Government, a state government, or one fourth of the Members of the Bundestag are entitled to file an application with the Court if there are disagreements or doubts concerning the compatibility of a federal or state law with the Basic Law.[48] It hence allows the Court, as the term 'abstract' indicates, to review the constitutionality of statutes, in full and independently of the facts of a particular case, and to resolve constitutional issues before they reach the specialized courts. In this highly visible and politicized procedure, political institutions enjoy privileged standing. It also expresses the Basic Law's clear preference that such politically sensitive controversies are resolved through the Court on the basis of the Basic Law. However, only very few fundamental rights cases reach the Court through that procedure. From 2000 to 2017, the abstract judicial review procedure only incurred 40 out of all constitutional cases, which amounts to only slightly more than two per year, and to only 0.04 percent overall.[49] In the dataset, 5 out of 114, or 4 per cent, of all cases are abstract review cases.

More, but still not many, cases come to the FCC through Organstreit proceedings that provide for a judicial procedure to resolve disputes between constitutional organs before the constitutional court.[50] Similar to the abstract judicial review procedure, Organstreit proceedings are characterized by privileged standing to particular federal institutions or parts thereof.[51] From 2000 to 2017, 98 Organstreit proceedings were initiated, which are, on average, 5.4 cases per year or 0.09 per cent of all cases.[52] In the dataset, 2 out of 114 decisions, or 2 per cent, were Organstreit proceedings.

Finally, the concrete judicial review procedure is designed to link the constitutional court with the judiciary. Ordinary and specialized courts are required to stay the proceedings and to obtain a decision from the Court if they conclude that a law on whose validity its decision depends is

48 See Article 93(1) no. 2 BL.

49 See Federal Constitutional Court, *Jahresstatistik 2017* (n 30) 9, for data between 2017 and 2008; and Federal Constitutional Court, *Jahresstatistik 2009* (n 44) 9, for data between 2008 and 2000.

50 See Article 93(1) no. 1 BL.

51 According to § 63 BVerfGG, applicants and respondents may only be the Federal President, the Bundestag, the Bundesrat, the Federal Government, and such parts of these organs that are vested with own rights pursuant to the Basic Law or the rules of procedure of the Bundestag and Bundesrat.

52 See Federal Constitutional Court, *Jahresstatistik 2017* (n 30) 9, for data between 2017 and 2008; and Federal Constitutional Court, *Jahresstatistik 2009* (n 44) 9, for data between 2008 and 2000.

unconstitutional. Over time, the FCC has raised the requirements for specialized court referrals.[53] As a result, only 535 cases of all cases from 2000 to 2017, roughly 30 per year, or 0.51 per cent of all cases, resulted from concrete judicial review.[54] In the dataset, 13 of 114 decisions, or 11 per cent, are concrete judicial review cases. The most important factor for the reduced role of the concrete judicial review procedure is that the Federal Constitutional Court prefers the constitutional complaint as the main procedural linkage to the judiciary. As we have seen, this procedure requires an alleged fundamental rights violation by a public authority. The Court interprets 'public authority' to include not only administrative or legislative acts but also judicial decisions. As procedural law requires for the admissibility of a constitutional complaint that the complainant has exhausted all available legal remedies in advance (*see* § 90(2) of the Federal Constitutional Court Act, hereinafter FCCA), the great majority of complaints are formally directed against judicial decisions even if the measure effectively contested is a legislative or administrative act. In the dataset, 80 out of all 114 FCC decisions, or 70 per cent, were initially decided by another court.[55]

This procedural linkage to the judiciary brings at least two distinct advantages for the FCC. First, it relieves the Court of many evidentiary issues because almost all constitutional cases brought before the Court have already proceeded through trial courts and a system of appeals where questions of evidence were already resolved before the case comes to the FCC. As a result, evidentiary issues play less of a role before the FCC than before ordinary courts. The reason for this heavy reliance on the fact-finding of ordinary and specialized courts is that the FCC is simply not a court for judging the facts.[56] As a specialized constitutional court, the FCC's focus is on resolving specific constitutional law issues

[53] Werner Hein, *Verfassung und Verfassngsgerichtsbarkeit im Vergleich* (Mohr Siebeck 2014) 192.

[54] See Federal Constitutional Court, *Jahresstatistik 2017* (n 30) 9, for data between 2017 and 2008; and Federal Constitutional Court, *Jahresstatistik 2009* (n 44) 9, for data between 2008 and 2000.

[55] For the purpose of having uniform data categories across jurisdictions that enable cross-country comparison, judicial decisions in the dataset that applied a legislative statute or upheld an executive measure were not coded as judicial but based on the underlying legislative or executive act.

[56] Oliver Lepsius, 'Die maßstabsetzende Gewalt' in Matthias Jestaedt and others (eds), *Das entgrenzte Gericht* (Suhrkamp 2011) 159, 206–07. Many of the provisions in the FCCA relating to evidence were drafted against the background of the dependence of the FCC on the evidence gathering of ordinary and specialized courts. For example, section 27

that arise based on the facts determined by the ordinary and specialized courts. Second, the linkage via the constitutional complaint procedure provides the FCC with a remarkable amount of control over the proper application of fundamental rights through the judiciary and serves as the procedural means for the constitutionalization of the entire legal order. Over the years, the FCC has also developed into a type of 'super-court of last resort' ('Superrevisionsinstanz') within the judicial system that determines and controls the legal practice in many areas of law. Although the Court has repeatedly denied this characterization and emphasizes that it is only competent to review violations of specific constitutional law ('spezifisches Verfassungsrecht'), the Court's overall impact on various areas of non-constitutional law should not be underestimated, particularly in administrative law.[57] The Court does not only give rough directions within the judicial system but its intra-chamber system enables the Court to review the constitutionality of countless specialized court decisions.

## III Structure of Limitation Analysis

### *A The Place of Proportionality in the Structure of Fundamental Rights*

In the doctrinal structure of German fundamental rights theory, PA is at the core of the last stage of a three-stage inquiry into whether a fundamental right has been violated. In the first stage, the Court determines the scope of protection ('Schutzbereich') of a fundamental right. The second stage concerns the question of whether governmental actions are considered to constitute an infringement of a fundamental right's protected

FCCA provides that all courts and administrative authorities shall afford the Federal Constitutional Court legal and administrative assistance. In addition, files of initial proceedings shall be directly submitted to the Court upon request. Moreover, section 33(1) FCCA entitles the Court to stay proceedings until a case pending before another court is terminated if the findings or the decision of such court might be of relevance to its own decision. According to section 33(2) FCCA, the Court may base its decision on the factual findings of a final judgment of another court in which the truth was to be established ex officio.

57 A famous assessment taught in most administrative law courses describes 'administrative law as concretized constitutional law', which implies that administrative courts tend to apply the principles and certain legal methods developed by the FCC. This famous statement was first made by the then-president of the Federal Administrative Court, see Fritz Werner, 'Verwaltungsrecht als konkretisiertes Verfassungsrecht' (1959) Deutsches Verwaltungsblatt 527.

scope ('Eingriff'). The scope of protection of fundamental rights is construed in a very broad and inclusive manner, and so is the notion of infringement. In other words, most human activities are encompassed by the scope of protection of a fundamental right in one way or another and most governmental actions that impair the exercise of that activity are deemed to constitute an infringement. Consequently, the full weight of the inquiry is on the third stage where the Court reviews whether the infringement of the fundamental right is justified ('Rechtfertigung'). It is fair to say that almost all governmental acts that interfere with individual liberties become fundamental rights issues and are subject to justification.[58] Although rights limitations analysis in Germany is predominantly geared towards assessing justifications for fundamental rights infringements, the Court generally does not brush over the scope of protection and infringement stages but only proceeds to the justification stage if the activity under review falls within a fundamental right's protected scope and if there has been an infringement.

Most fundamental rights provisions contain limitation clauses ('Schranken') that explicitly authorize the state to restrict the exercise of a fundamental freedom but require that this limitation is effectuated through or on the basis of a legislative statute ('Gesetzesvorbehalt'). While this formal requirement of a specific legislative enactment ensures the participation of parliament and that the executive only acts on the basis of laws, it does not impose any substantive limitations on the power of the legislature to limit the exercise of fundamental rights. This is where PA comes into play, which carries the main burden of fundamental rights protection in Germany.[59] PA limits the limitations that the state may impose on a fundamental right ('Schranken-Schranke') and ultimately determines whether a fundamental right has been violated or not.

### B *The Basic Contours of the Proportionality Test*

How exactly is PA applied in Germany? What are the different stages of analysis and how important are they? Over time, the FCC has – in close collaboration with legal scholarship – given PA a definite dogmatic

[58] Mattias Kumm, 'The Idea of Socratic Contestation and the Right to Justification: The Point of Rights-Based Proportionality Review' (2010) 4 Law and Ethics of Human Rights 141, 144.

[59] Grimm, 'Proportionality in Canadian and German Constitutional Jurisprudence' (n 7) 386.

structure within the context of fundamental rights and formed PA into an integrated and systematic test.[60] In this analytical framework of a four-part test (or three-part, depending on whether the first stage is considered distinctive), the FCC reviews step-by-step the legitimate purpose, the suitability, the necessity, and the proportionality in the strict sense of a measure.

First, the government measure is required to pursue a legitimate purpose ('legitimes Ziel'). In German constitutional scholarship, this inquiry into the 'legitimacy' of the measure is generally considered not to constitute a substantial hurdle and to primarily serve the purpose of preparing the ensuing means-ends comparison that lies at the heart of PA by identifying the objectives pursued by the government. However, a measure may already fail the PA test at this stage if the Court does not deem the state measure to pursue a worthy purpose. Second, the measure adopted by the government must be suitable to advance its objective ('Geeignetheit'). In constitutional scholarship, the suitability stage is deemed to be a technical stage that is a necessary precondition of the necessity test. Third, the judge reviews whether the measure is necessary for the achievement of the legitimate purpose in the sense that no equally suitable but 'less-restrictive means' are available ('Erforderlichkeit'). While some scholars in the 1970s demanded that the necessity test receive a more prominent role within the proportionality framework in lieu of the strict proportionality test,[61] this stage too is not considered to be a substantial hurdle. It is the strict proportionality stage that is at the core of the German conception of proportionality. In this final stage, which is called proportionality in the strict sense ('Verhältnismäßigkeit im engeren Sinn'), appropriateness ('Angemessenheit'), or reasonableness ('Zumutbarkeit'), the Court leaves the strictly understood means-ends analysis behind and broadens the scope of analysis by balancing the benefits gained by the contested measure and the costs incurred by the infringement of the fundamental rights.[62] According to the definition used by the Court, a measure is disproportionate when 'the resulting limitation of the affected

[60] Lepsius credits a legal textbook on fundamental rights (see Bodo Pieroth and Bernhard Schlink, *Grundrechte Staatsrecht II* (C. F. Müller 1985)) for having contributed significantly to the canonization of PA into a uniform framework. Oliver Lepsius, 'Die Chancen und Grenzen des Grundsatzes der Verhältnismäßigkeit' in Matthias Jestaedt and Oliver Lepsius (eds), *Verhältnismäßigkeit* (Mohr Siebeck 2015) 1, 16.

[61] See for a good overview: Schlink (n 3) 127–53.

[62] Grimm, 'Proportionality in Canadian and German Constitutional Jurisprudence' (n 7) 393–94.

individual's rights *clearly outweighs* the increased protection of legal interests which the measure attains'.[63] Dieter Grimm once observed that '[t]he vast majority of laws that failed to pass the proportionality test in Germany do so at the . . . [final stage, the balancing stage stricto senso]'.[64]

### C Contexts of Proportionality Analysis

The quantitative analysis on which this chapter is based takes into consideration the application of PA regarding different policy fields, different fundamental rights, and different measures being scrutinized. The data show the prevalence of PA in German constitutional law: it is applied across subject matters and across fundamental rights guarantees. It is used to review legislation and judicial decisions, federal and state measures.

Figure 1.1 shows the widespread application of PA in all branches of law and in various policy fields. In the 114 cases included in the dataset, PA was applied in the branch of public law in 66 cases, or 58 per cent,[65] in the realm of private law in 33 cases, or 29 per cent,[66] and in criminal law in 15 cases, or 13 per cent.[67] The data shows that the majority of PA cases are in the branch of public law from which the proportionality doctrine historically originated. But PA is also prevalent in private law and is used in criminal cases as well. This indicates that the application of PA is not limited to the traditional constellation of the intervening administration ('Eingriffsverwaltung') but occurs in all types of contexts in which fundamental rights are affected.

PA is also applied in numerous policy fields without a particular subject matter attracting the bulk of PA cases. PA was applied most in the field of health, social security, and pension law (19 cases, or 17 per cent), followed by commercial and economic regulation (15 cases, or 13 per cent), criminal law and criminal procedure (15 cases, or 13 per

[63] BVerfGE 90, 145 [146].

[64] Grimm, 'Proportionality in Canadian and German Constitutional Jurisprudence' (n 7) 389.

[65] Cases that were categorized as public law fall into the subject matters of commercial and economic regulation, health, social, and pension law, animal protection law, fiscal and tax law, national security law, administrative court procedure, constitutional and parliamentary law, education law, land, planning, and development law, and public holiday law.

[66] The private law branch includes cases in the subject matters of family law, labour law, legal services, corporate law, copyright law, real estate law, and traditional civil law such as torts and inheritance law.

[67] The branch of criminal law comprises substantive criminal law and criminal procedure.

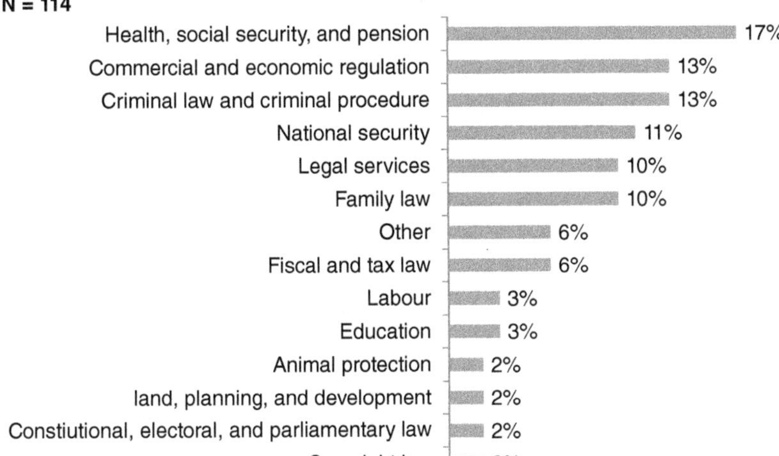


**Figure 1.1** Proportionality cases by subject matter[68]

cent), national security (12 cases, or 11 per cent), legal services (11 cases, or 10 per cent), and family law (11 cases, or 10 per cent). Rather than pointing to a particular centre of gravity, the data show the dispersion of PA across very different subject matters. Cases in the fields of criminal law and procedure and national security, and to some extent in commercial and economic regulation, tend to resemble the classical scheme of the intervening state and the individual rights-bearers. Health, social security, and pension law cases typically concern distributive state actions ('Leistungsverwaltung'). Legal services and family law constitute highly legalized, judicially driven policy fields in which the FCC adjudicates in a targeted manner by requiring limited modifications to particular provisions.

[68] The category of commercial and economic regulation is composed of all fields of economic administrative law ('Wirtschaftsverwaltungsrecht'). It includes laws in the fields of gambling, shop closing time, passenger transportation, public procurement, association, foreign trade, agriculture, energy, and telecommunications. The category of health, social security, and pension law comprises laws in the areas of medical supply, retirement, health insurance and other public insurances, social benefits, pharmacy, medical and psychiatric treatment, and anti-smoking. The category of national security includes laws in the fields of police law, telecommunications, and finance law. By contrast, criminal procedure laws designed to protect national security were exclusively coded as criminal procedure. The category of family law contains laws relating to gender identity, custody, personal statute, paternity, and traditional family law.

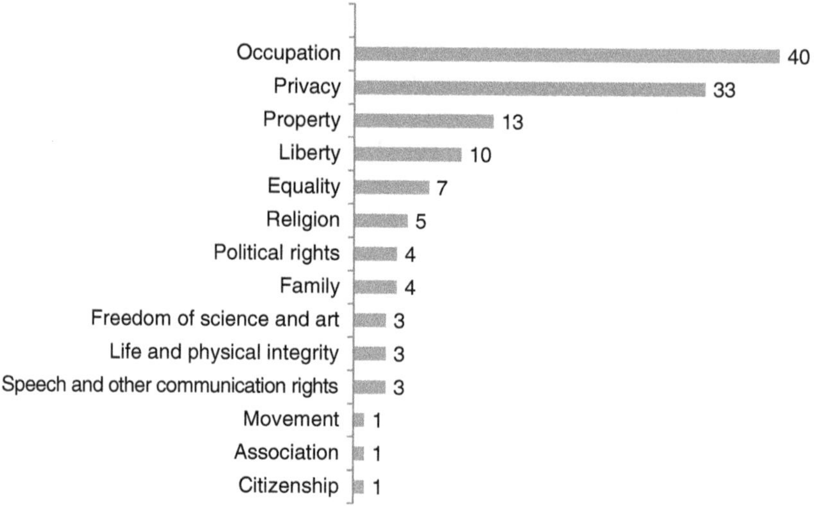


**Figure 1.2** Rights triggering proportionality analysis[69]

Figure 1.2 lists all fundamental rights that were analysed within the PA framework in the database and shows how often each right was analysed.[70] The data reveal on the one hand that PA is applied across almost all fundamental rights guarantees. Notable exceptions to which the Court generally does not apply PA are (i) procedural due process, (ii) access to courts set forth in Article 19(4) BL, (iii) certain criminal defendant rights such as *nulla poena sine lege* laid down in Article 103(2) BL, and (iv) the human dignity guarantee clause of article 1(1) BL for which the Court favours a strictly categorical form of reasoning. In addition, the Basic Law does not contain provisions regarding economic, social, and cultural rights. On the other hand, the data show concentration of PA in the contexts of the freedom of occupation, Article 12(1) BL and privacy rights. The PA framework was applied to either occupation or privacy rights or both in almost

[69] For purposes of comparability, the rights to personality (22), to privacy of correspondence (8), and to inviolablity of home (3) were grouped into the broader category of privacy. Liberty comprises the freedom of action (6) and the freedom of the person (4). Family rights comprise the distinct rights to marriage (2) and to parenthood (2). Speech and other communication rights comprise both freedom of speech (2) and of broadcast (1). Political rights comprise the rights to assembly (2) and to a free mandate (2).

[70] The number of fundamental rights (129) is higher than the number of cases (114) because, on a few occasions, the Court applied PA to more than one fundamental right within the same case.

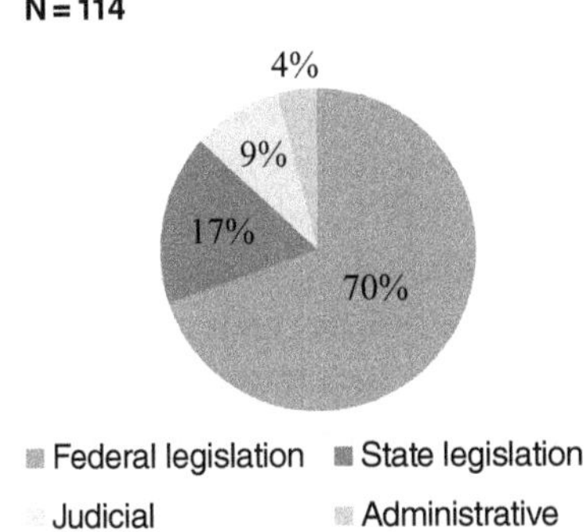


**Figure 1.3** Proportionality cases by contested measure

two thirds of all cases, specifically in 73 out of all 114 cases, or 64 per cent.[71] These data confirm the close correlation between PA and freedom of occupation in German constitutional adjudication. PA was first introduced as a systematic test in the *Pharmacy* judgment of 1958 concerning Article 12 (1) BL and it was initially primarily developed and refined in the context of occupational freedom. Today, the freedom of occupation still represents the fundamental right to which the proportionality test is, by far, most often conducted.

The data presented in Figure 1.3 show the spread of PA across different public acts, namely federal legislation, state legislation, judicial decisions, and administrative acts.[72] The data suggest that the Court sitting as a Senate to decide 'hard cases' is predominantly preoccupied with resolving constitutional issues regarding legislation, especially the

[71] In one case, the Court reviewed the compatibility of a federal statute with both guarantees, the freedom of occupation and the right to personality. See BVerfGE 128, 1.

[72] It is important to note that the delimitation of those public acts is based on substance and not on formal categories. In other words, the quantitative analysis only includes those acts to which the Court substantively applied PA. Judicial decisions were not included if they only served as a procedural vehicle to bring a case before the Court and if they were not addressed in the proportionality reasoning of the Court. The reason for this coding is that the great majority of FCC decisions formally review a judicial decision even though the substance of the review relates to legislative or administrative acts. Contested measures are only coded as judicial decisions if no prior administrative or legislative acts were being challenged. These are typically cases of horizontal clashes between private litigants and cases concerning the constitutionality of a statute and the constitutionality of the judicial application in the particular case of the statute in the particular case. In the latter type of cases, the legislation and the judicial decision counted half each. In contrast, if the complainant challenged a judicial decision that upheld a rights-limiting administrative decision, this was coded as an administrative act.

compatibility of federal statutes with the Basic Law. Although the FCC is, by virtue of a broadly conceived constitutional complaint procedure,[73] entitled to review legislative, administrative, and judicial acts so long as they raise constitutional issues, the focus of its review, at least insofar as Senate decisions are concerned, lies on legislation.[74] In 98 out of all 114 cases, or 86 per cent, the public acts reviewed by means of PA in the dataset were legislative statutes, 79, or 69 per cent, of which were federal statutes. A plausible explanation for this concentration of Senate activity on federal legislation is that fundamental rights issues regarding judicial decisions and administrative regulation and policy are likely resolved in most cases by the FCC's chamber system and by ordinary or specialized courts, implementing the constitutional standards by the FCC. It is important to note, however, that the Court's practice of proportionality had not always been concentrated on legislation but is the result of an evolution in the application of proportionality. Oliver Lepsius argues that the early case-law in the 1950s and 60s concerned predominantly administrative acts and judicial decisions.[75] It was not until the 1970s that federal legislation increasingly became subject to the Court's proportionality review.[76]

While the spread of PA across different public acts is indicative of a concentration on federal legislation, the rate of findings of unconstitutionality is substantially higher with respect to state legislation than regarding federal legislation. While the Court only found federal statutes to violate fundamental rights in 31 out of 79, or 39 per cent, of all cases included in the quantitative analysis, it struck down 14 out of 19, or 74 per cent, of the state statutes.[77] There are different possible explanations for these starkly different rates concerning federal and state legislation. They could be explained by a higher quality of lawmaking on the federal level where more personal resources and expertise in the ministerial bureaucracy and in parliament are available. They could also

[73] See Section II.

[74] While this study does not purposefully exclude the constitutional review of administrative acts from the analysis, the restriction of the quantitative analysis on Senate decisions has this effect because the great majority of public acts reviewed by the FCC Senates are statutes.

[75] Lepsius, 'Die Chancen und Grenzen des Grundsatzes der Verhältnismäßigkeit' (n 60) 14.

[76] ibid.

[77] This quantitative finding requires qualification. The dataset on which the finding is based is limited to cases in which the Court sitting as Senate applied PA in a fundamental rights context. As a consequence, the dataset does not include cases in which federal or state legislation was struck down on other grounds than with the proportionality test. The rate regarding state legislation is therefore based on a small sample of only 19 decisions.

be explained by the assumption that federal constitutional courts and supreme courts are institutionally inclined to support an allocation of powers in favour of the federal level even though they are set up as impartial arbiters to 'neutrally' adjudicate disputes between the different levels of government.[78]

### D *Division of Labour between the Different Proportionality Subtests*

As we have seen, the proportionality test is an integrated analytical framework that reviews the compatibility of a public act with a fundamental right on the basis of four different subtests, the worthy purpose, the suitability, the necessity, and the strict proportionality test, and that each approaches this issue from a different angle. If we seek to understand how PA works in judicial practice, it is necessary to analyse the division of labour between the different proportionality subtests and their respective roles within the broader proportionality framework.

The division of labour between the different subtests of the proportionality framework is best empirically analysed by looking at the cases in which the Court deemed the scrutinized measure disproportional, i.e. the measure violated a fundamental right.[79] Overall, the Court upheld the scrutinized measures in 56 out of all 114 cases in the dataset, or 49 per cent, and in 58 out of all 114 cases, or 51 per cent, it struck the measure down. It is important to note that in all the cases in the dataset in which legislation was concerned, there was not a single instance in which the Court found the entire statute or law to be unconstitutional.[80] In other words, the scrutinized legislation was only partially disproportional.[81]

[78] Christoph Möllers, 'Legalität, Legitimität und Legitimation des Bundesverfassungsgerichts' in Matthias Jestaedt and Others (eds), *Das entgrenzte Gericht* (Suhrkamp 2011) 281, 340–41.

[79] The reason is that in cases that pass the PA, at least the strict proportionality stage always passes. Therefore, these cases do not contribute to the question of division of labour between the different stages.

[80] This is in line with the general reluctance of the FCC to strike down a statute or a law in its entirety. The Court has since its inception found 748 statutes and administrative regulations (or parts thereof) to violate the constitution but only in 86 instances, or 11.5 per cent, did it declare the entire act unconstitutional. Since 2010, there was not a single statute, federal or state, that was struck down entirely. Federal Constitutional Court, *Jahresstatistik 2017* (n 30) 31.

[81] Against this background, the outcome of a case was coded as 'disproportional' even if only one out of several sections of a law or one out of several scrutinized measures were found unconstitutional.

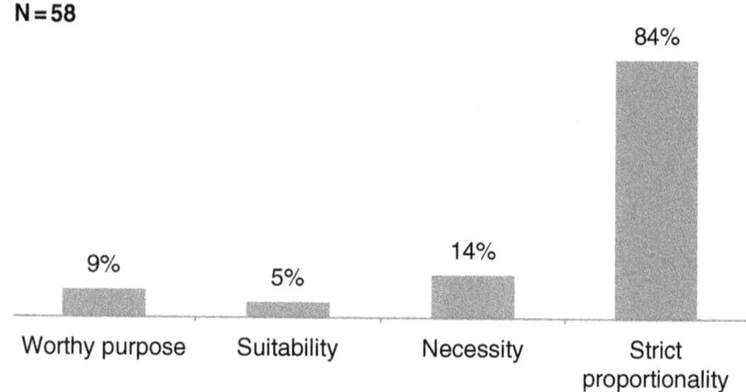


**Figure 1.4** Frequency of failure at each stage of proportionality analysis[82]

Figure 1.4 shows the frequency with which the Court reached a judgment of disproportionality with regard to each subtest of proportionality. These data show in quantitative terms the dominance of the final strict proportionality test in German proportionality practice. It demonstrates that in the great majority of cases deemed disproportional, in 49 out of 58, or 84 per cent, the Court makes this determination with the final test. In contrast, it is infrequent that a law fails the worthy purpose, suitability, or necessity tests

## *E Deviations from the Standard Sequential Model of Proportionality*

Notwithstanding a broad consensus on the structure of PA among the legal community in Germany, there are significant differences between PA in the books and PA in action, especially with regard to the sequential character of PA. In legal scholarship, there is a strong formal commitment to processing sequentially through the different subtests and, consequently, to reviewing, step-by-step, the worthy purpose, the suitability, the necessity, and the strict proportionality of a governmental measure. According to this sequential approach, each subtest is reached only after the previous test has been passed. If a measure fails, for example, the necessity stage, the inquiry does not proceed to the next stage, the strict proportionality test. In legal scholarship, this sequential approach is

[82] In Figure 1.4, the total sum of all percentage numbers is larger than 100 per cent because one measure can fail more than one stage of proportionality.

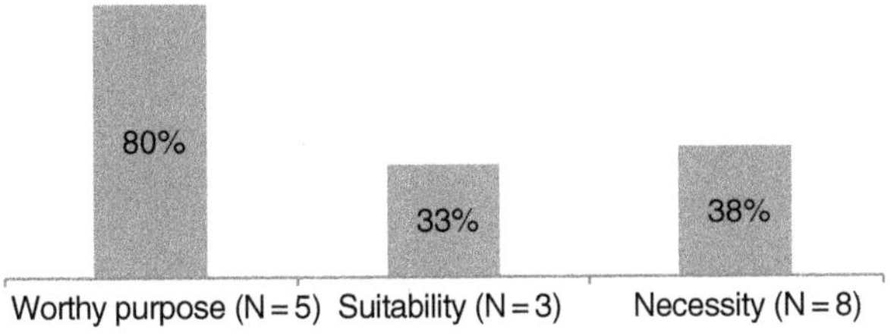


**Figure 1.5** Termination of proportionality analysis after failure

credited as having a 'disciplining and rationalizing effect'.[83] Although the Federal Constitutional Court would presumably not contest the sequential character of PA, there are three distinct phenomena in the Court's case-law that deviate from the sequential model of proportionality. First, the Court continues to perform the subsequent subtests even if it had already deemed a law to fail a previous stage.[84] Second, it skips the suitability and the necessity stages to jump straight to the strict proportionality stage.[85] Third, it refrains from making a final determination at an earlier stage before entering the strict proportionality stage.[86]

Figure 1.5 analyses the first phenomenon by looking at the likelihood that the PA ends, as the sequential model suggests, after it has failed one of the stages of proportionality. This analysis excludes all cases that failed for the first time at the strict proportionality stage because this is the final stage at which the analysis ends by definition. The remaining sample is small: there are only 15 cases in the dataset overall in which the Court found a measure to fail at a stage of proportionality other than the last stage. In 7 out of those 15 cases, or 47 per cent, the PA continued nonetheless.[87] These data indicate that the strict proportionality test is of special importance to the Court when it justifies a finding of unconstitutionality. In the majority of cases in which it had already deemed a measure to fail at the suitability or the necessity stage, the Court preferred to continue its analysis and to express its ultimate determination with the

[83] See Grimm, 'Proportionality in Canadian and German Constitutional Jurisprudence' (n 7) 397.
[84] See Figure 1.5.
[85] See Figure 1.6.
[86] See Section VIII.A.2.
[87] Specifically, PA continued in 1 out of 5 cases, or 20 per cent at the worthy purpose stage, in 2 out of 3 cases, or 67 per cent, at the suitability stage, and in 5 out of 8 cases, or 62.5 per cent, at the necessity stage.

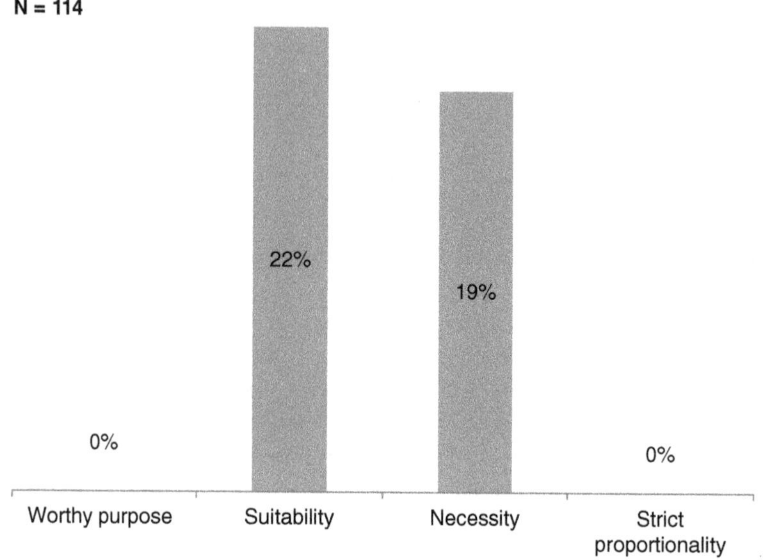


**Figure 1.6** Frequency of each stage being skipped in the analysis

strict proportionality test.[88] This unease with striking down a measure solely on the basis of the suitability and the necessity test is further bolstered by four additional cases in which the Court identified a serious problem with the measure at issue at the suitability and/or the necessity stages but nevertheless refrained from finding the measure to fail at those stages and, instead, made the fail judgment at the stage of proportionality in the strict sense.[89]

The diminished role of the suitability and necessity stages in the proportionality framework as applied by the FCC is further demonstrated by the phenomenon that the Court regularly skips the suitability and the necessity stages to jump straight to the strict proportionality stage. The reason for skipping a stage is arguably that the Court does not deem this stage to contribute meaningfully to solving the case at hand. Figure 1.6 shows the frequency with which a stage is being skipped in PA. While the worthy purpose and the strict proportionality stages were never skipped, the suitability stage was skipped in 25 out of all 114 cases in the dataset, or 22 per cent, and the necessity stage in 22 out of 114

[88] See for more detail Sections V.C, VII.C, and VIII.A.

[89] See BVerfGE 103, 1; BVerfGE 110, 33; BVerfGE 127, 132; BVerfGE 138, 296.

cases, or 19 per cent. Overall, the Court skipped either the suitability or the necessity stage in 28 out of all 114 cases in the dataset, or 25 per cent. Put differently, the Court determines in every fourth proportionality case that either the suitability or the necessity stage is not helpful for its PA.

A phenomenon similar to skipping a stage is that of glancing over a stage. It means that the Court deals with this stage in only a cursory fashion of not more than three sentences. The contribution of this glancing over a stage to PA is very limited. It closer resembles the 'ticking off' of a checkpoint than a meaningful analysis. In 32 out of all 114 decisions in the dataset, or 28 per cent, the Court glanced over the suitability stage and in 28 out of all 114 cases, or 25 per cent, it glanced over the necessity stage. If we combine the phenomena of skipping and of glancing over a stage, we see that the suitability stage was either entirely skipped or only glanced over in 57 out 114 cases, or 50 per cent, and the necessity stage in 50 out of 114 decisions, or 44 per cent.

Although the phenomena of skipping and glancing over a stage are similar in that they are indicative of the diminished role of the suitability and necessity tests, they reveal differences when analysing the outcomes of the cases. When the Court skips the suitability or the necessity stage, it will ultimately conclude that the scrutinized measure is disproportional in roughly three out of four of this type of cases.[90] By contrast, in cases in which the Court only glanced over the suitability or the necessity stages, this rate drops to slightly more than one third of the relevant cases.[91] Roughly speaking, the probability that a measure is struck down is almost twice as high after the suitability or necessity stages were skipped as when they were glanced over. This finding is especially significant from the perspective of a claimant that views each stage of proportionality as an opportunity to strike down the challenged right-limiting measure. If the measure ultimately passes the scrutiny of a PA, it is questionable to entirely skip a subtest that could have, at least in theory, led to the measure being struck down. The data suggest that the Court is at least subliminally aware of this problem. Overall, the Court found the scrutinized measure to pass the proportionality test in only 6 out of all 28 cases,

90 In 19 out of the 25 cases, or 76 per cent, in which the Court skipped the suitability stage, and in 16 out of the 22 cases, or 73 per cent, in which it skipped the necessity stage, the scrutinized measure was ultimately struck down by the Court.

91 The FCC only struck down the scrutinized measure in 13 out of all 32 cases, or 41 per cent, in which it had glanced over the suitability stage and only in 10 out of all 28 cases, or 36 per cent, in which it had glanced over the necessity stage.

or 21 per cent, in which either the suitability or the necessity stage was skipped.

While the reasons for deviating from the standard sequential model of PA can be manifold, the empirical analysis of the Court's case-law suggests that the Court deviates from sequentiality because it considers the strict proportionality test the stage that is best suited to address the issues posed by the particular case under review. The Court is especially reluctant to exclusively rely upon the suitability and necessity stages to strike down public acts. In cases in which the FCC deems the scrutinized measure to be unconstitutional, it prefers to express this determination with the strict proportionality test.[92]

## IV Limitation of a Fundamental Right

According to the prevailing dogmatic structure in German constitutional law, the infringement of a fundamental right requires that a human activity is covered by the scope of protection of that right (Section A) and that there is an infringement into that protected scope (Section B). The protected scope defines what activity is protected and the notion of infringement specifies against whom and against what the fundamental right provides protection. While limitation clauses authorize infringements of fundamental rights, they are themselves subject to constitutional limits (Section C).

### *A Scope of a Fundamental Right*

The FCC has traditionally construed the scope of protection broadly. In the famous *Elfes* decision,[93] the Court reconstructed the right to general freedom of action in Article 2(1) of the Basic Law into a 'catch all' provision that protects trivial activities such as feeding pigeons in public squares[94] and riding horses in public woods.[95] The Court's decision of 1957 concerns the case of Wilhelm Elfes, a political office holder and a member of the conservative CDU, who had publicly voiced harsh criticism of the politics of rearmament and reunification domestically and abroad pursued by Chancellor Adenauer, who also happened to be the

[92] See for more detail Sections V.C., VII.C, and VIII.A.
[93] BVerfGE 6, 32.
[94] BVerfGE 54, 143 [147].
[95] BVerfGE 39, 1; BVerfGE 88, 203.

CDU chairman at the time.[96] In reaction to Mr Elfes' political activities, the responsible authorities, based on Section 7(1) of the Passport Act, refused to renew his passport to prevent him from travelling to other countries, arguing that Mr Elfes' political activities abroad endangered public interests.[97] After losing before the Federal Administrative Court, Mr Elfes filed a constitutional complaint contending that this refusal violated his freedom of movement guaranteed by Article 11(1) BL. A problem with Elfes' claim was that Article 11 BL only guarantees the right to move freely inside but not outside (German) federal territory.

Although the FCC ultimately rejected Mr Elfes' constitutional complaint, the interesting part of the FCC's *Elfes* decision from the point of view of constitutionalist construction is how the Court created a fundamental right for the protection of Mr Elfes' concerns. In a shrewd strategic move, the FCC chose to interpret 'the right to free development of his personality' provided in Article 2(1) of the Basic Law as a subsidiary catch-all fundamental right to 'general freedom of action', in other words: as 'a right to do or not do as one pleases',[98] that provides fundamental rights protection for almost all human activity against state interference. While Bills of Rights are historically contingent documents that typically do not provide comprehensive protection, the *Elfes* decision transformed the Basic Law's fundamental rights section into 'a comprehensive system of rights protection without any gaps'.[99] The *Elfes* judgment illustrates an artful interplay of judicial reasoning and remedy,[100] as the Court combines a sweeping account of seamless fundamental rights protection, a masterpiece in constitutionalist construction, while, at the same time, upholding the administrative decisions to proscribe a German citizen from travelling to foreign countries to voice critical political opinions.[101] Complementing its *Elfes* approach concerning

[96] In post-war Germany, the questions of rearmament and reunification were among the most divisive political issues. In a controversial step, Mr Elfes participated in an all-German declaration with GDR representatives criticizing the 'revival of German militarism' as a threat to Europe.

[97] Section 7(1) of the Passport Act provided at the time that '[a] passport must be refused if facts justify the supposition that (a) the applicant threatens the internal or external security or other vital interests of the Federal Republic of Germany or one of the German states. . . '.

[98] Mattias Kumm, 'Constitutional Rights as Principles: On the Structure and Domain of Constitutional Justice' (2004) 2 International Journal of Constitutional Law 574, 582.

[99] Werner Heun, *The Constitution of Germany* (Hart Publishing 2011) 207.

[100] See Section III.

[101] Schönberger (n 24) 35.

Article 2(1), the Court also interprets the general equality clause of Article 3(1) very broadly by requiring legislative distinctions to be justifiable independently of specific grounds of discrimination.[102]

As a result, the scope of protection has become a threshold stage at which the 'hard cases' adjudicated by the First or Second Senate do not fail. There is only 1 case out of the 114 cases in the dataset, or 1 per cent, in which the Court denied that the activity at issue was protected by the scope of a fundamental right.[103] In 2 out of all 114 cases, or 2 per cent, the Court refrained from making a determination as to whether the protected scope was affected.[104] In all three of those cases, the Court proceeded with its PA and upheld the federal legislation under review. There is not a single case in the dataset in which the Court entirely brushed over the protected scope stage to directly proceed to PA.[105] The Court puts emphasis on properly defining the scope of protection and grapples with the criteria laid down in the various fundamental rights provisions such as 'property' in Article 14(1) BL, 'assembly' in Article 8 (1) BL, 'correspondence' in Article 10(1) BL, and 'home' in Article 13(1) BL. While the protected scope is hence a necessary analytical step in deciding fundamental rights cases, it only takes up a few sentences in most FCC cases.[106] The only cases in which the Court engages substantively with the scope of protection and discusses this stage over several paragraphs are landmark cases in which it defines the basic contours of a fundamental right.[107] Questions regarding the importance or the core of a right are generally addressed at the strict proportionality stage.[108]

102 Kumm, 'The Idea of Socratic Contestation and the Right to Justification' (n 58) 144.

103 BVerfGE 116, 96 [123]–[24]. It is necessary to point out, however, that the dataset is based on search terms for proportionality and therefore excludes cases that do not contain these search terms. The dataset is hence geared towards excluding cases that already failed the protected scope stage because the dogmatic structure of fundamental rights in Germany requires that an activity falls under the protected scope of a fundamental right before PA commences.

104 BVerfGE 110, 370 [393]; BVerfGE 122, 374 [391].

105 In the three cases in which the Court refrained from making a determination, it briefly discussed the issue of scope of protection and did not entirely brush over this stage.

106 See, e.g., BVerfGE 121, 175 [190]–[91]; BVerfGE 122, 89 [105]–[06]; BVerfGE 123, 90 [102]; BVerfGE 133, 277 [316]–[17].

107 See, e.g., BVerfGE 7, 198 [207]–[09] (freedom of expression); BVerfGE 30, 173 [188]–[91] (freedom of arts); BVerfGE 65, 1 [41]–[43] (right to informational self-determination); BVerfGE 69, 315 [342]–[47] (freedom of assembly); BVerfGE 120, 274 [297]–[309] (right to the guarantee of the confidentiality and integrity of information technology systems); BVerfGE 128, 226 [250]–[54] (freedom of assembly).

108 For an exception to this rule, see BVerfGE 110, 33 [52].

Distinctions between a right's core and its periphery are only peripherally touched upon when the Court justifies a broadly conceived uniform scope of protection that covers both the core activity and related activities that are both equally protected by the fundamental right.[109]

The consequence of the Court's broad conceptualization of the scope of protection is that almost any state intervention becomes a fundamental rights issue for which the FCC is competent and which individuals are entitled to bring before the FCC by filing a constitutional complaint.[110] As an institutional side-effect, the Court's power to review the constitutionality of public acts, legislative, executive, or judicial, becomes extremely broad. But if the scope of protection is interpreted virtually seamlessly, the protection provided cannot be absolute and not every infringement of that right will result in a fundamental rights violation, as Mr Elfes had to experience himself in his case before the Court.[111] As a consequence, it becomes necessary to find an alternative mechanism to decide which infringements are justified and which are not. In German fundamental rights adjudication, this vacuum is filled by PA, which ultimately decides in most cases whether a fundamental rights infringement constitutes a violation. Every public act that affects individuals is, in principle, subjected to the requirement of justification and the FCC is entitled to review the proportionality of all governmental action.

This generally broad interpretation of the protected scope makes sense conceptually because, as Kumm succinctly put it, '[i]f all you have in virtue of having a right is a position whose strength in any particular context is determined by proportionality analysis, there are no obvious reasons for defining narrowly the scope of interests protected as a

[109] In the context of the right to artistic freedom pursuant to Article 5(3) BL, the Court distinguishes between the work produced, the core artistic activity, and the effect produced, the presentation and dissemination of the work of Article 5(3). See, e.g., BVerfGE 119, 1, deeming the publisher to be entitled to rely on Article 5(3) BL by noting that '[t]he guarantee of artistic freedom covers the "work produced" and the "effect produced" by artistic creation in the same way' and that '[n]ot just the artistic activity (work produced), but also the presentation and dissemination of the work of art are important for the encounter with the work as an enterprise that is likewise specific to art'. ibid 21–22. In the context of the freedom of occupation, the Court distinguishes between the periphery of the exercise of a vocation and the core of the choice of a vocation. Both are covered by the protected scope of Article 12(1) BL. See BVerfGE 7, 377 [401].

[110] Heun (n 99) 180.

[111] See Section IV.A.

right.'[112] Defining the scope narrowly would exclude a big chunk of government measures from the outset from the requirement to justify the fundamental rights infringements in terms of proportionality. On the other hand, this reconstruction of Article 2(1) of the Basic Law into a 'catch all' provision also has downsides that were eloquently articulated by Judge Grimm. In his dissenting opinion in the *Equestrian* case, he blamed the majority on the Court for 'limitless' fundamental right protection and the 'trivialization of fundamental rights'.[113] He further argued that it is "neither historically nor functionally the purpose of the basic rights to put every conceivable kind of human conduct under their special protection" and that "[r]iding in the forest does not enjoy any fundamental right protection".[114] Rather than engaging in PA, Grimm concluded that the majority should have dismissed the case for not falling into any fundamental right's protected scope.[115] Furthermore, he warned about the procedural consequences of that approach, in particular the "escalation [in the use] of the constitutional complaint".[116]

Grimm presents strong arguments in favor of defining the scope of protection narrower. The broad *Elfes* construction provides every affected complainant with the opportunity to initiate a full-blown review of the infringing governmental act that includes review of competencies and procedure because infringements of a fundamental right are only constitutional so long as they are formally and materially in harmony with the Basic Law. Moreover, the broad understanding of the protected scope contributes significantly to the Court's high workload. It also shifts the judicial analysis to the justification stage and, therein, to the strict proportionality level where the Court's decision-making is less predictable than it would be if the protected scope was defined more narrowly.

On the other hand, however, if certain types of activities are entirely exempted from a fundamental right's protected scope, thorny

[112] Kumm, 'The Idea of Socratic Contestation and the Right to Justification' (n 58) 150–51.

[113] BVerfGE 80, 137 [165]–[66] (dissenting opinion Judge Grimm). The case concerned a state law that restricted the riding of horses in public woods to specifically designated trails. The complainant, the owner of several horses, challenged that law before the FCC, arguing that it interfered with his general freedom of action pursuant to Article 2(1) BL. Although the Court's majority ultimately upheld the state law, it held that horse riding in public woods falls into the protected scope of the complainant's freedom of action, that the law intruded on that freedom, and, consequently, reviewed the law's constitutionality and, in the process, conducted a PA.

[114] ibid 160–61.

[115] ibid 167.

[116] ibid 168.

demarcation issues tend to arise. It is also hard to contest that the Court's approach improves fundamental rights protection at least to some extent. Although the Court ultimately rejects most 'trivial' fundamental rights claims, the onerous state measure is still subjected to constitutional review and is therefore opened to different, more rights-friendly considerations than they would be otherwise. If certain cases were excluded from the protected scope, there would be no requirement to justify intruding governmental acts in the language of proportionality and, hence, there exists a risk that a practice evolves that lacks the necessary fundamental rights sensitivities.

That said, the main effect of the Court's broad construction is arguably not the improvement of fundamental rights protection but the expansion of the Court's power. By increasing the scope of protection and thus the scope of constitutional review, the Court increases the level of control over the practice of the specialized and ordinary courts and lays the foundation for the constitutionalization of the entire legal order. The Court uses a private attorney model in the sense that individuals are empowered to challenge all types of government measures before the Court that would otherwise have escaped the Court's jurisdiction, as the latter is – as any court – a passive institution that can only act if someone brings a claim.

### *B What Triggers the Infringement of a Fundamental Right?*

Conceptually, the notion of infringement of a fundamental right has an important hinge function between the protected scope and the justification stage.[117] It links the protected individual activity with the requirement to justify state interferences.[118] Traditionally, the concept of infringement was designed to encompass targeted state measures that directly interfered with the individual fundamental right position by means of command and coercion. This 'classical' notion of infringement had four elements: (i) the measure was an imperative command or prohibition, (ii) it was intentional, (iii) direct, and (iv) constituted a legal act.[119]

[117] Franz-Joseph Peine, 'Der Grundrechtseingriff' in Detlef Merten and Hans-Jürgen Papier (eds), *Handbuch der Grundrechte* (vol 3, C. F. Müller 2009) § 57, 87, 114. See also Herbert Bethge, 'Der Grundrechtseingriff' in *Veröffentlichungen der Vereinigung der Deutschen Staatsrechtler* (vol 57, de Gruyter 1998).

[118] Peine (n 117) § 57, 114.

[119] ibid [120].

In the process of transformation from the liberal state to the modern welfare state, the German courts significantly softened these requirements. The FCC does not limit its broad interpretation to the protected scope but also deems various governmental measures (and omissions) as infringements. Today, the notion of infringement also includes measures that are not directly aimed at the rights holder but that nonetheless have – an often unintended – indirect and factual detrimental effect on the fundamental right position.[120] It is sufficient that the measure is detrimental to the rights holder and attributable to the state in some form. The point behind this generous understanding is that these measures require a justification and therefore trigger PA. As a result, however, the notion of infringement largely loses the filter function in fundamental rights analysis that it once had.

Even if the Court did not positively find an infringement, it proceeded with the proportionality test to make the ultimate determination at the strict proportionality stage. In 3 out of 114 cases, or 3 per cent, the Court refrained from making a determination at the infringement stage, and in 2 out of 114 cases, or 2 per cent, the Court held that the measure at issue did not constitute an infringement. Nevertheless, the Court continued its examination with the ensuing PA in all five of those cases. Interestingly, the Court decided in all five cases that the measures being scrutinized were constitutional. This suggests that the Court feels uneasy about simply letting a fundamental rights claim fail at the infringement stage. It prefers to explain its reasoning by means of the strict proportionality test. In the same vein, the Court typically also does not establish the degree of severity of the infringement of the fundamental right at the infringement stage but prefers to conduct this evaluation at the strict proportionality stage.[121] The marginalization of the infringement stage is also reflected in the fact that the FCC typically deals with this stage in a brief manner – significantly briefer than with the scope of protection.[122]

## C *Limitation of Fundamental Rights*

In German constitutional law, the limitation of fundamental rights is effectuated through an interplay between limitation clauses that explicitly provide for the possibility of limitations enacted by statute

[120] ibid [129].
[121] See, e.g., BVerfGE 107, 299 [314]–[15] and [319]–[22]; BVerfGE 124, 43 [58], [62].
[122] See, e.g., BVerfGE 104, 337 347]; BVerfGE 128, 226 [254]–[55].

('Schranken') and certain constitutional limits upon these rights limitations ('Schranken-Schranken').

### 1 Limitation Clauses

The idea that fundamental rights have limits and that they can be limited on a regular basis to pursue public policy objectives is explicitly laid down in the Basic Law's constitutional limitation clauses. Although Germany's constitution does not contain a general limitation clause that specifies the requirements under which the limitation of a fundamental right can be justified, most fundamental rights provisions contain their own limitation clause. The Basic Law lays down three distinct ways to deal with limitations: fundamental rights with ordinary limitation clauses, fundamental rights with qualified limitation clauses, and fundamental rights without any limitation clause.

First, ordinary limitation clauses, such as Article 12(1) s. 2 BL or Article 2(2) s. 3 BL, authorize the legislator to restrict the fundamental right but only through or on the basis of a legislative statute. They do not provide for any additional requirements other than the existence of a statute. It is generally recognized that every restriction of a fundamental right requires the specific enactment of a parliamentary statute. The FCC has developed a doctrine according to which the 'essential' decisions in a law cannot be delegated to the executive but have to be made by parliament ('Wesentlichkeitstheorie').[123] The Court generally considers infringements into fundamental rights as essential decisions the formal justification of which requires legislation. Without such a legislative authorization, any interference with the individual freedom is unconstitutional. Moreover, the Court will strike down right-infringing laws that are based on a procedural mistake even though it would easily pass the proportionality test because the rights infringement is minor.[124] As a result, every 'law without the necessary legislative authority or in contradiction to procedural constitutional rules is an unconstitutional invasion

[123] See BVerfGE 49, 89. In addition, Article 80(1) BL provides that the delegation of legislative power to the executive requires that '[t]he content, purpose and scope of the authority' is specified in the law. In other words, a vague blanket authorization that enables the executive to act largely free of statutory constraints will not meet constitutional standards. See the detailed analysis of BVerfGE 8, 274 [305]–[22].

[124] The Court introduced this requirement of legality for rights-infringing laws in the aforementioned *Elfes* decision, holding that the general freedom of action is subject to limitation by any law that procedurally and substantially conforms to the constitution. BVerfGE 6, 32 [41].

of Article 2 I BL'.[125] In the context of every admissible fundamental rights case, the Court will review, amongst others, whether the fundamental right infringement has a sufficient legal basis and whether the federative competencies between the federal government and the states as well as the procedures of the lawmaking body have been observed.

Second, several fundamental rights provisions have so-called qualified limitation clauses, such as Article 5(2) BL, Article 11(2) BL, and Article 14(3) BL, which provide for stricter justification requirements than only the formal requirement of a statute. According to Article 5(2) BL, for example, not all parliamentary laws meet the substantive requirements of the limitation clause but only 'general laws' that are not directed against particular expressions but that are aimed at 'the protection of young persons' and laws protecting the 'right to personal honor'.

Finally, some fundamental rights provisions, such as the freedom of religion in Article 4(1) BL or the guarantees of artistic and scientific freedom in Article 5(3) BL, do not contain any reference about their limitability. With the notable exception of the right to human dignity, however, these textual niceties have not prevented the FCC from providing for the possibility of limitation of these textually unlimited fundamental rights. On the basis of the interpretive principle of the unity of the constitution, the Court argues that a fundamental rights provision must not be seen in isolation because other competing constitutional guarantees would otherwise be impaired.[126] As a result, fundamental rights without limitation clauses underlie the constitutional limitations inherent in the Basic Law ('verfassungsimmanente Schranken der Grundrechte'). In other words, they can be restricted through competing constitutional norms and principles.

In constitutional adjudication, the differences between rights with ordinary limitation clauses, rights with qualified limitation clauses, and rights without limitation clauses are significantly attenuated. The Court interprets the notion of inherent constitutional limitations broadly so that most public interests pursued by legislation that compete with a

[125] Heun (n 99) 206.

[126] The interpretive principle of constitutional unity was already introduced by the Court in its first major decision in the *Southwest State* case. The Court held that '[n]o single constitutional provision may be taken out of its context and interpreted by itself'. To the contrary, '[e]very constitutional provision must always be interpreted in such a way as to render it compatible with the fundamental principles of the constitution and the intention of its authors'. BVerfGE 1, 14 [32]–[33].

textually unlimited fundamental right are encompassed.[127] It has transferred the idea of inherent constitutional limitations to fundamental rights with limitation clauses.[128] And it tends to conduct elements of reasoning that ordinarily occur at the strict proportionality stage in the context of its analysis of qualified limitations clauses.[129] By attenuating structural and textual differences between the different fundamental rights provisions, the FCC has contributed to the harmonization of all fundamental rights guarantees into a largely uniform model of limitations analysis at the centre of which stands PA.[130]

### 2 Limits of Rights Limitations except Proportionality

The possibility of policy-makers to restrict a right is limited by certain norms and principles; some of them are explicitly set forth in the Basic Law and others, such as the proportionality principle, originate from judicial construction. Doctrinally, these norms and principles are located at the level of justification and, as so-called Schranken-Schranken, impose inherent constitutional limits on rights limitations. Article 19 BL lays down three general requirements that a law infringing upon a right needs to have to be considered constitutional. First, a rights-restricting 'law must apply generally and not merely to a single case' (Article 19(1) s. 1 BL). Second, 'the law must specify the basic right affected and the Article in which it appears' (Article 19(1) s. 2 BL). Third, the law may in no case affect 'the essence of a fundamental right' (Article 19(2) BL).

In the case-law of the FCC, these textual requirements have long faded into constitutional insignificance. In the long history of the Basic Law, it only happened 13 times that a statute was struck down based on the prohibition of private bill legislation laid down in Article 19(1) s. 1 BL.[131]

127 See for a detailed case-law analysis, Hans-Jürgen Papier, 'Vorbehaltlos gewährleistete Grundrechte' in Detlef Merten and Hans-Jürgen Papier (eds), *Handbuch der Grundrechte* (vol 3, C.F. Müller 2009) § 64, 365–404 [¶35]–[¶94].

128 See, e.g., BVerfGE 107, 104 [118]–[20].

129 See, e.g., BVerfGE 124, 300 [321]–[26]

130 This approach has evoked criticism inside the Court. Several justices objected that the differences between different fundamental rights provisions are levelled, the significance of text is reduced in favour of a uniform model of analysis, and that, as a consequence, the protection of fundamental rights is reduced. In particular, they argued that fundamental rights are transformed into balancing factors and that the criteria for balancing are not to be found in the constitution itself but only, on a case-by-case basis, in the judge's balancing judgment. See BVerfGE 69, 1 [57]–[92] (dissenting opinion).

131 See Joachim Lege, 'Verbot des Einzelfallgesetzes' in Detlef Merten and Hans-Jürgen Papier (eds), *Handbuch der Grundrechte* (vol 3, C. F. Müller 2009) § 66, 439–92 [¶31].

The majority of those cases is from the 1950s and 60s.[132] Among all 114 cases included in the dataset, there is only one single case that refers to the issue of private bill legislation.[133] Although the specification or citation requirement in Article 19(1) s. 2 BL is more relevant in constitutional practice, the FCC has consistently limited its scope of application, prompting German constitutional scholars to lament its 'shadowy existence'.[134] In the dataset, there are 8 out 114, or 7 per cent, that review the conformity of a statute with the specification requirement. In 4 out of those 8 cases, or 50 per cent, the statute under review failed this requirement.

Limited relevancy is also the fate of the essence guarantee of Article 19(2) BL. Out of the 114 PA Senate judgments rendered between 2000 and 2017 the essence guarantee is only mentioned in 4 cases, or 4 per cent. In those decisions, the possibility of a violation of this guarantee was succinctly dismissed.[135] The essence guarantee indicates that the drafters of the Basic Law preferred a model of fundamental rights protection that is more akin to the US-style strict scrutiny model, in which more narrowly defined rights function almost as categorical prohibitions, for its wording seems to leave no room for balancing. Interestingly, the Federal Administrative Court and the Federal Court of Justice had advocated such an understanding in the *Pharmacy* case.[136] However, the FCC explicitly rejected this approach in this matter arguing that 'the essence of a fundamental right' could not be an adequate standard of review because 'in no case' is an infringement admissible.[137] Instead, the FCC preferred PA as a decision-making technique and chose to largely neglect Article 19(2) BL. The motives for preferring PA over a categorical approach based on Article 19(2) BL were likely of practical and institutional nature. On the one hand, it is difficult for judges to cope with absolute fundamental rights protection because all constitutional conflicts involve the balancing of competing concerns in some way and decisional flexibility is paramount. On the other hand, the combination of a broad scope of protection and PA significantly increases the FCC's

[132] ibid [¶32]–[¶98].
[133] BVerfGE 143, 246.
[134] Peter Axer, 'Zitiergebot' in Detlef Merten and Hans-Jürgen Papier (eds), *Handbuch der Grundrechte* (vol 3, C.F. Müller 2009) § 67, 493–516, [¶35].
[135] See BVerfGE 109, 133 [155]–[56]; BVerfGE 109, 279 [312]; BVerfGE 115, 118 [164]–[65]; BVerfGE 125, 260 [322].
[136] BVerfGE 7, 377 [407]–[08].
[137] ibid [410]–[11].

institutional influence because it also allows the Court to adjudicate constitutional disputes in which the essence of a fundamental right is not concerned.[138]

In contrast to the limits on rights limitations explicitly set forth in the Basic Law, the judicially constructed Schranken-Schranken are of fundamental importance to German fundamental rights adjudication. Although the proportionality principle is, by far, the most important limit on rights limitations, the general principle of clarity or determinacy also assumes a prominent role in the context of fundamental rights adjudication. It requires that 'the clarity and determinedness of the provision ensure that the person concerned can realise the legal situation and can adjust to possible burdensome measures'.[139] In the dataset, the compatibility of the contested law with the clarity principle is reviewed in 28 out of 114 cases, or 25 per cent. In 9 out of those 28 cases, or 32 per cent, the Court did not only strike the scrutinized statute because it failed the proportionality test but, in addition, for a violation of the clarity principle.[140] At the same time, the likelihood that the Court strikes down legislation with the clarity principle is, at a rate of 32 per cent, substantially lower than with the proportionality test that has, as we have seen, a failure rate of 51 per cent.

The principle of clarity and the proportionality principle resemble each other in that they both set the concern for a fundamental right in proportion to a competing concern. In the context of proportionality, this concern is the public interest that the right-infringing law pursues; in the context of clarity, it is the degree of clarity that a right-infringing law is required to have.[141] Both principles differ in that proportionality is geared towards producing individual justice, while clarity is geared towards legal certainty.[142] In most constellations, individual justice and legal certainty represent opposing values. However, this has not stopped the FCC from incorporating the clarity principle into the proportionality

[138] *Grimm* rightly notes that 'it would be incompatible with the importance attributed to individual freedom that the legislature be entitled to limit fundamental rights until it reaches the ultimate borderline of its very essence'. Grimm, 'Proportionality in Canadian and German Constitutional Jurisprudence' (n 7) 387.

[139] BVerfGE 120, 274 [295]–[96].

[140] For a list of applicable FCC decisions, see Niels Petersen, *Proportionality and Judicial Activism: Fundamental Rights Adjudication in Canada, Germany and South Africa* (CUP 2017) 147 n. 170, 204–6

[141] Jakobs (n 3) 123.

[142] ibid 124.

framework. While the Court initially derived the clarity principle from the *Rechtsstaatsprinzip*, there are several decisions in the Court's recent case-law in which clarity explicitly forms part of proportionality.[143] In fact, it is possible to observe the larger historical trend that concepts which were initially developed apart from proportionality such as the principles of clarity or of practical concordance have become part of the proportionality framework.[144]

## V Worthy Purpose

The worthy purpose test is the only stage of the proportionality framework that is practically always addressed by the FCC. In all PA decisions by a Senate in a fundamental rights case from 2000 until 2017, the Court made a determination as to the worthy purpose in every single decision.[145] In general, the Court applies the requirement of a worthy or legitimate purpose generously. In the 58 cases in the dataset that failed the proportionality test, the measure under review was struck down with the worthy purpose test in only 5 out of those 58 cases, or 9 per cent. Only two of those decisions concerned federal legislation.[146] If the Court has determined that the measure fails the worthy purpose test, the PA likely ends: In 4 out of those 5 cases, or 80 per cent, the failure at the worthy purpose stage was determinate of the ultimate outcome of the case.

143 See, e.g., BVerfGE 110, 33 [52]; BVerfGE 113, 348 [386]–[87]; BVerfGE 131, 268 [306].

144 Petersen, *Verhältnismäßigkeit als Rationalitätskontrolle* (n 3) 211. See for the doctrine of practical concordance in particular Konrad Hesse, *Grundzüge des Verfassungsrechts der Bundesrepublik Deutschland* (20th ed., C. F. Müller 1999) ¶72, who has arguably been the most influential scholar in developing this doctrine. See for more detail on practical concordance Section VIII.B.

145 Specifically, the worthy purpose test was conducted in 114 out of 114 decisions in the dataset. These findings are further confirmed by a quantitative analysis conducted by Engel, who analysed all FCC decisions rendered in 2011, Senate and Chamber decisions, with respect to the question of the worthiness of the purpose. He finds that the FCC always determines the legitimate aim whenever it conducts a PA. See Christoph Engel, 'Das legitime Ziel in der Praxis des Bundesverfassungsgerichts' in Matthias Jestaedt and Oliver Lepsius (eds), *Verhältnismäßigkeit* (Mohr Siebeck 2015) 97, 105.

146 BVerfGE 107, 186; BVerfGE 147, 1. In two cases, the Court struck down state legislation with the worthy purpose test. See BVerfGE 106, 181 [193]–[200]; BVerfGE 133, 112 [133]–[42]. In one case, the Court overturned the contested judicial decision based on the worthy purpose test but upheld the federal legislation interpreted by that decision. BVerfGE 122, 190 [207]–[09].

Although not many laws fail the worthy purpose test, it still has several important functions in German proportionality practice. It is at the very least the reference point for the ensuing means-ends analysis and the subsequent PA subtests.[147] Moreover, in some judgments, the Court will deal with the worthy purpose stage over several paragraphs to explain the purposes of and considerations behind complex pieces of legislation.[148] Finally, the Court uses the worthy purpose test to weed out particular purposes as unworthy although the measure being scrutinized still passes the test because it can be based on a different (worthy) purpose.[149] As we will see in more detail later, the determination of unworthiness regarding one of several purposes has consequences for the subsequent PA. At the later stages, the Court will frequently evaluate implicitly whether the contested measure has been designed to accommodate the unworthy purpose.[150]

### *A Establishing What the Purpose Is*

In principle, defining the purpose of a law is a prerequisite to conducting PA, which, at its core, is a means-ends analysis. As we have seen, the Court meticulously observes this requirement: whenever it applies the PA framework it begins with defining the law's purpose. But what exactly the purpose of a law is can be in dispute. Conceptually, it is possible to determine the purpose of a law subjectively, i.e., based on either the true motivation of the decision-maker or the purpose stated by the decision-maker, or objectively, i.e., based on an objectivized interpretation undertaken by the Court. In practice, the Court blends subjective and objective elements. Starting points for determining a law's purpose are the purposes stated by the legislator in a statute itself or in a supplementary explanatory memorandum to the statute. Normatively, the Court justifies the legislative discretion in defining the purpose of a statute with the argument that 'in a democracy the legislature is entitled to pursue any purpose, provided it is not excluded by the constitution'.[151] The Court

[147] Grimm, 'Proportionality in Canadian and German Constitutional Jurisprudence' (n 7) 388.

[148] See, e.g., BVerfGE 117, 272 [294]–[96]; BVerfGE 120, 224 [243]–[49]; BVerfGE 121, 317 [349]–[54]; BVerfGE 128, 1 [47]–[49].

[149] See, e.g., BVerfGE 104, 357 [365]–[67]; BVerfGE 115, 276 [307]–[08]; BVerfGE 128, 226 [259]; BVerfGE 135, 90 [119].

[150] See Section V.C. and VIII.A.

[151] Grimm, 'Proportionality in Canadian and German Constitutional Jurisprudence' (n 7) 388. See, e.g., BVerfGE 77, 84 [106].

does not investigate the true motives of the legislator. The idea is that so long as the content and the stated purpose of a law pass constitutional muster, the motives of the legislator are not pertinent.

### 1 Reliance on Statutory Text and Legislative History

In the majority of PA cases, the Court relies on the text of the statute that sometimes explicitly sets forth the law's purpose in the first provision or in the legislative history such as the explanatory memorandum given by the federal government that introduced a draft bill into parliament.[152] Although there is no constitutional requirement for the legislator to define the purpose of a statute, it is accepted practice to include in a legislative proposal a definition of the bill's objective. Some scholars have argued that the legislator is constitutionally required to clarify the purpose of law.[153] The prevailing view dictum in German constitutional law is, however, that the legislator owes nothing but the law.[154] In an act of self-commitment, the German Bundestag and the Federal Government provide in their self-made rules of procedure that a legislative proposal must, in the former case, contain a 'short explanation',[155] and, in the latter case, an explanatory memorandum that explains 'the purpose and necessity of the bill'.[156]

Establishing a law's purpose is predominantly a pragmatic exercise that has not caught significant attention of constitutional judges or legal scholarship.[157] The FCC has not developed particular evidentiary rules or principles to ascertain the purpose of the policy or the legislation under review. Rather, the Court accepts most of the purposes laid down in the bill itself, stated in the explanatory memorandum, or identified in the legislative history – without necessarily referencing these sources. And if these sources do not contain sufficient information about the purpose, the Court generously allows the parties to submit a purpose during the proceedings.[158] While the emphasis of the respect of the democratic

[152] See, e.g., BVerfGE 37, 1 [19]–[20]; BVerfGE 104, 337 [347]; BVerfGE 117, 163 [182]; BVerfGE 119, 59 [83].

[153] See in favour of this so-called Zweckverdeutlichungsgebot: Görg Haverkate, *Rechtsfragen des Leistungsstaats* (Mohr Siebeck 1983) 290–92; Dechsling (n 3) 143–45.

[154] On this dictum, see Christian Bickenbach, *Die Einschätzungsprärogative des Gesetzgebers* (Mohr Siebeck 2014) 430–38.

[155] Section 76(2) Rules of Procedure of the German Bundestag (GOBT).

[156] Section 43(1) No. 1 of the Joint Rules of Procedure of the Federal Ministries (GGO).

[157] Engel, 'Das legitime Ziel in der Praxis des Bundesverfassungsgerichts' (n 145) 98.

[158] See, e.g., BVerfGE 30, 292 [318].

legislature hence motivates the FCC to define the purpose of a statute primarily subjectively from the point of view of the legislature,[159] the Court in some cases complements this approach with an 'objective' perspective.[160]

### 2 Purposes Supplied by the Court

It appears that there are two different sets of cases in which the Court defines the purpose of a law based on what the Court – and not the legislator – deems as the purpose of the law. On the one hand, the FCC often refrains from adopting the official phrasing when a law ultimately fails the PA test. In those types of cases, the Court deviates from the official phrasing to exclude some of several stated purposes of a law to limit the analysis to a single worthy purpose. By eliminating several worthy purposes the Court decreases the legitimating basis of the law. If the Court chooses this approach it is fair to assume that it will ultimately find the law under review to be unconstitutional.[161] Although the Court prefers to strike down such a law at a later PA stage, the point of the worthy purpose test is to pave the way for the critical analysis at a subsequent stage.[162]

On the other hand, the Court supplies a legitimate purpose itself if it seeks to preserve the constitutionality of a bill whose stated purpose is unworthy or otherwise insufficient.[163] The rationale behind this practice is that a law is constitutional so long as there is a worthy purpose to

159 See, e.g., BVerfGE 88, 145 [161].

160 See, e.g., BVerfGE 93, 386 [400].

161 In the *Separate Appeals Court Registration* case concerning the prohibition for attorneys admitted to a certain Appeals Court ('Oberlandesgericht') to take legal actions before another court, the FCC first noted several purposes that had been claimed to be legitimately pursued by this prohibition such as better attorney reachability, rapidity of court proceedings, and trustful cooperation between the court and locally residing attorneys. However, the Court found that these purposes had not been decisive for the legislature because the latter had recently abandoned the separate registration requirement for lower courts. In addition, the Court argued that improved mobility and modern communication technology ensured attorney reachability and speedy trials. Ultimately, the Court focused the PA on the legitimate purpose that the separate registration ensures that a second lawyer with a fresh look on the merits of the case examines whether an appeal is worthwhile. In that regard, the Court found that less intrusive means than entirely limiting an attorney to one court were available such as requiring an attorney change in appeals cases. BVerfGE 103, 1.

162 For an analysis of the interplay between the worthy purpose and the strict proportionality stages, see Section VIII.A.

163 See BVerfGE 75, 246 [268]; BVerfGE 115, 1 [17]–[18].

justify the law regardless of the purpose actually pursued by the legislator.[164] This approach can have the effect that old legislation, whose original objective is obsolete, can survive PA. In the *Sibling Incest* case,[165] two siblings who had lived separately during their childhood began an intimate relationship as young adults and had four children together. During this relationship, the older brother was repeatedly sentenced under § 173(2) of the German Criminal Code that threatens sexual intercourse between natural relatives with imprisonment. He filed a constitutional complaint, asking the Court to review the constitutionality of this punishable offence. While the incest prohibition has a long cultural history, the key question in the case was what exactly the legitimate purpose is that this restriction of the right to sexual self-determination of siblings pursues. The parliamentary debate in the 1970s when the law was enacted suggests that the aim was to protect the family order from the damaging effects of incest and to avoid serious genetic diseases in children of incestuous relationships. But because these moral and eugenic considerations would not have passed a thorough PA, the Court itself added an additional purpose, namely the protection of the sexual self-determination of the inferior or weaker partner in an incestuous relationship.[166] It concluded that these objectives legitimize 'in their totality' the limitation on the right to sexual self-determination.[167]

[164] This rationale is expressed in a case concerning the general equality clause in Article 3(1) BL: 'If it is not possible to gather from the legislative history sufficient grounds to justify an unequal treatment between the two groups, other considerations can be suitable to justify the challenged regulation. Not subjective but only objective arbitrariness of the legislator results in a finding of unconstitutionality of a norm.' BVerfGE 93, 386 [400].

[165] BVerfGE 120, 224.

[166] ibid [259] (dissenting opinion Hassemer).

[167] ibid [243]. This generous judicial practice of supplying a worthy purpose test led to a forceful dissenting opinion of Judge Hassemer. ibid [255]–[73] (dissenting opinion Hassemer). He argued that § 173 of the German Criminal Code is incompatible with the principle of proportionality. ibid [255]. In his opinion, '[t]he evidence seems to indicate that the provision in its existing version is solely aimed at attitudes to morality and not at a specific legally protected right'. ibid [264]. What the majority did, in his view, was to subsequently supplant worthy purposes to this provision. ibid [257]. He argued against this approach that clarity regarding the aims is an essential component of the legislature's decision that should not be left to subsequent supplementation by the courts. ibid. In his view, PA could not be performed methodologically correctly without clarity about the purpose of a rule. ibid. The subsequent insertion of a legitimate purpose that was not pursued by the legislature changed the coordination, contours, and context of PA. ibid.

### 3 Multiple Purposes

The fact that the FCC grants the legislator significant discretion in determining a legitimate purpose is not tantamount to a superficial examination of this PA step. The particular care with which the Court conducts the worthy purpose test is illustrated by cases with complex facts where a statute does not pursue a single purpose.[168] In these cases, the FCC conducts a thorough analysis of each of the multiple purposes separately.

There are two important constellations of bundles of purposes that need to be distinguished. In the first constellation, the Court reaches the differentiated conclusion that several stated purposes are worthy but that at least one – unstated but suspected – purpose is unworthy;[169] in the second, it deems all purposes to be worthy.[170] Although the law under review will ultimately pass the worthy purpose test under both scenarios, the fact that one purpose of the law was found to be unworthy in the first constellation typically does not bode well for the proportionality of that law.[171] In the first scenario, the Court suspects that the stated purpose actually covers an illegitimate purpose but is nevertheless reluctant to directly challenge a law with the legitimate purpose test. Instead, the Court accepts the officially stated purposes for a law but, at the same time, clarifies that a different objective, namely the purpose that the Court secretly suspects the law to actually pursue, would not constitute a worthy purpose. The Court then proceeds to conduct the analysis of the later PA stages in a particularly strict manner and, in most cases, strikes down the law with a subsequent subtest. In other words, whether or not the Court deems one of the various purposes unworthy is consequential for how the analysis at the later stages is conducted.

Examples for this practice are the *Sports Betting* and the *Casino Order* cases.[172] This is the background: in many areas of gambling and betting, German states have created government monopolies and operate

168 For an analysis of this phenomenon, see See Christoph Engel, 'Das legitime Ziel als Element des Übermaßverbots' in Winfried Brugger, Stephan Kirste and Michael Anderheiden (eds), *Gemeinwohl in Deutschland, Europa und der Welt* (Nomos 2002) 134–36; Haverkate (n 153) 26–28.

169 See, e.g., BVerfGE 102, 197 [215]; BVerfGE 103, 1 [12]–[14]; BVerfGE 104, 357 [365]–[67]; BVerfGE 115, 276 [307]–[08]; BVerfGE 128, 226 [259]; BVerfGE 135, 90 [119].

170 See, e.g., BVerfGE 21, 150 [155]–[56]; BVerfGE 28, 364 [375]; BVerfGE 30, 292 [323]–[24]; BVerfGE 37, 1 [19]–[20]; BVerfGE 77, 84 [107]–[08]; BVerfGE 120, 274 [313]–[14]; BVerfGE 120, 224 [243]–[49].

171 See in more detail Section V.C. and Section VIII.A.

172 BVerfGE 102, 197; BVerfGE 115, 276.

state-owned betting agencies against which private operators sued under the Basic Law's freedom of occupation guarantee. In *Sports Betting*, a public monopoly had existed for decades prior to the litigation. In *Casino Order*, casinos had been privately operated in the state for decades until a law established a monopoly in favour of the state. In both cases, the central purpose officially stated in favour of the monopoly was to combat gambling and betting addiction. Conveniently, the states also generated (or expected to generate) a sizeable amount of earnings in the process. At the worthy purpose stage, the Court conducted a thorough analysis of the applicable purposes. In the *Sports Betting* case, the Court found that the 'main purpose of creating a state betting monopoly ... is combating gambling and betting addiction'.[173] At the same time, '(f)urther legitimate goals are the protection of the gamblers against fraudulent schemes by the bookmakers and additional consumer protection, in particular protection against the danger of misleading advertising'.[174] Furthermore, '(a)nother legitimate goal of a state betting monopoly is the averting of dangers which arise from crime that accompanies betting and is consequential upon betting'.[175] Finally, it held that the 'state's public-revenue interest does not justify the creation of a betting monopoly'.[176] In other words, the Court accepted the official purpose but stated, at the same time, that fiscal considerations alone would not justify a state monopoly, thereby excluding the fiscal interests of the state as a worthy purpose in this context. Ultimately, the Court struck down the state laws creating a state monopoly for sports betting and for casinos in both cases at the strict proportionality stage. In both cases, the Court sensed, without explicitly stating so, that the true objective behind the state monopoly was not, as officially stated, to combat gambling addiction but to increase the state's source of revenue because the policies accompanying the monopoly were barely designed to prevent gambling addiction.[177] While the Court conducted the worthy purpose test generously, it proceeded with a strict analysis at the later stages that relied heavily on consistency arguments aimed at discrediting the legislature's regulatory scheme.[178]

[173] BVerfGE 115, 276 [304].
[174] ibid [306].
[175] ibid.
[176] ibid [307]. See also BVerfGE 102, 197 [215].
[177] BVerfGE 115, 276 [310]–[16]; BVerfGE 102, 197 [216]–[17].
[178] For an analysis of consistency arguments in constitutional adjudication, see Niels Petersen, 'Gesetzgeberische Inkonsistenz als Beweiszeichen' (2013) 138 Archiv des öffentlichen Rechts 108–34.

For example, in the *Sports Betting* case, the Court's reasoning focused especially on the contradiction between the stated purpose of combating betting addiction and the aggressive advertisement campaigns run by the state-owned betting agencies.[179] It follows that the legislature is entitled to enact a gambling monopoly to combat betting addiction but it must implement this regulatory purpose in a consistent manner.

In the second scenario, the Court, like in the first scenario, diligently reviews the worthiness of each purpose separately, but subsequently conducts the ensuing analysis in a more lenient fashion. Conceptually, PA in light of multiple purposes can be conducted separately, relative to each purpose, or combined, considering all purposes as a bundle. In practice, the Court refrains from untying the bundle of purposes and tends to conduct the analysis at the later stages based on the bundle of purposes or the law's dominant purpose. In the *Incest* case, for example, the Court distinguished the protection of the family order from the damaging effects of incest, the prevention of serious genetic diseases in children of incestuous relationships, and the protection of the sexual self-determination of the inferior or weaker partner in an incestuous relationship as distinct purposes pursued by the criminal incest prohibition under review.[180] However, it ultimately concluded that the purposes legitimize 'in their totality' the limitation on the right to sexual self-determination.[181] This bundling of purposes has a safeguarding effect for the law because the analytical clarity of the suitability and the necessity stages is blurred.[182] Another case in point is the *Oil Reserve* decision concerning a statutory oil-stocking obligation imposed on oil companies.[183] By requiring private petroleum companies to stockpile a certain amount of their oil, a federal law adopted in 1965 sought to prevent an energy crisis in the event of a supply shortage. At the worthy purpose stage, the Court distinguished carefully between the 'primary purpose', namely to ensure sufficient oil reserves, and the 'secondary purpose', namely protection of the struggling German coal industry vis-à-vis the rising oil industry on the German energy market.[184] Heating oil and coal

[179] Similarly, in the *Casino Order* case, an important supporting consideration for the Court to strike down that law was that the regulatory experience with private operators had been overwhelmingly positive. BVerfGE 102, 197 [217], [219]–[20].
[180] BVerfGE 120, 224 [243]–[49].
[181] ibid [243].
[182] See Engel, 'Das legitime Ziel als Element des Übermaßverbots' (n 168) 135.
[183] BVerfGE 30, 292.
[184] ibid [317]–[18].

were substitutable products but, while oil was imported, the coal industry was a major employer in Germany. The idea was that the financially burdensome oil-stocking obligation of the oil companies would increase their operational costs and hence decrease their competitive position vis-à-vis the coal industry. Rather than conduct the analysis separately relative to each purpose, the Court held that 'the different purposes pursued by the statute should not be considered in isolation; on the contrary, the regulatory instruments chosen by the legislator ought to be evaluated in light of the primary and the secondary purpose combined'.[185]

### B *What Are Worthy Purposes?*

Over the years, the FCC has assembled an extensive and open-ended list of goals that are considered worthy. In general, the Court defines those purposes at an intermediate level of generality.[186] In contrast, decisions defining the purpose at a highly abstract level such as national security, public order, or public health are rare today.[187] For example, in the *Smoking Ban* case concerning anti-smoking legislation that banned smoking in eating and drinking establishments, the Court did not choose the abstract purpose of public health, but, more specifically defined the protection of people from the health dangers of passive smoking as the worthy purpose.[188]

In the field of economic policy, the Court has, amongst others, recognized as worthy the purposes of preserving and promoting the professional performance of the handicraft business,[189] safeguarding professional independence and qualification,[190] protecting small and medium businesses,[191] ensuring sufficient oil reserves,[192] protecting consumers against

[185] ibid [318].

[186] The extent of generalization in formulating the purpose has real consequences for PA: the freer the legislator is in determining the purpose of its lawmaking, the weaker is the force of the proportionality principle. See for this statement in German: Grabitz (n 8) 600–1.

[187] They were more common in the 1960s and 1970s.

[188] BVerfGE 121, 317 [349]. Similarly BVerfGE 90, 145 [174] (defining the worthy purpose as protecting the health both of the individual and of the population as a whole against the dangers which flow from drugs, and preventing the population, especially the young, from becoming addicted to drugs).

[189] BVerfGE 13, 97 [114]–[15].

[190] BVerfGE 135, 90 [114]–[15].

[191] BVerfGE 14, 19 [23].

[192] BVerfGE 30, 292 [317]–[18].

deception,[193] reducing structural excess capacities in the German mills industry,[194] preserving the particular quality of German wine and stabilizing the wine market,[195] and ensuring effective judicial supervision of insolvency administrators.[196] Worthy purposes are typically more abstract when it comes to national security. Examples are the proper functioning of the military force,[197] security and proper functioning of airport operations,[198] investigation of serious criminal offences and improvement of legal instruments to combat organized crime,[199] facilitating the exchange of relevant information between different security authorities,[200] and protection of the liberal-democratic constitutional order[201] or of public peace.[202] Other worthy purposes defined by the Court in other policy fields are, in the field of cultural policy: the preservation of cultural monuments,[203] preservation of the identificational potency and generational succession of names by limiting the formation of double and composite names,[204] and making literary works as comprehensively accessible as possible to scientifically and culturally interested persons and giving future generations a comprehensive impression of the intellectual heritage from earlier epochs;[205] in the field of legal services: proper functioning of legal services,[206] proper functioning of the administration of justice,[207] and, more specifically, of tax justice;[208] in the field of social policy: preventing socially detrimental early retirement,[209] securing the financial stability of public health insurance funds,[210] and cutting of no longer justified tax subsidies;[211] in the

193 BVerfGE 53, 135 [145].
194 BVerfGE 25, 1 [13]–[14].
195 BVerfGE 21, 150 [155]–[56]; BVerfGE 37, 1 [19]–[20].
196 BVerfGE 141, 121 [¶42].
197 BVerfGE 28, 243 [261].
198 BVerfGE 128, 226 [259]–[60].
199 BVerfGE 109, 279 [335]–[36].
200 BVerfGE 133, 277 [321].
201 BVerfGE 30, 1 [21]; BVerfGE 120, 274 [319]; BVerfGE 134, 141 [179]–[80].
202 BVerfGE 124, 300 [331].
203 BVerfGE 100, 226 [242].
204 BVerfGE 123, 90 [103]–[04].
205 BVerfGE 58, 137 [149].
206 BVerfGE 78, 77 [85].
207 BVerfGE 103, 44 [64].
208 BVerfGE 21, 173 [179].
209 BVerfGE 81, 156 [191]–[92].
210 BVerfGE 68, 193 [218].
211 BVerfGE 105, 17 [34].

field of health policy: public health,[212] health of employees in the bakery business,[213] combating gambling and betting addiction,[214] and protecting the health both of the individual and of the population as a whole against the dangers which flow from drugs, and preventing the population, especially the young, from becoming addicted to drugs.[215]

### 1 Determining the Worthiness of a Purpose

In the event of a fundamental right infringement, a plausible requirement may be that the purpose pursued by the infringing measure must be explicitly set forth in the constitution. In German constitutional law, it depends on the structure of the limitation clause whether and to what extent the worthy basis must have its basis in the constitution. The structure of ordinary limitation clauses, such as Article 12(1) s. 2 BL, do not provide for any requirement to limit a fundamental right other than that the infringing measure is taken by or on the basis of a parliamentary statute. As a result, the FCC grants the legislator a wide margin of discretion in pursuing any purpose unless it is excluded by the constitution.[216] In other words, a purpose must not be based on the constitution to count as worthy. It must be in the public interest, which is primarily defined by the legislator.[217] For example, the FCC held repeatedly in the context of the freedom of occupation that 'appropriate and defensible public policy considerations' constitute a legitimate purpose[218] so long as the legislator 'does not misuse its legislative power to pursue extraneous considerations'[219] or 'contradicts the Basic Law's value order'.[220] According to the Court, 'it is primarily a matter of the legislator to decide on the basis of its political ideas and objectives which measure it intends to take in the public interest'.[221] The Court justifies this position with democratic considerations, arguing that 'the Basic Law primarily confers the legislator the decision regarding which public interests are of

212 BVerfGE 7, 377 [413]; BVerfGE 25, 236 [247].
213 BVerfGE 87, 363 [385]–[86].
214 BVerfGE 115, 276 [304].
215 BVerfGE 90, 145 [174].
216 See, e.g., BVerfGE 81, 156 [192]; BVerfGE 124, 300 [331].
217 Grimm, 'Proportionality in Canadian and German Constitutional Jurisprudence' (n 7) 388.
218 BVerfGE 30, 292 [316]; BVerfGE 37, 1 [18]; BVerfGE 39, 210 [225].
219 BVerfGE 30, 292 [316].
220 BVerfGE 39, 210 [225].
221 BVerfGE 116, 202 [224].

such magnitude that individual freedoms must recede' and that the public decision-making process within parliament is best suited to protect the public interest against particular interests.[222]

The existence of a qualified limitation clause or the non-existence of any limitation clause for that matter limit the discretion of the legislator in determining the worthiness of a purpose in the context of specific fundamental rights. Article 13(7) BL concerning the right of inviolability of the home provides that certain interferences and restrictions are only permissible 'to avert a danger to the public or to the life of an individual, or, pursuant to a law, to confront an acute danger to public safety and order, in particular to relieve a housing shortage, to combat the danger of an epidemic, or to protect young persons at risk'.[223] The expropriation clause of Article 14(3) of the Basic Law explicitly provides that expropriations are only permissible for the public good.[224] Moreover, fundamental rights without limitation clauses can, as we have seen,[225] only be restricted through competing constitutional norms and principles. In other words, not every public interest is considered worthy but only purposes that have their basis in the Basic Law. In constitutional practice, however, these qualifications typically do not amount to much more than slight differences. The Court has, as we have seen, attenuated these textual differences in favour of uniform structure of PA that provides the legislator with a broad discretion in determining the worthiness of a purpose.[226] Even if the worthy purpose must be based on the constitution because the fundamental right at issue does not contain a limitation clause, the Court generously reads statutory policy goals into the constitution.[227]

[222] BVerfGE 33, 125 [153].

[223] See Article 13(7) BL.

[224] The FCC interprets this requirement broadly, see BVerfGE 134, 242 [292]–[93].

[225] See Section IV.C.

[226] See Section IV.C.

[227] This practice was criticized by the constitutional judges Mahrenholz and Böckenförde in their dissenting opinions in the *Extended Alternative Service* case. BVerfGE 69, 1 [57]–[92] (dissenting opinion). The background of this case is the following: In the 1980s, Germany still had mandatory military service but, at the same time, Article 4(3) BL provided that the freedom of faith and conscience includes a person's right not to be 'compelled against [one's] conscience to render military service involving the use of arms'. For persons who refused to render military service, Article 12a(2) BL provided that they may be required to perform alternative service. In 1983, a CDU-led Bundestag passed a controversial law that required conscientious objectors to pass a recognition proceeding and to serve an extended period of civilian service that exceeded the alternative military service. The idea behind that law was that only those two

## 2 Importance and Urgency of the Worthy Purpose

The FCC generally does not require that the purpose of a law that infringes a fundamental right represents a pressing need. Instead, the Court prefers to address the question of whether a certain objective is sufficiently important to justify the restriction of a right at the strict proportionality stage. According to former federal constitutional judge *Dieter Grimm*, the Court views importance 'as a correlational notion that cannot be determined in abstract terms'.[228] Therefore, '[r]aising this question in connection with the purpose would be regarded as a premature anticipation of the final balance'.[229]

There is one important qualification to the claim that the importance and urgency of the worthy purpose is irrelevant for the worthy purpose stage. The so-called three-step theory created by the Court in *Pharmacy* in the context of the freedom of occupation already considers the intensity of the infringement on the legitimate purpose stage and categorizes, based on this intensity, what type of measures the legislator may legitimately take. In other words, the requirements for the importance of the worthy purpose increase with the increasing intensity of the regulation.[230]

requirements would ensure that the conscientious objection is real and not based on mere convenience. The right to conscientious objection in Article 4(3) BL does not contain any reference about its limitability. As a consequence, this fundamental right may only restricted through competing constitutional norms and principles. Based on a holistic constitutional interpretation, the majority of the Court read into several constitutional norms referencing aspects of military defence 'a basic constitutional decision in favor of effective national military defense'. BVerfGE 69, 1 [21]. As a result, it was constitutionally permissible to limit the right to conscientious objection to further that policy goal and to apply PA. While they did not put into doubt the possibility of limiting fundamental rights without reservation clauses in general, the dissenting opinion of judges Böckenförde and Mahrenholz questioned that the majority founded the limitation of the right to conscientious objection on a holistic collection of individual provisions including enabling norms in the area of national defence, arguing that the Court had created 'a very wide and vague arsenal of potential restrictions of fundamental rights'. ibid [62]. Put differently: What is the point of formulating fundamental rights without reservation clauses if almost any statutory policy goal is read into the constitution and vested with constitutional status.

228 Grimm, 'Proportionality in Canadian and German Constitutional Jurisprudence' (n 7) 388.

229 ibid.

230 More specifically, the Court distinguishes three forms of governmental regulations affecting the freedom of occupation with different degrees of intensity. These are from lowest to highest intensity (a) regulations concerning the freedom of exercise of certain occupations, (b) regulations concerning the freedom of choice based on subjective

### C What Are Unworthy Purposes?

Although the Court grants the legislator a wide margin of discretion in establishing the worthy purpose, the legislative discretion is not without limits. When a fundamental right is infringed, the FCC insists that the purposes pursued by the legislator are subject to judicial review.[231] As we have seen at the beginning of this section, a FCC Senate has only held in 5 out of all 114 PA cases in a fundamental right context between 2000 and 2017, or 4 per cent, that the measure being scrutinized failed the worthy purpose test. However, in significantly more cases the Court has identified a particular purpose as unworthy without striking the measure down with the worthy purpose test. The quantitative analysis shows that the Court has pointed out an unworthy purpose in 24 out of 114 decisions, or 21 per cent.[232]

It is possible to roughly distinguish three types of circumstances in which a purpose is deemed unworthy. First, the Court has found laws to lack a worthy purpose that further antiquated purposes.[233] The most important category of those cases concerns laws in the areas of family law and professional conduct that seek to protect antiquated moral standards or outdated professional rules.[234] In some of those cases, the Court explicitly considers a purpose to be insufficiently worthy to justify the infringement of a fundamental right such as 'strengthening the collegiality among attorneys'[235] or 'limiting the income of attorneys'.[236] In most

admission criteria depending on the personal qualification, and (c) regulations using objective admission criteria that are independent of the personal qualifications. Accordingly, regulatory interferences with the freedom of exercise 'can be restricted in so far this seems appropriate according to rational considerations of the common good', interferences based on subjective admission criteria 'can only be restricted to the extent that protection of particularly important interests of the community positively requires it', and the justification of objective admission criteria require 'the prevention of severe dangers for a community interest of paramount importance which are provable or highly probable'. BVerfGE 7, 377 [405]–[06].

231 BVerfGE 7, 377 [410]–[12]; BVerfGE 25, 1 [12]; BVerfGE 39, 210 [225].

232 The following analysis concern all references to unworthy purposes whether or not the measure under review failed the unworthy purpose test.

233 See Petersen, *Verhältnismäßigkeit als Rationalitätskontrolle* (n 3) 167–69.

234 See in the area of family law: BVerfGE 36, 146 [163]; BVerfGE 61, 358 [375]–[82]; BVerfGE 84, 168 [181]; BVerfGE 109, 256 [270]; BVerfGE 115, 1 [16]–[17]; BVerfGE 127, 132 [153]–[54]; See in the area of professional conduct: BVerfGE 103, 1 [15]–[19]; BVerfGE 104, 357 [365]–[67]; BVerfGE 118, 1 [22]–[23]; BVerfGE 122, 190 [207]–[08]; BVerfGE 135, 90 [114]–[15].

235 BVerfGE 122, 190 [207]–[08].

236 BVerfGE 118, 1 [22]–[23].

cases, however, the Court does not challenge the purpose set forth by the government in the judicial proceedings but questions the rational connection between the (legitimate) stated purpose and the (illegitimate) purpose apparently pursued by the law at the worthy purpose stage.[237] This is plausible if we assume that the point of the worthy purpose test is to distinguish between worthy and unworthy purposes, and hence, to force the political decision-maker to justify the policy on the basis of reasons that are justifiable in a liberal democracy.[238] A case in point is a 1973 decision concerning the general prohibition of marriage in the case that one partner previously had a sexual partnership with a parent of the other partner: the FCC found that this prohibition violates the right to marry.[239] Historically, such a marriage was found to be offensive and unnatural. The Court held that any infringement of the right to marry would require substantive rational reasons but it did not recognize the existence of such reasons with respect to the marriage prohibition for the sexual relationship.[240] In particular, the Court argued that 'outdated ritual ideas, rationally incomprehensible views or metaphysical reasons or religious-ecclesiastical would not meet this requirement'.[241] Only 'rationally comprehensible reasons' were capable of justifying infringements of the right to marry. In this matter, the FCC distinguished between the legitimate prevention of sexual relationships within the family and the illegitimate prevention of the foundation of a new family.[242]

Second, the Court does not accept the pursuit of purely fiscal or anticompetitive reasons as a worthy purpose to infringe a fundamental right.[243] As we have seen in the *Casino Order* and *Sports Betting* cases, the Court suspected that the state gambling monopoly was not predominantly aimed at combatting gambling addiction but primarily driven by

[237] See, e.g., BVerfGE 36, 146 [163]; BVerfGE 61, 358 [375]–[82]; BVerfGE 84, 168 [181]; BVerfGE 103, 1 [15]–[19]; BVerfGE 104, 357 [365]–[67]; BVerfGE 107, 186 [198]; BVerfGE 135, 90 [114]–[15].

[238] Kumm, 'The Idea of Socratic Contestation and the Right to Justification' (n 58) 142.

[239] BVerfGE 36, 146.

[240] ibid [163].

[241] ibid.

[242] Of course, the facts of the case at hand raised substantial concerns about sexual abuse or at least exploitation of power relationships. The male partner had a sexual relationship with the mother of the female partner. He had started the relationship with his female partner when he was 31 and she was 17. ibid [156].

[243] Examples of cases deeming purely fiscal reasons as unworthy are BVerfGE 102, 197 [215]; BVerfGE 115, 276 [307]; BVerfGE 134, 242 [292]–[93].

fiscal considerations. In *Sports Betting*, the Court held that 'the state's public-revenue interest does not justify the creation of a betting monopoly'.[244] While the Court does not generally deem fiscal considerations as illegitimate in the context of fundamental rights infringements, it does so if they constitute the predominant purpose of an infringing law.[245] Similarly, the Court has repeatedly stated at the worthy purpose stage that protection from competition is not a worthy purpose if it constitutes the predominant purpose of a regulation.[246] This market-based bias in favour of economic competition has a long tradition in the FCC's jurisprudence that dates back to the foundational period of the Basic Law when the Court invoked the liberal spirit of the 'new' fundamental rights provisions to strike down protectionist and dirigiste economic regulations that have a long history in Germany, dating all the way back to the traditional guild system.[247] At the same time, the Court has been generous in redefining the purpose into a legitimate objective that is pursued by an anti-competitive regulation.[248] It appears that even if the Court suspects a regulation to predominantly pursue an unworthy purpose, it is reluctant to directly challenge that regulation at the worthy purpose stage. Rather than directly questioning the intentions of the legislator, the Court limits its analysis at the worthy purpose stage to clarifying that fiscal reasons and protection from competition are unworthy if they are the predominant purposes of a right-infringing

244 BVerfGE 115, 276 [307].

245 Other examples: In the area of property law, the Court insisted in the *Retro Expropriation* case based on the wording of Article 14(3) of the Basic Law that expropriations are only permissible for the public good but not for fiscal reasons. Accordingly, the Court held that a complainant is entitled to the re-transfer of his expropriated property if the public project for which that property was expropriated (here: expansion of a public road) is not carried out. BVerfGE 38, 175 [180]. In the *Commuter Tax Allowance* decision concerning a popular tax relief for commuters in the car country of Germany, the Court struck down a federal law limiting the scope of that allowance arguing that it constituted 'a constitutionally not sufficiently well-founded, purely fiscally motivated and designed regulation'. BVerfGE 122, 210 [244].

246 BVerfGE 94, 372 [395]; BVerfGE 111, 10 [32]–[33].

247 See, e.g., BVerfGE 7, 377 (overturning a 'necessity clause' set forth in state legislation requiring that a permission for opening a new pharmacy will only be granted if (a) it is in the public interest that the pharmacy should be established in order to secure the provision of the public with medicines, and (b) it is to be assumed that the economic basis of the pharmacy is ensured and the economic basis of neighbouring pharmacies is not impaired by it).

248 BVerfGE 19, 330 [342]; BVerfGE 41, 360 [370]–[74]; BVerfGE 94, 372 [395]; BVerfGE 111, 10 [32].

regulation. Instead, the Court prefers to focus its analysis on certain inconsistencies of the regulation and to strike the regulation down at a later stage. This indicates that there is an interplay between the worthy purpose stage and the necessity and strict proportionality stages.[249] An example is a case concerning attorney admissions in East Germany, in which the entitlement of attorneys to take legal action before a court in East German states after reunification was restricted based on the law firm's seat.[250] While the Court stated that protection from competition (from West German law firms) is not a legitimate aim, it accepted as worthy the officially stated purpose of improving legal services in East Germany by compensating for the competitive disadvantages of East German law firms after reunification. How this official purpose is different from protection of competition is not easy to detect. In any event, the law failed at the necessity stage because the Court found that a less intrusive means would have been a temporary, time-limited restriction.[251]

Finally, the Court held that 'the repeal of the principle of freedom as such contained in a fundamental right is illegitimate'.[252] In other words, laws are distinctively unworthy if they contradict the essence of the freedom guarantee of a particular fundamental right. This idea is especially prominent in the context of the Basic Law's fundamental rights to freedom of expression and freedom of assembly. The Court argues that 'the intention to inhibit expressions with harmful or dangerous content repeals the principle of freedom of speech as such and is hence illegitimate'.[253] As a result of this view, the Court strikes down administrative measures prohibiting right-extremist demonstration only on the basis of the content of the expected statements made therein.[254] This approach is based on Article 5(2) of the Basic Law, according to which speech restrictions are only permissible by 'general laws' that pursue non–speech-related objectives and are not designed to suppress a particular viewpoint and on Article 21(2), according to which only the FCC is competent to rule on the question of unconstitutionality of political parties that seek to undermine or abandon the democratic order of the

[249] See Section VIII.A.
[250] BVerfGE 93, 362.
[251] ibid [371].
[252] BVerfGE 124, 300 [331]–[32].
[253] ibid [332].
[254] BVerfGE 111, 147 [155]–[56].

Federal Republic. On the basis of an *a contrario* reading of those provisions, the Court concludes that prohibiting the demonstration of a right-extremist party does not pursue a legitimate objective if it is not based on 'general laws' and if the party has not been deemed unconstitutional by the FCC.[255]

### D *Administrative Efficiency and Cost Savings as Worthy Purpose?*

Even though laws that infringe upon fundamental rights must not purely be based on fiscal reasons, the Court accepts fiscal considerations as legitimate so long as they complement other substantive worthy purposes.[256] In general, the Court is realistic and pragmatic about the significance of fiscal considerations in the policy process. It seeks to strike a fine balance between the protection of fundamental rights, on the one hand, and respect for parliament's budgetary needs, on the other hand.[257] Neither do budgetary constraints trump fundamental rights, nor do rights trump fiscal considerations. It appears that the Court avoids interferences with fiscal planning to the greatest extent possible – albeit without sacrificing substantial fundamental rights concerns.[258] As a general rule, the more intensively the goal of cost efficiency impairs the protected scope of a fundamental right, the less will the Court be willing to accept fiscal considerations to justify the cost-saving measure. When, for example, a state monopoly entirely excludes private operators from exercising a certain professional activity like in *Sports Betting* and in *Casino*, fiscal considerations may only have a supporting role and the policy under review must be strictly designed to pursue the other stated purposes such as combatting gambling addiction.

## VI **Suitability**

The formula consistently used by the FCC to describe the suitability prong is that 'a means is suitable if it is capable of attaining the desired

[255] In the *Rudolf Hess Memorial* case, the Court upheld the criminal prohibition of § 130 Abs. 4 StGB that holds everyone criminally liable who 'publicly or in a meeting disturbs the public peace in a manner that violates the dignity of the victims by approving of, glorifying, or justifying National Socialist rule of arbitrary force'.

[256] BVerfGE 68, 193 [218]; BVerfGE 114, 196 [243].

[257] Thomas Wischmeyer, *Die Kosten der Freiheit* (Mohr Siebeck 2015) 32–33.

[258] ibid.

purpose'.[259] In the FCC case-law, the suitability test is a threshold test that does not present a substantial hurdle in German PA practice.[260] According to former FCC judge Dieter Grimm, its main function is to eliminate a 'small number of runaway cases'.[261] This assessment is validated empirically by the quantitative analysis conducted for this book. In all PA cases concerning fundamental rights decided by a Senate from 2000 to 2017 that failed the proportionality test, the measure being scrutinized only failed the suitability stage in 3 out of those 58 cases, or 5 per cent. In addition, the Court either dealt with the suitability stage in only a cursory fashion or entirely skipped this stage in almost half of the cases.

### A *Establishing that the Measure Achieves the Purpose*

The FCC construes the suitability requirement leniently. The Court limits its review to whether the measure is 'objectively unsuitable',[262] 'simply unsuitable',[263] 'generally unsuitable',[264] or 'wholly unsuitable or totally inadequate'[265] to promote the pursued objective.[266] But finding that a measure is entirely unsuitable will be difficult. In fact, reflecting its generous suitability standards, the FCC has itself observed that a finding of 'objective unsuitability will be rare and limited to special categories of cases'.[267] The central argument put forward by the Court in favour of this broad definition of suitability is – similar to the legitimate purpose test – respect for the democratic legislature.[268]

259 See BVerfGE 30, 292 [316]; BVerfGE 113, 167 [234]; BVerfGE 120, 224 [240]; BVerfGE 126, 112 [144].

260 See also with this assessment: Hirschberg (n 3) 55–56; de Oliveira (n 3) 130.

261 Grimm, 'Proportionality in Canadian and German Constitutional Jurisprudence' (n 7) 389.

262 BVerfGE 16, 147 [181]; BVerfGE 17, 306 [317]; BVerfGE 73, 301 [317]; BVerfGE 81, 156 [192]; BVerfGE 126, 331 [361].

263 BVerfGE 19, 119 [127]; BVerfGE 71, 206 [216]; BVerfGE 81, 156 [192].

264 BVerfGE 70, 1 [26].

265 This formulation is especially used in the context of protective duties of the state. See BVerfGE 85, 191 [212]; BVerfGE 79, 174 [202]; BVerfGE 77, 170 [215]; BVerfGE 56, 54 [81].

266 BVerfGE 19, 119 [127]; BVerfGE 30, 250 [263]; BVerfGE 69, 1 [53]; BVerfGE 70, 1 [26]; BVerfGE 126, 331 [361]–[62].

267 BVerfGE 30, 250 [263].

268 Laura Clérico, *Die Struktur der Verhältnismäßigkeit* (Nomos 2001) 39.

### 1 Partial and Abstract Suitability

These democratic considerations have two important doctrinal consequences: on the one hand, the Court does not require that the means will achieve the pursued objective in its entirety. It is sufficient that the measure can partially promote the objective.[269] On the other hand, the Court only reviews the suitability of a measure in the abstract, focusing on the 'abstract possibility' that the measure under review will fulfil its purpose.[270] Put differently, there is no requirement that the measure adopted actually promotes the purpose. It suffices that there is a 'possibility of purpose attainment'.[271] Although such a broad interpretation could conceptually have the consequence that a serious fundamental rights infringement occurs for a marginal effect (for the objective pursued), it will not have such a consequence in Germany because the FCC will take a marginal effect into account at the strict proportionality stage.[272] The primary point of the suitability test is to plausibly establish the existence of an imagined causality between means and end.[273] It is not to analyse extensive empirical evidence about complex social correlations. If at all, such an analysis will typically be carried out at the strict proportionality stage.

[269] An example: in the *Night Baking Ban* decisions, the Court upheld the suitability of that ban for purposes of bakery employees' health protection even though the law did not comprehensively protect employees from night work by allowing work to start at 4 am. It sufficed, however, that the law 'contributed to health protection'. BVerfGE 87, 363 [385]–[86]. See also BVerfGE 23, 50 [57]; BVerfGE 41, 360 [370]; BVerfGE 73, 301 [317].

[270] See BVerfGE 67, 157 [173], [175], [178]; BVerfGE 79, 256 [270]; BVerfGE 81, 70 [90]; BVerfGE 81, 156 [192]; BVerfGE 83, 1 [19]; BVerfGE 100, 313 [373].

[271] BVerfGE 103, 293 [307]; BVerfGE 117, 163 [188]–[89]; BVerfGE 121, 317 [354]; BVerfGE 126, 112 [144]; BVerfGE 134, 204 [227]; BVerfGE 138, 136 [189]; BVerfGE 143, 246 [¶274].

[272] Take the following example: in a decision concerning the public notification of legal incapacitation due to waste of money and gambling addiction for the purpose of protecting legal transactions, the Court upheld the suitability of that incriminating measure, arguing that the unintended side-effect that the person affected was only informed subsequently to their incapacitation does not put the suitability of that measure into question. However, the Court later struck down that measure at the strict proportionality stage based on the severity of the infringement that could not be compensated through the importance of fulfilling the protection of legal services in this special circumstance. BVerfGE 78, 77 [86]–[87].

[273] Hirschberg (n 3) 50.

## 2 The Burden of Proof and the Limited Role of Evidentiary Issues

The outcome of many proportionality cases depends on evidentiary issues. In theory, the suitability and necessity test are the primary stages at which facts are incorporated into the means-ends framework that lies at the heart of the proportionality doctrine. In practice, however, an evidentiary issue rarely occurs at the suitability stage because the Court only reviews the suitability of a measure in the abstract and does not require that the measure adopted actually promotes the purpose of the law to be deemed suitable. In addition, the Court tends to allocate the evidentiary burden in favour of the legislature and to the detriment of the rights-bearer when complex legislation, particularly in the field of economic and social policy, is under review. While there is no general rule regarding the burden of proof such as a presumption of constitutionality in favour of parliamentary laws or, vice versa, an *in dubio pro libertate* in favour of the rights-bearer, there are three considerations that favour a legislation-friendly burden of proof allocation in German constitutional law.

First, the issues of burden of proof and of separation of powers are interrelated. How the constitutional court allocates the burden of proof impacts the legal power of the legislature to pass laws under conditions of factual uncertainty. Because courts, as the 'least dangerous branch', are typically careful not to overly restrict parliament's power to assess what policies could solve certain social problems, they tend to be wary of allocating factual uncertainties at parliament's expense. Second, legislative facts that underlie a policy are distinct from adjudicative facts that only concern the immediate parties. While it is a straightforward judicial task to adjudicate 'who did what, where, when, how and with what motive or intent' in the context of a particular legal dispute,[274] the determination of legislative facts is a much more multi-facetted task that requires collecting, processing, and evaluating complex empirical information, which is difficult for courts to accomplish.[275] Third, legislation is

[274] See for this famous phrase Kenneth Davis, *Administrative Law Treatise* (1st ed., K. C. Davis Pub. Co. 1958) § 15.03, 353.

[275] For example, in the *Codetermination* case, the Court was required to assess the impact of the extended employee representation on the power relationships in companies. BVerfGE 50, 290. In the *Smoking Ban* decision, the Court had to assess what economic effects anti-smoking legislation had on small one-room pubs that, in contrast to larger establishments, could not offer their customers any room for smoking purposes. BVerfGE 121, 317.

often based on prognoses, predictions, and forecasts about the future course of complex social causalities. But because no one can predict the future with certainty, the probability of legislative predictions required to persuade the FCC is typically lower than in other cases. The FCC insists that 'courts may not to substitute their own convictions about the expected course of economic developments'.[276]

Based on these considerations, the Court tends to grant the legislature a broad margin of appreciation in making predictions and in assessing legislative facts.[277] It is settled case-law that a legislative measure is *prima facie* suitable if the complainant does not establish that the law under review is 'objectively'[278] or 'generally unsuitable'[279]. This lowered judicial scrutiny effectively imposes the burden of proof on the individual because it bears the risk of factual uncertainties so long as the factual premises of the legislature are not evidently or manifestly false. A welcome side-effect of this distribution of burden of proof is that it largely relieves the Court of making its own evidentiary assessments. The Court either relies on a common-sense approach that does not require evidence to show the suitability of a measure[280] or, in more complex matters, only reviews whether the legislature diligently and comprehensively analysed the available facts when passing the law.[281]

### 3 The Preference for Ex-ante Review

When reviewing the suitability of a measure adopted by a policy-maker, a court has the choice between two different points in time: it can (at least try to) put itself into the shoes of the policy-maker and perform an *ex-ante* review based on the information available at the time of enactment, or it can use the superior knowledge about the suitability of the measure at the time of the legal proceedings and review the measure

276 BVerfGE 25, 1 [17].

277 For example, in the context of the freedom of occupation, the Court held that 'the FCC is not entitled to challenge the value judgments of the legislator so long as it is not evident that those are based upon incorrect factual premises or that they contradict the constitution'. BVerfGE 13, 97 [113].

278 BVerfGE 16, 147 [181]; BVerfGE 17, 306 [317]; BVerfGE 73, 301 [317]; BVerfGE 81, 156 [192]; BVerfGE 126, 331 [361].

279 BVerfGE 70, 1 [26].

280 See BVerfGE 67, 157 [175]; BVerfGE 81, 156 [192].

281 See BVerfGE 50, 290 [334] (imposing on the legislature the 'procedural requirements' of making 'sound and justifiable evaluation of the available material' and exploiting 'the accessible sources of information to assess the expected effects of its regulations as reliable as possible').

*ex post*. The FCC prefers the former approach and performs an *ex-ante* review. It bases its 'assessment on the circumstances that presented themselves to the legislature at the time of the drafting of the law'[282] and consistently holds that the 'constitutional assessment of the suitability of a measure depends on whether the legislature could assume *from its perspective* that the adopted measure fulfills its ideas'.[283] In other words, the Court prefers a subjectivized suitability review and limits its control to arbitrary misjudgments.[284] As a consequence, to show the unsuitability of a measure, it is not sufficient to establish *ex post* at the time of the judicial review that a measure has not actually promoted the purpose it was set out to promote.[285] The FCC holds that mispredictions regarding the suitability of a measure do not alone conclusively establish the unconstitutionality of that measure and accepts the possibility of forecast errors about future developments based on the legislative prerogative.[286] The Court 'is only entitled to challenge the adequacy and defensibility of the legislative prognosis regarding the assessment of economic policies if the measure can clearly be deemed unsuitable after the utilization of all epistemic possibilities at the time of the adoption of the law'.[287] As we have discussed previously, this fairly low standard of judicial scrutiny has the effect that the burden of proof regarding the suitability of the legislative policy shifts to the rights-bearer.[288]

### 4 Measures Deemed Unsuitable

It is surprising then that a law still fails the suitability test in some cases, for if the function of this test is limited to eliminating a few extreme cases in which there is no correlation between means and end, it is difficult to imagine that modern legislative processes still result in the adoption of laws that entirely fail to make any contribution to the achievement of the purpose that they were intended to achieve. Not surprisingly, the few

282 BVerfGE 30, 250 [263].

283 BVerfGE 39, 210 [230]. See also BVerfGE 30, 250 [263]; BVerfGE 118, 1 [24].

284 Klaus Meßerschmidt, *Gesetzgebungsermessen* (Berlin Verlag 2000) 996.

285 See, e.g., BVerfGE 67, 157 [175]. According to the FCC, 'the suitability of the means understood as the possibility to promote the pursued purpose does not require . . . that the objective is achieved in every single case or achievable. The abstract possibility of the fulfillment of the purpose suffices'. ibid.

286 BVerfGE 25, 1 [13]; BVerfGE 30, 250 [263]. See also BVerfGE 50, 290 [331]–[32]; BVerfGE 113, 167 [234]; BVerfGE 123, 186 [242].

287 BVerfGE 30, 250 [263]; BVerfGE 39, 210 [230].

288 See Section VI.A.

laws that failed the suitability test in the case-law were not indicative of the incapacity of the legislator but of a more stringent application of suitability. Today, most of those cases would likely be solved at the strict proportionality stage.

Generally speaking, the cases in which laws were deemed unsuitable are characterized by two different elements. On the one hand, these decisions go beyond the strict means-ends causality typically exercised at the suitability stage today and instead contain comparably strong normative elements that would typically be addressed at the strict proportionality stage.[289] On the other hand, these cases contain marked elements of over- and under-coverage or over- and under-inclusiveness.[290] In some of those cases, the Court struck down the law under review at the suitability stage;[291] in other cases, the Court merely raised doubts about the suitability of the measure but ultimately decided to strike down the over-inclusive measure with the necessity test.[292] Over-inclusiveness can become an issue for the FCC at the suitability stage if, for example, a law seeks to reduce pension benefits granted to a certain group of public servants in exchange for political loyalty with the authoritarian regime of the German Democratic Republic but reduces these benefits for all public servants in this group irrespective of their political loyalty;[293] requires an applicant for a falconry license to have sufficient knowledge about weapons law and technology even if that applicant is a hawker that has never used a gun in his life;[294] or strictly limits the grounds for a child's challenge of legitimacy that would allow it to find out about its descent to contribute to stable family relationships even if all family members support the child's challenge.[295] In other words, the Court implicitly blames the responsible policy-maker for having designed an overbroad policy that is not sufficiently narrowly tailored to its core purpose.[296]

289 Hirschberg (n 3) 55.

290 A law is over-inclusive if it includes persons or situations that do not need to be included to achieve the purpose of the law. It is under-inclusive if it fails to include persons or situations that would need to be included to achieve the purpose.

291 BVerfGE 17, 306; BVerfGE 55, 159.

292 See, e.g., BVerfGE 19, 330; BVerfGE 61, 291; BVerfGE 100, 59; BVerfGE 99, 341.

293 BVerfGE 100, 59.

294 BVerfGE 55, 159.

295 BVerfGE 79, 256.

296 For a more detailed analysis of narrow tailoring cases, see Section VIII.B.

An example for a decision from 1964 that contains elements of under-inclusiveness is the *Carpool Agency* decision[297] in which the FCC struck down a burdensome, criminally sanctioned authorization requirement for car drivers that offered a ride to passengers via a carpooling company. To put this practice into historical context: in the post-war period, carpooling had become an important means of transportation in Germany. The stated purposes of the challenged law were road safety and the protection of the individual passenger. The FCC held that 'the authorization requirement was unsuitable to achieve either purpose', arguing that the density and security of the traffic would not be significantly affected because the car driver likely makes the planned trip with or without an added passenger. While this point addresses the empirical question of whether the measure achieves the goal that lies at the heart of the suitability test, the FCC expands its analysis regarding the purpose of the individual passenger's protection and relies on considerations of equal treatment and non-arbitrariness,[298] arguing that it is not evident why passengers publicly recruited by a carpooling company are particularly vulnerable compared to privately recruited passengers. The decision to strike down the statutory authorization requirement for car drivers is primarily driven by two objections that go beyond the suitability test understood in a technical sense and that the Court would today typically address at the strict proportionality stage: first, the FCC seems to hold the view that the law primarily serves the illegitimate purpose to protect the then state-owned national railway company from competition from the widely established car sharing practice. This view is directly expressed and further substantiated by exposing the inconsistencies of the statutory arrangement.[299] In that regard, there is a strong parallel to the *Sports Betting* and *Casino Order* cases discussed earlier.[300] Second, the FCC is especially critical of the legislative use of criminal sanctions, which it calls a 'misuse of legal criminal arrangements'.[301]

[297] BVerfGE 17, 306.
[298] Clérico (n 268).
[299] The law only protected publicly recruited passengers and did not prohibit carpooling as such but only required prior authorization.
[300] See Section V.C.
[301] BVerfGE 17, 306 [317]–[18].

### B *Effectiveness of Purpose Achievement*

As we have seen, the Court only reviews the suitability of a measure in the abstract.[302] But if it is not required that the law actually and verifiably furthers its purpose, the question of effectiveness of purpose achievement only has a subordinated role. As a consequence, a low probability or a lack of effectiveness in achieving the purpose of a law virtually never has the consequence that a law fails the suitability test. This does not mean that issues of effectiveness are not addressed at the suitability stage. There are a significant number of cases in which a lack of effectiveness of a law raised by the plaintiff is considered by the Court.[303] But these considerations typically end with reference to the low threshold of partial and abstract suitability. The Court recites that the legislative measure passes the suitability stage so long as the measure is not 'generally unsuitable' to promote the pursued purpose and concludes that it was not shown that the law was generally unsuitable.[304] The combination of this limited standard of review and the burden of proof in favour of the state render it difficult for a plaintiff to establish the unsuitability of a law.

Similar to effectiveness considerations, considerations of negative consequences other than the infringement of the right and arguments of counter-effectiveness of the adopted means are typically dismissed or not even addressed by the Court at the suitability stage. The locus for these considerations in German proportionality practice is typically the strict proportionality stage that serves as a sponge in which all types of considerations are weighed against each other. However, there are some cases in which considerations of counter-effectiveness play a central part in judicial suitability analysis. Most of these decisions ultimately uphold the legislative assessment that the law under review furthers the intended purpose despite contentions of counter-effectiveness brought forward by the plaintiffs in the case. For example, in the *Cannabis* decision concerning the criminal prohibition of the possession of marijuana,[305] the lower courts referring the case to the FCC had argued that the criminalization of cannabis was unsuited to achieve the purpose pursued by the legislator, namely health protection, because it was counter-effective.[306] Studies in other countries had shown that the decriminalization of marihuana

302 See Section VI.A.
303 See, e.g., BVerfGE 112, 255 [266].
304 See, e.g., BVerfGE 70, 1 [26].
305 BVerfGE 90, 145. See on this judgment in more detail Section VII.B.
306 ibid [162].

had resulted in a decrease of consumption.[307] Moreover, the criminalization of cannabis would force those who want to get intoxicated to rely on alcohol, which was more harmful to health than marihuana.[308] However, the FCC did not specifically address these arguments but stressed more generally that '[i]n forming a judgement as to whether the chosen means is suitable and necessary for achieving the desired goals the legislator has a certain degree of discretion'.[309] Because 'there remain not insignificant dangers and risks' resulting from the consumption of marijuana, 'comprehensive penalties on illegal dealings with Cannabis products . . . are suitable to limit the distribution of the drug in society and thus limit the dangers which flow from it as a whole'.[310]

A rare counter-example is the *Parental Duty of Contact* decision, in which the FCC struck down a federal family law provision at the suitability stage based on considerations of counter-effectiveness.[311] In this matter, the mother of an illegitimate child sought to force the father of the child to have contact with his extramarital child. The father, who was married to a different woman with whom he had two marital children, refused because of the negative effect this would have on his family. However, Section 1684(1) of the German Civil Code, aimed at the protection of children's welfare, entitles the child to contact with his parents and, correspondingly, obligates the parents to engage in such contact. The FCC reviewed the conformity of this provision with the general right of personality guaranteed by article 2(1) i.c.w. 1(1) BL. The central issue in the context of PA was whether the compulsory enforcement of the duty of contact was truly suitable to further the child's welfare or whether forcing a parent against his will to engage in contact with his child was, in reality, detrimental to the child's best interest – and thus counter-effective to the purpose pursued by the legislator. The Court found that the statutory enforcement was 'not suitable for achieving the sought purpose', for '[i]f coercive measures are necessary to force an unwilling parent to have contact with a child, this contact is not usually in the best interests of the child'.[312] Based on empirical evidence presented by several NGOs in the oral hearing, the Court argued that in the

307 ibid [154]–[55].
308 ibid [161].
309 ibid [173].
310 ibid [182]. For a similar approach, see BVerfGE 61, 291 [313]; BVerfGE 77, 84 [108]–[09]; BVerfGE 50, 290 [350]–[51].
311 BVerfGE 121, 69.
312 ibid [98].

case of an uncooperative parent the child would 'not experience the parental warmth and affection which is the purpose of the contact, but instead experiences personal rejection', which 'poses a big risk that the child's self-esteem could be damaged' and which, ultimately, 'does not benefit the child's well-being, but instead damages it'.[313]

### C *Substantiation over Time*

As a result of the abstract and *ex-ante* review of the suitability test performed by the FCC, judicial scrutiny regarding legislative predictions is low. The Court prioritizes the legislative ability to act and to experiment under conditions of uncertainty over strict judicial control of factual assumptions. However, the Court combines the generous legislative margin of appreciation with a legislative duty to monitor the future development of assumed facts and predictions and to rectify laws if the predictions prove to be false and the laws passed on their basis violate a fundamental right.[314] If the legislature is entitled to intrude into fundamental rights despite factual uncertainties, it must at least react to this uncertainty by institutionalizing learning processes about these facts.[315] Abiding by the constitution becomes a dynamic concept[316] and the timeframe considered for the suitability of the means to achieve the goal is hence long term. As a result of changing factual circumstances or false predictions, a law that was deemed constitutional by the Court at a certain point in time may later become unconstitutional without legislative rectifications.

Most of these decisions deal with the legislative monitoring and rectification briefly. How the legislature is expected to fulfil this duty is not specified. In some decisions, however, the Court is more specific.

[313] ibid [99]–[100].

[314] See, e.g., BVerfGE 49, 89 [130]–[33]; BVerfGE 50, 290 [331]–[33]; BVerfGE 56, 54 [78]–[80]; BVerfGE 95, 267 [314]; BVerfGE 110, 141 [158]. See generally on this constitutional duty of the legislature: Christian Mayer, *Die Nachbesserungspflicht des Gesetzgebers* (Nomos 1996); Daniel Oliver-Lalana, 'Due Post-legislative Process? On the Lawmakers' Constitutional Duties of Monitoring and Revision' in Klaus Meßerschmidt and Daniel Oliver-Lalana (eds), *Rational Lawmaking under Review* (Springer 2016) 257–94; Ino Augsberg and Steifen Augsberg, 'Prognostische Elemente in der Rechtsprechung des Bundesverfassungsgerichts' (2007) 98 VerwArch, 290, 205–309; Marion Albers, 'Evaluation sicherheitsbehördlicher Kompetenzen: Schritte von der symbolischen Politik zum lernenden Recht' (2008) 99 VerwArch 481.

[315] ibid 485.

[316] ibid 484.

It requires of the legislature, as part of 'the duty to observe', that 'the necessary data be collected and evaluated regularly'.[317] Or it requests the legislature to conduct an examination after a deadline of 10 years to assess whether the desired purpose may be attained on the chosen path within the next10 years.[318] In the *Telecommunication Surveillance Act* decision concerning acoustic surveillance measures by the German intelligence agency BND, the Court held that the statute was suitable for achieving its purpose despite 'the fact that it is possible to encrypt messages'.[319] The statute under review provided for a wide interception of private international telecommunications in the fight against international terrorism and organized crime based on computerized searches. The Court ultimately found the statute to be constitutional on most grounds and only deemed specific provisions to be incompatible with the privacy of telecommunications guarantee of article 10(1) BL. A concern raised by the Court at the suitability stage was, however, that 'it is likely that exactly the individuals or organisations that are the targets of monitoring are, due to their high degree of organisation and their use of modern infrastructure, in a position to evade telecommunications monitoring whereas unsuspected individuals who cannot make use of encryption technologies ... become subjects of monitoring'.[320] The Court concluded that 'the question whether monitoring for the objective of early recognition of the respective threats fails due to the use of encryption technologies cannot ... be answered on an abstract level but only on account of practical experience'. As a consequence, it required the BND – without giving a specific time period – 'to ensure

[317] BVerfGE 88, 203 [313]. Similarly, in the *Cannabis* decision, the Court took the open-natured criminological and academic debate 'about the dangers presented by the consumption of Cannabis and the correct way of combating them' as an occasion to impose on the legislature 'a duty to monitor and check the effects of the laws currently in force'. In particular, the Court required the legislature to have 'due regard to experiences in other countries' and, in doing so, to monitor 'to what extent a legalisation of Cannabis could lead to a separation of the market in drugs, and thus to a reduction in drug consumption as a whole; or whether on the contrary only resistance to the drug market as a whole and the organised crime which determines it, backed up by criminal penalties, offers reasonable chances of success'. See BVerfGE 90, 145 [194]. Other examples are BVerfGE 109, 279 [340]; BVerfGE 110, 177 [194].

[318] BVerfGE 95, 267 [314]–[15]. The so-called *Old Debts* case concerned the different treatment of the debt burden of former East German and West German companies, which the Court found, in a nutshell, to be justified because of the particular circumstances of German reunification but only for a limited period of time.

[319] BVerfGE 100, 313 [373].

[320] ibid [374]–[75].

that in spite of the possibility of encryption, the suitability of the measures . . . is maintained'.[321]

## VII Necessity

While the necessity, minimal impairment, or least restrictive means test presents more than only a technical hurdle, its role in German proportionality practice is limited. The quantitative analysis shows that a measure failed the necessity test in only 8 out of all 58 'failure' cases, or 14 per cent. Although the number of laws that failed the necessity test is as large as the number of laws failing the previous two stages combined,[322] what nevertheless sticks out is the low overall number of measures deemed unnecessary. Moreover, it is also not the case that – notwithstanding this low number of struck down measures – the necessity test would occupy a prominent place in the PA judgments of the Court. In 50 out of 114 decisions, or 44 per cent, the FCC either only glanced over this stage, stating that the existence of less intrusive alternatives was not evident, or entirely skipped the necessity stage.[323]

The FCC views a measure as necessary for the achievement of its purpose if 'the legislator could not have chosen a different means which would have been equally effective but which would have infringed on fundamental rights to a lesser extent or not at all'.[324] This formula contains two distinct comparisons between alternative means: on the one hand, a comparison between the suitability of the available means to achieve the purpose and, on the other hand, a comparison of the intensity of the infringement into a fundamental right. With regard to both comparisons, the FCC limits the stringency of its necessity test in favour of the strict proportionality stage. A key factor for the reduced role of the necessity step is that the FCC stresses the prerogative of the

321 ibid [375].

322 In the 114 cases included in the dataset, a contested measure failed the worthy purpose test in five instances and the suitability test in three instances. In his comparative analysis of German and Canadian constitutional adjudication, Grimm observes that in Germany, 'the proportion of laws failing at the second [necessity] step is considerably larger than the number of laws failing at the first [suitability] step'. Grimm, 'Proportionality in Canadian and German Constitutional Jurisprudence' (n 7) 389.

323 In the 114 cases included in the dataset, the Court deals with the necessity stage in a cursory fashion in 28 cases. It entirely skips the suitability stage in 22 cases.

324 BVerfGE 90, 145 [172]; BVerfGE 30, 292 [316]; BVerfGE 113, 167 [252]; BVerfGE 117, 163 [189]; BVerfGE 120, 224 [240]; BVerfGE 126, 112 [144]–[45].

legislature at this stage and enhances the legislative margin of discretion in deciding what measures are equally suitable or effective. Overall, the FCC is determined to keep value-laden elements out of the necessity stage and, accordingly, does not consider the intensity of the infringement at this stage but reserves a more comprehensive costs-benefits analysis of the effects of the law to the strict proportionality stage that is at the heart of German PA practice.[325]

### *A Is There a Less Restricting Alternative?*

The FCC performs the comparison of the intrusiveness of the legislative and of the alternative means in a manner similar to the suitability test. It grants the legislator a substantial margin of appreciation to choose the least restrictive regulatory means.[326] The means chosen by the legislature need not be the least intrusive measure in every single case but only 'in general'[327] or 'as a general rule'.[328] In most cases, the Court requires that 'it must *clearly* be established that a less restrictive means is available'.[329] Limiting the standard of review to cases of obviousness has the effect that the complainant – and not the state – bears the burden of proof to show that a less restrictive means is available.[330] As a consequence, there is no accepted practice that the state is required to present before the Court other alternatives that it considered in the legislative process. In most cases, the complainant will submit alternative measures that, in his view, would have been readily available to the legislature. In addition, the FCC asserts itself that it does not engage in an extensive search for alternative means but confines 'its review of whether other alternatives can achieve the pursued objective in an equally effective but a less fundamental rights intruding manner to the alternatives pointed out by the complainants and discussed in professional circles'.[331]

325 Grimm, 'Proportionality in Canadian and German Constitutional Jurisprudence' (n 7) 390.

326 BVerfGE 126, 112 [145]. See also BVerfGE 81, 156 [193]; BVerfGE 102, 197 [218]; BVerfGE 115, 276 [309].

327 BVerfGE 30, 292 [316]; BVerfGE 37, 1 [22].

328 BVerfGE 68, 155 [172].

329 BVerfGE 30, 292 [319]; BVerfGE 37, 1 [21]; BVerfGE 39, 210 [231]; BVerfGE 40, 196 [223]; BVerfGE 53, 135 [145].

330 See Section III.

331 BVerfGE 40, 196 [222]; see also BVerfGE 77, 84 [109]; BVerfGE 80, 137 [160].

### 1 Strict Exclusion of Less Restrictive but More Expensive Means

The Court also does not accept fiscally more expensive but less right-infringing measures as less restrictive alternatives at the necessity stage. In other words, it will not require government at the necessity stage to assume a significant financial burden for a less intrusive means.[332] Means that require additional financial resources are strictly excluded from the necessity test.[333] The Court emphasizes that the individual cannot expect that limited public funds are used beyond reasonably expected measures to ease fundamental rights limitations.[334] A measure is only less restrictive if it is 'as cost-effective for the public purse'.[335] A case in point is the *Deposit Copy* decision concerning a state law obliging publishers to provide a free copy of every publication to the state library. The purpose of the law – deemed as worthy by the Court – was to make literary works as comprehensively accessible as possible to scientifically and culturally interested persons and to give future generations a comprehensive impression of the intellectual heritage from earlier epochs.[336] Although the decision effectively dealt with the distribution of financial resources between the state and private publishers, the Court did not even mention the less restrictive alternative of a purchase obligation by the state. Instead, the Court mostly accepted the fiscally motivated deposit copy for private publishers but also eased the burden for publishers at the strict proportionality stage by requiring the state to compensate in excessive cases of very small and very expensive editions.[337] This provision of redress in hardship cases is a central theme in the Court's jurisprudence.[338]

### 2 Comparative Law as Proof for the Existence of Less Restrictive Means

In a few cases, the FCC has relied on comparative law from other countries and from German states, the Länder, to prove the existence

[332] Grimm, 'Proportionality in Canadian and German Constitutional Jurisprudence' (n 7) 390. See, e.g., BVerfGE 77, 308 [334].
[333] Wischmeyer (n 257) 60–61.
[334] See, e.g., BVerfGE 77, 84 [110]–[11]; BVerfGE 81, 70 [91]–[92]; BVerfGE 118, 168 [194]; BVerfGE 119, 59 [86].
[335] BVerfGE 125, 260 [360].
[336] BVerfGE 58, 137 [149].
[337] ibid [150].
[338] See in more detail Section VIII.B.

of less restrictive means.[339] By outlining different regulatory solutions from different jurisdictions, the Court shows that less restrictive means are indeed practically possible. In the *Pharmacy* case,[340] in which the Bavarian legislature had adopted a rigid 'necessity clause' scheme for the admission of new pharmacies that was justified with the argument that unregulated competition between pharmacies would likely inhibit the proper operation of the pharmacy business, the Court relied on a comparison with the pharmacy business in Switzerland, where no such regulatory scheme existed, to show that the legislative assumptions were flawed and that less restrictive alternatives existed to regulate pharmacy admission than a strict system of necessity clauses.[341]

In the *Milk Distributor* case,[342] the Court compared the regulatory effects of German states that applied legislation requiring milk companies to produce minimum quotas of milk with states that did not apply that legislation.[343] The purpose of the minimum quotas was to protect the health of milk consumers. Minimum milk quotas were viewed as a necessary regulatory means to ensure the quality of milk because a large amount of milk companies would be harder to monitor and would compromise the economic performance and operational profitability of milk companies. Based on the experience of the states that had not applied the quota system, the Court concluded that 'neither the degree of probability nor the intensity of the alleged health dangers were serious enough to justify the establishment of minimum quotas'.[344]

[339] See Petersen, *Verhältnismäßigkeit als Rationalitätskontrolle* (n 3) 170–71.
[340] BVerfGE 7, 377.
[341] ibid 415–16.
[342] BVerfGE 9, 39.
[343] ibid 52–57.
[344] ibid 52. In the *Separate Appeals Court Registration* case, concerning the prohibition for attorneys admitted to a certain Appeals Court to take legal actions before another court, the FCC also used comparisons between different German states to prove the existence of less restrictive means. On the basis of the different experiences in different states, the Court noted that deficits in the administration of justice had not occurred, suggesting that this restriction of attorneys' freedom of occupation was not necessary. BVerfGE 103, 1 [11]–[16]. Similarly, in the *Right of Reply* case, an important consideration supporting the decisions to find the law under review unconstitutional was that most provisions in the field of press and broadcasting did not contain such a short time limit. BVerfGE 63, 131 [145]–[46].

## *B Comparative Effectiveness of Alternatives*

Assessing the comparative effectiveness of regulatory alternatives is a complex judicial task. The FCC exercises this particular task with judicial restraint. While it will always be possible to think of a less intrusive measure, the hardest part about the necessity test is to assess the equivalent effect of that measure. The Court is generally cautious in presuming that an alternative measure is as effective as the measure chosen by the government.

### 1 Degree of Comparative Effectiveness Required

The classic formulation of the necessity prong that requires the legislator to choose less restrictive means if they are equally effective suggests a simplicity that typically does not exist with regard to real-life regulatory alternatives.[345] In a legal laboratory, one can conceive of a simple scale of various equally effective measures that is sorted by the intensity of the infringement for the rights holder and choose the least intrusive of these alternatives.[346] In reality, however, matters are more complex. It is hard to think of two different regulatory alternatives that are of identical effectiveness. Every regulation causes distinct effects, has particular disadvantages, or requires additional resources.[347] If courts were literally to insist on identical or equal effectiveness the necessity test would be rendered worthless. The decisive question for the significance of the necessity test is therefore to what extent courts require the legislator to adopt less restrictive alternatives that are less effective than the adopted measure.

In general, the Court is reluctant to assume that an alternative is as effective as the means chosen by the policy-maker.[348] In most decisions that review the necessity prong, the Court virtually requires an identical degree of effectiveness.[349] If a less intrusive measure results in an additional burden for a third person or the general public, it is disregarded in the framework of the necessity test. Any doubts about the effectiveness of

[345] Kai Möller, 'Proportionality: Challenging the Critics' (2012) 10 International Journal of Constitutional Law 709, 714.
[346] Hirschberg (n 3) 65.
[347] Möller (n 345) 714.
[348] See Wischmeyer (n 257), 57; n. 206; Dechsling (n 3) 55–56.
[349] See, e.g., BVerfGE 120, 274 [321]; BVerfGE 128, 1 [51]–[52]; BVerfGE 134, 204 [227]–[28].

an alternative are to the detriment of the complainant. An example for this strict construction of necessity is the *Employee Leasing* decision, in which the Court dismissed a less restrictive alternative as not equally effective due to a lack of practicability.[350] The case concerned a statutory prohibition for private operators to lease employees to construction companies that, among other purposes, sought to combat illegal employment in the construction sector. The Court upheld the prohibition in its entirety. The government representatives had argued that conditions of frequently changing employment furthered illegal employment. Against the contention of the complainants that less restrictive measures than a total ban of employee leasing were readily available, as illegal employment could as effectively but less restrictively be combated by means of inspection and control measures, the Court held that it is not reasonable to expect the legislature to adopt such measures.[351] The Court again emphasized the wide discretion of the legislature and found that the alternatives were less practicable than the measure chosen by the legislature.[352] It was defensible to assume for the legislature that it requires an unduly heavy burden to effectively perform administrative construction site inspections.[353] If we recall that regulatory alternatives rarely come without some disadvantages, the exclusion of measures that cause additional financial resources or raise issues of administrative practicability significantly limits the scope of the necessity test.

However, as will be later discussed in detail,[354] the Court lowers the degree of comparative effectiveness required in cases in which a law is struck down with the necessity test. In those cases, the alternative was slightly less effective than the means adopted. In other words, the required degree of effectiveness varies between cases in which a law was upheld or struck down. This variation is closely related to the degree of factual uncertainty posed by a case. The more uncertain and complex social causalities are, the more the Court tends to defer to the assessment of the legislator.

[350] BVerfGE 77, 84.

[351] ibid [110]–[11].

[352] ibid [111].

[353] ibid [110]–[11]. See also BVerfGE 115, 276 [309]. But see, exemplary for a stricter scrutiny regarding the comparative effectiveness of alternatives in the Court's early jurisprudence, BVerfGE 13, 290 [317].

[354] See Section VII.C.

### 2 Conditions of Uncertainty and Deference to Policy-Makers

When assessing the comparative effectiveness of alternatives under conditions of uncertainty, the FCC applies a standard of review that is generous for the legislature and strict for the complainant. While the legislature is only required to show that its factual assessments were 'defensible',[355] a complainant challenging a statute will only prevail on the necessity stage before the FCC if the equivalence of an alternative measure is 'evident'.[356] This required showing of obviousness is tantamount to imposing the burden of proof on the complainant.[357]

How the Court grants deference to policy-makers and deals with uncertainty in the framework of the necessity test can be illustrated with the decisions in *Cannabis*[358] and in *Oil Reserve*.[359] At the time of the *Cannabis* decision, the Federal Intoxicating Substances Act made the possession of marijuana a criminal offence even if it was only for personal use and irrespective of the amount. This criminal regime has been challenged by some scientists that argue that the negative medicinal effects of the use of marijuana are exaggerated and that the different treatment of marijuana and alcohol has no sufficient scientific basis. Against this background, some lower criminal courts concluded that this law is unconstitutional and sought to obtain a decision from the FCC via the concrete judicial review procedure of Article 100(1) of the Basic Law. The FCC upheld the relevant provisions of the Intoxicating Substances Act in its *Cannabis* judgment.[360] The criminally sanctioned prohibition of cannabis possession pursues the legitimate purpose 'to protect the health both of the individual and of the population as a whole against the dangers which flow from drugs' and 'to prevent the population, especially the young from becoming addicted to drugs'.[361] The key question in the case was whether based on new scientific findings 'the unbanning of Cannabis would be a milder instrument with better chances of achieving

[355] See, e.g., BVerfGE 77, 84 [109]–[11].
[356] See, e.g., BVerfGE 126, 331 [362].
[357] Section III.
[358] BVerfGE 90, 145.
[359] BVerfGE 30, 292.
[360] At the time, the Court conducted an interpretation in conformity with the Constitution with respect to the relevant criminal procedure provisions concerning the prosecution of minor crimes that required the public prosecutor's office to refrain from prosecution in cases of personal consumption. BVerfGE 90, 145 [198].
[361] ibid [193].

those aims'.[362] The Court held that 'the legislature has a degree of discretion' when 'forming a judgment as to whether the chosen means is suitable and necessary for achieving the desired goals' and that the 'Court can only review the exercise of this discretion to a limited extent'.[363] Although the Court recognized that the 'legislature's original assessment of the health risks is contentious',[364] it observed that '[t]here is no scientifically based information indicating firmly that the one view or the other is correct'.[365] 'In these circumstances', the Court stated, 'if the legislature remains of the view that a general ban on Cannabis backed up by criminal penalties will scare off more potential users than will a suspension of the criminal penalties . . . then this must be accepted from a constitutional point of view',[366] adding that the conclusions of this debate 'have not reached such *a level of clarity*' required to strike down legislation at the necessity stage.[367]

There are two important takeaways from this decision for how the Court performs the necessity test as to the equivalence of the means. First, the defensibility standard applied by the Court in the context of the equivalence of a measure signifies in essence a procedural approach. This becomes apparent when the Court stresses that 'the legislature has repeatedly re-considered its view',[368] which is effectively a diligence argument in the sense that so long as the legislature makes diligent factual assessments, the Court will let them stand. Of course, there is a risk that procedural rationality requirements overburden the compromise-seeking nature of the political process that often cannot be broken down to a single purpose pursued by a policy.[369] Second, the Court applies a burden of proof rule in favour of the legislature. A showing that an alternative measure is equally effective requires a sufficient 'level of clarity'.[370] In other words, it must be evident. In contrast, if the criminological evidence does not firmly support 'one view

362 Response to this question in the negative: ibid [181].
363 ibid [172].
364 ibid [177]. In particular, the Court noted that the 'threat to health posed by Hashish products is today seen as being smaller than the legislature was assuming when it passed the Act'. ibid [181].
365 ibid [181].
366 ibid.
367 ibid.
368 ibid.
369 Matthias Jestaedt, 'Verhältnismäßigkeit als Verhaltensmaß' in Matthias Jestaedt and Oliver Lepsius (eds), *Verhältnismäßigkeit* (Mohr Siebeck 2015) 293, 300–2.
370 BVerfGE 90, 145 [181].

or the other', the legislative assessment generally prevails so long as that assessment appears 'defensible'.[371]

The Court used the same approach in the *Oil Reserve* decision concerning the stockholding obligation of oil companies in order to ensure sufficient oil reserves and to prevent an energy crisis.[372] In that case, independent oil importers had filed a constitutional complaint because they were excessively burdened by the stockholding obligation as they had very limited storage capacities. While larger oil companies already had such capacities, the law would have required the smaller and more specialized independent oil importers to make significant investments. Against this background, the independent oil importers proposed several less restrictive alternatives, in particular that (i) the federal government should assume the stockholding obligation, (ii) the obligation of the oil industry should be limited to specific periods of high demand or (iii) to crude oil instead of finished oil, and (iv) the obligation should be imposed on other companies than independent oil importers. However, the FCC stated that all these alternatives would have to be equally effective with regard to both purposes and emphasized the broad legislative discretion in the area of economic policy.[373] As a result, the Court concluded that a preference for an alternative means would not necessarily result in the unconstitutionality of the means elected by the legislature.[374] Accordingly, the Court required that the equivalence of the alternative measure must be 'evident' and the measure passed the necessity test but was then struck down on the strict proportionality stage insofar as independent oil importers were excessively burdened.[375]

### C Can the Chosen Means Be More Narrowly Tailored?

The decisions in which the FCC has struck down laws at the necessity stage effectively require the legislator to choose a less effective

[371] ibid.

[372] BVerfGE 30, 292. See analysis of this decision in Section V.A.

[373] ibid [319].

[374] ibid.

[375] ibid. See also BVerfGE 25, 1 [19]–[20]. Similarly, in the *Vineyard* decision concerning the constitutionality of a public stabilization fund for wine intended to contribute to the maintenance of the quality of German wine, for which the grape growers were required to pay a levy, the Court rejected the argument of the complainant wine companies that they could perform the fund's tasks of advertisement and storing 'at least as effectively as the Fund', arguing that the legislature was only required to show the generalized necessity of the legislative regulation. See BVerfGE 37, 1 [21]–[22].

alternative.[376] They use different narrowly tailored techniques that require policy-makers to adopt more nuanced categories, exception mechanisms, or individual assessment possibilities.

### 1 What Characterizes Laws That Fail the Necessity Test?

Most laws that failed the necessity test constituted excessive prohibitions or sweeping bans that are in some sense reminiscent of 'shooting sparrows with cannons'.[377] These laws severely restricted the access to certain professions or economic sectors through excessive health,[378] safety,[379] client,[380] or consumer protection laws[381] or through overbroad economic needs tests[382] that effectively amounted to a protection from competition. In all of these cases, the regulatory purpose could still be achieved with a much less intrusive policy than with a total ban. But the policy-maker had to accept a moderately higher degree of risk that the regulatory purpose would not be achieved in all instances. An example: in the *Chocolate Candy Bunny* decision concerning the freedom of occupation guaranteed by Article 12(1) of the Basic Law,[383] the Court struck down an excessive consumer protection regulation that prohibited the marketing of Easter bunnies and Santa clauses primarily made of puffed rice but covered with chocolate icing creations. The prohibition was based on the assumption that those puffed rice creations were capable of being confused by consumers with chocolate Easter bunnies and Santa clauses. With a reasoning that closely resembles the jurisprudence of the Court of Justice of the European Union (ECJ),[384] the FCC argued that 'such a danger [of consumer deception] can be countered in an equally

[376] See, e.g., BVerfGE 7, 320; BVerfGE 7, 377; BVerfGE 9, 39; BVerfGE 11, 30; BVerfGE 11, 168; BVerfGE 17, 269; BVerfGE 30, 227; BVerfGE 30, 336; BVerfGE 41, 378 ; BVerfGE 53, 135; BVerfGE 63, 88; BVerfGE 63, 131; BVerfGE 69, 209; BVerfGE 90, 263; BVerfGE 92, 158; BVerfGE 93, 362; BVerfGE 99, 341; BVerfGE 101, 106; BVerfGE 102, 197; BVerfGE 103, 1; BVerfGE 130, 151; BVerfGE 135, 90.

[377] See for this famous phrase first Fritz Fleiner, *Institutionen des deutschen Verwaltungsrechts* (8th ed., Mohr Siebeck 1928) 404.

[378] BVerfGE 9, 39; BVerfGE 17, 269; BVerfGE 102, 197.

[379] BVerfGE 40, 371 [383].

[380] BVerfGE 41, 378; BVerfGE 93, 362; BVerfGE 103, 1; BVerfGE 135, 90.

[381] BVerfGE 53, 135.

[382] BVerfGE 7, 377; BVerfGE 11, 30; BVerfGE 11, 168.

[383] BVerfGE 53, 135.

[384] For a detailed analysis of the ECJ's proportionality practice concerning internal market regulations, see Oliver Koch, *Der Grundsatz der Verhältnismäßigkeit in der Rechtsprechung des Gerichtshofs der Europäischen Gemeinschaften* (Duncker and Humblot 2003) 369–95.

effective but less intruding way with a labelling requirement'.[385] Strictly understood, a labelling requirement is never as effective as a total marketing prohibition because certain consumers will only give the labelling a cursory look and not read it carefully. Interestingly, the FCC recognized that fact but still found the marketing prohibition to fail the necessity test by redefining the purpose of the regulation more narrowly. The Court specified who is indeed worthy and who is unworthy of protection, noting that the protection of the 'cursory consumer' is not 'an interest that is legitimately pursued in the context of consumer protection'.[386] This decision indicates not only the far-reaching penetration of constitutional adjudication into remote areas of economic regulation but also shows that the FCC is required to concretize the purpose of the law that was defined broadly at the legitimate purpose stage to conduct a meaningful necessity test.[387]

A very similar set of cases, in which the FCC has struck down laws at the necessity stage, concern provisions that gave preference to legal certainty over providing a mechanism or a forum to realize individual justice.[388] Typically, the challenged laws provided for clear-cut rules that did not leave any room for exceptions. In reaction, the Court requested provision for individualized procedures that leave room to do justice to the particular facts of the individual case. In a case concerning testamentary dispositions, the Court deemed a provision unconstitutional that denied the right to testate to persons who were unable both to write and to speak.[389] Under the German civil law at the time, testamentary

[385] BVerfGE 53, 135 [145]–[46].

[386] ibid.

[387] Similarly, in the *Association's Name* case concerning electoral rules for elections to the self-governing bodies of social security agencies, the Court found a law unconstitutional that required those associations participating in the elections the name of which featured elements of the social security agency to change their name in order not to confuse voters. The Court argued that instead of providing for a general name change requirement, it would be less intrusive to verify on an individualized basis whether voters are truly misled. See BVerfGE 30, 227 [245]–[46]. Another area of relevancy is demonstrations law, where the Court consistently held that it is unconstitutional to entirely ban a demonstration before the less restrictive means to restrict the demonstration with particular requirements has not been exhausted. In those cases, the concern to prevent dangers to public safety resulting from demonstrations could be effectively pursued in a much less intrusive way than with a total ban. See in particular the Court's decision in *Brokdorf* that was foundational for the law of assembly. BVerfGE 69, 315 [353].

[388] See, e.g., BVerfGE 7, 320; BVerfGE 30, 227; BVerfGE 30, 336; BVerfGE 41, 378; BVerfGE 63, 131; BVerfGE 90, 263; BVerfGE 99, 341; BVerfGE 108, 150; BVerfGE 101, 106.

[389] BVerfGE 99, 341 [354]–[55].

dispositions were accomplished either by the testator declaring his last will to the notary or by the testator handing the notary a self-written last will. Persons who are mute and illiterate are incapable of performing either alternative. These strict requirements have the purpose of ensuring legal certainty with regard to last wills, in particular reliably ascertaining the content of a deceased person's will, and protecting persons who lack the ability to decide in a self-determined way. While the Court found that the legislature pursued legitimate public interests and that the denial to make testamentary dispositions was suitable to further those interests,[390] it concluded that less intrusive but equally effective means to reliably ascertain the last will were available, such as providing for a procedure that included a special confidant and a second notary.[391] Generally excluding all mute and illiterate persons from the right to testate exceeded what was necessary to protect their self-determination because, in some cases, persons with those disabilities are able to decide about their last will in a way that is self-determined and that conforms to the requirements of legal certainty.[392]

As those examples show, the FCC requires policy-makers with the necessity test to accept that the regulatory purpose will not be achieved in all cases (as some cursory consumers will inadvertently purchase puffed rice instead of chocolate and some mute and illiterate persons will get to testate even though they lack the ability to decide in a self-determined way). In exchange, there is a substantial gain for the concerns of the affected rights-holders (the puffed rice producer continues its business activities and mute and illiterate persons are granted the right to testate

[390] ibid [353]–[54].

[391] ibid [353]–[55].

[392] Similarly, in the *Challenge of Legitimacy* case, the Court struck down a provision according to which the time limit for the challenge of legitimacy through a child started strictly with the age of majority even if the child had no knowledge of the relevant facts before the expiry of that time limit. BVerfGE 90, 263. The challenge of legitimacy was the only way for the child to find out about its descent. The primary legislative objective behind this rule was to ensure legal certainty and, thereby, to contribute to stable family relationships. ibid [271]–[72]. However, the Court found that a less restrictive way to achieve those purposes was, for example, to allow for a declaratory judgment to ascertain a child's descent without legal effects on the family relationships. ibid [272]. In any event, the Court concluded that a strict rule with strict time limits intended to further legal certainty did not pay due regard to the child's general personality right and the special circumstances of each individual case. ibid [272]–[73]. Interestingly, he Court deemed it necessary to back up its reasoning with strict proportionality stage considerations, arguing that the public interest in legal certainty is not sufficiently significant to justify such far-reaching restrictions of the child's personality right.

themselves). Put differently, the Court implicitly balances the public benefits of a total ban with the costs incurred by the fundamental rights infringement. While legal certainty is most effectively served with a clear-cut rule without exceptions, the Court restricts the legislative margin of manoeuvre to pursue considerations of practicability and of legal certainty to the greatest extent possible if fundamental rights are affected. If this is the case, the legislature must leave sufficient room for the realization of individual justice.

This raises the question of delineation between the necessity and the strict proportionality test: which types of cases are dealt with at the necessity stage and which are ultimately decided at the strict proportionality stage? In my view, there are at least four factors that characterize cases that are struck down with the necessity test. First, there is an apparent disparity between the slight public benefit of a total ban and the substantial cost of rights infringement. In *Chocolate Candy Bunny* and in *Testamentary Dispositions*, a total ban clearly presents a drastic and exaggerated measure that could easily be remedied through an exception mechanism that did not impede the purpose of the law. Second, the laws were based on questionable factual assumptions about the buying habits of consumers or the self-determination of mute and illiterate persons that are characterized by an element of irrationality. Third, a comparatively high number of laws that fail the necessity test are placed in highly judicialized fields such as legal profession law,[393] family law,[394] media law,[395] and judicial procedure law.[396] This suggests that the Court is more confident in striking down laws with the factually driven necessity test in lawyer-dominated areas in which it has special experience and expertise. Finally, the majority of those cases concern the right to occupation provided by Article 12 BL,[397] which is characterized by the particular dogmatic structure of the three-step theory that requires considering the intensity of the infringement on the legitimate purpose stage.[398] The three-step theory expands the scope of the necessity test

393 BVerfGE 41, 378; BVerfGE 69, 209; BVerfGE 93, 362; BVerfGE 103, 1; BVerfGE 135, 90; BVerfGE 141, 82.

394 BVerfGE 63, 88; BVerfGE 90, 263; BVerfGE 92, 158.

395 BVerfGE 7, 320; BVerfGE 30, 336; BVerfGE 63, 131.

396 BVerfGE 101, 106.

397 BVerfGE 7, 377; BVerfGE 9, 39; BVerfGE 11, 30; BVerfGE 11, 168; BVerfGE 17, 269; BVerfGE 41, 378; BVerfGE 53, 135; BVerfGE 69, 209; BVerfGE 93, 362; BVerfGE 102, 197; BVerfGE 103, 1; BVerfGE 135, 90; BVerfGE 141, 82.

398 See for the three-step theory Section V.B.

because part of the balancing exercise that typically occurs at the strict proportionality stage will already be conducted with the worthy purpose test.

### 2 A Narrow Conception of Necessity

What does this tell us about the role of the necessity test in German proportionality practice? The FCC takes a narrow understanding of the necessity test. Indeed, a confined means-ends analysis contains a particular rationality. In legal scholarship, the necessity test is described 'as the doctrinally most secure part of proportionality analysis'.[399] The Court is determined not to overload necessity with value-laden elements in order not to compromise the restricted but rationalized necessity test. As a consequence, considerations that go beyond this narrow rationality test are moved to the strict proportionality stage, where the Court comprehensively takes into account all relevant factors of the case.

Judge Graßhof objected to this narrow conception of necessity in her dissenting opinion in the *Cannabis* case.[400] The decision represents one of the few instances in which a member of the Court conceptually challenged the Court's PA practice. In general, there seems to be a broad consensus among constitutional justices regarding the basic structure of PA. *Graßhof* criticized the Court's preference for the strict proportionality stage, arguing that the emphasis of PA should be on the suitability and the necessity stages and not on proportionality in the strict sense that should only serve as a corrective to prevent evidently unacceptable results.[401] While the suitability and the necessity test made proportionality palpable and provided precise argumentation patterns, the appropriateness stage would set less rational and reliable standards.[402] In particular, Graßhof criticized with regard to the treatment of the necessity prong that the Court should have borne in mind the serious infringement of the freedom of the person that comes with a criminal offence, which should only be necessary to pursue 'community interests of fundamental importance'.[403] What Graßhof proposes resembles in some aspects the three-step theory developed by the Court in *Pharmacy*

[399] Christoph Möllers, 'Wandel der Grundrechtsjudikatur' (2005) 58 Neue Juristische Wochenschrift 1973, 1975.

[400] BVerfGE 90, 145 [198]–[226] (dissenting opinion Graßhof). See also critical Schlink (n 3) 59–79.

[401] BVerfGE 90, 145 [200].

[402] ibid.

[403] ibid [201]–[02].

concerning the freedom of occupation.[404] Rather than defining the legitimate purpose generously, the *Pharmacy* decision and Graßhof's dissenting opinion prefer to consider the intensity of the infringement already on the legitimate purpose stage and to conduct a strict necessity review in which regulations must be made at the level which causes the smallest interference with the affected fundamental right. Accordingly, Graßhof describes criminal law as an 'ultima ratio' that should only be the utilized if administrative liability is clearly insufficient.[405]

## VIII Strict Proportionality

In the final stage, which is alternatively called proportionality in the strict sense ('Verhältnismäßigkeit im engeren Sinn'), appropriateness ('Angemessenheit') or reasonableness ('Zumutbarkeit'), the Court leaves the strictly understood means-ends analysis behind and broadens the scope of analysis by balancing the benefits gained by the increase in the achievement of the public interest and the costs incurred by the degree of infringement into the fundamental right.[406] Here, the Court assesses in a concretized and contextual manner the relative weight of the purpose pursued by the law under review and the likelihood that the law will actually protect that public interest effectively against the degree of infringement into the fundamental right.[407]

The 'vast majority' of laws that fail the PA test do so at the strict proportionality stage.[408] In 49 out of all 58 cases in the dataset that failed the proportionality test, or 84 per cent, the measure being scrutinized failed the strict proportionality subtest. Even more cogent is the fact that the Court made the ultimate determination regarding the constitutionality of the contested measure at the strict proportionality stage in 106 out of 114 cases, or 93 per cent. These data clearly show that the strict proportionality test constitutes the epicentre of proportionality practice in Germany. The reason that the FCC excessively relies on the

404 See about the three-step theory Section V.B. and Section VII.C.

405 BVerfGE 90, 145 [201]–[02]. This example seems to confirm a popular criticism of the generous application of the legitimate purpose test, namely that it significantly limits the stringency of the necessity test. See for an overview of this critique: Dechsling (n 3) 145–46.

406 Grimm, 'Proportionality in Canadian and German Constitutional Jurisprudence' (n 7) 393.

407 ibid 396.

408 See already with this assessment: ibid 389.

strict proportionality test to decide fundamental rights cases is likely because it provides the Court with a maximum degree of latitude and flexibility to make the most sensible decision possible under the particular circumstances of a case, considering the political and institutional context. While one of Jeremy Waldron's central objections against judicial review is that judges would often not tackle the real moral issues at stake but get side-tracked, 'focusing on precedent, text, doctrine, and other legalisms',[409] this criticism does not seem to hold its own against the FCC, as PA has largely enabled the Court to sever the bonds of legalism.

### *A Interplay between the Strict Proportionality Test and the Other Tests*

The interplay with the other subtests is an important factor for the dominant role of balancing within the proportionality framework. The strict proportionality test functions as a sponge that absorbs considerations from the worthy purpose, suitability, and necessity tests and combines them with additional considerations. Although the Court makes, as we have seen, the ultimate determination regarding the constitutionality of a contested measure in 93 per cent of all decisions in the dataset at the strict proportionality stage, the importance of considerations from the other tests is higher than this number suggests. These considerations regularly play a role at the strict proportionality test, where they are regularly re-evaluated in some form or another. In many cases, however, the Court does not seem to consider arguments from the worthy purpose, suitability, and necessity tests to justify in themselves striking down a law but, instead, deems it necessary to underpin these arguments with additional considerations that are best addressed at the strict proportionality stage.

#### 1 Interplay with the Worthy Purpose Stage

As we have discussed,[410] the FCC is reluctant to directly challenge a law with the legitimate purpose test even if it suspects that the stated purpose actually covers an illegitimate purpose. Instead, it prefers to strike down

[409] Jeremy Waldron, 'The Core of the Case against Judicial Review' (2006) 115 Yale Law Journal 1346, 1386.

[410] See Section V.C.

such a law with the strict proportionality test. The data confirm this preference.[411] While the Court has only struck down a measure at the worthy purpose stage in 5 out of 114 decisions, or 4 per cent,[412] it has pointed out an unworthy purpose in 24 out of 114 decisions, or 21 per cent.[413] In some of those decisions, the measure under review was based on that unworthy purpose but also on other (worthy) purposes; in other decisions, the Court only stressed in the abstract that the pursuit of a particular purpose would be deemed unworthy. What is striking is that the rate of findings of unconstitutionality is much higher when the Court has referred to an unworthy purpose, even if it did so only abstractly, than on average. As we have seen, the average rate of measures deemed unconstitutional was 51 per cent of all cases in the dataset. By contrast, there was a finding of unconstitutionality in 21 out of the 24 cases, or 88 per cent, in which the Court had pointed to an unworthy purpose whether it was pursued by the law or not.[414] In other words, whenever the Court mentions an unworthy purpose at the worthy purpose stage, the prospect of the contested measure to be deemed proportionate is slim. But although the data suggest that the unworthiness of a purpose that either is, amongst other worthy purposes, or could be pursued by the law is critical for the ultimate judgment on proportionality, the Court prefers the strict proportionality stage to make this ultimate determination. While a measure was struck down at the worthy stage in 5 out of those 21 decisions, it failed the strict proportionality stage in 13 of those decisions.[415] In 10 out of those 13 decisions, the reasons for the

411 See Section V.C.

412 These decisions are BVerfGE 106, 181 [193]–[200]; BVerfGE 107, 186 [198]–[205]; BVerfGE 122, 190 [207]–[09]; BVerfGE 133, 112 [133]–[42].

413 Considering the significant number of decisions, I limited myself in this and in the following footnotes to the short citation form that is commonly used in German legal scholarship. See BVerfGE 102, 197 [215]; BVerfGE 103, 1 [15]–[19]; BVerfGE 104, 357 [365]–[67]; BVerfGE 106, 181 [97]–[100]; BVerfGE 107, 186 [198]–[205]; BVerfGE 109, 256 [270]; BVerfGE 111, 10 [32]; BVerfGE 111, 289 [302]–[03]; BVerfGE 112, 255 [264]; BVerfGE 115, 1 [16]–[17]; BVerfGE 115, 276 [307]; BVerfGE 117, 163 [185]–[86]; BVerfGE 118, 1 [22]–[23]; BVerfGE 122, 190 [207]–[09]; BVerfGE 124, 300 [331]–[32]; BVerfGE 125, 260 [316]–[17]; BVerfGE 127, 132 [153]–[54]; BVerfGE 128, 226 [259]; BVerfGE 130, 151 [187]; BVerfGE 133, 112 [133]–[42]; BVerfGE 134, 141 [181]; BVerfGE 134, 242 [292]–[93]; BVerfGE 135, 90 [114]–[15].

414 From the cases listed in the n 413, the only three cases that ultimately passed the PA stage are BVerfGE 111, 10; BVerfGE 118, 1; BVerfGE 124, 300.

415 See BVerfGE 102, 197; BVerfGE 104, 357; BVerfGE 109, 256; BVerfGE 111, 289; BVerfGE 112, 255; BVerfGE 115, 1; BVerfGE 115, 276; BVerfGE 117, 163; BVerfGE 125, 260; BVerfGE 127, 132; BVerfGE 128, 226; BVerfGE 134, 141; BVerfGE 134, 242. In

unworthiness of the purpose reappear in the reasoning at the strict proportionality stage.[416] This suggests that if the Court senses an illegitimate purpose it will perform a particularly strict PA review, but it will likely not strike down the measure with the worthy purpose test.[417] A case in point is the FCC's decision concerning the prohibition of advertisement for a sanatorium run by a medical doctor.[418] In its judgment, the Court found that 'it is not apparent which reasonable public interests would justify this restriction'.[419] Still, the Court viewed it as necessary to move to the strict proportionality stage to back up its position, arguing that 'even if it was possible to justify the current rules for sanatorium advertisement with sufficient public interests, the comprehensive weighing of the severity of the infringement and the weight of the justifying reasons would result in the conclusion that the limits of reasonableness were exceeded'.[420]

### 2 Interplay with the Suitability and Necessity Stages

How the interplay between strict proportionality and the other PA subtests works and how it affirms the dominance of the strict proportionality stage is best illustrated by the interplay with the suitability and especially the necessity test.[421] A careful analysis of the case-law suggests

three decisions, the measure failed at the necessity stage. See BVerfGE 135, 90; BVerfGE 130, 151; BVerfGE 103, 1. In one case, the Court found the measure to fail the necessity test but still continued its PA and also deemed the measure to fail the strict proportionality stage. See BVerfGE 111, 289.

416 The three decisions in which the reasons for the unworthiness are not re-evaluated are: BVerfGE 102, 197; BVerfGE 109, 256; BVerfGE 127, 132.

417 Similarly Hirschberg (n 3) 55, n 54.

418 BVerfGE 71, 183. In Germany, there was a strict prohibition on the advertising by doctors, but not for sanatoriums, at the time. The issue was whether this prohibition extended to doctors.

419 ibid [198].

420 ibid [200]. Another example is the famous *Pharmacy* case. BVerfGE 7, 377. It appears that a central motivation for the FCC to strike down the law under review was that the predominant purpose of the regulation appeared not to be protection of public health but establishing of protective barriers against competition. However, the Court struck down the law on a later stage after a thorough PA.

421 In the *Cannabis* decision discussed previously, in which the FCC had upheld the legislative assessment as to the necessity of the criminal prohibition of Cannabis possession at the necessity stage, the Court explained the relationship between the necessity and the strict proportionality stages, arguing that '[t]he test of proportionality in the strict sense can thus lead to the conclusion that a means of protecting legal interests which is in itself suitable and necessary may not be resorted to because the resulting infringement of the fundamental rights of the affected person significantly

that the Court prefers the strict proportionality over the necessity stage even in cases that seemed well-suited to strike down a measure with the necessity test.[422] While many PA cases can be presented as either a necessity or strict proportionality problem, the Court construes the necessity test narrowly and uses the strict proportionality stage to disclose the underlying normative considerations of its decision and to support the decision by invoking the normative authority of the Basic Law. Behind this preference for the strict proportionality over the necessity stage lies a deeper point: The Court is reluctant to find that an alternative measure is generally less intrusive than the measure adopted by the legislature because this would constitute a significant infringement into the legislative realm. Instead, the Court prefers to accept the solution adopted by the legislature in principle but to request limited modifications of the policy being scrutinized.[423]

A decisional technique commonly used by the Court is to defer the ultimate determination regarding the constitutionality of the contested measure to the strict proportionality stage. This deferral can be conducted in two ways. In some cases, the Court will deem a law to fail the suitability or necessity stages but still continue its analysis through the strict proportionality stage despite failing at an earlier stage. In other cases, the Court will point out a problem with the measure under review at the necessity stage but still refrain from making a final determination until the strict proportionality stage.

As we have previously seen,[424] the Court has deemed a measure to fail the suitability test in three cases and the necessity test in eight cases. In almost two thirds of those cases, however, specifically in 7 out of those 11 cases, the Court continued its analysis with the strict proportionality test,

outweighs the increased protection of legal interests which is thereby achieved, with the result that the use of the protective measure is disproportionate'. BVerfGE 90, 145 [185].

422 See, e.g., BVerfGE 102, 197 [216]–[18]; BVerfGE 104, 357 [367]–[70]; BVerfGE 108, 150 [167]–[68]; BVerfGE 112, 255 [266]–[68]; BVerfGE 113, 348 [387]–[88]; BVerfGE 115, 1 [19]–[24]; BVerfGE 119, 59 [87]–[89]; BVerfGE 121, 175 [194]–[202]; BVerfGE 128, 109 [130]–[36].

423 This approach, according to which the Court accepts the basic decision of the legislature but requires certain modifications to better respect constitutional principles, is characteristic for the practice of constitutional courts. They operate as guides that push the legislative decision in a certain direction without questioning the original legislative goal. For details, see Andrej Lang, 'Wider die Metapher vom letzten Wort: Verfassungsgerichte als Wegweiser' in Dominik Elser and others (eds), *Das letzte Wort – Rechtsetzung und Rechtskontrolle in der Demokratie* (Nomos 2013) 15.

424 See Section VI.

where it ultimately struck down the measure even though it had already found the measure to fail the suitability test (in two cases) or the necessity test (in five cases). These data clearly show the limited role of the suitability and necessity tests in proportionality practice in Germany. How the Court proceeds in those types of cases can be illustrated by two examples.[425] In the *Legal Counsel* case concerning geographical restrictions on the occupational activities of legal counsels representing conscientious objectors before inspection committees,[426] the Court had already found this restriction to fail the necessity test[427]. While the purpose of the law was to ensure the monitoring of legal counsels who were non-lawyers by the justice administration system, the Court argued that proscribing them to appear before inspection committees outside their court district extended the restriction further than necessary.[428] In the view of the Court, it was sufficient for proper monitoring that legal counsels had a registered office in the court district.[429] Interestingly, the Court moved on to the strict proportionality stage to support its finding with normative value considerations. In particular, the Court argued that it contradicted the conception of the Basic Law about the fundamental status of the citizen to subject him to unreasonable restrictions of the freedom of occupation only to facilitate governmental control.[430] In the *Tax Consultant Exam* case,[431] the regulation under review required tax officials to resign before they were entitled to take the tax consultant exam. The purpose of the regulation was to prevent conflicts of loyalty in the administration of tax justice.[432] The Court held that the rule was unnecessary because it would have been sufficient to require tax officials to resign once they had been appointed as tax consultants.[433] Rather than leaving it at that, the Court continued its PA, observing that 'in any event, considering all the relevant circumstances of the case, the overall balancing between the weight of the infringement into the freedom of occupation and the weight of the justifying reasons, the limits of reasonableness

[425] See also BVerfGE 71, 183 [200]; BVerfGE 90, 263 [272].
[426] BVerfGE 41, 378.
[427] ibid [395].
[428] ibid.
[429] ibid.
[430] ibid [396].
[431] BVerfGE 69, 209.
[432] ibid [218]–[19].
[433] ibid.

have been exceeded'.[434] In view of the uncertainty of the examination, it would be unreasonable to require tax officials to quit the basis of their livelihood before they are even admitted to the exam.[435] Both cases suggest that the Court regarded it as necessary to underpin the arguments from the necessity test with more flexible and normative considerations.

A similar pattern can be observed in those cases in which the Court only identifies a problem with the law being scrutinized at the suitability or the necessity stage and makes the final determination with the strict proportionality test. In some of those cases, the Court explicitly refrains from making a decision at the suitability or the necessity stage;[436] in other cases, it points out a problem with the measure being scrutinized but still deems the measure to barely pass this stage.[437] Overall, there are eight of those cases in the dataset. In all of those cases, the scrutinized measure was struck down. In 7 out of those 8 cases, the determination of disproportionality was made at the strict proportionality stage.

The following two examples from the FCC case-law illustrate that the ultimate decision at the balancing stage is not based on entirely different considerations than the suitability and necessity concerns articulated at the respective stages but that these concerns are re-evaluated and supplemented with additional considerations at the strict proportionality stage. The FCC's preference for the strict proportionality over the necessity stage becomes especially apparent in the context of the German gambling monopoly when it is contrasted with the jurisprudence of the ECJ.[438] The FCC reviewed the conformity of this arrangement with the freedom of occupation guarantee under Article 12(1) of the Basic Law, the ECJ with the freedom to provide services and the freedom of establishment protected by Articles 56(1) and 49(1) of the Treaty on the Functioning of the European Union. Both, the FCC and the ECJ found the monopoly in its present structure to violate those freedoms. Although both courts engaged in very similar considerations, focusing especially on the contradiction

434 ibid [219].

435 ibid.

436 In the dataset, there are four cases that fall under this description: BVerfGE 103, 1; BVerfGE 110, 33; BVerfGE 127, 132; BVerfGE 138, 296.

437 In the dataset, there are four cases that fall under this description as well: BVerfGE 102, 97; BVerfGE 112, 255; BVerfGE 117, 163; BVerfGE 128, 157.

438 See Nicholas Emiliou, *The Principle of Proportionality in European Law* (Kluwer 1996); Koch (n 384); Tor-Inge Harbo, *The Function of Proportionality Analysis in European Law* (Brill 2015).

between the stated purpose of combating betting addiction and the aggressive advertisement campaigns run by the state-owned betting agencies,[439] a lot can be learnt from the differences between the approaches of the two courts. While the language of the ECJ is more technical and the approach more structural, the considerations set forth by the FCC are broader and take the individual position of the affected companies and the infringement into their individual freedom more strongly into account.

The ECJ solved the case at the suitability stage, arguing that the suitability of a measure as restrictive as a monopoly requires that 'they must serve to limit betting activities in a consistent and systematic manner'.[440] Ultimately, the Court found that 'in so far as the authorities of a Member State incite and encourage consumers to participate in lotteries, games of chance or betting to the financial benefit of the public purse, the authorities of that State cannot invoke public order concerns relating to the need to reduce opportunities for gambling in order to justify restrictive measures'.[441] In contrast, the FCC kept its analysis of the suitability and necessity stages brief, stressing the legislature's 'scope for assessment and prognosis'.[442] It did not address the inconsistency between the stated purpose of betting prevention and the actual practice of betting incitement at those stages and moved relatively quickly to the strict proportionality stage. Here, the Court found that 'the state betting monopoly . . . is a disproportionate encroachment on occupational freedom' as '[c]itizens who are interested in working in this area can reasonably be expected to suffer the effects of the exclusion of commercial betting [. . .] only if the existing betting monopoly serves to avoid and avert gambling addiction and problematic gambling behaviour, not only on paper, but as specifically implemented in practice'.[443] However, when the FCC stresses that a proportionate state betting monopoly would be required to avert gambling addiction in practice and not only on paper, the Court implicitly re-evaluates a suitability concern, namely if the policy is truly designed to further the objective of averting gambling addiction.

In a similar case a few years earlier, the *Casino Order* decision,[444] the FCC struck down a state law creating a state monopoly for casinos that

[439] See for more detail Section V.C.

[440] Cases C-316/07 et al., *Stoß v Land Baden-Württemberg* [2010] ECLI:EU:C:2010:504 [88].

[441] ibid [99].

[442] BVerfGE 115, 276 [309].

[443] ibid [309]–[10].

[444] BVerfGE 102, 197.

was justified by the public interest in controlling the dangers of gambling addiction. In contrast to the *Sports Betting* case, casinos had been privately operated in the state for decades. But although the Court voiced concerns as to the necessity of this monopolization as the regulatory experience with private operators had been overwhelmingly positive, it concluded that '[i]t cannot evidently be ruled out that the control of casinos and the containment of gambling addiction is more effective if casinos are operated by the government'.[445] The Court then found that the law creating the monopoly is not proportionate in the strict sense because 'the limits of reasonableness are no longer respected when balancing between the severity of the infringement and the weight of the justifying reasons'.[446] In particular, the Court argued that the total exclusion from the business of casino operation is inappropriate considering that casinos had been privately operated in the states for decades without giving cause for complaint,[447] thereby putting into doubt the necessity of the monopoly.

## *B Formulations and Applications of the Strict Proportionality Test*

While the role of the other subtests, worthy purpose, suitability, and necessity, is functionally limited within the proportionality framework, the strict proportionality test is at the heart of PA in Germany, providing the FCC with a high degree of flexibility to accommodate very different concerns and interests. Given its central role in resolving different types of 'hard' constitutional cases, it is hardly surprising that the strict proportionality test consists of an amalgam of various formulations and applications.

### 1 Formulas of Strict Proportionality

There are basically three different types of definitions that the FCC uses to describe the strict proportionality test. Most commonly, the Court describes proportionality in the strict sense with the standard of reasonableness.[448] It formulates that the challenged provisions 'must not excessively burden the person affected and be therefore

445 ibid [219].
446 ibid [218].
447 ibid [221].
448 In the dataset, the Court describes the strict proportionality test in this way in 57 out of 114 decisions.

unreasonable',[449] that 'in a comprehensive weighing between the gravity of the interference on the one hand and the weight and urgency of the reasons justifying it, the limits of reasonableness must be observed',[450] or that the complainant can 'be reasonably expected to accept' the measure being scrutinized[451]. Slightly less often but still frequently, the Court uses the term 'appropriateness', requiring that a measure must be 'appropriate',[452] referring to the 'standard of appropriateness',[453] or noting that 'an appropriate balance must be struck between the gravity of interference of the provision and the objective pursued by the legislator, between individual and collective interest'.[454] In contrast to a common perception in German public law, the standards of reasonableness and appropriateness are significantly more commonly used by the FCC than the formulation that legal scholarship arguably considers to be the preeminent description of the strict proportionality test. According to that formulation, the principle of proportionality in the strict sense 'requires that the gravity of the encroachment, in an overall evaluation, may not be disproportionate to the gravity of the reasons justifying it'.[455]

These different definitions of the strict proportionality test can be grouped into a continuum confined by two poles. On one end of the continuum, the reasonableness standard suggests that the Court respects the legislative decision so long as the latter is not clearly unreasonable or does not exceed what can be demanded from a rights-bearer. On the other end of the continuum, the appropriateness standard indicates that the Court seeks to optimize the competing fundamental right and the public interest concerns at stake under the particular facts of the individual case.[456] Overall, most cases fall somewhere in the middle of this

[449] BVerfGE 128, 138 [153].
[450] BVerfGE 126, 112 [152]–[53].
[451] BVerfGE 122, 89 [116].
[452] BVerfGE 125, 260 [316]; BVerfGE 128, 226 [260], [267].
[453] BVerfGE 128, 157 [185].
[454] BVerfGE 133, 277 [322]. See also BVerfGE 124, 43 [62]. Overall, there are 48 out of 114 cases in the dataset in which the Court characterizes the strict proportionality test in that manner.
[455] BVerfGE 115, 320 [345]–[46]; BVerfGE 120, 274 [315]–[16].
[456] The leading German legal theorist on proportionality, *Robert Alexy*, has characterized fundamental rights as optimization requirements. Robert Alexy, *A Theory of Constitutional Rights* (Julian Rivers tr, OUP 2002) 47–48. With reference to *Ronald Dworkin*, *Alexy* distinguishes sharply between norms and principles. While '*rules* are norms which are always either fulfilled or not', ibid 48, 'principles are norms which require that something be realized to the greatest extent possible given the legal and factual possibilities'. ibid 47. According to Alexy, '[p]rinciples are optimization requirements,

continuum. In other words, many cases seek to optimize competing concerns but, in general, the Court's approach is more restrained and focuses on remedying instances in which the limits of proportionality, appropriateness, or reasonableness are crossed. Which definition the Court uses in a particular case to describe the strict proportionality test is typically not indicative for the type of balancing subsequently exercised by the Court. In fact, the Court regularly uses different definitions of the strict proportionality test in the same decision.[457]

The central element of the strict proportionality test is a comparison between the severity of the infringement on one hand and the importance of the purpose on the other.[458] How the Court specifically structures the balancing process in its written judgments varies but in an ideal-type decision, the Court typically begins its analysis of the strict proportionality test with carving out the specific harm imposed by the contested measure on the complainant. Noting that the interference 'carries much weight', the Court describes how the intruding measure constrains the exercise of the activity protected by the fundamental right at issue.[459] In a second step, the Court outlines the importance of the purpose pursued by the policy-maker.[460] In a third step, the Court analyses to what extent the contested measure is capable of furthering the objective pursued by the policy and to what degree the realization of that objective would be compromised without the measure and, with even more emphasis, whether and to what extent the policy limits the severity of the infringement via exemption rules, hardship clauses, or other mitigating factors.[461] Overall, strict proportionality is a concrete, situational,

characterized by the fact that they can be satisfied to varying degrees, and that the appropriate degree of satisfaction depends not only on what is factually possible but also on what is legally possible'. ibid.

457 See BVerfGE 113, 29 [53]–[54]; BVerfGE 119, 59 [87]; BVerfGE 125, 260 [283], [360], [368]; BVerfGE 128, 1 [53]–[54], [60], [65].

458 See BVerfGE 102, 197 [218]; BVerfGE 103, 1 [10]; BVerfGE 104, 357 [368]; BVerfGE 106, 181 [191]–[92]; BVerfGE 109, 256 [270]; BVerfGE 109, 64 [85]; BVerfGE 112, 255 [262]–[63]; BVerfGE 113, 167 [260]; BVerfGE 113, 29 [54]; BVerfGE 115, 320 [345]–[46]; BVerfGE 118, 168 [195]; BVerfGE 120, 224 [241]; BVerfGE 120, 274 [315]–[16]; BVerfGE 121, 317 [355]; BVerfGE 126, 112 [152]–[53]; BVerfGE 130, 372 [392]; BVerfGE 133, 277 [322]; BVerfGE 134, 141 [181]; BVerfGE 138, 261 [285].

459 See, e.g., BVerfGE 102, 197 [218]-[19]; BVerfGE 104, 337 [350]; BVerfGE 107, 299 [319]; BVerfGE 116, 243 [261]; BVerfGE 120, 274 [337]–[38]; BVerfGE 124, 43 [62].

460 See, e.g., BVerfGE 102, 197 [220]; BVerfGE 104, 337 [351]; BVerfGE 107, 299 [322]–[23].

461 See, e.g., BVerfGE 102, 197 [220]; BVerfGE 104, 337 [352]–[53]; BVerfGE 107, 299 [322]–[24].

case-oriented process that does not resemble an abstract weighing of the competing concerns at issue.[462] Neither the fundamental right concern nor the public interest at stake enjoys precedence per se over the other but the decisive question is always under what conditions and circumstances one concern takes precedence over the other.[463]

How the Court depicts the strict proportionality process can be nicely illustrated by the *Ritual Slaughter* decision.[464] In that decision, the Court upheld the relevant provision of the Animal Protection Act that required an exceptional permission for ritual slaughter of animals without prior stunning but overturned the decisions of the lower administrative courts that had refused the complainant the grant of such permission. By interpreting this provision in conformity with the constitution, the Court held that Muslim butchers are generally entitled to receive an exceptional permission.[465] The strict proportionality test concerning the competing occupational and religious concerns of Muslim butchers and of animal protection commenced with the holding that '[t]he legal regulation that is in question here is also proportional in a strict sense' because, '[i]n an overall weighing of the severity of the encroachment upon fundamental rights . . . and the importance and the urgency of the reasons that justify the encroachment, it can be reasonably required of the person concerned . . . to conduct the slaughter of warm-blooded animals without stunning only on the basis of an exceptional permission'.[466]

The Court subsequently noted that the 'encroachment upon Muslim butchers' fundamental right to occupational freedom . . . carries much weight', observing that without an exemption, 'it would no longer be possible for pious Muslims like the complainant to practice the occupation of a butcher in the Federal Republic of Germany'.[467] The *Ritual Slaughter* judgment demonstrates that the FCC broadly considers factors that increase the severity of the infringement by not only reflecting the (Muslim) minority status of the complainant but also taking into account the consequences of banning ritual slaughter to the customers of Muslim butchers.[468]

[462] Lepsius, 'Die Chancen und Grenzen des Grundsatzes der Verhältnismäßigkeit' (n 60) 6.
[463] Alexy (n 456) 51.
[464] BVerfGE 104, 337.
[465] ibid [356].
[466] ibid [349]–[50].
[467] ibid [350].
[468] The Court argued that '[i]f they were required to, basically, forgo the consumption of meat, this would not sufficiently take the eating habits in the Federal Republic of

The Court then directed its attention to the importance of the public purpose, noting that '[t]hese consequences for pious Muslim butchers and their pious customers must be weighed against the fact that the protection of animals constitutes a public interest that is attached high importance among the population'.[469] Analysing the regulatory concept for the protection of animals, the Court found that 'parliament has regarded it as compatible with a protection of animals that is based on ethical principles to move away from mandatory stunning in cases where factual considerations or reasons of tradition and social acceptance suggest exemptions'.[470] Against this background, the Court concluded that '[w]ithout such exemptions, the fundamental rights of those who want to perform slaughter without stunning ... would be unreasonably restricted, and the interests of the protection of animals would, without a sufficient constitutional justification, be given priority in a one-sided manner'.[471]

### 2 Modes of Strict Proportionality

What the FCC does at the strict proportionality stage can be roughly grouped into three distinct modes of reasoning. These modes partially overlap with each other, and they correspond, to some extent, with the strict proportionality formulas outlined previously. However, as the use of strict proportionality formulas by the Court is largely random, it does not, in fact, signal the use of a particular balancing mode. The first mode of reasoning consists of what is most commonly understood by balancing in the proper sense. It is the straightforward balancing of the benefits of a measure for the public interest against the costs incurred by the rights infringement. Balancing in the proper sense typically involves the optimization of competing constitutional concerns, either of two competing fundamental rights or of a fundamental right and a public concern. It corresponds with the formula of 'appropriateness', suggesting that the Court seeks to strike a balance between competing values.

The majority of proportionality decisions, however, are based on narrower considerations than on balancing in the proper sense. The

Germany into consideration'. ibid [350]–[51]. For another decision in which the Court takes into account negative consequences other than those affecting the rights-bearer, see BVerfGE 117, 163 [194]–[97] (basing the violation of the freedom of occupation of attorneys on a total ban on attorney contingency fees).

469 BVerfGE 104, 337 [351].

470 ibid [352].

471 ibid.

second mode aims at remedying excessive burdens and hardships of the measure being scrutinized for a particular group of addressees. Its dominant focus is on the effects of a measure on the individual rights-bearer. It demarcates a 'red line' that may not be crossed by the state. This mode is congruous with the formula of reasonableness, requiring that a measure 'must not excessively burden the person affected and be therefore unreasonable'.[472] In the third mode of reasoning, the Court requires policy-makers to narrowly tailor rights-infringing measures in order to minimize the intensity of the infringement. The focus is on the scrutinized measure and on ways to design the measure in a more rights-friendly manner. There are certain similarities of the narrowly tailoring mode with the formulation that 'the gravity of the encroachment . . . may not be disproportionate to the gravity of the reasons justifying it'[473] because both are geared towards policies that provide for a disproportionate fit between the measure and the objective.

How the Court balances competing values can be best illustrated by the most pronounced form of balancing in German constitutional law, the technique called 'practical concordance' that concerns balancing between two competing fundamental rights. It was initially developed as a concept distinct from proportionality but has, over time, morphed into the proportionality framework. The doctrine of practical concordance is built on the idea that fundamental rights are optimization requirements.[474] According to the Court, a 'conflict among various bearers of a fundamental right guaranteed without reservation, and between that fundamental right and other constitutionally protected objects, is to be resolved on the principle of practical concordance, which requires that no one of the conflicting legal positions be preferred and maximally asserted, but all given as protective as possible an arrangement'.[475]

In many ways, the doctrine of practical concordance is prototypical for German legal and political theory, which has a strong preference for communitarian ideas and emphasizes the existence of shared common

[472] BVerfGE 128, 138 [153].

[473] BVerfGE 115, 320 [345]–[46]; BVerfGE 120, 274 [315]–[16].

[474] *Konrad Hesse*, who was influential in the formation of the doctrine of practical concordance, has argued that the basic idea of practical concordance is that both competing 'legal values need to be limited so that each can attain its optimal effect'. Hesse (n 144) ¶72. Translation taken from Kommers and Miller (n 39) 68.

[475] BVerfGE 93, 1 [21]. See also BVerfGE 28, 243 [260]–[61]; BVerfGE 52, 223 [247], [251].

values that must be coordinated.[476] Accordingly, the balancing of competing constitutional concerns is not a zero-sum game but requires optimization of the competing concerns. Norm conflicts between different fundamental rights are not solved through hierarchy but addressed through balancing. Even though Article 1(1) of the Basic Law lends itself to a hierarchical understanding by providing emphatically that '[h]uman dignity shall be inviolable', the FCC does not recognize a hierarchy among the various fundamental rights.[477] To the contrary, the Court holds that all fundamental rights are concretized forms of the principle of human dignity.[478] Practical concordance therefore requires that when a norm conflict between different fundamental rights occurs, no fundamental right shall be realized at the expense of a competing fundamental right but both fundamental rights shall be harmonized with one another and preserved in creative unity. Although the FCC limits the scope of the doctrine of practical concordance to cases of competing fundamental rights lacking a limitation clause such as the freedoms of art, scholarship, and religion,[479] this type of optimization is also regularly conducted when balancing between fundamental rights and public interests.[480] In German constitutional practice, both concerns are generally treated as equal types of parameters, compete on the same plane, and are meant to be optimized by the decision maker.

How the FCC optimizes competing fundamental rights concerns can be illustrated by its judgments in the *Crucifix* and in the *Muslim Headscarf* cases.[481] In both cases, the Court emphasized the optimization requirement to harmonize the competing fundamental rights concerns.[482] In both cases, no fundamental rights concern prevailed over

476 See Cohen-Eliya and Porat (n 1) 50. In the same vein, one of the most important constitutional interpretive principles is the unity of the constitution according to which the various provisions of the Basic Law are not to be construed in isolation but must be harmonized with each other.

477 See from the early case-law: BVerfGE 3, 225 [231]–[32]; BVerfGE 12, 45 [52]–[53]; BVerfGE 19, 135 [138]. See also Grimm, 'Proportionality in Canadian and German Constitutional Jurisprudence' (n 7) 393–94.

478 BVerfGE 93, 266 [293].

479 BVerfGE 93, 1 [21].

480 See only BVerfGE 104, 337.

481 BVerfGE 93, 1; BVerfGE 108, 282 [302]; BVerfGE 138, 296.

482 In *Muslim Headscarf*, the Court noted that '[t]he provisions must be seen together, and their interpretation and their area of influence must be coordinated with each other'. BVerfGE 108, 282 [305]–[06]. In *Crucifix*, the Court argued that '[b]oth provisions have to be seen together and reconciled with each other through interpretation, since it is only

the other but the Court forged a compromise in which both concerns were validated and the outcome depended on the particular facts of the case.[483] The *Muslim Headscarf* case involved a state prohibition on teachers wearing a headscarf at school and in lessons. In its judgment, the Court sought to reconcile the positive freedom of faith of a teacher on the one hand and the state's duty of religious and ideological neutrality, the parents' right of education, and the negative freedom of faith of the pupils on the other hand.[484] It demanded that any prohibition for a public teacher to wear a headscarf in the classroom required explicit legislation that had been absent in this case. Beyond that particular case, the Court required state legislatures pursuing such a prohibition to enact legislation that 'seek[s] a compromise that is reasonably acceptable to everyone'.[485] According to the FCC, '[t]his includes the possibility that the individual Länder [states] may make different provisions, because the middle course that needs to be found may also take into account school traditions, the composition of the population by religion, and whether it is more or less strongly rooted in religion'.[486] The similarly situated *Crucifix* Case concerned a constitutional complaint against the mandatory affixation of crosses or crucifixes in public elementary schoolrooms in Bavaria. In *Crucifix*, the Court required public schools to remove the crucifix from schoolrooms only under the condition that students in a school had objected to its presence.[487]

The second mode of reasoning conducted at the strict proportionality stage concerns the redress of hardship. The Court seeks to remedy cases of hardship to a clearly definable group of persons or companies. While the law causing hardship is unobjectionable vis-à-vis most addressees, it places an excessive burden on a small minority. The Court therefore does not typically question the law in its entirety but requires the legislature to enact certain exceptions, hardship clauses, or transitional measures to prevent hardship. In hardship cases, the contested law typically contains rigid rules that fail to leave sufficient room for exceptions for a subgroup of addressees that are affected by the law in a particularly severe way.[488]

concordance of the objects of legal protection under both articles that can do justice to the decision contained in the Basic Law'. BVerfGE 93, 1 [22]–[23].

483 See also BVerfGE 35, 202 [220]–[21].
484 BVerfGE 108, 282 [302].
485 ibid.
486 ibid.
487 BVerfGE 93, 1 [24].
488 See Petersen, *Verhältnismäßigkeit als Rationalitätskontrolle* (n 3) 155–57.

The majority of those cases are in the different fields of family law and economic regulation. What characterizes hardship cases in family law is that the provision being scrutinized pursues objectives associated with traditional family values such as 'heterosexuality of marriage'[489] or 'lineage of family names'[490] but that it neglects the excessive effect on a particular group of persons. For example, in the *Transsexuals V* decision, the FCC stressed that the legislator pursued a worthy purpose when it sought to preserve the heterosexuality of marriage when legally recognizing the new gender of a transsexual person.[491] The Court found, however, that it constituted an unreasonable hardship for married transsexuals to make the gender recognition contingent upon a divorce without allowing them to continue their cohabitation in a different but equally secure union.[492]

A prototypical hardship case in the area of commercial law and economic regulation is the *Smoking Ban* case.[493] In its judgment, the Court deemed the anti-smoking legislation enacted by the two German states Baden-Württemberg and Berlin to violate the constitutional freedom of occupation guarantee because it found that the owners and operators of small single-room pubs and bars were subject to an especially heavy economic burden. The laws under review pursued the purpose of health protection by banning smoking in eating and drinking establishments to protect people from the dangers of passive smoking but exceptionally granted operators the opportunity to establish separate rooms in which smoking is allowed. The rationale seems to have been to allow exceptions to the ban on smoking only to the extent that this does not endanger the protection of non-smokers. However, the Court assumed on the basis of statistical evidence that this legislative scheme would burden single-room corner pubs which primarily serve alcoholic beverages in an unreasonable way. The concern was that an economically vital chunk of their customer-base would prefer larger establishments with an extra-smoking room where smoking was allowed. While large establishments were in a position to satisfy the smoking demands of their customers, the regulation had the effect of a total ban on small pubs and

489 BVerfGE 121, 175 [193].
490 BVerfGE 109, 256 [269]–[70].
491 BVerfGE 121, 175 [193].
492 ibid [194]–[95].
493 BVerfGE 121, 317.

bars.[494] The Court held that the legislature would not be prevented from imposing a strict ban on smoking without any exceptions.[495] But if the legislature chooses a less vigorous concept for the pursuit of public health protection, it is required to take into account the special burdens on individual areas of the eating and drinking sector and to afford equal treatment.[496]

The third mode of strict proportionality relates to measures that are not sufficiently narrowly tailored. The term 'narrow tailoring' stems from US constitutional law where it describes a stringent requirement for racial classifications.[497] Without seeking to transplant a concept from US into German constitutional law, the basic idea behind the requirement of narrow tailoring that regularly surfaces in the jurisprudence of the FCC is that a rights-infringing law should only include those cases in its scope of application that are strictly required to achieve its purpose. Put differently, the law should minimize the infringement of the right to the greatest extent possible without compromising the purpose of the policy. Narrow tailoring cases can be divided into two subgroups of cases. One type of cases is closely related to the necessity or least restrictive means test. They often involve a re-evaluation of the necessity test and the strict proportionality is regularly conducted relative to an alternative. Those cases could have also been overturned at the necessity stage if the Court did not follow a strict interpretation of the requirement of equal effectiveness of an alternative measure.[498] At the strict proportionality stage, however, the Court does not deem a slight deviation of an alternative in terms of effectiveness sufficient to justify a substantially greater intrusion into a fundamental right.[499] An example is the *Tax Consultant Exam* case discussed previously,[500] in which a regulation required tax officials to resign before they were even entitled to take the tax consultant exam. The Court found that it constituted an unreasonable burden on tax

494 ibid [365]–[66].

495 ibid [357].

496 In this same category falls the discussed *Oil Reserve* decision, in which the Court found that the general scope of the stocking obligation that did not provide for any exceptions did not allow to properly take into account the particularly adverse economic effects of the legislation for independent oil importing companies. BVerfGE 30, 292. Another example is BVerfGE 14, 19 [23]–[24].

497 See Ian Ayres, 'Narrow Tailoring' (1996) 43 UCLA Law Review 1781.

498 See Section VII.C.

499 Petersen, *Verhältnismäßigkeit als Rationalitätskontrolle* (n 3) 150–53.

500 BVerfGE 69, 209. See also BVerfGE 71, 183; BVerfGE 90, 263.

officials to quit the basis of their livelihood before they were even admitted to the exam. In order to prevent conflicts of loyalty in the administration of tax justice, it would have been sufficient to require tax officials to resign once they had been appointed as tax consultants.[501] The difference of narrow tailoring cases to the hardship group is that equality considerations are of less concern. In the former category, the legislative scheme affects different types of addressees very differently. Particular groups such as single-room corner pubs bear an especially heavy economic burden. In the latter, all addressees are affected in essentially the same way. The problem with the legislation is that it does not take sufficient measures to minimize the infringement into the fundamental rights of *all* addressees.

The other type of cases in the narrow tailoring category concerns decisions in which the Court imposes substantive and procedural constraints on the contested policy to minimize the fundamental rights infringement.[502] It does not, however, analyse the policy relative to an alternative or put into doubt the basic legitimacy of the policy. This type of decisions frequently concerns surveillance measures in the realm of national security and also contains an element of balancing between the public interest of security and fundamental right to informational self-determination guaranteed in Article 2(1) in connection with Article 1(1) of the Basic Law.[503] The Court will typically accept new surveillance measures in principle but nevertheless find the law to be unconstitutional for a lack of substantive and procedural restrictions on police and intelligence authority.[504] A case in point is the *Antiterrorism Database* decision.[505] The matter concerned a federal law that set up a

[501] BVerfGE 69, 209 [218]–[19].

[502] See, e.g., BVerfGE 109, 279; BVerfGE 113, 348; BVerfGE 115, 320; BVerfGE 120, 274; BVerfGE 120, 378; BVerfGE 125, 260; BVerfGE 130, 151; BVerfGE 133, 277; BVerfGE 141, 220.

[503] The right of informational self-determination is one of several manifestations of the right to personality. The FCC, as the guardian of the constitutional order, has creatively invented new fundamental rights to protect individuals against government surveillance. The aim of those rights is not to outlaw new surveillance technologies but to keep their use in check. Over time, the Court and the political process have developed a constructive interaction as part of which the FCC routinely scrutinizes laws providing a legal basis for new surveillance measures and imposes substantive and procedural limits on the exercise by police and intelligence services.

[504] Safeguards demanded by the Court are, for example, a stricter requirement of a judicial order, a heightened gravity of the criminal offence investigated or degree of specificity of the suspicion required, and the deletion of inadvertently retrieved data.

[505] BVerfGE 133, 277.

standardized central antiterrorism database of police authorities and intelligence services of the federal government and the states to facilitate the exchange of information to effectively combat the threat of terrorism. The joint database was established to allow all participating agencies to identify which agency has relevant information about a suspected terrorist.[506] Assessing the constitutionality of the antiterrorism database according to the right to informational self-determination, the FCC held that the database is in its fundamental structures compatible with the Basic Law but that certain provisions of the database do not meet all 'the requirements of the principle of proportionality in the strict sense'.[507] In particular, the Court found that the scope of people who the database may cover was overly broad and not sufficiently narrowly tailored. It criticized that persons were covered (i) who merely support a support group organization that seems unsuspicious to them, without clarifying that a conscious support of activities which support terrorism is required, (ii) who advocate violence, thus using only subjective convictions as a yardstick, and (iii) who are contact persons but do not know about the protagonist's connection to terrorism. Moreover, the Court required a stricter duty of documentation and publication duties and mandatory checks in definite intervals.[508]

The quantitative analysis of all PA decisions by a FCC Senate from 2000 until 2017 shows that of the three, partially overlapping, modes of reasoning applied with the test of proportionality in the strict sense, the narrow tailoring mode is the one most commonly used by the Court. In 28 out of all 49 cases, or 57 per cent, in which the measure under review failed the strict proportionality test, the measure was not sufficiently narrowly tailored. In 14 out of 49 cases, or 29 per cent, the measure caused excessive hardship to rights holders. In 20 out of those 49 cases, or 41 per cent, the Court engaged in balancing and challenged the value choices of policy-makers. In 7 out of those 20 decisions, the Court applied the doctrine of practical concordance.[509]

506 It is essentially limited to initiating the receipt of information via data that have already been collected.

507 BVerfGE 133, 277 [335]–[36].

508 As a remedy, the Court did not void the law but made a declaration of incompatibility and gave the legislature until the end of 2014 to amend the relevant legislation. ibid [375].

509 In 4 out of those 49 cases, the reasoning at the strict proportionality stage did not fit into any of the three categories.

These results correlate with a similar empirical analysis of the FCC's case-law regarding PA conducted by Niels Petersen. Based on an analysis of all Senate decisions from 1951 until the end of 2015, in which the FCC held a legislative statute to violate a fundamental right on substantive grounds,[510] he finds that '[f]rom 1978 onwards, the Constitutional Court based about one third of the decisions in which it declared a law as unconstitutional on balancing'.[511] In his view, famous FCC judgments characterized by straightforward balancing, like the *Crucifix* case,[512] are outliers that do not truly represent the Court's PA practice.[513] Instead, he conceives PA as a form of 'rationality control', as part of which the Court ensures and monitors the rationality of political decisions.[514]

But while the proportionality case-law of the FCC is too multi-faceted to be reduced to a rationality control, it is true that the Court does not primarily use the final stage of proportionality in the strict sense to verify or correct legislative value decisions.[515] Notwithstanding the dominance of the strict proportionality test in PA in Germany,[516] the quantitative analysis shows that the FCC uses a more restrained approach than balancing in the proper sense if it strikes down federal legislation. We have seen at the beginning of this chapter that while the vast majority of measures in which a FCC Senate applied the proportionality framework concern federal legislation (69 percent compared to 17 per cent state legislation, 10 per cent judicial decisions, and 4 per cent administrative acts),[517] the Court is much more reluctant to overturn federal legislation than state legislation or judicial decisions. The data show a

[510] Petersen, *Proportionality and Judicial Activism* (n 140) 99.

[511] ibid 14. According to Petersen, in almost all of the remaining decisions the Court uses the strict proportionality test for four distinct purposes: (1) correcting the assignment of financial burdens from individual rights-bearers to either the state or the primary beneficiaries of the measure, (2) analysing the fit of the measure and the purpose, (3) applying a consistency test, and (4) correcting cases of individual hardship. ibid 15–16. Petersen's second category largely correlates with my category of narrow tailoring cases. His fourth category is congruent with my category of hardship cases. Moreover, Petersen acknowledges that many of the cases in his first category could be captured by the hardship category. ibid 243. It is important to note that Petersen's quantitative analysis is not limited to cases in which the Court applied the proportionality framework but encompasses all decisions in which the Court struck down legislation.

[512] BVerfGE 93, 1.

[513] Petersen, *Proportionality and Judicial Activism* (n 140) 10.

[514] ibid 10–11.

[515] ibid 246–49.

[516] See Section VIII.

[517] See Section III.

success rate in PA cases for complainants of 39 per cent when contesting federal legislation compared to 74 per cent with regard to state statutes.[518]

This restraint with respect to the outcome corresponds with a restraint concerning the mode of reasoning. The Court only used balancing in the proper sense in 8 out of 31 decisions, or 26 per cent, in which it has struck down a federal statute.[519] In 7 out of 8 of those decisions, balancing in the proper sense is combined with either narrow tailoring or prevention of hardship. Put most starkly, the Court relied exclusively on balancing in the proper sense to overturn federal legislation in 1 out of the 114 Senate decisions from 2000 until 2017 in which the Court applied the proportionality framework.[520] To clarify this point, these data do not put into question the important role of balancing in the proper sense, including the doctrine of practical concordance, in German proportionality practice. The reasoning of many of the most important decisions in German constitutional law, such as *Lüth*, *Mephisto*, *Crucifix*, *Ritual Slaughter*, *Esra*, or *Muslim Headscarf*, is tantamount to full-blown judicial balancing of competing constitutional values. These judgments, however, all concern the judicial review of ordinary courts or state legislation. By contrast, the Court is wary of engaging in a highly normative optimization exercise when it reviews federal legislation. Instead, it concentrates on identifying clearly defined constitutional shortcomings in order to preserve the margin of manoeuvre of the federal legislator.

## 3 Rules of Thumb

It is possible to identify several rules of thumb in the case-law of the Court that guide decision-making at the strict proportionality stage and that are indicative, yet rarely determinative, of the ultimate decision at this stage. A basic rule is that fundamental right concerns need to be accommodated by the contested policy in some form. Because the strict proportionality process is geared towards finding a workable

[518] See Section III.

[519] In 17 of those decisions, the Court relied, either exclusively or in combination with another mode of reasoning, on narrow tailoring, in 11 decisions, on hardship considerations. Six of those 31 decisions had already failed conclusively at a prior stage, 2 at the worthy purpose stage, 1 at the suitability stage, and 3 at the least restrictive means stage.

[520] In comparison, the Court relied on balancing in the proper sense as a mode of reasoning to overturn state legislation in 6 out of 12 cases (50 per cent) and to overturn judicial decisions in 5 out of 13 cases (38 per cent).

compromise between the competing concerns, a policy is susceptible to being disproportionate if the fundamental right concern does not come to bear. In the *Ritual Slaughter* case discussed earlier,[521] it was critical for the constitutionality of the policy that the Animal Protection Act provided for the possibility of an exemption. Otherwise, the occupational and religious concerns of Muslim butchers would have been entirely disregarded.[522] In the *Casino Order* case, the Court struck down the state law creating a state monopoly for casinos because private casino operators were invariably precluded from exercising their freedom of occupation in this field.[523]

Furthermore, there are several rules of thumb that concern the linkage between the severity of the infringement and the importance of the legislative purpose that is critical to the strict proportionality test. First and foremost, the more important a certain aspect of the right and the more severe the infringement, the more justified and important the purpose pursued by the infringing measure must be.[524] The Court held in several decisions that a measure is disproportionate if the resulting fundamental rights infringement weighs more heavily than the public

521 BVerfGE 104, 337.

522 Similarly, in the *University Lecturers of Theology* case discussed earlier, the Court upheld the transfer of teaching duties of a theology professor that had lost his faith because the administrative decisions being scrutinized validated fundamental rights concerns to some extent. While his teaching duties were transferred, the complainant retained his position as a university lecturer and was allocated a subject largely similar to his original subject. BVerfGE 122, 89 [116]. Other examples are: BVerfGE 123, 90; BVerfGE 124, 300.

523 BVerfGE 102, 197 [219]–[20]. In the same manner, the Court held in its *Frankfurt Airport Demonstration* judgment, concerning the constitutionality of demonstration bans at Frankfurt International Airport, that a general ban imposed by the Fraport stock corporation that operates Frankfurt airport and in which the majority of shares are publicly owned violates the freedom of demonstration guarantee of Article 8(1) of the Basic Law. The Court found that a publicly owned entity is bound to observe the fundamental rights guarantees of the Basic Law. Although the FCC recognized that the security and functioning of airport operations is a legitimate purpose that can justify certain limitations on demonstration, it concluded that a general demonstration ban is overbroad and found it necessary to limit the ban 'to averting specific imminent dangers to fundamental legal interests which are equivalent to freedom of assembly'. BVerfGE 128, 226 [263]–[64].

524 BVerfGE 103, 1 [10], noting in the context of the freedom of occupation that 'the more severely affected professionals and practictioners are in their freedom of occupation, the stronger the public interests must be that the regulation is meant to pursue'. This rule of thumb was initially formulated by Alexy, who famously stated that '[t]he greater the degree of non-satisfaction of, or detriment to, one principle, the greater must be the importance of satisfying the other'. Alexy (n 456) 102.

interests pursued by that measure.[525] Conversely, a measure 'might have to be accepted as proportionate considering important legislative objectives if the intensity of the infringement is minor'.[526] The problem with this logical axiom is that it is designed to solve 'easy cases': it is self-evident that a clear disproportionality between the intensity of the infringement and the importance of the public interest will direct the decision in favour of the more pressing concern. However, the Senates of the FCC generally deal with 'hard cases' in which no evident disproportionality exists. But if both the intensity of the infringement and the importance of the public interest meet on an equal plane, this rule of thumb provides no help to the judicial decision-maker.

Moreover, the Court has developed different criteria that have a bearing on the strict proportionality process by impacting either the severity of the infringement or the importance of the public interest. For example, the Court has identified several factors concerning surveillance measures in the context of national security that tend to increase the severity of the infringement, including the covertness and long-term character of a surveillance,[527] a vast number of persons affected,[528] a broad range of possible uses of the collected data,[529] and the extent to which the surveillance is beyond the control and conduct of the rights-bearer.[530] By contrast, the importance of the public interest decreases when the contested measure is only of marginal benefit to the worthy purpose that it is designed to further. The extent to which the measure actually suits the public interest is disregarded at the suitability stage but it reappears at the strict proportionality stage and impacts the weight of the public interest at stake.[531] The Court held in the context of the freedom of occupation that 'the closer a provision is related to the protected public good, the more is an infringement of the freedom of occupation justifiable'.[532] Conversely, 'if a fundamental rights limitation

[525] See, eg, BVerfGE 120, 274 [315]–[16]; BVerfGE 118, 168 [195]; BVerfGE 120, 378 [428]; BVerfGE 133, 277 [322].
[526] BVerfGE 118, 168 [195].
[527] BVerfGE 124, 43 [62].
[528] BVerfGE 107, 299 [321]; BVerfGE 115, 320 [347].
[529] BVerfGE 124, 43 [62].
[530] ibid; BVerfGE 115, 320 [354]–[55].
[531] See, e.g., BVerfGE 110, 226 [263]; BVerfGE 112, 255 [266]–[68]; BVerfGE 134, 141 [187]–[88].
[532] BVerfGE 107, 186 [197].

is only remotely connected to the public good, then the latter cannot generally claim precedence over the freedom of occupation'.[533]

Finally, the FCC has crafted detailed rules of thumb in the area of national security and police law that address issues of probability and uncertainty. They are derived from principles of police law and impose substantive restrictions on police authority.[534] In essence, they establish a linkage between the importance of the public interest at stake and the degree of probability required that a danger to a public interest leads to an impending loss. First, the Court has held in several decisions that 'the more weighty the imminent or completed violation of a public good and the less weighty the fundamental rights infringement at issue, the lower are the required degree of probability of a violation and the required degree of substantiation of the facts inducing the suspicion'.[535] At the same time, the Court noted that 'under no circumstances is it permissible to dispense with the requirement of sufficient probability even if the imminent violation of a public good is of highest importance'.[536] In several decisions, the severity of infringement caused by police measures, including data mining, online computer surveillance, and data retention, prompted the Court to insist on the requirement of a concrete danger to a public good or, at the very least, factual indications for such a concrete danger.[537] As a consequence, the use of these police instruments must be based on facts that substantiate a prognosis of danger given the severity of the fundamental rights infringement involved; by contrast, neither 'presumptions or general experience' nor 'diffuse indications of possible dangers' are sufficient to justify the use of this police authority.[538]

533 ibid.

534 An exception to this rule is the *Unfitness to Stand Trial* decision that deals with the probability of a fundamental rights infringement – and not the probability of harm to the public interest. In a nutshell, the central issue in this case concerned the permissibility of a trial of an accused person who was in danger of suffering a stroke and heart attack from the stress of the trial. In its judgment, the FCC instructed the ordinary court that 'if there is a proximate and specific danger that if the trial is continued, the accused person will lose his life or suffer serious injury to his health, then continuing the legal process breaches his fundamental rights'. BVerfGE 51, 324 [346].

535 BVerfGE 110, 33 [59]; BVerfGE 113, 348 [387]; BVerfGE 115, 320 [360]–[61]; BVerfGE 120, 378 [428]–[29]. See also BVerfGE 124, 300 [333]–[34] concerning the degree of probability required for expressions of opinion to violate a public interest.

536 BVerfGE 115, 320 [360]–[61]; BVerfGE 120, 378 [428]–[29].

537 See, e.g., BVerfGE 115, 320 [364]; BVerfGE 120, 274 [323]; BVerfGE 125, 260 [330]–[31].

538 BVerfGE 120, 274 [323]–[24].

### C Interplay between Strict Proportionality and Remedy

The function and consequence of PA cannot be properly understood without consideration of the interplay between the strict proportionality test and the remedy. An important factor for the success story of PA in German constitutional practice is that the FCC skilfully strikes the balance between PA and remedy. While German sociologist Niklas Luhmann characterizes the dichotomous code of the law as lawful/unlawful,[539] implying that only one side can win the trial, the outcome of the Court's reasoning at the strict proportionality stage is generally not that one concern entirely prevails and the conflicting concern entirely loses out. Instead, the Court will typically 'split the difference' between the parties,[540] seek a middle ground between the fundamental right concern and the public interest concern, and try to realize both concerns to some extent. Alec Stone Sweet has argued that the motive of constitutional judges behind the careful crafting of remedies is to ensure that the constitution continues to be 'the essential reference point for the settlement of like cases that may arise in the future'.[541] This requires that litigants feel their concerns are taken seriously and, at least to some extent, are validated by the Court. The primary stage at which the FCC strikes the balance between the competing constitutional concerns raised by the case at hand is the strict proportionality stage that provides the Court with a maximum degree of latitude and flexibility to make the most sensible decision possible under the particular circumstances of a case.

The FCC has been particularly successful at implementing this strategy. It has established itself as an institution of balance, compromise, and reason in Germany's political system that attracts litigants and is respected by government institutions. On the one hand, the Court identifies and carves out the normative concerns of both parties and emphasizes in textbook fashion the importance of the abstract constitutional values at stake but, on the other hand, it chooses the remedies sensibly. The standard case if the Court finds a law unconstitutional is that it addresses particular constitutional concerns regarding the specific design of a law and requires certain rectifications from the legislature.

539 Niklas Luhmann, *Law as a Social System* (OUP 2004) 178.
540 Alec Stone Sweet, *Governing with Judges* (OUP 2000) 142.
541 ibid 141.

In all those cases, the typical end result will be that a modified law can still stand and help to address the objective that the legislature initially pursued.

## IX Overview of the Means Struck Down

Anyone who expects from the foregoing analysis of the FCC's proportionality case-law clear guidance and predictability for policy-makers must be disappointed. It is one thing to request from policy-makers that they pass laws that are proportionate, and another thing to answer what this means concretely. The two Senates of the FCC typically decide 'hard cases' whose outcome is difficult to predict. Unambiguous rules on what would constitute proportionate or disproportionate policy-making do not exist. As we have seen, the Court generally favours a flexible case-by-case approach over predictable rules and standards. While PA provides a useful analytical framework to identify and tackle difficult constitutional issues, it does not transform 'hard cases' into 'easy cases'. Its virtue lies in the flexibility that it provides to the Court – not in its predictability.

Nevertheless, this analysis has shed light on the type of measures and their characteristics and defects that are deemed disproportionate. Taken together, they enable us to formulate in broad strokes a typology of disproportionate policy-making. The analysis confirms that the Court does not generally use PA to challenge the basic value decision of the legislature.[542] Although full-blown judicial balancing of competing constitutional values, as exemplified by the doctrine of practical concordance,[543] has a significant role in German constitutional practice when it comes to reviewing decisions of ordinary courts or state legislatures, or even upholding federal legislation, the Court seldom relies on balancing in the proper sense to overturn federal legislation.[544] Instead, the Court uses a more restrained approach that concentrates on identifying clearly defined constitutional shortcomings in order to limit restrictions of the legislator's margin of manoeuvre to the margins. In conformity with this restrained approach, a finding of unconstitutionality will typically only require certain limited modifications by policy-makers and, in essence,

542 Petersen, *Proportionality and Judicial Activism* (n 140) 246–49.

543 See on this doctrine Section VIII.B.

544 See Section VIII.B.

allow a modified policy to pursue the objectives that it was designed to achieve.[545]

What are, based on a generalized view, the characteristic defects of measures that are struck down by the FCC with the proportionality test? First, the Court regards certain purposes with suspicion. A law that pursues such a purpose, even if it constitutes only one out of several worthy purposes, will likely fail the proportionality test.[546] Although the Court rarely strikes down measures with the worthy purpose test and generously allows the legislator to define what purposes are in the public interest so long as they are not excluded by the Constitution, rights-infringing laws that predominantly pursue antiquated moral standards or outdated professional rules and fiscal or anti-competitive reasons are susceptible to being overturned at a later PA stage.[547] While the Court typically accepts the officially stated purposes in those cases, its subsequent analysis will focus on discrediting the legislature's regulatory scheme by pointing out inconsistencies between the stated and suspected purpose. Inconsistencies and contradictions in the regulatory scheme are frequently considered to indicate that the policy-maker pursues a different than officially stated purpose.[548]

Second, policy-makers should ensure that fundamental rights concerns do not lose out entirely as a result of the contested policy but are accommodated by the policy in some form.[549] As we have seen, the Court conceptualizes fundamental rights as optimization requirements and the balancing process is geared towards finding a workable compromise between the competing concerns. Consequently, policy-makers should generally design their policies in a way that allows fundamental rights concerns to be validated to at least some extent in any particular case setting. A policy will likely be deemed disproportionate if the fundamental right concern does not come to bear.

Third, and more specifically, the Court has a preference for individual justice over legal certainty.[550] If policy-makers seek to avoid that their policies are found to violate constitutional fundamental rights guarantees they are better off crafting rules that provide for exception mechanisms

[545] See Section III.
[546] See Section V.C.
[547] ibid.
[548] ibid.
[549] See Section VIII.B.
[550] See Section VII.C.

and individualized procedures that leave room to do justice to the particular facts of the individual case. In contrast, laws with clear-cut rules that leave no room for individual assessment possibilities have repeatedly been deemed unconstitutional by the Court.

Fourth, the proportionality test as conducted by the Court is focused on remedying excessive burdens and hardships for a particular group of addressees of the policy being scrutinized.[551] Even if the law causing hardship is unobjectionable vis-à-vis most addressees, it will be found disproportionate if it places an excessive burden on a small minority. Policy-makers should therefore think long and hard whether the policy imposes an unreasonable burden on particular addressees. Of course, the judicial process is arguably better equipped than the political process from an institutional perspective to detect special burdens on particular individuals. While courts adjudicate individual cases on external initiative retrospectively, in other words with additional information about how a policy is applied in practice, the political process is not geared to the individual hardship but to legislative agendas and electoral prospects.[552] However, policy-makers can compensate this disadvantage by including certain exceptions, hardship clauses, or transitional measures into the policy to prevent hardship. Findings of unconstitutionality in hardship cases are typically the result of rigid rules that fail to leave sufficient room for exceptions for a subgroup of addressees that are affected by the law in a particularly severe way. Policy-makers may be able to prevent such a verdict even in cases in which they are unsure of the societal consequences of their policy if they enact hardship clauses to prevent an excessive burden on a small minority.

Fifth, policy-makers should ask themselves whether they have narrowly tailored their policy.[553] If they are determined to avoid the risk of a judicial finding of unconstitutionality, the policy should minimize the infringement into the fundamental rights of all addressees to the greatest extent possible without compromising the purpose of the policy. The policy should not be over-inclusive but limit the scope of application to those addressees or circumstances that are strictly required to achieve the purpose. Designing a measure in such a way would signal to the Court that the government has duly taken fundamental right concerns into account. Against this background, policy-makers should be particularly

[551] See Section VIII.B.

[552] See Christoph Möllers, *The Three Branches* (OUP 2013) 84–96.

[553] See Section VIII.B.

mindful of the constitutional ramifications if they impose total bans on any conduct that falls within the scope of protection of a fundamental right.[554] As we have seen, it is not characteristic for FCC decisions that one side entirely prevails and that the other side entirely loses. As a result, the Court is not reluctant to require policy-makers to choose over a total ban a less effective alternative or to accept a moderately higher degree of risk that the regulatory purpose is not achieved in all instances so long as the regulatory purpose can still be achieved, especially in cases of a disparity between a slight public benefit of a total ban and a substantial cost of rights infringement. Policy-makers should therefore think carefully whether the public interest that they pursue can be attained effectively in a less intrusive way than with a total ban. If they fail to do so, the Court is not shy of specifically outlining an alternative policy in its judgment that would have been less intruding even if it is slightly less effective.

Sixth, policy-makers should take into consideration that particular policy fields are subject to particularly high judicial scrutiny. If they prepare a policy in these fields, they should be especially determined, for the sake of passing constitutional muster, to minimize the infringement of a fundamental right. As we have seen, the subject matters of national security, family law, and legal services seem to experience findings of disproportionality at a significantly higher rate than average.[555] The fields of family law and legal services can be characterized as highly judicialized, lawyer-dominated areas in which constitutional judges are arguably more knowledgeable about factual issues and may therefore be more inclined to show less deference to policy-makers in assessing the facts of a case. The policy field of national security is characterized by a high vulnerability of rights-bearers who are subject to covert surveillance and data collection measures. If policy-makers intend to draft legislation regarding new surveillance measures in the realm of national security, they should know that the Court, while being unlikely to question the basic legitimacy of security policies, will require strict substantive and procedural constraints on security policies to minimize the fundamental rights infringement.[556] They should therefore seriously consider expanding the scope of judicial orders, to increase the level of gravity of the criminal offence investigated, to provide for the deletion of

[554] See Section VII.C.
[555] See Section III.
[556] See Section VIII.B.

inadvertently retrieved data, or to enact safeguards to ensure that criminal investigations do not intrude into the protected core of the right to personality in its various manifestations.

Finally, the Court has made it clear that diligence and consistency in the legislative enactment process are significant factors in its constitutionality review.[557] Starkly put, process matters to the Court. If the legislative process displays diligent factual assessments and full exploitation of the accessible sources of information, the policy has generally better chances of surviving judicial scrutiny, particularly if the facts on which the policy is based are disputed. In contrast, laws based on questionable factual assumptions contain an element of irrationality and are more likely to be found unconstitutional.

[557] See Section VII.B.

# 2

## Proportionality Analysis by the Canadian Supreme Court

LORIAN HARDCASTLE

### I Introduction

Proportionality review plays a crucial role in Canadian constitutional law and, more broadly, in public decision-making. The first section of the Canadian Charter of Rights and Freedoms enshrines the government's authority to place reasonable limits on constitutionally protected rights: the Charter 'guarantees the rights and freedoms set out in it subject only to such reasonable limits prescribed by law as can be demonstrably justified in a free and democratic society'. Given that the Charter provides no definitions for any of these terms employed in section 1 or additional guidance or qualifications on this provision, constitutional drafters left its interpretation and application to the courts. Section 1 is the most important part of the Charter, with one commentator noting that it 'has become the hungriest, the greediest of Charter provisions, absorbing most issues of genuine constitutional dispute into its analytic grasp'.[1]

The legal test for determining whether section 1 has been satisfied was first set out by the Supreme Court of Canada in *R v Oakes*.[2] Although this test has certainly evolved over time, legal scholars and courts throughout Canada continue to refer to section 1 as requiring an application of 'the *Oakes* test'. Under this test, once a claimant proves that a constitutionally protected right has been infringed, the burden shifts to the government to justify the rights infringement. The *Oakes* test is described by the Supreme Court of Canada as follows:

[1] Benjamin L Berger, 'Section 1, Constitutional Reasoning and Cultural Difference: Assessing the Impacts of Alberta v. Hutterian Brethren of Wilson County' (2010) 51 Supreme Court Law Review 25, 26.

[2] [1986] 1 SCR 103.

1. Does the government have a pressing and substantial objective?
2. Was the means by which the government addressed this objective proportional?[3]
   a. Are the means chosen by the government rationally connected to the objective?
   b. Is there a minimal impairment of rights?
   c. Is there proportionality between the effect of the infringement and the objective?

The *Oakes* test built upon prior statements made by the Supreme Court of Canada in *R v Big M Drug Mart*, which suggested that the crux of the test would be a form of proportionality analysis (PA) requiring judges to balance a sufficiently important governmental interest against the reasonableness of the means chosen to achieve that goal:

> Principles will have to be developed for recognizing which government objectives are of sufficient importance to warrant overriding a constitutionally protected right or freedom. Once a sufficiently significant government interest is recognized then it must be decided if the means chosen to achieve this interest are reasonable – a form of proportionality test. The court may wish to ask whether the means adopted to achieve the end sought do so by impairing as little as possible the right or freedom in question.[4]

This chapter is based on a qualitative and quantitative analysis of 120 Supreme Court cases, which are all cases in which a Charter right was alleged to have been breached and the Court conducted a PA, since the Court's articulation of the test in *R v Oakes* and until the end of 2017, a period of 31 years.[5] This dataset of cases was arrived at by reading the

[3] Stone Sweet and Matthews suggest that a proportionality approach did not necessarily flow from the language of the test and that 'reasonable limits' could just as easily have been interpreted to require a 'more relaxed "reasonableness" or "irrational basis" standard'. However, the authors note that Canadian history supports the more rigorous standard. Specifically, it was necessary in order to forestall opposition to the Charter by the provinces (who had blocked previous human rights instruments). Alec Stone Sweet and Jud Matthews, 'Proportionality, Balancing and Global Constitutionalism' (2008) 47 Columbia Journal of Transnational Law 68, 116–17.

[4] [1985] 1 SCR 295 [139].

[5] The dataset does not include cases in which the courts borrow from the *Oakes* test but do not apply the test in the same manner (i.e. in the adjudicaton of aboriginal rights or claims under human rights laws). It also does not include cases involving a rights infringement that do not involve the application of the *Oakes* test, such as cases in which evidence is obtained in an unconstitutional manner and the courts use another balancing approach to determine whether to exclude that evidence. Finally, it does not include cases in which

headnote (a brief summary) of all of the Supreme Court of Canada cases from the Court's official website during this 31-year period (2,688 cases) to determine which involved the adjudication of a Charter right and the application of the *Oakes* test.

## II Legal and Institutional Context

Prior to 1982, Canada had a system of parliamentary sovereignty, subject to the division of powers set out in the Constitution Act. The courts had the power to strike down both federal and provincial laws that were ultra vires the level of government responsible for their enactment. Prior to the enactment of the Charter, Canada also had a Bill of Rights, which was enacted in 1960. The scope of this law was quite limited, as it only applied to federal laws, it was easily amended by Parliament (in contrast to the amending formula required to change the Charter[6]), and the courts were quite reluctant to declare laws of no force and effect.

In 1982, Canada's constitution was amended to include the Charter, which arguably had the effect of shifting Canada from a system of parliamentary supremacy to one of constitutional supremacy. The enactment of the Charter expanded the power of the courts considerably, as it authorized judges to review federal and provincial laws for compliance with the Charter. Specifically, section 32 states that the Charter applies to 'the Parliament and government of Canada in respect of all matters within the authority of Parliament' and 'the legislature and government of each province in respect of all matters within the authority of the legislature of each province'. This has been interpreted to include the policies of all branches of government (federal and provincial), rules or regulations created by 'government actors', and the courts.

In *McKinney v University of Guelph*,[7] the Supreme Court of Canada articulated the 'effective control test' to determine whether a particular entity constituted a 'government actor' for the purposes of the Charter.

claiments alleged a violation of charter rights, but the court found there to be no violation and the decision comes to an end.

6 The general amending formula, which is set out in s 38 of the *Constitution Act, 1982* requires resolutions of the Senate and House of Commons (federally) and resolutions of the legislative assemblies of at least two-thirds of the provinces that have, in the aggregate, at least 50 per cent of Canada's population.

7 [1990] 3 SCR 229. This case related to a mandatory retirement age for university professors and whether that rule was discriminatory on the basis of age, contrary to section 15 of the Charter.

This test requires an examination of whether the government has statutory authority to exercise substantial control over the day-to-day operations of the entity, the government's responsibility for policy-making respecting the entity, and whether the government provides substantial funding to the entity. In an absence of 'effective control', an entity can still be considered a 'government actor' for the purposes of the Charter if it provides services that are in furtherance of a specific government policy or programme.[8] Regardless of whether the impugned conduct is a law or a policy, or whether the actor is government itself or a government actor, the framework for proportionality review remains the same. The Charter does not apply to private actors and, although the Charter does not strictly apply to the application of the common law, it is to be interpreted in light of Charter values.[9]

Charter questions can reach the courts in a variety of ways. First, a person to whom a law is applied can allege that the law is unconstitutional. This occurs, for example, when an individual charged with a criminal offence claims that the provision setting out the criminal offence is contrary to a Charter right (such as the presumption of innocence, the right to liberty, or the right to a fair trial). Charter review might also occur when an individual seeks a declaration that a law is contrary to his or her rights. For example, a media company may apply for a declaration that a law limiting cameras in the courtroom is contrary to freedom of speech, or an individual may apply to the court for a declaration that a law restricting spousal support benefits to married couples is discriminatory.

Canada has very broad standing laws, allowing even those who are not directly affected to bring a challenge to a law. An individual need not be directly affected by the impugned law to assert public interest standing. The courts will ask three questions in determining whether someone has standing to bring a challenge. First, is there a serious issue raised as to the invalidity of the legislation in question? Second, has it been established that the plaintiff is directly affected by the legislation or, if not, does the plaintiff have a genuine interest as a citizen in its validity? Third, is there another reasonable and effective way to bring the issue before the court?[10]

[8] As was the case, for example, in *Eldridge v British Columbia (Attorney General)* [1997] 3 SCR 624, in the context of a hospital delivering publicly funded health care services.

[9] *RWDWU v Dolphin Delivery Ltd* [1986] 2 SCR 573.

[10] *Canadian Council of Churches v Canada (Minister of Employment and Immigration)* [1992] 1 SCR 236. Notably, in this case, the Court framed standing as an issue of striking a balance 'between ensuring access to the courts and preserving judicial resources'. This

It is not necessary that a dispute be 'ripe' to bring a challenge. For example, there have been constitutional challenges to new criminal laws that no one has yet been charged under. Similarly, a case can proceed even if it is rendered moot prior to trial. Canadian courts do not require that a rights infringement has actually occurred, nor are they concerned whether an infringement is certain. The courts are satisfied if a hypothetical rights violation (as opposed to any real rights violation before them) is possible in order to proceed with the Charter analysis. For example, in *R v Bedford*,[11] the Supreme Court of Canada found that the criminalization of several activities that are ancillary to prostitution infringed the right to life, liberty, and security on the basis that their criminalization could expose sex workers to safety risks (for example, making it illegal to operate a brothel means that prostitution must happen in less safe places without security, such as cars, hotel rooms, or the customer's apartment). There was no evidence before the Court that the laws had, in fact, made prostitution less safe than it would otherwise be, but the Court was willing to accept the possibility that the laws increased risk.

Another way that Charter questions can reach the courts is through a reference question. Reference questions occur when the government seeks an opinion directly from a court on the constitutionality of a piece of federal or provincial legislation. For example, when the federal government enacted comprehensive legislation governing assisted reproduction (i.e. cloning, surrogacy, egg donation, the use of embryos in research, the regulation of reproductive health facilities), it was the subject of a reference question on whether the law properly fell within the federal government's criminal law power.[12] Reference questions are quite uncommon.[13]

quotation suggests that the primary focus may be on keeping frivolous or vexatious cases out of the courts, rather than a desire to ensure that the party is the best litigant to raise a particular issue. Several authors have argued in support of broad and purposive standing rules as a vehicle for improving access to justice, as it enables individuals with sufficient resources to ensure judicial scrutiny of laws, as those affected may not have the capacity to bring legal challenges. See e.g. Lorne Sossin, 'The Justice of Access: Who Should Have Standing to Challenge the Constitutional Adequacy of Legal Aid?' (2007) 40 UBC Law Review 727.

[11] [2013] 3 SCR 1101.

[12] *Reference re Assisted Human Reproduction Act* [2010] 3 SCR 457.

[13] The Supreme Court of Canada has heard only 19 reference questions that mentioned the Charter since its enactment. Where reference questions met my criteria (i.e. involved the adjudication of a right and the application of the proportionality test), they were included in the dataset.

There is no constitutional court in Canada, but rather Charter questions can be raised before trial courts or appellate courts at either the provincial or the federal levels. Occasionally, cases may begin before an administrative body. However, the process by which most Charter cases reach the Supreme Court of Canada is to begin in a provincial superior court, to be appealed to the applicable provincial appellate court,[14] and finally to be appealed to the Supreme Court of Canada. For example, a recent case in which a claimant sought a declaration that the prohibition on assisted suicide violated the Charter rights to life and security of the person originated in the British Columbia Supreme Court, proceeded through the British Columbia Court of Appeal, and then finally to the Supreme Court of Canada.[15] If a party intends to raise a constitutional issue before the courts, then a notice of a constitutional question is sent to the government. In general, appellate courts are deferential to the findings of fact made by trial courts, as those judges have had the opportunity to hear the full factual record and are able to assess the credibility of witnesses. As such, appellate level courts generally focus on legal arguments rather than factual issues.

The Supreme Court of Canada grants very few leaves to appeal each year.[16] For example, in 2016, the Court released judgments in 56 cases.[17] In that same year, the Court issued 546 decisions on leaves to appeal.[18] Although the Supreme Court is a court of general jurisdiction and can thus hear appeals on any type of legal question including private law cases (i.e. negligence, contracts between private parties, family law), many of the cases granted leave to appeal involve constitutional law. For example, in 2016, the Court heard 14 private law disputes and 42 public law cases, the latter of which can be further subdivided into 14 administrative law cases, 14 Charter cases, 12 criminal law cases (not involving the Charter), 1 division of powers case, and 1 indigenous law case.

[14] At the provincially appellate level, the case is typically heard by between three and five justicies (usually three). The Supreme Court of Canada has nine justices and most frequently hears cases with a full panel of all nine justices.

[15] *Carter v Canada (Attorney General)* [2015] [2013] BCCA 435.

[16] In certain, limited, criminal law cases, there is a right of appeal.

[17] This number is relatively consistent: 69 in 2015, 78 in 2014, 73 in 2013, 75 in 2012, and 66 in 2011.

[18] This number is also relatively consistent: 503 decisions in 2015, 502 in 2014, 520 in 2013, 581 in 2012, and 541 in 2011.

The Supreme Court of Canada and Canadian courts more broadly are relatively non-political.[19] Comparing the Canadian judiciary to the American judiciary, Macfarlane notes that Canada has a less overtly partisan (and thus less politicized) appointment process, 'a more collectivist and deferential political and legal culture', and strong behavioural norms.[20]

There is little separation of powers between the executive and the legislative branches of the Canadian federal and provincial governments.[21] However, the ability of judges to review legislation for its compliance with the Charter entrenched the separation of powers between the judiciary and government. Due to the broad scope of Charter review and the way that it has been interpreted by Canadian courts, there is a great deal of discussion in the Canadian legal and policy literature on judicial activism.[22] There is a concern that Charter adjudication gives judges

[19] See CL Ostberg and Matthew Wetstein, 'Dimensions of Attitudes Underlying Search and Seizure Decisions of the Supreme Court of Canada' (1998) 31 Canadian Journal of Political Science 767; Matthew E Wetstein and CL Ostberg, 'Search and Seizure Cases in the Supreme Court of Canada: Extending an American Model of Judicial Decision Making across Countries' (1999) 80 Social Science Quarterly 757; CL Ostberg, Matthew E Wetstein and Craig R Ducat, 'Attitudinal Dimensions of Supreme Court Decision Making in Canada: The Lamer Court, 1991–1995' (2002) 55 Political Research Quarterly 235; CL Ostberg and Matthew E Wetstein, *Attitudinal Decision Making in the Supreme Court of Canada* (UBC Press 2007).

[20] Emmett Macfarlane, 'Consensus and Unanimity at the Supreme Court of Canada' (2010) 52 Supreme Court Law Review 379.

[21] In Canada, the legislative and executive branches are basically fused. The executive branch originates from the legislative branch (that is, the Prime Minister is the leader of the party with a majority of the seats in Parliament), is part of the legislative branch, and is responsible to the legislative branch (in that the Prime Minister must retain the 'confidence' of the legislative branch in order to stay in power, which is assured, in part, by strict party discipline).

[22] Some Canadian scholars are critical of the term 'judicial activism'. For example, Roach argues that judicial activism is not a helpful way to structure a debate about judicial review. He argues that the label allows commentators to criticize the Court and the *Charter* without explaining their reasons. Kent Roach, 'The Myths of Judicial Activism' (2001) 14 Supreme Court Law Review 297. Other commentators do not see 'judicial activism' as a clear concept, without something more. For example, Bruce Ryder notes that the term 'judicial activism' is an unhelpful way of formulating the debate about the appropriate uses of judicial power:

> Often an unspoken set of assumptions animate allegations of judicial activism. The expression carries negative connotations – it suggests an illegitimate usurpation of the powers of the legislative or executive branches. It presupposes a baseline, an appropriate stance regarding judicial power that has been exceeded by a court. But how do we go about defining that baseline and thus determining what kinds of exercise of judicial power are appropriate?

an opportunity to substitute their policy preferences with those of government.

Courts themselves often disagree in this area, with some judges using their role as 'the guardians of the Constitution'[23] to justify broad judicial review. In justifying what might be seen as judicial policy-making, some commentators argue that by enacting the Charter, the government explicitly tasked courts with reviewing its policies. Weinrib argues that the Charter 'effected a revolutionary transformation of the Canadian polity from legislative supremacy to constitutional supremacy . . . The Supreme Court became the major agent of this transformation, mandated to bring the entire legal system into conformity with a complex new structure of rights-protection'.[24] Monahan takes another approach to questioning whether constitutional adjudication demands judicial policy-making, noting that the Charter does not require courts 'to test the substantive outcomes of the political process against some theory of the right or the good', but rather the *Charter* guarantees the integrity of the process by enhancing 'the opportunities for public debate and collective deliberation'.[25]

Another theoretical school of thought that is often invoked to explain judicial review is dialogue theory. Proponents of this theory argue that Charter interpretation represents a dialogue between courts and the government. Specifically, governments pass legislation, courts respond (sometimes with advice on how to make laws constitutionally permissible),[26] and governments respond with amended laws. In some cases, the

Ryder argues that judges should not be labelled as active or passive, 'until we have made clear what our standard or background theory is regarding the appropriate approach of judicial power'. Bruce Ryder, 'Unavoidable Judicial Power and Inevitable Charter Controversy' (2001) 14 Supreme Court Law Review 289, 290.

23 *Hunter v Southam Inc* [1984] 2 SCR 145 [44].

24 Lorraine Weinrib, 'Canada's Charter of Rights: Paradigm Lost?' (2002) 6 Review of Constitutional Studies 119. For a contrary view, see, e.g., Jamie Cameron, 'The Original Conception of Section 1 and Its Demise: A Comment on *Irwin Toy Ltd v Attorney-General of Quebec*' (1989–90) 35 McGill Law Journal 253, 258.

25 Patrick J Monahan, 'Judicial Review and Democracy: A Theory of Judicial Review' (1987) 21 UBC Law Review 87, 89.

26 This is a point of some debate in the Canadian legal commentary. For example, Monahan argues that dialogue theory is best served by the courts producing 'minimalist rulings', which would leave 'the greatest scope possible for potential responses by the legislative and executive branches'. Patrick J Monahan, 'The Supreme Court of Canada in the 21st Century' (2001) 80 Canadian Bar Review 374, 392. In contrast, Roach refers to these rulings as 'unfortunate', arguing that constitutional dialogue permits the government to respond to 'even bold and broad judicial rulings'. Kent Roach, *The Supreme Court on Trial: Judicial Activism or Democratic Dialogue* (Irwin Law 2001) 154.

amended legislation may be subject to challenge, giving courts another opportunity to engage with the judiciary. In other words, Charter decisions should not be conceptualized 'as imposing a veto on desired legislative policies, but rather as starting a "dialogue" with the legislative branch as to how best to reconcile the individualistic values of the Charter with the accomplishment of social and economic policies for the benefit of the community as a whole'.[27]

There are many critics of dialogue theory in Canada. For example, Petter argues that it discounts the extent to which judicial decision-making drives public policy-making. He argues that dialogue theorists tend to exaggerate the influence of legislatures in responding to judicial decisions, noting that many legislative responses are better characterized as merely reflecting judicial decisions rather than actually responding to them. Second, he argues that dialogue theorists downplay the powerful position held by courts, as they are able to speak in the rhetoric of rights, while legislatures are left to speak about limits on those rights. Third, he argues that dialogue theory ignores the extent to which Charter rights shape public debate, regardless of dialogue.[28]

It is likely that public support for the Canadian judiciary fluctuates depending on a number of factors, including the political party in power and high-profile legal cases. That would be particularly true of the Supreme Court, which has, in recent years, opined on such controversial issues as the legalization of assisted suicide and decriminalization of prostitution. However, 2013 data from Statistics Canada indicate that 57 per cent of Canadians have confidence in the justice system, compared to only 38 per cent confidence in the federal Parliament.[29] Other recent polls show similar results. For example, in a recent study, 58 per cent of those surveyed reported that the Court generally had a positive effect on

[27] Peter W Hogg, *Constitutional Law of Canada* (Looseleaf 5th edn, Carswell 2007). See also Roach, 'The Myths of Judicial Activism' (n 22) 298–99. See also Kent Roach, 'Constitutional and Common Law Dialogues between the Supreme Court and Canadian Legislatures' (2001) 80 Canadian Bar Review 481.

[28] Andrew Petter, 'Twenty Year of Charter Justification: From Liberal Legalism to Dubious Dialogue' (2003) 52 University of New Brunswick Law Journal 187. See also Christopher P Manfredi, 'Judicial Power and the Charter: Three Myths and a Political Analysis' (2001) 14 Supreme Court Law Review 336. Citing two cases that are often given as an example of the dialogue between the courts and the government, he notes that '[i]f any dialogue occurred in these two instances, it was among the justices themselves'.

[29] Adam Cotter, 'Public Confidence in Canadian Institutions' (Statistics Canada, 7 December 2015) <www.statcan.gc.ca/pub/89-652-x/89-652-x2015007-eng.htm> accessed 23 June 2019.

individual rights and freedoms, while 57 per cent reported that the Supreme Court of Canada generally had a positive effect on the country as a whole.[30] In contrast, few Canadians had 'a great deal' or 'quite a lot' of confidence in the federal government (28 per cent), politicians (12 per cent), political parties (13 per cent), and the Senate (10 per cent). When asked about specific recent Supreme Court decisions, more Canadians supported than opposed controversial decisions on medical assistance in dying, prostitution, and aboriginal land title. However, more Canadians opposed than supported a decision to strike down mandatory minimum sentences for firearm offenses.

## III Structure of Limitation Analysis

### *A Overview*

The Charter protects several types of rights and freedoms: fundamental freedoms (i.e. freedom of religion, association, expression), democratic rights (i.e. the rights to vote and run for government), mobility rights, legal rights (i.e. freedom from unreasonable search and seizure, freedom from arbitrary detention, the right to a fair trial, the right to the presumption of innocence), equality rights, and language rights (i.e. the requirement that laws are printed in French and English and the right to public education in either official language).

The first stage of a Charter analysis requires the plaintiff to establish that the government breached his or her rights. The standard of proof is a balance of probabilities, which is the civil standard of proof.[31] As I describe in greater detail later, Canadian courts are often likely to find

[30] BJ Siekierski, 'Vast Majority of Canadians Trust Supreme Court, Including Most Tories' (*iPolitics*, 16 August 2015) <https://ipolitics.ca/2015/08/16/vast-majority-of-canadians-trust-supreme-court-including-most-tories/> accessed 23 June 2019.

[31] As the majority noted in *Oakes* (n 2),

> Within the broad category of the civil standard, there exist different degrees of probability depending on the nature of the case ... The case may be proved by a preponderance of probability, but there may be degrees of probability within that standard. The degree depends on the subject-matter. A civil court, when considering a charge of fraud, will naturally require a higher degree of probability than that which it would require if considering whether negligence were established. It does not adopt so high a degree as a criminal court, even when it is considering a charge of a criminal nature, but still it does require a degree of probability which is commensurate with the occasion.

that a right has been breached and to allow the claim to proceed to the justification stage, although there is often significant debate and even disagreement on this question, particularly for certain rights (such as the right to be free from discrimination), and a significant amount of cases that do terminate at this point ot the analysis. According to Choudhry, section 1 was initially conceived of as a 'stringent standard of justification', in which 'rights are the norm and are of presumptive importance' and cannot be limited unless 'exceptional criteria which justify their being limited' are met.[32]

In addition to establishing a rights infringement, a claimant must also demonstrate that the right is limited by a governmental actor. Second, according to section 1, rights are subject to ' ... reasonable limits prescribed by law ... ' Although the question of whether something is 'prescribed by law' is rarely raised by a claimant in Charter jurisprudence, there are judicial interpretations of this requirement. For example, in *R v Nova Scotia Pharmaceutical Society*, the defendant was charged under the Combines Investigation Act for conspiring to lessen competition. Although the Supreme Court ultimately upheld this statute, the Court found that an enactment could theoretically be so vague that it is not 'prescribed by law'. They found that the standard for determining whether a law was too vague was one of 'intelligibility'.[33] There has been little recent discussion of the 'prescribed by law' requirement, and the court tends to address issues of vagueness elsewhere.[34]

Once a claimant proves a violation of his or her rights the burden shifts to the government to justify the limit on the right, and the burden of proof is the balance of probabilities. Section 1 of the Charter requires a court to determine whether the government has a pressing and

[32] Sujit Choudhry, 'So What Is the Real Legacy of Oakes? Two Decades of Proportionality Analysis under the Canadian Charter's Section 1' (2006) 34 Supreme Court Law Review 501, 506. During the drafting of the Charter, section 1 initially allowed for limits on rights that were 'generally accepted in a free and democratic society'. Later 'reasonable' and 'demonstrably justified' were added, which Bredt and Pessione argue reflects the 'intention that limitations on Charter rights be held to what the Supreme Court of Canada later referred to [in *Oakes*] as a "stringent standard of justification"'. Christopher D Bredt and Heather K Pessione, 'The Death of Oakes: Time for a Rights-Specific Approach?' (2013) 63 Supreme Court Law Review 285, 285.

[33] [1992] 2 SCR 606.

[34] For example, Section 7 of the Charter can elicit discussion of vagueness, since laws that are vague will not satisfy the principles of fundamental justice. In addition, vagueness can arise in the context of PA under Section 1 of the Charter, as vague laws will seldom be minimally impairing.

substantial objective, whether its law or policy is rationally connected to that objective, whether the means of achieving that objective is minimally impairing of the claimant's rights, and finally, whether there is proportionality between the effect of the infringement and the objective.

There is scholarly debate as to whether the *Oakes* test should consistently be applied across all cases, or whether it should be flexible as to context, with the courts tending to adopt the latter approach. For example, in *Edmonton Journal v Alberta (Attorney General)*, Justice Wilson stated that a contextual approach is preferable, as it recognizes that a particular right or freedom may have a different value depending on the context:

> The contextual approach attempts to bring into sharp relief the aspect of the right or freedom which is truly at stake in the case as well as the relevant aspects of any values in competition with it. It seems to be more sensitive to the reality of the dilemma posed by the particular facts and therefore more conducive to finding a fair and just compromise between the two competing values under s. 1.[35]

Ponomarenko criticizes this flexible approach, noting that 'by meandering amidst a welter of contentious evidentiary requirements and digressing into the vicissitudes of judicial deference, the proportionality test

[35] [1989] 2 SCR 1326. See also *Rocket v Royal College of Dental Surgeons of Ontario* [1990] 2 SCR 232. In that case, the Court stated that in undertaking a section 1 analysis, the Court must place conflicting values in their factual and social context. Similarly, as Justice McLachlin stated in *R. v Keegstra* [1990] 3 SCR 697,

> The task which judges are required to perform under s. 1 is essentially one of balancing ... The exercise is one of great difficulty, requiring the judge to make value judgments. In this task logic and precedent are but of limited assistance. What must be determinative in the end is the court's judgment, based on an understanding of the values our society is built on and the interests at stake in the particular case ... [T]his judgment cannot be made in the abstract. Rather than speak of values as though they were Platonic ideals, the judge must situate the analysis in the facts of the particular case, weighing the different values represented in that context.

See also Paul G Murray, 'Section One of the Canadian Charter of Rights and Freedoms: An Examination at Two Levels of Interpretation' (1989) 21 Ottawa Law Review 631, 635–36, in which the author states that the balance between the value of protected rights and permitting certain limits 'reflects the view that the least important exercise of a right, when weighed in the balance, justifies a stringent review'. He later argues that an 'abstract notion of importance ... fails to reflect the fact that infringement of Charter rights may vary in their significance' (at 641).

became so contextual and diluted that many ... assert that section 1 justification has been rendered ad hoc'.[36]

Cameron also criticizes this flexible approach in which the interpretation of rights and the application of section 1 varies depending upon the context. She cites *Irwin Toy Ltd v Quebec (Attorney General)*,[37] in which the Court suggested that a strict standard of proportionality should apply when the government acts as the 'singular antagonist', as it does in the criminal context, as opposed to the socio-economic context, in which a more deferential standard should apply. According to Cameron, '[t]his distinction assumes that government authority is presumptively less insidious when it is invoked to protect a vulnerable group or otherwise allocate scarce resources than when it is exercised to prosecute and punish individuals', 'which has enabled the Court to engage in a case-by-case manipulation of Oakes' as it 'chooses between strict and deferential standards of justification on purely subjective grounds'.[38]

### B The Relationship between Section 1 Limitation Analysis and Internal Balancing Clauses

In addition to the justification stage contained in section 1 of the Charter, several rights include specific, internal balancing clauses. Although section 1 still applies to these rights, their resolution will often be determined largely by these internal balancing clauses. This section will specify the rights that include such a clause, how the court has interpreted these balancing clauses, and how they relate to the PA. I define rights with internal balancing clauses as those rights in which the courts do not merely look at the impact of the provision on the plaintiff, but rather also evaluate the government's policy in some fashion.

36 Iryna Ponomarenko, 'The Unbearable Lightness of Balancing: Towards a Theoretical Framework for the Doctrinal Complexity in Proportionality Analysis in Constitutional Adjudication' (2016) 49 UBC Law Review 1103–4.

37 [1989] 1 SCR 927.

38 Jamie Cameron, 'Abstract Principle v. Contextual Conceptions of Harm: A Comment on *R. v Butler*' (1992) 37 McGill Law Journal 1144. Murray details some of the other kinds of cases in which the courts will show deference. Specifically, he notes that objectives which relate to social or economic policy or matters generally relating to public policy are more likely to receive a deferential application of section 1. The measures which attract deference are also often regulatory or administrative in nature. However, when the objective relates to the suppression of crime or administration of justice or when the measures formed part of a judicial or quasi-judicial process, the Oakes criteria have been strictly applied. Murray (n 35) 674.

The first and most important right with an internal balancing clause is the right to life, liberty, and security of the person, which is qualified by 'the right not to be deprived thereof except in accordance with the principles of fundamental justice'. This is arguably the most important right in the Canadian constitution, with a variety of important governmental policies being challenged under this right.[39]

Canadian courts have articulated several principles of fundamental justice which serve to qualify the rights to life, liberty, and security of the person. First, and most commonly, an arbitrary law does not accord with the principles of fundamental justice. Similarly, laws that are grossly disproportionate or overbroad can also run afoul of the principles of fundamental justice. There is considerable overlap between these principles and the PA. For example, determining whether a law is arbitrary requires examining whether it targets the government's objective, which is somewhat similar to the question of whether there is a 'rational connection' between the law and the government's objective, as required by the PA. Similarly, a law that is 'grossly disproportionate' requires asking whether it goes further than is necessary, which overlaps with the minimal impairment stage of the proportionality test. Because of this overlap, when analysing a claim regarding the right to life, liberty, and security of the person based on section 7, the court tends to more closely scrutinize the impugned law at the rights infringement stage of the analysis and then to conduct a very brief PA that reiterates its earlier conclusions.[40]

The second right with an internal balancing clause is the freedom from unreasonable search and seizure. This requires a court to determine, at the infringement stage, whether the government violated the expectation of privacy that a reasonable individual would have in the situation at issue in the cases. This again creates some overlap with the PA, as it is difficult to envision how an unreasonable search could satisfy the requirements of the *Oakes* test. For example, in *R v Tse*,[41] the Court held that a law permitting warrantless wiretaps in certain circumstances constituted an unreasonable search and seizure, given the lack of oversight mechanisms and the lack of mechanisms to notify persons whose

[39] For example, section 7 was used to decriminalize prostitution and assisted suicide and to legalize abortion.

[40] In the dataset, cases with an internal balancing test were coded like other cases: although the PA in such cases is often brief and repetitive of the rights infringement analysis, the courts do still apply the *Oakes* test.

[41] [2012] SCR 531.

communications have been intercepted. These criticisms played directly into the minimal impairment analysis, in which the Court found that these shortcomings constituted examples of how the government might have enacted a less restrictive regime.

The third right with an internal balancing clause is the right to be free from arbitrary detention. After deciding that a law is arbitrary, the court often conducts a very brief PA,[42] having stated that it is difficult to imagine a law that is arbitrary but is somehow rationally connected to a pressing government objective. However, there are counter-examples in which laws deemed to be arbitrary in the context of arbitrary detention have been found to meet the rational connection test's requirements. For example, in *R v Ladouceur*,[43] an individual challenged a law that provided for random police stops. A majority of the Court found that this detention was arbitrary, in that there were no criteria for the selection of drivers to be stopped. However, the Court found that the law was justified under section 1. The law had the pressing objective of protecting the public and reducing highway-related injuries and deaths, it was 'rationally connected and carefully designed to achieve safety on the highways', it impaired the rights of drivers as little as possible, and the stops did not so severely interfere with individual rights as to outweigh the legislative objective.

The fourth right with an internal balancing clause is the right to be free from cruel and unusual punishment. The justification required in applying this section goes well beyond internal balancing clauses such as 'reasonableness' or 'arbitrariness' and actually requires that governmental policies are 'so excessive as to outrage standards of decency' or 'grossly disproportionate to what would have been appropriate'.[44] Again, this links with the PA, as it is difficult to envision something that outrages the standards of decency or is grossly disproportionate, but which is minimally impairing of an individual's rights.

### C *Contexts of Proportionality Analysis*

Of the cases in the dataset, a majority of the claims are challenges to federal laws or policies (56 per cent). This can be explained, in part, by

42 The arbitrariness analysis requires asking 'whether there is a direct connection between the purpose of the law and the impugned effect on the individual, in the sense that the effect on the individual bears some relation to the law's purpose'. *Bedford* (n 11) [111].

43 [1990] 1 SCR 1257.

44 *Miller and Cockriell v The Queen* [1977] 2 SCR 680.

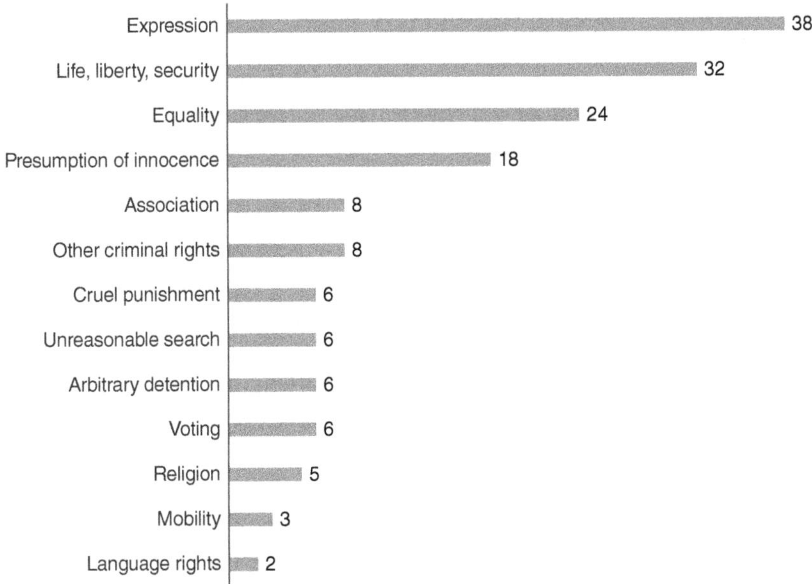


**Figure 2.1** Rights triggering proportionality analysis[45]

the fact that criminal law is a matter of federal jurisdiction and numerous Charter rights are largely exclusive to the criminal law context. There are also certain types of criminal cases for which the defendant has an appeal as of right (as opposed to requiring leave of the Court), which may also increase the number of criminal decisions. Provincial laws or policies are responsible for 33 per cent of the cases included in the dataset. The remaining 11 per cent of the cases are a mix of challenges to the common law, municipal laws, court orders, and administrative decisions.

The rights that most frequently trigger PA are freedom of expression (32 per cent of the cases in the dataset), the right to life, liberty, and security of the person (27 per cent), equality (20 per cent), and the presumption of innocence (15 per cent). In contrast, rights and freedoms relating to religion, mobility, voting, and minority language rights are very seldom the basis of PA. Figure 2.1 details the rights claimed to have been infringed in the proportionality cases in the dataset, taking into

[45] The 'Other Criminal Rights' category includes a variety of criminal law rights that have only been discussed in a few cases, such as habeus corpus, the right to a jury trial, the right to counsel, and the right to reasonable bail.

account that a single case can include claims of infringement of more than one right.

As Figure 2.1 illustrates, the right that most frequently triggers PA in the dataset is freedom of expression, which appeared in 38 cases, or 32 per cent. A partial explanation for this is that freedom of expression claims are often invoked alongside other rights. Although there are certainly some cases whose primary focus is free speech (i.e. restrictions on tobacco advertising or cases relating to publication bans in the courtroom), the number of expression cases is driven up by the fact that cases focusing primarily on freedom of association or voting rights often include a freedom of expression claim or a voting rights claim. This number is also driven up by a number of fairly duplicative cases around publication bans in criminal cases and another set of largely similar cases around unionization in the labour law context.

There are also a significant number of cases involving the right to life, liberty, and security of the person, and this right is raised in 27 per cent of the cases in the dataset. The rationale for this is perhaps, in part, the wide-ranging nature of the right, given that it can encompass everything from criminal law to various areas of social policy. Because 'liberty' is at stake in most criminal law cases (i.e. any offence with the possibility of imprisonment), this right is often litigated in conjunction with other criminal law rights, such as arbitrary detension or the presumption of innocence. The 'security of the person' portion of this right is also quite broad, which may also help to explain the large number of cases in this category. This has been interpreted to include state-imposed psychological stress, which can arise in a variety of contexts. For example, waiting to access health services, being at risk of having one's child seized by the state, or waiting to have one's immigration status determined could all engage security of the person.

There are many areas of policy-making that are rich in proportionality analyses, particularly criminal law (43 per cent of the cases in the dataset) and, to a lesser extent, labour law (13 per cent), and elections (8 per cent). Figure 2.2 categorizes the cases by subject matter.

As Figure 2.2 indicates, criminal law comprises the majority of the proportionality cases in Canada. There are several possible reasons for this. The first is that the federal criminal law power is defined quite broadly, arguably extending beyond what would traditionally be thought of as criminal law. For example, recent criminal cases have included Charter challenges to the criminalization of prostitution and medical assistance in dying, the latter of which is an area of shared jurisdiction

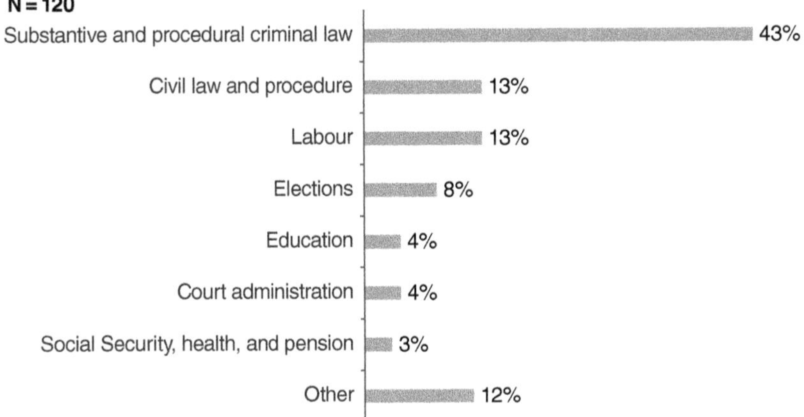


**Figure 2.2** Proportionality cases by subject matter[46]

between the federal government's criminal law power and the provincial power to regulate health pofessionals and health facilities. The criminal law power has also been used to regulate areas such as controlled drugs and substances and highway safety, the latter of which is also an area of shared responsibility with the provinces and represents many cases in the dataset.

Another explanantion for the large number of criminal cases is that the Charter guarantees numerous rights that are largely unique to the criminal context, such as the presumption of innocence, the right to be

[46] The civil law category is a hodgepodge of different types of cases that do not easily fit into any other category but are not plentiful enough to constitute their own category. This includes, for example, family law and regulation of retail stores. Although many labour laws apply to private actors, I did not include these cases within the private law category for two reasons. First, many of the labour law cases are more in the public realm (i.e. relate to government unions). Second, there were a sufficient number of cases to comprise its own category. Labour law cases relate to disputes between employers and their employees (whether public or private) regarding such issues as the right to form unions, the right to strike, wages, and other collective agreement issues. The rights generally invoked in these cases are freedom of association and freedom of expression. Court administration cases relate primarily to publication bans challenged on the basis of freedom of expression. Social benefit cases relate to access to social programmes such as welfare or employment benefits. These cases generally allege that the government's current means of allocating benefits is discriminatory on the basis of, for example, gender, marital status, or age. The other category includes cases addressing language rights, immigration (apart from cases also involving criminal law, such as extradition cases), transportation, or human rights laws.

free from arbitrary detention, and the right to be free from unreasonable search and seizure. Furthermore, criminal law generally inherently implicates the right to liberty, and so any deficiencies with those laws can be the subject of a Charter claim.

In terms of the outcome of PA, in the dataset government laws or policies subject to the review were declared unconstitutional in whole or in part in 70 per cent of the cases (84 out of 120 cases). It is important to note that striking down a law in whole or in part can be relatively minor: in some cases, the Court found that a relatively small aspect of a larger statutory scheme was unconstitutional. This success rate may also be driven in part by the fact that these are Supreme Court of Canada cases. There are several reasons that the level of court may make a difference to the outcome of the cases. First, the Supreme Court of Canada may be more inclined to grant leave to appeal when it is concerned about the constitutionality of a particular governmental law or policy. Second, if an individual loses a claim at trial that will often be the end of the litigation due to resource issues. However, if the government loses at trial, they are much more likely to continue to appeal all the way to the Supreme Court of Canada. In other words, these numbers might be skewed by the fact that this sample includes many cases that the government was likely to lose (and indeed had lost at both the trial and the appeal court levels).

### *D Division of Labor between the Stages of the Analysis*

This section will explore the way in which the Canadian Supreme Court has approached the PA since articulating the *Oakes* test. Using the dataset, I will examine the division of labor between the different stages of the test. According to the bulk of the scholarly commentary, the minimal impairment stage of the *Oakes* test is the touchstone of the PA.[47] Two empirical analyses of the *Oakes* test have been previously published: the first empirical analysis of proportionality in Canada was conducted by Trakman, Cole-Hamilton, and Gatien.[48] The key difference between this analysis and that contained in this chapter is the time period

47 David M Beatty, 'The Canadian Charter of Rights: Lessons and Laments' (1997) 60 Modern Law Review 481; Hogg (n 27) 128; Dieter Grimm, 'Proportionality in Canadian and German Constitutional Jurisprudence' (2007) 57 University of Toronto Law Journal 383.

48 Leon E Trakman, William Cole-Hamilton, and Sean Gatien, '*R. v Oakes* 1986–1998: Back to the Drawing Board' (1998) 36 Osgoode Hall Law Journal 83.

covered by the cases: while the paper published by Trakman and his collaborators was published in 1998, covering the first decade of the *Oakes* test, this chapter is based on a dataset that captures cases to the end of 2015. Although their results do not differ significantly from the findings in this chapter, the differences may be indicative of some trends in the jurisprudence between the earlier cases and later cases, which will be addressed later.

The second empirical analysis of the Canadian Supreme Court's application or proportionality is that conducted by Niels Peterson.[49] He relies on a similar sample of cases covered by this chapter – Supreme Court cases from the articulation of the *Oakes* test until the end of 2015.[50] The key difference between his analysis and the analysis in this chapter is that the focus of this chapter is on what occurs within each of the different stages of the *Oakes* test. Any blending between the stages or considering arguments made under one stage of the analysis that relate more to another (i.e. balancing arguments made within the minimal impairment analysis) are reflected not in the empirical analysis, but rather in the discussion following this empirical section of this chapter. Petersen is less concerned with the formal stages of the test and instead categorizes the arguments made in the cases as falling into categories, some of which mirror the *Oakes* test (i.e. balancing, rational connection) and others of which do not (i.e. overbreadth, consistency/coherency, procedural). In contrast, the methodological approach taken in this chapter, which focuses on the stages of the test as articulated by the Court itself, has the benefit of greater certainty, despite possibly sacrificing some nuance in terms of the disconnect between what the Court says it is doing and what it is actually arguing. In sum, while there is overlap between the two approaches, they are complementary rather than duplicative. Despite the differences in our methodological approaches, the results, which are discussed later, are relatively consistent.

Figure 2.3 illustrates the frequency of failure at each stage of the PA for the cases in the dataset. Of the 120 cases in which the Court conducted a

[49] Niels Petersen, *Proportionality and Judicial Activism: Fundamental Rights Adjudication in Canada, Germany and South Africa* (CUP 2017).

[50] Petersen restricts his analysis to legislation struck down by the Supreme Court of Canada. The analysis in this chapter takes a broader definition, and considers the constitutionality of policies, court orders, and the common law (i.e. any time that the Court does a PA), and therefore the dataset includes a few additional cases, but these few cases are unlikely to sway the results significantly.

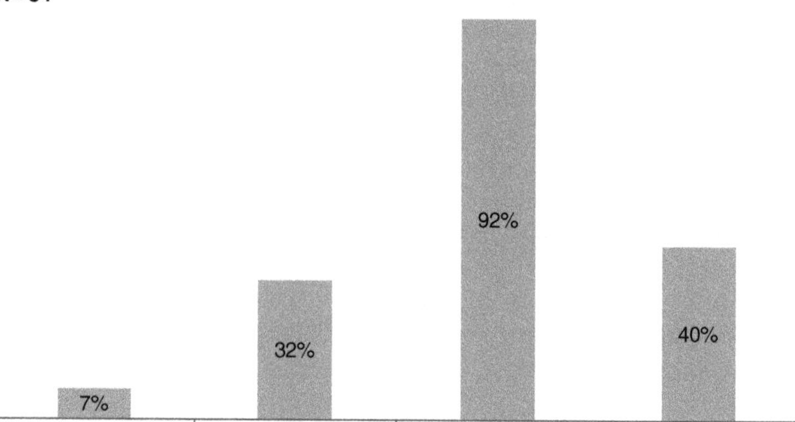


**Figure 2.3** Frequency of failure at each stage of proportionality analysis

PA, the figure reflects the 84 cases in which the government failed to justify its law or policy.

As Figure 2.3 illustrates, a relatively low – although not miniscule – number of cases fail at the worthy purpose stage. Of the cases in the dataset that ended with a finding of disproportionality, the government's purpose was found unworthy in 6 cases, or 7 per cent. This does not differ significantly from the findings of Trakman and his collaborators and Petersen's analyses, which both found 6 per cent of cases to fail the worthy purpose test.[51]

Of the cases in the dataset that ultimately failed the proportionality test, the measure failed the rational connection stage in 27 cases, or 32 per cent. This finding is highly surprising in light of the scholarly literature, which generally downplays the importance of this stage of the test. Interestingly, as will be shown later, failures at the suitability stage rarely serve as the sole basis for failure, with the Court almost always continuing to discuss minimal impairment for further support of the

[51] Petersen (n 49) 118; Trakman, Cole-Hamilton, and Sean Gatien (n 48) 94–97. The data presented in the Trakman article were adjusted in order for the percentages to be comparable to the dataset in this chapter: in the article, the percentages presented were calculated out of all *Oakes* cases in the examined period, both pass and fail (87 cases), finding 3 per cent failure at the worthy purpose test. For the sake of comparison, the failure rates were recalculated out of the fail cases only (3 out of 52 cases), reaching 6 per cent.

finding of the government's law or policy to be disproportionate. A quarter of the cases that failed at the suitability stage of the test are cases invoking section 7 of the charter – life, liberty, and security of the person, which itself includes an internal balancing clause.[52] Once a law has been held to fail to satisfy the internal balancing clause of section 7 because it is arbitrary, it will almost certainly fail to satisfy the rational connection test as well.

These figures are higher than those found in the analyses of the first 10 years of the *Oakes* test by Trakman and his collaborators, which documented only 17 per cent of cases failing the rational connection stage of the test.[53] A few possible reasons can be offered as possible causes for the differences in the failure rates at the rational connection test. The first relates to the types of cases that tended to characterize early Charter jurisprudence. Many of these cases related to criminal laws that very clearly suited their purpose but were not in accordance with newly articulated rights. For example, there were several cases in which the accused bore the burden of proof in a criminal matter, which clearly violates the Charter right to the presumption of innocence. Several of these cases were either struck down or upheld on minimal impairment. However, with respect to rational connection, it is fairly clear that these laws are well suited to their purposes. In contrast, the Court is hearing an increasing number of cases relating to complex areas of social policy such as the social harms associated with prostitution or the benefits of private health care when comparing Canada to other jurisdictions. When the Court looks at conflicting social science evidence in an area with several possible policy choices, it is much easier to disagree about whether the government's law is rationally connected to its objective.

A related explanation for the increase in failures at the rational connection stage is that as the Court has delved into these areas of social policy, it has often attracted criticisms of judicial activism. This may encourage the Court to bolster its conclusions at minimal impairment by also emphasizing that other stages of the proportionality test were not met. In other words, the Court may be attempting to add legitimacy to its conclusions.

[52] See Section III.B.

[53] Trakman, Cole-Hamilton, and Sean Gatien (n 48) 97–100 (9 cases failed rational connection out of 52 failure cases). Petersen's figures are not comparable here, as he does not separate rational connection from minimal impairment, but rather notes that these arguments, together, were significant in 63 per cent of the cases in his sample. Petersen (n 49) 118.

Of the cases in the dataset in which the challenged law was ultimately determined to be disproportionate, the law was found to not be minimally impairing in 77 cases, or 92 per cent. This is consistent with the findings of Trakman and his collaborators, who found that in the first decade of *Oakes* jurisprudence a similar rate of 96 per cent of the cases failed at the minimal impairment stage,[54] and is generally in line with the scholarhip on Canandian application of the proportionality framework.[55]

The final stage of the test is an overall assessment of proportionality (i.e. whether the salutary effects outweigh the deleterious effects of the law being challenged). Of the cases in which the Court ultimately found that the policy was disproportionate, 34 cases failed at this stage of the test (40 per cent). Importantly, however, nearly none of these cases failed based on the analysis at the final stage alone, but rather also failed previously at an earlier stage of the analysis. In the analysis of Trakman and his collaborators of the first 10 years of the *Oakes* test the number of cases that failed at this final stage was smaller – only 27 per cent of the failure cases failed the final balancing stage. They similarly found that none of the failure cases was based solely on a failure at this final stage, but rather were all preceded by failure at the minimal impairment stage.[56] The notion that the final balancing stage generally does not contribute significant independant value to the decision is bolstered by Petersen's findings, according to which balancing arguments affected a case being dismissed in only 6 per cent of the cases in his sample.[57] Petersen does, however, note that this stage of the test seems to be more relevant in recent years, with balancing arguments showing up more often in Supreme Court jurisprudence.[58]

Additional important insights regarding the relationship between the different stages can be gained from the termination rate after failure. Figure 2.4 illustrates the rate at which the Court terminates its analysis after failure at each stage of the *Oakes* test. It indicates, quite surprisingly,

[54] Trakman, Cole-Hamilton, and Sean Gatien (n 48) 100–2 (50 cases failed at the minimal impairment stage out of 52 failure cases). As mentioned previously, Petersen's figures are not comparable here, as he does not separate rational connection from minimal impairment. He finds that these two arguments, together, were significant in 63 per cent of the cases in his sample, which is quite lower than the findings of Trakman, as well as the current study. See Petersen (n 49) 118.

[55] See n 47.

[56] Trakman, Cole-Hamilton, and Sean Gatien (n 48) 102–5 (14 cases failed at the final balancing test, out of 52 failure cases).

[57] Petersen (n 49) 118.

[58] ibid 142–47.

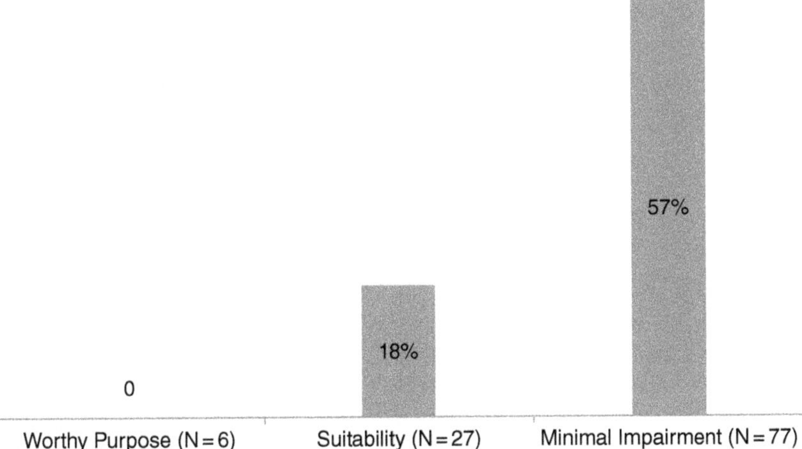


**Figure 2.4** Termination of proportionality analysis after failure

that cases that fail at the worthy purpose stage never come to an end based solely on that finding, and that cases that fail at the rational connection stage overwhelmingly progress to the minimal impairment analysis. In contrast, in less than half of the cases in which the court determines that there has been no minimal impairment does the court go on to consider strict proportionality.

In sum, the quantitative analysis reinforces the perception existing among Canadian legal scholars that minimal impairment is the central stage of the PA, while adding additional nuance to it. Indeed, the minimal impairment stage is that in which the largest number of cases fail for the first time. In addition, though, even when cases fail at either the pressing or substantial objective or rational connection stage, which happens more often than generally acknowleged, in the large majority of these cases (83 per cent) the court continues the analysis to the minimal impairment stage, for an additional failure. Finally, in more than half of the cases in which a law or policy fails the minimal impairment test the Court does not go on to consider the final balancing stage.

## IV Limitation of a Constitutional Right

### *A The Scope of a Constitutional Right*

The party alleging a Charter violation must demonstrate that his or her right has been infringed on a balance of probabilities. The general tendency of Canadian courts is to interpret rights quite broadly and thus to resolve cases through proportionality.[59] However, this does not mean that this stage is merely a formality. The court often engages in significant deliberation on the question of right limitation, and even with the court taking a broad rights interpretation the claimant fails to prove a right violation more often than not: in the examined timeframe, alongside the 120 cases in which a Charter right was found to have been violated, thus triggering PA, an additional 134 cases were identified in which the majority of the court held that the the claimant failed to establish the allegation that a Charter right had been breached, thus bringing the case to an end without proceeding to limitation analysis.

Table 2.1 indicates the rate in which a claimant succeeded to establish a limitation, per right.[60] The table demonstrates that with the exception of freedom of expression and arbitrary detention, the court is generally highly likely to find that the Charter right had not in fact been limited.

In a small number of cases the Court has spoken of some rights having a 'core' versus a 'periphery',[61] but this is quite uncommon. One area in which the Court does refer to a right's core occurs in the context of freedom of speech, where political speech goes to the core of the right (given its importance to democracy) versus commercial speech (given that it is done to further economic interests).

In *Harper v Canada*, Chief Justice McLachlin stated that '[t]his Court has repeatedly held that liberal democracy demands the free expression

[59] There are scholarly critiques of this approach. For example, some argue that readily finding that a right has been infringed but then finding that these violations are routinely justified cheapens those rights. See, e.g., Bradley W Miller, 'Justification and Rights Limits' in Grant Huscroft (ed), *Expounding the Constitution: Essays in Constitutional Theory* (CUP 2008).

[60] Table 2.1 only includes rights that were alleged in at least 10 different cases. The calculation in Table 2.1 is based on the rights invoked in a total of 163 cases in the examined period: 134 cases in which none of the rights alleged by the claiments were found to have been limited, bringing the analysis to an end; 120 cases in which at least one of the alleged rights was found to have been limited and limitation analysis was conducted; and 9 cases in which a right was held to have been limited but the courts' analysis was based on reasoning other than PA.

[61] The words 'core' and 'periphery' are used almost exclusively in the context of freedom of speech. For example, *R. v Zundel* [1992] 2 SCR 731 addressed the protection of false speech, which was at the periphery of the protected right; *R. v Bryan* [2007] 1 SCR 527 addressed the publication of election results prior to the closing of polls, which was at the periphery of the right to free speech; and *Saskatchewan (Human Rights Commission) v Whatcott* [2013] 1 SCR 467, in which hate speech was at the periphery of the protected right, while political speech was at its core.

Table 2.1 *Success rates in establishing a limitation of a right*

| Right invoked | Percent of cases in which the claimant was successful (%) |
|---|---|
| Expression | 74.5 |
| Arbitrary detention | 60 |
| Presumption of innocence | 50 |
| Unreasonable search and seizure | 50 |
| Association | 42 |
| Equality | 37.5 |
| Life, liberty, security of the person | 34 |
| Religion | 33 |
| Cruel and unusual punishment | 33 |

of political opinion, and affirmed that political speech lies at the core of the Canadian Charter of Rights and Freedoms' guarantee of free expression'.[62] However, it is important to note that this does not mean that a government may not infringe on that right, but rather it may influence the court's PA. For example, in *Rocket v Royal College of Dental Surgeons of Ontario*, the Supreme Court held that:

> Although it has been clearly held that commercial expression does not fall outside of the ambit of s. 2(*b*), the fact that expression is commercial is not necessarily without constitutional significance. Regulation of advertising may offend the guarantee of free expression in s. 2(*b*) of the Charter, but this does not end the inquiry. The further question of whether the infringement can be justified under s. 1 of the Charter must be considered. It is at this stage that the competing values – the value of the limitation and the value of free expression – are weighed in the context of the case. Part of the context, in the case of regulation of advertising, is the fact that the expression at issue is wholly within the commercial sphere.[63]

There is nothing in the constitution to suggest that certain rights are more important than others. In addition, in commenting on the rights infringement in the PA, the court generally does not distinguish between the different kinds of interests protected by the right. One exception to this occurs in cases relating to life, liberty, and security of the person. Although the Court has not created any sort of explicit hierarchy

[62] [2004] 1 SCR 827 [1].
[63] *Rocket* (n 35).

between these three rights, it is clear that they are particularly concerned when a government action potentially threatens the right to life as opposed to liberty or security of the person (the latter of which protects such interests as serious state-imposed psychological harm). The Court also speaks about the importance of political rights, and free speech in particular,[64] in many cases, but it is not clear how the importance of these rights would compare to other rights.

### B *What Triggers the Limitation of a Constitutional Right?*

In general, with the exception of rights with an internal balancing clause, any degree of rights infringement is sufficient to trigger the PA. For example, whether freedom of expression has been violated is merely a question of whether the government has limited expressive content in some way. Virtually any restriction on speech, regardless of the value of that speech (i.e. whether it is political or commercial) or the potential harms flowing from that speech, infringes the Charter right.[65] Similarly, freedom of religion 'has, for example, become so capacious as to be analytically vacant, with almost all meaningful analysis taking place under s 1'.[66] In other words, when a claimant alleges a breach of his or her religious freedoms, the court subjects that claim to very little analysis, instead summarily concluding that there has been an infringement.

64 See, e.g., *Harper v Canada (Attorney General)* [2004] 1 SCR 827 [20], in which one of the justices referred to political speech as 'one of the most valuable forms of speech' and noted that 'Canadians cherish the unimpeded diffusion of political ideas and opinions', which is 'essential to the working of a parliamentary democracy'.

65 It should be noted that freedom of speech is one of the rare circumstances in which the courts occasionally refer to the right having a protected core of activity. This protected core would include things like political speech, but would exclude things like hate speech or commercial speech. However, these considerations are discussed at the proportionality stage of the analysis rather than the infringement stage. For example, in *Zundel* (n 61), a case in which an individual challenged laws limiting certain kinds of false statements, three of the judges noted that this law limited expression which is only peripheral to the core values of the *Charter*. They also commented that falsehoods can actually hinder or detract from democratic debate.

66 Benjamin L Berger, 'The Abiding Presence of Conscience: Criminal Justice against the Law and the Modern Constitutional Imagination' (2011) 61 University of Toronto Law Journal 579, 584. He also states that '[f]inding an infringement of a Charter right has become, for a number of rights, an increasingly brief and cursory pit stop to the key analytic point', which is the PA. See also Christopher J Evans, 'Adjudicating Contested Values: Freedom of Religion and the Oakes Test' (2013) 10 Journal of Law and Equality 5, in which the aurhor argues that the most appropriate place for the adjudication of value disputes involving freedom of religion is the final stage of the *Oakes* test.

In most cases, the court does not focus on the degree of infringement prior to the PA, but merely states that the requirements have been met, whereas in some cases, the courts will note the degree of infringement. Whether this occurs or not is rather haphazard, with no clear pattern emerging from the cases. *R v Morelli* exemplifies a case in which the Court discussed the degree of infringement to point out the special degree of severity of the right limitation. This case related to the constitutionality of a search of an individual's computer. According to the majority, 'it is difficult to imagine a more intrusive invasion of privacy than the search of one's home and personal computer'. This is because computers contain 'our most intimate correspondence', such as financial and medical records and personal information.[67]

An exception to the relatively straightforward analysis of rights infringement that occurs in many cases is that relating to the equality guarantee, which can be complex and often a matter of dispute among the members of the Court. As Table 2.1 indicates, it is a rights claim that is likely to succeed before the Court only slightly over a third of the time. The equality analysis involves a contextual analysis that explores the impact of the law on the individual's dignity, whether the individual is part of a historically disadvantaged group, and whether the law reflects stereotypes about that group. Furthermore, when analysing whether a law is discriminatory, justices often disagree about the appropriate comparator group (to determine whether the government is drawing a discriminatory distinction between two groups) and whether a particular distinction is discriminatory. According to Truesdale, there has been considerable analytical blurring, as considerations better suited to the section 1 analysis are often addressed under the section 15 contextual analysis.[68] This may help to explain the low success rates for equality claims.

It is not necessary that the claimant personally suffered any rights violation, but rather the potential for a rights violation suffered by a hypothetical person is sufficient. In this regard, the Supreme Court has stated that 'laws may be struck out on the basis of hypothetical situations, provided they are reasonable'.[69] This, when combined with Canada's

[67] 2010 SCC 8 [2010] 1 SCR 253 [105].

[68] Claire Truesdale, 'Section 15 and the Oakes Test: The Slippery Slope of Contextual Analysis' (2012) 43 Ottawa Law Review 511.

[69] *R. v Sharpe* [2001] 1 SCR 45.

broad standing laws,[70] creates a fairly low bar for constitutional challenges to reach the courts. Because Canadian courts have interpreted standing laws broadly, and they are not necessarily concerned with whether the particular claimant has had his or her rights infringed but may also look to hypothetical rights violations, it is clear that they are not merely concerned with the effect of laws on the individual parties but rather their broader societal effect. In this regard, the courts do not just look at how a rights infringement may impact the party to the litigation but also how rights infringements may impact the public at large. For example, in *Canadian Broadcasting Corp v Canada (Attorney General)*,[71] a broadcasting company challenged limits on media in certain courthouse locations and the limited ability to televise court hearings. Although the Court discussed the fact that this law impeded individual rights by restricting expressive conduct, they were also concerned with the effect of this rights violation on the public at large, noting that the media enhances democratic discourse, self-fulfillment, and truth finding.

## V Worthy Purpose

In *Oakes*, a majority of the Supreme Court of Canada stated that the objective must be 'of sufficient importance to warrant overriding a constitutionally protected right or freedom'.[72] In addition, the Court stated that,

> The standard must be high in order to ensure that objectives which are trivial or discordant with the principles integral to a free and democratic society do not gain s. 1 protection. It is necessary, at a minimum, that an objective relate to concerns which are pressing and substantial in a free and democratic society before it can be characterized as sufficiently important.[73]

In essence, there are two questions at issue here. The first is to determine what the government's purpose is and the second is to determine whether that purpose is worthy. Although these are two distinct questions, the Court tends to blur them together. Although 7 per cent of the cases in the dataset failed at this stage of the analysis, it was seldom

[70] See discussion of *Canadian Council of Churches* (n 10).
[71] [2011] 1 SCR 19.
[72] *Oakes* (n 2) [69].
[73] ibid.

determinative, with the Court going on to consider the remainder of the PA in all of the cases.

### A Establishing What the Purpose Is

Although it is officially up to the government to prove, on a balance of probabilities, that it had a pressing and substantial objective, the low standard set by the court means that little evidence is introduced at this stage of the analysis. Indeed, in several cases the claimant conceded that the government's objective was pressing.[74] In many other cases, the Court merely assumed that the objective offered by the government is pressing, noting that they prefer to decide the case at other stages of the test. Although the 'pressing and substantial' language from Oakes is still widely used and has not been overruled, it has been relaxed in some subsequent cases, with the court referring to a 'valid' objective or a 'sufficiently important' objective.[75]

In most cases, the Court does not require evidence of a particular problem to consider there to be a pressing and substantial problem worthy of overriding a protected right, but rather will use common sense to determine if a particular issue is pressing. At times, the government will assert its purpose at the time of litigation. The Court may look to such sources as the preamble to the legislation, the legislative scheme itself, the parliamentary debates, and other relevant government documents.

For example, in *Harper v Canada (Attorney General)*, the Court was called upon to assess the constitutionality of limits on third-party election spending and advertising. In that case, a majority of the Court noted that the issue sought to be addressed was election fairness. They stated that '[t]he legislature is not required to provide scientific proof based on concrete evidence of the problem it seeks to address in every case … Given the difficulties in measuring this harm, a **reasoned apprehension** that the absence of third party election advertising limits will lead to electoral unfairness is sufficient'.[76]

[74] See, e.g., *B(R) v Children's Aid Society of Metropolitan Toronto* [1995] 1 SCR 315, in which the claimant accepted that the govenment had a pressing and substantial reason to enact a law allowing for the state to take temporary custody of a child in order to consent to medical treatment on that child's behalf.

[75] Andrew J Petter and Patrick J Monahan, 'Developments in Canadian Constitutional Law: The 1986–1987 Term' (1988) 10 Supreme Court Law Review 61.

[76] *Harper* (n 64) [77], [88].

The three dissenting judges in *Harper* went even further, and, in essence, said that the government need not show any proof that they have a worthy purpose at all, but rather must merely assert one: 'the proper question at this stage of the analysis is whether the Attorney General **has asserted** a pressing and substantial objective . . . A theoretical objective asserted as pressing and substantial is sufficient for purposes of the s 1 justification analysis'.[77]

In *R v Bryan*, another Supreme Court Justice cited this statement from *Harper v Canada* with approval, noting that'[t]he law is clear that the first stage of the s 1 analysis is not an evidentiary contest'.[78] Given that this stage of the test represents a low hurdle for government, the fact that government generally need only assert a pressing objective, and the wide variety of acceptable 'pressing and substantial objectives', the Court has made no distinction as to which objectives are sufficient to override certain rights. In other words, one can assume that an objective that is sufficiently pressing could, in theory, be used to override any other Charter right.

Although it is open to a Court to ultimately disagree with the government's stated purpose, this is somewhat rare, and the starting point of the analysis is generally the manner in which it was asserted by the government. If the Court disagrees with the government's purpose, they will restate it. Several of the other cases in which the government did not have a pressing and substantial objective relate to legislation that was designed before changes in social attitudes, for example, towards same-sex marriage. In some cases, the government had not extended social benefits or other legal protections to those groups at a time when that decision was in congruence with the thinking of the time. However, when called upon to justify those laws many years later, their legislative objectives are flimsy and the Court may find that they are not pressing. For example, in one case in which the government had not included sexual orientation as a ground of prohibited discrimination under a human rights law, the government did not really attempt to justify such underinclusion, but rather pointed to the laudable nature of the legislative scheme as a whole and seemed to hope that the Court would come up with a worthy purpose on its own.[79]

[77] ibid [24]–[26].
[78] *Bryan* (n 61) [32].
[79] *Vriend v Alberta* [1998] 1 SCR 493.

Most often, even when the Court is skeptical of the government's purpose, they will nonetheless accept the objective and move on to conduct the remainder of the analysis. In other words, the cases very seldom turn on the issue of whether the government's purpose was worthy, but rather other stages of the PA are determinative. For example, *Eldridge v British Columbia (Attorney General)* was a challenge to a decision not to fund sign-language interpreters for hospital patients receiving medically necessary insured services. The Court stated that 'assuming without deciding that ... the objective of controlling health care expenditures is pressing and substantial'.[80] The Court went on to conclude that the decision not to fund interpreters was not made in furtherance of controlling health care expenditures, as interpretation services would constitute a miniscule share of the annual provincial health care budget and because the government had never adequately considered whether those services should be funded.[81]

The case of *Sauve v Canada (Chief Electoral Officer)*[82] is another example of one of a few cases in which the Court disagreed as to whether the government had a pressing objective. This case was a challenge to a law that limited the rights of prisoners to vote. The objectives introduced by the government were that the law enhanced civic responsibility and respect for the rule of law and that it provided additional punishment beyond the criminal sanction. The majority found that the first objective would be true of most laws and determined that there was nothing to suggest why additional punishment was required, and thus this was not a pressing and substantial objective. However, they still chose to go on and consider the remainder of the proportionality test. In contrast, the dissent accepted these legislative objectives, despite acknowledging that they were abstract and symbolic. After expressing scepticism as to the government's purpose, the majority of the Court went on to find that there was no rational connection between the law and the objectives, given that denying the right to vote is likely to undermine respect for law and democracy rather than enhance it and given that the law did not serve

[80] *Eldridge* (n 8) [84]. See also *Sharpe* (n 70), in which a defendant charged with possession of child pornography conceded that the possession of some pornographic materials should be prohibited, but argued that the law went too far (in other words, he accepted that the government had a pressing objective to limit certain types of pornographic material). See also *R. v Ruzic* [2001] 1 SCR 687.

[81] For discussion of whether cost containment can ever be a worthy reason for overriding a Charter right see Section V.D.

[82] [2002] 3 SCR 519.

a legitimate punitive function. The majority also felt that the law did not minimally impair the right to vote as it was overbroad (i.e. it caught too many people who, on the government's own arguments, should not be denied this right) and the negative effects of denying the right outweighed the 'tenuous' benefits that might ensue.[83]

The government's objective can often be phrased with varying levels of generality, which may affect the rest of the PA. The appropriate level of generality is the subject of some academic debate and has, on occasion, divided the members of the Court. Typically, the more broadly phrased an objective is, the more likely it is to be deemed pressing and substantial. By adopting a very broad conception of the harm to be remedied by the law, the government is also likely to pass the rational connection stage of the test. Citing *R v Butler*, a case relating to criminal prohibitions on obscene material, Cameron notes that 'by adopting a generalized conception of harm, [Justice Sopinka] made it virtually impossible for the statutory definition of obscenity to fail the rational connection test'.[84] Indeed, the Court went on to find that the criminalization of certain kinds of material was rationally connected to harm such as 'potentially victimize[ing] women' and negatively affecting 'attitude and behaviour'. However, an objective stated with a high level of generality may be more likely to fail the minimal impairment test. In this regard, when an objective is stated with specificity, it may be difficult for a court to think of another way, let alone a less impairing way, that the goal could be achieved.[85]

Although the justices tend to agree that the government had a pressing and substantial objective, they sometimes disagree on the specificity of the objective. For example, in *Reference re ss 193 and 195.1(1)(c) of the Criminal Code*,[86] the Court considered laws criminalizing certain aspects of prostitution. The justices disagreed as to whether the purpose of the laws was more narrow – taking prostitution out of public view, thereby eradicating nuisances like street congestion, noise, an harassment – or whether the purpose was broader and related to harms less directly linked to prostitution, such as violence, drugs, and other crimes, and the elimination of victimization and economic disadvantage.[87]

[83] ibid.
[84] Cameron (n 38) 1150.
[85] Hogg (n 27) 38-19.
[86] [1990] 1 SCR 1123.
[87] See also *R. v Seaboyer* [1991] 2 SCR 577, in which the justices considered the purpose of a law restricting the right of defence to cross-examine or lead evidence of a rape victim's sexual history. Some of the justices categorized the purpose as preventing sexist-based use

Another issue that has arisen in some cases is the extent to which a purpose can shift over time. In other words, even if a law was enacted for one purpose, can it be justified on its applicability to more modern social concerns? Because of the typically low burden at this stage of the analysis, the issue of shifting purposes has received relatively little discussion. However, in *R v Zundel*,[88] the majority of the Court criticized the government's failure to identify a current social problem that was addressed by laws prohibiting false statements that were likely to cause mischief or to injure the public interest (given that there were other laws already protecting against concerns arising from hate speech). The impugned law was initially justified on the basis of preventing 'slanderous statements against nobles', and the government suggested that it would now cover problems such as hate speech. However, a majority of the Supreme Court found that the new objective was too far from the initial objective that had motivated the legislation. Because the initial legislative objective was no longer pressing and substantial in modern society, the government failed this stage of the proportionality test.

### B *What Are Worthy Purposes?*

Because most cases easily pass this stage of the analysis, it is difficult to develop any sort of hierarchy of pressing objectives, and the court generally does not speak of varying degrees of worthy objectives (in terms of how they might affect the rest of the analysis). Similarly, because the Court is, in essence, finding that an objective is sufficiently important to override a Charter right, the tendency is generally to speak about most objectives as though they are reasonably pressing (rather than speaking about some as though they are more important than others).

Despite wording linking the objectives to those that are pressing 'in a free and democratic society', there is generally little reference to what kinds of objectives would satisfy that criteria. In other words, the Court does not require the government make any specific connection between the objective and democracy or democratic values. The focus has become whether the objective is sufficiently 'pressing and substantial', with the court seeming to accept that any concern that falls into that category also satisfies the second part of the test (that it is pressing and substantial in a

of sexual conduct evidence, while a minority of the Court focused on the broader social purposes of minimizing discrimination and encouraging women to report sexual assaults.

88 *Zundel* (n 61).

free and democratic society). In addition, the objectives do not have to be grounded in constitutional rights or other constitutional provisions.

There is no exhaustive list of acceptable objectives in Canadian Charter jurisprudence, but rather the court has accepted dozens of different objectives as sufficiently pressing and substantial. Some examples of the wide variety of objectives upheld by the Supreme Court include preserving freedom of choice (in terms of choosing to be legally married versus remaining common law spouses and the family law benefits that flow from that choice),[89] reducing the harmful effects and social costs of discrimination (by passing laws to prohibit hate speech),[90] protecting individual information (by passing laws governing personal information protection),[91] preventing serious harm to persons or property (in the context of laws permitting warrantless wiretap searches in limited, exceptional circumstances),[92] promoting public health and safety (in the context of laws prohibiting possession of drugs),[93] and maintaining order in court and protecting the privacy of litigations (with regard to limits on media in certain courthouse locations and courtroom broadcasting).[94] Notably, this list includes purposes that relate to individual rights (i.e. freedom of choice and protecting individual privacy), as well as those protecting public interests (i.e. promoting public health and maintaining safety).

Two categories of objectives that the court sometimes speaks more strongly about (in terms of their importance) are the protection of public health and safety (which often arises in the criminal law context) and the protection of speech (which the Court often links to broader objectives, such as fostering democracy). Interestingly, one of these constitutes a fairly clear harm (i.e. a threat to safety), while the other one is more symbolic or intangible (i.e. a threat to democracy). The Court does not distinguish between these two kinds of objectives.

### C *What Are Unworthy Purposes?*

In theory, an objective can be problematic on its face, but this is extremely rare. There are cases, however, in which the Court has found

89 *Quebec (Attorney General) v A* [2013] 1 SCR 61.
90 *Saskatchewan* (n 61).
91 *Alberta (Information and Privacy Commissioner) v United Food and Commercial Workers, Local 401* [2013] 3 SCR 733.
92 *Tse* (n 41).
93 *Canada (Attorney General) v PHS Community Services Society* [2011] 3 SCR 134.
94 *Canadian Broadcasting Corp* (n 71).

that the government's purpose is actually antithetical to Charter rights. For example, in *R v Big M Drug Mart*, the Supreme Court held that the purpose of legislation requiring a business to remain closed on a Sunday was to compel the observance of the Christian Sabbath.[95] The Court found that this was not a pressing and substantial objective, as it was directly contradictory to the Charter right being claimed (freedom of religion). Similarly, in *Vriend v Alberta*, a claimant challenged the failure of a provincial human rights statute to include sexual orientation as a prohibited ground of discrimination. The Court found that there was no pressing objective to justify this law.[96]

### D *Administrative Efficiency and Cost Savings As Worthy Purpose?*

Governments may face difficulty in justifying a law motivated by considerations of cost containment or administrative efficiency. Weinrib argues that it is difficult to justify limiting rights for financial reasons because 'it is inherent in the nature of constitutional rights that they must receive a higher priority in the distribution of available government funds than policies or programmes that do not enjoy that status'.[97] Similarly, Hogg argues that utilitarianism is incompatible with Charter rights because the cost of rectifying a breach can be calculated, whereas the benefit derived from enjoying a Charter right cannot.[98]

In *R v Schwartz*, the Court reviewed a provision reversing the onus of proof, requiring the accused to show proof of registration of a restricted weapon. A minority of the Court found that the law could have called upon the Crown to prove that the firearm had not been registered, and thus the reverse onus was merely for administrative convenience, which was not a purpose worthy of overriding a constitutional right.[99] However,

95 *Big M Drug Mart Ltd* (n 4).
96 *Vriend* (n 79).
97 Lorraine Weinrib, 'The Supreme Court of Canada and Section 1 of the Charter' (1986) 10 Supreme Court Law Review 469, 478.
98 Hogg (n 27) 38–30.
99 [1988] 2 SCR 443. Chief Justice Dickson also felt that there was a lack of rational connection, given that the proved fact (possession of a restricted weapon) did not prove the presumed fact (lack of registration). Furthermore, a scheme that called upon the Crown to demonstrate a lack of registration would be less impairing. See also *R. v Lee* [1989] 2 SCR 1384, which challenged a law deeming an accused to waive a right to a jury trial after he or she did not appear. The majority found the worthy purpose was to protect the administration of justice and to secure public respect for the trial process. However, a two-judge minority argued that the government had showed no evidence that

the majority in that case found the law to be aimed at restricting possession of weapons and, more broadly, to discourage firearm use, which they found justifiable. Furthermore, they found that the accused was in a better position to demonstrate possession of a valid registration certificate than the state. They also questioned whether this even constituted a true reverse onus, given that an accused was not being called upon to establish his innocence (as there were other elements of the offence that the Crown had to prove).[100]

In *Singh v Minister of Employment and Immigration*, Justce Wilson, writing on behalf of the minority,[101] responded to the government's argument that oral hearings for all people seeking refugee status would be an unreasonable burden by expressing 'considerable doubt' that this 'utilitarian consideration . . . can constitute a justification for a limitation on the rights set out in the Charter'. She went on to say that '[n]o doubt considerable time and money can be saved by adopting administrative procedures which ignore the principles of fundamental justice but such an argument, in my view, misses the point of the exercise under s. 1'.[102]

However, in some cases, it has been difficult for the court not to take into account the costs of recognizing a Charter right, for example, when the government is experiencing a 'fiscal crisis', as occurred in *Newfoundland (Treasury Board) v NAPE.*[103] In that case, the government had signed a Pay Equity Agreement such that female employees in the health sector would receive comparable wages with their male counterparts. However, due to a 'financial crisis unprecedented in the Province's history' the government had to pass legislation to delay the commencement of this increase and to cancel payment arrears (which would have cost the province approximately $24 million). The Court was persuaded, in part, by the fact that the government had also enacted many other cost saving measures to reduce the province's deficit, including freezing the

non-appearing individuals were a major problem and said this amounted to administrative inconvenience (as it would involve setting another date and summoning additional jurors).

[100] The majority also found that the provisions were rationally connected to the objective (given that the accused was in a better position to demonstrate proof of registration), impaired the right as little as possible (given the existence of an exemption), and the law adequately balanced the community interests and the interests of those wanting to legally possess firearms.

[101] The remaining two justices resolved the case without relying on the Charter.

[102] [1985] 1 SCR 177 [70].

[103] *Newfoundland (Treasury Board) v NAPE* [2004] 3 SCR 381.

wages of all public sector employees, de-listing services from the public health insurance plan, closing hospital beds, freezing student grants and equalization grant payments to school boards, and laying off almost 2,000 employees.

Another context in which it has been difficult for the Court to disregard budgetary concerns as 'pressing' occurs when individuals allege that a particular social benefit or programme is underinclusive (generally on the basis of discrimination). In those cases, although the Court could resolve inequality by cancelling the programme rather than allow underinclusiveness to persist, their preference is to expand the inclusion criteria.[104] However, they have recognized that opening eligibility to a programme or benefit to hundreds or even thousands of people can have significant fiscal implications.

Lessard offers two principled justifications for judicial reluctance to find in favour of plaintiffs where the result would be significant government expenditures. First, is the 'institutional limitations concern, namely, that courts lack the institutional competence to make complex budgetary decisions'. Second, is the 'legitimacy or separation of powers concern, namely, that decisions with a significant budgetary impact lie outside the appropriate constitutional role of the judicial branch'.[105] He notes that, in general, the successful Charter cases are the ones in which rights recognition is costless, is of comparatively low cost, or is characterized by the Court as an inexpensive or even money saving outcome.

It is important to note that even if a Court finds that financial concerns are not a sufficiently pressing objective to override a right, they can certainly form a legitimate part of the minimal impairment analysis.[106] I will address the relationship between cost and deference in the minimal impairment analysis later.[107]

[104] See, e.g., *Tétreault- Gadoury v Canada (Employment and Immigration Commission) [1991] 2 SCR 22*, *Schachter v Canada* [1992] 2 SCR 679, *Eldridge v British Columbia* (n 8).

[105] Hester A Lessard, 'Dollars versus [Equality] Rights: Money and the Limits on Distributive Justice' (2012) 58 Supreme Court Law Review 299, 302. See also Hugh Mellon, 'Charter Rights and Public Policy Choices: The Supreme Court and Public Finance' (2006) 15 Constitutional Forum 135.

[106] As Chief Justice Lamer stated in *Reference re Remuneration of Judges of the Provincial Court of Prince Edward Island* [1997] 3 S.C.R 3, '[w]hile purely financial considerations are not sufficient to justify the infringement of *Charter* rights, they are relevant to determining the standard of deference for the test of minimal impairment when reviewing legislation which is enacted for a purpose which is not financial'.

[107] See Section VII.C.

## VI Suitability or Rational Connection

In a surprisingly high number of cases – 32 per cent of all proportionality cases ending in failure – the government fails to prove that the impugned law is rationally connected to its pressing and substantial objective. In contrast to this relatively high failure rate, however, in only 18 per cent of those cases was the Court content to resolve the PA at this stage of the analysis. In the overwhelming majority of the cases, the court continued its analysis beyond the failure at the rational connection test at least to one additional failure at the minimal impairment stage of the analysis.

### *A The Standard for Establishing Suitability*

The question asked by the court at this stage is whether there is a link between the law and its purpose, with little evaluation of questions regarding the law's efficancy, fairness, or overbreadth. In *Oakes*, the Court stated that 'the measures must be fair and not arbitrary, carefully designed to achieve the objective in question and rationally connected to that objective'.[108] As with the test of whether the objective is worthy, the government must prove a rational connection between that objective and the means of achieving it on a balance of probabilities.[109]

The standard set by the court for this stage is not particularly demanding: the Court has not articulated a need for there to be a clear link between the harm and the law, but rather it will be sufficient for Parliament to have a 'reasoned apprehension of harm' that is linked to the impugned law or policy.[110] As a majority of the Court stated in *Alberta v Hutterian Brethren of Wilson Colony*, the government must show 'that it is reasonable to suppose that the limit may further the goal, not that it will do so'.[111] In that case, a religious group sought an

[108] *Oakes* (n 2) [70].

[109] Murray emphasizes this link, stating that 'it is noteworthy that we are concerned with the rationality of this connection and not with whether the law is rational . . . there may be a number of reasons for passing a particular law, all of which may be good reasons that therefore make the law rational. However, our concern is with that aspect of the law which impairs a right and with the reason or objective related to it'. Murray (n 35).

[110] The majority of the Supreme Court of Canada made this comment in the context of discussing the link between obscenity and harm to society. The Court found that Parliament was entitled to have a 'reasoned apprehension of harm' resulting from the desensitization of individuals exposed to materials depicting violence, cruelty, and dehumanization in sexual relations.

[111] [2009] 2 SCR 567 [48].

exemption from the requirement that drivers' licenses be accompanied by a photograph, which the government refused.

The Court has at times been willing to assume the presence of a rational connection despite doubts that arise. For example, *Quebec (Attorney General) v A* related to a law that did not extend family law benefits to common law spouses.[112] The government justified this law on the basis that individuals should have the autonomy to choose how their financial relationships would be structured. Several of the justices noted that the connection between the law and this objective was 'tenuous', but were willing to assume that the connection existed and to proceed with the minimal impairment analysis. One member of the Court noted that despite a tenuous connection, it could not be said that 'excluding common law spouses is wholly unconnected to choice'.

In the cases in which this stage is successfully passed, there is often very little engagement with this stage, with the Court being willing to assume the presence of a rational connection with no further analysis.[113] The Court generally does not engage in a significant scrutiny of whether the law meets the goal at this stage, but rather merely expects that there be a logical connection. There tends to be relatively little evidence introduced at this stage. When faced with conflicting expert evidence as to the effectiveness of a policy, the Court generally prefers to examine that evidence at the following stage of minimal impairment. In several cases the court has been satisfied with a 'common sense' link between the harm and the law, preferring to actually scrutinize the evidence at the minimal impairment stage of the test.[114] As Justice Iacobucci wrote in

[112] *Quebec (Attorney General) v A* (n 89).

[113] See eg *Tse* (n 41). See also *Canadian Broadcasting Corp* (n 71), in which the Court was willing to assume that limits on filming in certain part of the courthouse 'would have a positive effect on the maintenance of and administration of justice'. See also Carissima Mathen, 'Rational Connections: Oakes, Section 1 and the Charter's Legal Rights' (2013) 43 Ottawa Law Review 49, who notes that post-*Oakes*, the rational connection criteria proved to be 'a fairly low one for the state to meet'. She argues for a return to a 'stronger version of rational connection', but notes that how this is to be accomplished is beyond the scope of the paper. However, she sees two advantages to a more rigorous approach to this aspect of the PA. First, it would catch the rare case where there is a 'misfit between the law and objective'. Second, it provides a counterbalance to an 'ever expansive resort to criminal law at a time where evidence-based reasoning appears to have fallen out of favour in criminal justice policy'. In other words, it would enhance the accountability of the current conservative government, which has been expanding the scope of criminal law.

[114] See David Schneiderman, 'Common Sense and the Charter' (2009) 45 Supreme Court Law Review 3.

*RJR-MacDonald Inc v Canada (Attorney General)*, '[r]ational connection is to be established, upon a civil standard, through reason, logic or simply common sense'.[115]

### B Effectiveness of Purpose Achievement

One of the reasons that this stage of the test presents such a low threshold is because the Court does not generally engage in a significant scrutiny of whether the law actually meets its goal at this stage, but rather often expect only that a logical connection be established. In other words, there tends to be relatively little evidence introduced at this stage as compared to the minimal impairment stage of the test. Where issues such as conflicting expert evidence as to effectiveness are before the Court, they tend to prefer to examine that evidence at the minimal impairment stage. In several cases, the court has been satisfied with a 'common sense' link between the harm and the law, preferring to actually scrutinize the evidence at the minimal impairment stage of the test.[116]

For example, in *RJR-Macdonald Inc v Canada*, the Supreme Court of Canada was asked to determine whether the government was justified in enacting a comprehensive ban on tobacco advertising. In that case, Justice McLachlin found that 'reason or logic' indicated that there was a rational connection between banning tobacco advertisement and suppressing tobacco consumption.[117] Three other justices similarly found a rational connection based on 'a common sense observation', noting that 'it is difficult to believe that Canadian tobacco companies would spend over 75 million dollars every year on advertising if they did not know that advertising increases the consumption of their product'.[118] Instead, the various members of the Court subjected the government's evidence to much more rigorous scrutiny at the minimal impairment stage of the PA. In the minimal impairment stage, a majority of the Court found that the government failed to provide convincing scientific evidence that such an extensive advertising ban was necessary.

Similarly, in *Lavoie v Canada*, the majority noted that 'Parliament's view is supported by common sense and widespread international

[115] [1995] 3 SCR 199 [364]. See also *Bryan* (n 61).
[116] See Schneiderman (n 114).
[117] *RJR-Macdonald Inc* (n 115) [153].
[118] ibid [84].

practice, both of which are relevant indicators of a rational connection'.[119] In that case, the Supreme Court upheld rules preferring Canadian citizens for employment in the federal public service as a reasonable limit on equality rights. Because the Court is merely looking for a link between the law and the objective, there is generally no need to assess the effectiveness of the law at this stage of the analysis. In other words, the court is not looking at how suitable a particular law is for achieving a goal, but rather merely that it be capable that the law furthers the goal that they accepted as pressing and substantial in the previous stage of the test.

In most cases, the Court does not require any sort of scientific or empirical proof of a connection, but rather is willing to base its conclusion on 'logic', 'rationality', or 'common sense' or to take 'judicial notice'[120] of the necessary facts. Panaccio refers to this as 'minimal instrumental rationality', in which rational connection merely 'requires that the rule be causally able to achieve the accepted objective'. Panaccio contrasts this with a more demanding test that he contemplates might involve 'more extensive moral balancing' in which a court would ask whether 'the balance of reasons favours other alternatives'.[121] As noted previously, the Canadian Court has preferred to leave this evaluation of policy alternatives until the next stage of the PA.

Although the general approach is to ask whether there is a mere connection between the law and the objective and not to conduct in any searching review of the evidence, there are cases that display a different, more scrutinizing approach. For example, in *Chaoulli v Quebec (Attorney General)* the Court was asked to determine whether prohibiting private health insurance was rationally connected to the protection of the public health care system and its allocation of health resources on the basis of need rather than ability to pay.[122] Surprisingly, in the face of

[119] [2002] 1 SCR 769 [59].

[120] For example, in *R. v Edwards Books and Art Ltd* [1986] 2 SCR 713 [195]–[196], one of the justices stated that 'The admonition in *Oakes* and other cases to present evidence in *Charter* cases does not remove from the courts the power, where it deems it expedient, to take judicial notice of broad social and economic facts and to take the necessary steps to inform itself about them.' He went on to state that 'it is a constitution that we are interpreting. It is undesirable that an Act be found constitutional today and unconstitutional tomorrow simply on the basis of the particular evidence of broad social and economic facts that happens to have been presented by counsel.'

[121] Charles-Maxime Panaccio, 'In Defence of the Two-Step Balancing and Proportionality in Rights Adjudication' (2011) 1 Canadian Journal of Law and Jurisprudence 109.

[122] *Chaoulli v Quebec (Attorney General)* [2005] 1 SCR. 791.

conflicting evidence, a minority of the Court found that the government had failed to meet the rational connection test. Cases like this are considered anomalies, however, and are subject to a great deal of criticism.[123] It seems to be more common for the court to find a lack of rational connection between the means and the goal in the context of cases invoking section 7 of the Charter – the right to life, liberty, and security of the person, where the internal balancing test asks whether the law is in accordance with the principles of fundamental justice.[124] One of the most common principles at issue is whether the law is arbitrary. As noted previously, if the Court concludes that a law is arbitrary, it would be illogical for them to then go on to conclude that the law is rationally connected to the government's objective.

Similarly, in *RJR-MacDonald v Canada (Attorney General)*,[125] the Court was asked to consider various regulations on tobacco advertising, promotion, sponsorship, marketing, and packaging, including a near-total ban on advertising. As noted previously, a majority of the justices were willing to assume that tobacco consumption was linked to advertising (citing, for example, the common sense principle that companies would not spend millions of dollars to advertise if it was not increasing demand for the product). However, one of the justices questioned whether the government had actually adduced sufficient evidence to establish a link between decreasing consumption and advertising.

In general though, the cases in which there was no rational connection did not involve the sort of conflicting evidence at issue in *Chaoulli*, but rather the Court was critical of the government's failure to adequately introduce any proof or argument in support of the connection between the law and the objective. For example, in *Greater Vancouver Transportation Authority v Canadian Federation of Students British Columbia Component*, the government prohibited political advertising on buses in furtherance of the objective of a safe and welcoming transit system.[126] The Court found that it was difficult to see how an advertisement on the side of a bus that constitutes political speech might create a safety risk or unwelcoming environment. As noted earlier, a significant number of the

[123] Colleen M Flood, Lorne Sossin, and Kent Roach (eds), *Access to Care, Access to Justice: The Legal Debate over Private Health Insurance in Canada* (University of Toronto Press 2005).

[124] See Section III.B.

[125] *RJR-Macdonald Inc* (n 115). See also *R. v Andrews* [1990] 3 SCR 870 and *Irwin Toy Ltd* (n 37).

[126] [2009] 2 SCR 295.

cases that fail at this stage are also from the section 7 context where the laws have already been declared arbitrary, which will also result in failing the rational connection test.[127]

## VII Necessity or Minimal Impairment

Almost all proportionality cases in Canada turn on the issue of minimal impairment. Even when the Court could have resolved a case after failure at an earlier stage of the *Oakes* test (i.e. finding that the law did not have a pressing objective or that the law was not rationally connected to that objective), in 83 per cent of the cases the Court did not do this, instead preferring to continue the analysis and resolve those cases based on the minimal impairment issue. In contrast, in less than half of the cases in which the Court finds that the law was not minimally impairing do they go on to consider proportionality. Judges require the most evidence from government at this stage of the analysis and subject the law or policy to the closest scrutiny at this stage. The bulk of a judge's PA will almost always consist of his or her discussion of minimal impairment. There are frequently deep disagreements among the justices relating to minimal impairment. For example, judges often differ on how to interpret conflicting evidence or on what level of deference to give to the government.

Several explanations can be offered for why this stage of the PA has eclipsed all others in terms of its importance in Canadian law. One reason that it is likely viewed as more important than rational connection is because implicit in a discussion of whether an existing law is the least restrictive way to achieve a particular goal is a consideration of whether that law is connected to that goal. Commentators suggest that minimal impairment is likely more important than proportionality, as the latter is duplicative. In this regard, Hogg argues that '[i]f the objective of a law is sufficiently important ... and if the law is rationally connected to the objective ... and if the law impairs the Charter right no more than is necessary to accomplish the objective ... how could its effects then be judged to be too severe?'[128] Similarly, Hickman notes that 'it is artificial in practice to divorce the question of overall proportionality from the potential availability of less-intrusive means'.[129] Critics of judicial

[127] See Section III.B.
[128] Hogg (n 27) 38–44.
[129] Tim Hickman, 'Proportionality: Comparative Law Lessons' (2007) 12 Judicial Review 31.

policy-making[130] have argued that the reason the Canadian court places so much emphasis on minimal impairment is because it allows them to weigh competing policy options and select which they feel is most appropriate. In contrast, other stages of the test merely call upon the court to assess the government's existing law.

In *Oakes*, the Supreme Court of Canada stated this part of the test very stringently, noting that 'the means should impair the right in question **as little as possible**'.[131] As with all of the other stages of the proportionality test, the burden is on the government to show minimal impairment on a balance of probabilities. As discussed earlier, tension often arises in the context of social policy, where there may be conflicting evidence or where evidence may be non-existent. Chief Justice McLachlin has spoken to the application of the burden of proof in this context: 'proof to the standard required by science is not required',[132] although the Court must demand 'the civil standard of proof on a balance of probabilities at all stages of the proportionality analysis'. However, she went on to explain that the 'discharge of the civil standard does not require scientific demonstration; the balance of probabilities may be established by the application of common sense to what is known, even though what is known may be deficient from a scientific point of view'.[133]

The Court almost immediately retreated from the initial phrasing of this test in *Oakes*, stating that the law should impair the rights 'as little as **reasonably** possible'.[134] This reflected a fear that the court would 'substitute judicial opinions for legislative ones'.[135] Similarly, the Court has stated that 'the state must have a margin of appreciation in selecting the means to achieve the objective'.[136] In other cases, the Court has stated the

[130] See, e.g., Petter (n 28). See also Manfredi (n 28) 336.

[131] *Oakes* (n 2) [70].

[132] As Murray notes,

> It is important to recognize the difficulties inherent in the nature of the factual evidence necessary to establish the section 1 criteria. The type of evidence typically utilized to establish factual matters in this context is of a social science nature. There are a number of difficulties associated with the use of such evidence, including availability, comprehensiveness, reliability, weight and cost. In addition, such evidence is usually tentative and seldom addresses directly the fact in dispute.

Murray (n 35) 656.

[133] *RJR-Macdonald* (n 115) [133].

[134] *Edwards Books and Art Ltd* (n 120) [196].

[135] ibid [147].

[136] *Quebec (Attorney General) v A* (n 89) [439].

minimal impairment standard with an even higher degree of deference. For example, in *Canadian Broadcasting Corp v Canada*, the Court considered a policy limiting media to certain courthouse locations and prohibiting hearings from being broadcast. The Court found that this policy fell within a range of 'reasonable alternatives'.[137] As discussed in greater detail later, certain kinds of cases will attract a more deferential approach than others.

### A *Factors Influencing the Resolution of the Test*

The Court is very reluctant to find that a total ban is minimally impairing, even though it will often be more effective than a partial ban. The fact that a total ban may capture conduct beyond what is justified is often sufficient to find a law unconstitutional. For example, in *RJR-Macdonald v Canada (Attorney General)*, a majority of the Court struck down a near-total ban on tobacco advertising as it was not minimally impairing.[138] However, when the government returned with new legislation that carved out very minimal exceptions to the ban in *Canada (Attorney General) v JTI-Macdonald Corp*, the Court upheld that law.[139]

Similarly, in *Ramsden v Peterborough*, the Court was critical of a total ban on putting up posters on public property. The Court accepted that this ban was linked to such objectives as the avoidance of littering, aesthetic blight, traffic, and hazards to persons engaged in repair of utility poles. However, they stated that there were many alternatives short of a total ban.[140] Similarly, in another case, an individual challenged a school

[137] *Canadian Broadcasting Corp* (n 71).

[138] *RJR-Macdonald* (n 115).

[139] [2007] 2 SCR 610. These two cases demonstrate one of the dominant theories of Canadian constitutional law – dialogue theory. Proponents of this theory argue that Charter interpretation is a dialogue between courts and the government. Specifically, governments pass legislation, courts respond (sometimes with advice on how to make laws constitutionally permissible), and governments respond with amended laws or, in extremely rare cases, invoke the notwithstanding clause. In some cases, the amended legislation may be subject to challenge, giving courts another opportunity to respond. In other words, Charter decisions should not be conceptualized 'as imposing a veto on desired legislative policies, but rather as starting a "dialogue" with the legislative branch as to how best to reconcile the individualistic values of the Charter with the accomplishment of social and economic policies for the benefit of the community as a whole.' Hogg (n 27) 36–14.1.

[140] [1993] 2 SCR 1084.

board's ban on students carrying kirpans to school.[141] A kirpan is a ceremonial dagger carried by Sikhs, which must be worn at all times. The Court accepted that banning kirpans was rationally connected to the pressing and substantial goal of school safety. However, the Court found that various alternatives short of a total ban would be sufficient. Specifically, they stated that the risk of violence would be very low if it was worn under certain conditions.

### *B Is There a Less Restricting Alternative?*

Practically speaking, it is often difficult for a party to prove something in the negative (i.e. to prove that there is not a law or policy that could have been less impairing), so while the government will often introduce proof that it considered other laws before arriving at the impugned one, the rights claimant will also frequently point to other policies (or variations on the chosen policy) that may have been less impairing. In addition, the Court itself may raise hypothetical less impairing alternatives to the law that was adopted. However, the Court itself has stated that a judge must be cautious not to 'second-guess Parliament and try to identify the least intrusive solution'.[142] In some cases, the Court will look to other jurisdictions, either in Canada or abroad, for less impairing alternatives to the one adopted.

The suggestions offered by the Court at the minimal impairment stage are sometimes seen as suggestions as to how the government might respond to the Court's decision and craft a constitutionally permissible law. The number of alternatives considered depends upon the case, although it is rare that more than one or two would be discussed to emphasize the Court's point. For example, in criticizing the government's adoption of a total ban on something, the court might point out a handful of ways in which exceptions may have been carved out from that total ban. In some cases, however, there may only be one less impairing alternative (for example, in a situation where a statute places part of the burden of proof on the accused, the only less impairing law may be to place that burden on the Crown).

One factor that seems to militate in favour of greater deference is when the government can show that it considered various approaches before settling on the current policy. For example, in *R v Bryan*, the Court

141 *Multani v Commission Scolaire Marguerite-Bourgeoys* [2007] 1 SCR 256.
142 *R. v St-Onge Lamoureux* [2012] 3 SCR 187 [39].

considered a law prohibiting the transmission of election results if polling stations in other districts were still open.[143] In this case, one of the justices (with whom several others concurred to form the majority) noted that the government had debated several approaches before arriving at this one. In contrast, in *Black v Law Society of Alberta*, the Court was critical of the Law Society (to which the Charter applied in this situation) for failing to consider anything less than a blanket prohibition on its members forming a partnership with other non-resident lawyers.[144]

The Court will consider a wide range of evidence during the minimal impairment inquiry, including evidence from other jurisdictions, medical evidence, social science evidence, etc. One factor that may work against a government is if they have legislation that is more restrictive than other Canadian provinces.[145] For example, in *Adler v Ontario*, several of the justices were critical of the limits on funding for private religious schools, noting that many other provinces provided partial funding.[146] Similarly, in *Professional Institute of the Public Service of Canada v Northwest Territories (Commissioner)*, three justices noted that other provinces struck a better balance of power between the government and unions.[147] In this case, an employee organization was challenging the government's refusal to enact the legislation required for the organization to bargain on behalf of its members.

### C Comparative Effectiveness of Alternatives

One area that lacks some clarity is whether a judge could find that there are less impairing alternatives that a government ought to have adopted, in situations where those less impairing alternatives are less effective (or efficient) than the impugned law, or more expensive than the impugned

[143] *Bryan* (n 61).

[144] [1989] 1 SCR 591.

[145] However, the Supreme Court has discussed uniformity between provinces in the context of federalism concerns, noting that the

> ... minimum impairment test is informed by the values of federalism. The uniformity of provincial laws that would be entailed by a stringent requirement of least drastic means is in conflict with the federal values of distinctiveness, diversity and experimentation ... The test must not be applied in a manner that amounts to identifying the Canadian province that has adopted the 'preferable' approach to a social issue and requiring that all other provinces follow suit.

*Quebec (Attorney General) v A* (n 89) [440].

[146] [1996] 3 SCR 609.

[147] [1990] 2 SCR 367.

law. With respect to the latter, the Court generally seems to have little concern with finding that the government could have adopted a more expensive and less impairing alternative. For example, as noted earlier, the Court is frequently critical of the government's adoption of a total ban, when exceptions could have been carved out of that ban. It is arguably generally the case that a ban subject to exceptions is going to be more administratively complex and expensive to oversee than a total ban.

Less clarity arises as to whether a government should adopt a less impairing measure, where that measure would be less effective. The Court has made conflicting statements on this point. For example, in *R v Downey*, which related to the criminalization of offences related to prostitution, the Court stated that 'Parliament is not required to choose the absolutely least intrusive alternative in order to satisfy this branch of the analysis. Rather the issue is whether Parliament could reasonably have chosen an alternative means which would have achieved the identified objective **as effectively**.'[148] In this regard, Panaccio argues that 'if a less impairing solution were to jeopardize the realization of the objective to whatever extent, the government would, in principle, satisfy this part of the proportionality test'.[149]

In *Alberta v Hutterian Brethren of Wilson Colony*, Chief Justice McLachlin, writing on behalf of herself and three other justices, clarified that the less restrictive alternative must also be able to achieve the government's objective: 'less drastic means which do not actually achieve the government's objective are not considered at this stage … the minimum impairment test requires only that the government choose the least drastic means of achieving its objective'. However, she went on to add that 'the court need not be satisfied that the alternative would satisfy the objective to exactly the same extent or degree as the impugned measure.' The question to be asked is 'whether there is an alternative, less drastic means of achieving the objective in a real and substantial manner.'[150] This case involved a refusal by a religious group – the

[148] [1992] 2 SCR 10 [39].

[149] Panaccio (n 121).

[150] *Hutterian Brethren of Wilson County* (n 111) [54]. Weinrib compares this case to Israel's version of the PA. She argues that Chief Justice McLachlin explicitly affirmed the Israeli version of proportionality with its 'diminished role' for the minimal impairment test and its corresponding relatively expansive role for the final stage of the test. However, Weinrib argues that Chief Justice McLachlin did not embrace 'the particular concerns [President Barak] called for the third step to address'. Sara Weinrib, 'The Emergence of

Hutterites – to be photographed for a drivers' license, as required by provincial law. They had the genuinely held religious belief that it was contrary to the Second Commandment to have one's photo taken. Although they had historically been exempted from this requirement on the basis of this religious exemption, a new law required all drivers' licenses to include a photo.

The majority of the Court found that the government had justified its limits on religious freedom. They found that the government's objective of maintaining the integrity of the driver's licensing system in a way that minimized the risk of identity theft was connected to the requirement of photo driver's licenses. They also found that the law was minimally impairing, as there were no alternative measures that would substantially satisfy the objective. At the final stage of the analysis, the majority found that there were a variety of benefits of photo driver's licenses, including limiting identity fraud, assisting in roadside identification by police, and harmonization of licensing with other jurisdictions. In contrast, the rights infringement was limited, given that the colony could avail themselves of alternatives such as hiring a driver.

In this same case, Justice Abella, one of three dissenting justices, noted that 'it is not difficult for the state to argue that only the measure it has chosen will maximize the attainment of the objective and that all other alternatives are substandard or less effective ... But at the minimal impairment stage, we do not assess whether the infringing measure fulfills the government's objective more perfectly than any other, but whether the means chosen impair the right no more than necessary to achieve the objective'.[151] While the Chief Justice believed that the law was

the Third Step of the Oakes Test in Alberta v. Hutterian Brethren of Wilson County' (2010) 68 University of Toronto Faculty of Law Review 77, 88. Specifically, while she did adopt Barak's 'conception of the limited role the [minimal impairment] step plays in rights protection to support her lack of scrutiny of the risks these alternatives each posed' and 'like President Barak, she inferred that the [final balancing] step would enable her to conduct a less restricted assessment of these alternatives'. However, unlike Barak, who at the final balancing stage, 'quantified the difference in effectiveness between [policy] alternatives and the impugned measure', Chief Justice McLachlin failed to do so. Instead, she repeated her minimal impairment analysis and 'explicitly declined to quantify the contrast in effectiveness' between policy alternatives, see page 91.

151 *Hutterian Brethren of Wilson Colony* (n 111) [147]. Weinrib characterizes Justice Abella's decision as one that affirms the significance of the third step without making it clear why she did so. In other words, a straightforward minimal impairment test ('even a less rigorous one, as set out in the Israeli cases') would have reached the same result. Weinrib (n 150) 88.

minimally impairing, Justice Abella demanded a more exacting standard of evidence at this stage, noting that the government had failed to adduce evidence that the integrity of the licensing system had been harmed during the 29 years in which Hutterites could claim an exemption from being photographed. She also noted that more than 700,000 people in the province had no driver's license (and are thus not in a facial recognition database), and questioned whether adding the photographs of approximately 250 Hutterites would really enhance protection from identity theft. She called the benefits of the law 'slight and largely hypothetical', whereas the infringement on religion was serious and much more concrete.[152]

Justice LeBel agreed with most of what Justice Abella said in her decision. However, he appeared to want to strike a middle ground between Chief Justice McLachlin and Justice Abella in the deference granted to the government's policy choices. He criticized the majority's approach, noting that 'the reasons of the Chief Justice treat the law's objective as if it were unassailable once the courts engage in the proportionality analysis. No means that would not allow the objective to be realized to its fullest extent could be considered as a reasonable alternative.'[153] Unlike Justice Abella, he emphasized the need to give the government some flexibility in developing policy responses. However, he ultimately agreed that a religious exemption from the law could satisfy the government's purposes while still protecting religious rights.[154]

[152] According to Sara Weinrib, if the salutary effects of Alberta's regulation truly lacked any discernible impact, then this measure should fail at the minimal impairment stage. Weinrib argues that this approach 'displaced rather than followed the minimal impairment test'. Weinrib (n 150) 93.

[153] *Hutterian Brethren of Wilson Colony* (n 111) [197]. Weinrib characterizes Justice LeBel's approach as most consistent with the Israeli approach, noting that his decision 'most fully invoked the distinctive methodology President Barak envisioned for the final step of the proportionality analysis'. Weinrib (n 150) 88. Specifically, he suggested that 'even if the alternative measures considered under the minimal impairment test did not fully achieve the government's objective, the court might nevertheless sanction them on the basis that they infringed rights less'. In other words, he 'seemed to contemplate a scenario in which a measure met the minimal impairment test (Because the proposed alternative did not fully achieve the government's objective), but was considered disproportionate under the final *Oakes* step' (at 94).

[154] The final justice, Justice Fish, wrote a two-line judgment concurring with both Justices Abella and LeBel.

## VIII Balancing

### A The Interplay between the Balancing Test and the Other Tests

In *Oakes*, the Supreme Court stated that '[e]ven if an objective is of sufficient importance, and the first two elements of the proportionality test are satisfied, it is still possible that, because of the severity of the deleterious effects of a measure on individuals or groups, the measure will not be justified by the purposes it is intended to serve. The more severe the deleterious effects of a measure, the more important the objective must be if the measure is to be reasonable and demonstrably justified in a free and democratic society.'[155]

Despite the suggestion from the language of *Oakes* that the final balancing stage may form an important part of the analysis, proportionality in the strict sense is never determinative of the section 1 analysis. In this regard, Hogg argues that proportionality duplicates other steps of the test: '[i]f the objective of a law is sufficiently important to justify overriding a Charter right (first step), and if the law is rationally connected to the objective (second step), and if the law impairs the Charter right no more than is necessary to accomplish the objective (third step), how could its effects then be judge to be too severe?'[156] Similarly, Hickman notes that 'no Canadian case has turned solely on proportionality … probably because it is artificial in practice to divorce the question of overall proportionality from the potential availability of less-intrusive means'.[157] Justice Iacobucci has described the last step of the test as a 'resume of previous analysis'.[158] According to Hogg, the last step 'has no work to do, and can safely be ignored'.[159] Similarly, Blanche argues that '[t]he third step has no real weakening impact on the first two steps. It comes too late in the process … it seems that it is a step that should almost never be reached.'[160]

In the vast majority of cases, the court is extremely brief in its proportionality analyses and says little about the legal test at this stage

155 *Oakes* (n 2) [71].
156 Hogg (n 27) 38–44.
157 Hickman (n 129)
158 Frank Iacobucci, 'Judicial Review by the Supreme Court of Canada under the Canadian Charter of Rights and Freedoms: The First Ten Years' in David M Beatty (ed), *Human Rights and Judiial Review* (Martinus Nijhoff 1994) 93, 121.
159 Hogg (n 27) 153.
160 Pierre Blanche, 'The Criteria for Justification under Oakes: Too Much Severeity Generatied through Formalism' (1991) 20 Manitoba Law Journal 437, 443.

of the analysis. In many cases, the court merely reiterates its previous findings. It will often briefly restate the importance of the objective (largely repeating its conclusions from the first stage of the analysis) and briefly restate the way the law affects the individual's right and the interests of the public (largely repeating their conclusions from the rational connection stage of the analysis), and it will emphasize that one outweighs the other, depending on the outcome of the other stages of the analysis. For example, if the plaintiff is to succeed with his or her claim, the court will emphasize how intrusive the law is on individual rights. It often also notes that the government had less impairing alternatives. However, if the law being challenged is to be upheld, the court will emphasize how important the government's objective is. Numerous cases contain merely a coulple of lines stating that a limit is either proportional or not.[161]

Close to half of the cases in the dataset contain no reference at all to the final stage of proportionality.[162] In all cases in the dataset that did include analysis at the final strict proportionality stage, the result at that stage was identical to the result of the minimal impairment analysis. In *RJR-Macdonald v Canada (Attorney General)*, one of the justices questioned whether something that impairs more than required 'contradicts the assertion of proportionality'.[163] In other words, the conclusion at the minimal impairment stage of the analysis may pre-empt a PA.

### *B A Larger Role for the Balancing Test?*

Although the Court does not employ a rigorous balancing test, at least one justice of the Supreme Court has suggested a role for the balancing test within the *Oakes* analysis, in the above-mentioned case involving religious exemptions from drivers' license photos. In this regard, Chief Justice McLachlin insisted that the fourth step of the analysis is distinct: 'the first three stages . . . are anchored in assessment of the law's purpose. Only the fourth branch takes full account of the

[161] *Greater Vancouver Transportation Authority* (n 126); *Nguyen v Quebec (Education, Recreation and Sports)* [2009] 3 SCR 208.

[162] 51 out of 120 cases, or 42.5 per cent. See eg *Trociuk v British Columbia (Attorney General)* [2003] 1 SCR 835, *Tse* (n 41), *Ruby v Canada (Solicitor General)* [2002] 4 SCR 3, *Charkaoui v Canada (Citizenship and Immigration)* [2007] 1 SCR 350.

[163] *RJR-Macdonald Inc* (n 115).

"severity of the deleterious effects of a measure on individuals and groups."'[164] In this regard, one could envision a hypothetical situation where a legislative objective is sufficiently important, but the least impairing means of accomplishing that objective has too serious an effect on rights to be a reasonable limit.

One commentator has interpreted this statement by Chief Justice McLachlin as calling for a more deferential approach towards the minimal impairment stage of the test and a 'corollary admonition' that more matters should be decided under the overall balance stage.[165] There is nothing in particular about this case that demanded a more exacting PA, and there is some informal speculation as to why Chief Justice McLachlin made these comments. One theory is that she was concerned with the general trend towards close scrutiny of governmental policy choices at the minimal impairment stage of the test and wished to point the Court in the opposite direction.

Zion has also argued strongly in favour of a more rigorous final stage of the PA. He argues that the other phases of the test should be modified, such that cases should routinely be determined at the final stage. Much like Chief Justice McLachlin, and unlike some other Canadian constitutional law scholars, he sees the final stage of the analysis as being distinct from the others. While most cases easily meet the first and second stages of the test as the court generally readily finds that the government's objective was pressing and that the law was connected to

[164] *Hutterian Brethren of Wilson Colony* (n 111) [76]. Chief Justice Lamer similarly hinted at some role for the PA in *Dagenais v Canadian Broadcasting Corporation* [1994] 3 SCR 835 [889]:

> In my view, characterizing the [final stage of the proportionality analysis] as being concerned solely with the balance between the objective and the deleterious effects of a measure rests on too narrow a conception of proportionality. I believe that even if an objective is of sufficient importance, the first two elements of the proportionality test are satisfied, and the deleterious effects are proportional to the objectives, it is still possible that, because of a lack of proportionality between the deleterious effects and the salutary effects, a measure will not be reasonable and demonstrably justified in a free a democratic society. I would therefore rephrase the third part of the *Oakes* test as follows: there must be a proportionality between the deleterious effects of the measures which are responsible for limiting the rights or freedoms in question and the objective, and there must be a proportionality between the deleterious and the salutary effects of the measure.

[165] Berger, 'Section 1, Constitutional Reasoning and Cultural Difference' (n 1) 32.

that objective, he states that at the final stage, 'the government no longer receives the benefit of the doubt'.[166] He notes that Canadian courts have tended to blend the stages of the analysis which, as I discussed previously, has often turned the PA into a recapitulation of what the court has already said at previous stages of the analysis. The Court itself has acknowledged this. For example, Justice Abella has stated that 'the stages of the *Oakes* test are not watertight compartments: the principle of proportionality guides the analysis at each step. This ensures that at every stage, the importance of the objective and the harm to the right are weighed.'[167] Zion argues that the problem with this blending is that it may allow judges to 'cloak the "policy" reasoning demanded by stage four in the neutral trappings of stage three.'[168] There is support for Zion's hypothesis in the empirical work of Petersen, which categorizes the arguments made in Supreme Court cases and finds that these types of arguments are made in 6 per cent of the cases in his sample.[169]

Although there was initially some speculation that this case, and Chief Justice McLachlin's comments in particular, represented a turning point in the Canadian proportionality jurisprudence, this does not seem to have been the result. This case has been cited by judges in 85 subsequent publicly reported cases in Canada, all of which I reviewed. After eliminating cases that only cited *Hutterian Brethren* for its discussion of freedom of religion rather than for its discussion of proportionality or for other reasons unrelated to proportionality,[170] and cases that merely cited this case in passing, a mere five cases remain.[171] It seems that the

[166] Mark Zion, 'Effecting Balance: Oakes Analysis Restaged' (2013) 43 Ottawa Law Review 431, 446.

[167] *Hutterian Brethren of Wilson Colony* (n 111) [134].

[168] Zion (n 166) 447.

[169] Petersen (n 49).

[170] For example, several cases cite this case as authority for the proposition that the government must be given deference to respond to social problems, a point that has been made in scores of other appellate and Supreme Court of Canada decisions. In addition, numerous cases cite the statement of Chief Justice McLachlin that 'the government must show that it is reasonable to suppose that the limit may further the goal, not that it will do so'. In stating this, she is indicating that the rational connection analysis is not a rigorous one.

[171] In *R. v Allen* [2014] SKQB 402, although the Court quoted Chief Justice McLachlin's comments about the final balancing stage at length, it went on to conduct its usual brief analysis that largely reiterated its previous comments. Another case with a somewhat similar approach is *Bennett v Canada (Attorney General)* [2011] FC 1310. In this case, the Federal Court quoted *Hutterian Brethren* and conducted a longer than usual PA. However, ultimately, the Court basically just said what was said or what might have been

precedential value of this case, at this time, has been its discussion of freedom of religion rather than its discussion of proportionality.

*R v Pawlowski*[172] is an example of a case in which a Court did cite *Hutterian Brethren* for its PA. This case involved restrictions on protesting (i.e. bylaws preventing the defendant from using sound modification devices or blocking the sidewalk with signs without a permit) and a resulting freedom of expression challenge. In this case, the Alberta Provincial Court (the trial level court) quoted Chief Justice McLachlin and then went on to paraphrase and interpret the Chief Justice's statements:

> In some circumstances the incidental effect of a law passed for the general good on a particular individual or group may be so great that they effectively deprive that individual or group of meaningful choice ... [rendering] the impact of the limit very serious. However, the incidental effects of a law passed for the general good on a particular individual or group may be less serious ... A limit on the right that extracts a cost of inconvenience but nevertheless leaves the individual or group with a meaningful choice about the expressive activity issue will be less serious than a limit that effectively deprives the individual or group of such choice.

Interestingly, following this relatively lengthy discussion of proportionality, the Court went on to conduct a very brief analysis:

> While it is true that the incidental effects of the bylaw include imposing upon [the Plaintiff] the inconvenience of obtaining the permission of the Calgary Stampede[173] before participating in the Calgary Stampede Parade, in my view, the limitations on expressive activity imposed by the bylaw do not effectively deprive [the Plaintiff] of a meaningful choice

said in more detail in previous stages of the test. In this case, an individual member of the 'Church of the Universe' believed that marijuana was the 'tree of life' and thus asserted that smoking marijuana was linked to freedom of religion. See also *Canadian Broadcasting Corp* (n 71).

172 [2014] ABPC 126.

173 The Calgary Stampede is the city's premiere event each year. It draws thousands of tourists to the city and includes many events, including numerous rodeo events, concerts, community events (such as pancake breakfasts hosted by businesses), and a fairground (with rides, demonstrations, etc.). It also includes a sizeable parade through the city's downtown area. The individuals in this case had a history of 'inserting themselves' into the Calgary Stampede Parade without permission in the name of religious protest in contravention of a bylaw that prohibited 'joining in or interfering with a parade or roadway event'. They disputed the constitutionality of this law.

> in the exercise of his right to freedom of expression. I therefore conclude that limits on freedom of expression imposed by [the bylaw] are proportionate in their effect.

The most detailed judicial analysis and application of the PA since *Hutterian Brethren* is found in *Carter v Canada (Attorney General).*[174] In this case, individuals sought to again challenge the criminal prohibition on assisted suicide, which the Supreme Court of Canada had already ruled was constitutional in a previous case. The claimants argued, and the trial judge had accepted, that both the factual context surrounding assisted suicide (i.e. that other countries had legalized it and that Canadian public opinion had shifted) and the legal context (i.e. the way courts analyse the right to life, liberty, and security of the person and the way courts conduct the PA) had sufficiently evolved such that it was open to her to reopen the issue (despite clearly being bound by Supreme Court of Canada jurisprudence). At the final stage of the analysis, the trial judge stated that:

> Courts are to widen their perspective at the final stage to take full account of the deleterious effects of the infringement on individuals or groups, and determine whether the benefits of the legislation are worth the cost. That is a different question than whether the legislation is rationally connected to the government's objective or impairs the rights as little as possible ... The clarification in *Hutterian Brethren* regarding the final step in the *Oakes* test has significant consequences in this case.[175]

On appeal, the Court of Appeal thus directly considered the issue of the extent to which the PA has evolved over time (i.e. whether cases such as *Hutterian Brethren* actually changed the analysis). Interestingly, the dissenting (on other issues) judge found that in *Hutterian Brethren,* the Chief Justice 'was not attempting to change the s. 1 analysis' but rather 'her points on the proportionality stage serve to counter academic commentary [from Peter Hogg] which suggested the final stage was now redundant ... '[176] Justice Finch went on to state that since *Hutterian Brethren*, 'courts have, on occasion, continued to see the final stage as connected to the work done at earlier stages of the proportionality analysis', with the Supreme Court of Canada even concluding in a subsequent case that the result of the final proportionality stage was

[174] *Carter* (n 15).
[175] [2012] BCSC 886 [994], [1003].
[176] *Carter* (n 15) [104].

'apparent from the ... analysis' at the earlier stages.[177] The remaining two judges agreed with the analysis of Chief Justice Finch, stating that they agreed 'with the reasoning and conclusion ... that it did not represent a change in the law'.[178] Although the Court discussed the PA, the majority did not actually conduct such an analysis.

There are a few isolated examples of the Court attempting a bit more of a balancing exercise at the proportionality stage of the analysis. For example, *Alberta (Information and Privacy Commissioner) v United Food and Commercial Workers, Local 401* was a challenge to a law restricting the collection, use and disclosure of personal information. During that case, both the Union and the employer videotaped and photographed individuals crossing the picketline. These individuals complained to the Information and Privacy Commissioner, which resulted in a challenge to legislation governing information collection. In that case, instead of merely reiterating its earlier conclusions, the Court looked at the various beneficial effects of such a privacy protection scheme (such as enhancing individual control and safeguarding privacy), but concluded that the law was disproportionate. The Court connected this conclusion to the minimal impairment stage of the analysis, noting that there was no mechanism in the act to accommodate expressive purposes.[179]

Similarly, *R v Lucas* challenged a criminal prohibition on defamatory libel. The Court found that certain aspects of the law were too broad and were thus not minimally impairing. In this case, the majority of the Court noted that when freedom of expression is at issue, the nature of the violation should be taken into consideration in determining whether an appropriate balance has been struck between the deleterious effects of the law on the right and the salutary goals of that legislation. In other words, courts could theoretically require more from government to justify a particularly egregious rights violation. They noted that the further a particular form of expression departs from the values underlying free speech, the lower the level of constitutional protection it will be afforded. In this case, defamatory libel, which was considered to be speech of low value, was sufficiently far removed from the core values of free speech that it merited little protection. The Court then went on to consider the benefits of the law, for example, its salutary effect on reputation.[180]

[177] *Carter* (n 15) [105], citing *Saskatchewan* (n 61).
[178] *Carter* (n 15) [270].
[179] *United Food* (n 91).
[180] [1998] 1 SCR 439 [88].

Because of the few cases in which a true PA occurs, it is difficult to draw many generalizations about the kinds of factors that are taken into account. As noted previously, the majority of the analysis is mere repetition. However, the court will consider any relevant factors, both those relevant to the degree of the rights infringement and those relevant to the justification. For example, the Court will mention the way in which the infringement affects the particular party at issue but also its effects on society more broadly, and any benefits arising from that law (be they benefits that occur to the public in general or to private actors, benefits that are purely financial or benefits that are more symbolic, etc.). Similarly, when considering the negative effects of the law, a court might consider any relevant factors. Although the starting point is generally on the way in which the law negatively affects the particular claimant, they often go on to consider other sorts of negative impacts. For example, in the context of a freedom of expression challenge, the court will not only consider the fact that a particular individual's speech was restricted but also the restriction's negative effects on values furthered by free speech such as democracy.

3

# Proportionality Analysis by the South African Constitutional Court

RICHARD STACEY

## I Introduction

South Africa's 1993 interim Constitution[1] and the 1996 Constitution[2] are transformative documents.[3] They set out the commitment to fundamental human rights for the first time, and aim to build a 'historic bridge between the past of a deeply divided society characterized by strife, conflict, untold suffering and injustice, and a future founded on the recognition of human rights, democracy and peaceful co-existence … for all South Africans'.[4]

Making good on this transformative commitment requires positive policy action on the part of the executive, legislative action by Parliament, and administrative action by the bureaucracy. Transforming South Africa from a society based on racism, injustice, and a massively unequal distribution of resources and opportunity into a society based on dignity, equality, and freedom may require the executive and legislative branches of government to act in ways that limit the constitutional rights of some members of society. The inclusion of limitations clauses in section 33 of the interim Constitution and section 36 of the 1996 Constitution recognizes that rights are never absolute, and that under certain circumstances the limitation of rights in the bill of rights may be justified by the pursuit of these broader transformative objectives. Section 36 therefore allows the limitation of rights, but closely controls these limitations: rights may be limited only by way of a law of general application, and only if doing

1 Constitution of the Republic of South Africa, Act 200 of 1993 (the 'interim Constitution').

2 Constitution of the Republic of South Africa, 1996 (the '1996 Constitution').

3 Karl Klare, 'Legal Culture and Transformative Constitutionalism' (1998) 14 South African Journal on Human Rights 146.

4 This 'post-amble' to the interim Constitution is an un-numbered section of the text that appears after the numbered sections but before the schedules appended to the text.

so is 'reasonable and justifiable in an open and democratic society based on human dignity, equality and freedom'.

The principle of proportionality has emerged in South African jurisprudence as the mechanism by which the dual commitment to transformation and respect for constitutional rights is fulfilled. While the limitations clauses of neither the interim nor the 1996 Constitutions include the word 'proportionality', the Constitutional Court made it clear in *S v Makwanyane*, one of its earliest cases decided under the interim Constitution, that the 'limitation of constitutional rights for a purpose that is reasonable and necessary in a democratic society involves the weighing up of competing values, and ultimately an assessment based on proportionality'.[5] *Makwanyane* concerned the constitutionality of the death penalty, a criminal sentence allowable in the criminal code which was found to limit rights to life, dignity, and not to be subjected to cruel, inhuman, or degrading treatment or punishment. In setting out an approach to determining the justifiability of rights limitations, the court remarked that the assessment of proportionality is an inherently case-specific practice, which 'calls for the balancing of different interests'.[6] 'In the balancing process', the court went on,

> the relevant considerations will include the nature of the right that is limited, and its importance to an open and democratic society based on freedom and equality; the purpose for which the right is limited and the importance of that purpose to such a society; the extent of the limitation, its efficacy, and particularly where the limitation has to be necessary, whether the desired ends could reasonably be achieved through other means less damaging to the right in question.

The 1996 Constitution adopted this approach almost verbatim, including it as a non-exhaustive list of factors relevant to the assessment of the reasonableness and justifiability of rights limitations. Section 36 provides, in full:

**Limitation of rights**

(1) The rights in the Bill of Rights may be limited only in terms of law of general application to the extent that the limitation is reasonable and justifiable in an open and democratic society based on human

[5] *S v Makwanyane & Another* 1995 (3) SA 391 (CC) [104].
[6] ibid [104].

dignity, equality and freedom, taking into account all relevant factors, including-

(a) the nature of the right;
(b) the importance of the purpose of the limitation;
(c) the nature and extent of the limitation;
(d) the relation between the limitation and its purpose; and
(e) less restrictive means to achieve the purpose.

(2) Except as provided in subsection (1) or in any other provision of the Constitution, no law may limit any right entrenched in the Bill of Rights.

The factors that section 36 requires courts to take into account in working towards an assessment based on proportionality reflect the model of proportionality analysis (PA) followed in other jurisdictions, consisting of four distinct inquiries. These inquiries go to the value or importance of the limitation's objective (the worthy purpose test); whether there is a rational connection between the limitation and its objective (the rational connection or suitability test); whether the limitation restricts rights as little as necessary to achieve the objective, or if there are less restrictive means available (the necessity or less restrictive means test); and whether the limitation is proportionate 'in the strict sense' – that is, whether the benefits achieved by the limitation justify the deleterious consequences of limiting a right (the balancing or strict proportionality test).

This chapter examines the reasoning of 100 Constitutional Court decisions and one High Court decision[7] over the 22 years between April 1995 and December 2017. During this period, the Constitutional Court has handed down 703 decisions. The 101 cases included in the chapter represent nearly all of the decisions in which the court both found that some government conduct limited constitutional rights and went on to consider whether the limitation was justifiable in terms of section 33 of the interim Constitution or section 36 of the 1996 Constitution.[8]

[7] *De Lille & Another v Speaker of the National Assembly* 1998 (3) SA 430 (C). I have included this decision because it is one of only five cases where a rights limitation was imposed by a measure other than a law of general application and no PA was called for. The High Court judgment was confirmed on appeal in the Supreme Court of Appeal, although the speaker did not challenge the High Court's finding that the limitation of constitutional rights to freedom of speech was unjustifiable (*Speaker of the National Assembly v De Lille & Another* 1999 4 All SA 241 (A)).

[8] The judgments left out of the analysis are those which consider challenges to statutory provisions that are so similar to the court's previous decisions that the analysis is very brief

In these 101 judgments, the court concluded that 83 of the rights limitations were not justifiable and were struck down. In 18 cases, it found the limitations to be justifiable and allowed the impugned measures to stand. In all but 5 of the 83 decisions striking down limitations as unjustifiable, the court conducted a PA to determine whether or not that limitation was justifiable. The 5 cases where the Court struck down limitations without conducting the PA involved limitations imposed by measures other than laws of general application, to which the limitations clause does not apply.[9]

This chapter aims to illustrate more precisely how the courts' decisions in rights cases rely on the principle of proportionality. The Constitutional Court frequently claims that its approach to adjudicating rights limitations focuses on the values and normative commitments at the heart of the Constitution.[10] The chapter uses a quantitative analysis of the case law in South Africa to argue that it is indeed the case that the jurisprudence relies more heavily on the evaluative and normative balancing of rights and competing objectives than on the formal or value-neutral elements of the PA which minimize this evaluative balancing. In practical terms, the data indicate that in striking down rights limitations as unjustifiable, the courts rely more on the inquiry into whether the value or benefits achieved by limiting a right are proportionate to or justify the harm of limiting the right in the first place than they do on any other inquiry that makes up the PA. The inquiries into how likely a limitation

and merely repeats or refers to its analysis in those earlier case. One such case is *First National Bank of South Africa Ltd v Land and Agricultural Bank of South Africa & Others; Sheard v Land and Agricultural Bank of South Africa & Another* 2000 (3) SA 626 (CC), in which the court relied heavily on its reasoning in *Lesapo v North West Agricultural Bank & Another* 2000 (1) 409 (CC) and conducted only a cursory recital of the PA. Indeed, in *First National Bank v Land and Agricultural Bank*, the state parties responsible for the impugned legislation admitted its unconstitutionality and sought only a suspension of the order of invalidity.

9 In one additional case, the court found that the limitation was not imposed by a law of general application and did not fall within the purview of the limitations clause, but conducted a PA in the course of considering whether the discrimination complained against was unfair or not: *Hoffmann v South African Airways* 2001 (1) SA 1 (CC). The prohibition against unfairness in section 9(3) of the Constitution thus acts as an internal limitations clause, requiring a PA in the context of working out if the discrimination complained against is justifiable.

10 See, e.g., *S v Manamela & Another* 2000 (3) SA 1 (CC) [32]; *Coetzee v Government of the Republic of South Africa, Matiso & Others v Commanding Officer Port Elizabeth Prison & Others* 1995 (4) SA 631 (CC) [46]; *Makwanyane* (n 5) [104.a].

is to achieve its goals, or whether the impugned measure adopts the least restrictive approach, are less influential in the court's approach to PA.

The data do present a challenge, however, to the court's accounts of its jurisprudence as 'global'[11] or holistic. Although the court describes the PA as a judgment that depends on a conspectus of all of the distinct inquiries in the PA, it is not uncommon for the court to rely on just one or two of the inquiries in the analysis to conclude that a limitation is disproportionate and unjustifiable. This chapter therefore suggests a more nuanced understanding of the court's 'global' judgment on proportionality: it is not that the analysis depends on a conspectus of all of the distinct considerations in the PA, but rather that the analysis is concerned to uncover how South Africa's constitutional commitments and values can be best realized and fulfilled. It may be that reaching this conclusion requires consideration of just one or two inquiries in the analysis, or it may be that it requires consideration of all four. But throughout the analysis, whether that analysis turns on one, two, three, or four inquiries, the fundamental question remains whether upholding the right or allowing its limitation better advances core constitutional commitments.

## II Legal and Institutional Context

### *A From Apartheid to the Human Rights Era*

The system of apartheid ended in South Africa on 27 April 1994 with the coming into effect of the interim Constitution. Civil and political rights were extended to all in South Africa for the first time, regardless of race or colour; and economic and social rights were made justiciable in an effort to remedy apartheid's legacy of massive inequality. Parliamentary supremacy was replaced by constitutional supremacy, and any official conduct inconsistent with the Constitution would henceforward be invalid. Before 1994, the government in South Africa had been able to pursue its racist policies free from the constraints of rights. Some judges in some courts made a valiant effort to restrain the excesses of government power through the common-law principles of administrative law, but these attempts were ultimately undermined by the government's appointment of executive-minded appellate judges.[12] South Africa's

[11] *Manamela* (n 10) [32].

[12] For an account of contrasting approaches to adjudication during the apartheid era, see David Dyzenhaus, *Hard Cases in Wicked Legal Systems: Pathologies of Legality* (2nd ed, OUP 2010).

rights revolution, codified in the bills of rights in the interim Constitution and then the 1996 Constitution, supplements these common-law principles with the substantive protections of rights.

The preamble to the 1996 Constitution commits South Africans generally and the government specifically to establishing a society based on democratic values, equality, and social justice, and to healing the divisions of the past. While the apartheid system was based on inequality and the denial of human dignity of millions of people, section 1 of the 1996 Constitution affirms that South Africa is a democratic state founded on the values of human dignity, equality, and freedom.

The South African Constitutional Court has described its inquiry into the reasonableness and justifiability of rights limitations as one that aims at a 'global judgment on proportionality'. The outcome of the analysis rests on a conspectus of all of the factors set out in section 36(1), rather than on a single factor or stage in the analysis. But in many cases, the court does appear to rely on just one or two of these inquiries – certainly not all four – in deciding that a limitation is unjustifiable.[13] The data therefore indicate that the court's 'global' analysis should not be understood as demanding consideration of each of the inquiries. Rather, we should understand the global analysis as one that seeks to determine whether allowing a rights limitation or striking it down is more congruent with the transformative character of South Africa's constitutional project. In some easy cases, the court need rely only on the evidence-based inquiries into suitability or necessity, but in other hard cases the court will need to confront the morally difficult and value-based question of whether the benefit achieved by limiting a right outweighs or is more important than the good served by upholding the right against any limitation.[14]

[13] See, e.g., Niels Petersen, *Proportionality and Judicial Activism: Fundamental Rights Adjudication in Canada, Germany and South Africa* (CUP 2017). A handful of scholars, including Petersen, argue that the fourth leg of the analysis in particular, the inquiry into proportionality in the strict sense, is at best unnecessary because it duplicates elements of the other inquiries, and logically untenable or unpredictable, subjective, and ad hoc at worst. See, e.g., Stavros Tsakyrakis, 'Proportionality: An Assault on Human Rights?' (2009) 7 International Journal of Constitutional Law 468; Grégoire N Webber, 'Proportionality, Balancing and the Cult of Constitutional Rights Scholarship' (2010) 23 Canadian Journal of Law and Jurisprudence 179; Francisco J Urbina, 'Is It Really that Easy? A Critique of Proportionality and "Balancing and Reasoning"' (2014) 27 Canadian Journal of Law and Jurisprudence 167.

[14] I have argued elsewhere that in conducting the balancing exercise the court does not, however, come to some measurable or quantified assessment of the value of the affected

### *B Access to Courts*

The 1996 Constitution provides that the courts must declare any legislation that is inconsistent with the Constitution invalid to the extent of its inconsistency.[15] Between 1994 and 2012, the Constitutional Court had jurisdiction to hear only constitutional matters and issues connected with constitutional matters, and it was the court of final appeal in all constitutional matters. The Supreme Court of Appeal remained the final court of appeal for all non-constitutional matters,[16] although it had jurisdiction to consider constitutional matters after 1996. The Constitution Seventeenth Amendment Act 2012 amended the Constitution and removed the jurisdictional limitation on the Constitutional Court, making it the court of final appeal for both constitutional and non-constitutional matters.[17]

Although generally a court of appeal, the Constitutional Court acts as a court of first instance in two situations. First, only the Constitutional Court may hear cases dealing with the matters listed in s 167(4) of the Constitution.[18] Second, the court will entertain applications for direct

right on one hand and the objective pursued by limiting the right on the other. Rather, the court assesses which of the two competing policy alternatives represented by upholding the right and limiting the right in pursuit of some other objective is more consistent with the transformative project of the Constitution, and better advances the constitutional commitment to the values of dignity, equality, and freedom. This 'balancing as reasoning' seeks to justify one course of action over another against the principles and values that are at the heart of South Africa's constitutional project. It is not a form of 'interest balancing', or some exercise in the numerical comparison or utilitarian calculus of the value of competing policy alternatives. See Richard Stacey, 'The Magnetism of Moral Reasoning and the Principle of Proportionality in Comparative Constitutional Adjudication' (forthcoming) American Journal of Comparative Law.

15 Section 172(2)(a) of the 1996 Constitution provides that High Courts have the power to make a declaration of constitutional invalidity, but when they do so the matter must be referred to the Constitutional Court for confirmation. Magistrates' Courts have no competence to inquire into the constitutionality of legislation (s 170).

16 *S v Boesak* 2001 (1) SA 912 (CC).

17 1996 Constitution, section 167(3)(b).

18 Section 167(4) of the 1996 Constitution provides:

Only the constitutional Court may-

(a) decide disputes between organs of state in the national or provincial sphere concerning the constitutional status, powers or functions of any of those organs of state;
(b) decide on the constitutionality of any parliamentary or provincial Bill, but may do so only in the circumstances anticipated in section 79 or 121;
(c) decide applications envisaged in section 80 or 122;
(d) decide on the constitutionality of any amendment to the Constitution;

access and may decide to hear a matter as a court of first instance if it is in the interests of justice to do so. The Constitution also provides for direct appeal to the Constitutional Court, allowing an applicant to leapfrog intermediate courts in the appellate hierarchy.[19]

Rule 18 of the Constitutional Court Rules in turn sets out in detail the procedure for making an application for direct access to the Constitutional Court. An applicant for direct access must set out the grounds on which it is contended that the interests of justice demand direct access to the court, the nature of the relief sought, whether the matter can be dealt with by the court without the hearing of oral evidence and if evidence must be adduced how this should be done, and how disputes of facts should be resolved.

A long line of the Constitutional Court's jurisprudence indicates that direct access will be granted only where there are exceptional circumstances,[20] requiring an applicant to show that there is either 'sufficient urgency or public importance' that justifies direct access, 'proof of prejudice to the public interest or the ends of justice and good government' that would be caused were direct access not granted,[21] or the need for finality based on a long-standing dispute and an existing history of litigation before the Constitutional Court and other courts.[22] The court is reticent to hear matters as a court of first instance, because it is not a trier of fact and its proceedings are not well-suited to resolving factual disputes.[23]

(e) decide that Parliament or the President has failed to fulfil a constitutional obligation; or

(f) certify a provincial constitution in terms of section 144.

19 1996 Constitution, section 167(6).

20 *Bruce & Another v Fleecytex Johannesburg CC & Others* 1998 (2) SA 1143 (CC) [9]; *Christian Education South Africa v Minister of Education* 1999 (2) SA 83 (CC) [4]; *Dormehl v Minister of Justice & Others* 2000 (2) SA 987 (CC) [5]; *National Gambling Board v Premier, KwaZulu-Natal & Others* 2002 (2) SA 715 (CC) [29]; *Van der Spuy v General Council of the Bar of South Africa* 2002 (5) SA 392 (CC) [7]; *Satchwell v President of the Republic of South Africa & Another* 2003 (4) SA 266 (CC) [6]; *Richter v Minister of Home Affairs & Others* 2009 (3) SA 615 (CC) [101]–[104].

21 *Bruce* (n 20) [19].

22 *Independent Newspapers (Pty) Ltd v Minister for Intelligence Services In Re Masetlha v President of the Republic of South Africa & Another* 2008 (5) SA 31 (CC).

23 *Bruce* (n 20) [8]. On the court's reluctance to hear direct appeals from courts of first instance without a judgment from an intermediate appellate court, see *Magajane v Chairperson, North West Gambling Board* 2006 (5) SA 250 (CC).

### C Judicial Review of Administrative Action

In the era of parliamentary supremacy before the coming into force of the interim Constitution in 1994, administrative law and the common-law principles of natural justice were the only tools through which to challenge the apartheid government's abuses of power. It is perhaps unsurprising that the interim and 1996 Constitutions entrenched a right to administrative justice. Section 33 of the 1996 Constitution provides that everyone has the right to administrative action that is lawful, reasonable, and procedurally fair, and enjoined the state to enact legislation giving effect to this right within three years of 4 February 1997, the date on which the 1996 Constitution came into force (section 33(3) read with schedule 6, item 23(1)).

The Promotion of Administrative Justice Act 3 of 2000 (PAJA) accordingly sets out in great detail what the right to lawful, reasonable, and procedurally fair administrative action means in practice, and how the right requires administrators to act. Since the coming into effect of PAJA and a number of other statutes giving effect to constitutional rights, including the Promotion of Equality and Prevention of Unfair Discrimination Act 4 of 2000 (PEPUDA) required by section 9(4) of the Constitution, the court has followed the principle of 'constitutional subsidiarity'. This requires claimants relying on constitutional rights given effect to in statutes to proceed on the basis of the provisions of the statute, rather than by relying on the Constitution directly.[24] Thus, wherever a complainant alleges that public conduct, other than legislation, is inconsistent with the right to administrative justice or constitutes unfair discrimination, he or she must proceed in terms of PAJA or PEPUDA. Section 6 of PAJA, for example, sets out no fewer than 20 distinct grounds of review of administrative actions including the catch-all ground of review for 'otherwise unconstitutional or unlawful' administrative action (section 6(2)(i)). Only where a complainant challenges PAJA or PEPUDA as inconsistent with constitutional rights could he or she rely directly on the Constitution, without going through the gateway of the subordinate legislation.

Challenges to administrative action brought under PAJA or PEPUDA thus do not require courts to consider the justifiability of rights limitations in terms of section 36. Cases brought under PAJA are thus not included in the quantitative analysis in this chapter because they involve

[24] *Mazibuko & Others v City of Johannesburg & Others* 2010 (4) SA 1 (CC) [73].

no PA. There are two cases in the dataset that concern administrative action, but they arose prior to the coming into effect of PAJA in 2000 and were thus disposed of in terms of the constitutional right to administrative justice.[25] A third case – *Pillay* – deals with a claim of unfair discrimination under PEPUDA – the only occasion on which the Constitutional Court has considered a claim under PEPUDA.[26] *Pillay* is included here because its analysis of whether the discrimination was unfair is so similar to the inquiry into whether or not a rights limitation was proportional.

### D Horizontal Application of the Bill of Rights

The Bill of Rights binds 'the legislature, the executive, the judiciary and all organs of state' (section 8(1)), but it also binds 'a natural or a juristic person, if and to the extent that, it is applicable' (section 8(2)). In six cases included in this analysis, the complainants allege that a rule of the common law, as it regulates the relationship between private parties, infringes constitutional rights. In *Khumalo v Holomisa,* for example, the court considered whether the common law of defamation unjustifiably infringed the right to freedom of expression protected by section 16, and should accordingly be developed by the court to eliminate this infringement. This chapter considers the source of rights limitation in these cases to be judicial, to the extent that the common law is a product of judicial decisions.

By far, though, the majority of cases included in the analysis here involve rights infringements constituted by legislation (87 per cent). Only 8 per cent of infringements were the result of administrative conduct (regulations or other subordinate legislation, policy, or administrative decision), and 5 per cent the result of a common-law rule or a rule of court.

### E Criticisms of Judicial Activism in South Africa

The debate about judicial activism in South Africa has been cast as the question of the appropriate level of deference that judges should pay to

[25] *Larbi-Odam & Others v MEC for Education (North-West Province) & Others* 1998 (1) SA 745 (CC) (challenging regulations made by a member of a provincial executive) and *Hoffmann* (n 9) (challenging an employment decision by a state-owned enterprise).

[26] *MEC for Education: KwaZulu-Natial v Pillay* 2008 (1) SA 747 (CC).

the policy decisions or administrative actions of government. Between about 2009 and 2013, the government made moves – largely unsuccessful – to restructure the judiciary and to limit the Constitutional Court's reach. Early versions of the Superior Courts Bill and attendant proposed amendments to the Constitution sought to make the courts, and especially the Constitutional Court, more accountable to the government.[27] The central feature of these bills would have placed the administration of the courts under the direction of the Minister of Justice rather than the Chief Justice. After significant opposition to this position, the Superior Courts Act 10 of 2013 was passed, ensuring that the administration of the courts remains the responsibility of the Chief Justice.

Much of the fuel for the debate about judicial deference has been provided by the ruling party, the African National Congress (ANC), rather than by the government itself. In 2005, the ANC's National Executive Committee complained that 'many within our judiciary do not see themselves as being part of these masses, accountable to them, and inspired by their hopes, dreams and value systems'. This, the statement continued, could lead to 'popular antagonism' against the judiciary.[28] In 2008, ANC Secretary-General Gwede Mantashe remarked that certain judges of the Constitutional Court were 'counter-revolutionary', although the ANC later distanced itself from these comments.[29] At the 'Access to Justice' conference in 2011, however, President Jacob Zuma stated that

> The Executive must be allowed to conduct its administration and policy making work as freely as it possibly can. The powers conferred on the courts cannot be superior to the powers resulting from the political and consequently administrative mandate resulting from popular democratic elections. Political disputes resulting from the exercise of powers that have been constitutionally conferred on the ruling party through popular vote must not be subverted, simply because those who disagree with the ruling party politically, and who cannot win the popular vote during elections, feel other arms of State are avenues to help them co-govern the country.[30]

[27] Cathy Albertyn, 'Judicial Independence and the Constitution Fourteenth Amendment Bill' (2006) 22 South African Journal on Human Rights 126.

[28] African National Congress, 'Statement of the National Executive Committee on the Occasion of the 93rd Anniversary of the ANC' (8 January 2005) .

[29] Franz Kruger, 'You Said It, Mantashe', *Mail & Guardian* (14 October 2008) <www.mg.co.za/article/2008-10-14-you-said-it-mantashe> accessed 21 June 2016.

[30] President Jacob Zuma, 'Keynote Address' (Access to Justice Conference, 8 July 2011) <http://constitutionallyspeaking.co.za/president-zumas-keynote-address-to-access-to-justice-conference/> accessed 21 June 2016.

In February 2012 President Zuma called for a process to review the Constitutional Court's decisions, and intimated that this process would lead to a revision of the court's powers.[31] To my knowledge, no such review has ever taken place, and the court's powers have not been reduced. On the contrary, the Superior Courts Act 10 of 2013 and the Constitution Seventeenth Amendment Act 2012 expanded the Constitutional Court's jurisdiction, making it the country's apex court in all matters – not just constitutional matters as before. Despite all of the government's posturing against what it sees as the Constitutional Court's activism, the government has never openly defied the Constitutional Court. For the most part, the government has complied with court orders even in those cases where it indicated its displeasure with the order.[32] In March 2016, for example, the Constitutional Court found that President Zuma violated the constitutional obligations to uphold, defend, and respect the Constitution as the supreme law of the land (s 83(b)) and to respect the independence of organs of state (s 181(3)), by refusing to comply with orders made by the Public Protector that he pay back public funds improperly spent on renovations to his own home.[33] After the judgment, opposition parties tabled an ultimately unsuccessful motion of no confidence in President Zuma, and then launched another court challenge complaining that the Speaker of the National Assembly had failed to fulfil her constitutional obligations by failing to make rules regulating the removal of a president for misconduct. A majority of the Constitutional Court agreed, but the Chief Justice in dissent would have found that ordering the National Assembly to make rules was a 'textbook case of judicial overreach – a constitutionally impermissible intrusion by the Judiciary in to the exclusive domain of Parliament'.[34]

[31] Moshoeshoe Monare, 'Concourt's Powers Need Reviewing, Says Zuma', *The Star* (13 February 2012) <www.iol.co.za/the-star/concourt-s-powers-need-reviewing-says-zuma-1.1232428#.U8ACTKifgeI> accessed 21 June 2016.

[32] See, e.g., the comments of Health Minister Manto Tshabalala-Msimang at an AIDS conference in Barcelona following the Court's judgment in the landmark decision requiring the government to provide anti-retrovirals to HIV-positive pregnant women in *Minister of Health & Others v Treatment Action Campaign & Others (No 2)* 2002 (5) SA 721 (CC): 'S Africa Must Supply Nevirapine, Court Rules', The Pharma Letter (15 July 2002) <www.thepharmaletter.com/article/s-africa-must-supply-nevirapine-court-rules> accessed 21 June 2016.

[33] *Economic Freedom Fighters v Speaker of the National Assembly & Others; Democratic Alliance v Speaker of the National Assembly & Others* 2016 (3) SA 580 (CC).

[34] *Economic Freedom Fighters & Others v Speaker of the National Assembly & Another* 2018 (2) SA 571 [223].

As a result of the general lack of outright defiance of court orders, the debate about judicial activism has been translated into the consideration of the proper amount of deference that the judiciary should show to government. The court has shown deference to the legislature in the area of remedy, if not in the extent to which it is prepared to find state conduct unconstitutional. In cases where the defect in rights-limiting legislation could be remedied in any number of ways, the court will tend to defer to the legislature to determine how to amend or replace the legislation so as to serve the purpose sought to be achieved without limiting rights. In a handful of cases, the court has held that there is only one way that a constitutional defect could be cured, and has made an order effecting that change itself. There is no pattern to these cases, or a class or type of legislation that fits into this category.

Where the court finds only one solution to the defect and does not defer to the legislature, it may choose to 'read in' a cure to the offending provision; 'read out' offending terms; or 'read down' or reinterpret legislation in a way that remedies the constitutional defect.[35] The court is often reluctant, however, to perform the quasi-legislative task of reading in significant changes to legislative provisions or reading them down in ways that stretch the plausible meanings of the statutory language.[36] The *Fourie* decision suggests that in matters of policy where public opinion is divided, where government policy is strongly opposed by NGO groups or civil society, or where the policy field is generally contested within government or society, the court will refrain from introducing the remedy itself. This is generally so even if only a single possible remedy exists. In *Fourie*, the subject matter was the controversial issue of same-sex marriage.[37]

There is some empirical evidence that the Constitutional Court enjoyed relatively little institutional legitimacy early on, and that unpopular, counter-majoritarian decisions such as declaring the death penalty unconstitutional led to low levels of popular support for the

[35] *University of Stellenbosch Legal Aid Clinic & Others v Minister of Justice and Correctional Services & Others; Association of Debt Recovery Agents NPC v University of Stellenbosch Legal Aid Clinic & Others; Mavava Trading 279 (Pty) Ltd & Others v University of Stellenbosch Legal Aid Clinic & Others* 2016 (6) SA 596 (CC); *Bato Star Fishing (Pty) Ltd v Minister of Environmental Affairs and Tourism & Others* 2004 (4) SA 490 (CC) [42]–[45].

[36] *Tronox KZN Sands (Pty) Ltd v KwaZulu-Natal Planning and Development Appeal Tribunal & Others* 2016 (3) SA 160 (CC).

[37] *Minister of Home Affairs & Another v Fourie & Another* 2006 (1) SA 524 (CC).

court.[38] However, this lack of diffuse and widespread popular support for the court in South Africa has not stopped it from playing a veto role in South African politics, blocking government conduct that it concludes is inconsistent with the Constitution regardless of the level of support for the government's proposals.[39] More recent empirical work finds that public confidence in the Constitutional Court has grown, and although public confidence may not be the same thing as popular support, it nevertheless appears to be a source of institutional legitimacy for the court.[40]

## III Structure of Limitation Analysis

### *A Overview*

In *S v Makwanyane*, the Constitutional Court set out five factors to take into account when considering whether a rights limitation is justifiable under the limitations clause of the interim Constitution.[41] The 1996 Constitution codified these factors: section 36 provides that all the rights in the Bill of Rights may be limited by law of general application (see Section III.F), if the limitation is 'reasonable and justifiable in an open and democratic society based on human dignity, equality and freedom'. Whether a limitation meets this test of reasonableness or justifiability in the context of South Africa's core constitutional values depends on a consideration of the same factors the court pointed to in *Makwanyane*. These factors are now listed in paragraphs (a–e) of section 36(1).

While the burden of proving that the rights in question have been limited falls to the plaintiff,[42] the burden of convincing the court that the

[38] James L Gibson and Gregory A Caldeira, 'Defenders of Democracy: Legitimacy, Popular Acceptance, and the South African Constitutional Court' (2003) 65 Journal of Politics 1. Surveys conducted by these scholars in 1996, 1997, and 2001 found that around 28 per cent of South Africans supported the court.

[39] Theunis Roux, *The Politics of Principle: The First South African Constitutional Court, 1995–2005* (CUP 2013) 27–35. More recent empirical work finds that public confidence in the Constitutional Court has grown, which may in turn translate into institutional legitimacy.

[40] See James L Gibson, 'Reassessing the Institutional Legitimacy of the South African Constitutional Court: New Evidence, Revised Theory' (2016) 43 Politikon 53.

[41] *Makwanyane* (n 5) [104].

[42] *Ferreira v Levin NO & Others; Vryenhoek & Others v Powell NO & Others* 1996 (1) SA 984 (CC) [44]: 'The task of interpreting . . . fundamental rights rests, of course, with the courts, but it is for the applicants to prove the facts upon which they rely for their claim of infringement of a particular right'.

limitation is justified in terms of section 36 falls to the state.[43] In *Makwanyane*, the court said: 'It is for the legislature, or the party relying on the legislation, to establish this justification, and not for the party challenging it to show that it was not justified.'[44] In *Moise*, the court pointed out that often the state has exclusive and privileged access to the information relevant to justifying a limitation on the basis of policy or factual grounds.[45] The standard of proof in both respects is the civil standard of the balance of probability. Questions of the kind of evidence that will be relevant to discharging the burden at each stage of the limitations analysis are considered in Sections V–VII.

### *B Challenges to Rights Limitation by Right Affected*

Figure 3.1 indicates the frequency with which claimants have relied on infringements of particular rights to challenge the constitutionality of government action. Note that the number of rights-based challenges reflected here exceeds 101 because in some cases the court considered whether violations of more than one right could be justified.

The nature of the transition to democracy in South Africa helps to explain the data reflected in Figure 3.1. The enactment of the interim Constitution did not displace the existing system of law in South Africa. Indeed, it was the minority white parliament that passed the interim Constitution through the existing processes of law making. There was thus no rupture or break in the legal system before and after 1994, even though the interim Constitution made the crucial shift from system of parliamentary supremacy with a minority government to a system of constitutional supremacy with a democratically elected government. This legal continuity between the apartheid-era and the democratic era after 1994 meant that all the laws existing in force before 27 April 1994 remained in force after that date.

However, many of the laws enacted by the apartheid government prior to 1994 were racist laws intended to maintain the economic, social, and political segregation of white and non-white South Africans. Given the transformative project of the Constitution we might expect a great deal of the courts' work, at least in the period immediately after the end of the

[43] *Moise v Greater Germiston Transitional Local Council* 2001 (4) SA 491 (CC) [19]; *Scagell v Attorney General, Western Cape* 1997 (2) SA 368 (CC) [9].

[44] *Makwanyane* (n 5) [102]. See also *Ferreira* (n 42) [44].

[45] *Moise* (n 43) [19].

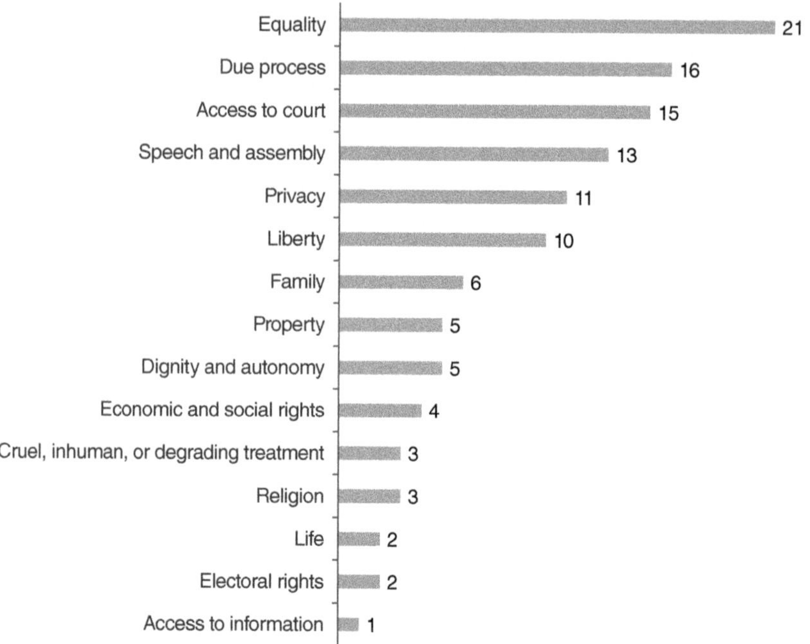


**Figure 3.1** Rights triggering proportionality analysis

apartheid era, to revolve around remedying the injustices of that era and to concern challenges based on rights most commonly affected by legislation from the apartheid era.[46] Figure 3.1 highlights how the rights to equality, fair trial, and access to court have dominated the court's docket since 1994.

These data are not surprising. The apartheid system was built on inequality entrenched in law, with much of that law inconsistent with the equality provisions of the interim Constitution (section 8) and the 1996 Constitution (section 9). At the same time, the apartheid government sought to quell opposition to its racist regime with oppressive and draconian criminal procedures, for example allowing detention without trial, limited fair trial procedures, and strict criminal sentencing. With

[46] Of the 101 cases analysed here, 62 involve legislation enacted prior to 1994. Of the 83 rights the court found to be unjustifiable, 52 (62.7 per cent) were contained in statutory provisions enacted prior to 1994. Further, these 52 cases in which apartheid-era legislation was found to impose unjustifiable limits on rights represent 85.2 per cent of all the apartheid-era provisions that were challenged.

these criminal procedure provisions still on the books in 1994, the court faced several challenges to these provisions on the grounds that they infringed the right to fair trial (section 35). Similarly, the right of access to court (section 34) made the legal process available as a way of redressing grievances for many people who had heretofore been unable to rely on the law for protection: laws limiting access to court have been challenged only slightly fewer times than criminal procedure provisions. Finally, the apartheid government also relied on laws restricting freedom of expression and association as a means to undermine anti-apartheid organizations. Challenges to these apartheid-era laws, combined with challenges to post-apartheid legislation regulating speech, raise the right to freedom of expression and association to the fourth-most relied on right in South Africa's constitutional jurisprudence.

It is also worth noting that all 21 limitations of the right to equality were found to be unjustifiable and struck down. A similar pattern is true for the right to property, where in four out of five cases included in the analysis the court found the infringement to be unjustifiable.[47] The explanation for this lies in the fact that the constitutional protections against both discrimination and deprivation of property are subject to 'internal' limitations: section 9(3) of the Constitution prohibits unfair discrimination, and section 25(1) prohibits arbitrary deprivation of property. These qualifications – the prohibitions on *unfair* discrimination and *arbitrary* deprivation – allow the state to discriminate fairly and to deprive people of property non-arbitrarily. In other words, discrimination is justifiable if it is fair, and deprivation of property is justifiable if it occurs non-arbitrarily.

The court's inquiries into the unfairness of discrimination and the arbitrariness of deprivation of property have come to rely on the same kind of PA the court conducts under the 'external' limitations clause in section 36. Indeed, the Constitutional Court observed in *National Credit Regulator*, a case alleging an arbitrary deprivation of property by statute, that the inquiry into proportionality at the limitations stage would merely duplicate the inquiry into arbitrariness at the infringement stage:

> The immediate question is: can the deprivation of property which is indeed arbitrary, ever be a reasonable and justifiable limitation in an open

[47] In the fifth case, *Transvaal Agricultural Union v Minister of Land Affairs & Another* 1997 (2) SA 621 (CC), the court assumed for the sake of argument that the deprivation had been arbitrary, and thus was a limitation of the right, but dismissed the appellants case on the basis that the limitation was justifiable.

> and democratic society, in terms of section 36(1)? . . . When considering the concept of arbitrariness, Ackermann J opined in *S v Makwanyane and Another* that '[n]either arbitrary action nor laws or rules which are inherently arbitrary or must lead to arbitrary application can, in any real sense, be tested against the precepts or principles of the Constitution.'[48]

The court's approach to determining unfair discrimination considers, similarly, the nature and extent of the discrimination, whether the discrimination serves a legitimate purpose, whether and to what extent the discrimination achieves that purpose, and whether there are less restrictive means to achieve that purpose.[49] The court recognizes explicitly that the inquiry into unfairness contemplates 'questions normally relevant to a limitation analysis under s 36(1) of the Constitution'.[50]

This chapter includes all of the cases where the rights to property or equality were found to have been infringed. PA in these cases thus occurs both in the context of determining that the right has been violated in the first place and whether that limitation is justified, although the latter analysis usually adds little to the former. I have not included any of the cases where discrimination was found to be fair or where the deprivation of property was not arbitrary. In these cases – of which there are several – the rights to equality and property were not infringed and no limitations analysis followed.[51] These cases thus fall outside the scope of this volume.

[48] *National Credit Regulation v Opperman & Others* 2013 (2) SA 1 (CC) [73], quoting *Makwanyane* (n 5) [156].

[49] *Pillay* (n 26) [167] (O'Regan J).

[50] *Pillay* (n 49) [70] (Langa CJ). See also *Shoprite-Checkers (Pty) Ltd v MEC for Economic Development, Environmental Affairs and Tourism, Eastern Cape* 2015 (6) SA 125 (CC) [80]–[83].

[51] See, e.g., *President of the Republic of South Africa & Another v Hugo* 1997 (4) 1 (CC); *Union of Refugee Women & Others v Director: Private Security Industry Regulatory Authority & Others* 2007 (4) SA 395 (CC); *Reflect-All 1025 CC v MEC for Public Transport, Roads and Works, Gauteng* 2009 (6) SA 391 (CC); *Shoprite-Checkers* (n 50); and *City of Tshwane Metropolitan Municipality v Link Africa (Pty) Ltd & Others* 2015 (6) SA 440 (CC). The court does not always rely on PA to find that the rights to equality or property have not been infringed, because the analysis does not necessarily reach the inquiry into the fairness of discrimination or the arbitrariness of a deprivation of property. In *Prinsloo v Van der Linde & Another* 1997 (3) SA 1012 (CC) and *Harksen v Lane NO* 1998 (1) SA 300 (CC), for example, the court found that there was no differentiation between the complainant and other persons which would have obliged the court to consider whether the discrimination was unfair. In *S v Jordan* 2002 (6) SA 642 (CC), the Constitutional Court rejected an argument that the criminal proscription of prostitution unfairly discriminated against women, on the basis that the impugned provision applied equally to male and female sex workers and thus did not discriminate against women at all (paras 8–20). On the other hand, the court has taken an expansive

The three limitations of the right to be free from cruel, inhuman, or degrading treatment or punishment were also all found to be unjustifiable and struck down. While this is an admittedly small sample from which to draw any conclusions, it may be that the state will be hard pressed to convince a court that cruel, inhuman, or degrading treatment is ever justifiable. Indeed, the international law right against torture is explicitly absolute, and admits of no limitation whatsoever. This may have influenced the South African courts' approach to understanding limitations of the right against cruel, inhuman, or degrading treatment.

In contrast, in all three cases alleging infringements of the right to freedom of religion and conscience, the court found the limitations to be justifiable and upheld the impugned measures. This may suggest that the legislature will find it easier to justify limitations of the right to religion than limitations of the right not to be subjected to cruel, inhuman, or degrading treatment or punishment – although, again, the sample size in both cases is very small here. While the court has consistently rejected any suggestion that there is a hierarchy of rights in the Bill of Rights, the PA nevertheless requires that the more serious the infringement, the more compelling the justification for the infringement must be. Perhaps the explanation lies in the view that the infringement of some rights, by the very nature of those rights, will inevitably be severe or serious and thus more difficult to justify (see Section IV.B).

There are relatively few cases – just five – adjudicated on the basis of a limitation of the right to property. Part of this may be due to the internal limitations clause in the property provision, prohibiting only arbitrary deprivation of property. There are at least three cases I am aware of in which the Constitutional Court found that the deprivations complained of were not arbitrary, and thus did not violate the prohibition against arbitrary deprivation of property.[52] There may well be more cases where the deprivation was found to be non-arbitrary in the lower courts and not

approach both to what constitutes property for the purposes of section 25(1) (*see First National Bank of SA Limited t/a Wesbank v Commissioner for the South African Revenue Services & Another; First National Bank of SA Limited t/a Wesbank v Minister of Finance* 2002 (4) SA 768 (CC), *Transkei Public Servants Association v Government of the Republic of South Africa* 1995 (9) BCLR 1235 (Tk), and to what constitutes a deprivation of property (see, e.g., *Shoprite-Checkers* (n 50) and *Reflect-All* (n 51)). Most of the analytical weight with respect to whether section 25(1) has been limited is carried by the question of whether any deprivation has been arbitrary.

52 *Reflect-All* (n 51), *Shoprite Checkers* (n 51), and *City of Tshwane Metropolitan Municipality* (n 51).

appealed. This may explain why there are fewer cases considering the proportionality of property rights limitations.

The 1996 Constitution's equality provisions are also structured with an internal limitation, however, and there are 21 cases that consider the justifiability of limitations of this right. The existence of an internal limitation cannot entirely explain why there are relatively few cases involving property rights in South Africa. A second speculative explanation is that while there was a vast body of apartheid-era legislation that discriminated unfairly against non-white people and women, there are fewer statutory instruments that permit deprivation of property. Indeed, the apartheid government was committed to legally entrenching unfair discrimination between white and non-white people, and to protecting the land and property white people owned. We should accordingly not expect to see laws allowing arbitrary deprivation of property prior to 1994, precisely because legislation of that era was consistent with the objective of protecting white-owned property. On the contrary, the property right has been seen as an obstacle to land reform: in *Transvaal Agricultural Union*, a group of white farmers argued that the Restitution of Land Rights Act 22 of 1994 infringed the right against arbitrary deprivation of property, but the court concluded that any such limitation of the right was justified by the objective of a more just distribution of land rights.[53] Of the five cases alleging infringement of property rights, four of them attack legislation enacted after 1994. The fifth case, *First National Bank v Minister of Finance*,[54] dealt with movable property and customs duties and thus did not engage the redistributive objectives of the Restitution of Land Rights Act.

[53] *Transvaal Agricultural Union* (n 47). Beyond this, there has not been a concerted legislative effort to redistribute land in a way that limits the right against arbitrary deprivation of property. In early 2018, however, Parliament voted in favour of a motion to introduce a draft constitutional amendment that would remove the clause in section 25(2)(b) that requires the payment of compensation for public-interest oriented the expropriation of land (Wendell Roelf, 'Vote in South Africa's Parliament Moves Land Reform Closer' *Reuters* (27 February 2018) <www.reuters.com/article/us-safrica-land-exproriation/vote-in-south-africas-parliament-moves-land-reform-closer-idUSKCN1GB22I> accessed 29 May 2019). It remains to be seen whether the proposed amendment will affect the prohibition on arbitrary deprivation of property in section 25(1), and whether any legislation allowing expropriation without compensation is subsequently challenged as an unjustifiable limitation of rights.

[54] *First National Bank of SA Limited t/a Wesbank* (n 51).

### C Challenges to Rights Limitations by Subject Area of Limiting Measures

Although the right to equality is the most frequent basis for challenges to the constitutionality of legislation, there is no direct correlation to a particular subject area of legislation that limits the right to equality. Statutory provisions or government decisions that discriminate unfairly and limit the right to equality, in other words, occur in the context of legislation that deals with a diverse range of subjects, including for example family law, health and social security law, labour law, fiscal and tax law, and constitutional, electoral, and parliamentary law, as well as the criminal law. The majority of these equality challenges, however, go to discriminatory elements of the private or civil law (14 out of 21 cases). This is because the apartheid system sought to segregate the economic, social, and family lives of black, Indian, coloured, and white people, as much as it sought to create separate political systems for each. Because the civil law was a tool the apartheid legislature used heavily in the attempt to separate racial groups in South Africa, many of the statutes impugned as infringing rights fall into the category of civil law.

The category of civil law reflected in Figure 3.2 includes, for example, statutes regulating family law (12 cases), labour law (3 cases), company law (3 cases), and the common law of defamation (2 cases). After

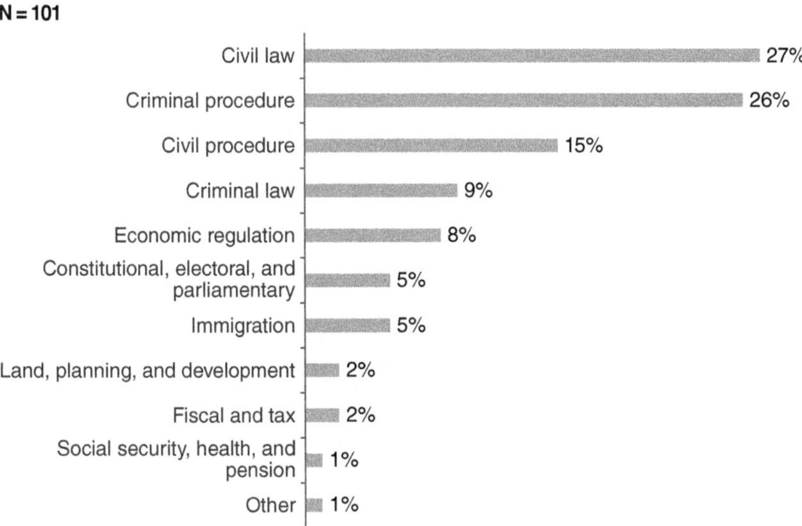


**Figure 3.2** Proportionality cases by subject matter

equality, the most common rights adjudicated under the branch of civil law are the guarantees of freedom of speech and freedom of association (5 cases). These cases involve, for example, challenges to speech-limiting contempt-of-court provisions,[55] the common law of defamation,[56] and the imposition of liability for destruction of private property on the organizers of protected protest action.[57]

In addition, the apartheid government relied on strict criminal procedures to suppress opposition to the system and maintain the political dominance of the white minority. Figure 3.2 illustrates the categories of subject matter into which the 101 cases fall, and the top of the chart is accordingly dominated by challenges to substantive civil law and criminal procedures.

Criminal procedure is a capacious subject category, including challenges to procedural provisions such as 'reverse onus' presumptions of criminal intent upon proof of certain facts,[58] prescribed sentences and punishments, bail requirements, asset forfeiture, and the admissibility of evidence. Only 9 per cent of the cases in this analysis concern challenges to substantive provisions of the criminal law, for example statutory provisions criminalizing sodomy, obscenity, and corporal punishment in schools, and regulating liquor sale through criminal law. The cases in the subject category of civil procedure involve challenges based on the right to access to court (7 cases),[59] liberty (4 cases),[60] due process and access to information, speech and association, and economic, social and culture rights (1 case each).

These subject categories themselves fall into three broad branches of law: criminal law (35 cases), civil or private law (43 cases), and public law (23 cases).[61]

55 *S v Mamabolo* 2001 (3) SA 409 (CC).

56 *Khumalo v Holomisa* 2002 (5) SA 401 (CC); *Johncom Media Investments v Minister for Justice and Constitutional Development* 2009 (4) SA 7 (CC).

57 *South African Transport and Allied Workers Unions & Another v Garvas & Others* 2013 (1) SA 83 (CC).

58 *Manamela* (n 10); *S v Bhulwana, S v Gwadiso* 1996 (1) SA 388 (CC).

59 See, e.g., *Lesapo* (n 8) (statute allowing banks to seize a debtors property on default without a court order); and *Mohlomi v Minister of Defence* 1997 (1) SA 124 (CC) (time bars to civil action against the state).

60 See, e.g., *Coetzee* (n 10) (involving provisions allowing the imprisonment of judgment debtors for civil debts); *Bernstein v Bester NO* 1996 (2) SA 751 (CC) (involving the master of the High Court's power to compel witnesses in bankruptcy proceedings to appear before him or her).

61 The branch of criminal law includes the subject categories of substantive criminal law and criminal procedure. The branch of civil or private law includes the subject categories of

### D South Africa's 'Global' Proportionality Analysis

The limitations analysis mandated by section 36(1) of the Constitution focuses the court's attention on four distinct inquiries. Section 36(1)(b) enjoins an inquiry into 'the importance of the purpose of the limitation' (a worthy purpose test); section 36(1)(d) requires courts to consider the 'relation between the limitation and its purpose' (a rational connection test); and section 36(1)(e) requires an inquiry into whether there are 'less restrictive means to achieve the purpose' (a necessity or less restrictive means test). The fourth leg of the analysis, the inquiry into proportionality in the strict sense, arises from the injunction to consider the importance of the purpose of the limitation alongside the nature of the right (s 36(1)(a)) and the nature and extent of the limitation (s 36(1)(c)). The seriousness or extent of the limitation, considering also the nature of the right on one hand, and the importance of the objective pursued by limiting the right on the other hand, fill the two pans in the scales of a strict PA.

The Constitutional Court has expressly eschewed a sequential approach to PA. All of the factors listed in section 36, the court has said, are relevant in coming to a 'global judgment on proportionality'.[62] No single factor or stage of the analysis is seen by the court as determinative of a rights-limiting measure's proportionality. Instead, the court sees each of the factors as playing a role in the broader consideration of whether a limitation strikes the balance required by the limitations clause. The key question to which all of the separate inquiries of the PA are directed is whether the seriousness of the rights limitation is justified – or balanced – by the value of the objective achieved by limiting it. 'The more substantial the inroad into fundamental rights', the court said in *S v Bhulwana* in 1996, 'the more persuasive the grounds of justification for the infringing legislation must be'.[63]

civil law and civil procedure, as well as one case in the subject category economic regulation (*Chevron v Wilson* 2015 (10) BCLR 1158 (CC), dealing with credit arrangements between private parties). The branch of public law includes cases in the subject areas of economic regulation (except for *Chevron v Wilson*), constitutional, electoral and parliamentary law, immigration, land, planning &development, fiscal & tax law, social security, health and pension, and the single case in the 'other' category (*Glenister v President of the Republic of South Africa & Others* 2011 (3) SA 347 (CC), dealing with the independence of a special police unit).

62 *Manamela* (n 10) [32] (involving a challenge to the constitutionality of a statutory provision providing that a person found in possession of stolen property would be presumed to have known the goods were stolen until the contrary is proven).

63 *Bhulwana* (n 58) [18]. The case dealt with the constitutionality of 'reverse onus' provisions of the Drugs and Drug Trafficking Act 140 of 1992, which provided that a person found in possession of a certain quantity of marijuana (itself a controlled substance under

The limitations analysis would thus appear to turn on a conspectus of the considerations listed in section 36. Consider this account of the court's understanding of the analysis required by the limitations clause in *Manamela*, echoing the dictum in *Bhulwana*:

> It should be noted that the five factors expressly itemised in s 36 are not presented as an exhaustive list. They are included in the section as key factors that have to be considered in an overall assessment as to whether or not the limitation is reasonable and justifiable in an open and democratic society. In essence, the Court must engage in a balancing exercise and arrive at a global judgment on proportionality and not adhere mechanically to a sequential check-list. As a general rule, the more serious the impact of the measure on the right, the more persuasive or compelling the justification must be. Ultimately, the question is one of degree to be assessed in the concrete legislative and social setting of the measure, paying due regard to the means which are realistically available in our country at this stage, but without losing sight of the ultimate values to be protected.[64]

The court's comments here reflect the view that PA should strive to protect and uphold the values at the heart of South Africa's constitutional project. The target of the PA, on this view, is the pursuit and protection of the Constitution's fundamental normative commitments: openness, democracy, equality, freedom, and dignity. The distinct inquiries listed in section 36 are the pillars of a heuristic framework by which the court decides whether striking down a limitation or allowing it will better protect and uphold those values.

Here and elsewhere, the court describes its approach as a rejection of a formalistic, routinized application of the inquiries in the limitations analysis. By considering the factors together in a global PA, the analysis is better able to focus on how upholding or striking down rights-limiting measures upholds the values and normative commitments at the heart of the Constitution. But the court neither proceeds sequentially through the PA until the limitation is found to fail one of the inquiries, nor mechanically considers all four inquiries as a matter of routine. Rather, the court considers as many or as few of the distinct inquiries as are required for it

the Act) would be presumed, until the contrary is proven, to be a 'dealer' of marijuana and guilty of a more serious offence than merely possession. The provision was challenged and consequently struck down as an unjustifiable limitation of the right to be presumed innocent (section 25(3)(c) of the interim Constitution). See also *Manamela* (n 10) [69].

64 *Manamela* (n 10) [32].

to reach a conclusion about how fundamental constitutional values are best served. In *Coetzee*, Sachs J emphasized the foundations of this global PA in the relationship between fundamental constitutional values and the legitimacy of statutory provisions:

> The notion of an open and democratic society is thus not merely aspirational or decorative, it is normative, furnishing the matrix of ideals within which we work, the source from which we derive the principles and rules we apply, and the final measure we use for testing the legitimacy of impugned norms and conduct. If I may be forgiven the excursion, it seems to me that it also follows from the principles laid down in *Makwanyane* that we should not engage in purely formal or academic analyses, nor simply restrict ourselves to ad hoc technicism, but rather focus on what has been called the synergetic relation between the values underlying the guarantees of fundamental rights and the circumstances of the particular case.[65]

Every rights limitation must be justifiable against these constitutional norms and values: this is the understanding of a 'global' model of PA that drives the Constitutional Court's rights limitations jurisprudence.

### *E Division of Justificatory Labour in the Court's Proportionality Jurisprudence*

Of the 101 judgments in the database, the court concluded that 83 of the rights limitations were not justifiable and were struck down. In 18 cases, the court found the limitations to be justifiable and allowed the impugned measures to stand. This section of the chapter considers how the various elements of the PA have operated in these cases, paying particular attention to the 83 cases where rights limitations were struck down as unjustifiable.

In light of the court's professed preference for value-based reasoning and global analysis rather than sequential technicism, we might expect to see the elements of the PA that focus on value-based reasoning carrying comparatively more weight in the court's jurisprudence. In practical terms, we would expect that the court's assessment of the justifiability of rights limitations will only rarely rely on the conclusion that a rights limitation is not rationally connected to its purported objectives or does not restrict rights as little as possible as the sole reason for striking down a rights limitation. We expect that the court will more frequently rely on

[65] *Coetzee* (n 10) [46] (footnotes omitted).

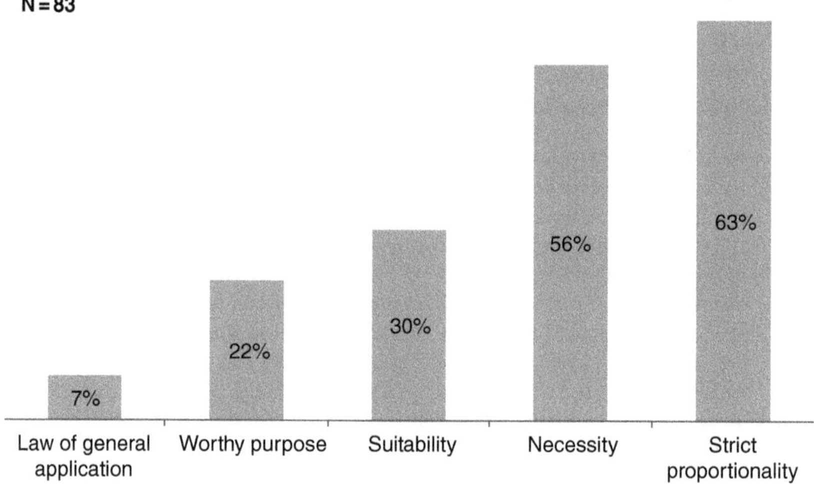


**Figure 3.3** Frequency of failure at each stage of proportionality analysis

the inquiry into whether the objective is consistent with the values at the foundation of the constitutional project, and whether the limitation of rights advances the constitutional project more effectively than prohibiting the limitation of the right.

This expectation is largely borne out by the quantitative data in Figure 3.3. The court found rights-limiting measures to be disproportionate in the strict sense in nearly two thirds of all cases where the limitation was found to be unjustifiable (52 cases out of 83, or 63 per cent). It found limitations to be more restrictive than necessary to achieve the objective pursued (or not to be minimally impairing) in over half of these cases (46.5 cases, or 56 per cent).[66] The court found 30.1 per cent of limitations

[66] I should briefly explain how the data include a half of a case. A handful of the 101 judgments analysed here consider more than one constitutional claim: for example, some cases involve separate challenges to more than one statutory provision or rule of common law, and other cases involve separate challenges based on infringements of more than one constitutional right. These multi-faceted decisions have been coded as single observations. Where more than one provision in a statute was challenged, the case is coded according to whether any part of the impugned statute was struck down as an unjustifiable limitation of a constitutional right. In both *Bhe & Others v Khayelitsha Magistrate & Others* 2005 (1) SA 580 (CC) and *De Vos N.O & Others v Minister of Justice and Constitutional Development & Others* 2015 (9) BCLR 1026 (CC), for example, two separate legal provisions were challenged as unjustifiably limiting rights, and struck down because they failed to meet the requirements of different elements of the PA. The two

to have no rational connection to a worthy purpose (25 cases), while 22.3 per cent of limitations were found to pursue no purpose important enough to justify the limitation of a right (18.5 cases). In 7 per cent of cases (6 cases) the court did not embark on a full PA because the rights limitation was not imposed by a law of general application and could not be saved by the application of section 36.

These data confirm that disproportionality in the strict sense forms part of the court's overall conclusion that the limitation is unjustifiable more often than any other element of the PA. However, in light of the court's emphasis on value-based reasoning and the need to reach an overall or global assessment on proportionality, we might have expected the court to consider proportionality in the strict sense in 100 per cent of cases. Against this expectation, considering proportionality in the strict sense in just 63 per cent of cases is actually surprisingly low. It is worth examining this datum briefly. Of the 31 cases out of 83 (37 per cent) in which the court found the limitation unjustifiable without considering its proportionality in the strict sense, five cases (6 per cent) are those where no PA was conducted at all because the limitation was not imposed by a law of general application.

Moreover, a further 12 of the remaining 26 cases are those where the court concluded the limitation pursued a purpose that is not important enough to justify the limitation of rights at all. In these 12 cases, the court did not need to consider proportionality in the strict sense in order to reach an evaluative judgment as to whether the limitation advanced constitutional values or not, because it had already made an evaluative judgment in the context of the worthy purpose inquiry.

Of the remaining 14 cases where the court did not consider proportionality in the strict sense, in only one case (i.e. less than 1 per cent of all 83 cases) did the court conclude that the limitation was unjustifiable without considering either the importance of the objective or proportionality in the strict sense. In this single outlying case, *Minister of Home Affairs v NICRO*,[67] the court was presented with the argument that not making provisions for convicted prisoners to vote is justified by the

failures in each case have been coded as half of an observed failure. In all of the cases where the court considered more than one rights infringement, the outcome of the PA was the same for each right (i.e., each right infringement was found to be justifiable or to fail the limitations test at the same stage of the analysis), meaning that there are no half-observations in this respect.

67 *Minister of Home Affairs v National Institute for Crime Prevention and the Re-integration of Offenders (NICRO) & Others* 2005 (3) SA 280 (CC).

objective of saving costs and logistical expenses. The court preferred not to confirm or deny that this was an important objective consistent with constitutional values in this case, noting that in a developing country facing resource constraints there may be occasions where saving costs might be an important government objective. But the court concluded that there was no evidence establishing in fact that extending to prisoners the voting arrangements already in place for people of limited mobility would impose any significant additional costs or burdens on the government.[68] The court disposed of the matter on the basis that there was no rational connection between the state's failure to act and the objective of cost-savings.

On a related note, the rates at which measures fail the suitability (rational connection) and necessity (least restrictive means) tests are themselves high: they are certainly not inconsequential to the court's reasoning. The court's emphasis on value-based reasoning, and its rejection of formality and technicism in its reasoning, should not be understood to imply that it will not consider suitability and necessity in assessing the justifiability of rights limitations. Rather, the implication is that the court will rely more frequently on the overall balance that the limitation strikes between competing values. This is reflected in the fact that while the court does rely on findings that a limitation is unsuitable or unnecessary in 30 and 56 per cent of cases, respectively, it still relies more frequently on the finding that a limitation is disproportionate in the strict sense to conclude that it is unjustifiable.

However, we also might have expected that the court's preference for global rather than formal reasoning, and for holistic rather than sequential or technical reasoning, would lead the Court to consider all the elements of the PA in every judgment. This is not the case: in 47 cases out of 83 (57 per cent) the court strikes a limitation down without considering at least one of the inquiries in the PA. This controverts any claim on the part of the court to be conducting a truly global analysis, if global is understood to mean the Court considers each of the inquiries that form part of the PA. The court's 'global' judgment on proportionality should therefore be understood in a more nuanced fashion, to refer to a mode of analysis that considers whether the limitation advances South Africa's constitutional commitments rather than simply insisting on a mechanical or perfunctory inquiry into each of the legs of the analysis.

[68] ibid [47]–[51].

The inquiries into the suitability or necessity of the mechanisms by which the legislature pursues its objectives are largely evidence-based or technical inquiries going to the efficacy of the limitation and whether the limitation is narrowly tailored to its objectives. They do not consider directly whether allowing or striking down the limitation best promotes constitutional values (although an ineffective or unnecessarily broad limitation is of course unlikely to do so). By contrast, the inquiry into the importance of the purpose of the limitation allows courts to examine whether there are justifications or compelling reasons for limiting a right in the first place, and the inquiry into proportionality in the strict sense investigates whether the seriousness of the rights limitation is warranted by the benefits that the limiting measure delivers. These elements of the limitations analysis turn on and operationalize constitutional values, and rely on value-based reasoning.

The data in Figure 3.3 present an incomplete picture, however. While these data indicate that the court relies on both value-neutral and value-based considerations in reaching its overall conclusion on proportionality, they do not indicate the weight that the court attaches to these different considerations in reaching this overall conclusion. It is therefore important to identify those cases in which the court relies on a single inquiry in the PA to conclude that a limitation is unjustifiable, and to identify how frequently the court relies exclusively on the technical, evidence-based inquiries compared to the value-based elements of the PA.

Figure 3.4 reflects the cases in which the court decides that a limitation is unjustifiable without considering all the elements of the PA, and in particular without considering whether the limitation is disproportionate in the strict sense. Each column indicates the percentage of the limitations found to fail a particular stage of the PA, where that failure was sufficient for the court to conclude that the limitation was unjustifiable and to dispense with the other inquiries. In other words, the chart indicates how frequently the court terminated its PA after reaching the conclusion that the impugned measure failed a particular inquiry. The sample size for each column is thus the total number of failures on each leg of the analysis – i.e. the failures illustrated in each column in Figure 3.3 – and is accordingly different for each column.

Figure 3.4 does not include data for analyses that end after the inquiry into proportionality in the strict sense, because this inquiry usually ends the analysis in any case and often follows on from inquiries into whether the limitation meets the other three elements of proportionality. Overall,

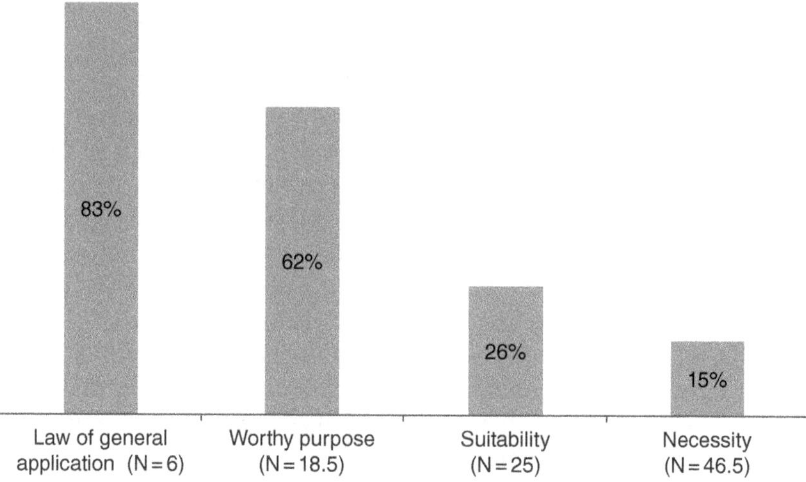


**Figure 3.4** Termination of proportionality analysis after failure

there are 29 cases out of 83 where the limitation was struck down, where the PA did not include consideration of all the legs of the PA. In other words, in 34.9 per cent of cases the limitation was found to be unjustifiable without the court considering proportionality in the strict sense.

It is also worth noting here that in only 4 cases out of the 83 where the impugned limitation was struck down (5 per cent) did the court rely solely on the inquiry into strict proportionality.[69] In none of these cases did the court consider the other legs of the analysis in any meaningful sense. On the strength of the court's commitment to value-based reasoning, however, we might have expected this number to be far higher. The implication here is that while the court sees the PA as an inherently value-oriented exercise focused on constitutional values, it nevertheless relies on the inquiry into proportionality in the strict sense more to confirm the normative conclusions of the other inquiries than as a stand-alone reason for striking down a limitation. The fact that these four cases exist, alongside a single case where the limitation was found to adopt an unnecessarily restrictive approach but was upheld as

[69] *S v Mbatha* 1996 (2) SA 464 (CC); *S v Niemand* 2002 (1) SA 21 (CC); *Ex Parte Minister of Safety and Security & Others: In Re S v Walters & Another* 2002 (4) SA 613 (CC); *DE v RH* 2015 (5) SA 83 (CC).

proportionate nevertheless,[70] indicates that the inquiry into proportionality in the strict sense is conceptually distinct from the other inquiries in the analysis. It remains important to emphasize, however, that disproportionality in the strict sense is rarely the only basis on which the court concludes that a limitation does not advance constitutional values as faithfully as protecting constitutional rights against limitation.

In similar fashion, in 83 per cent of cases where the limitation was imposed by means other than a law of general application (five out of six cases), the court struck the measure down without embarking on the PA at all. This is to be expected, since the imposition of a limitation by way of a law of general application is a gateway into the PA in section 36: the section does not apply, and limitations cannot be justified in its terms, if the limitation is imposed by means other than a law of general application.[71]

In 62 per cent of cases in which the court found that the objective sought by the limitation was not consistent with constitutional values (11.5 out of 18.5 cases), it struck down the limitation without considering any other elements of the PA. This is a high termination rate – higher than for any other inquiry in the analysis – and indicates that the inquiry into the importance of the objective of a rights limitation is more likely to be fatal to the government's attempt to justify a rights limitation than any other element of the PA.

This is consistent with the court's view of limitations analysis as being focussed on upholding constitutional values. The Constitution is a transformative document, and we should expect that the rights it protects can only be limited in pursuit of purposes that are congruent with the core values that the Constitution entrenches. A rights limitation that is premised on the pursuit of an objective that is inconsistent with constitutional values can never be proportionate, even if that limitation itself is, on the evidence, the least restrictive means to achieve that purpose and is likely to achieve that purpose. In these cases, there is nothing to be gained from conducting the rest of the PA.

[70] *S v Dlamini; S v Dladla and Others; S v Joubert; S v Schietekat* 1999 (4) SA 623 (CC) (Schietekat case).

[71] The one case where the court proceeded with a PA is *Hoffmann* (n 9), where the court relied on the principle of proportionality to find that the impugned measure amounted to unfair discrimination and was thus a limitation of equality rights. The court did note that section 36 did not apply and that the state could not rely on section 36 to justify the limitation of the right.

By contrast, the court terminates the analysis and does not proceed to consider other elements of the inquiry in just 26 per cent of limitations that fail the suitability test (6.5 cases out of 25), and in only 15 per cent of limitations that fail the necessity test (7 cases out of 46.5). The comparatively lower rates at which these analyses are terminated indicate that the inquiries into suitability and necessity carry less argumentative weight for the court. That is, a conclusion that a limitation is unsuitable or unnecessarily restrictive is unlikely to be sufficient for the court to conclude that the limitation is unjustifiable. In most cases where the court finds that a limitation is unsuitable or unnecessarily restrictive, it will continue the PA anyway.

What about the 38 per cent of cases (7 cases out of 18.5) in which the court continued the analysis even though it found the limitation to fail the worthy purpose test? This is not an insignificant number, and it raises the question of why the court continued with the analysis at all if the purpose was not important. In three of these seven cases, the court did not consider the suitability or necessity tests: the only other element of the analysis it considered was proportionality in the strict sense. In these three cases, then, the court did not consider the factual or value-neutral elements of the inquiry. It relied entirely on the value-centric elements of the inquiry.

And similarly, in the majority of cases where a limitation was found to fail either the suitability or the necessity tests and was struck down, the court nevertheless considered other elements of the PA to reach the conclusion that the limitation was unjustifiable. The inquiries into proportionality in the strict sense and the importance of the purpose of the limitation contributed to the court's conclusion that the limitation was unjustifiable in about 80 per cent of cases where the limitation was found to fail the suitability test, and in about 90 per cent of cases where the limitation was found to be unnecessarily restrictive.

These data indicate that the court tends to rely more heavily on evaluative rather than evidentiary considerations in concluding that a limitation is unjustifiable. This is consistent with the court's position that a global proportionality assessment must strive to protect fundamental constitutional values. Even where the court finds, as a matter of fact, that a measure is unlikely to achieve its objectives (i.e. that it fails the suitability test) or that there are less restrictive alternatives to achieving its objective (i.e. that it fails the necessity test), it usually relies also on the value-based assessments that the importance of the objective does not justify the rights limitation or that the balance between the extent of the limitation and the values advanced by the limitation is disproportionate, to conclude that the limitation is not justifiable in an open and democratic society based on dignity, equality, and freedom.

The court's global approach is not one that insists in every case that each element of the PA be considered. Rather, the court's focus is on whether, on balance, allowing a particular limitation or striking it down and protecting the right advances constitutional values more faithfully. A limitation that is unnecessarily restrictive of rights or is unlikely to achieve its objective will not advance those values faithfully, since it imposes limits on rights with little to gain in return. But even in these cases where a limitation fails the suitability or necessity tests, the court usually proceeds to consider the balance between the values sought by the limitation and those protected by the right affected.

In nearly all cases, a rights-limiting measure that fails the necessity or suitability tests will also fail the test of proportionality in the strict sense. In one case – although it is the only one of its kind in South Africa of which I am aware – a rights limitation was upheld even though the Court found it to be unnecessarily restrictive. In *S v Dlamini; S v Dladla; S v Joubert; S v Schietekat* ('*S v Schietekat*'), the court found that even though the limitation had not adopted the least restrictive means to achieve an important purpose, the balance the limitation struck between the values protected by the right and the values advanced by the limitation was nevertheless proportionate.[72] The data generated by the court's case law, and reasoning such as in *S v Schietekat*, illustrate that the court does indeed rely primarily on value-based reasoning, supplemented by formal or evidence-based analysis, to reach a global assessment on proportionality.

## F *Justification Requirements other than Proportionality*

The limitations clause allows the limitation of rights only in terms of a 'law of general application'. This definitional threshold has two components: whether the limiting measure is 'law', and whether the law is of 'general application'.

[72] Schietekat case (n 70). The case concerned limitations to due process rights in order to provide magistrates with information on which to determine bail conditions. The court looked to foreign jurisdictions for examples of similar provisions that restrict due process rights less, but nevertheless concluded that limitations in question were nevertheless proportionate in South Africa.

Case law reveals the following sources of public authority to constitute law for the purposes of section 36: provincial regulations;[73] presidential decrees;[74] municipal by-laws;[75] common law;[76] customary law;[77] rules of court;[78] rules of parliament;[79] and international conventions.[80] In six cases, limitations were imposed by means other than a law of general application and fell outside the scope of section 36.

In *De Lille*, the High Court and the Supreme Court of Appeal (SCA) concluded that the suspension of a Member of Parliament for comments made in a session of Parliament infringed the MP's rights to freedom of expression, just administrative action, and access to court, and that Parliament's decision to suspend the MP was not authorized by any law.[81] The High Court noted specifically that no authority for the suspension of the MP could be found in 'the Constitution, the Powers and Privileges of Parliaments Act of 1963 or the Standing Rules of the National Assembly'.[82] In *Hoffmann*, the state-owned airline decided not to employ an HIV-positive job applicant, without any statutory authority,[83] and in *Dladla and Others v City of Johannesburg*, the applicants complained that a state-run shelter for homeless people had established rules of conduct, not authorized by any law of general application, which infringed rights.[84]

In *Pretoria City Council v Walker*, the selective enforcement of rates and tax assessments against the residents of only predominantly white neighbourhoods was not authorized by a law of general application, even though the court suggested that the broader policy framework by which rates were assessed differently against residents of historically white and black neighbourhoods would have been a law of general application for

[73] *Larbi-Odam* (n 25).
[74] *Hugo* (n 51).
[75] *Du Toit v Minister of Transport* 2006 (1) SA 297 (CC).
[76] *Du Plessis & Others v De Klerk & Another* 1996 (3) SA 850 (CC); *Shabalala & Others v Attorney-General of the Transvaal & Another* 1996 (1) SA 725 (CC); *S v Mamabolo* 2001 (3) SA 409 (CC).
[77] *Bhe* (n 66); *Taylor v Kurtstag NO & Others* 2005 (1) SA 362 (W).
[78] *Ingledew v Financial Services Board: In re Financial Services Board v Van der Merwe & Another* 2003 (4) SA 584 (CC).
[79] *De Lille* (1998) (n 7) [37].
[80] *Sonderup v Tondelli & Another* 2001 (1) SA 1171 (CC); *Chief Family Advocate & Another v G* 2003 (2) SA 599 (W).
[81] *De Lille* (1998) (n 7); De Lille (1999) (n 7).
[82] *De Lille* (1998) (n 7) [37].
[83] *Hoffmann* (n 9).
[84] (2) SA 327 (CC).

the purposes of section 36.[85] Whether broader policy with general application will constitute law of general application is open to debate, however.[86] The question of policy is particularly relevant in the case of the economic and social rights in South Africa's bill of rights. While 'negative' civil and political rights restrain government from interfering in the public's exercise of rights except in terms of laws of general application, the Constitution's economic and social rights impose positive obligations on government to take legislative and other steps, including policy steps, to progressively realize rights to housing, food and water, health care, and social security. The limitation of these positive rights is thus as likely to occur through policy as through legislation. If policy is not recognized as 'law of general application' for the purposes of section 36(1), then a policy that limits the economic and social rights set out in section 26 and section 27 will not be capable of being saved by the limitations clause. This sets a very high bar for the state to meet in its attempts to meet positive rights obligations. In practice, however, most policy commitments to progressively realize economic and social rights are implemented through legislation in any case, making the consideration of whether policy itself constitutes law of general application largely academic.

Omissions that infringe rights may not be authorized by a law of general application and thus will not be capable of being justified under section 36. In *Modderklip*, the state had failed to ensure the enforcement of a court order and infringed the applicant's right of access to court. No law authorized this omission, and section 36 was held to be inapplicable 'since no law of general application' limited the applicant's right.[87] In *August*, similarly, the court held that the state's failure to provide a mechanism for prisoners to vote limited political rights. No law of general application could be relied on to authorize this omission.[88]

The requirement that a law that limits rights be a 'law of general application' is, broadly speaking, meant to ensure that the limitations

[85] 1998 (2) SA 363 (CC).

[86] Stu Woolman and Henk Botha, 'Limitations' in Stu Woolman and Michael Bishop (eds), *Constitutional Law of South Africa* (2nd ed, Juta 2005) 53; Iain Currie and Johan De Waal, *The Bill of Rights Handbook* (5th ed, Juta, 2005) 173; Danie Brand, 'Food' in Stu Woolman and Michael Bishop (eds), *Constitutional Law of South Africa* (2nd ed, Juta 2005).

[87] *President of the Republic of South Africa v Modderklip Boerdery* 2005 (5) SA 3 (CC) [52].

[88] *August & Another v Electoral Commission* 1999 (3) SA 1 (CC) [23].

clause does not allow bills of attainder that limit the rights of specific individuals or groups of individuals.[89] The jurisprudence on this element of the section 36 limitations analysis in South Africa is not extensive. Generally, once a court has found that rights have been limited in terms of law, it will go on to find that the law in question has the characteristic of general application. There are two primary considerations in which the courts engage in reaching this conclusion.

The first is whether the law meets a requirement of parity, or whether it applies equally to all classes of persons in similar situations.[90] In *De Lille*, in which an MP was suspended from parliament following a speech in the lower house to which members of the majority party objected, the Supreme Court of Appeal described parliament's actions in punishing an opposition MP for comments critical of the government as an exercise of power targeted specifically at a single individual.[91] This exercise of power was not of general application.

The second consideration going to general application is whether the law is publicly available and accessible. Where members of the public are unaware of the legal rules in terms of which their rights may be limited, they will be unable to regulate their conduct in light of the provisions of the law.[92] In *President of the Republic South Africa v Hugo* Justice Mokgoro asked, but did not answer, whether directives or guidelines that are not broadly available to the public but nevertheless govern officials in their interactions with members of the public meet the requirement of

[89] In *Gainsford & Others NNO v Tiffski Property Investments (Pty) Ltd & Others* 2012 (3) SA 35 (SCA), the Supreme Court of Appeal lent support to this view in the context of section 25(1) of the Constitution, which provides that 'No one may be deprived of property except in terms of law of general application'. The court quoted favourably the following passage: 'As it occurs in s 25(1), the requirement that any deprivation of property must occur in terms of law of general application is intended to protect individuals from being deprived of property by bills of attainder or other laws that single them out for discriminatory treatment'. See Theunis Roux, 'Property' in Stu Woolman and Michael Bishop (eds), *Constitutional Law of South Africa* (2nd ed, Juta 2005) 46–21. In addition, support for this proposition can be found in the interim Constitution's drafting history. Previous versions of the provision stated that limitations may occur only in terms of 'a law applying generally and not solely in an individual case'. Technical Committee on Fundamental Rights, 'Seventh Report' (29 July 1993).

[90] See the disagreement between the High Court and the Constitutional Court in the application of this principle in *Joubert v Van Rensburg* 2001 (1) SA 753 (W), 797 and *Mkangeli & Others v Joubert & Others* 2001 (2) SA 1191 (CC).

[91] *Speaker of the National Assembly v De Lille* (1999) (n 7) [17].

[92] *Sunday Times v Handyside* (1979) 2 EHRR 245.

general application.[93] She warned that if such directives and guidelines serve important social objectives and limit rights in order to do so, but do not constitute laws of general application, courts might be persuaded to uphold the directives by defining the scope of rights more narrowly in order to find that there is no rights limitation. This would enable a court to 'save' the impugned internal directive or guideline and ensure it achieves its important purpose, even though the limitations provisions of section 36 do not apply.

Woolman and Botha suggest that laws of general application must display characteristics of precision, clarity, and non-arbitrariness.[94] In practice, however, the courts have considered whether a rights-limiting provision has these characteristics during the PA, once the threshold requirement of general application has been cleared. Rights-limiting laws that are imprecise, unclear, or arbitrary have usually been found not to be rationally connected to the purposes for which the limitation is imposed, and unjustifiable on that basis (see Section VI). Provisions that are overbroad as a result of imprecision, lack of clarity, or arbitrariness – in other words, provisions that are not narrowly tailored to the objective sought to be achieved – are often found to be unnecessary and thus unjustifiable (see Section VII). For example, in *Case*, the court found the prohibition on 'obscenity' in the Indecent or Obscene Photographic Matter Act 37 of 1967 to be overbroad, and thus not minimally impairing or necessary for the achievement of its objectives. The indeterminacy of the provision resulted in its application to forms of expression beyond only those connected to the statute's objectives.[95]

### G *Conflict between Rights and Conflict with Public Interest*

The Constitutional Court sees the content of constitutional rights as 'delimited by the rights of the community as a whole'.[96] A conflict between rights will usually be resolved at the initial stage of rights analysis rather than at the limitations stage, with the scope of activity protected by a constitutional right defined or constrained in such a way

93 *Hugo* (n 51) [100] (considering whether a decision to pardon female prisoners with children under a certain age unfairly discriminated against make prisoners with children under a certain age).

94 Woolman and Botha (n 86) 62–65.

95 *Case & Another v Minister of Safety and Security; Curtis v Minister of Safety and Security & Others* 1996 (3) SA 617 (CC) [61].

96 *Bernstein* (n 60) [79].

that the exercise of the right does not infringe on the exercise of other rights by other people (see Section IV. A). The purpose of a law of general application, however, may be the protection of a constitutional right. If this law of general application limits a second right, then the law can only be upheld if the limitation of the second right can be shown to be reasonable and justifiable in terms of section 36. The strict PA then weighs the importance of the right sought to be protected, as the limitation's objective, against the seriousness of the infringement of the second right.

In *Christian Education*, for example, the court considered the prohibition of corporal punishment of school pupils in terms of the South African Schools Act 84 of 1996.[97] The objective of the prohibition was the protection of children's rights to dignity and to be free from physical and mental anguish (the latter is an element of the right to freedom and security of the person). The applicants complained that the prohibition infringed the right to religious freedom, to the extent that their religious convictions required them to discipline their children through beatings. The court agreed the prohibition limited the right to religious freedom, but that the importance of the objective served by the limitation – that is, upholding the rights of children – justified that limitation.

In *Khumalo v Holomisa*, the court had to consider whether the common law of defamation, which is aimed at protecting rights to dignity and privacy, imposed a justifiable limitation on the freedom of expression. Resolving the dispute required the court to decide whether the extent of the limitation on freedom of expression was proportional to the need to protect people against negative or unflattering media coverage. In *Fourie*, the court held that while the prohibition on same-sex marriage was an unjustifiable limitation of the right to equality, ministers of religion could not be compelled to consecrate same-sex marriages if that offended their religious views.[98]

In all of these cases, the limitations analysis is reduced to a weighing up of the seriousness of the infringement of one right against the value of upholding another right. The court noted in *Christian Education* that the protection of a particular constitutional right or rights provides a compelling reason for the limitation of other rights,[99] but since the court holds to the view that there is no hierarchy of importance in

[97] *Christian Education* (n 20).
[98] *Fourie* (n 37) [90]–[98].
[99] *Christian Education* (n 20) [50].

constitutional rights (see further Section IV-B), the balancing exercise involved in determining whether to uphold or strike down the impugned law cannot simply compare the value of each right. Rather, the court must compare the extent or the seriousness of rights infringements that would occur without the protections of the impugned law, with the extent or the seriousness of rights infringement imposed by the impugned law. In this light, the court has admitted that while there is no hierarchy of rights, 'there are circumstances in which one right will take precedence over others'.[100]

This approach is consistent with the court's global assessment of proportionality, guided by the question of which of two competing policy options better advances the constitutional commitment to the values of openness, democracy, equality, dignity, and freedom. The rights in the Bill of Rights are closely connected to these values, with the result that a law that seeks to protect rights – even if it poses a threat to other rights – will be seen as a compelling or persuasive reason for the limitation of the second right. Where the objective of rights limitation is not the protection of some other right, however, the state will have to show that the objectives pursued by the impugned measure advance or fulfil core constitutional values in other ways, in order to justify the rights limitation.

## IV Limitation of a Constitutional Right

In 95 of the 101 cases considered in this chapter, the court decided that the rights the applicants relied on had been infringed, and then proceeded to the limitations analysis. In six cases, however, the court refrained from reaching a finding that the impugned law infringed the rights concerned, instead assuming for argument's sake that they were infringed.[101] In all these cases, the court went on to conclude that the impugned measure would not have been justifiable had it limited rights, striking the measures down for that reason. In the cases where the court

[100] *South African Broadcasting Corp Ltd v National Director of Public Prosecutions* 2007 (1) SA 523 (CC) [55].

[101] ibid; *National Director of Public Prosecutions v Mohamed* 2003 (4) SA 1 (CC); *Sonderup* (n 80); *Metcash Trading Limited v Commissioner for the South African Revenue Service and Another* 2001 (1) SA 1109 (CC); *Christian Education* (n 20); *Transvaal Agricultural Union* (n 47).

concludes that rights have been limited, the extent of the limitation is crucial to the PA by which the justifiability of the limitation is assessed.

### *A The Scope of a Constitutional Right and the Seriousness of Rights Infringements*

The Constitutional Court determines the scope of a right with reference to core constitutional values and the established content of other rights. Early decisions debated two competing approaches. The prevailing approach has evolved out of the second of these approaches.

The first approach proposed that rights should be interpreted extremely broadly, on the understanding that any activity that could notionally fit within the meaning of a right is protected by the right.[102] In a minority judgment in *Ferreira v Levin*, Ackermann J preferred to interpret the right to freedom in section 11 of the interim Constitution broadly and generously and to allow restriction of the right under the limitations clause rather than through a restricted definition of the right to freedom.[103] Ackermann J's expansive reading of the right was rejected by a majority of the court, however.

A second approach proposed to interpret the right more narrowly, based on the values that the South African Constitution aims to serve. Section 39(1) of the Constitution prompts this 'value-based' approach to the interpretation of the text of the Constitution:

> When interpreting the Bill of Rights, a court, tribunal or forum-
>
> (a) must promote the values that underlie an open and democratic society based on human dignity, equality and freedom.

On this approach, rights are to be interpreted and their scope circumscribed in light of five core values of South Africa's constitutional project: openness, democracy, human dignity, equality, and freedom. Of course, the limitation of rights under section 36 also depends on a consideration of these five values, leading Sachs J to comment in *Coetzee* that there are commonalities that run through the logic of rights interpretation and rights limitation, and that 'faithfulness to the Constitution is best achieved by locating the two-stage balancing process within a holistic, value-based and case-oriented framework'.[104]

[102] Woolman and Botha (n 86) ch 34, 17.
[103] *Ferreira* (n 42) [45].
[104] *Coetzee* (n 10) [46].

In *Bernstein v Bester*, the court reiterated that rights adjudication remains a two-stage inquiry, whatever the commonality between the inquiries into infringement and justification.[105] In a majority judgment, Ackermann J turned away from the notional approach he took in *Ferreira*, and defined the scope of the right to privacy as 'delimited by the rights of the community as a whole'.[106] The scope of a right is not absolute, protecting everything to which it notionally pertains, but depends at least on the extent to which other rights are affected by the exercise of that right. The court has relied on this approach in subsequent cases such as *Beinash*, where the court defined the scope of the right of access to court subject to the competing right to fair trial and the constitutional imperative on the state to ensure the effectiveness of the judicial system (see section 165(4) of the Constitution). The Court held that clogged court rolls undermine an effective judicial system and the right to a speedy trial, with the result that vexatious litigation is not protected within the scope of the right of access to court.[107]

The scope of each right is thus circumscribed by the underlying values of South Africa's Constitution on one hand, and by the content of other rights on the other hand. This shift in focus onto the Constitution's core values has at the same time provided the courts with a matrix for assessing the seriousness or extent of each rights infringement. This development is tied to the distinction between the core and the peripheral content of rights. Section 33(1)(b) of the interim Constitution, like article 19 of Germany's Basic Law, prohibited limitation of the 'essential content' of rights. But the Constitutional Court was reluctant to engage with the concept of essential content in adjudicating limitations under the interim Constitution, and went as far as to express an inability to understand the concept:

> Negating the essential content of a constitutional right is, however, a concept that I have never understood. Nor can I fathom how one applies it to a host of imaginable situations. Baffled as I am by both conundrums, I would have been at a loss to hold that the denial of the right in question either had or had not negated its essential content.[108]

105 *Bernstein* (n 60) [71].
106 ibid [79].
107 *Beinash & Another v Ernst & Young & Others* 1999 (2) SA 116 (CC).
108 *Azanian Peoples Organisation (AZAPO) & Others v President of the Republic of South Africa & Others* 1996 (4) SA 671 (CC) [66].

Section 36 of the 1996 Constitution does away with the protection of the 'essential content' of rights; but to the extent that the global assessment of proportionality means that more substantial inroads into fundamental rights must be justified on more persuasive grounds, the analysis requires courts to consider the extent of infringements to rights. Section 36(1)(c) itself requires the consideration of the 'nature and extent of the limitation'. Both the court's approach and the implicit structure of section 36 call for distinction between more and less serious infringements of rights.

The test for the seriousness or insignificance of the rights violation follows the structure of the inquiry into whether the core or the periphery of a right has been affected. While neither the court's jurisprudence nor the Constitution imposes an absolute prohibition on limitations to the core of a right, the justifications for a serious infringement of a right – or a limitation of the core of the right – must be very compelling indeed to pass muster.[109] The court's approach has been to identify the core of rights in order to determine the seriousness of the limitation, and thus to identify how compelling the justification for the limitation must be, rather than to protect absolutely the core of each right.

The court has relied on the language of core and periphery to describe serious rights limitations in a handful of cases. 'The way in which we give expression to our sexuality', for example, lies at the core of the right to privacy,[110] while the privacy interest in 'the commercial interests of the prostitute' are at the periphery of the right.[111] In *De Lange v Smuts* the court held that a core component of the right to fair trial is to face the possibility of detention only as an outcome of a process presided over by a judicial officer, and that a civil process that created the possibility of detention without the oversight of a judicial officer struck at the core of the right to fair trial.[112] In *Manamela*, the court held that provisions requiring criminal accused to disprove the presumption that mere possession of stolen property denoted intent to receive stolen property struck

[109] *Manamela* (n 10) [49]; *De Reuck v Director of Public Prosecutions (Witwatersrand Local Division) & Others* 2004 (1) SA 406 (CC) [59].

[110] *National Coalition for Gay and Lesbian Equality & Another v Minister of Justice & Others* 1999 (1) SA 6 (CC) (NCGLE 1 case) [32]–[36].

[111] *Jordan* (n 51) [27]–[29].

[112] 1998 (3) SA 785 (CC) [89] (concerning the constitutionality of provisions of the Insolvency Act 24 of 1936 empowering the presiding officer of a creditors' meeting to commit to prison any person who refuses to cooperate with insolvency investigators).

at the core of the right to be presumed innocent until proven guilty.[113] In each of these cases, it is apparent that the interests that lie at the core of the right, limitation of which would be serious, are those that are closely linked to the rationale for constitutionally protecting a right in the first place.[114] This approach is consistent with the section 36(1)(a) requirement that courts consider 'the nature of the right' in the limitations analysis.

Two other considerations are relevant to inquiry into the 'nature and extent' of the limitation. First, the impact of limitations on vulnerable sections of the community – minorities, historically disadvantaged people, the poor – may be greater than the impact on other members of society (see further Section VIII.C(ii)). It is this disproportionate impact that should be taken into account in determining the extent of the limitation. In *Prince*, for example, the dissenting minority judgments noted that limitation of the right to religious freedom experienced by adherents of the Rastafari faith as a result of the criminalization of marijuana was compounded by the fact that the Rastafari are a politically powerless group which is vulnerable to stigmatization in society as a result of the criminalization of marijuana.[115] In *Coetzee*, the court noted that the limitation on the right of freedom and security of the person imposed by provisions allowing imprisonment for the failure to pay judgment debts impacted the poor and unemployed more severely than other groups in society,[116] and in *Jaftha*, the court concluded that sales in execution of debts of the homes of people who fail to pay trifling debts are more likely to affect the poor and indigent.

[113] *Manamela* (n 10) [49]. See also *De Reuck* (n 109) [59] (prohibitions on child pornography limits 'expression of little value which is found on the periphery of the right'); *South African National Defence Union (SANDU) v Minister of Defence & Another* 1999 (4) SA 469 [7] (holding that the core of the right to freedom of expression involves the right's instrumental value as a guarantor of democracy, its recognition and protection of individual moral agency, and its facilitation of the search for truth by individuals and society). See also *Khosa & Others v Minister of Social Development & Others; Mahlaule & Others v Minister of Social Development & Others* 2004 (6) SA 505 (CC) [119].

[114] The Supreme Court of Canada has taken a similar approach, holding for example that hate speech lies at the periphery of the right to freedom of expression because it is not closely related to the reasons we value free expression. The court listed these underlying justifications for free expression as the facilitation of the democratic process, the search for truth, and self-fulfilment (*R v Keegstra* [1990] 3 SCR 697).

[115] *Prince v President of the Law Society of the Cape of Good Hope* 2002 (2) SA 794 (CC) [52] (Ngcobo J) and [157]–[163] (Sachs J).

[116] *Coetzee* (n 10) [66]–[67].

Second, a total denial of a right will demand more compelling justification than a partial limitation. In considering the constitutionality of the death penalty in *Makwanyane*, the court drew a distinction between 'encroaching upon rights for the purpose of punishment and destroying them altogether'.[117] By contrast, in *Christian Education*, the court held that the prohibition on corporal punishment in schools imposed only a partial limitation of the right to religious freedom. Although the applicants' religious beliefs required corporal punishment of children, parents remained free to impose corporal punishment on their children in their own homes even though the impugned law prohibited corporal punishment in schools.[118]

Third, a temporary limitation of a right is less serious than a long-term or permanent limitation of a right. In *Metcash Trading*, the court held that a rule in the Value Added Tax Act 89 of 1991 that prohibits vendors from challenging the Commissioner of Revenue's tax assessment until after paying the assessed taxes was a justifiable limitation of the right of access to court, because the limitation is temporary.[119] In *Makwanyane*, in contrast, the court emphasized the permanence of the deprivation of the right to life involved the execution of a death sentence.[120]

The court's prevailing approach to determining the scope of a right, as well as how seriously a right has been infringed, is to look into the connection between the right, core constitutional values, and other rights. Once the court has established that an impugned law does intrude on the scope of a right, the seriousness of the intrusion can be determined with reference to three principles that have crystallized in the case law: a serious rights violation is one which strikes at the core rather than the periphery of a right, which constitutes a total rather than a partial denial of the right, and which permanently rather than temporarily infringes the right.

### *B Hierarchy of Rights*

The Constitutional Court remains ambiguous about whether some rights are more important than others, both in the express statements it has

117 *Makwanyane* (n 5) [143].
118 *Christian Education* (n 20) [48]–[51].
119 *Metcash Trading* (n 101) [58]–[62].
120 *Makwanyane* (n 5) [269].

made on the matter and in the logic by which limitations analysis proceeds. On one hand, in *Makwanyane*, Chaskalson P stated quite plainly that

> The rights to life and dignity are the most important of all human rights, and the source of all other personal rights in [the Bill of Rights]. By committing ourselves to a society founded on the recognition of human rights we are required to value these two rights above all others.[121]

On the other hand, the court has held that there is no hierarchy of rights in the South African Constitution and that no one right is more important than others.[122] According to the court, any attempt to set out a fixed hierarchy of rights under the 1996 Constitution would be textually unsupported and uncertain.[123]

In its practice of PA, however, the Constitutional Court has lent some support to the notion of a hierarchy of rights with suggestions that the limitation of some rights, because of the nature of those rights, may be justified only by very compelling reasons. Rights to life, human dignity, bodily integrity, and the right not to be treated in cruel, inhuman, or degrading ways, are central to the society envisaged by the Constitution, and only compelling and persuasive grounds will justify their infringement.[124]

This view is rooted in the interim Constitution, which established a scale of judicial scrutiny of rights infringements with the requirement that the limitation of only certain rights must be 'necessary' in addition to being reasonable and justifiable (s 33(1)(b)(aa) and (bb)). The rights listed in sub-paragraphs (aa) and (bb) included rights to human dignity, freedom and security of the person, freedom of religion and opinion, political rights, fair trial, various children's rights, and the protection against servitude and forced labour.

The additional requirement of 'necessity' in the limitation of certain rights gave rise to disagreements between members of the Constitutional Court:

121 *Makwanyane* (n 5) [144].

122 *The Citizen 1978 (Pty) Ltd & Others v Mcbride (Johnstone & Others, Amici Curiae)* 2011 (4) SA 191 (CC) [148]; *South African Broadcasting Corporation* (n 100) [55], [91], [125]; *Mamabolo* (n 76) [41].

123 *Ferreira* (n 42) [77], [82].

124 *S v Williams* 1995 (3) SA 632 (CC) [76]; *Walters* (n 69) [28]; *National Coalition for Gay and Lesbian Equality & Others v Minister of Home Affairs & Others* 2000 (2) SA 1 (CC) (NCGLE 2 case) [58]; *Bhe* (n 66) [71].

> I respectfully disagree with the [Chief Justice's] view that those freedoms (and by implication other rights) whose limitation is made subject to the 'necessary' test by s 33 of the Constitution are necessarily of a 'higher order' than those freedoms which are not subjected to such an onerous test. A limitation of the s 8 equality right, for example, is not made subject to the more stringent 'necessary' test, yet in my view it could scarcely be said that this right is of a 'lower' order.[125]

These disagreements may have provided the impetus for the removal of the clause in the 1996 Constitution and the court's subsequent declaration that no one right in the Constitution is more important than others.

Despite the court's statements that there is no hierarchy of rights in the Constitution, the injunction in section 36(1)(a) of the Constitution to consider the nature of the right in the limitations analysis suggests that the importance of the right will play some role in the PA.[126] The inquiry into the nature of the right has allowed something like a hierarchy to develop, in the sense that infringements of some rights will only be justifiable on the basis of very compelling reasons. Considering the right to life, the court held in *Makwanyane* that infringements of the right to life will always be very serious, demanding correspondingly compelling reasons to justify any infringement.[127] While neither section 33 of the interim Constitution nor section 36 of the 1996 Constitution refer to the

[125] *Ferreira* (n 42) [58].

[126] The Constitution itself sets out something of a hierarchy of rights in the 'table of non-derogable rights' in section 37. During a state of emergency, the table indicates that some rights cannot be derogated at all (human dignity, life, protections against slavery and servitude) while other rights can be derogated with respect only to certain elements of the right (equality; freedom and security of the person; children's rights; and arrested, accused, or detained persons). All the other rights in the Bill of Rights (i.e. those not listed on the table of non-derogable rights) can be derogated during states of emergency with no restriction.

[127] Halton Cheadle, 'Limitation of Rights' in Halton Cheadle, Dennis Davis, and Nicholas Haysom (eds), *South African Constitutional Law: The Bill of Rights* (Butterworths 2002) 707–8. Compare the South African jurisprudence on the right to life with the jurisprudence of the Indian Supreme Court. The Indian court has interpreted the right to life enshrined in article 21 of the Indian Constitution to include access to a range of economic and social goods including housing and shelter and clean water. Deprivations of access to these goods may infringe the right to life, to the extent that these goods are material to the enjoyment of life, but such deprivations will not completely extinguish life. In South Africa by contrast, access to economic and social goods is entrenched in sections 26 and 27 of the Constitution. The upshot is that South Africa has not had to read the right to life expansively, to include access to the resources guaranteed by other rights in the South Africa Constitution. Any limitation of the right to life in South Africa is a necessarily serious threat to life itself.

'importance' of the right, in *Makwanyane* the court listed 'the nature *and importance* of the right' as a factor to be taken into account in the PA in the context of limitations analysis under the interim Constitution.[128] That the importance of the right has permeated post-1996 limitations analysis is clear from the court's statement in *National Coalition for Gay and Lesbian Equality I*: 'the importance of the right . . . is a factor which of necessity must be taken into account in any proportionality enquiry'.[129]

In the court's view, the importance of some rights means that any limitation will require extremely persuasive or compelling justification. The nature of the right not to be tortured (section 12(1)(d)) is such that any limitation of the right will have to be justified on very persuasive grounds indeed, if it is possible at all to identify certain kinds of torture as less serious than others.[130] But the nature of other rights suggests that, while any infringement of the right must still be justified, some infringements are not that serious and need not be justified on as persuasive grounds. It is conceivable, for example, that the right against cruel, inhuman, or degrading treatment or punishment (section 12(1)(e)) may admit of different degrees of infringement, and indeed, treatment that infringes this right may be less extensive or serious than acts that qualify as torture. Although in the South African case law none of the infringements of the right against cruel, inhuman, or degrading treatment or punishment have been upheld, it is possible that limitations of this right will prove to be more readily justifiable than the right against torture.

In practice, the Constitutional Court has held that certain rights are central to the society envisaged by the Constitution, and only compelling and persuasive reasons will justify their infringement. These are the rights to life, human dignity, bodily integrity, and the right not to be treated in cruel, inhuman, or degrading ways.[131] Despite these rights' centrality, they are not inviolable. The proposal that certain rights would be expressly inviolable was rejected during the constitutional drafting process in the 1990s.[132] This position differs to some extent from the

[128] *Makwanyane* (n 5) [104] (emphasis added).

[129] NCGLE 1 case (n 110) [34].

[130] The South African Constitutional Court has never been asked to adjudicate an argument that torture was justifiable. The international law states plainly that the right against torture is an absolute right that admits of no limitation. Whether the South African court takes this approach, if it is faced with a section 12(1)(d) complaint, remains to be seen.

[131] *Makwanyane* (n 5) [144]; *Williams* (n 124) [76]; *Walters* (n 69) [28]; NCGLE 2 case (n 124) [58]; *Bhe* (n 66) [71].

[132] Woolman and Botha (n 86) 11.

position in international law, where the right not to be tortured is cast in absolute terms and brooks no limitation whatsoever.[133]

The court has held that other rights are 'vital' to constitutional democracy – freedom of religion, freedom of expression, the right to vote, right of access to adequate housing, the right of access to court, and the right to be presumed innocent.[134] Presumably these rights, distinguished from rights 'central' to the society envisaged by the Constitution, can be limited on less compelling grounds. Indeed, the very description of certain rights as 'central' or 'vital', rather than the blanket assumption that all rights are central or vital, reinforces the conclusion that the nature of a right influences the degree of persuasiveness necessary to justify its limitation.

### C What Triggers the Limitation of a Constitutional Right?

Section 7 of the 1996 Constitution provides that 'the rights in the Bill of Rights are subject to the limitations contained or referred to in section 36'. All of the rights in the Constitution are thus in principle capable of being limited, but any such limitation can only take place in accordance with the principles set out in section 36. Any rights limitation that fails the PA under section 36 is unconstitutional and invalid, and the section 36 PA must be undertaken whenever a law of general application limits a right, even to a minor extent. There is no minimal infringement necessary to trigger PA, and indeed, as illustrated by the six cases where the court assumed a rights limitation only to strike down the impugned measure on the basis of its unjustifiability, PA sometimes proceeds even in the absence of a rights limitation.

## V Worthy Purpose

Section 36(1)(b) of the 1996 Constitution points to the 'the importance of the purpose of the limitation' as a factor to be taken into account in the global judgment on proportionality. The inquiry mandated by this

[133] See, e.g., article 3 of the European Convention on Human Rights. The Convention does not contain a general limitations clause of the kind represented by section 36 of the 1996 Constitution or section 1 of the Canadian Charter of Rights and Freedoms. Rather, discrete articles in the Convention contemplate the limitation of the specific right to which they pertain. The right against torture is stated in absolute terms.

[134] *Fourie* (n 37); *SANDU* (n 113) [7]; *NICRO* (n 67) [47]; *Jaftha v Schoemann & Others; Van Rooyen v Stoltz & Others* 2005 (2) SA 140 (CC) [39]; *Lesapo* (n 8) [22]; *S v Ntsele* 1997 (11) BCLR 1543 (CC) [4]; *First National Bank of South Africa Ltd* (n 8) [6].

paragraph of section 36(1) corresponds to the 'worthy purpose' test. The court held in *Magajane*:

> The second factor, the importance of the purpose of the limitation, is crucial to the analysis, as it is clear that the Constitution does not regard the limitation of constitutional rights as justified unless there is a substantial state interest in requiring the limitation ... The court must carefully review the public interest served by the statutory provision and determine the weight that this purpose should carry in the proportionality review.[135]

A respondent's failure to identify a worthy purpose for the limitation of a right puts an immediate end to the PA in over three-fifths of all cases in which the limitation is found not to pursue a worthy purpose (11.5 out 18.5 cases, or 62 per cent). In the remaining cases, the court proceeded to consider other legs of the PA even though no worthy purpose had been established, but in all 18.5 cases the court struck down the impugned measure.

### A *Establishing the Purpose of the Limitation*

#### (i) The Legislature's Stated Purpose

It is a fairly standard practice in South Africa for legislation to set out its purpose in the preamble. When inquiring into the purpose of rights-limiting legislation, South African courts will consider these statements, but have preferred to read the relevant legislation objectively rather than rely exclusively on legislative or governmental assertions of the purpose of the legislation. In *Larbi-Odam*, for example, a provincial education department sought to justify the employment of only South African citizens rather than permanent residents on the argument that doing so advanced the objective of reducing unemployment among South African citizens. The Court accepted that while this might be a legitimate purpose for the state to pursue, the primary aim of a provincial education department is the provision of quality education to learners. The pursuit of the secondary aim of reducing unemployment among South Africans, even though legitimate, must never be allowed to compromise the primary aim of ensuring quality education. In light of this primary objective, the Court concluded that 'the government's aim should be to reduce unemployment among South African citizens *and permanent residents*'.[136]

[135] *Magajane* (n 23) [65].
[136] *Larbi-Odam* (n 25) [27]–[31].

In a handful of cases, complainants argued that the stated purposes of the legislation in question were merely pre-textual, and that the real or underlying reason for the legislation was in fact another, illegitimate purpose. In *United Democratic Movement* ('*UDM*') the court considered the constitutionality of legislation allowing parliamentary floor-crossing, in which an MP changes party allegiance, having been elected in a party-list proportional representation system under the banner of another party.[137] The opposition United Democratic Movement argued that the 'legislation is designed to and in fact serves the interests of the ANC, which is the governing party'.[138] In response, the court drew a distinction between the purposes of legislation and the motives for introducing it. While the former is well within the realm of judicial scrutiny, the latter is not: 'Courts are not . . . concerned with the motives of the members of the legislature who vote in favour of particular legislation.'[139] The court ultimately dismissed the challenge and upheld the legislation.

In the *Glenister* litigation, the Constitutional Court was seized with the question of whether legislation disestablishing a corruption-fighting agency was motivated by the motives of the ANC to 'shield high-ranking ANC politicians and their associates from prosecution'.[140] The court affirmed its decision in *UDM* that the motives of the government in introducing legislation are irrelevant to the consideration of the purposes of the legislation itself. The court held in this regard that 'there is nothing wrong, in our multiparty democracy, with Cabinet seeking to give effect to the policy of the ruling party'.[141]

In *S v Jordan*, a minority of the court considered whether the purpose of legislation can change over time.[142] In this case, the criminal prohibitions on prostitution were challenged as an infringement of rights to privacy and equality. The minority concluded that although the statute's

[137] *United Democratic Movement v President of the Republic of South Africa & Others (African Christian Democratic Party & Others Intervening; Institute for Democracy in South Africa & Another as Amici Curiae) (No 2)* 2003 (1) SA 495 (CC) (UDM case).

[138] ibid [54].

[139] ibid [56]. See also *Poverty Alleviation Network & Others v President of the Republic of South Africa & Others* 2010 (6) BCLR 520 (CC) [75].

[140] *Glenister* (n 61) [59].

[141] *Glenister v President of the Republic of South Africa & Others* 2009 (1) SA 287 (CC) [54]. The complaint was eventually upheld on the basis that the structural changes to the anti-corruption investigative services weakened their independence in ways that were contrary to international law commitments and undermined the government's financial capacity to meet economic and social rights obligations under the Constitution.

[142] *Jordan* (n 51) [104]–[14].

original purpose was to enforce a traditional and patriarchal conception of morality, the purposes of legislation are not unchangeable and should, where possible, be reinterpreted in a way that is consistent with the Constitution. This is consistent with the presumption of constitutionality, a rule of statutory interpretation that directs public officials to prefer the interpretation of a statute that is consistent with the Constitution over interpretations that are inconsistent with it.[143] The minority recast the objective of the statute criminalizing prostitution as controlling commercial sex, rather than enforcing a particular view of social morality. The majority in this case did not reach a limitations analysis because it held that the impugned provisions did not infringe constitutional rights.

In *S v Lawrence*, a minority of two judges made a similar move in reframing the purpose of restricting the sale of liquor on Sundays as reducing the ill effects of alcohol use on certain rest days that are coincidentally associated with religious celebrations, rather than recognizing those days for their religious significance.[144]

A danger of this 'shifting purpose' doctrine is that overzealous reliance on it may result in courts ascribing constitutionally legitimate purposes to legislation that is nevertheless directed towards the achievement of an illegitimate purpose.[145] This danger is overstated, however, for two reasons. First, the inquiry into purposes is just one of several elements that constitute the limitations analysis. Even if a constitutionally legitimate purpose can be ascribed to legislation, the legislation may not be related closely enough to that purpose to satisfy the section 36(1)(d) requirement that a limitation be closely related to its purpose. A measure that is initially intended to achieve one unworthy purpose may not be rationally connected to the achievement of a second, worthy but unintended, objective. Second, the Constitutional Court is alive to the danger, and has rejected attempts to recast racist and sexist statutory provisions as serving objectives less offensive to the Constitution.[146]

[143] See the injunction in s 39(2) of the Constitution to interpret legislation in a manner that it consistent with the spirit, purport and objects of the Bill of Rights, and *Investigating Directorate: Serious Economic Offences & Others v Hyundai Motor Distributors (Pty) Ltd & Others: In re Hyundai Motor Distributors (Pty) Ltd & Others v Smit NO & Others* 2001 (1) SA 545 (CC) [21]–[23].

[144] 1997 (4) SA 1176 (CC) [175].

[145] Woolman and Botha (n 86) 78.

[146] *Moseneke & Others v The Master & Another* 2001 (2) SA 18 (CC) [20]–[23].

### (ii) Evidence

The court is unequivocal that evidence relevant to meeting the justificatory burdens of section 36 must be put up by the state. While the state's failure to present argument or evidence on justification will not be fatal to the justification of a rights limitation, the court has said that it may 'tip the scales against the state'.[147] Since the evidence tending to establish the objective of a limitation and thus the worthiness of the limitation is usually in the hands of the state,[148] the state's failure to adduce any evidence of the worthiness of the objective will usually result in the court concluding that the limitation does not pursue an objective that justifies the limitation of a right. In *S v Lawrence* O'Regan J commented (for a minority):

> [I]n this case, little evidence was placed before us by government of the precise purpose and effect of the provisions. It is not the first time that this Court has been left with little assistance in this regard. Inevitably, the absence of such evidence is an obstacle to the exercise we have to conduct in terms of [the limitations clause]. It makes it far less likely that we will conclude that the infringement is justified.[149]

A dozen years later in *Centre for Child Law*, the court upheld a complaint that imposing minimum sentences on offenders aged 16 and 17 at the time they committed the offence unjustifiably limits children's rights. The court rebuked the state for its failure to adduce evidence to show that the limitation of children's rights could be justified against the purpose that the limiting law sought to achieve: 'The difficulty is that the Minister's affidavit tenders no facts from which the legitimacy of this purpose, and the efficacy of its execution, can be assessed.'[150] The Court instead examined the views given about the legislation in the proceedings of parliament when the bill was first introduced in the legislature.[151] The court referred to its earlier judgment in *NICRO:*

[147] *Moise* (n 43) [18]–[19]; *Phillips & Another v Director of Public Prosecutions* 2003 (3) SA 345 (CC) [20].

[148] *Minister for Welfare and Population Development v Fitzpatrick & Others* 2000 (3) SA 422 (CC), 2000 (7) BCLR 713 (CC) [20]; *Potgieter v Lid van die Uitvoerende Raad: Gesondheid, Provinsiele Regiering, Gauteng* 2001 (11) BCLR 1175 (CC); *Satchwell v President of the Republic of South Africa* 2002 (6) SA 1 (CC) [26]; *S v Steyn* 2001 (1) SA 1146 (CC) [32]–[36]; *Niemand* (n 69).

[149] *Lawrence* (n 144) [130].

[150] *Center for Child Law v Minister for Justice and Constitutional Development* 2009 (6) SA 632 (CC) [54].

[151] ibid [52].

> The party relying on justification should place sufficient information before the Court as to the policy that is being furthered, the reasons for that policy and why it is considered reasonable in pursuit of that policy to limit a constitutional right. That is important, for if this is not done the Court may be unable to discern what the policy is, and the party making the constitutional challenge does not have the opportunity of rebutting the contention through countervailing factual material or expert opinion.[152]

In *Mohlomi v Minister of Defence*, concerning legislation which required claims against the state to be instituted within six months, the state relied on reports of the South African Law Reform Commission, a publicly funded entity tasked with the investigation of specific questions of legislative drafting, for the argument that the purpose of the limitation was to avoid the logistical and practical difficulties occasioned by claims against the state. The court gave this argument short shrift, however, because even the Law Commission had discounted this as an uncompelling justification for the time bar. The court went on to hold that this was not a purpose that could justify the infringement of a right (see Section V.C.).[153]

### (iii) General v. Specific Statements of Purpose

The South African courts have not offered a guide as to the level of specificity at which the purposes of legislation should be stated. The more generally or widely the purpose of legislation is described, the more likely it will be that it includes worthy and important purposes within its scope. However, commentators argue that if the objective of a limitation is described generally or widely it may be more difficult to convince a court that a specific limitation is rationally connected to or likely to achieve that very broadly stated objective.[154] For example, the correction of the legacy of apartheid and the pursuit of social justice is, of course, an important objective, but there is little to suggest that charging different rates for services as between the residents of historically black and white neighbourhoods is likely to achieve that broad and vaguely articulated objective.[155] Although a rights limitation may partially achieve a broadly stated goal, or move society towards it in some incremental or piecemeal

[152] *NICRO* (n 67) [36].
[153] *Mohlomi* (n 59) [16].
[154] Woolman and Botha (n 86) 74; *Manamela* (n 10) [35]–[49].
[155] See *Walker* (n 85).

way, those small gains towards broadly stated objectives are likely to justify only minimal limitations of rights. In contrast, very extensive or serious rights limitations are unlikely to be justifiable against incremental or partial steps towards a broadly stated or aspirational objective.

In *NICRO*,[156] a government minister sought to defend limitations of certain prisoners' rights to vote imposed by the Electoral Act 73 of 1998 as a means of protecting the integrity of the voting process – an objective the pursuit of which is surely legitimate.[157] But rights limitations can only be justified if they are rationally connected to a legitimate or worthy purpose. To pass muster on this second element of the limitations analysis, the government had to convince the court that the limitation of prisoners' rights did in fact protect the integrity of the voting process. The government submitted that the cost and expense of making voting stations available to prisoners would stretch the resources of the Electoral Commission and threaten the entire voting process, but no evidence was presented to suggest that making arrangement for prisoner voting would place an undue burden on the Electoral Commission's resources.

In *NICRO*, the government's primary objective in limiting prisoner's rights was to reduce costs and lower the administrative burden on the Electoral Commission – an objective the legitimacy of which the court declined to comment on. The government then tried to parlay this objective into the broader, and legitimate, objective of protecting the integrity of elections as a whole. A majority of the court held that even if the cost-saving objective was connected to the broader objective of protecting the integrity of elections, it held that there was in any case no rational connection between the limitation and this objective because the government had not established that there was any threat posed to the integrity of the elections by making arrangements for prisoners to vote.

In *Mohlomi v Minister of Defence*, in contrast, the government argued that the rights-limiting measure achieved a much more narrowly defined goal. The complaint was that a six-month time limit within which civil actions against the state must be commenced unjustifiably limited the right of access to court.[158] The Court noted that while there were good reasons that other statutes set a time bar at three years for ordinary civil actions, such as ensuring speedy resolution of cases and ensuring that evidence remains reliable and available, the government had relied instead

[156] *NICRO* (n 67).
[157] ibid [40].
[158] *Mohlomi* (n 59).

on the argument that a more restrictive time bar relieves the state of the logistical burdens and difficulties associated with civil actions. The court acknowledged that this quite narrowly circumscribed objective would be well-served by a restrictive time bar because it would likely reduce the number of civil claims against the state, but suggested at the same time that this was not a sufficiently important objective to justify the limitation of the right of access to court. The limitation was thus rationally connected to its objective, but the objective itself was not an important or worthy one. The court also found that there were less restrictive alternatives available to achieve the worthy purposes that the limitation might have served – i.e. speedy resolution and the preservation of evidence – as was clearly demonstrated by the less restrictive three-year limit for ordinary civil actions.

It may be that *NICRO* and *Mohlomi* are cases with unique facts from which it is difficult to draw general conclusions about how the court will approach broadly or narrowly defined goals of rights limitations. The cases do, however, serve to illustrate how the attempted justification of a rights limitation may be unable to overcome either the broad or narrow articulation of its objective.

### *B Worthy and Unworthy Purposes*

The 1996 Constitution's limitations clause requires courts to consider the importance of the purpose of a rights limitation in coming to a global judgment on proportionality. An answer to this question is crucial to the inquiry into proportionality in the strict sense, as a restatement of *Bhulwana*'s touchstone of limitations analysis reveals: the more important the purpose of the limitation is to the project of constitutional democracy in South Africa, the greater the intrusion into a constitutional right that it will justify. We can see the court's approach to PA not as an attempt to balance the separate and independent values of rights on one hand and public interests or state objectives on the other, but rather as a mechanism of working out which of two competing policy options – upholding the right and striking down its limitation or limiting the right in pursuit of some objective – best advances the underlying constitutional commitment to openness and democracy in a society based on dignity, equality, and freedom.[159] In this light, the urgency of determining the importance of the objective of the limitation is patent.

[159] There is a large literature that is critical of the very idea of balancing because constitutional rights on one hand and the public interests pursued by their limitation on the

Following this approach, the court assesses the importance of the purpose of limitations in light of the values of the Constitution itself, holding that rights limitations that aim to promote these constitutional values provide compelling and persuasive reasons for the limitation of rights. For example, the court has identified the following purposes as tending to promote constitutional values:

- the promotion of equality, dignity, and national reconciliation as the country transitions from a society based on racism and segregation and seeks to overcome the conflicts and divisions of the past;[160]
- the protection of children from the degradation and indignity of corporal punishment[161] and child pornography;[162]
- the efficiency and integrity of the judicial process;[163]
- maintaining a disciplined defence force that acts in a politically impartial and non-partisan manner.[164]

Conversely, rights limitations the objectives of which are inconsistent or incompatible with the values of the Constitution will never justify the infringement of a right. Consistency or at least compatibility with the values of the Constitution is thus a threshold requirement for a purpose or objective that is capable of justifying infringement of rights. In this light the court has held that:

- While the expression of society's moral outrage is a legitimate objective of criminal punishment, retribution understood as vengeance or

other hand are incommensurable goods. It makes no sense to talk of weighing or balancing goods the value of which cannot meaningfully be compared. But if we are concerned to work out which of two options best advances the pursuit of a given set of objectives – openness, democracy, dignity, equality, and freedom in South Africa's case – then we need not be troubled by any incommensurability between the values of those two options. For statements of the incommensurability thesis, see for instance Niels Petersen, 'How to Compare the Length of Lines to the Weight of Stones: Balancing and the Resolution of Value Conflicts in Constitutional Law' (2013) 14 German Law Journal 1387; John Finnis, 'Natural Law and Legal Reasoning' in Robert P George (ed), *Natural Law Theory: Contemporary Essays* (Clarendon Press 1992); James Griffin, 'Incommensurability' in Ruth Chang (ed), *Incommensurability, Incomparability and Practical Reason* (HUP 1997); Tsakyrakis (n 13); Webber (n 13); Urbina (n 13).

160 *Islamic Unity Convention v Independent Broadcasting Authority* 2002 (4) SA 294 (CC) [45]–[46]; *AZAPO* (n 108) [48].

161 *Christian Education* (n 20) [39]–[50].

162 *De Reuck* (n 109) [61]–[67].

163 *Beinash* (n 107) [17].

164 *SANDU* (n 134) [11].

retaliation is inconsistent with the constitutional commitments to protect the human rights of all, to end the state-sponsored violation of human rights, and to promote reconciliation rather than retaliation;[165]
- Re-inscribing historical patterns of prejudice and disadvantage among racial groups is inconsistent with the commitment to equality and dignity;[166]
- The enforcement of laws animated by bigotry or intolerance dressed up as morality is inconsistent with the commitment to equality and dignity;[167]
- Differentiating between black and white South Africans following patterns of apartheid law is inconsistent with the commitment to equality and dignity.[168]

Between these two polar categories sit purposes for rights limitation which neither promote constitutional values directly nor are inconsistent with them. While the court is unlikely to conclude that purposes of this kind are unworthy or illegitimate, precisely because they do not undermine the values of the Constitution, these purposes inevitably carry less persuasive force in the strict proportionality inquiry than purposes that directly advance constitutional values. A non-exhaustive list of purposes that fall into this intermediate category includes:

- taking effective action against crime;[169]
- ensuring that bail proceedings protect the public from the risk of criminal activity;[170]
- preventing the abuse and trade in harmful drugs;[171]
- reducing the negative consequences of liquor consumption in public places;[172]
- protecting the institution of marriage;[173]
- the full and speedy settlement of tax debts;[174]

165 *Makwanyane* (n 5) [129]–[31].
166 *Bhe* (n 66) [72].
167 NCGLE 1 case (n 110) [37].
168 *Moseneke* (n 146) [23].
169 *Manamela* (n 10) [41]–[42]; *Investigating Directorate* (n 143) [53]–[54]; *S v Dodo* 2001 (3) SA 382 (CC); *Walters* (n 69) [44]; *National Director of Public Prosecutions* (n 101 ) [14]–[15].
170 Schietekat case (n 70) [55]–[56].
171 *Bhulwana* (n 58) [52]–[53].
172 *Phillips* (n 147) [24], [46]–[48].
173 NCGLE 2 case (n 124) [55].
174 *Metcash Trading* (n 101) [60].

- debt recovery – except where the debt is of a 'trifling nature';[175]
- recovery of the assets of a company under liquidation.[176]

Along with the category of purposes that directly advance constitutional values, this intermediate category of cases presents a fruitful line of inquiry into the strict PA. The category of cases dealing with purposes that are inconsistent with the values of the Constitution offers little insight into the strict proportionality or balancing stage of the inquiry, because upholding a constitutional right necessarily always advances constitutional values better than upholding a statutory purpose that undermines constitutional values. In the other two categories of cases, on the other hand, the court's conclusion on proportionality must depend on a case-specific inquiry into which of the two policy alternatives – i.e. upholding the right or limiting the right to achieve some other purpose – better advances the commitments and values of the Constitution. This balancing exercise is at the heart of the court's global judgment on proportionality.

### C *Administrative Efficiency and Cost-Saving as a Worthy Purpose*

A question that has come before the courts a handful of times is whether avoiding the administrative burden that would be imposed by not limiting a right is a legitimate purpose for which a right may be limited. The South African Constitutional Court has concluded that saving time and reducing bureaucratic costs may be a legitimate purpose, especially in a developing country where difficult choices about resource allocation must be made, but that a limitation that pursues this objective must still do so in a proportionate way.[177] Cost-saving or administrative inefficiency is not incompatible with the values of the Constitution, but it may be difficult to argue that it directly promotes the achievement of core constitutional values.

In *NICRO*, the court found that while avoiding additional administrative costs involved in making provision for prisoners to vote could be a legitimate objective – the court refrained from explicitly confirming that this was so – the evidence did not indicate that there were significant

[175] *Jaftha* (n 134) [40].
[176] *Ferreira* (n 42) [126].
[177] *Williams* (n 124) [79].

costs to be saved by not making these arrangements anyway.[178] In *Chief Lesapo*, the court held that reducing administrative burdens in the recovery of a bank's property did not justify limitation of the right of access to court.[179] In *Mohlomi v Minister of Defence*, the court held that even though statutory time bars for civil actions against the state may reduce the costs and logistical burdens that civil suits impose on the state, there were less restrictive means to limit these costs.[180] And in *Lawyers for Human Rights v Minister of Home Affairs* (2017), the Court held:

> A limitation of rights like physical freedom cannot be justified on the basis of general facts and estimates to the effect that there will be an increase in costs. The mere increase in costs alone cannot be justification for denying detainees the right to challenge the lawfulness of their detention.[181]

As yet, there have been no cases in which the avoidance of administrative burdens has been clearly held to justify the limitation of a right.

Two cases consider administrative burdens and public funds in a more favourable light. In *Prince*, the court held that prohibitions on the use of cannabis pursued the legitimate objective of controlling the use of dangerous narcotics.[182] The court held that the prohibition infringed the right to religious freedom, and a majority held that that this was a justifiable limitation. In rejecting the argument that a permit system was a less restrictive means of achieving the objective than a blanket prohibition, the majority accepted that a permit system would impose significant administrative burdens on enforcement officials and undermine the efficacy of the law in achieving the objective. Note, however, that this judgment is not authority for the proposition that the reduction of administrative burdens is a legitimate or worthy purpose for the limitation of a right. Rather, the majority held that the permit system proposed as an alternative to the blanket prohibition on the use of cannabis would not achieve the purpose of controlling dangerous narcotics, precisely because it would have imposed greater administrative burdens on enforcement officials.

[178] *NICRO* (n 67) [47]–[50].

[179] *Lesapo* (n 59) [23]–[24].

[180] *Mohlomi* (n 59) [16].

[181] *Lawyers for Human Rights v Minister of Home Affairs & Others* 2017 (5) SA 480 (CC) [61].

[182] *Prince* (n 115).

In *Law Society of South Africa v Minister for Transport*,[183] the court agreed that limiting the amount of compensation available from the publicly funded Road Accident Fund to victims of road accidents, and abolishing the common-law right to seek additional compensation from at-fault drivers, limited the right to security of the person and freedom from violence (section 12(1)(c) of the Constitution). The Minister for Transport argued that the limits on compensation and the abolition of the common-law action were needed as part of a broader overhaul of the road accidents compensation scheme from one based on driver fault to a comprehensive, no-fault, social security system meant to offer life, disability, and health insurance cover for all accidents.[184] The court held that ensuring the financial viability of the Road Accident fund was central to its ability to provide this social security safety net, and that limiting the amount of compensation payable to individual road accident victims was therefore a legitimate objective. The 'prime purpose of the legislative scheme', the court said,

> is to provide reasonable, fair and affordable compensation to all innocent victims of motor accidents. It is to be expected that a scheme which depends on public funding would at times have income less than the compensation victims may be entitled to. It is thus fair and reasonable that the scheme should have a cap as to the character and extent of the compensation each victim is entitled to.[185]

Where the availability of public funds or public resources are thus central to the government's ability to deliver important services to the public, in other words, cost-saving might be a legitimate objective that could justify the limitation of a right. What emerges from the case law, then, is that the onus will rest on the government to show a direct link between any cost savings that flow from rights limitations and the government's capacity to provide discrete and identifiable services to the public.

## VI Suitability or Rational Connection

### *A The Significance of the Suitability Test*

Section 36(1)(d) requires the court to consider 'the relation between the limitation and its purpose'. The case law on this provision has solidified

[183] 2011 (1) SA 400 (CC).
[184] ibid [45].
[185] ibid [77].

into the rule that 'there must be a rational connection between the purpose of the law and the limitation imposed by it'.[186]

Among the 83 rights limitations that the court ultimately struck down, it found that 25 did not meet the requirement of a rational connection between means and ends (30 per cent).[187] The impugned measures were struck down in all 25 of these cases. In 6.5 of these cases the court did not consider any further elements of the proportionality inquiry, resting its conclusion that the limitation was unjustifiable on the determination that it was not rationally connected to its objective. These 6.5 cases represent 8 per cent of all 83 limitations the court struck down, but make up 26 per cent of the 25 cases where no rational connection was found to exist.

The implication here is that the inquiry into rational connection is important: in almost a third of cases in the dataset it forms part of the court's conclusion that the limitation is unjustifiable. However, it is rare that the court will rely entirely on the lack of a rational connection to conclude that a limitation is unjustifiable, without considering the other legs of the analysis, and in 26 cases out of 83 (31 per cent) the court reached no conclusion on whether there was a rational connection or not.

### B Suitability as Rational Connection

As part of the inquiry into the relation between the limitation and its purpose, or the existence of a rational connection between the purpose of a limitation and the limitation itself, the courts sometimes consider whether the limitation is overbroad and goes further than is necessary to achieve its purpose. In *Case v Minister of Safety and Security*, a matter concerning whether criminal proscriptions on pornography justifiably infringed the right to freedom of expression, the court explicitly imported the consideration of overbreadth into this element of the analysis. It said: 'To determine whether a law is overbroad, a court must consider the means used ... in relation to its constitutionally legitimate underlying objectives.'[188]

186 *Gaertner & Others v Minister of Finance & Others* 2014 (1) SA 442 (CC) [67]; *Union of Refugee Women* (n 511) [34].

187 The conclusion that there is no rational connection between means and ends actually appears in 32 cases, but in two cases the lack of rational connection related to one of two statutory provisions challenged in those cases as limiting a right (*Bhe* (n 66) and *De Vos* (n 66)). Each of these conclusions is thus counted as half an observation for the purposes of the quantitative analysis.

188 *Case* (n 95) [49].

Approaching the relation between the limitation and its purpose in this way flows into the consideration of whether there are less restrictive means available to achieve the purpose of the limitation, which section 36 (1) explicitly mentions as a separate consideration in paragraph (e) (see Section VII). The court thus fails on occasion to distinguish clearly between what paragraphs (d) and (e) of section 36(1) actually require. When it understands paragraph (d) to prohibit overbreadth and goes on to conclude that a provision is overbroad, I understand it to be concluding that the measure is more restrictive than necessary to achieve its objective. Consider this passage in *Twee Jonge Gezellen*, a case about whether the common-law remedy of provisional sentence unjustifiably infringes the right to fair trial:

> The next question is whether there is an appropriate relationship between the limitation and its purpose. The limitation imposed by provisional sentence certainly achieves its purpose. It does enable the plaintiff armed with a liquid document to obtain a speedy remedy . . . Moreover, the restriction of the court's discretion to 'special circumstances' would contribute to these purposes. But, while provisional sentence is an important remedy, the restriction of the court's discretion to special circumstances goes too far. Without affording the court a discretion to refuse provisional sentence where the result may be patently unfair to the defendant, the remedy goes further than is necessary to protect any concomitant interests of the plaintiff. The limitation is out of balance with its purpose.[189]

In one sense of the term, a limitation that goes further than is necessary is indeed 'unsuitable'. An overbroad limitation is unsuitable in the same way that a sledgehammer is not well suited to cracking a nut.[190] But using a sledgehammer to crack a nut is nevertheless rationally connected to that objective. There is little doubt that a sledgehammer will crack a nut, but the concern is that a sledge hammer is unsuitable for cracking nuts despite its effectiveness in doing so, because it will cause other broader harms as it does so.

It is worthwhile, then, to make clear the conceptual distinction between overbreadth and the lack of a rational connection. The rational connection test is more focussed than this capacious understanding of unsuitability. It is concerned to identify when a statutory measure limits a right but fails to produce any countervailing benefits that might, on

[189] *Twee Jonge Gezellen (Pty) Ltd & Another v Land and Agricultural Development Bank of South Africa t/a The Land Bank & Another* 2011 (3) SA 1 (CC) [64].

[190] *Manamela* (n 10) [34].

balance, justify the limitation. A limitation may be justifiable by the good it is supposed to produce, but if it fails to produce that good there is nothing to weigh in the balance against the extent of the rights limitation, and it cannot be justifiable at all. The rational connection test is designed to consider whether the benefits that a limitation purports to achieve are likely to be achieved at all.

In this analysis, I count only those measures which the court clearly concludes are unlikely to achieve their purported objectives as failures of the rational connection or suitability test. Where the court conducts what is in effect an inquiry into overbreadth or the availability of less restrictive means under the colour of inquiring into the 'relation between the limitation and its purpose', I nevertheless count these as cases decided on the basis of overbreadth and not on the basis of the lack of a rational connection.

### C Determining Whether a Rational Connection Exists

The Constitutional Court does not have a one-size-fits-all test for when a limitation satisfies the rational connection test. Broadly, however, there are two modes of reasoning the court has tended to adopt in assessing whether a measure meets the rational connection test. The first is to consider whether, on its face, the measure is directed towards the achievement of a legitimate objective or not, or whether it is directed to achieving some other purpose. In *Larbi Odam*, a regulation limiting teaching positions to South African citizens was found to discriminate unfairly against permanent residents. The provincial education department responsible for the regulation argued that the objective of the limitation was to reduce unemployment among citizens, and although the court accepted that this may be a secondary aim of an education department, its primary aim must be the provision of quality education for learners. The exclusion of competent teachers from employment on the basis that they are permanent residents rather than citizens, the court found, is not rationally connected to the primary aim of providing quality education and provided no justification for the discrimination against permanent residents.[191]

In *Lawyers for Human Rights v Minister of Home Affairs* (2004), the court considered the constitutionality of provisions of the Immigration

[191] *Larbi-Odam* (n 25) [27]–[35].

Act 13 of 2002, allowing persons attempting to enter South Africa illegally, by sea, to be detained on the arriving ship indefinitely without a court order. The court agreed that the legitimate objective of the statutory scheme as a whole is to prevent people gaining entry to South Africa illegally, but held that 'no legitimate governmental purpose is served by ensuring that this safeguard [a court order for detention beyond 30 days] is not applicable to a person detained on a ship'.[192]

And in *Fourie*, the state sought to justify the exclusion of same-sex partnerships from the definition of marriage on the basis that limiting marriage to heterosexual couples would preserve the institution of marriage as a 'pillar of society' and 'protect the religious beliefs and convictions of many South Africans'. However, the court concluded that excluding same-sex partnerships from the institution of marriage in no way threatened marriage as a pillar of society or 'attenuate the capacity of heterosexual couples to marry in the form they wished and according to the tenets of their religion'.[193]

The second mode of reasoning accepts that the limitation is directed towards the achievement of a legitimate objective, but considers how likely it is, on the evidence, that the limitation will actually achieve that objective. Whether a rights-limiting measure is considered rationally connected to a legitimate purpose is thus often a question of what the evidence shows to be the effects or consequences of the measure's implementation. The court's jurisprudence in turn suggests that ex post evidence may be required to prove that a limitation has been effective in achieving its purpose over time. The judgment in *Teddy Bear Clinic v Minister of Justice and Constitutional Development* is instructive. Once the violation of a right has been established, the burden to prove that there is a rational connection between the limitation and its purpose lies with the party arguing that the limitation is justifiable:

> As a starting point, it is important to note that where a justification analysis rests on factual or policy considerations, the party seeking to justify the impugned law – usually the organ of state responsible for its administration – must put material regarding such considerations before the court.
>
> ...

[192] *Lawyers for Human Rights & Another v Minister of Home Affairs* 2004 (4) SA 125 (CC) [37], [43].

[193] *Fourie* (n 37) [110]–[11].

> What the [organs of state] need to demonstrate is that the existence and enforcement of the impugned provisions can reasonably be expected to control the aforementioned risks. The minister, however, has not tendered any evidence, expert or otherwise, to corroborate these claims.[194]

In this case, the impugned provisions of the Criminal Law (Sexual Offences and Related Matters) Amendment Act 32 of 2007 imposed criminal liability for consensual sexual conduct between persons under the age of sixteen. The state suggested, equivocally, that the purpose of the provisions was either to deter sexual conduct at a young age and thus minimize the associated risks, or to prohibit conduct that gives sexual gratification to children regardless of its consequences.[195] The court rejected the latter purpose as unworthy, concluding that deterring sexual conduct at a young age and minimizing its risks must have been what the legislature intended to achieve. But in considering whether this purpose was likely to be achieved by the impugned provisions, the court relied on an expert psychological report:

> The expert report clearly demonstrates that the impugned provisions cultivate a society in which adolescents are precluded from having open and frank discussions about sexual conduct with their parents and care-givers. Rather than deterring early sexual intimacy, the provisions merely drive it underground, far from the guidance that might otherwise be provided by parents, guardians and other members of society.[196]

Quite contrary to the objective of deterring sexual conduct at a young age, the evidence suggested that the legislation was unlikely to achieve that end. Worse, because the evidence suggested that criminalizing underage sex would discourage younger persons from talking openly about sex or seeking guidance from elders, the criminal prohibition on underage sex was actually likely to increase its risks. With no countervailing evidence of the efficacy of the provisions, the court had little option but to conclude that there was no rational connection between the limitation and its objective.

In *South African National Defence Union v Minister of Defence*, the court was asked to consider whether statutory provisions prohibiting members of the armed forces from forming, joining, and participating in the activities of trade unions unconstitutionally infringed the right to

[194] 2014 (2) SA 168 (CC) [84], [87]; *Moise* (n 43) [19].
[195] *Teddy Bear Clinic* (n 194) [80].
[196] ibid [89] (footnote omitted).

fair labour practices in sections 23(2)(a) and (b) of the Constitution. The applicant did not assert the right to strike (section 23(2)(c)) on behalf of members of the armed forces. The government argued that any limitation of activities other than striking protected by the right to fair labour practices was justified by the need to ensure a 'disciplined military force'.[197] The court considered a social science research report adduced by the union suggesting that allowing members of the armed forces to form and join trade unions in other countries (the Netherlands, Germany, Sweden) had not led to a reduction in the levels of discipline or effectiveness of the armed forces. This was sufficient evidence to persuade the court that the limitation was not rationally connected to the purpose it sought to achieve.

In both *SANDU* and *Teddy Bear* the parties seeking to vindicate the right led evidence to show that there was no rational connection between the limitation and its purpose. This should not be taken to mean that the party seeking to vindicate the right bears the burden to prove that there is no rational connection between the limitation and its purpose, but it does indicate that the courts will respond favourably to evidence tending to show an absence of such a connection. In contrast, if the state or some other party wants to defend a rights limitation as justifiable, it bears the burden of convincing the court that the limitation is demonstrably connected to the achievement of the purpose of the limitation. In *De Lange v Smuts*, considering the justifiability of provisions allowing officers presiding over creditors' meetings in terms of the Insolvency Act to commit persons to prison for non-cooperation, the court noted that there was no evidence establishing, either 'statistically or by way of informed expert opinion', that the limitation was at all effective in securing the repayment of debts in cases of insolvency.[198] The state's failure to adduce evidence 'tipped the scales' in favour of the party seeking to vindicate the right.

In *Makwanyane*, the state entities seeking to defend the death penalty as a justifiable limitation of the rights to life, dignity, and to be free from cruel, inhuman, or degrading treatment or punishment submitted that the imposition of the death penalty was a more effective deterrent against crime than other punishments. The court rejected this argument on the strength of substantial sociological, criminological, and psychological evidence and on a comparison of crime statistics during periods while

[197] *SANDU* (n 134) [32].
[198] *De Lange* (n 112) [94].

sentences of death were carried out and when they were suspended by a moratorium after 1990. The court looked at similar data from the United States in the wake of *Furman v Georgia*,[199] in which the US Supreme Court struck down the death penalty for a period as inconsistent with the right not to be subjected to cruel and unusual punishment, and at academic studies examining the sociological effect of the death penalty as a deterrent against crime in the United States. On reviewing all this evidence, the court concluded that evidence showed the death penalty to have been no more effective in deterring crime than long prison sentences.[200]

In most cases where the court accepts that a rights limitation is rationally connected to its objective, it does so on the basis of at least some evidence. In a small handful of cases, however, the court has accepted with very little argumentation or evidence that the objective is likely to be achieved. In *Christian Education*,[201] for example, the objective of the limitation on corporal punishment in schools was the protection of school pupils' rights to dignity and bodily integrity. It is apparent from the judgment that the court saw it as self-evident that prohibiting corporal punishment in schools will promote this objective. Indeed, the state tendered no evidence in support of the rational connection between the prohibition and this objective, and the judgment includes no discussion of the efficacy of the prohibition in achieving this objective.

Similarly, the following paragraph from *Gaertner v Minister of Finance* represents the court's entire inquiry into the rational connection between the limitation of the right to privacy and the revenue-generating objectives of customs and excise law:

> There must be a rational connection between the purpose of the law and the limitation imposed by it. In broad terms, that rational connection does exist between the limitation at issue here and the provision's purpose. The tight regulation of the customs-and-excise industry is enforced through inspections. Intrinsically, inspections of this kind are still intrusive, although they must be somewhat tolerable in respect of business premises. But this is something that participants in the industry must be content with if compliance with the Customs and Excise Act is to be achieved.

[199] *Furman v Georgia* 408 US 238 (1972).
[200] *Makwanyane* (n 5) [119]–[26], [180]–[81], [287]–[95].
[201] *Christian Education* (n 20).

In some cases, then, the court adopts a common-sense approach to whether an impugned provision will achieve its purported objectives, and concludes that the limitation meets the suitability test even without evidence tending to establish a rational connection.

In turn, the failure of a party challenging the limitation to present evidence of the ineffectiveness of the limitation is not necessarily fatal, and the court has shown itself to be willing to accept common-sense or abstract arguments that the limitation is unlikely to achieve its objective without any evidence of ineffectiveness. Indeed, the onus of showing that a limitation is justifiable – and that the limitation is rationally connected to a worthy purpose – falls on the state. This means that a rational connection must be established by the party seeking to justify the limitation, but the party seeking to have the limitation struck down may not need to bring evidence demonstrating the lack of a rational connection in order to succeed with a challenge.

At least two cases illustrate the court's flexibility in this regard. In *Bhulwana,* the court struck down as an unjustifiable limitation of due process rights a presumption of the criminal intention to deal in cannabis, based merely on possession of a certain amount of cannabis. To the court, it did 'not appear to be logical' that presuming an intention to deal in cannabis would achieve the objective of reducing illicit cannabis sales.[202] As well, in *National Coalition for Gay and Lesbian Equality*, the court held without any consideration of evidence that there was no rational connection between the objective of protecting the institution of marriage and limiting marriage to heterosexual couples.[203] However, the court's openness to common-sense arguments like these should not detract from the more general point that – as in *Makwanyane* – evidence of a statutory measure's ineffectiveness in achieving its purpose will far better serve the party challenging the constitutionality of that measure.

[202] *Bhulwana* (n 58) [23].

[203] NCGLE 2 case (n 124). The rational connection test has been relied on by the High Courts to strike down rights-limiting legislation in a number of cases. See *Dodo* (n 169) (no rational relationship between a mandatory sentence of life imprisonment and the purpose of deterring crime); *Walters* (n 69) [29] (no rational connection between the authorization of deadly force to prevent the escape of a suspect, and the purpose of bringing the suspect before a court of law); *Lawyers for Human Rights v Minister of Home Affairs* 2003 (8) BCLR 891 (T), 902H-I (neither the arbitrary powers granted to immigration officials nor the absence of procedural safeguards in s 34(8) of the Immigration Act alleviated the strain on state resources).

## VII Necessity or Less Restricting Means

### A *The Significance of the Less Restrictive Means Test*

Section 36(1)(e) directs courts to consider whether there are 'less restrictive means to achieve the purpose' of the limitation. The test has not been interpreted to establish a distinct hurdle or test that a limiting law must pass. Rather, the availability of less restrictive means is 'but one of the enumerated considerations which have to be weighed in conjunction with one another, and with any others that may be relevant'.[204]

As Figure 3.3 indicates, the court finds in more than half of all cases that fail the limitations analysis (46.5 out of 83 cases, or 56 per cent) that there are less restrictive means available to achieve a legitimate objective.[205] This suggests that adopting the least restrictive means is important to showing the limitation of constitutional rights to be justifiable. Indeed, in all 15 cases where the court found that the state had adopted the least restrictive means to achieve a worthy purpose, it went on to uphold the limitation as justifiable.

In contrast, a finding that the impugned measures do not adopt the least restrictive means is not crucial to a finding that the limitation is unjustifiable: in 39.5 cases in the dataset the court did not decide whether less restrictive means were available, but nevertheless struck down the limitations in 37.5 of them.[206]

In one case among the 18 cases where the limitation was upheld as justifiable, *S v Dlamini; S v Dladla; S v Joubert; S v Schietekat*,[207] the court found that even though the impugned law had not selected the least restrictive means to achieve its objective, the provision nevertheless struck a proportionate balance between the objective and the extent of the limitation. The failure to adopt the least restrictive means is thus not necessarily fatal to the justifiability of a rights limitation either: a measure

204 *Mamabolo* (n 76) [49].

205 In *De Vos* (n 66) the court considered challenges to two separate statutory provisions, finding one provision to lack a rational connection to a worthy purpose and the other to be more restrictive than necessary to achieve a limitation. I have thus counted the findings on these tests, with respect to different rights limitations, as half an observation each.

206 In the other two cases, *Beinash* (n 107) and *Road Accident Fund & Another v Mdeyide* 2011 (2) SA 26 (CC), the court upheld the impugned limitations as justifiable, finding them to be proportionate in the strict sense, even though it did not consider whether less restrictive means were available.

207 Schietekat case (n 70).

can be proportional in the strict sense and justifiable on balance even if it does not adopt the least restrictive means.

*S v Schietekat* indicates how the inquiry into less restrictive alternatives places the courts on the horns of a dilemma. On one hand, courts must allow the legislature some room to choose between competing 'reasonable policy options' but should not, on the other hand, give the legislature an 'unrestricted licence to disregard an individual's rights'.[208] In *Manamela*, the court put the problem succinctly:

> The problem for the Court is to give meaning and effect to the factor of less restrictive means without unduly narrowing the range of policy choices available to the legislature in a specific area.[209]

Against this background the court has tended to consider two primary factors: whether the impugned measure is more broad than necessary to achieve its objective (or by contrast whether it is narrowly tailored to that objective), and whether any less restrictive measures are 'sufficiently effective' in achieving the objective of the impugned measure.

### B Narrow Tailoring of Means

In *Print Media v Minister of Home Affairs*, the Constitutional Court emphasized that statutory provisions that are more broadly stated than is necessary to achieve their objectives, and limit rights in doing so, are more likely to fail the less restrictive means test. The consideration of the 'relation between the limitation and its purpose' in section 36(1)(d) overlaps with the less restrictive means in this regard, because a provision that goes further than it needs to in order to achieve its purpose fails to display a close or rational connection to that purpose.[210]

In *Mamabolo*, the court elaborated on the requirement that the legislature choose from among the 'reasonable' less restrictive means, by noting that reasonableness requires a legislative measure to be carefully and narrowly tailored to achieve its objectives.[211] If there are less restrictive means available, it follows that the limitation was overbroad and that it was not narrowly tailored to its purpose. While the rationality test asks whether the limitation is likely to achieve the stated objective, the less

[208] *Makwanyane* (n 5) [107].
[209] *Manamela* (n 10) [95].
[210] 2012 (6) SA 443 (CC) [62]–[71]; *Case* (n 95) [62].
[211] *Mamabolo* (n 76) [48]–[50].

restrictive means test asks whether the limitation, despite being likely to achieve its purpose, goes beyond what is necessary to achieve the purpose and limits rights unnecessarily.

The court's case law discloses three broad kinds of limitations that are not narrowly tailored. The first involves cases where the limitation imposes a blanket or total prohibition on an activity or conduct, or applies indiscriminately to a category of people without distinguishing between their circumstances. In *Coetzee & Matiso*, the court held that provisions authorizing the imprisonment of judgment debtors for non-payment of judgment debts applied more broadly than necessary to achieve the purpose of ensuring the payment of judgment debts, because they included in their sweep not only judgment debtors who refused to pay but also those who failed to establish in court proceedings that they were not able to pay.[212] The court held that the legislature should have crafted a more focused piece of legislation that limits rights only in specifically identified cases.

In *Christian Education*, the complainant organization argued that the prohibition on corporal punishment in schools infringed religious freedom, because the people the organization represented sincerely believe that their faith commands them to employ 'corporal correction' in raising and educating children. The organization argued for an exemption to the blanket prohibition on religious grounds. The objective of the legislation banning corporal punishment, the court stated, was to protect the dignity and physical and emotional integrity of children.[213] The court held, however, that any exemption to the ban would undermine the purpose of the ban: allowing corporal punishment at all would compromise the dignity and physical and emotional integrity of children subjected to corporal punishment. There was no way to uphold the objective of the ban on corporal punishment other than a complete ban, meaning that there were no less restrictive means available to achieve the purposes of protecting the rights to dignity and security of the person.

In *Sonderup v Tondelli*,[214] a mother removed her minor child to South Africa from Canada without the consent of the father, and in violation of a court order made by the Supreme Court of British Columbia that the child's father retains custody. The Hague Convention on the Civil

[212] *Coetzee* (n 10).
[213] *Christian Education* (n 20) [50].
[214] *Sonderup* (n 80).

Aspects of International Child Abduction, incorporated into South African Law by The Hague Convention on the Civil Aspects of International Child Abduction Act 72 of 1996, provides that where a child is wrongfully removed from his or her habitual country of residence and taken to another country, the courts of the latter country 'shall order the return of the child forthwith', unless certain countervailing considerations exist. The mother argued that the mandatory return order was an overbroad blanket rule that did not allow the full enjoyment of a child's constitutional right to have his or her best interests paramount in decisions affecting him or her.[215] The court held, however, that the provisions of the Convention already included exemptions to the general rule that children be returned to the country of their habitual residence. This substantially mitigated the extent of any limitations to the section 28(2) right.[216] The limitation was thus not a blanket rule, and was in fact narrowly tailored to protecting the interests of children.

A second kind of unnecessarily broad rights limitation involves exemptions to blanket rules that are so narrow as to have little impact on the application of the blanket rule. In *Dawood*, a statutory provision created an exception to the rule that non-residents may not be physically present in South Africa while their applications for permanent residence are processed. The exception conferred a discretion on officials to allow non-resident spouses of permanent residents to remain in South Africa while their own applications for permanent residence were processed. However, the empowering legislation contained no guidelines directing officials how to exercise this discretion, and exceptions were rarely granted. A less restrictive scheme, the court said, would be one that clearly states what considerations are relevant to the exercise of the discretion.[217] Further, legislation should establish regulatory schemes that guides officials to act in ways that tend to promote rights, rather than schemes that compel or encourage officials to act in ways that tend to limit rights.[218]

A third type of overbroad limitation is legislation that allows administrative action that significantly limits rights, without the prior

[215] 1996 Constitution, section 28(2).

[216] *Sonderup* (n 80) [32].

[217] *Dawood & Another v Minister of Home Affairs & Others; Shalabi & Another v Minister of Home Affairs & Others; Thomas & Another v Minister of Home Affairs & Others* 2000 (3) SA 936 (CC).

[218] *Nel v Le Roux No & Others* 1996 (3) SA 562 (CC).

involvement of courts. Examples are criminal procedure provisions that authorize officials responsible for criminal investigations to gather evidence of criminal activity in ways that may constitute limitations of the right to privacy. In cases testing such provisions, the court has identified the requirement of a court-issued warrant as a less restrictive means of gathering this evidence.[219]

### C *Sufficiently Effective Alternatives*

The practice that has developed in the Constitutional Court is for the party challenging a rights-limiting measure as unconstitutional to suggest less restrictive alternatives that might have been adopted, as in *Christian Education*. Even so, the court has never stated unequivocally that it is a claimant's obligation to offer these alternatives. However, once less restrictive means to achieve the purpose of the limitation have been described, the burden falls on the party seeking to justify the limitation – usually the state – to show that the adoption of the less restrictive means would be less effective than the impugned measure in achieving the given objectives.[220] The state is thus obliged to prove that although the alternatives might be less restrictive, they will not actually achieve the purpose that justifies limiting the right in the first place. This is in many ways an evidentiary question that depends on the likelihood or probability that various policy options will in fact achieve a particular purpose. As with all evidentiary burdens in the limitations analysis, the state's failure to present evidence that less restrictive alternatives are less effective will not be fatal to the justification of the limitation, but it will 'tip the scales' in favour of the claimant.

In *De Reuck*, the court clarified the approach, holding that less restrictive alternatives need not be equally effective in achieving the stated purpose as the impugned measure. Rather, less restrictive alternatives need only be 'sufficiently effective'. This implies that the efficacy of less restrictive alternatives is not to be assessed on the basis of comparison with the policy as adopted in the impugned legislation, but must meet a free-standing criterion of sufficient efficacy in achieving the purpose. The applicant in *De Reuck*, a documentary film-maker, was charged under a provision of the Film and Publication Act with possession of prohibited

[219] *Mistry v Interim Medical and Dental Council of South Africa & Others* 1998 (4) SA 1127 (CC); *Magajane* (n 23); *Gaertner* (n 186).

[220] Woolman and Botha (n 86) 92.

child pornography. He challenged the provision of the statute as inconsistent with rights to privacy and freedom of expression, arguing in particular that the legislative objective of protecting children and stamping out a market for child pornography could as effectively be achieved if the provisions included an exemption for possession for a 'legitimate purpose' such as research or journalism.

The court held that the limitation was justifiable, however, in particular because the 'legitimate purpose' alternative proposed by the applicant was unlikely to be sufficiently effective in achieving the objectives of the impugned legislation: The court held:

> The result of a 'legitimate purpose' defence would then be that people may exploit the defence as a cover. Such persons pose a reasonable risk of harm. The assessment of risk does not attach to the particular person who is charged, but considers the average probability that, among all the people who possess child pornography, some will use it to harm children. The proposed 'legitimate purpose' defence seeks to undo this form of risk assessment by requiring an individualised risk to be proved on the part of a researcher, a film-maker or someone pursuing a similar project. Drawing an analogy with other possession offences may illustrate how the 'legitimate purpose' defence would undermine the effectiveness of the general prohibition. Consider, for example, a 'legitimate purpose' defence which allowed amateur chemists to possess dangerous drugs. In my view, the less restrictive means suggested by the applicant are not sufficiently effective to warrant their adoption.[221]

In *Prince*, a member of the Rastafari religion challenged the constitutionality of the ban on the use of cannabis on the grounds that it unjustifiably limited the right to religious freedom. The judgment turned on whether an exemption for religious cannabis use, regulated by a permit system, would be as effective as a blanket ban in achieving the objective of reducing the harmful effects of narcotic drug use. A minority of the Court concluded that the government's purpose in controlling the use of cannabis could be achieved by a permit system, and that the blanket prohibition on the use of cannabis was overbroad.[222]

The majority of the court disagreed, holding instead that a permit system would be difficult to enforce, would impose significant financial and administrative burdens on the state, and would require police officers charged with enforcing the ban to investigate and decide whether a

221 *De Reuck* (n 109) [82]–[83].

222 *Prince* (n 115) [65]–[70]. See also *Union of Refugee Women* (n 51), where the existence of exceptions in a blanket prohibition was held to meet the requirements of section 36.

person's use of cannabis was for lawful religious or sacramental purposes or for unlawful or illegal recreational purposes. The complications involved in enforcing the permit scheme, the majority concluded, would impair law-enforcement agencies' ability to effectively enforce the legislation.[223] The less restrictive alternative, in other words, was insufficiently effective to achieve the objective.

*Prince* raises the question of how much deference the courts should show to the legislature and government when analysing their policy choices. A finding that less restrictive alternatives should be adopted may affect the state's prioritization of social demands and compel the state to reallocate resources in order to meet court orders.[224] In *Prince*, the court showed itself willing to defer to the state's judgment that adopting a less restrictive but administratively complex and burdensome alternative would not be sufficiently effective.

Moreover, in *Schietekat*, the court showed itself willing to uphold a rights limitation as proportionate in the strict sense, even though the complainants were successful in arguing that less restrictive alternatives were available.[225] The question was whether the right to bail while awaiting trial was compromised by the requirement that the accused adduce evidence establishing that the interests of justice require release on bail. The court noted that the statutory rules setting out the kinds of evidence required for a successful bail application compromised the due process right to silence, and did so more extensively than in other countries. The court nevertheless held that the objectives of maintaining public order and avoiding public outrage occasioned by the release on bail of persons charged with heinous crimes was important enough in the social and political climate of South Africa's high incidence of violent and outrageous crime to justify a limitation of the right to silence, even though less restrictive approaches had been adopted elsewhere.[226]

The logic of these cases explains why the availability of 'less restrictive means' is seldom determinative of the outcome of a limitations analysis. The court made plain in *Mamabolo* that the availability of less restrictive means is merely one of the factors relevant to the determination of the reasonableness and justifiability of a rights limitation:

223 *Prince* (n 115) [129]–[42].
224 *Manamela* (n 10) [95].
225 See *Schietekat* case (n 70).
226 ibid [55].

> Where section 36(1)(e) speaks of less restrictive means it does not postulate an unattainable norm of perfection. The standard is reasonableness. And in any event, in theory less restrictive means can almost invariably be imagined without necessarily precluding a finding of justification under the section. It is but one of the enumerated considerations which have to be weighed in conjunction with one another, and with any others that may be relevant.[227]

Even in the context of the less restrictive means inquiry, then, the court relies on a standard of reasonableness rather than a purely formal or evidentiary conclusion about whether there are less restrictive alternatives available. And as *Schietekat* indicates, a limitation may be reasonable even though there are less restrictive alternatives. Ultimately, courts, policy-makers, and law makers will have to consider whether a mechanism that purports to achieve some worthy objective is reasonable. The existence of less restrictive alternatives is just one factor that may be relevant to reaching this more global conclusion.

## VIII Balancing or Strict Proportionality

### *A The Interplay between the Balancing Test and the Other Tests*

The lodestar of the court's limitations jurisprudence since 1996 has been the principle that more extensive infringements of rights need to be justified by more compelling and persuasive reasons. All the factors set out in section 36 are relevant to reaching this global judgment on proportionality: it is difficult to imagine how a court or a lawmaker might decide that a limitation is compelling enough to justify the limitation of a right without thinking about the nature of the right and how seriously the right is infringed (s 36(1)(a) and (c)), without evaluating the importance of the objective the limitation seeks to achieve (s 36(1)(b)), without examining whether the measures will actually achieve the stated objective, or without considering whether that objective could be achieved through mechanisms that limit rights less extensively (s 36(1)(d) and (e)). The court does not see these inquiries as freestanding determinants of a limitation's justifiability, however. Rather, these inquiries all inform a global, multifaceted, and well-rounded judgment about whether a limitation is consistent with the constitutional commitment to 'an open and democratic society based on human dignity, equality and freedom'.

[227] *Mamabolo* (n 76) [49].

Section 1 of the Canadian Charter of Rights and Freedoms contains a similar expression of the values against which rights limitation must be evaluated. In *Oakes*, the seminal Canadian case on limitations, the Supreme Court of Canada held that a free and democratic society must be taken to mean, at least, a society that values and protects dignity, social justice, equality, participation in the democratic process, respect for individual and group identity, and accommodation of a variety of different beliefs.[228] *Oakes* set out a sequential, cumulative approach to the PA, indicating that a failure at any stage of the analysis would be sufficient to conclude that a limitation is unjustifiable.

The sequential approach of *Oakes* has been rejected in South Africa. The Constitutional Court has affirmed that it is the quest for an 'open and democratic society based on human dignity, equality and freedom' that drives the PA, rather than the outcome of each individual stage of that analysis. Speaking of the section 36 limitations analysis in *Coetzee v Government of the Republic of South Africa*, Sachs J said in a minority judgment:

> The values *that must suffuse the whole process* are derived from the concept of an open and democratic society based on freedom and equality, several times referred to in the Constitution.[229]

And even in Canada, there is some support for a global rather than sequential approach: in *R v Keegstra*, the Supreme Court of Canada warned against the mechanical application of the *Oakes* test and emphasized that the concept of a free and democratic society links the guarantee of rights and freedoms to their limitation.[230]

In *Prince*, the court remarked that the process of limitations analysis requires the 'maximum harmonisation of all the competing interests . . . without losing sight of the ultimate values highlighted by our Constitution'.[231] PA in South Africa is thus directed at upholding core constitutional values of openness, democracy, dignity, equality, and freedom, and the analysis turns on whether limitations can be justified against those values. Rights limitations are justified, in other words, when pursuing the objective served by limiting a right advances these constitutional values more faithfully than would prohibiting the limitation and

228 *R v Oakes* [1986] 1 SCR 103 [64].
229 *Coetzee* (n 10) [46] (footnotes omitted, my emphasis).
230 *Keegstra* (n 114) [735]–[36].
231 *Prince* (n 115) [155].

upholding the right. This approach has been described as 'balancing as reasoning', as opposed to the more formal 'interest balancing' that attempts to weigh or compare the value of the purposes of a limitation directly against the value of the right that is limited.[232] The focus of the inquiry is not whether the objectives served by the limitation are more important or more valuable than the right, but rather which option is most congruent with the normative commitments at the foundation of South Africa's constitutional order.[233]

The court's statement that more extensive infringements of rights need to be justified by more compelling reasons needs to be understood in light of this conception of balancing as reasoning. The persuasiveness or compelling force of the justifications given for a rights limitation depends on the extent to which it can be shown that the limitation advances or fulfils core constitutional values. A limitation that pursues an objective that is inconsistent with constitutional values, or which is not rationally connected to a constitutionally valuable objective, or which infringes a right more than is necessary to achieve that objective, is unlikely to present a compelling case that a rights limitation advances core constitutional values. But the court sees these inquiries as elements constituting the broader, more global inquiry into whether upholding or striking down a right advances constitutional values more faithfully.

In the 83 cases where rights-limiting measures were struck down, the limitation was held to be strictly disproportionate in 52 cases (63 per cent). In four of these cases, the court struck down limitations on the sole basis that they were not proportionate in the strict sense. In these cases, the court found that the impugned limitations were rationally connected to worthy objectives and used minimally restrictive means to achieve them (or did not reach a conclusion on those questions) but were unjustifiable because, in the court's view, achieving the objectives sought by the limitation would not align as faithfully with constitutional values as protecting the threatened constitutional right against the limitations involved.[234]

In 31 cases of the 83 where limitations were struck down (37 per cent), the court determined that the limitations in question were unjustifiable without directly considering whether they were proportionate in the

232 Kai Möller, 'Proportionality: Challenging the Critics' (2012) 10 International Journal of Constitutional Law 709.

233 Stacey (n 14).

234 See the cases listed at n 69: *Mbatha; Niemand; Walters; DE.*

strict sense (i.e. the court found the limitation to be unjustifiable on one of the other inquiries in the analysis or not to be imposed by law of general application). By contrast, in all 18 cases where the limitation was upheld, the court concluded that it was proportionate in the strict sense. These data suggest that while it is not necessary to find a measure disproportionate in the strict sense in order to strike it down as unjustifiable, a rights limitation can be justifiable only if it is proportionate in the strict sense. No limitation that is disproportionate in the strict sense is justifiable.

The relationship between the least restrictive means inquiry and the strict proportionality inquiry is important. In all 15 cases where the court found that the limitation was the least restrictive means to achieve the objective, it went on to conclude that the limitation was proportionate in the strict sense and upheld the limitation.[235] But there are 13.5 cases where the court made no finding as to whether the limitation was minimally impairing yet found it to be disproportionate in the strict sense. Similarly, there are two cases where the court did not consider whether the limitation was the least restrictive means available to achieve the objective, and yet found that the limitation was proportionate in the strict sense and upheld it.[236]

In a third similar case, *S v Schietekat*, the court noted that even though the impugned statutory measure did not adopt the least restrictive means to achieve the purpose, it was nevertheless a proportionate and justifiable limitation. The impugned provisions required accused persons to disclose certain information in order to be considered for release on bail, even though they would be entitled to withhold that information at trial. The fact that these disclosures became part of the record at trial compromised the right to silence. The court acknowledged that bail proceedings in other jurisdictions do not limit due process rights to the same extent – indicating that there are less restrictive alternatives available– but nevertheless held that in the context of South Africa's high crime

[235] In *De Vos* (n 66), the court decided that one of two impugned provisions failed to show a rational connection to a worthy purpose, while the other failed to adopt the least restrictive means to achieve the purpose. With respect to the first provision the court made no finding as to minimal impairment, hence counting this decision as half of an observation. The court went on to find both provisions to be disproportionate in the strict sense.

[236] In *Beinash* (n 107) and *Mdeyide* (n 206), the court reached no conclusion on the least restrictive means test; in the *Schietekat* case (n 70), it found the limitation to be proportionate in the strict sense even though it failed to adopt the least restrictive means.

rates and the public outcry against the release on bail of people accused of violent and heinous crimes, it was justifiable to limit the right to silence in order to ensure public safety and instil confidence in the criminal justice system.[237]

There are seven cases in which the court struck down the impugned measure on the basis that it did not adopt the least restrictive means available (i.e. the measure failed the necessity test), but made no finding about proportionality in the strict sense.[238]

All of these cases illustrate that the inquiries into necessity and proportionality in the strict sense are conceptually distinct. The finding that a measure fails to adopt the least restrictive means to achieve a worthy objective is thus not a necessary precondition for a conclusion that the limitation is disproportionate in the strict sense. Neither will it follow from a conclusion that a measure does not adopt the least restrictive means that it will be either proportionate or disproportionate in the strict sense. The court's conclusions on proportionality in the strict sense are independent of the inquiry into the availability of less restrictive means.

I understand this jurisprudence differently than the analysis Niels Petersen presents in a 2017 book.[239] He finds that the court considers proportionality in the strict sense in only four cases.[240] In all the other cases Petersen analyses (his sample size is 44), he finds that the court ends its analysis after finding the limitation to fail one of the other legs of the PA – usually the rational connection or less restrictive means test – and does not go on to consider proportionality in the strict sense. I do not disagree with Petersen that the court's conclusions on the rational connection and less restrictive means inquiries are often material to its

[237] *Schietekat* case (n 70) [55].

[238] *S v Ntuli* 1996 (1) SA 1207 (CC); *Brink v Kitshoff* 1996 (4) SA 197 (CC); *Hoffmann* (n 9); *Nyathi v Member of the Executive Council for the Department of Health Gauteng & Another* 2008 (5) SA 94 (CC); *Print Media SA* (n 210); *J v National Director of Public Prosecutions* 2014 (7) BCLR 764 (CC); *Chevron* (n 61).

[239] Niels Petersen, 'Proportionality and the Incommensurability Challenge in the Jurisprudence of the South African Constitutional Court' (2014) 30 South African Journal on Human Rights 405; and Petersen, *Proportionality and Judicial Activism* (n 13).

[240] Petersen, *Proportionality and Judicial Activism* (n 13) 82–86, 106–116, 208–9. The cases Peterson sees as decided on proportionality in the strict sense are *Makwanyane* (n 5), *Niemand* (n 69), *Walters* (n 69), and *De Vos* (n 66). I agree with Petersen that the court reaches a finding of disproportionality in the strict sense in these cases, and that this is the sole reason for striking down the limitation in two of these cases (*Niemand* and *Walters*). However, in *Makwanyane* and *De Vos*, I believe the court found the impugned limitations to fail other legs of the analysis as well.

global assessment of proportionality, but in most of these cases, as I read them, the court goes on to consider proportionality in the strict sense even if it finds a measure to fail one of the other legs of the PA.

Consider, for example, *National Credit Regulator*, which involved a challenge to certain provisions of the National Credit Act 34 of 2005. The Act required all persons making certain loans to register as credit providers with a national regulatory body, and provided that any qualifying loans made by unregistered lenders were unlawful and therefore unenforceable in law. The objective of the legislation was to protect consumers from predatory credit lending practices. The court held, however, that these provisions limited the right not to be arbitrarily deprived of property by restricting the ability of non-registered credit providers to recover unpaid debts. Petersen sees the court's reasons for finding the measure to be disproportionate as limited to the less restrictive means and rational connection tests, with no attention paid to proportionality in the strict sense. But the court's reasoning displays a focus on proportionality in the strict sense alongside the recognition that less restrictive means were available to achieve the objective:

> Though one can be sympathetic to the objects of the provision, I am not persuaded that the importance and purpose of the limitation, including deterrence and protection of the public, *provide sufficient reason for the deprivation embodied in this provision* . . . Given that the extent of deprivation here is far reaching, the purpose should be stated clearly, and the means chosen to accomplish it must be narrowly framed. In this case the means chosen are disproportionate to the purpose, as is further demonstrated by the less restrictive means analysed below under the justification enquiry.[241]

The court's reasoning here stands on two legs. First, it found that the objectives of deterring unregistered credit arrangements and protecting the public from predatory lenders were not sufficiently important to justify the extent to which property rights were infringed in this case. This is a conclusion based entirely on a strict balancing of the importance of two alternatives, assessed according to underlying constitutional values. Second, the court noted that the disproportionality of the measure was highlighted by the fact that less restrictive means could have been selected to achieve these purposes. Both proportionality in the strict sense and the availability of less restrictive means were relevant to the court's

[241] *National Credit Regulator v Opperman & Others* 2013 (2) SA 1 (CC) [71] (my emphasis).

conclusion that, as a matter of proportionality, the impugned measure was an unjustifiable limitation of constitutional rights.[242]

The judgment is a useful example of both the court's global approach to the analysis and of balancing as reasoning. The inquiry into whether the impugned measure is minimally impairing supplements the inquiry into whether it is proportionate in the strict sense, and the court does not rest its conclusion on just one leg of the analysis. And the inquiry into proportionality in the strict sense is itself aimed at determining whether allowing a rights limitation or striking it down better serves core constitutional values. If we understand proportionality in the strict sense to require the kind of 'interest balancing' that weighs the inherent value of a right on one hand against the value of its limitation on the other, we will indeed struggle to find examples of the court's reliance on proportionality in the strict sense. But if we understand the question that drives the PA to be whether there are sufficiently compelling reasons, when assessed against constitutional values, to justify the limitation of a right, there are several examples of this kind of reasoning in the court's record. The next section highlights a few examples of the court's reasoning in this regard.

### *B Formulation and Application of the Strict Balancing Test*

The conceptual distinctiveness of the inquiry into proportionality in the strict sense is most apparent in those cases where the limitation passes all of the other tests (or the court does not reach a conclusion on the other tests), and strict proportionality is determinative of the conclusion that the limitation is not justifiable. The judgment in *In re S v Walters* provides a useful example. Here, the court considered the constitutionality of section 49(2) of the Criminal Procedure Act 51 of 1977, which provided that where a police officer is attempting to arrest a person on a reasonable suspicion that he or she has committed one of a number of

[242] Of the 44 cases Petersen considers, I agree with his analysis of 13 of them. We agree that the court reaches no conclusion on proportionality in the strict sense in nine cases (*NICRO* (n 67); *Bhe* (n 66); *Fourie* (n 37); *Richter* (n 20); *C & Others v Department of Health and Social Development, Gauteng* 2012 (2) SA 208 (CC); *Print Media SA* (n 210); *J v NDPP* (n 238); and *Chevron* (n 61); *Sarrahwitz v Maritz* 2015 (4) SA 491 (CC); and we agree that the court's conclusion includes a finding about proportionality in the strict sense in four cases (see cases listed at n 240). In the other 31 cases – like *National Credit Regualtor* – I find that the court does reach a finding about proportionality in the strict sense in addition to a finding that the impugned measure fails one of the other inquiries.

offences listed in a schedule to the Act, and the police officer cannot effect the arrest or prevent the suspect from fleeing by any means other than by killing the suspect, 'the killing shall be deemed to be justifiable homicide'.

The court found the measure to serve a worthy purpose ('to protect the safety and security of all through the deterrence of an effective criminal justice system' and 'to ensure that suspects do not readily flee from arrest and are brought to justice'), and to be rationally connected to that purpose.[243] The court did not consider at all whether non-deadly force – i.e. means less restrictive of the right to life – could achieve the objective of ensuring people suspected of crimes face justice. Instead, the court concluded that in failing to distinguish between serious crimes, for which the use of deadly force may be appropriate, and 'relatively petty offences like pickpocketing', there is 'manifest disproportion' between the seriousness of the infringement of rights to life, dignity and bodily integrity and the interests sought to be advanced by the provisions.[244] The court tied this conclusion explicitly to constitutional values:

> What looms large in both the threshold and the limitation phases of the exercise in the present case is that the right to life, to human dignity and to bodily integrity are individually essential and collectively foundational to the value system prescribed by the Constitution. Compromise them and the society to which we aspire becomes illusory. It therefore follows that any significant limitation of any of these rights would for its justification demand a very compelling countervailing public interest.[245]

In *S v Niemand*, the court found that statutory requirements that persons declared to be 'habitual criminals' serve at least seven years of a prison sentence before being considered for parole was a limitation of the right to liberty that was 'grossly disproportionate' in relation to the purpose for which the limitation was imposed.[246] In *S v Ntsele*, the question was whether a presumption that a person has committed the crime of dealing

[243] *Walters* (n 69) [36].

[244] ibid [41]–[46].

[245] ibid [28].

[246] *Niemand* (n 240) [19], [24]–[25]. The Criminal Procedure Act 51 of 1977 and the Correctional Services Act 8 of 1959 provided that a court may declare a person to be a habitual criminal if convinced that the person habitually commits crimes, that the community needs protection from the person and that a period of detention of seven years is appropriate , that the person is over the age of 18, and that the crime does not warrant a sentence of more than 15 years imprisonment. Beyond these restrictions, however, the declaration is at the discretion of the court (para 9).

in cannabis merely upon a showing that a person is in control of land on which cannabis plants are cultivated justifiably infringes the right to be presumed innocent. In this case the court did not go through the sequential checklist of the standard PA, instead resting its conclusion on this pithy analysis of strict proportionality:

> The fundamental rights bound up with and protected by the presumption of innocence are so important, and the consequences of their infringement potentially so grave, that compelling justification would be required to save them from invalidation. None is apparent here. On the contrary, the importance of the values in issue and the extent and nature of the risk involved in their erosion outweigh any societal interest likely to be advanced by the presumption.[247]

The same approach to disproportionality in the strict sense is apparent in cases where the court found the impugned limitation to fail one or more of the other tests as well. In *Dawood*, for example, the court found that the government's failure to issue guidelines for the exercise of a regulatory discretion to allow spouses of permanent residents to remain in South Africa while applying for residence status impeded people's ability to live with their loved ones and amounted to an unjustifiable limitation of the right to dignity. The court accepted that controlling immigration into South Africa is an important legislative objective and that the impugned limitation was rationally connected to that objective. Issuing guidelines as to when and how officials should exercise their discretion, however, would have been a less restrictive means to achieve that objective. More than this, the court went on, the absence of such guidelines provided no guarantee that the discretionary powers conferred on immigration officials would be exercised in a way that is congruent with constitutional values:

> It is therefore not ordinarily sufficient for the legislature merely to say that discretionary powers that may be exercised in a manner that could limit rights should be read in a manner consistent with the Constitution in the light of the constitutional obligations placed on such officials to respect the Constitution. Such an approach would often not promote the spirit, purport and objects of the Bill of Rights. Guidance will often be required to ensure that the Constitution takes root in the daily practice of governance.[248]

[247] *Ntsele* (n 1344) [4].
[248] *Dawood* (n 217) [54].

An unguided discretion that provided no guarantee that officials would respect or be cognisant of constitutional values, the court held, could not be justified by the extent to which it promoted the objective of controlling immigration.

In all of these cases, the court found that the objectives served by the rights limitation were less closely connected to the constitutional values of dignity, equality, and freedom than the constitutional rights at stake. It follows that for any broad, public objective to justify the infringement of a right, it must be rooted in the same value system prescribed by the Constitution. This understanding of proportionality in the strict sense is especially visible in some of the cases where the Constitutional Court upheld rights limitations as justifiable.

In *SATAWU v Garvas*, for example, the court considered the constitutionality of imposing liability for property damage or physical harm on the organizers of a street protest, when damage or harm occurs during the course of the protest. While the court agreed that such liability had a chilling effect on free speech and freedom of assembly, and thus limited those constitutional rights, it held that the limitation was reasonable and justifiable when balanced against the need to protect vulnerable members of society against threats to their physical integrity, lives, and sources of livelihood. For the court, the constitutional commitment to human dignity, equality, and freedom was better served by protecting vulnerable members of society from physical and economic harm, than by avoiding the chilling effect on free speech and freedom of assembly occasioned by imposing liability on protest organizers.[249]

In *Law Society of South Africa v Minister for Transport*, the court held that abolishing a road accident victim's common-law right to recover compensatory damages from an at-fault driver, and establishing a comprehensive, publicly funded, no-fault road accident compensation scheme did limit the right to bodily integrity and to be free from violence. But the purpose of replacing common-law civil actions with a comprehensive compensation scheme, the court said, was to ensure that rights to bodily integrity and security of the person were adequately protected for everyone:

> The right to security of the person is of great importance. The adequate protection of bodily integrity is often a prerequisite to the enjoyment of all other guaranteed rights [and] the right is protected by the State in a

[249] *SATAWU v Garvas* (n 57) [67], [80]–[84].

> myriad of ways. The protection includes providing a publicly funded insurance to compensate accident victims. However, the State's constitutional duty to protect and enforce the right to security of the person need not always include a civil claim for damages in delict or indeed any private-law remedy ... The impugned scheme puts in the place of the common-law residual right a compensation regime that is directed at ensuring that the Fund is inclusive, sustainable and capable of meeting its constitutional obligations towards victims of motor vehicle accidents.[250]

In the court's view, an inclusive and sustainable Road Accident Fund from which all victims of road accidents can seek compensation – albeit compensation that is capped at fixed amounts – better serves the right to bodily integrity and all other rights in the Constitution than a scheme where only those with means are able to seek compensation through litigation in the civil courts. Justifying the compensation cap in terms of the constitutional commitment to equality, the court said: 'Public funds to finance the liability of the Fund are finite. The scheme must be sustainable, open and fair to every victim.'[251]

Finally in this respect, in *Christian Education*, the court upheld a blanket prohibition on corporal punishment in school as a justified limitation on the right to religious freedom, because the elimination of state-sponsored violence, particularly against school learners, was closely connected to the restoration of dignity in the post-apartheid era.[252] The new South African government, the court said,

> ... wished to make a radical break with an authoritarian past. As part of its pedagogical mission, the Department [of Education] sought to introduce new principles of learning in terms of which problems were solved through reason rather than force. In order to put the child at the centre of the school and to protect the learner from physical and emotional abuse, the legislature prescribed a blanket ban on corporal punishment. In its judgement, which was directly influenced by its constitutional obligations, general prohibition rather than supervised regulation of the practice was required.[253]

The court recognized the importance that corporal correction held to the religious beliefs of the complainants, but held the balance came down 'firmly in favour of upholding the generality of the law in the face of the

[250] *Law Society of South Africa* (n 183) [79]–[80].
[251] ibid [103].
[252] *Christian Education* (n 20).
[253] ibid [50].

appellant's claim for a constitutionally compelled exemption'.[254] While the court recognized the importance of corporal correction to the complainants' religious ethos, it went on to emphasize that since the complainants' schools 'of necessity function in the public domain' and are involved in preparing learners for 'life in the broader society',[255] allowing a religious exemption to the ban on corporal punishment in order to protect their religious rights from infringement would undermine the constitutional values that motivated the ban in the first place.

Whether the court ultimately allows or strikes down a rights limitation, its approach to proportionality in the strict sense is to inquire into whether upholding the right and protecting it against limitation, or allowing its limitation in the pursuit of some broader social objective, better reflects the constitutional values of openness, dignity, equality, and freedom against which section 36 explicitly requires rights limitations to be justified. The court's conclusions to its inquiries on this approach to proportionality in the strict sense are sometimes supported or supplemented by its conclusions on other legs of the inquiry. It is less common, though, for the court to rely on a direct balancing of the value of rights and the value of the objectives sought by limitation.

### *C Additional Factors Taken into Account*

#### (i) Broader Harms

While the primary considerations in the balancing exercise are the extent to which the limitation infringes rights and the importance of the purpose of the limitation, in some cases the court has considered the wider effects on democracy or the constitutional project as secondary considerations. For example, in considering limitations on the right to vote, the court has also considered the effects on electoral democracy more broadly.[256] In considering limitations on the right to freedom of expression and freedom of assembly, the court has also considered the 'chilling effect' on public discourse more broadly.[257] Cases in which these considerations have carried weight are those that involve rights central to democracy. The right to vote and other political rights are directly connected to democracy, while the rights to freedom of expression and

[254] ibid [52].
[255] ibid [51].
[256] *August* (n 88); *NICRO* (n 67).
[257] *South African Transport and Allied Workers Union* (n 57); *Print Media SA* (n 210).

freedom of assembly, the court has said, are important to the spread of information and the formation of social consciousness that supports thriving and vibrant constitutional democracy.

#### (ii) Vulnerable Groups

In assessing the 'nature and extent' of the infringement of rights in terms of section 36(1)(c), the Constitutional Court does consider the social position of the affected individuals or group. When legislation has a disproportionate impact on the rights of vulnerable sections of the population, such as religious minorities,[258] the poor,[259] or children born out of wedlock,[260] the level of justification needed to show that the infringement is reasonable and justifiable in terms of section 36 may be higher. Similarly, the court has held that the violation of the rights of a vulnerable person by a powerful person in a position of authority is a more serious violation of rights.[261] The court has also held that attention must be given to the extent to which the rights of 'permanent minorities', which have suffered from established patterns of discrimination, are affected.[262] The case law has not drawn a distinction between whether legislation targets vulnerable populations intentionally and whether the effect on vulnerable groups is incidental and unintentional. For the court, what is important is that the infringement is experienced equally seriously by the victims.

## IX Overview of the Means Struck Down

There is a distinction to be drawn in the Constitutional Court's limitations jurisprudence, based on the data analysed in this chapter, between cases in which value-based analysis carries the conceptual burden in the conclusion that a limitation is disproportionate, and cases where the inquiries into suitability and necessity do the heavy conceptual lifting. There are, then, some generalizations that can be drawn about the reasons for which limitations fail each of the inquiries in the PA.

[258] *Prince* (n 115) [51].

[259] *Coetzee* (n 10) [8], [66]–[67]; *Jaftha* (n 134) [39], [43]; *Manamela* (n 10) [44].

[260] *Petersen v Maintenance Officer & Others* 2004 (2) SA 56 (C) [22].

[261] *Le Roux & Others v Dey (Freedom of Expression Institute and Restorative Justice Centre as Amici Curiae)* 2011 (3) SA 274 (CC) [46].

[262] NCGLE 1 case (n 110).

Purposes that are generally not considered important enough to justify the limitation of a right are those that are inconsistent with the values and fundamental norms of the Constitution. Many racist and sexist laws from the apartheid era remain on the books in South Africa, and although the number of these statutes is decreasing with time, the objective of discriminating between people and treating them differently on the basis of race, colour, sex, or gender is clearly inconsistent with the values of a transformative constitution based on dignity and equality.

Apartheid-era laws are not the only place where rights limitations have been found to serve purposes inconsistent with underlying constitutional values. Although at this point still a minority, there are several examples of statutory provisions enacted, or government action taken since 1994, that the court has found to pursue objectives that are not capable of justifying the rights limitation those measures impose. In *Lawyers for Human Rights v Minister of Home Affairs* (2017), for example, the court roundly rejected the government's reliance on reducing costs and administrative burdens as a justification for limitations of the right to physical freedom.[263] *C v Department of Health* concerned provisions allowing for the removal of children from the care of their parents without judicial oversight limited rights to family and of access to court. A majority of the court found that the impugned provisions served no purpose, legitimate or otherwise, on the basis of which a justifications analysis could begin, noting as well that the state had not offered any purposes in argument.[264]

The provisions challenged in both *Lawyers for Human Rights* and *C* were enacted after 1994. As fewer and fewer apartheid-era laws survive into the democratic era, there will presumably be fewer and fewer challenges to rights limitations that are motivated by motives that are patently inconsistent with constitutional values and norms. However, there is evidence that government will nevertheless impose limitations on rights that serve no purpose at all, or which serve purposes that the court thinks are not important enough to justify the limitation of rights. From this we can conclude that while limitations that fail the PA because they pursue objectives directly inconsistent with the values of the

[263] *Lawyers for Human Rights* (2017) (n 181) [61].

[264] *C & Others* (n 242) [81]–[82]. A minority judgment would have found that the measure's served the objectives, stated in another part of the legislation, of 'protect [ing] children from discrimination, exploitation and any other physical, emotional or moral harm or hazards' and 'provid[ing] care and protection to children who are in need of care and protection' (para 31).

Constitution may begin to drop in number, we may yet expect to see government action that limits rights for no good reason, or in pursuit of objectives that, while not inconsistent with constitutional values, are nevertheless not important enough to justify rights limitations.

Limitations that have been found to fail the suitability test often lack sufficient evidence tending to establish that an otherwise important objective will even be achieved. In *Makwanyane*, the court concluded that the evidence tendered in support of the death penalty did not indicate that it was no more effective in deterring crime than less restrictive alternatives like sentences of life imprisonment. In *Teddy Bear*, similarly, the court relied on expert evidence to conclude that criminalizing consensual underage sex was not only unlikely to achieve the objective of reducing the risks associated with underage sex, but might actually increase them.

With respect to the necessity test or the availability of less restrictive means to achieve a worthy purpose, the court has often looked to whether a rule that does not allow for exemptions is the only way to achieve that purpose. For example, in *Prince*, the court considered whether a blanket ban on the use of cannabis, with no exemption for religious use of the drug, was the least restrictive means to reduce the harms associated with cannabis use. The court has also considered, however, whether less restrictive alternatives are 'sufficiently effective' in achieving the stated purpose of the limitation to indicate that the impugned limitation was not the least restrictive means.[265] It is often easy to conceive of an exemption to the operation of a blanket ban, and to suggest therefore that the government has not chosen the least restrictive means to achieve its objective. And even if the proposed exemption is likely to be less effective in achieving the purpose than the means chosen, if it is nevertheless sufficiently effective in achieving that purpose the court may conclude that the limitation is unnecessarily restrictive and should be struck down.

In *De Reuck*, a criminal accused argued that the criminal prohibition on the possession of child pornography was an unnecessary or overly restrictive limitation of the right to freedom of expression. His primary argument was that an exemption to the blanket ban, for journalistic use, would be just as effective in reducing the harms of child pornography while preserving journalists' free speech. The court rejected this

[265] *De Reuck* (n 109).

argument on the basis that this alternative would not be sufficiently effective in eliminating the market for child pornography or preventing harm to children that child pornography poses.

A different approach to challenging rights limitations as unnecessarily or overly restrictive has been to look to foreign jurisdictions where less restrictive means have been adopted to pursue the same or similar objectives. In *Ferreira v Levin*,[266] for example, the court concluded that the United States and Canada had enacted measures just as effective in securing full information from witnesses in bankruptcy proceedings, but without limiting rights protecting people against self-incrimination as extensively. As *S v Schietekat* shows, however, the court may agree that there are less restrictive means available but that the means selected is nevertheless proportionate in the strict sense and justifiable.

The court's approach to proportionality in the strict sense is hardest to generalize. In many cases, the court reaches the conclusion that a limitation is disproportionate – that the good served by limiting a right does not outweigh the harm that limiting the right causes – on the back of a failure of one of the other inquiries. But in a handful of cases, the court simply concludes that even though a rights limitation does not fail the tests set by each of the other three inquiries, the impugned rights limitation does not strike a reasonable balance between the good it achieves and the harm it produces. Consider again *Ex parte Minister of Safety and Security; In re S v Walters*.[267] Here, the court held that the use of deadly force to prevent the escape of people suspected of minor crimes is disproportionate, irrespective of the unavailability of less restrictive means to effect arrest. In many cases, as Aharon Barak has pointed out, it may be impossible to prevent a person escaping from the scene of a minor crime without the use of deadly force.[268]

The statutory amendments that followed *Walters* made a PA central to the authorization of deadly force. The amended section 49(2) of the Criminal Procedure Act 51 of 1977 provides that an arresting officer may 'use such force as may be reasonably necessary *and proportional* in the circumstances to overcome the resistance or to prevent the suspect from fleeing', and only if the suspect poses a threat of violence to others and there is no other reasonable means of effecting the arrest. The

266 *Ferreira* (n 42) [127].
267 *Walters* (n 69).
268 Aharon Barak, 'Proportional Effect: The Israeli Experience' (2007) 57 University of Toronto Law Journal 369.

amendment itself draws a distinction between necessity and proportionality, affirming that the distinction between the two inquiries is now well rooted in South African jurisprudence.

And if this distinction is well rooted in South African law, it means that the proportionality of a rights limitation cannot depend just on whether it is likely to achieve a worthy goal or restricts the right no more than is necessary to achieve that goal. More than this, proportionality depends on some degree of evaluative justification that is independent of these factual and evidentiary inquiries. The evaluative question at the core of South Africa's PA, then, is whether upholding a right and striking down a limitation or allowing the limitation of the right in order to pursue some other objective, advances South Africa's constitutional values more faithfully.

# 4

# Proportionality Analysis by the Israeli Supreme Court

TALYA STEINER

## I Introduction*

Over the past two and a half decades the proportionality doctrine (*'mid-atiyut'*) has emerged as a foundational principle in Israeli public law. The three-pronged proportionality test has been adopted as the framework for judicial review of right-limiting legislation. Additionally, proportionality has been adopted as a framework in administrative review, although not replacing but rather complementing other pre-existing doctrines. Celebrated by some, sharply critiqued by others, proportionality has become the basis for reasoning and debating about the limitation of rights across branches of government.

The doctrine was officially adopted by the court as the framework for review of legislation in the landmark *Mizrahi Bank* decision handed down in 1995, which is seen as Israel's 'constitutional revolution', first establishing the judiciary's authority to review legislation. In that case the limitation clause of Basic Law: Human Dignity and Liberty was interpreted as to include a proportionality requirement, concretized by the three-pronged test.[1] Almost simultaneously, the proportionality doctrine was adopted as a standard of review in administrative cases, as a supplement to the less structured 'reasonableness' test.[2]

* I wish to thank Raanan Sulitzeanu-Kenan and Keren Weinshall-Margel for their guidance in the quantitative methodology; Miriam Grinstein for assistance in the data analysis; and Doron Karasenty, Achikam Lazovitz, and Amit Haim for their research assistance. I would also like to thank Mordechai Kremnitzer, Andrej Lang, and Barak Medina for their helpful comments.

1 CA 6821/93 *United Mizrahi Bank Ltd v Migdal Cooperative Village* [1995], IsrSC 49(4) 221, available in English at <https://supremedecisions.court.gov.il/Home/Download?path=EnglishVerdicts%5C93%5C210%5C068%5Cz01&fileName=93068210_z01.txt&type=4> All on-line sources referenced throughout this chapter were last accessed in November 2017.

2 The precise relationship between PA and reasonableness in administrative review has not been clearly determined, and both doctrines continue to be applied, at times separately

The rise in judicial application of proportionality has brought about a growing academic interest in the doctrine. Chief Justice Aharon Barak, who was instrumental in the adoption of the doctrine, spent the immediate years after his retirement composing a comprehensive book devoted entirely to proportionality.[3] The centrality of Barak's decisions as a Justice, coupled with his encyclopaedic book, has positioned him as the benchmark on the topic; it is to him scholars refer and with which they argue when they address Israeli proportionality. Despite the fact that Barak has not been on the court for more than a decade, his normative understanding of the doctrine and the court's application of the doctrine in practice are often conceived of as one and the same.

This chapter portrays a detailed portrait of proportionality in the practice of Israeli Supreme Court case law, and uncovers certain gaps between the way proportionality has been framed in Israeli academic literature and its actual practice. As opposed to the more traditional focus on a small number of prominent cases, the chapter is based on both a qualitative and quantitative analysis of a large sample of case law, scrutinizing both legislation and administrative actions.

The qualitative analysis is based on approximately 100 cases spanning nearly a quarter of a century, since the adoption of the proportionality test in 1995 until 2017. These cases were chosen based on references in secondary literature, primarily Barak's book, with an addition of cases handed down in the seven years subsequent to its publication.

The quantitative analysis is based on a database including all Supreme Court cases handed down in the ten-year period of 2006–15, decided based on the multi-stage proportionality framework. The cases were drawn from the results of an initial search of all cases decided in the relevant timeframe including the word 'proportional'.[4] The results were reviewed individually to identify the cases where the outcome was based upon multi-stage proportionality analysis (PA),[5] resulting in a database

and at times in a joint manner. See Daphne Barak-Erez, *Administrative Law*, vol 2 (Israel Bar Publishing House 2010) 771–75 (in Hebrew).

3 Aharon Barak, *Proportionality: Constitutional Rights and Their Limitations* (CUP 2012). The book was previously published in Hebrew, see Aharon Barak, *Proportionality: The Infringement of Constitutional Rights and Its Restrictions* (Nevo Publishing 2010); references below are to the English edition, unless otherwise mentioned.

4 The search was conducted in the 'Nevo' database. The search term was the word 'מידתי' in Hebrew, including morphological conjugations. The search resulted in 2,698 cases.

5 The criterion of a decision being based on the multi-stage proportionality framework was applied relatively broadly, meaning that the titles of the sub-tests (such as worthy purpose,

of 161 cases.[6] These were coded in multiple dimensions, including subject-matter, adjudicated right, contested measure, the outcome in the various sub-tests of proportionality analysis, and the final outcome.[7]

To place the database in broader context, the Israeli Supreme Court handles an exceptionally heavy caseload, due to its dual function as a court of final resort for appeals on civil, criminal, and administrative matters, and a High Court of Justice (HCJ) hearing petitions against state authorities as a court of first and only instance. In 2015, for example, the Supreme Court disposed of over 4,000 cases, of which slightly over 2,000 were public law cases (approximately 1,850 HCJ cases and 300 appeals from administrative courts).[8] Although research has shown that nearly 60 per cent of HCJ cases are settled out of court,[9] hundreds of public law decisions are written by the court each year. Nevertheless, the average number of cases a year in our database is only 16. This illustrates that the

suitability, or necessity) did not need to be explicitly mentioned. Rather, when proportionality was referenced as the principle guiding the decision, together with analysis of the effectiveness of the means, the existence of less-restricting alternatives or a weighing of the costs and benefits, the case was included in the database. The screening process was conducted by two research assistants, both fourth year law school students. To ensure the reliability of the screening, 10 per cent of the results were reviewed by both research assistants and the author. The agreement level on inclusion in the database was 97 per cent.

The additional search results – cases that included the word 'proportionality' that were not included in the database – belonged to one of four main categories: (1) the court quoted the parties' reference to proportionality in their arguments, but the court itself did not invoke proportionality in its decision; (2) incidental references to proportionality, not as part of the justification of the outcome of the case; (3) reference to proportionality in the criminal context, such as proportionality between crime and punishment or between threat and response in self-defence; and (4) use of proportionality as a concept rather than a multi-stage doctrine, and see elaboration on this category at the end of the introduction.

6 In nine additional cases the proportionality framework was applied only by the minority, while the majority decided the case using an alternative doctrine. These nine cases were not included in the database.

7 To ensure the reliability of the coding process, 10 per cent of the cases were coded by both research assistants, and were found to have a high level of internal consistency and reliability (kappa value 0.93).

8 See The Judicial Authority of Israel, *Annual Report 2015* (in Hebrew) <www.gov.il/he/departments/publications/reports/statistics_annual_2015> 13. The average of public law cases (HCJ and administrative appeals) disposed of between 2008 and 2015 was 1,995 cases a year. See periodic reports of the Judicial Authority of Israel <www.gov.il/he/departments/publications/?OfficeId=b7f4cf74-9ceb-454d-a057-e9bdc1dcdae9&blockCollector=true&skip=0&limit=10>.

9 Yoav Dotan, *Lawyering for the Rule of Law: Government Lawyers and the Rise of Judicial Power in Israel* (CUP 2013) 97–101.

frequency that structured proportionality is applied by the Supreme Court is low relative to the full extent of its activity in the realm of public law. However, despite constituting only a small segment of the overall judicial activity, the cases applying PA seem to be ones of relatively great importance: 16 per cent of the cases in the database were handed down by an extended panel,[10] which are only used in cases of particular public importance, while the general average of extended panels is only around 3 per cent.[11]

It is important to acknowledge the boundaries of the database by pointing out two types of cases which were not included in it and are beyond the scope of this chapter. The first group is cases that use the words 'proportional' or 'proportionality' as an abstract concept as part of the justification of the outcome, without conducting the multi-stage analysis.[12] These cases highlight the fact that the penetration of proportionality into the public law discourse extends beyond the application of the structured doctrine.[13]

[10] The Supreme Court consists of 15 justices, who typically sit in panels of three, but the panels can be enlarged by the Chief Justice to constitute any uneven number from 5 to 15.

[11] Weinshall-Margel found a general average of 3 per cent extended panels, which rose in particular sensitive topics (in security-related cases she found 5 per cent, and in religion and state cases 17 per cent). Keren Weinshall-Margel, *Law and Ideology in Supreme Court Decision-Making: A Comparative and Quantitative Analysis* (in Hebrew, Hebrew University Sacher press 2016). Another more anecdotal measure that demonstrates the importance of these cases is that the database includes six out of the eight 'retirement decisions' handed down in the period of the database – decisions read by justices at their retirement ceremony, traditionally reserved for high profile cases.

[12] In such cases proportionality is used by the court as a concept rather than a doctrine, and it will often be coupled with additional words, such as 'reasonable', 'fair', 'worthy', or 'balanced' or together with an additional doctrine. See, e.g., LCA 3808/15 *Ploni v Ministry of Health* (7 June 2015, unpublished) concerning forced hospitalization in handcuffs in a prison-operated facility of a homeless person with tuberculosis to prevent hazard to public health, due to his resistance to treatment. The court stated that 'the decrees of liberty and proportionality required seeking alternate arrangements that were better in terms of proportionality'.

[13] The extent of this phenomenon was not comprehensively analysed quantitatively, but some evaluation of its prevalence can be provided: of all cases including the word 'proportional' from the year 2015, beyond the 12 decisions that applied the multi-stage proportionality framework that were included in the database, 28 additional cases included the word 'proportional' as part of the basis for the decision without an application of the doctrine – i.e. more than twice as many. For a general discussion on the distinction between the proportionality principle and doctrine see Margit Cohn, 'Proportionality in Israel and Beyond: Four Aspects' in Gideon Sapir, Daphne Barak-Erez and Aharon Barak (eds), *Israeli Constitutional Law in the Making* (Hart Publishing 2013) 189.

The second group includes cases where judicial balancing is practised without invoking proportionality. The concept of balancing precedes the adoption of the proportionality doctrine and in some cases continues to be practised independently.[14] It is therefore important to keep in mind that the findings are confined to applications of the proportionality doctrine in its structured multi-stage form, rather than the broader use the court makes of the concepts of balancing and proportionality.

After a brief description of the Israeli legal and institutional context, the chapter opens with an overview of limitation analysis in Israel, presenting the central findings of the quantitative analysis. The chapter continues with sections devoted to each one of the stages of the analysis, based primarily on a qualitative evaluation of the application of these stages in the case law. An overview of means struck down concludes the chapter.

## II Legal and Institutional Context

The rise of the proportionality principle in Israeli public law is intricately related to the historical development of the Israeli constitution and the status of the Supreme Court in Israeli society.

### *A The Pre-constitutional Era*

Israel is one of the few countries that does not have a single document that acts as a formal and comprehensive constitution. Upon the establishment of the state in 1948 a Constitutional Assembly was elected, but since consensus on the content of the constitution or even the need for one could not be reached, a compromise decision was made according to which the constitution would be constructed gradually, by adopting individual Basic Laws that would ultimately be united to create a full constitution.[15] To this date, the constitution-making process was never completed and a full constitution is yet to be formed.

[14] See, e.g., HCJ 979/15 *Yisrael Beiteinu Party v Chairman of the Central Elections Committee for the 20th Knesset* (25 February 2015, unpublished), on whether distribution of the *Charlie Hebdo* magazine constitutes a prohibited gift in a political campaign. The case was decided based on a balancing between freedom of speech and the restrictions on political campaigns using different balancing formulas rather than the structure of the proportionality doctrine (Although the word 'proportional' appears in the decision).

[15] Dotan (n 9) 14.

Until 1992, all Basic Laws were of strictly institutional nature, establishing governmental institutions and defining the division of powers between the branches of government such as Basic Law: the Knesset (i.e. Parliamant), and Basic Law: the Judiciary. During the course of these years a bill of rights was judicially developed through rulings and precedents, using various creative interpretative techniques such as drawing upon the country's Declaration of Independence despite it lacking formal legal status, referencing the democratic system's unwritten 'fundamental principles' and referring to foreign jurisprudence. Despite there being no judicial review of legislation prescribed by law, the Supreme Court established its authority to review administrative actions, developing doctrines such as the rule of law and ultra vires; the principles of equality, anti-discrimination, and arbitrariness; and the fairness principle which led to various procedural requirements.[16] In the course of reviewing executive limitations of fundamental rights, the courts placed limits on the goals that could justify such actions and required some form of substantive justification for the limitation. Recognizing the need to balance between the public interest and individual rights the court introduced formulas, such as the need to show probability amounting to near-certainty that serious harm will be caused to justify the limitation of speech for the sake of national security.[17]

## B *The Rise in Judicial Activism and the Constitutional Revolution*

The constitutional reality changed when in 1992 two Basic Laws regarding rights were enacted – Basic Law: Human Dignity and Liberty, and Basic Law: Freedom of Occupation.[18] In 1995 the Supreme Court handed down

[16] Aeyal M Gross, 'The Politics of Rights in Israeli Constitutional Law' (1998) 3 Israel Studies 80, 81–85; Dotan (n 9) 32–36.

[17] See the seminal Kol Haam case, regarding a decision to shut down newspapers that had published critique of government policy: HCJ 73/53 *'Kol Ha'am' Co LTD v Minister of Interior* [1953], IsrSC 7 87, available in English at <https://supremedecisions.court.gov.il/Home/Download?path=EnglishVerdicts\53\730\000\Z01&fileName=53000730_Z01.txt&type=4>. More generally see Gila Stopler and Moshe Cohen-Eliya, 'Probability Thresholds as Deontological Constraints in Global Constitutionalism' (2010) 49 Columbia Journal of Transnational Law 75, 99–101, and recently Gila Stopler, 'The rise of proportionality, fall of probability, and the unexpected consequences of the Constitutional Revolution on Israeli constitutional law' (2018) 19 Mishpat U'Mimshal 187 (in Hebrew).

[18] Available in English at <www.knesset.gov.il/laws/special/eng/basic3_eng.htm>. The enactment of the two Basic Laws followed failed attempts to enact a comprehensive Basic

the *Mizrahi Bank* decision, declaring that the Basic Laws hold constitutional status relative to regular legislation. The court went on to hold that it was in its power to review parliamentary legislation to ensure its consistency with the Basic Laws and nullify legislation that is incompatible, despite there being no explicit textual basis for such power.[19] The decision was subsequently termed Israel's 'constitutional revolution', shifting it from a model of parliamentary supremacy into a model of strong judicial review. It was in this decision that the limitation clauses of the Basic Laws were interpreted to require a three-pronged proportionality test.

The constitutional revolution of the mid-1990s occurred at the height of a shift in judicial approach that begun a decade earlier. Up until then, the court refrained from explicitly involving itself in the political arena by using various doctrines and evasion tactics, and was characterized by a more formalistic mode of reasoning. During the 1980s and throughout the 1990s a process of change brought about an increased involvement of the court in the public sphere. This process was multi-faceted, including: the waiving of the standing requirement, declaring that essentially any petitioner could bring an issue of constitutional merit before the court; the erosion of the non-justiciability doctrine, essentially declaring all policy matters – including political questions and national security policy which had previously been outside the scope of judicial review – as potentially subject to legal evaluation; an increase in the intensity of review of executive judgement through requirements such as rationality and reasonableness; and changes in the style of judicial rheotoric, including a more explicit reference to values and direct discussion of policy considerations.[20]

Law on Human Rights. As part of the political compromise that enabled the enactment of these Basic Laws, each contained a preservation clause restricting their application to new legislation only, providing existing legislation immunity from review. The preservation clause was subsequently deleted from Basic Law: Freedom of Occupation, but remains intact with regard to Basic Law: Human Dignity and Liberty.

19 *Mizrahi Bank* (n 1) [74]–[82] (Justice Barak). Acknowledging that the Basic Laws do not address what the remedy should be when regular legislation is passed in contradiction to the Basic Laws, Barak sought the answer in the 'legal culture and tradition'. Starting with the American *Marbury v Madison*, Barak traced the development of the concept of judicial review of legislation in modernity. He referred to the handful of cases where the Israeli Supreme Court had previously held legislation void when in contradiction to formal requirements of Basic Laws. He also offered a row of theoretical justifications for judicial review, all supporting his conclusion that the remedy in cases of contradiction between legislation and a Basic Law was invalidation by the courts.

20 Dotan (n 9) 36–41. For analysis of the causes for this shift see Ran Hirschl, *Towards Juristocracy: The Origins and Consequences of the New Constitutionalism* (HUP 2004);

### C The Backlash against the Court

The constitutional revolution and the increased involvement of the court in controversial questions of policy triggered harsh criticism. Opposition to the court began to gain traction during the 1990s and reached an unprecedented peak in the mid-2000s, in an open battle between the Minister of Justice and the Chief Justice over the court's status and powers.[21] General criticism of the court has since crystalized into a comprehensive agenda for rolling back the court's power and changing the method of judicial appointments. Legislative initiatives along these lines have been proposed consistently over the past decade, although to date no significant change has yet been implemented. Nevertheless, some believe that the threatening climate has led the court to practice a greater level of self-restraint, including the re-introduction of evasion tactics such as the ripeness doctrine, to avoid decisions in sensitive cases thus protecting itself from the materialization of the threats.[22]

The Supreme Court has historically enjoyed a high level of prestige and respect in the eyes of the Israeli public. However, during 2000–09 a sharp decline was registered in the levels of trust in the court in public polling (dropping from 84 to 52 per cent). While a similar decline was suffered by all public institutions over the same time period, the court's level of decline was the sharpest, considering its previously high status.[23] Nevertheless, the Supreme Court continues to be afforded a level of public trust which surpasses other branches of government.[24]

Menachem Mautner, *Law and Culture of Israel* (OUP 2011); Assaf Meydani, *The Israeli Supreme Court and the Human Rights Revolution: Courts as Agenda Setters* (CUP 2011).

21 Isabel Kershner, 'Friends Clash Reflects Battle over Israeli Court' *New York Times* (New York, 22 November 2007) <www.nytimes.com/2007/11/22/world/middleeast/22israel.html?mcubz=0>.

22 Michal Loft, 'Fell as a Ripe Fruit In His Hands – the Ripeness Doctrine in the Supreme Court and the Admittance Committees Act' (2015) 35 Law Online: Human Rights 22 (in Hebrew); Ilan Saban, 'The Political Counter-Attack to the Constitutional Revolution' (2017) ICON-S-IL Blog (in Hebrew).

23 Yael Hadar, 'Israeli Public's Trust in Governmental Institutions over the Past Decade' (2009) 63 Parliament (in Hebrew).

24 In 2016 the level of trust in the court was 56 per cent, whereas the government and the Knesset both enjoyed only some 28 per cent. Among Israel's Arab Citizens the court secured only 52 per cent trust, but it is by far the institution to which they afford the highest level of trust. Generally, the Supreme Court was outranked only be the non-partisan and symbolic President, and the military (Israeli Defence Forces). See Tamar Hermann and others, *The Israeli Democracy Index 2016* (Israel Democracy Institute 2016), available in English at <en.idi.org.il/publications/11985>.

### D The Ways Cases Are Brought before the Supreme Court

The Supreme Court receives criminal, civil, and administrative appeals from courts of lower instances and direct petitions against state authorities in its capacity as the High Court of Justice (HCJ).[25] Although the Supreme Court has ruled that all courts are authorized to hear and decide on constitutional challenges to legislation, in practice such challenges are predominantly submitted directly to the Supreme Court.[26] In 2015 50 per cent of the cases decided by the Supreme Court were direct challenges to the court acting as HCJ against state authorities, 24 per cent civil and 18 per cent criminal appeals, and 8 per cent administrative appeals.[27] In contrast, in our database of cases applying the multi-stage PA, 87 per cent are direct petitions to the HCJ, while civil and administrative appeals are merely 5.5 per cent each, and only 2 per cent are criminal appeals.

Since proportionality as a structured doctrine is predominantly applied by the court in HCJ cases, a brief description of these proceedings is in order. In HCJ cases the Supreme Court is both the first and last judicial instance, and the procedure is significantly flexibile. Hearings before the court are based on affidavits submitted by both sides with nearly no examination of witnesses.[28] The court applies a variety of judicial remedies, allowing it at times to intervene extremely quickly – hearing arguments and ruling within 48 hours on an impending government action, and in other cases allowing proceedings to go on for over a decade – when the submission of the petition sets in motion a governmental policy-making process which the court receives periodical updates on, essentially bringing about change in policy without an explicit judicial ruling ever being written.[29] Research has documented that the majority of HCJ petitions are resolved in out-of-court settlements since the state partially or fully

[25] Prior to the year 2000 all petitions against public agencies were filed directly to the HCJ. A reform introduced in 2000 due to overload on the Supreme Court defined certain categories of cases that were to be filed to administrative courts at the level of district courts, with right to appeal to the Supreme Court. Still, a substantial portion of administrative actions remains under the sole jurisdiction of the HCJ.

[26] Considering that the judicial authority to review legislation was created by the Supreme Court itself, a more conservative practice has evolved in applying this authority in lower instances. See Ori Aronson, 'The Democratic Argument for Decentralized Judicial Review' (2015) 16 Mishpat U'Mimshal 9 (in Hebrew).

[27] Judicial Authority Annual Report 2015 (n 8) 13.

[28] Dotan (n 9) 26–29.

[29] This format has been termed in scholarship 'judicial babysitting'. See Ariel Bendor, 'Trends in Israeli Public Law: Between Law and Adjudication' (2012) 14 Mishpat U'Mimshal 377, 379–89 (in Hebrew).

accepts the petitioners claims, exposing that the HCJ's indirect influence on public policy extends beyond its written decisions.[30] Our database, however, is naturally made up of written and reasoned judgements, and therefore reflects only a fragment of HCJ's activity in the public domain.

## III Structure of Limitation Analysis in Israel

### *A Overview*

Israeli limitation analysis is based on the two-stage model: first, the court investigates whether the contested legislation or administrative action indeed limits a protected right.[31] Once a limitation has been established, the court evaluates the justification of the limitation. Both Basic Law: Human Dignity and Liberty, and Basic Law: Freedom of Occupation contain limitation clauses stating that the rights numerated in these laws can be infringed only 'in a law that is in accordance with the values of the State of Israel, for a worthy purpose, and to an extent that is not beyond necessary'.[32] The court has derived four requirements from this clause.

The first is that right limitations must be by law, reflecting the principles of legality and rule of law.[33] Beyond the formal requirement that the limitation be enacted in law, substantive requirements have been included as well, such as publicity, accessibility, generality, and clarity, although in practice these have not been significantly developed.[34] The

[30] Dotan (n 9) 97–101.

[31] The first stage is a more central component in judicial review of legislation, since the court is only authorized to review legislation if it limits a right protected by the Basic Laws. When reviewing administrative actions the the review power of the court is broader and it is therefore less important to establish whether the petitioner's interest constitutes a constitutionally protected right or not. For this reason, the first stage tends to be less structured or explicit in cases of administrative review.

[32] Section 8 of Basic Law: Human Dignity and Liberty, and section 4 of Basic Law: Freedom of Occupation. The court has stated that the logic of these limitation clauses could be applicable to rights guaranteed by other Basic Laws, despite the fact that they do not contain such clauses, such as the right to vote and the right to stand for election according to Basic Law: The Knesset. See EA 92/03 *Shaul Mofaz v Chairman of Central Elections Committee for the 16th Knesset* [2003], IsrSC 57(3) 793, available in English at <https://supremedecisions.court.gov.il/Home/Download?path=EnglishVerdicts\03\920\000\f06&fileName=03000920_f06.txt&type=4>.

[33] Barak Medina, *Human Rights Law in Israel* (Nevo Publishing 2016) (in Hebrew) sections 1.103–1.110.

[34] See HCJ 10203/03 *Hamifkad Haleumi Ltd. v Attorney General* [2008], IsrSC 62(4) 715 [9] (Justice Beinisch). available in English at <https://supremedecisions.court.gov.il/Home/Download?path=EnglishVerdicts\03\030\102\c22&fileName=03102030_c22.txt&type=4>.

main deliberation in the case law on this requirement relates to the delegation of authority to limit rights from the legislature to an administrative body. The court has adopted the 'non-delegation doctrine',[35] according to which the legislature cannot broadly delegate power to administrative authorities, but is required to detail the guiding priciples of the delegated authority. However, the court's application of this principle is not uniform: in some cases it has struck down right-limiting administrative actions, requiring more explicit or detailed authorization from the legislature;[36] whereas in others it accepted broad authorization clauses as sufficient sources for administrative right limitations.[37] The proper interpretation of the 'non-delegation doctrine' is the subject of ongoing academic debate.[38]

The second requirement is that the law limiting rights must be 'in accordance with the values of the State of Israel'. Both Basic Laws include opening statements according to which their goal is to establish the values of the State of Israel 'as a Jewish and democratic state'. It is therefore widely accepted that the requirement that the law be in

On the principle of generality see HCJ 6971/11 *Eitanit Construction Products Ltd. v State of Israel* (April 2, 2013, unpublished), dismissing a petition against a law that applied to a single company while rejecting the claim that it failed the generality requirement.

35 The Hebrew term is the 'Primary Regulation Rule'.

36 See, e.g., HCJ 3267/97 *Rubinstein v Minister of Defence* [1998], IsrSC 55(2) 255 (holding that the Defence Minister cannot broadly exempt an entire segment of society from compulsory military service without explicit authorization by law), available in English at <https://supremedecisions.court.gov.il/Home/Download?path=EnglishVerdicts\97\670\032\A11&fileName=97032670.A11.txt&type=4>; HCJ 7803/06 *Abu Arfa v Minister of Interior* (13 September 2017, unpublished) (setting boundaries to the discretion of the Minister of Interior to deprive permanent residency permits).

37 HCJ 2887/04 *Abu Madigam v Israel Land Administration* [2007], IsrSC 62(2) 57 (approving state authority to aerial spray of pesticides on illegally planted crops inferred from authority to prevent transgressions; however, see dissent by Justice Joubran), available in English at <https://supremedecisions.court.gov.il/Home/Download?path=EnglishVerdicts\04\870\028\h05&fileName=04028870_h05.txt&type=4>; *Hamifkad Haleumi* (n 34) (approving authority of the public broadcaster to set rules for content limitations on advertisements; however, see dissent by Justice Beinisch; HCJ 769/02 *Public Committee against Torture v Government of Israel* [2006], IsrSC 62(1) 507 (approving state authority for targeted killings against terrorists), available in english at <https://supremedecisions.court.gov.il/Home/Download?path=EnglishVerdicts\02\690\007\A34&fileName=02007690_A34.txt&type=4>.

38 See Gideon Sapir, 'Non-delegations' (2010) 32 Iyunei Mishpat 5 (in Hebrew); Yoav Dotan, 'Non-delegation and the New Legality Principle' (2012) 42 Mishpatim 379 (in Hebrew); Barak Medina, 'The Constitutional Rule Obliging to Set Non-delegations in Law – A Response to Yoav Dotan and Gideon Sapir' (2012) 42 Mishpatim 449 (in Hebrew).

accordance with the values of the state should be interpreted to include both Jewish and democratic values. The challenge, however, is to define what the nature of these values are, particularly when at times Jewish values may coflict with universal democratic principles. Probably due to the contested nature of such questions this requirement has not been significantly developed in the case law and is typically either ignored, quickly brushed over, or merged with the next requirement, that the law promote a worthy purpose.[39] In the small number of cases where the court has addressed this as a separate stage, it has typically emphasized the harmony between the Jewish and democratic values promoted by the governmental policy under review.[40]

The third requirement is that the law must promote a worthy purpose. This has been understood as a threshold requirement, according to which the policy must pursue a legitimate social goal.[41] The fourth and final requirement is that the limitation be to an extent no greater than necessary, which was interpreted in *Mizrahi Bank* as the proportionality requirement. Based on reference to both German and Canadian law, the court adopted a three-pronged test: suitability, necessity, and

[39] An exceptional evocation of this stage was that of Justice Levy dissenting in *Galon,* striking down policy based on lack of coherence with the values of the Jewish and democratic state. This was an a-typical use of this stage, which has not occurred since. See HCJ 466/07 *MK Zehava Galon v Attorney General* [2012], IsrSC 65(2) 44, available in English at <http://versa.cardozo.yu.edu/opinions/gal-v-attorney-general-summary>.

[40] See, e.g., *Solodkin* (regarding municipal bans on the selling of pork, Justice Barak demonstrated how the protection of national and religious feelings with regard to pork, which is an non-kosher product, was in coherence with both Jewish and democratic values). HCJ 953/01 *Solodkin v Beit Shemesh Municipality* [2004], IsrSC 58(5) 595, available in English at <https://supremedecisions.court.gov.il/Home/Download?path=EnglishVerdicts\01\530\009\A19&fileName=01009530_a19.txt&type=4>; *Design 22* (regarding the requirement for a special permit to employ Jewish employees on Saturdays, the court emphasized that a common day of rest on Saturday serves both social-democratic goals and goals related to Jewish heritage). HCJ 5026/04 *Design 22 v Rosenzweig* [2005], IsrSC 60(1) 38, available in English at <http://versa.cardozo.yu.edu/opinions/design-22-shark-deluxe-furniture-ltd-v-rosenzweig>; See also HCJ 3752/10 *Rubinstein v Knesset* (17 September 2014, unpublished) [69]–[70] (Justice Arbel) (regarding the exemption of ultra-orthodox schools from teaching core general education; the Core Education case).

[41] *Mizrahi Bank* (n 1) [91]–[92]; HCJ 4541/94 *Miller v Minister of Defence* [1995], IsrSC 49 (4) 94 [21] (Justice Dorner) (regarding a prohibition on women to enroll in Air Force pilot training). Available in English at <https://supremedecisions.court.gov.il/Home/Download?path=EnglishVerdicts\94\410\045\Z01&fileName=94045410_Z01.txt&type=4>; HCJ 1661/05 *Hoff Azza Regional Council v Knesset* [2005], IsrSC 59(2) 481 [98]; Barak (n 3) 246–47.

proportionality in the strict sense.[42] The suitability test requires that the means chosen be rationally connected to the policy's goal and capable of its achievement.[43] The necessity test, also termed 'the less-restricting means test', is meant to ensure that the limitation of rights is indeed necessary, and cannot be minimized or avoided entirely. It requires the policy-maker to select, from the means that can effectively attain the policy's goal, that which is least-restricting.[44] The final test, proportionality in the strict sense – also termed balancing – requires the weighing of the public benefit arising from the achievement of the policy goal, against the harm caused to the constitutional right, to ensure that the benefit outweighs the harm.[45]

### B *Contexts of Proportionality Analysis*

The cases in the database can be divided based on the types of public acts they review: parliamentary legislation, administrative action of a variety of governmental ministries and public bodies, and judicial decisions.[46] Considering that petitions against public bodies are significantly more common than constitutional challenges to legislation, one would expect that cases of administrative review would be more prevalent in the database.[47] The data confirm this indeed: the significant majority of cases in the database are reviews of administrative action (70 per cent), relative to review of legislation (27 per cent). Only a small minority of cases (3 per cent) were reviews of judicial right limitation.

42 *Mizrahi Bank* (n 1) [95] (Justice Barak).

43 See HCJ 3477/95 *Ben Atiya v Minister of Education* [1996], IsrSC 49(5) 1, 11; HCJ 1715/97 *Investment Consultants Bureau v Minister of Finance* [1997], IsrSC 51(4) 367, 385; Barak (n 3) 303–4.

44 *Mizrahi Bank* (n 1) [95]; HCJ 7052/03 *Adalah Legal Centre for Arab Minority Rights v Minister of Interior* [2006], IsrSC 61(2) 202 (regarding prevention of family unification within Israel for Palestinians; the Family Unification case) [68] (Justice Barak). available in English at <https://supremedecisions.court.gov.il/Home/Download?path=EnglishVerdicts\03\520\070\a47&fileName=03070520_a47.txt&type=4>; Barak (n 3) 317–19.

45 *Mizrahi Bank* (n 1) [95] (Justice Barak); *Adalah* (Family Unification) (n 44) [29] (Justice Barak); Barak (n 3) 341–42.

46 Judicial decisions are cases without a legislative or administrative right limitation prior to the judicial decision. This includes cases involving two private parties with conflicting rights that reach the Supreme Court on appeal from the magistrate level, and cases where the primary authority for right limitation is the judiciary's (such as extradition).

47 In Dotan's sample of HCJ litigation in the 1990, only 7.9 per cent of the petitions were of constitutional nature, the rest were administrative. Dotan (n 9) 91–92.

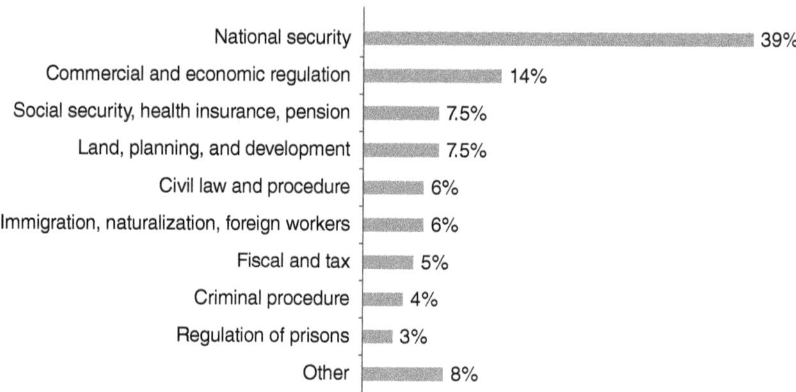


**Figure 4.1** Proportionality cases by subject matter

The majority of cases are public law cases (89.5 per cent), encompassing a relatively broad array of topics, reflecting that proportionality was adopted as a general principle in public law. Only ten cases (6 per cent) in the database can be defined as private law cases, including civil procedure, torts, and libel. An additional seven cases (4 per cent) are criminal, including principled challenges to criminal procedure, investigation powers, detention, and challenges to prosecutorial discretion. The database does not include any cases challenging substantive criminal law. A central cause for the limited number of criminal law is probably the immunity from judicial review granted to legislation enacted prior to 1992, which leaves the majority of criminal law legislation outside the scope of constitutional challenge.

Figure 4.1 displays the distribution of the cases in the database between subject-matters. The most dominant subject-matter that the proportionality framework is applied to is national security, including 62 cases (39 per cent).[48] The size of this category is partially due to a group of 42 security fence cases, which themselves are 26 per cent of the entire database. In 2002 the Israeli Government decided to establish a strategic barrier over 100 kilometres along the 'seamline' between Israel and the

[48] This includes only national security cases which were coded as 'public law'. When taking into consideration two civil law cases and two criminal law cases that also relate to national security, this category grows to 41 per cent of the database. To put this number in context, a study that analysed HCJ cases in the 1990s found security-related cases to constitute 22 per cent of HCJ cases. Dotan, ibid.

Occupied Territories, to prevent passage of terrorists. The legality of the fence from the perspective of both Israeli and International law was upheld by the court in 2004, while holding that the specific route of the fence in each segment was to be subject to PA.[49] This subsequently led to a flood of petitions, each challenging a specific segment of the fence, resulting in the court applying PA in a recurring manner over the course of the decade.

Besides national security, the central subject-matters that proportionality is applied to include commercial and economic regulation (14 per cent),[50] social security, health insurance, and pension (7.5 per cent), and land and infrastructure (7.5 per cent). Additional public law subjects that have only minimally invoked PA include immigration and foreign workers,[51] fiscal and tax issues,[52] and regulation of prisons, each constituting between 3 and 6 per cent of the database.[53]

Figure 4.2 shows the rights whose limitation evoked the use of proportionality in the database, taking into account that a single case can include claims of limitation of more than one right. There are four rights that stand out as the most dominant in the database: property (74 cases, 46 per cent), equality and freedom of movement (each 42 cases, 26 per cent), and freedom of occupation (30 cases, 19 per cent). The large group of security fence cases described earlier, together with additional national security cases that include limitation of free movement, are the cause for

[49] HCJ 2056/04 *Beit Sourik Village Council v The Government of Israel* [2004], IsrSC 58(5) 807, available at <https://supremedecisions.court.gov.il/Home/Download?path=EnglishVerdicts\04\560\020\A28&fileName=04020560_a28.txt&type=4>. It should be mentioned that according to the advisory opinion of the International Court of Justice, delivered only one month after the *Beit Sourik* decision, the establishment of the fence is contrary to International Law. See International Court of Justice, 'Legal Consequences of the Construction of a Wall in the Occupied Palestinian Territory' [2004] *Advisory Opinion, I.C.J. Reports* 2004, 136, available at: <www.icj-cij.org/en/case/131>.

[50] Including regulation of specific branches, such as agriculture, transportation, communication, pension consultants, mail, marketing of products, and foreign worker permits (but note that cases on the employment conditions of foreign workers were included in the immigration category).

[51] Including detention policy of illegal migrants, conditions for foreign workers, naturalization and registration of family members (although family unification of Palestinians was included in national security), and official documentation.

[52] Including budget allocation and tax policy.

[53] The 'other' category includes three cases on employment in the public sector; two cases on exemptions from military draft; two cases on public broadcast; one case on collection of tax debt; one case on a demonstration; one case on a permit for private armed guard; one case on egg donation policy; one case on government intervention in a non-functioning municipality; and one case on revocation of a MKs citizenship; compiling altogether thirteen cases.

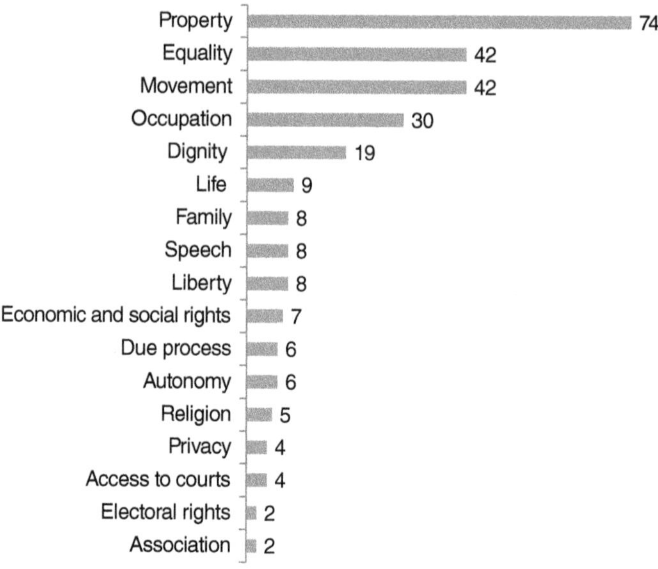


**Figure 4.2** Rights triggering proportionality analysis

the prevalence of freedom of movement in the database.[54] The security fence cases are also partially responsible for the centrality of the right to property.[55] The combination of property, freedom of occupation, and equality – at times separately and at times jointly – are the predominant rights invoked in the contexts of economic regulation and social benefits. Notably, the right to equality is not confined to discrimination of particular protected groups, but is invoked with regard to any form of distinction, and carries the broadest sense of arbitrariness.[56]

Human dignity functions in Israeli constitutional law as both a 'mother-right', from which the majority of other rights are derived, and an independent right in the narrower sense of protection from

[54] To clarify, freedom from detention was included under liberty, not under freedom of movement.

[55] The security fence often involved appropriation of privately-owned Palestinian land, and restricted passage between villages or accessibility to agricultural land. Out of all freedom of movement cases in the database, 70 percent were security fence cases, and 45 percent of all property cases were security fence cases.

[56] 61 percent of the cases in the database involving claims for limitation of equality did not involve a special population.

humiliation and derogatory treatment.[57] Dignity was coded only when it was mentioned as an independent limitation,[58] and yet it is still relatively common, invoked in 12 per cent of the cases.

Interestingly, rights that are nearly absent from the database include freedom of association, election rights, freedom of speech, and privacy. This does not mean that these rights are peripheral in HCJ case law, only that they are not often resolved using the proportionality framework.[59]

As for final outcomes of the analysis,[60] in 27 per cent of the cases the challenged measure was struck down fully or partially, as opposed to 73 per cent where the measure was upheld.[61] Previous empirical research conducted on Israeli Supreme Court case law in different contexts has shown similar acceptance rates.[62] The extent to which measures are upheld as proportional may make the Supreme Court seem relatively 'government-friendly'. It is important, however, to take into account that the database only includes cases that ended with a

57 This is due to the partial nature of the written bill of rights. See subsequently Section IV regarding the stage of establishing a limitation of a right, and generally Aharon Barak, *Human Dignity: The Constitutional Value and the Constitutional Right* (CUP 2015).

58 Thus, for example, cases regarding limitations of freedom of speech or equality were not coded as dignity cases even if the court mentioned the fact that these rights are derived from the right to dignity in Israeli constitutional law.

59 In the context of privacy and election rights specific pieces of legislation exist, which in cases of administrative review can provide a focal point for the decision, minimalizing the need to rely upon the multistage proportionality framework as an organizing structure. In the context of freedom of speech and privacy, these rights often conflict with other rights rather than with a public interest, leading the court to conduct balancing without invoking proportionality. See subsequently Section V.B, regarding horizontal rather than vertical balancing.

60 The final outcome of PA should be distinguished from the final outcome of the case, since at times a case can be accepted based on a different aspect of the analysis other than proportionality. Thus, although 26 per cent of the cases had a finding of disproportionality, 30 per cent of the cases in the database were partially or fully accepted.

61 26 per cent of the administrative measures in the database were struck down, and 29.5 per cent of legislation in the database was struck down. The final outcome was determined based on the majority opinion. Out of the 43 cases ending in a finding of disproportionality, 15 cases (35 per cent) included minority opinions.

62 Weinshall-Margel found a 26 per cent acceptance rate in religion and state matters. Weinshall-Margel (n 11) 72; she found a lower acceptance rate of 12 per cent in counter-terrorism cases, where the court is generally expected to be more pro-government. ibid 88. Eisenberg et al. found an average 30 per cent acceptance rate in appeals decided by the Supreme Court. Theodore Eisenberg, Talia Fisher and Issi Rosen-Zvi, 'Israel's Supreme Court Appellate Jurisdiction: An Empirical Study' (2011) 96 Cornell Law Review 693; Gliksberg found an overall 31 per cent acceptance rate in tax cases. David Gliksberg, 'Does the Law Matter? Win Rates and Law Reforms' (2014) 11 Journal of Empirical Legal Studies.

written judicial decision, while research has shown that at least in terms of review of administrative authority, over 80 per cent of petitioner successes were reached as a result of the state fully or partially accepting the petitioners claims without HCJ having to make an official ruling.[63]

### C Division of Labour between the Stages of the Doctrine

When analysing the application of a multi-stage doctrine, a natural question is the relationship between the stages of the analysis. An underlying assumption in the literature on proportionality is that the different stages do not hold equal weight. This is expressed in discussions over the location of the 'centre of gravity' of the analysis, or in distinctions made between 'threshold' stages and substantive stages.

In *Mizrahi Bank*, Barak argued the necessity stage was the heart of PA.[64] However, later on his position shifted, and in his book on proportionality he officially retracted this position, declaring the last stage of proportionality in the strict sense to be the crown jewel of the analysis – 'the most important of the three sub-tests'.[65] The concrete meaning of the final stage being the most important in Barak's view seems to be that decisions should be deferred, to the extent possible, to the final stage. This is achieved by setting a relatively low standard for passing the previous stages, causing them to be fulfilled more easily. Barak has characterized the worthy purpose and rational connection stages as threshold stages that are not meant to pose significant hurdels but rather sift out a

63 Dotan (n 9) 97; Israel State Attorney's Office annual report for 2016, at 65 (in Hebrew) <www.justice.gov.il/Units/StateAttorney/Documents/Annual-Report-2016.pdf>. The high prevalence of settlements in HCJ litigation is a phenomenon that increased dramatically starting in the 1990s, and has been attributed to the growth in caseload of the court, caused, among other things, by the court's own flexible standing and justiciability standards. This has caused a shift in the role of the HCJ department in the Ministry of Justice, which is central in these settlements. See Dotan (n 9) 119–72.

64 *Mizrahi Bank* (n 1) [95] (Justice Barak): 'It should be stated that among the sub-tests of proportionality the most important is the second sub-test. The requirement that legislation limit a protected right at the least possible level is the heart of the proportionality requirement . . . In many cases the purpose is worthy, and there is rational connection between the goal and the means chosen. The decision focuses on the question of whether the legislature chose the least restricting means' (my translation, T. S).

65 Barak (n 3) 340; Ariel Bendor and Tal Sela, 'On the Proportionality of Proportionality: Following Aharon Barak's Book on Proportionality' (2012) 42 Mishpatim 1113 (in Hebrew).

small number of extreme cases.[66] He has also provided a relatively strict interpretation of the necessity stage, according to which only the existence of an alternative of equal effectiveness can be cause for failure.[67]

Barak's interpretation of the stages and the centrality he affords to the final stage have been criticised in Israeli literature and alternative approaches have been advocated for, including using the worthy purpose more extensively,[68] and emphasizing the first two sub-tests of proportionality, which are more evidence-driven.[69] Nevertheless, at the descriptive level it is almost an unchallenged convention in Israeli scholarship that Barak's conception reflects the practice in Israeli case law, and that the final stage of proportionality in the strict sense is indeed the dominant one.

In order to empirically evaluate the division of labor between the stages, measures for a stage's importance must be defined. Since the debates in the literature revolve around the role of the different stages in invalidating measures and the division of responsibility for justifying the failure,[70] this

[66] Barak (n 3) 246, 315 including a discussion on whether the suitability test is even needed, stating that it is not of great importance. Barak does go on to say that even the small contribution provided by this stage should not be taken lightly.

[67] Barak (n 3) 321–24, and see subsequent section on the necessity test.

[68] Barak Medina and Ilan Saban have advocated that more substantive work be done at the worthy purpose test. Barak Medina and Ilan Saban, 'On Human Rights and Risk-Taking: Democracy, Ethnic Profiling, and the Requirements of the Limitation Clause (Following the Decision re the Citizenship and Entry into Israel Act)' (2009) 39 Mishpatim 47 (in Hebrew); Also see Barak Medina, 'On "Infringement" of Constitutional Rights and "Worthy Purpose": Following Aharon Barak's Book on Proportionality' (2012) 15 Mishpat Ve Asakim 281 (in Hebrew).

[69] Moshe Cohen-Eliya has criticized the value-oriented balancing of the final stage, and advocated for most cases to be decided using the more formalistic and evidence-based necessity stage. In cases of severe right infringement he believes some degree of substantive balancing can be done within the confines of the necessity test. Moshe Cohen-Eliya, 'The Formal and Substantive Meanings of Proportionality in the Supreme Court's Decision Regarding the Security Fence' (2005) 38 Israel Law Review 262. Gideon Sapir has formulated a conception according to which the necessity stage should be used for reaching a compromise between the right and the public interest, whereas the proportionality in the strict sense stage should be used for determinating one over the other. Gideon Sapir, 'Proportionality and compromise' in Shulamit Almog, Dorit Beinisch, Yaad Rotem (eds), *Dorner Book* (Nevo Publishing 2009) 397, 412–13 (in Hebrew).

[70] For example, see Dieter Grimm's comparative discussion on Canada and Germany focusing on the differences in importance between the minimal impairment and balancing stages, which is framed in terms of where the majority of failures occur. Dieter Grimm, 'Proportionality in Canadian and German Constitutional Jurisprudence' (2007) 57 University of Toronto Law Journal 383. In the Israeli context see Cohen-Eliya (n 69), who advocates for justifying failure decisions in terms of suitability and necessity rather than strict proportionality. Medina (n 68), advocates for more significant use of the preliminary worthy

seems to be viewed as the primary way in which the relative importance of the stages is expressed. Therefore, the empirical analysis of the stages will focus on the 41 failure cases in the database.[71] In analysing these failure cases two central measures for each stage will be addressed: the frequency of failure and the termination rate (whether the analysis ends after a failure at that stage). Jointly, these measures capture the notion of importance as expressed previously: the frequency of failure addresses the extent to which each stage takes part in the failing of the measure, and the termination rate addresses whether the stage was sufficient to justify the outcome, or whether additional justification was needed.

Based on the conception of the stages in the literature, the expectation would be for a negligible number of failures at the threshold stages of worthy purpose and suitability, a moderate rise in the number of failures at the necessity stage, and the vast majority of failures at the final stage. Considering that the stages of the doctrine are all understood to be necessary and cumulative requirements, failure at any stage is presumably sufficient to nullify a measure.[72] Therefore, the decision would be expected to come to an end after a failure, regardless of the stage at which it occurs. Especially considering that the threshold stages are viewed as sifting out extreme cases, the expectation would be that such rare failures would immediately bring the analysis to an end.

Interestingly, the quantitative findings are quite different. Figure 4.3 shows the percentage of failures at each one of the stages of the analysis for the 41 cases in the database where measures were struck down.[73] In five cases (12 per cent) the measure failed at the preliminary stage of

purpose stage in the sense that it serve as a more substantial gateway – meaning, having fewer measures pass this stage.

71 For the sake of this analysis two atypical cases were excluded: HCJ 2245/06 *Dobrin v Prison Services* (13 June 2006, unpublished), available in English at <https://supremedecisions.court.gov.il/Home/Download?path=EnglishVerdicts\06\450\022\r02&fileName=06022450_r02.txt&type=4> and RCA 10520/03 *Ben Gvir v Dankner* (12 November 2006, unpublished).

72 Barak (n 3) 131–33.

73 The coding of the outcome at each stage of the analysis was based upon the majority opinion. In the rare cases of differences within the majority opinion, the coding was based on the majority of the majority. When a single case included more than one application of proportionality, these were aggregated and counted as a single coding. In the two cases that reviewed the constitutionality of several sections and some were upheld and some struck down, the coding for the sake of this section was based upon the section that was struck down.

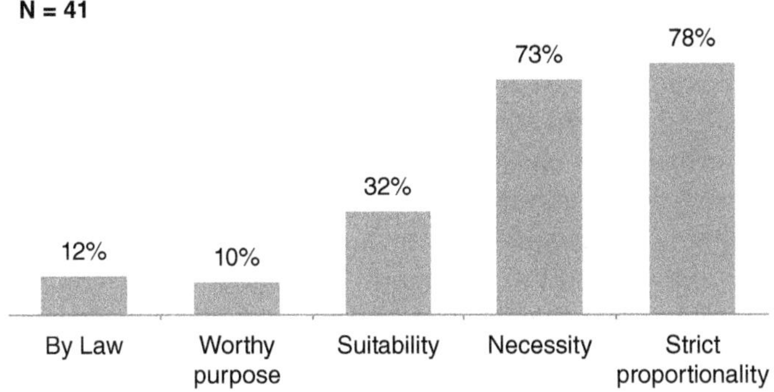


**Figure 4.3** Frequency of failure at each stage of proportionality analysis

requiring the limitation to be authorized by law.[74] As expected, the smallest amount of failures occurred at the worthy purpose stage, with only four cases (10 per cent) failing at this stage. Surprisingly, 13 cases (32 per cent) failed at the suitability stage. The number of failures leaps to 30 cases (73 per cent) at the necessity stage, extremely close to the 32 cases of failure (78 per cent) at the final stage of proportionality in the strict sense.

These findings reveal two surprising phenomena in PA in Israel: first, in the vast majority of cases that result in invalidation, the measure fails at a stage prior to the final stage. Second, in the majority of these cases the analysis continues until the final stage, despite previous failures.

In terms of the frequency of failures prior to the final stage, the data reveal the suitability and necessity tests as more substantial hurdles than typically perceived. Overall, 85 per cent of the cases that failed in the database (35 out of 41 cases) failed at a stage prior to the final stage, while only 15 per cent failed solely at the final stage. This finding is significant considering that in some of the main cases that have become

[74] To clarify the data regarding the stage of 'by law': nearly all cases of administrative review address the question of whether the administrative body was legally authorized to act, as a preliminary question before reviewing the application of authority. Our database only included cases that evaluate this question and subsequently apply the proportionality doctrine, or cases that evaluate this question, fail the measure due to lack of legislative authority, and end the analysis at that stage, but after acknowledging that the analysis was meant to follow the stages of the limitation clause. See HCJ 6745/15 *Abu Hashia v Commander of IDF in the West Bank* (1 December 2015, unpublished); HCJ 6824/07 *Mana v Tax Authority* [2010], IsrSC 64(2) 479. In cases of legislative review this stage is generally assumed to be fulfilled by definition.

canonical examples for the application of the proportionality doctrine in Israel, particularly *Beit Sourik*[75] and *Adalah (Family Unification I)*,[76] the reviewed measure passed all stages and failed only in the final evaluation of proportionality in the strict sense. The database demonstrates that this pattern is actually the minority of invalidation cases,[77] and that contrary to the general perception the balancing stage typically does not bear the entire weight of the failure on its own.

To fully understand this finding, it is important to re-emphasize the selection criteria that the database was founded upon: as detailed in the introduction, the court can conduct judicial balancing without reference to proportionality. In such cases the judicial outcome is based entirely on the outcome of balancing, but since the proportionality doctrine was not applied such cases were not included in the database. Therefore, the data presented should not be construed to mean that it is rare for the Israeli Supreme Court to strike down measures based solely on balancing. What the data do demonstrate is that when the court chooses to apply the multi-stage proportionality framework as the basis for striking down a reviewed measure, the suitability and necessity stages play a significant role in the justification, and only rarely is the full weight of the justification placed solely on the final stage.

[75] *Beit Sourik* (n 49). The prominence of this decision is not confined strictly to Israeli literature. See, e.g., Tom Hickman, 'Proportionality: Comparative Law Lessons' (2007) 12 Judicial Review 31, 50–54, using the case as an illustration of the fact that the use of the necessity test in Israeli case law is limited relative to the final stage of proportionality in the strict sense; Alec Stone Sweet and Jud Mathews, 'Proportionality Balancing and Global Constitutionalism' (2008) 47 Columbia Journal of Transnational Law 74, 136–37, elaborating on the fact that this case turned entirely on the balancing test; David Bilchitz, 'Necessity and Proportionality: Towards a Balanced Approach' in Liora Lazarus, Christopher McCrudden, and Nigel Bowles (eds), *Reasoning Rights: Comparative Judicial Engagement* (Hart Publishing, 2014) 41, 49, 56–57, and Paul Yowell, 'Proportionality in US Constitutional Law' in *Reasoning Rights*, ibid 87, 91 (both referring to the case as an example of a strict interpretation of the necessity test, leading the result of the case to turn solely on balancing); Francisco J Urbina, *A Critique of Proportionality and Balancing* (CUP 2017) 6.

[76] *Adalah* (Family Unification) (n 44).

[77] The division of labour between the sub-tests as applied in *Beit Sourik* does not seem to be representative even of security fence cases: the database includes three cases where segments of the fence were struck down, all of which failed the necessity test. See HCJ 8414/05 *Yassin v Government of Israel* [2007], IsrSC 62(2) 822, available in English at <https://supremedecisions.court.gov.il/Home/Download?path=EnglishVerdicts\05\140\084\n25&fileName=05084140_n25.txt&type=4>; HCJ 2577/04 *El Khawaja v Prime Minister* (19 July 2007, unpublished); HCJ 1748/06 *Mayor of Daharia v Commander of IDF in the West Bank* (14 December 2006, unpublished).

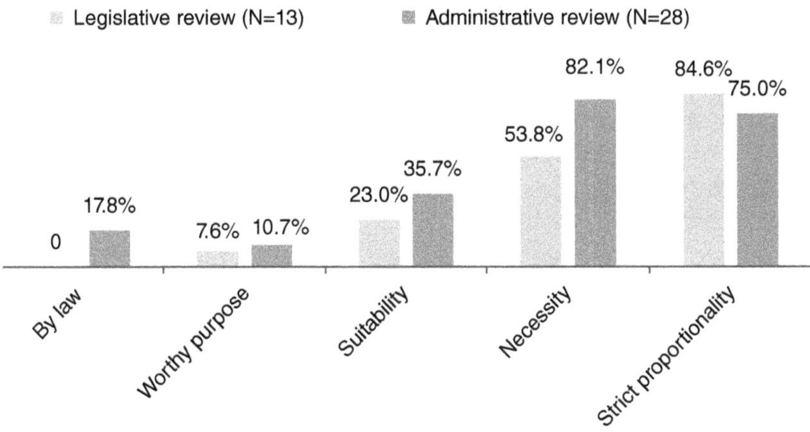


**Figure 4.4** Frequency of failure at each stage by type of reviewed measure

Interestingly, the data reveals differences between cases of legislative review and cases of administrative review in terms of the frequency of failure at each stage, which are shown in Figure 4.4. Failure at the worthy purpose stage occurs at a similar, low frequency in both forms of review, and the failure rates at the suitability stage are generally similar, with nearly 36 per cent failure in administrative review and 23 per cent in legislative review. This gap widens, however, at the necessity stage, with 82 per cent of administrative review cases that result in invalidation failing this stage as opposed to only 54 per cent in legislative review. Both types of review display high frequencies of failure at the final stage, with legislative review leading with 84.6 per cent relative to 75 per cent in administrative review. Overall, in cases that reviewed legislation nearly two thirds (62 per cent) of the cases failed in a stage prior to the final stage. However, in cases of administrative review an overwhelming 96.5 per cent failed prior to the final stage.

These differences between legislative and administrative review may objectively reflect that administrative actions are more likely to be deeply flawed, considering the differences in enactment procedures. An additional explanation would suggest that effectiveness and alternatives can be more easily evaluated in administrative review, which is often characterized by more narrow policy, as opposed to legislation which can be broader and more complex. Finally, this difference may reflect a tendency of the court to apply the sub-tests differently depending on the type of measure under review. The court may critique an administrative body more freely for choosing a means that lacks rational connection or point to an alternate measure that should have been chosen. When reviewing the legislature the court may slightly prefer to frame its decision in terms of an imbalance between social benefit and harm to rights.

The second surprising phenomenon revealed is the tendency of the analysis to continue beyond the first failure. Overall, 28 of the 41 failure cases (68 per cent) include failures at more than one stage, and of the 35 cases that failed at a stage prior to the final stage, in 26 (74 per cent) the analysis continued until the final stage. This practice seems contradictory to the theory of the doctrine, according to which failure at any stage is sufficient for invalidation.

A qualitative evaluation of the cases with multiple failures reveals variety in the dynamics between the first failure and the subsequent failures: in some cases the emphasis is clearly placed on the first failure, which contains the greatest level of detail and may even be concluded with an explicit statement that this failure provides sufficient basis to strike down the measure. The continuation of the analysis beyond this stage in such cases is presented as beyond what is officially required and the reasoning in the subsequent failures is significantly shorter.[78] In other cases, however, the continuation from one failure to the next is done in an uninterrupted sequence with similar levels of detail at each stage, seemingly granting equal weight to all failures in the justification.[79] Finally, in a few cases the final failure is presented in the greatest level of detail and the court may state that doubts that remain regarding previous failures can be put to

[78] For examples of cases with explicit statements that the analysis beyond the first failure is not required and significantly shorter subsequent failures see; *Yassin* (n 77); HCJ 10662/04 *Hassan v National Insurance Institute* [2012], IsrSC 65(1) 782 [31], available in English at <https://supremedecisions.court.gov.il/Home/Download?path=EnglishVerdicts\04\620\106\n44&fileName=04106620_n44.txt&type=4>; HCJ 9593/04 *Morar v IDF Commander in Judaea and Samaria* [2006], IsrSC 61(1) 844 [25] (Justice Beinisch), available in English at <https://supremedecisions.court.gov.il/Home/Download?path=EnglishVerdicts\04\930\095\n21&fileName=04095930_n21.txt&type=4>; HCJ 5870/14 *Hashavim v Judiciary Administration* (unpublished, 12 November 2015).

[79] For examples of cases with an equal level of detail and an uninterrupted sequence between failures see *El Khawaja* (n 77); HCJ 4124/00 *Yekutieli v Minister of Religious Affairs* [2010], IsrSC 64(1) 142; HCJ 4264/02 *Ibillin Breeders Partnership v Ibillin Local Council* (12 December 2006, unpublished).

rest by the failure in the final test, thus attributing greater significance to the final failure relative to earlier ones.[80]

This variety gives rise to two complementary explanations for the prevalent practice of continuing the analysis until the final stage despite previous failures. The first is that the doctrine is primarily applied as a whole unit rather than a modular combination of independent tests. When considering the 74 per cent of cases in which the reviewed measure is upheld where by definition all stages are applied, it is reasonable that inertia can cause discontinuation of the analysis to seem slightly unnatural, even when the additional justification is not truly necessary. The second is that the final stage is generally perceived as having more persuasive power, providing added value to the justification.

A rare objection to the practice of continuing the analysis until the final stage despite previous failure was voiced by Justice Levy, who believed that the final stage of the analysis should be avoided, due to its broadness and lack of clear definition. In his judgements he indeed refrained from continuing the analysis to the final stage.[81]

Figure 4.5 shows the termination rate for each stage – the percentage of cases that came to an end after failing at that stage. Although the overall termination rates are low, the suitability stage presents an exceptionally low rate of only 8 per cent: only a single case out of 13 that failed the suitability stage concluded after that failure. This finding demonstrates that failure at the suitability stage is generally not perceived as sufficient justification for invalidation, requiring it to be supported by at least one additional failure.

[80] For examples of cases where the emphasis is placed on the final failure see Justice Arbel in *Abu Madigam* (n 37) and HCJ 7146/12 *Neget Adam v Knesset* (16 September 2013, unpublished), available in english at <https://supremedecisions.court.gov.il/Home/Download?path=EnglishVerdicts\12\460\071\b24&fileName=12071460_b24.txt&type=4>.

[81] See *Adalah* (Family Unification) (n 44) [9] (Justice Levy); *Galon* (n 39) [19] (Justice Levy); *Hoff Azza* (n 41) [37]–[39] (Justice Levy); HCJ 2150/07 *Abu Safiyeh v Minister of Defence* [2009], IsrSC 63(3) 331 [6] (Justice Levy) (discussing the closure of a road in the West Bank for Palestinians, due to security measures, and holding it unnecessary at the present circumstances), available in English at <https://supremedecisions.court.gov.il/Home/Download?path=EnglishVerdicts\07\500\021\m19&fileName=07021500_m19.txt&type=4>. A single exception is HCJ 4542/02 *Kav Laoved v Government of Israel* [2006], IsrSC 61(1) 346 (the Binding Workers case) [51]–[60] (Justice Levy) (holding that 'binding' foreign labourers to their employers is a disproportional infringement of their rights), available in English at <https://supremedecisions .court.gov.il/Home/Download?path=EnglishVerdicts\02\420\045\o28&fileName=020454 20_o28.txt&type=4>.

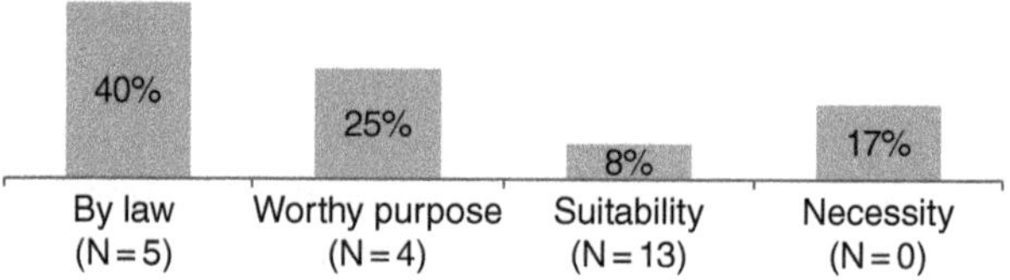


**Figure 4.5** Termination of proportionality analysis after failure

Although theoretically the analysis at each stage must end with an outcome of either pass or fail, in practice justices can at times point out problems at a certain stage of the analysis while refraining from explicitly failing the measure at that point. They may state that despite the difficulties they are willing to assume for the sake of the analysis that the measure passes the stage, or that it 'barely passes'. Alternatively, they may leave the issue undecided, stating that a determination is not required due to a subsequent failure. Such practices can collectively be termed 'negative signalling', and in all such cases the measure subsequently fails a later test.[82] Negative signals can be found in all stages of the analysis prior to the final stage, and overall over one quarter of the failure cases (11 out of the 41) included a negative signal prior to the first explicit failure. Signalling is a partial retreat from the strict sequential character of the test, since doubts from one stage are carried over to later stages.[83] The phenomenon of negative signalling, as well as the practice of continuing the analysis beyond the first failure, both point to a hesitation on the part of the court with regard to the earlier tests, viewing

[82] See, e.g., *Adam* (n 80) [19], [23] (Justice Vogelman) and [10] (Justice Joubran); HCJ 7385/13 *Eitan Israel Migration Policy v Government of Israel* (22 September 2014, unpublished) [52], [59], [68]–[71], [111]–[13], [193] (Justice Vogelman) (striking down a year-long detention of illegal immigrants); HCJ 4644/15 *Raai v Prisons Service* (15 June 2016, unpublished) (Justice Vogelman); HCJ 2605/05 *Academic Center of Law and Business v Minister of Finance* [2009], IsrSC 63(2) 545 [47] (Justice Beinisch) (Prison Privatization), available in English at <http://versa.cardozo.yu.edu/opinions/academic-center-law-and-business-v-minister-finance>.

[83] A downside of this practice is that a less precise message is conveyed to the decision-maker regarding the nature of the flaw in the policy, decreasing the potential of the decision to accurately guide future behaviour. Critique of this kind was voiced by Justices Hendel and Naor in HCJ 8665/14 *Naga Dasta v Knesset* (11 August 2015, unpublished) (regarding the detention of illegal immigrants); *Eitan* (n 82) [12] (Justice Hendel); Talya Steiner, 'Improving the Dialogue between the Court and the Parliament in light of the Infiltrators' Cases' (2015) 29 Israel Bar Journal (in Hebrew).

them as weaker bases for judicial determinations, subsequently seeking to support the outcome in subsequent stages.

To summarize, the empirical analysis reveals that in contrast to the common conception, failure under the proportionality doctrine in Israeli Supreme court case law seldom relies solely on the final stage. It is overwhelmingly common for measures to fail before the final stage, including the suitability stage and especially the necessity stage. Nonetheless, the prevalent judicial practice is to continue until the final stage, regardless of previous failures. This seems to reflect a certain weakness of the earlier stages, which in some cases may not be perceived as a sufficient basis for concluding the decision. It also seems to reflect the general perception of the final stage as one that adds value, contributing to the persuasiveness of the decision.

The findings clearly reflect that not only does the Israeli court not try to avoid balancing, to the contrary: it chooses to engage in balancing voluntarily, even when it is not doctrinally required. However, the centrality of balancing in the judicial application of proportionality does not cause the earlier stages to be easily dismissed. The justification of the invalidation of measures is typically made up of a combination of disproportional harm relative to benefit together with additional flaws in the policy, as reflected by the other sub-tests of the doctrine.

## IV Limitation of a Constitutional Right

Israeli constitutional review is made up of two stages:[84] the first determines whether the state action under review limits a constitutionally protected right. At this stage the plaintiffs bear the burden of proof.[85] Once the limitation is established, the analysis proceeds to the second stage to determine whether the limitation is justified, at which point the burden of proof shifts to the respondants.[86] The first stage of the analysis requires addressing the content and scope of the constitutionally

84 Barak (n 3) 17–25.

85 ibid 438.

86 In the *Mizrahi Bank* case (n 1), it was left undecided whether there should be a presumption of constitutionality that would need to be reversed by the plaintiffs, or whether the plaintiffs would only need to prove the limitation of a right in order for the burden to shift to the state to then prove, in the balance of probabilities, that the limitation was justified. A general convention has since evolved that the state bears the burden to justify the limitation at the second stage of the analysis. See Barak (n 3) 442–49.

protected right and demonstrating that the government action indeed causes a limitation of a right.[87]

## A The Scope of Constitutional Rights

As detailed previously, Israel does not have a comprehensive constitution or a full-fledged bill of rights, and instead relies on two Basic Laws: Human Dignity and Liberty, and Freedom of Occupation. The first explicitly mentions the rights to life and bodily integrity, property, privacy, personal liberty and human dignity, and freedom of movement in and out of the country. Starkly missing are the explicit recognition of the rights to equality, freedom of speech, and freedom of religion. Following the constitutional revolution, the Supreme Court interpreted the concept of human dignity as a 'framework right' or 'mother-right', from which 'daughter-rights' are derived. Over the past two decades the court has recognized an array of 'daughter-rights' as derivatives of human dignity, including freedom to develop one's personality, freedom of speech, freedom of religion, freedom of movement, the right to equality, right to due process, right to family, right to health, right to education, and right to dignified human subsistence.[88] The list of derivative rights is not considered exhaustive and therefore the limits of the right to human dignity continue to evolve on a case-by-case basis.[89]

Justice Barak has been a strong advocate for placing the emphasis of the constitutional analysis on the second stage – the justification of the limitation – rather than on the first stage.[90] This is indeed the dominant approach in the case law, and it is rare for a decision to end with a finding

[87] As mentioned previously, in administrative review it is not necessary to establish that the interest limited is a protected constitutional right.

[88] For a description of the historical process of interpreting the right to human dignity in Israeli case law, see the Hebrew version of Barak's book on *Human Dignity* (n 57) – Aharon Barak, *Human Dignity: The Constitutional Value and the Constitutional Right*, 2 vols (vol I, Nevo Publishing 2014) 139–59. For a more detailed description of the 'daughter rights' recognized in Israeli case law, see ibid at pp. 537–872.

[89] Barak (n 88) vol I, 312–13. One of the areas in which the scope of the right to dignity has been evolving is socio-economic rights, such as health and education. For a review of the development in the recognition of these rights under the scope of human dignity, see Barak (n 88) vol II, 566–98.

[90] Barak (n 3) 45–106. For academic writing criticizing Barak's broad interpretation of the first stage of limitation of the right, see Medina, 'On "Infringement"' (n 68); Bendor and Sela (n 65) 1113–17; Moshe Cohen-Eliya, 'Towards a Procedural Limitation Clause' (2007) 10 Mishpat U'Mimshal 521, 540–61 (in Hebrew).

that a right has not been limited. In the decade of case law analysed for the quantitative analysis, only nine cases were identified in which the court held that no right had been limited and then terminated the decision without proceeding to conduct limitation analysis.[91] In slightly under 20 per cent of the cases in the database the court found that no right of the petitioner was restricted, but still continued to demonstrate that even if a right had been limited, the limitation would be considered proportional. In the majority of cases (80 per cent) at least one right was found to have been limited, and the conflict between rights and interests was resolved at the second stage of justification.

Occasionally, the court will avoid explicitly ruling on whether there was indeed a right limitation. Instead, the court can hold that even if it were to be assumed that there was a limitation – it could be justified.[92] Justice Barak explicitly justified this practice in *Silgado*, stating that if the determination of a limitation is difficult and unnecessary – it can be skipped.[93] Justice Hendel recently criticized this practice, stating that the court should make the effort to decide whether a right has been limited rather than leave this unresolved, to help clarify the contours of rights and develop guidelines for the future.[94]

An outlier approach has been expressed by former Chief Justice Grunis, who applied a stricter standard and refrained from considering every negative effect on a plaintiffs' interest to be a limitation of a

[91] These cases were not included in the database, since they did not apply multi-stage PA.

[92] See, e.g., *Rubinstein* (Core Education) (n 40); HCJ 7245/10 *Adalah Legal Centre for Arab Minority Rights v Ministry of Welfare* (4 June 2013, unpublished) (discussing welfare deductions due to failure to immunize children and the right to equality; the child immunization case); HCJ 5998/12 *Ronen v The Knesset* (25 August 2013, unpublished) (discussing the right to property and pension endowments); HCJ 3071/05 *Luzon v Government of Israel* [2008], IsrSC 63(1) 1 (discussing whether public funding for special medical treatments is part of the right to live in dignity); HCJ 5627/02 *Seif v Government Press Office* [2004], IsrSC 58(5) 70 (discussing the freedom of press of Palestinians in the Occupied Territories); HCJ 3734/11 *Davidian v The Knesset* (15 August 2012, unpublished) (discussing change in taxation of future oil production and the right to property).

[93] CrimA 4424/98 *Silgado v Israel* [2002], IsrSC 56(5) 529, [21] (Justice Barak) (in the context of whether a criminal offence constitutes a limitation of the constitutional right to liberty). An additional phenomenon is when petitioners claim that several rights have been limited, and the court chooses to focus its discussion on one particular right. A disproportional limitation of that right will lead to nullification of the legislation, making the decision regarding the other rights unnecessary. See, e.g., HCJ 1030/99 *MK Haim Oron v Knesset Chairman* [2002], IsrSC 56(3) 640.

[94] *Rubinstein* (Core Education) case (n 40) [6] (Justice Hendel).

constitutional right. This led him to reject petitions at the first stage more often, grounding his approach in the concern that a broad conception of constitutional rights may result in a 'watering down' of rights, ultimately promoting disrespect for the constitutional discourse.[95] However, as detailed earlier, this is not the prevelant practice.

### *B Government Actions as Limitations of Rights*

After establishing that the affected interest is included within the scope of the constitutionally protected right, it must also be established by the petitioners that the government action under review limits the right. In the majority of cases this is straightforward and does not elicit much discussion. However, there have been cases where the effect of the government action on rights was not clearly evident, and the court may require the plaintiffs to produce evidence to support their claim that the government action will indeed limit rights.

For example, in *Commitment to Social Justice*, the plaintiffs claimed that a 30 per cent reduction of government income support was a limitation of the constitutional right to minimum conditions for dignified human subsistence, a derivitive of human dignity. The majority of the court accepted the right as a derivative, but held that the plaintiffs had not established that the challenged reduction would result in the limitation of the right. They further specified that to factually support such a claim all forms of government assistance would have to be considered, and that rights limitations could be ascertained only on an individual basis as opposed to a general finding regarding the reduction as a whole.[96]

The impact of a policy on rights may be uncertain at the point of judicial review, since it is dependant upon the discretion and interpretation of the administrative body implementing the policy. Traditionally,

[95] For a general statement of Justice Grunis's approach see the *Rubinstein* (Core Education) case, ibid [29] (Justice Grunis); *Ronen* (n 92); HCJ 2334/02 *Shtanger v Knesset Chairman* [2003], IsrSC 58(1) 786 (the Lawyers case); HCJ 5578/02 *Manor v Minister of Finance* [2004], IsrSC 59(1) 729; HCJ 5975/12 *Cigarette vendors v Ministry of Health* (3 July 2013, unpublished). Also, see Ittai Bar Siman Tov, 'John Hart Grunis?: The jurisprudence of Chief Justice Grunis in Light of Ely's Constitutional Theory' (2015) 9 Din U-dvarim 67 (in Hebrew).

[96] HCJ 366/03 *Commitment to Peace and Social Justice Society v Minister of Finance* [2005], IsrSC 60(3) 464, available in English at <https://supremedecisions.court.gov.il/Home/Download?path=EnglishVerdicts\03\660\003\a39&fileName=03003660_a39.txt&type=4>, but see dissenting opinion by Justice Levy.

the court has accepted prima facie challenges to a policy even before its implementation, finding that the right limitation is inherent in the policy itself.[97] However, in recent years the court has increased its use of the 'ripeness doctrine', pointing to the uncertainty in how the policy would be applied, leading to rejection of the petition.[98]

There has been limited discussion in the case law on whether demanding payment as a pre-condition to fulfill a right or withdrawing governmental funding in reaction to behaviour that is fulfillment of a right are to be considered limitations of rights.[99] These questions have not been sufficiencly developed, and a clear doctrine is still lacking.

### C *The Severity of the Limitation*

Typically, the assessment of the severity of limitation is done at the final balancing stage, in comparison to the benefit of the policy. However, occasionally the first stage of analysis can include some form of reference to the severity. Such a practice makes much sense: it has been stated that the level of scrutiny with which the limitation analysis is conducted should depend upon the importance of the right – the more important the right, the higher the standard for passing each stage.[100] For this

[97] See, e.g., in the *prison privatization* case (n 82), the majority of the court held that the construction of a first privatized prison facility was by definition a limitation of the rights to liberty and human dignity of the future inmates held in that facility, regardless of the way the privatized authority would be executed. See Justice Beinisch, at para. 19. Justice Levy agreed that the privatization limited rights, but held in the minority that PA could not be conducted until the privatization is implemented, since the benefit to prisoners' rights could not yet be evaluated.

[98] See, e.g., HCJ 3429/11 *Alumni Association of the Arab Orthodox School v Minister of Finance* (5 January 2012, unpublished) (maintaining that a law authorizing the finance minister to withdraw government support for anyone commemorating the Palestinian Nakba cannot be reviewed in abstract), available in English at <http://versa.cardozo.yu.edu/opinions/alumni-association-arab-orthodox-school-haifa-v-minister-finance>; HCJ 2311/11 *Sabach v Knesset* (17 September 2014, unpublished) (maintaining that a law allowing for small communities to set criteria for accepting residents cannot be reviewed in abstract). For the debate over the use of the ripeness doctrine see Ronen Poliak, 'Relative ripeness: Applied or abstract constitutional judicial review' (2014) 37 Iyunei Mishpat 45 (in Hebrew); Medina (n 33) 1.69–1.74.

[99] HCJ 2651/09 *Association for Civil Rights in Israel v Minister of Interior* (15 June 2011, unpublished) (discussing whether charging increased payment for renewal of passports in case of loss is an limitation of freedom of movement; the Passports case); *Adalah* (Child Immunization) (n 92); *Nakba* case (n 98); Medina (n 33) 1.62.

[100] HCJ 6427/02 *The Movement for Quality Government v Knesset* [2006], IsrSC 61(1) 610 (the Ultra-Orthodox Exemption 2006) [53] (Justice Barak); HCJ 6298/07 *Ressler*

purpose the importance of the right and the severity of the limitation need to be established in advance of limitation analysis. In practice, however, it is difficult to identify a clear pattern that explains when the first stage of the analysis includes a detailed analysis of severity of limitation.[101] The degree of detail seems to ultimately be a stylistic decision made by individual justices, used at times as a way to frame their subsequent analysis and even foreshadow their decision.[102]

There are different methods for evaluating severity of limitation: one involves ranking the importance of the right relative to other rights, despite a clear and explicit hierarchy of rights never being established.[103] It has been stated in different opportunities that human dignity in its core sense of non-humiliation, the right to life and bodily integrity,

*v Knesset* (21 February 2012, unpublished) [52]–[53] (Justice Beinisch). Available in English at <https://supremedecisions.court.gov.il/Home/Download?path=EnglishVerdicts\07\980\062\n18&fileName=07062980_n18.txt&type=4>; Dalia Dorner, 'Proportionality', in Aharon Barak and Haim Berenson (eds), *Berenson Book,* 3 vols. (in Hebrew, Nevo Publishing 2000) vol. II, 281.

101 In cases where the limitation is undisputed a detailed evaluation of severity is generally not conducted. See CrimA 6659/06 *Ploni v State of Israel* [2008], IsrSC 62(4) 329 (regarding a law authorizing internment of 'unlawful combatants', i.e. those who are not eligible for prisoner of war status under international law; the Unlawful Combatants case), available in English at <https://supremedecisions.court.gov.il/Home/Download?path=EnglishVerdicts\06\590\066\n04&fileName=06066590_n04.txt&type=4> and HCJ 450/97 *Tnufa Human Resources v Minister of Labour and Welfare* [1998], IsrSC 52(2) 433 (discussing requirement for substantial cash deposit as prerequisite for human resources sub-contractor license). However, there are exceptions including detailed evaluation of severity despite the limitation being uncontested, such as *Adam* (n 80). When the state holds that no right was limited, naturally the analysis is more extensive. See *Kav Laoved* (Binding Workers) (n 81) [29]–[33] (Justice Levy), and [35]–[43] (Justice Procaccia); CrimApp 8823/07 *Ploni v State of Israel* [2010], IsrSC 53(3) 500 (the Due Process case) available in English at <https://supremedecisions.court.gov.il/Home/Download?path=EnglishVerdicts\07\230\088\p25&fileName=07088230_p25.txt&type=4>. However, even in light of disagreement on the question of limitation and severity the discussion may be conducted at the final balancing stage, such as *Abu Safiyeh* (n 81) [33] (Justice Vogelman).

102 See, e.g., in the *Avneri* case that reviewed legislation that established tort liability upon individuals who call for a boycott on political grounds. There was agreement among the justices that the law limited freedom of speech, but this stage already revealed the differences between the justices: the characterization of the limitation as pertaining to the core or periphery of the right foreshadowed the differences in outcome of the proportionality analysis. HCJ 5239/11 *Avneri v Knesset* (15 April 2015, unpublished), available in English at <http://versa.cardozo.yu.edu/opinions/avneri-v-knesset>.

103 Justice Hendel has recently pointed out that it would be helpful to develop such a hierarchy as a standard that would guide the court in its balancing. See *Galon* (n 39) [4] (Justice Hendel).

freedom of political speech, liberty from detention, and the right not to be discriminated against based on specific group classifications, enjoy a more strict level of protection. In contrast, rights to property, freedom of occupation, and privacy are generally afforded a lower level of protection.[104]

A second method for evaluating severity of right limitation is classifying it as affecting either the core or the periphery of the right. Reference to the right's core, or even 'hard core', does not refer to an absolutely protected aspect of the right but rather to more important aspects which make the limitation more severe. When limiting a core aspect of a right, a higher level of justification and a more substantial benefit to the public interest are required, whereas limitation of a peripheral aspect will require a lower level of justification.[105] The terms 'core' and 'periphery' have been used, for example, with reference to the right to due process,[106] liberty,[107] dignity,[108] freedom of speech,[109] family,[110] health,[111] and water.[112]

Certain rights have particular models for distinguishing between more and less severe aspects of limitations. For example, a structural

[104] See Medina (n 33) 1.94; *Davidian* (n 92); HCJ 7956/10 *Gabai v Minister of Finance* (19 November 2012, unpublished) [22]–[24] (Justice Rubinstein).

[105] *Adalah (Family Unification)* (n 44) [398]–[99] (Justice Cheshin). This is also stated by Justice Barak in HCJ 5016/96 *Horev v Minister of Transportation* [1997], IsrSC 51(4) 1, at 49 (discussing legality of blocking roads on the Sabbath for religious reasons), available in English at <https://supremedecisions.court.gov.il/Home/Download?path=EnglishVerdicts\96\160\050\A01&fileName=96050160.A01.txt&type=4>; Justice Beinisch in *Hassan* (n 78); AAA 5493/06 *Emanuel Peled v Prisons Service* (12 October 2010, unpublished); and see Barak (n 57) 362–63

[106] *Ploni* (Due Process) (n 101) [29].

[107] *Adam* (n 80) [72] (Justice Arbel).

[108] HCJFH 204/13 *Salech v Prisons Service* (14 April 2015, unpublished) [3]–[4] (Justice Hendel) (maintaining that prisoners' core rights to dignity include food and medical treatment and conditions of imprisonment, as opposed to peripheral aspect, such as education); HCJ 4634/04 *Doctors for Human Rights v Minister of Internal Security* [2007], IsrSC 62(1) 762 (maintaining that sleeping on a bed is part of prisoner's core right to dignity).

[109] *Dobrin* (n 71); *Peled* (n 105); *Hamifkad Haleumi* (n 34).

[110] *Adalah* (Family Unification) (n 44); HCJ 4293/01 *New Family v Minister of Labour and Welfare* (24 March 2009, unpublished) (discussing whether the right to adopt is part of the constitutional right to family), available in English at <https://supremedecisions.court.gov.il/Home/Download?path=EnglishVerdicts\01\930\042\r07&fileName=01042930_r07.txt&type=4>.

[111] *Luzon* (n 92) [16].

[112] CA 9535/06 *Abu Musaed v Water Commissioner* (5 June 2011, unpublished) [24] (discussing accessibility to water as a human right, and its core and peripheral aspects).

differentiation in the context of freedom of occupation was adopted from German law, distinguishing between a limitation on the entrance into a field of occupation and regulation of the occupation, with the first being considered more severe.[113] In the context of the right to property, limitations relating to an individual's home are treated as especially severe, as opposed to other forms of property.[114]

The severity of the right limitation may be a contested issue, and the court may critique the state for taking too narrow a perspective on the effect of a policy. In *Abu Safiyeh* and *Dir Samet*, both reviewing restrictions on Palestinian use of particular roads due to security reasons, the state presented the limitations of movement as minimal – merely causing slight detours. However, the court categorized the limitations as significantly more substantial, pointing out the collateral effects of the restriction of movement on livelihood, access to school and health care, social isolation, effects on accessibility to water due to transfer costs and more. The court also emphasized the fact that the ban was absolute, applied for a prolonged period of time affecting thousands of residents, all of which increased the severity of the limitation.[115]

## V Worthy Purpose

This stage is typically presented as a threshold requirement, primarily meant to weed out clearly illegitimate goals, and therefore not a substantial hurdle to pass.[116] The quantitative analysis indeed confirms that the smallest number of failures occures at this stage – only 10 per cent of the cases that ultimately failed. However, the importance of this stage goes

[113] HCJ 4769/95 *Menachem v Minister of Transportation* [2002], IsrSC 57(1) 235 [18]–[20] (Justice Beinisch) (regarding charging high fees for taxi licenses); AAA 4436/02 *Tishim Kadurim Restaurant v Haifa Municipality* [2004], IsrSC 58(3) 782 (regarding regulation of gambling and freedom of occupation); *Cigarette vendors* (n 95) [9] (Justice Grunis).

[114] *Gabai* (n 104) [22] (Justice Rubinstein); HCJ 7015/02 *Ajuri v Commander of IDF in the West Bank* [2002], IsrSC 56(6) 352 (discussing restriction of movement for families of Palestinian terrorists), available in English at <https://supremedecisions.court.gov.il/Home/Download?path=EnglishVerdicts\02\150\070\A15&fileName=02070150_a15.txt&type=4>; *Hoff Azza* (n 41).

[115] *Abu Safiyeh* (n 81) [33]–[35] (Justice Vogelman); HCJ 3969/06 *Dir Samet Village Council v Commander of IDF in the West Bank* (22 October 2009, unpublished) [29]–[32] (Justice Beinisch). In both cases, the discussion of the severity of the right limitation was conducted as part of proportionality in the strict sense. Since these are cases of administrative review, there wasn't a preliminary stage establishing the limitation of a constitutionally protected right.

[116] Barak (n 3) 246.

beyond the handful of cases where the goal was held unworthy: the very determination of what the policy goal is structures the discussion in a way that may ultimately effect the outcome.

The worthy purpose stage theoretically includes two internal requirements: the content of the goal must be worthy of pursuit; and there must be a degree of importance or urgency in attaining the goal.[117] However, before determining whether the goal is both worthy and important, there is an implicit preliminary stage of defining what the goal of the policy is.

## A *Establishing What the Purpose Is*

This preliminary stage is at times the most substantial, though inexplicit, aspect of this test. Definition is a creative act, involving choices of what to include and exclude, what to emphasize and what level of abstraction to use. The act of definition begins with the parties and then passes on to the court, and as will be demonstrated these often implicit and unannounced choices can have substantial effects on the analysis.

This section will begin by addressing two aspects in the process of goal definition that have the effect of avoiding difficult decisions at this stage: the relationship between the officially declared goal and unofficial motivations, and the level of abstraction used in the goal definition. These will be followed by a discussion regarding the phenomenon of goal multiplicity and its effects on the subsequent analysis.

### 1 Official Declarations of Objective as Opposed to Unofficial Goals and Motivations

One of the choices that determine the definition of the policy's goal is what sources are relied upon. In simple cases all sources point towards the same goal, which is often undisputed between the parties. However, in some cases there are discrepancies between sources: the official goal as appears in the legislation's explanatory notes or declared by the Attorney General as opposed to unofficial goals expressed on different occasions by ministers, members of parliament, or high-ranking public officials. In such cases the question arises whether the court should address these other sources and how the discrepancies should be resolved.

[117] Justice Levy in *Galon* (n 39) [22]–[23], added a third requirement – that the goal be sufficiently sensitive to the existence of rights, and see a more elaborate discussion on Justice Levy's position in the subsequent section on multiple goals.

In *Mizrahi Bank* – the first case of judicial review of legislation in Israel – Chief Justice Shamgar set a presumption that the legislature acts in good-faith, and therefore the court's analysis should be based on the official statement of the legislature, rather than an analysis of the subjective intentions of particular members of parliament.[118] Justice Barak, pointing to the complexity of the question, left it undecided. Since then it has generally become a matter of consensus that the court focuses on the officially stated goal of the legislature, and does not address the unofficial motivations of individuals involved in the process.[119] This position has been summarized in the saying that the court must 'analyze the law and not psychoanalyze the legislature',[120] which has often been coupled with the reservation that the intent of a collegial body cannot be inferred from the expressions of individual members.[121]

Only in a single case has the court explicitly concluded at the worthy purpose stage that the legislature's goal was different than that officially stated, and subsequently illegitimate: in *Oron*, legislation setting the

[118] *Mizrahi Bank* (n 1) [81] (Justice Shamgar).

[119] In the *Guttmann* case, which challenged legislation raising the electoral threshold, the official goal was to increase governance by limiting the number of small parties. However, statements by leading politicians specifically targeted the Arab parties, in an attempt to exclude them from parliament. Most justices refrained from discussing these statements. Justice Rubinstein was the only justice to include an analysis of the motivations, but he was ultimately persuaded by the sincerity of the official goal. HCJ 3166/14 *Guttman v Attorney General* (March 12, 2015, unpublished) [1]–[2] (Justice Rubinstein). In *Adalah* (Family Unification) (n 44) the majority rejected the claim that the legislation was motivated by demographic considerations of maintaining the Jewish majority in the state. See Justice Barak [79]–[81], and [24] (Justice Cheshin); *Galon* (n 39) [6] (Justice Arbel). Only Justice Joubran addressed the evidence on this matter but chose not to make a determination on this question.

[120] HCJ 246/81 *Agudat Derekh Eretz v Broadcasting Authority* [1981] IsrSC 35(4) 001 [12] (Justice Barak) (regarding the preference of parties already represented in the Knesset over contenders in the allocation of broadcast time in advance of the elections), available in English at <https://supremedecisions.court.gov.il/Home/Download?path=EnglishVerdicts\81\460\002\Z01&fileName=81002460_Z01.txt&type=4>; Quoted by Justice Grunis in *Sabach* (n 98) [26].

[121] *Sabach* (n 98) [5] (Justice Melcer). In *Seif* (n 92), the evidence included an explicit statement by the head of the Government Press Office that the motivation for the newly introduced ban on issuing journalist cards for Palestinian journalists was a principled response to the expression of anti-Israeli views by Palestinian journalists. Despite acknowledging this evidence, the court conducted its analysis based on the officially stated goal of security, considering that the journalist card provides access to press conferences in sensitive locations. However, the scepticism that the court expressed at the necessity stage regarding the security justification for a complete ban seems to reflect its scepticism regarding the sincerity of this goal.

terms for selection of radio channels for broadcasting licenses through an auction provided automatic licenses for channels that fulfilled certain conditions, one of which was that the channel had been broadcasting for the previous five years. The objectively stated goal was diversifying the radio channels to fulfil the needs of different sections of society. However, the court reviewed the legislative history – including the explanations of the member of Knesset who initiated the amendment – and found that the concrete goal was to provide a license to 'Channel 7', which had previously been illegally broadcasting, and whose operators were facing criminal charges. The court held this goal unworthy: it did not promote a public goal and was contrary to the concept of rule of law since it rewarded law breakers.[122] This case was unique, since the Attorney General himself sided with the plaintiffs, and took the position that the law was unconstitutional.

A rare example where the legislative motivation was a pivotal issue that divided the court was the *Sabach* case, reviewing legislation regulating acceptance committees to community villages. The justices in the minority addressed the legislative history and statements by the law's initiators, some of whom explicitly stated that the goal was to block the acceptance of Arabs to community villages.[123] Because of these statements they found the law to facilitate discrimination despite it including a non-discrimination clause.[124] However, the position of the majority, following the court's general tradition, was that statements made by particular members of the Knesset regarding the goals of the law should not be considered in the constitutional analysis, thus side-stepping this issue.[125]

[122] *Oron* (n 93) [33]–[40]. However, out of precaution, the court was willing to accept the claim that there was an additional and more abstract goal of diverse representation in the media. The court then proceeded to conduct PA based on the more abstract definition of the goal, and struck down the legislation at the suitability stage. It is interesting to note that even in this clear-cut case, and with the backing of the Attorney General who objected to the law, the court was still hesitant to strike down legislation based solely on the worthy purpose stage.

[123] *Sabach* (n 98) (Justices Joubran and Arbel).

[124] This case is slightly complex since this discussion did not take place at the worthy purpose stage, but at the preliminary stage of determining whether the legislation limited rights. However, the debate was clearly focused on whether the interpretation of the law's purpose should address sources other than the official texts accompanying the legislation.

[125] *Sabach* (n 98) (Justices Grunis and Melcer).

## 2 The Level of Abstraction Used in the Definition of the Goal

It is typical to find goals defined at high levels of abstraction, such as national security,[126] rule of law,[127] public health,[128] preventing crime,[129] and public order.[130] As I will demonstrate, phrasing the goal at a high level of abstraction can enable avoiding problematic issues at this early stage, postponing their resolution to later stages, subsequently affecting the way they are discussed.

In cases involving problematic means, choosing a more abstract definition postpones the discussion of the issue. For example, in *Adam* the court reviewed a three-year detention period for illegal migrants. Justices who framed the goal in an abstract manner as the prevention of unlawful migration held it to be worthy; but justices who included prolonged detention for the sake of deterrence of future migrants as part of the goal had to then address the problematic nature of these means.[131]

Another context where the level of abstraction can lead to avoiding problematic issues is when the plaintiffs' challenge is directed at a subsection of a law or an amendment of a pre-existing law. If the goal is defined in terms of the overarching legislation, this stage of the analysis becomes irrelevant, since the concrete goal of the particular section or the

[126] *Ploni* (Unlawful Combatants) (n 101); *Ploni* (Due Process) (n 101); *Dir Samet* (n 115); *Abu Safiyeh* (n 81); and LHCJA 6956/09 *Yonas v Prisons Service* (October 7, 2010, unpublished) (regarding limitation of visits to security prisoners).

[127] AAA 4614/05 *State of Israel v Oren* [2006] 61(1) 211 [12]; *Abu Madigam* (n 37) [33]–[34] (Justice Arbel); *Abu Musaed* (n 112) [41]–[42] (Justice Procaccia); HCJ 1953/09 *Elwalidi v Minister of Agriculture* (8 July 2009, unpublished) [25] (Justice Danziger) (regarding a requirement to present proof of tax payments as a pre-condition for receiving service from the state).

[128] *Adalah* (Child Immunization) (n 92); *Cigarette vendors* (n 95).

[129] HCJ 3809/08 *Association for Civil Rights in Israel v Israel Police* (28 May 2012, unpublished) [11] (regarding legislation allowing security authorities to receive communication metadata from phone and internet providers; the Data Communication case), available in English at <http://versa.cardozo.yu.edu/opinions/association-civil-rights-israel-v-israel-police>.

[130] HCJ 316/03 *Bakri v Israel Film Council* [2003], IsrSC 58(1) 249 (regarding the banning of a controversial film presenting supposed lies), available in English at <https://supremedecisions.court.gov.il/Home/Download?path=EnglishVerdicts\03\160\003\L15&fileName=03003160_L15.txt&type=4>; *Horev* (n 105); HCJ 7311/02 *Association for Support and Defence of Bedouin Rights in Israel v Beer Sheva Municipality* (22 June 2011, unpublished) (Discussing the decision of the municipality to turn an old unused mosque into a museum; the Mosque case).

[131] *Adam* (n 80) [85]–[91] (Justice Arbel) and [9]–[10] (Justice Joubran). For a full discussion on whether deterrence is to be considered a worthy purpose, see later section on unworthy purposes.

amendment will only arise at the necessity stage or the final balancing stage. For example, *Adalah (tort liability)* challenged an amendment in a series of amendments dealing with state tort liability for damages caused in the Occupied Territories. The challenged amendment held that damage caused by the state in certain areas and during certain dates would categorically be presumed to have been caused by combat, absolving the state. At the worthy purpose stage the court accepted the state's abstract definition of the legislative goal as creating compatibility between tort liability and the state of combat.[132] Only at the necessity stage did the court find that this goal had already been attained by the previous amendment, and therefore the additional step taken in the current amendment towards relieving the state entirely from its duty to prove causation to an act of combat was beyond necessary. This discussion could have been conducted at the worthy purpose stage, had the goal been defined concretely in reference to the specific amendment under review.[133]

Another issue affected by the level of abstraction is the issue of administrative efficiency and financial saving. A more concrete definition of the goal can reveal that the underlying objective is that of financial saving or efficiency, which may at times not be considered a worthy enough goal. A high level of abstraction can cause the financial nature of the goal to arise only at the necessity stage, in the context of evaluating alternatives.[134]

To conclude these last two points, the fact that it is rare for the court to strike down policy at the worthy purpose stage is often a result of choices made regarding the goal definition, such as focusing on the objectively stated goal and using a high level of abstraction, both resulting in problematic issues being avoided at this stage. At times these issues are deflected to later on in the analysis, resurfacing more or less explicitly, particularly at the suitability and necessity stages.[135]

132 HCJ 8276/05 *Adalah Legal Centre for Arab Minority Rights v Minister of Defence* [2006], IsrSC 62(1) 1 (the Tort Liability case) [32]–[33] (Justice Barak), available in English at <https://supremedecisions.court.gov.il/Home/Download?path=EnglishVerdicts\05\760\082\a13&fileName=05082760_a13.txt&type=4>.

133 ibid [35]–[41] (Justice Barak).

134 See elaboration on this point in Section V.D, regarding efficiency as a worthy purpose.

135 For examples of problematic goals resurfacing at the suitability stage see n 191 and accompanying text. As for problems with the goal resurfacing at the necessity test, in some of the challenges to segments of the security fence the court rejected claims raised at the worthy purpose stage that the objective of the fence was the annexation of

Although explicit failures at the worthy purpose stage are uncommon, expressions of unease may still be echoed by way of negative signalling.[136] Frequent signalling can attest to a reluctance to actively determine failure. The stage that stands out with the largest gap between explicit failures and negative signals is the worthy purpose stage: while only 4 of the 41 failure cases in the database (10 per cent) explicitly failed at the worthy purpose stage, in an additional six cases a problematic signal was expressed by at least one of the justices of the majority at this stage, all of which resulted in the measure being struck down later on.[137] This is an additional testament to the reluctance of the court to fail a measure at the worthy purpose stage, even when difficulties in the analysis do arise.

## 3 Multiple Goals

Typically, policy goals are defined in single form (e.g. national security, public order, or consumer protection). However, some policies have multiple goals. There are simple cases where the policy is objectively geared at two separate public interests – such as raising passport issuance fees both to cover costs and increase deterrence,[138] or prohibiting cigarette dispensers to both minimize accessibility and restrict advertising by eliminating the machines themselves.[139] In such cases, the multiplicity does not have any particular effect on the analysis.

The more complex cases are those where the multiplicity of goals seems to result from a conscious choice of framing. This raises the question of whether the framing originates from the policy-maker or the court, and what the ramifications of this framing are on the analysis.

settlements, instead relying solely upon the official goal of prevention of terrorism. However, when analysing alternative routes as part of the necessity test, the court addressed evidence that the specific route was chosen based on plans for future expansion of settlements and held these considerations to be illegitimate. See *El Khawaja* (n 77); *Yassin* (n 77); HCJ 7957/04 *Marabe v Prime Minister of Israel* [2005], IsrSC 60(2) 577 (the Alfei Menashe case); HCJ 2645/04 *Nasser v Prime Minister of Israel* (April 25, 2007, unpublished). Discussion of illegitimate motivations can even resurface at the final balancing stage. See *Adalah* (Family Unification) (n 44) [1], [13]–[18] (Justice Procaccia).

136 See n 82.

137 In comparison, at the stage requiring the limitation to be by law there were 5 failures and 3 cases of negative signalling; at the suitability stage there were 13 failures and 4 cases of negative signalling; and at the necessity stage there were 30 failures and only 2 cases of negative signalling.

138 *ACRI* (Passports) (n 99).

139 *Cigarette vendors* (n 95).

As will be demonstrated, in some cases choosing a multiple-goal framing can act as a gentle manipulation of the subsequent review process.

One type of goal multiplicity is caused by the considerations that were taken into account in the policy-design being framed as goals. This can be accompanied by the definition of an overarching goal of striking a balance between all the competing considerations. For example, in the context of reform of the taxi licensing market that replaced the quota-based system with a fee-based system, the goals were defined as opening the market to competition while continuing to limit the number of drivers to prevent traffic congestion, while striking a balance between the interest groups in the taxi market – the freedom of occupation of new taxi drivers and the financial interests of existing license holders.[140] An additional example is a reform setting a uniform retirement age, where the goal was defined in terms of striking a balance between the competing interests, including dignity of older workers, interests of employers, and interests of younger workers.[141]

The origin of this type of framing may authentically originate from the policy process: when the groups affected by the policy are an integral part of the process, the focus of the policy can be to mediate the conflicting interests in a way that blurs the distinction between goals and side-effects, interests and rights. This framing of the goal, however, subtly affects the analysis. Proportionality is a structure constructed upon core components – public goals and rights, means and ends. Each stage is meant to evaluate certain components in reference to others. By clumping components together and including the balance between them as part of the goal, the analytical power of the analysis is weakened: the suitability stage becomes redundant, since any balance attains the goal of striking a balance; it is difficult to evaluate alternatives in reference to an abstract goal of balancing; and the final stage in such cases will typically not weigh harm against benefit but merely assert that the policy strikes a balance, locating it within the 'proportional range'.[142]

140 *Menachem* (n 113) [18]–[20] (Justice Beinisch).

141 HCJ 9134/12 *Gavish v Knesset* (21 April 2016, unpublished) [38]–[40] (upholding the mandatory retirement age), available in English at <http://versa.cardozo.yu.edu/opinions/gavish-v-knesset>.

142 This was the case in both examples brought – in *Menachem* (n 113) [26]; and *Gavish* ibid [38]–[40] (Justice Naor). See elaboration on the phenomenon of placing the policy in the 'proportional range' at the necessity stage in Section VII.C, and at the proportionality in the strict sense stage in Section VIII.B.

When the policy-maker defines multiple goals including a goal of compromise between several considerations, the court can somewhat restore the analytical power of the analysis by introducing a hierarchy between the goals, rather than treating them all as equally important. It should be noted, however, that this gives a normative edge to a supposedly factual determination: instead of establishing what the goal is and evaluating if it is worthy, the court determines what the goal should be in order for it to be deemed worthy.[143]

Such a dynamic was interestingly demonstrated in the series of cases reviewing legislation on recruitment of the ultra-orthodox population to the military. Following decades of a complete exemption from draft for the ultra-orthodox, a new legislation scheme was passed, with a goal defined in terms of compromise between respecting different lifestyles in Israeli society on the one hand, and equally distributing the burden of military service on the other. This was then concretized into sub-goals of gradually increasing ultra-orthodox enlistment in a non-coercive manner to promote greater equality, as well as increasing the integration of the ultra-orthodox in the workforce.[144] The court accepted this formulation, but added that increasing equality was to be viewed as the policy's dominant goal, and that the law's constitutionality would be established primarily relative to this aspect.[145] This assertion set the stage for the policy to subsequently fail the suitability stage, since it did not sufficiently increase the number of ultra-orthodox being recruited.[146]

[143] With similar critique see Bradley W Miller, 'Proportionality's Blind Spot: "Neutrality" and Political Philosophy' in Grant Huscroft, Bradley W Miller, and Grégoire Webber (eds), *Proportionality and the Rule of Law: Rights, Justification, Reasoning* (CUP 2014).

[144] Since the condition for the exemption from the military was full-time religious study, the effect was non-participation of ultra-orthodox men in the workforce. For the formulation of the goal in this manner see *Movement for Quality Government* (Ultra-Orthodox Exemption 2006) (n 100) [54]–[56] (Justice Barak); *Ressler* (n 100) [10], [19] (Justice Beinisch) and [4] (Justice Arbel).

[145] *Ressler* (n 100) [38] (Justice Beinisch). The list of goals and the hierarchy between them were repeated by the court in its third round of review, setting the stage for another failure of the legislation at the suitability stage. HCJ 1877/14 *The Movement for Quality Government v Knesset* (12 September 2017, unpublished) (the Ultra-Orthodox Exemption 2017 case).

[146] In the minority in the first round of judicial review Justice Cheshin rejected the goal as unworthy and in gross contradiction to democratic principles. In his opinion the only worthy formulation of the goal was the promotion of equality. In the second round of judicial review the court chose to define equality as the central goal, leading to failure at the suitability stage. *Movement for Quality Government* (Ultra-Orthodox Exemption 2006) (n 100) [43]–[48] (Justice Cheshin).

A second type of goal multiplicity can originate from the court, using the definition of the policy goal to introduce rights which in the court's opinion were not accorded sufficient weight by the policy-maker. In *Solodkin*, the court reviewed legislation authorizing municipalities to regulate, as well as ban, the sale of pork in their area of jurisdiction.[147] The Attorney General claimed that the policy goal was protection of religious feelings and protection of a national symbol.[148] However, Justice Barak framed the legislation as a compromise between conflicting political powers, and beyond the protection of religious and national feelings he included the goals of protecting liberty and individual autonomy, as well as a goal of having this issue balancing at the local rather than the national level.[149] These aspects could have been discussed later on, but introducing them as part of the goal increased their salience and pre-empted the possibility of 'balancing them away'.

In this context, it is interesting to mention the position voiced by Justice Levy in the context of the ban on naturalization of Palestinian spouses of Israeli citizens, according to which a goal defined solely in terms of maximizing the public interest should be deemed unworthy, since the definition of the goal itself must be framed in a way that reflects respect for rights. He found the goal of obtaining maximal security to be unworthy since it afforded no 'breathing room' for the rights severely limited by it.[150] Justice Levy essentially held that goals should always be defined in a multiple manner, since protection of rights must always be part of the policy goal itself, as a way to empower rights by treating their protection as a goal rather than merely a side-constraint.

A final type of multiplicity can be caused by framing certain characteristics of the means as part of the goal. In *Eitanit*, legislation

Also see *Menachem* (n 113) [21]–[22] (Justice Beinisch), where she emphasizes traffic improvement as the dominant goal, and the interests of the current license holders as merely secondary, and even goes further to state that the consideration of such interests, on their own, would not constitute a worthy public goal.

147 Originally, a business license was conditioned upon a prohibition on the sale of pork, until the legislation passed left the question to be decided by the individual municipalities. For a full historic account of the development of the sale of pork in Israel, see Daphne Barak-Erez, *Outlawed Pigs: Law, Religion and Culture in Israel* (University of Wisconsin Press 2007).

148 *Solodkin* (n 40) [13].

149 ibid [17]–[22]. The outcome of the case was that the court ordered the municipalities that had banned the sale of pork to conduct a renewed decision-making process based on demographic data and evaluation of alternatives.

150 *Galon* (n 39) [22]–[23] (Justice Levy).

establishing an asbestos dumping site and placing half of the building costs on the asbestos manufacturing company was reviewed. Both sides agreed the legislation advanced the worthy goal of promoting public health. However, the state added an additional goal: the 'polluter pays' principle. Justice Hendel pointed out this was not an independent goal but merely a justification for the payment scheme chosen. He warned against 'upgrading the means to the status of a goal', in an attempt to immunize this aspect from judicial scrutiny.[151]

To conclude, the phenomenon of goal multiplicity shines a light on the fact that the status of the components that make up PA is not always clear: the restricted right, the characteristics of the means and policy considerations may all find themselves included in the definition of the policy goal.[152] These framing choices can originate from the parties or the court and have subtle effects on the subsequent analysis.

### B *What Are Worthy Purposes?*

After defining the goal, the court addresses its worthiness. The worthy purpose stage theoretically includes two internal requirements: the content of the goal must be worthy of pursuit, and there must be a certain degree of importance in attaining the goal.

In terms of content, two major categories of worthy goals have been recognized in the jurisprudence of the court: protecting constitutional rights and promoting important public interests.[153] Protecting constitutional rights is unequivocally considered a worthy goal.[154] However, the classification of a policy as protecting rights as opposed to promoting a public interest is far from clear-cut, and classification may at times be subject to disagreement between justices.[155] Framing the goal in terms of

[151] He ultimately upheld the policy. *Eitanit* (n 34) [24]–[25] (Justice Hendel).

[152] Similarly, on this point see Julian Rivers, 'Proportionality and Variable Intensity of Review' (2006) 65 Cambridge Law Journal 174, 187–88.

[153] *Menachem* (n 113) [14] (Justice Beinisch); Barak (n 3) 251–56.

[154] Barak (n 3) 261–63. An example of a policy aimed at protecting constitutional rights is the policy providing a waiver for ultra-orthodox high schools from teaching the government core curriculum. The whole panel agreed that the goal of the policy was to allow the realization of the parental right to autonomy over child education, and the collective right to culture. See *Rubinstein* (Core Education) (n 40) [69]–[71] (Justice Arbel) and [6] (Justice Naor).

[155] For an explicit engagement with the distinction between constitutional rights and public interests for the first time, see the *Ganimat* case (whether in the criminal procedure the public interest in public order should be treated in terms of the right to security of the

protecting individual rights rather than promoting a public interest can potentially change the methodology of the analysis, and tilt the outcome to one direction or another.[156]

A distinction was developed by Barak regarding two modes of balancing: Horizontal balancing for resolving conflicts between considerations of equal status, such as two constitutional rights, that aims to provide the greatest level of manifistation for each of the conflicting considerations in a typically unstructured manner; and vertical balancing for conflicts between unequal types of considerations, such as rights and public interests, which follows the full structure of the limitation clause and is meant to ensure that the infrigment of a right is necessary and limited.[157]

Although the distinction between the two modes seems straightforward, the case law and scholarship include a degree of confusion and disagreement regarding the categorization of the types of considerations

potential victims, which should then be horizontally balanced against the defendant's right to liberty). CrimFH 2316/95 *Ganimat v State of Israel* [1995], IsrSC 49(4) 589 [2]–[3] (Justice Shamgar) and [2] (Justice Dorner). See also *Adalah* (Family Unification) (disagreement whether the public interest in security should be treated as the accumulation of the right to life and bodily integrity of the members of the public, which should then be horizontally balanced against the right to family); *Adalah* (Family Unification) (n 44) [15], [17] (Justice Rivlin) and [5] (Justice Grunis). Additional examples of classifying security in terms of the right to life are Justice Turkel's opinions in HCJ 2753/03 *Kirsch v IDF Chief of Staff* [2003], 57(6) 359; and CrimFH 7048/97 *Plonim v Minister of Defence* [2000], IsrSC 54(1) 721, available in English at <https://supremedecisions.court.gov.il/Home/Download?path=EnglishVerdicts\97\480\070\a09&fileName=97070480_a09.txt&type=4>.

The protection of feelings is also difficult to classify: it could be considered part of the interest in public order, or part of the individual right to dignity or freedom of religion in the case of religious feelings. This goal has been recognized as problematic, since a broad interpretation could potentially justify vast limitation of rights. See Barak (n 3) 274–76; Barak (n 88) vol. II, 778; *Horev* (n 105) [56]–[58] (Justice Barak).

156 Barak (n 3) 253–57; Michael Birnhack, 'Constitutional Geometry: The Supreme Court's Methodology in Value Judgments' (2003) 19 Mechkarei Mishpat 591 (in Hebrew); Alexander Ailenkoff, 'Constitutional Law in the Age of Balancing' (1987) 96 Yale Law Journal 943, 981.

157 HCJ 2481/93 *Dayan v Yehuda Wilk Jerusalem District Commissioner* [1994], IsrSC 48(2) 456 [480]–[82] (Justice Barak) (discussing protests in front of homes of public figures), available in English at <http://versa.cardozo.yu.edu/opinions/dayan-v-wilk>; HCJ 5432/03 *SHIN Israeli Movement for Equal Representation of Women v Council for Cable and Satellite Broadcasting* [2004], IsrSC 58(3) 65 [19] (Justice Dorner) (discussing the broadcasting of pornography), available in English at <http://versa.cardozo.yu.edu/opinions/shin-israeli-movement-equal-representation-women-v-council-cable-tv-and-satellite>.

and the determination of which mode is to be applied in each case.[158] Without delving into this complexity, it can be said that in practice the multi-staged PA is rarely applied to resolve conflicts between two individual human rights, but rather such cases invoke unstructured balancing. In only 8 per cent of cases in the database the framing of the conflict included a right on both sides of the conflict, as opposed to 92 per cent that contrasted a right and a public interest.

Beyond protection of rights, worthy goals are those promoting the public good. This can be done 'positively' by increasing citizen welfare, or 'negatively' by preventing threats to it.[159] Barak defines the public good as any interest that is not a constitutionally protected right, while recognizing that this is a very broad and ill-defined category.[160]

The goal of national security is a central and recurring goal in both legislation and administrative action.[161] Public order and safety are also commonly cited goals, and are usually concretized to include goals such as preventing crime[162] or promoting public health.[163] An additional aspect of public order that can be found in the case law is the enforcement of immigration policy – ensuring that foreign workers leave at the end of their work permit and that those present in the country illegally be deported.[164] A final variation on the theme of public order is the enforcement of zoning law against unlawful construction.[165] Some of

[158] Barak Medina and Hagar Segev, '"Clash" between Rights: A New Characterization of Horizontal and Vertical Balancing' (2018) 46 Mishpatim 535 (in Hebrew); Oren Gazal-Ayal and Amnon Reichman, 'Public Interests as Constitutional Rights' (2011) 41 Mishpatim 97 (in Hebrew).

[159] *Beer Sheva Municipality* (Mosque) (n 130) [18] (Justice Procaccia).

[160] Barak (n 3) 253, 265–67.

[161] See, e.g., *Beit Sourik* (n 49); *Marabe* (n 135); *Hoff Azza* (n 41); *Ajuri* (n 114); *Adalah* (Family Unification) (n 44); *Targeted Killings* (n 37); HCJ 3239/02 *Marab v IDF Commander in the West Bank* [2003], IsrSC 57(2) 349, available in English at <https://supremedecisions.court.gov.il/Home/Download?path=EnglishVerdicts\02\390\032\A04&fileName=02032390_a04.txt&type=4>.

[162] *Beer Sheva Municipality* (Mosque) (n 130); *ACRI* (Data Communication) (n 129); *Adam* (n 80); *Eitan* (n 82); *Dasta* (n 83).

[163] *Adalah* (Child Immunization) (n 92); *Cigarette vendors* (n 95); *Ibillin Breeders* (n 79).

[164] *Oren* (n 127); first and second infiltrators cases – *Adam* (n 80) and *Eitan* (n 82); *Kav Laoved* (Binding Workers) (n 81); HCJ 11437/05 *Kav Laoved v Ministry of Interior* [2011], IsrSC 64(3) 122 (requiring pregnant foreign workers to leave the country after giving birth; the Pregnant workers case); HCJ 2355/98 *Stamka v Minister of Interior* [1999], IsrSC 53(2) 728, available in English at <http://versa.cardozo.yu.edu/opinions/stamka-v-minister-interior>.

[165] This goal recurs in the context of the Bedouin community in Israel, see *Abu Madigam* (n 37); *Abu Musaed* (n 112).

the other interests that have been recognized in the case law as worthy are consumer protection,[166] development of public infrastructure,[167] and efficiency of the legal system.[168]

In terms of the exact level of importance required to pass the worthy purpose stage, this was debated for the first time in *Mizrahi Bank*. Justice Shamgar was of the opinion that the goal was required to be important and vital in order to justify right limitation. Conversely, Justice Barak preferred to leave the exact level of importance to be developed in the future.[169] Since then it seems that the consensus that has developed is that there is not a uniform standard of importance, but rather it is dependent upon the importance of the right: the more important the right, the more substantial or pressing the goal must be.[170] Yet, despite the general agreement on this concept, neither a clear definition of a hierarchy of rights nor a hierarchy of goals has been developed.[171]

In practice, the idea of different levels of importance of worthy purposes serves primarily as a rhetorical mechanism, used only in one direction: stating that the right at stake is very important, therefore requiring a substantially important goal, and then finding that the goal at hand is indeed important, thus satisfying the standard and successfully passing the hurdle.[172] A case has yet to occur where the goal was recognized as worthy but not sufficiently important considering the limited right, causing the policy to be struck down at this preliminary stage.[173]

166 *Shtanger* (Lawyers) (n 95); *Investment consultants* (n 43); *Tnufa* (n 101); *Menachem* (n 113).

167 HCJ 4636/07 *Alaksa Almubarak Ltd. v Israel Electricity Company* (29 October 2007, unpublished).

168 HCJ 2442/11 *Shtanger v Knesset Chairman* (unpublished, 26 June 2013) (the Suspects case).

169 *Mizrahi Bank* (n 1) [81] (Justice Shamgar) and [91] (Justice Barak).

170 See references (n 100).

171 See references (n 103) and (n 104).

172 See, e.g., *Menachem* (n 113); *Hoff Azza* (n 41); *Adalah* (Family Unification) (n 44); *Movement for Quality Government* (Ultra-Orthodox Exemption 2006) (n 100) [53] (Justice Barak).

173 In his chapter on future developments of PA Barak has suggested a two-tiered standard for the worthy purpose stage. According to his suggestion, the higher standard of a 'vital and pressing social need' would be required in cases of limitation of rights of special importance. He bases the list of these important rights on the declaration of independence: equality and freedom of religion, language, education, and culture. All other rights will need to meet the lower standard of an 'important' goal. See Barak (n 3) 531–33. This approach has not been mentioned in the case law. Also see criticism in Medina (n 68).

When the goal of the policy is to prevent risk to the public, the importance may also involve a question of probability, namely what the chances are that substantial damage would be caused to the public interest if the measure is not taken.[174] Although the dominant position is that probability should be incorporated in the final balancing stage,[175] in a number of cases it has been considered at the worthy purpose stage. The result of the consideration of probability at the worthy purpose stage seems to always be positive: the probability is found high enough to justify the need for the policy.[176]

### C *What Are Unworthy Purposes?*

There is hardly any explicit conceptual development in the case law of what unworthy goals are. As demonstrated previously, potentially problematic aspects of the policy goal are typically bypassed using different methods, such as refraining from addressing unofficial statements of motivation or using high-level abstractions. Therefore, it is difficult to compile a coherent view, based on the case law, on what unworthy policy goals are.

One consensus extracted from the case law is that policy aimed at targeting a particular population with the intention of purposefully harming them by limiting their rights – be they equality, speech, or religion – is an unworthy purpose. However, in reality such intentional harm or discrimination is never declared as the official goal. Therefore, this feeds into the complexity discussed previously regarding how unofficial statements concerning the policy goal should be treated. Considering, though, that in the context of discrimination there is no requirement to

[174] Probability formulas were developed in the period before the Basic Laws were enacted and the limitation clauses were introduced, as a framework for analysing the need to limit rights for the sake of public interests.

[175] *Miller* (n 41) [14] (Justice Dorner); *Prison Privatization* (n 82) [46] (Justice Procaccia). On the other hand, Barak Medina's position is that the worthy purpose stage is their appropriate location. See Medina (n 68), and see elaboration in Section VIII.

[176] *Horev* (n 105) [63], [73] (Justice Barak) (high probability of substantial harm to feelings); *Ajuri* (n 114) [25] (Justice Barak) (reasonable possibility of substantial danger); HCJ 951/06 *Stein v Police Commissioner* (30 April 2006, unpublished) [18]–[19], [25] (Justice Barak) (near certainty to cause harm, substantial danger that the public good will be harmed). An exception is Justice Joubran's opinion in the *Beer Sheva Municipality* (Mosque) (n 130) [17], finding that the claim that the existence of an active mosque would lead to conflict was pure speculation, and that no evidence was presented to demonstrate a high probability of realization of this threat.

prove discriminatory intention but rather it is sufficient to show a discriminatory outcome, the question of whether the goal was discrimination becomes of little practical importance. The court is generally willing to assume that the goal was not intentionally discriminatory, and focus instead on the question of the law's effect. For example, in *Guttman*, which challenged the raising of the minimal electoral threshold for inclusion in parliament, all justices agreed in principle that legislation which intentionally targeted excluding Arab parties would be considered illegitimate. However, they accepted the official legislative goal of increasing governance stability, and continued to analyse the question of the discriminatory effects on the Arab political parties.[177] Similarly, in *Sabach*, all justices agreed that legislation aimed at excluding Arabs from community villages would be considered illegitimate, but the discussion focused on the discriminatory effects of the policy rather than on its goal.[178]

In certain contexts deterrence has been treated as an unworthy goal: the court has held that the sole goal of detention of a defendant during criminal proceedings must be prevention of danger posed by the defendant, rather than general deterrence of others;[179] and the majority opinion held in the context of prolonged detention of illegal migrants, that the sole goal of such detention must be to facilitate their deportation, not to deter future migrants.[180] In contrast, regarding house demolitions of terrorists, the court repeatedly accepted deterrence of future terrorists

177 *Guttman* (n 119).

178 *Sabach* (n 98). See also the *Supreme Monitoring Committee for Arab Affairs* case where despite suspicion of discriminatory intent the court struck down based on discriminatory effect. HCJ 11163/03 *Supreme Monitoring Committee for Arab Affairs v Prime Minister of Israel* (27 February 2006, unpublished) [12] [17] (Justice Barak) (discussing government plans for 'national priority areas' which entail various benefits). Available in English at <https://supremedecisions.court.gov.il/Home/Download?path=EnglishVerdicts\03\630\111\a18&fileName=03111630_a18.txt&type=4>.

179 *Ganimat* (n 155). This was similarly held in the context of assigning families of terrorists from Judea and Samaria to live in the confines of the Gaza strip. *Ajuri* (n 114) [24], [27] (Justice Barak).

180 *Adam* (n 80) [85]–[90] (Justice Arbel) and [18] (Justice Vogelman); *Eitan* (n 82) [52] [193] (Justice Vogelman), [5] (Justice Arbel) and [2] (Justice Naor); in the minority in *Adam* [2]–[5], Justice Hendel was willing to accept deterrence as a legitimate consideration together with additional goals. In *Eitan*, Justice Amit, at para. 10, distinguished between detention of one group to deter others which is morally problematic, and having a threat of detention for the purpose of deterrence which is applied to those who were not deterred, which in his opinion was legitimate.

as a worthy purpose, while rejecting as an unworthy purpose the use of demolition as a form of punishment or revenge.[181]

Another unworthy purpose is the protection or promotion of a narrow individual interest at the expense of the public good. For example, in *Oron*, legislation aimed at securing a license for a specific illegally operating radio station politically affiliated with the party leading the legislation efforts was found to fail to promote the general public good and offend the rule of law. In *Ibillin Breeders*, the court stated that banning privately owned slaughter houses to ensure the publicly owned slaughter house would retain its monopoly status and increase municipal profit is unworthy.[182]

As mentioned earlier, a unique interpretation of an unworthy purpose was put forward by Justice Levy: a goal defined solely as maximizing the public interest should be considered unworthy in his view, since a worthy goal must include respect for rights, providing them with 'breathing room'. Other justices have also expressed the idea that a worthy purpose is one that respects rights,[183] but there has been no other application of the idea that a goal phrased in terms of maximizing public interests is by definition unworthy.

[181] See, e.g., HCJ 4597/14 *Awada v Commander of IDF in the West Bank* (1 July 2014, unpublished); HCJ 5290/14 *Kawasma v Commander of IDF in the West Bank* (11 August 2014, unpublished); HCJ 8091/14 *Centre for the Defence of the Individual v Minister of Defence* (31 December 2014, unpublished), available in English at <http://versa.cardozo.yu.edu/opinions/hamoked-center-defense-individual-v-minister-defense> [17] (Justice Rubinstein), [4] (Justice Solberg), and [4] (Justice Hayut). Justice Hayut (similar to Justice Joubran in *Adam* (n 80)) distinguishes the goal from the means – the goal is worthy, the means may not be. Deterring of future terrorists in the abstract, without regard to the means of house demolition is worthy. In HCJ 5839/15 *Cedar v Commander of IDF in the West Bank* (15 October 2015, unpublished) [3] Justice Vogelman accepts the legitimacy of deterrence and only questions its effectiveness.

However, a minority opinion has rejected the clear distinction between deterrence and punishment in this context. See HCJ 4772/91 *Hizran v Commander of IDF in the West Bank* [1992], IsrSC 46(2) 150, Justice Cheshin, before the proportionality test was introduced; and more recently HCJ 7220/15 *Aliwa v Commander of IDF in the West Bank* (1 December 2015, unpublished) [7] (Justice Mazuz). For elaboration on recent developments see Guy Harpaz and Amichai Cohen, 'House Demolitions in HCJ Review: There are Judges in Jerusalem' (2018) 19 Mishpat U'Mimshal 43 (in Hebrew).

[182] *Ibillin Breeders* (n 79). Since the claim regarding the goal was not substantiated by hard evidence, the court accepted the municipality's goals for the sake of the analysis and struck down the ban later on. Also see *Menachem* (n 113) [21]–[22] (Justice Beinisch).

[183] *Movement for Quality Government* (Ultra-Orthodox Exemption 2006) (n 100) [52] (Justice Barak); *Oron* (n 93) [662] (Justice Or); *Menachem* (n 113) [264] (Justice Beinisch).

Interestingly, all four cases in the database that explicitly failed at the worthy purpose stage included seemingly arbitrary inequalities in the context of budget distribution. Budget design requires prioritization, which can in turn cause inconsistencies and inequality. The state is expected to tread with care to ensure that the ramifications of budget allocation choices are intentional and justifiable. All four failures at the worthy purpose stage were not situations where the state defended its purpose as worthy and the court rejected the state's position, but rather no clearly formulated purpose was even presented to justify the inequality.[184] These cases may reflect havoc and unintentionality, or alternatively, indifference to discriminatory effects.

### *D Administrative Efficiency and Financial Saving as Worthy Purposes*

A distinction can be found in the case law between large-scale and small-scale financial goals. There is agreement that large-scale goals, such as maintaining the governmental budget frame, ensuring national financial stability, and preventing financial crises are legitimate policy goals.[185] However, discrepancies arise in the court's approach to smaller-scale goals of administrative efficiency and resource saving. At the outset, inconsistency exists in including such considerations as part of the definition of the goal, as opposed to raising them at the necessity or balancing stages as considerations which affected the

[184] All four cases were cases of discrimination, three of which involved the Arab minority. *Nasser* (n 135) (the original policy had a worthy goal of drawing population to the periphery. However, the list of settlements for receiving the benefit lacked clear criteria, settlements were included despite having no connection to the goal while others that were identical in all aspects were not. The court found that the discriminatory result of nearly only Jewish settlements being included served no worthy purpose); *Supreme Monitoring Committee for Arab Affairs* (n 178) (no explanation was provided regarding the criteria used, resulting in blatant discrimination between Jewish and Arab settlements); HCJ 5373/08 *Abu Labda v Minister of Education* (5 February 2011, unpublished) (the state had no goal that could justify the prolonged lack of funding for new classrooms in East Jerusalem); HCJ 8487/03 *IDF Disabled Veterans Organization v Minister of Defence* [2006], IsrSC 62(1) 296 (the state failed to provide justification for a distinction between types of disabled veterans for benefit rates).

[185] See *Manor* (n 95) [13] (Justice Barak); *Commitment to Peace and Social Justice* (n 96); *Kav Laoved* (Pregnant workers) (n 164); AAA 7335/10 *Rehabilitation Officer – Ministry of Defence v Lupo* (December 29, 2013, unpublished) [27]–[38], [51]–[53] (Justice Rubinstein); HCJ 2911/05 *Elhanati v Minister of Finance* [2008], IsrSC 62(4) 406 [31]–[32] (Justice Hayut); HCJ 4947/03 *Beer Sheva Municipality v Government of Israel* (10 May 2006, unpublished).

policy design. These differences in the stage at which the consideration of resources is discussed depend on the level of abstraction chosen in framing the goal rather than an inherent difference in the policy itself. It is also not necessarily correlated to the final result.[186]

More troubling is the fact that there is not a consistent position on whether resource efficiency is considered a worthy goal justifying right limitation or not. While there have been some cases clearly stating that mere financial saving would not be considered a worthy purpose for the sake of limitation analysis,[187] in other cases the court accepted goals that were defined in terms of efficiency and saving as legitimate.[188] Generally speaking, the tendency of the court is to address considerations of efficiency as questions of weight leading to their resolution as the necessity or balancing stages rather than through a categorical statement of illegitimacy at the worthy purpose stage. In some cases the court has expressed scepticism regarding the sincerity of the budgetary constraints presented as motivating the policy, noting that such claims may cover up other less worthy goals or arbitrary actions, and has therefore required evidence to support such claims.[189]

[186] See, e.g., *Shtanger* (Suspects) (n 168), and *Tzemach* that both dealt with the length of time before a detainee was to be brought before a judge. In *Shtanger*, the goal was phrased in terms of efficiency and resources of the judiciary, and the policy was ultimately upheld. In *Tzemach*, the goal was phrased in terms of protection of the public peace and the issue of resources only arose in the necessity stage, where the policy was ultimately struck down. HCJ 6055/95 *Tzemach v Minister of Defence* [1999], IsrSC 53(5) 241.

Both *Hassan* and *Hoff Azza* dealt with generalizations in payment mechanisms, and in both they were struck down, but in *Hassan* the goal was defined as preventing abuse of the income support system which was held worthy and resources were discussed only at the necessity stage, whereas in *Hoff Azza* the goal was defined as administrative efficiency which was found unworthy. *Hassan* (n 78) [56]–[57], [69] (Justice Beinisch); *Hoff Azza* (n 41) [235]–[37]. Also see differences between Justices Beinisch and Naor as opposed to Procaccia and Levy in addressing the financial aspect of the goal in the *Prison Privatization* case (n 82).

In one example the consideration of efficiency was discussed in determining the scope of the right. See *Eitan* (n 82) [176]–[79] (Justice Vogelman).

[187] *Manor* (n 95) [13] (Justice Barak); *Hoff Azza* (n 41) [235]–[37] (Justice Barak).

[188] *Prison privatization* case (n 82), where Justice Beinisch explicitly rejected the plaintiffs' claim that the financial nature of the goal should deem it illegitimate, emphasizing that the appropriate question was that of weight; *Lupo* (n 185); HCJ 4797/07 *Association for Civil Rights in Israel v Airports Authority* (3 March 2015, unpublished) (regarding racial profiling at security checks in airports; the Profiling case) [13] (Justice Grunis). Although the case was not decided, the court mentioned that considerations of efficiency could prevent adopting a solution of a unified level of screening for all.

[189] *Lupo* (n 185) (where the court found no up-to-date evidence to support the claim of over-extension of the budget); *Miller* (n 41) [19]–[20] (Justice Mazza) (the justification

## VI Suitability or Rational Connection

The suitability stage is generally perceived as the least substantial of the three sub-tests of proportionality, aimed at weeding out a small number of irrational means by providing an expedited analysis for particularly problematic cases.[190] However, the quantitative analysis demonstrates that this stage fulfils a more significant role than commonly perceived: 32 per cent of cases that ultimately failed did so at this stage.

This gap between conception and practice may stem from an overlooked role the suitability stage plays in relation to the worthy purpose stage. When a disconnect exists between means and ends, this may implicitly indicate that the policy was designed with an different goal in mind. Considering that at the worthy purpose stage the court tends to accept the policy goal as officially declared by the state, the suitability stage can be indirectly utilized to undermine the sincerity of the official goal. In other words, the weakness of the worthy purpose stage causes spillover on to the suitability stage, providing it with an additional function beyond the relatively narrow role afforded it in theory.

*Ibillin Breeders* can illustrate this dynamic: a local municipality prohibited the operation of privately-owned slaughter houses based on the goal of reducing environmental hazards, ensuring strict supervision over sanitation conditions and preventing the formation of a private monopoly. The court accepted these declared goals as worthy, but subsequently found that the means were not rationally connected to some of these goals, and later held that clearly there were less restricting means to achieve the others. Without explicitly saying so, the court essentially validated the plaintiffs' claim that the actual motivation behind the prohibition was to allow the municipally owned slaughter house to operate as a monopoly and maximize its profit.[191]

for not accepting women to the pilot training course had changed throughout the hearings from social and military constraints to logistic and planning considerations, and the court held that such claims could not be made hypothetically but required evidence).

190 Barak (n 3) 315–16.

191 *Ibillin Breeders* (n 79) [22]–[26] (Justice Procaccia); Additional examples include the *Oron* case (n 93) (the policy was failed at the suitability stage after the court stating explicitly at the worthy purpose stage that the policy was motivated by illegitimate goals but accepting the plaintiffs' formulation for the sake of the analysis); *Sabach* (n 98) [25]–[61], [77]–[79] minority opinion of Justice Joubran (accepting the officially stated goal of ensuring the candidates compatibility to the social fabric for the sake of the worthy purpose stage, despite his rejection of the sincerity of this goal, and subsequently

### A The Formulation of the Suitability Test

In a significant number of cases this stage is summed-up briefly, essentially stating that the means is rationally connected to the goal. This briefness can be found in cases where the means are upheld,[192] as well as in cases where the means are ultimately struck down.[193] The briefness may often be a result of the question of suitability being undisputed between the parties.

Conflicting statements can be found regarding the standard set by this stage. On the one hand, Barak has stated that any contribution of the means to the policy's goal is sufficient for passing the suitability stage.[194] In this vein, the case law is full of negative statements regarding the requirements of this stage – what the threshold is *not* or what is *not* required of the means: the means are not required to be optimal or ideal, but merely suitable and rational.[195] Alternatively, the standard has been framed in terms of probability, with different levels being voiced: some have required there to be a decent chance that the means will have a reasonable contribution to the goal, or that the chance that the means will contribute to the goal should not be slim and strictly theoretical.[196] Others have required a 'real and significant' probability for change caused by the measure.[197]

These differences in formulation of the test seem to be grounded in a position that the proportionality sub-tests in general, and specifically suitability, are not to be applied in a uniform fashion but rather as a function of the importance of the limited right. The more important the right and severe the limitation. a greater probability of the policy

failing the suitability test); HCJ 616/11 *Students Association of Israel v Government of Israel* (25 May 2014, unpublished) [50]–[57], [73] (Justice Rubinstein) (The policy was officially struck down at the suitability stage, but included severe remarks regarding the sincerity of the declared goal at the worthy purpose stage).

192 See, e.g., *Design 22* (n 40); *Cigarette vendors* (n 95); *Hamifkad Haleumi* (n 34); *Shtanger* (Suspects) (n 168); HCJ 2171/06 *Cohen v Knesset Chairman* (29 August 2011, unpublished) (regarding a law barring class actions against the state).

193 *Kav Laoved* (Pregnant workers) (n 164); *Ploni* (Due Process) (n 101); HCJ 9198/02 *Israeli Medical Association v Attorney General* [2008], IsrSC 63(1) 352 (regarding rules of conduct prohibiting doctors working in government-owned hospitals from providing expert testimony against any government hospital; the Testimonies case).

194 Barak, *Proportionality* (n 3) 305–6.

195 *Menachem* (n 113) [25].

196 *Adam* (n 80) [101] (Justice Arbel) and [21] (Justice Vogelman).

197 *Movement for Quality Government* (Ultra-Orthodox Exemption 2017) (n 145) [75] (Justice Naor), citing Beinisch in [4] [65]–[66].

achieving the goal is expected.[198] Barak has presented a two-tiered hierarchy: the general requirement should be one of low probability, but in cases where important rights are at stake a slightly higher probability standard should be applied. In his opinion, however, a level of near certainty should never be required.[199]

In practice, the requirements at this stage do indeed differ, although not necessarily in relation to the severity of the right limitation, but rather dependant on the nature of the policy evaluated and the point in time that judicial review is conducted. I will differentiate between cases that focus at the suitability stage on the logical connection between the measure and the goal in terms of common sense, as opposed to cases that focus on the actual effectiveness of the policy, that may require engagement with evidence.

### B Establishing Rational Connection: Logic and Common Sense

There are cases where the state relies on certain logical assumptions in asserting that the means will achieve the goal, which the court mostly does not challenge. For example, in *Abu Musaed*, the state claimed that prohibiting individual water connections for residents in unrecognized Bedouin settlements would incentivize their transition to permanent legal settlements, which was the state's goal;[200] in *Kav Laoved (Pregnant workers)*, the state maintained that requiring foreign workers that were pregnant to leave the country after giving birth, conditioning their return for the remainder of their work permit period only without the newborn child, would secure their leaving the country at the end of the permit.[201]

In rare cases the court will reject the logic presented by the state regarding the connection between means and ends. In *Ben Atiya*, certain schools were excluded from a new policy that exempted students from three matriculation exams, allowing them to have their internal grades in those topics serve as their final grade. The exclusion was based on the number of incidents of cheating at the school over the previous three years. The goal of the policy was defined as ensuring the reliability of the matriculation grades, and the rationale for the measure was that the there

198 *Investment consultants* (n 43) [4] (Justice Dorner); [4] [52]–[53] (Justice Beinisch) and citations there.

199 Barak (n 3) 309–16, 539.

200 *Abu Musaed* (n 112) [45] (Justice Procaccia).

201 *Kav Laoved* (pregnant workers) (n 164) [61] (Justice Levy). The policy was subsequently struck down at the necessity stage.

was mistrust in those schools' internal grading system. The court found no rational connection: the copying incidents had occurred in previous years by students other than those currently being examined, and the external exams were supervised by non-school related personnel, and therefore could not reflect the reliability of the school's internal exam system.[202]

Over-breadth and under-breadth are both claims that can be brought by plaintiffs at the suitability stage that are based on logic rather than evidence, in an attempt to reveal flaws in the policy design that undermine the rational connection to the goal.

Over-breadth occurs when the policy's scope is broader than needed to fulfil the goal. Policy over-breadth typically does not make for a lack of rational connection, but more of a claim regarding necessity. However, drastic over-breadth could be considered a form of arbitrariness or irrationality which could be relevant to suitability. Typically, the court will not strike down a policy at the suitability stage based on over-breadth, but it may point out doubts regarding the choice of means which will recur at the next stage. For example, in *Hassan* an irrefutable presumption that ownership or permanent use of a car were equivalent to a certain amount of income, which in turn disqualified recipients for income-support, was challenged. At the suitability stage Chief Justice Beinisch pointed out that the policy achieved its goal only relative to those for whom the ownership or use of the car indeed reflected the equivalent income. However, the policy was not relevant to those individuals, such as the plaintiffs, for whom the car use did not reflect equivalent income, and in this sense the policy was over-broad. Despite the over-breadth, the measure was passed at the suitability stage only to subsequently be struck down at the necessity stage based on similar reasoning.[203]

Under-breadth refers to cases where the policy applies only to a small portion of the issue (such as certain people or certain cases), so that by definition it cannot fully attain the policy goal. Although it is the state's prerogative to define the extent of its policy intervention, the more

[202] *Ben Atiya* (n 43) [8] (Justice Barak).

[203] *Hassan* (n 78) [59]–[61] (Justice Beinisch). Similarly, see *Stamka* (n 164) [54] (Justice Cheshin). In a similar situation in the *Commitment to Peace and Social Justice Society* (n 96) [17], Justice Levy held in a minority opinion, that a uniform cut in social benefit rates as an incentive to integrate into the workforce could potentially be rationally connected only relative to beneficiaries who were capable of work, but not to beneficiaries incapable of work. He found this form of over-breadth to be arbitrary and deemed the policy to fail this stage.

drastic the under-breadth of the policy the more doubts may be raised. Although under-breadth is rarely a basis for striking down a policy at the suitability stage,[204] such claims may be taken into consideration later on. For example, in *Adam* and *Eitan*, cases reviewing prolonged detention periods of illegal migrants, the court remarked that the detention center's capacity was limited to several thousand out of more than 50,000 migrants present in Israel at the time, thus having only marginal influence on the effects of the massive presence of illegal migrants in city centers, which was the officially stated goal. This limited potential of effectiveness subsequently affected the analysis at the necessity and balancing stages.[205]

An additional claim that can be raised by plaintiffs at the suitability stage is counter-effectiveness. According to this argument, not only are the means incapable of promoting the goal set by the policy-maker, but they are actually detrimental to it. Claims of counter-effectiveness can be found in the context of prevention of terrorism, holding that certain drastic steps aimed at preventing terror actually incentivize it,[206] and in the context of suppression of certain kinds of speech.[207] Broadly speaking, the court does not tend to accept such claims, and requires the plaintiffs to carry a heavy evidentiary burden.[208] One exception is *Bakri*, where the court accepted the claim that the supression of a position by banning a film will backlash, by increasing publicity and causing exposure to a larger audience.[209] Additionally, in *Stamka*, the court accepted the plaintiffs' claim that requiring a citizen's foreign spouse who applied for naturalization to exit the country for the period of the investigation of the relationship was counter-productive, since not

[204] But see the *Kirsch* case (n 155).

[205] *Adam* (n 80) [97] (Justice Arbel); *Eitan* (n 82) [128]–[29] (Justice Vogelman).

[206] Such as *Beit Sourik* (n 49), regarding the route of the security fence; and in the context of house demolitions, *Centre for the Defence of the Individual* (n 181).

[207] Such claims were made in the *Nakba* case (n 98), regarding expressing mourning on Israel's independence day; and *Avneri* (n 102), regarding calls for boycott of Israel or the settlements.

[208] In the *Avneri* case the claim of counter-productivity was rejected by the court despite the position of the ministry of foreign affairs cited by the plaintiffs that the law would only fuel boycott attempts. *Avneri* (n 102) [13] (Justice Danziger). But see *Galon* (n 39) [36] (Justice Levy), accepting the claim that the absolute ban on naturalization of Palestinians spouses of citizens could be counterproductive considering its long-term ramifications: entrenching inequality between Jewish and Arabs citizens festers frustration which could be channeled towards violence, thus undermining security.

[209] *Bakri* (n 130) [14] (Justice Dorner).

only did it fail in deterring fictious requests but it diminished the ability to actually verify the sincerity of the relationship, which was the policy's goal.[210]

### C *Establishing Policy Effectiveness: The Use of Evidence*

Although in the majority of cases the discussion at the suitability stage is brief and remains at the level of logic and common sense, there are cases where the court engages with expert opinions or evidence at this stage. The nature of this engagement and the party bearing the burden of proof may differ, depending upon whether the evaluation of the measure's suitability is *ex-ante* (prior to implementation) or *ex-post*.

A reminder is in place: proportionality is primarily invoked by the Supreme Court in HCJ cases where it is the court of first instance, and its ability to deeply engage with evidence, relative to a trial court, is limited. For example, there is no cross-examination of witnesses. Additionally, because HCJ petitions are directly submitted to the Supreme Court, the review process can occur very quickly, at times within less than one year of the introduction of a new law or policy, so that evidence regarding the policy effectiveness may not yet exist.

#### 1 Establishing Effectiveness *Ex Ante*

When judicial review is conducted relatively shortly after the initiation of a policy, the court will generally accept a great level of uncertainty at the suitability stage. As a rule, the court will defer to the state's expert opinion on the expected effectiveness of the measure, and view it as fulfilling the respondent's burden of proof. Only if the plaintiffs bring evidence casting serious doubt regarding the plausibleness or reasonableness of the government position will the state be required to respond with counter-evidence. This seems to be effectively impossible.

For example, in *Beit Sourik*, the route of the security fence was based on the military's conception of the optimal way to ensure security, which was founded on certain working assumptions (e.g. strategic high points, maximum distance from Israeli settlements to allow reaction time in case of penetration). The plaintiffs submitted an expert report prepared by former military officials, based on alternative assumptions on how to optimally obtain security (i.e. high points were not necessary, vicinity of

[210] *Stamka* (n 164) [55] (Justice Cheshin).

the fence to Palestinian houses would make it difficult to differentiate between citizens and terrorists, substantial discomfort to the Palestinian population caused by the fence would increase motivation for terrorism). Based on this position, the plaintiffs claimed lack of rational connection between the chosen route and the goal of increasing security, but the court held that in a situation of contradicting expert security opinions, the military's position would be given precedence, unless the plaintiffs prove this position to be unreasonable, which they had not.[211]

Other examples of the court's deference to the state's expertise at the suitability stage include the acceptance of the estimations of the effects of the new regulation of the taxi driving market on traffic, despite alternative estimations presented by experts for the plaintiffs;[212] and the acceptance of the state's position regarding the extent of financial saving that would be achieved by the construction of a privatized prison, despite pessimistic estimations presented by the plaintiffs.[213]

In certain cases of evaluation of a policy *ex-ante*, the state will present data from other countries that have implemented such policy successfully. For example, in *Adalah (child immunization)*, the state presented the court with evidence from other countries in the world showing that financial incentives have been found to raise immunization rates, as support for the adoption of such policy in Israel.[214] In some instances the court will explicitly state that its deference to the state's assertion of effectiveness holds only for the *ex-ante* stage, but that the state is expected to collect data regarding the actual effects of the policy and re-evaluate these assessments against reality.[215]

There have been outlier positions of justices that have criticized speculations of effectiveness presented by the state, requiring more significant evidence to support them. Justice Levy failed policy at the suitability stage despite the fact that the review was *ex-ante*, holding that a sufficient factual basis to support rational connection had not been presented. In the *Commitment to Social Justice* case, his minority opinion

[211] However, the route of the fence was found to cause disproportionate harm at the final stage. *Beit Sourik* (n 49) [47] (Justice Barak).

[212] *Menachem* (n 113) [13] (Justice Beinisch).

[213] *Prison Privatization* case, (n 82) [47]; [52] (Justice Beinisch). The policy was ultimately struck down by at the final stage of balancing.

[214] *Adalah* (Child Immunization) (n 92) [60] (Justice Arbel).

[215] ibid (Justice Arbel); *Adalah* (Family Unification) (n 44) (Justice Barak-Erez); *Menachem* (n 113) (Justice Beinisch).

was that the state had failed to prove that a significant cut in social benefit rates would minimize the number of benefit recipients who were unjustifiably supported. Since no data had been presented regarding the estimated scope of the phenomenon of 'willfully unemployed', nor was data presented regarding the projected decrease in the phenomenon following the cut in benefits, he concluded that rational connection had not been established.[216]

### 2 Establishing Effectiveness *Ex Post*

When a policy already in place for some time is subjected to judicial review, the question of its effectiveness generally changes from a matter of estimation to a matter of fact. Therefore, the expectation from the state to provide data to support its claim of effectiveness is higher.[217] When the state does not provide such data the court may no longer be willing to defer to its estimations.

For example, in *Stamka*, the state presented no data to support its claim that the policy requiring a spouse requesting naturalization to leave the country actually decreased the number of requests based on fictitious relationships or made it easier for these to be discovered.[218] When it is clearly evident from the data that a policy is inefficient it will fail the suitability test, as occured in *Kav Laoved (binding workers)*, when a policy binding foreign workers' permits to one particular employer was claimed to serve the goal of ensuring the workers' exit from the country at the end of the permit period. However, the data presented to the court showed an increase rather than a decrease in the number of foreign workers remaining in the country beyond the period of their permit, and the policy was subsequently failed at the suitability test.[219]

In evaluating policy effectiveness, the question may arise of what is the correct timeframe for demonstrating effectiveness. In the case of ultra-orthodox enlistment in the military the same piece of legislation was reviewed by the court twice: the first instance was three years after the policy had been introduced, and at the suitability stage the data presented to the court reflected that only very small amounts of ultra-orthodox

[216] *Commitment to Peace and Social Justice Society* (n 96) [17]–[19] (Justice Levy). The justices of the majority in this case held that the plaintiffs had not proven a limitation of the right to dignity, and therefore did not conduct PA. Similarly, see *Hoff Azza* (n 41) [33]–[37] (Justice Levy); *Raai* (n 82) (Justice Vogelman).

[217] See also Barak (n 3) 312–15.

[218] *Stamka* (n 164) [54] (Justice Cheshin).

[219] *Kav Laoved* (Binding Workers) (n 81) [50]–[51] (Justice Levy).

were enlisting. The court held that the data pointed to lack of rational connection between the means and the goal of increasing equality in army service. However, the court refrained from striking down the policy at that point, accepting the state's position that a broader timeframe was needed to test effectiveness, considering the complexity of the social change required.[220] The second round of judicial review was nearly 10 years after the introduction of the policy, and the data continued to show insignificant change. At that point the court concluded that it had become evident that the legislation was fundementally uncapable of becoming effective, and struck it down.[221]

Even when data exists, it may be inconclusive. In such cases the court may defer to the state's interpretation of the data, considering the generally low threshold required for suitability. However, the inconclusiveness of the data may affect the weight afforded to the policy benefit at the final balancing stage. For example, in *Adam*, reviewing a three-year detention period for illegal migrants, the data presented by the state pointed to a drastic drop in infiltration from Africa through the Southern border that coincided with the passage of the legislation. However, while the state attributed this decrease to the legislation, the plaintiffs attributed it to the completion of critical sections of the wall built on the border. The court found the situation to be one of causal ambiguousness, and for the sake of the suitability stage was willing to accept the premise that the detention had had some contribution to preventing infiltration,[222] though the policy was ultimately struck down later on.

Despite the generally more demanding stance towards the state to prove the effectiveness of policy already in place for some time, the nature of the evidence and the level of proof required are not always clear. In the context of house demolitions in the Occupied Territories and East Jerusalem as a tool for deterring future terrorists, plaintiffs have

[220] *Movement for Quality Government* (Ultra-Orthodox Exemption 2006) (n 100) [63]–[69] (Justice Barak). There were also problems revealed in the implementation mechanism, which made it difficult for the court to assess whether the ineffectiveness was due to an inherent flaw in the legislative framework or due to administrative issues which could be resolved.

[221] [4] [57] (Justice Beinisch). In a minority opinion [7], [10], [17]–[18] Justice Arbel suggested more time should be afforded to prove effectiveness, based on some encouraging positive trends in the data. A slightly revised law came before the court a third time, and the court concluded again, based on the data accumulated, that the new legislation had not had any substantial effect on recruitment rates. *Movement for Quality Government* (Ultra-Orthodox Exemption 2017) (n 145).

[222] *Adam* (n 80) [99]–[101] (Justice Arbel); *Eitan* (n 82) [57]–[59] (Justice Vogelman).

recurringly challenged the effectiveness of the policy. Although anecdotal evidence pointing to some level of a dettering effect has been presented, a more systemic picture of the effects of the policy is lacking. For several years the court accepted the state's expert position that the policy was effective without much challenge, considering the importance of preventing terrorism.[223] Recently, however, some justices have stated that considering the extreme nature of the right limitation caused by the policy, the claim for its effectivness would not be taken as a given indefinitely, and that the state was expected to actively re-evaluate the effectiveness from time to time.[224]

In summation, evaluation of policy suitability *ex-post* may lead to a more substantial engagement with evidence. Nevertheless, the substantitiation required by the data is not necessarily significant, and there generally is willingness to defer to the governmental interpretation of the data.[225]

223 In the *Ghanimat* case, Justice Goldberg held that so long as there was the slightest possibility that such demolitions saved even one life – the use of policy was justified. See HCJ 2006/97 *Ghanimat v IDF Central Command* [1997], IsrSC 51(2) 651. See also HCJ 7040/15 *Hamad v Commander of IDF in the West Bank* (12 November 2015, unpublished) [1] (Justice Solberg).

224 In the words of Justice Rubinstein: 'The principle of proportionality does not allow us to continue to assume forever that choosing the drastic option of house demolition, or even of house sealing, achieves the desired purpose of deterrence, unless all of the data that properly confirms that hypothesis is presented to us for our review. (. . .) However, as aforesaid, I believe that using means that have considerable consequences on a person's property justifies an ongoing review of the question of whether or not it bears fruit. (. . .) Thus, I believe that state authorities must examine the measure and its utility from time to time, including conducting follow-up research on the matter, and insofar as possible, should, as may be necessary in the future, present this court with the data demonstrating the effectiveness of house demolition as a means of deterrence that justifies the infliction of damage to parties who are not suspected nor accused.' *Centre for the Defence of the Individual* (n 181) [27] (Justice Rubinstein). Also see Justice Hayut, at para. 6, quoted in agreement by Justice Naor in HCJFH 360/15 *Centre for the Defence of the Individual v Minister of Defence* (12 November 2015, unpublished) (denying a request for further hearing of the HCJ on house demolitions); and *Cedar* (n 181) [3] (Justice Vogelman).

The military itself decided to suspend the use of this measure in 2005, based on the recommendations of an expert commission questioning its effectiveness. Three years later, in light of a new wave of terrorism, the military reintroduced the measure, and the court rejected a petition challenging this decision, stating it would not intervene with the security bodies' expert opinion that the measure was effective. HCJ 9353/08 *Abu Dheim v GOC Home Front Command* (5 January 2009, unpublished) [8]–[11] (Justice Naor).

225 Changes in circumstances over time may also be addressed by the court as part of the final balancing stage, stating that the original balance struck at the adoption of the policy must be updated periodically. See *Elhanati* (n 185) [32] (Justice Hayut); *Abu Safiyeh* (n 81) (Justice Levy).

It should be briefly noted that beyond requiring that the means be rational in the technical sense of causality, an additional aspect has been added to this stage, at least in principle: if the means are distinctly unfair or arbitrary they will also fail the test.[226] This requirement was established in *Morar*, where the goal of preventing violent clashes between Palestinian farmers and Jewish settlers was attained by preventing Palestinian access to agricultural plots located in 'friction areas'. Justice Beinisch held that although preventing Palestinian access would prevent attacks from settlers, thus technically fulfilling the rational connection requirement, it blatantly violated the most basic sense of fairness by punishing the innocent party.[227] The requirement that the means not be distinctly unfair or arbitrary continues to be quoted in the case law, although it has not been substantially implemented.[228]

## VII Necessity or Less-Restricting Means

The necessity stage plays a significant role in Israeli PA, as demonstrated by the quantitative data, with 73 per cent of the measures that were ultimately struck failing this stage. Interestingly, there is a relatively large degree of variation in the way this stage is applied, both between cases and between justices. In this section I will categorize the approaches and offer initial explanations for some of the variations.

At the outset, it is helpful to distinguish between two aspects included within the necessity test, despite the fact that they are not explicitly differentiated by the court, and at times are blurred together: the first is the evaluation of whether the scope of the chosen measure could have been narrowed, minimizing the extent of the right limitation. The second is the evaluation of whether alternative measures, that are less rights-restricting, could have been chosen.[229]

226 *Menachem* (n 113) [23] (Justice Beinisch).

227 *Morar* (n 78).

228 See, e.g., *Abu Madigam* (n 37) (Justice Arbel); *Eitanit* (n 34) [29] (Justice Hendel). In Barak's opinion fairness should not be a relevant factor at this stage of the analysis. See Barak (n 3) 307. Gideon Sapir also joins in the critique of the approach adding a normative aspect to the suitability stage. See Sapir (n 69).

229 This distinction has not been explicitly recognized in the case law. Recently, Justice Hendel distinguished between the necessity test in the negative sense – is there a less-restricting means, and in the positive sense – is the means itself narrowly tailored. *Eitanit* (n 34) [33] (Justice Hendel).

### A Can the Chosen Means Be More Narrowly Tailored?

The state typically focuses its claims at the necessity stage on the efforts that were made to design the means in a way that minimizes the right limitation. It tends to point out ways the policy could have been broader or *more* rights-restricting, to assert that the measure is currently narrowly tailored, rather than demonstrating why it could not have been narrower and *less* rights-restricting – in essence creating a mirror image of the necessity test.

Some of the central aspects discussed in the context of narrowly tailoring the means are the scope of the measure, the frequency in which the measure is applied, and the time period of the limitation.[230]

#### 1 Narrowing the Scope of the Measure

The broader the scope of the policy, the more severe the right-limiting effect. Therefore, a central aspect of narrowly tailoring a policy is narrowing the scope of people or situations to which it applies. The broadest scope of application is a sweeping and absolute application to an entire group. An exception mechanism can slightly narrow this broad application by allowing a small amount of unjust limitations to be excluded. Tailoring the categories of application in a way that is sensitive to differences between individuals within the group is a more nuanced way to design policy. The most narrowly tailored design is one based on individual assessment.

**Exception Mechanisms** Exception mechanisms are used when the policy is applied in a sweeping manner, as an outlet for dealing with exceptional cases and preventing unnecessary right limitation for individuals to whom the policy need not apply. The court has criticized the use of broad restrictions without any outlet for exceptions.[231] However, the court has also been critical of exception mechanisms when they are used instead of a more nuanced design of the policy itself. The court has

[230] The design of the right limitation is not always analysed solely at the necessity test, but may also appear at the final stage as the basis for the court's evaluation of the harm to the right. There are some cases where the reasoning presented at the necessity stage as fulfiling the condition of narrowly tailoredness is repeated at the final stage to establish the marginal nature of the limitation. See, e.g., *Shtanger* (Suspects) (n 168) [42]–[43] (Justice Grunis); *Avneri* (n 102) [43]–[53] (Justice Melcer).

[231] *Adalah* (Family Unification) (n 44) [72] (Justice Barak), [126] (Justice Cheshin) and [24] (Justice Naor); *Raai* (n 82) [27] (Justice Vogelman); *Salech* (n 108) [26]–[28] (Justice Naor), but see [11] (Justice Grunis).

stated that an exception mechanism cannot, on its own, transform an over-broad means into a narrowly tailored one, since this turns the limitation of rights into the norm and protection of rights into an exception. If a policy systemically fails to take particular circumstances into consideration, the rule itself needs to be refined.[232]

At times the court will extend its scrutiny beyond the mere existence of an exception mechanism, and evaluate the standard used in granting exceptions to assess whether it indeed substantially narrows the extent of limitation. If the exception committee applies its discretion too narrowly, the court may find its existence insufficient.[233]

**The Categories of Application** In the positive, the court may point to the design of the categories in the policy as evidence that it is indeed narrowly tailored and thus mitigates the severity of the limitation. In the negative, the court may criticize the categories' lack of sufficient sensitivity, and question whether a certain category should indeed be included in the scope of the policy at all.

An example of the court referring to the way in which the policy categories are designed as a mitigating factor is the *Adalah (family unification I)* case, which reviewed the absolute ban on naturalization of Palestinian spouses of Israeli citizens for security reasons. The ban was applied to women under the age of 25 and men under the age of 35, based on the evaluation of the security authorities that this represented the profile that posed the greatest risk of involvement in terrorism. Some of the justices of the majority viewed this definition as representing a narrow tailoring of the policy.[234] In *Menachem*, which reviewed the high fee for purchasing a

232 *Adam* (n 80) [114] (Justice Arbel); *Kav Laoved* (Pregnant workers) (n 164) [65] (Justice Levy); *Adalah* (Tort Liability) (n 132) [42]; *Hassan* (n 78) [65] (Justice Beinisch). The court is especially critical where it is evident that the exception mechanism was created as a superficial effort to make the legislation seem more proportional. See *Oren* (n 127) [29].

233 See *Medical Association* (Testimonies) (n 193) [57] (Justice Naor). In the *Galon* (n 39) case the record of the exceptions committee – 33 out of 600 requests granted – was addressed by some of the justices. Interestingly, however, some inferred from this that the law is indeed narrowly tailored (see Justice Melcer), whereas others inferred that the framework is too restrictive (see Justices Levy and Hayut). Also see HCJ 5771/12 *Moshe v The Board for Approval of Embryo Carrying Agreements under the Embryo Carrying Agreements Law* (18 September 2014, unpublished) [31]–[32] (Justice Hayut), available in English at <http://versa.cardozo.yu.edu/opinions/moshe-v-board-approval-embryo-carrying-agreements-under-embryo-carrying-agreements-law>.

234 *Adalah* (Family Unification) (n 44) [116] (Justice Cheshin). The justices who struck down the policy criticized the fact that it was not based on individual assessment. Their

taxi-driving license, the court pointed out that a reduced rate had been set for those who had been working as taxi drivers for over six years as one of the considerations for finding the limitation proportionate.[235]

An example of the court deeming a policy too broad due to lack of nuance in the definition of categories is the *Medical Association (testimonies)* case: the civil service rules of conduct prohibited doctors working in government-owned hospitals from providing expert testimony against any government hospital for fear of conflict of interests. The prohibition had a narrow exception – when the doctor was the sole expert in the field. The court held that the prohibition should be limited to providing testimony against the hospital where the doctor is employed, and that the exception to the rule should be broadened to include situations where the field is dominated by government doctors.[236]

**Individual Assessment** A recurring question in the context of narrowing the application of a policy is whether a policy based on generalized categories can be replaced by individual-based assessment. The choice of design typically involves considerations of policy effectiveness as well as considerations of cost and resources.

The court will typically not accept considerations of costs and administrative resources as a sufficient justification for choosing a broad generalization. For example, in *Hassan*, the court struck down an irrefutable presumption that ownership or permanent use of a car disqualified beneficiaries from receiving income support, despite recognizing that individual evaluation of car value or car-use patterns would increase administrative burden.[237] In *Mustaki*, the court struck down a categorical decision not to recognize academic degrees from a particular foreign institution after the discovery of fraudulent behaviour, instead requiring the state to create an administrative mechanism to individually evaluate the authenticity of each degree.[238]

reasoning, however, was located at the final stage of proportionality in the strict sense rather than at the necessity stage.

235 *Menachem* (n 113) [27] (Justice Beinisch) (although this consideration was discussed as part of the proportionality in the strict sense stage).

236 *Medical Association* (Testimonies) (n 193) [59]–[61] (Justice Naor). For an additional example of requiring more nuanced categories, see *Investment consultants* (n 43) [61]–[63] (Justice Barak).

237 *Hassan* (n 78) [62]–[68] (Justice Beinisch).

238 HCJ 3379/03 *Mustaki v State Attorney* [2004], IsrSC 58(3) 865; See also *Adalah* (Tort Liability) (n 132) [37] (Justice Barak); *Raai* (n 82); *Hoff Azza* (n 41) [88]–[194]. For an

However, a recurring theme in cases regarding security is that policy must be based on generalizations, since individual evaluations are incapable of providing the same level of security. This poses a real challenge to the principle that policy must be narrowly tailored rather than broad and categorical. The court's general tendency is, at least in evaluation of necessity, to accept this as a justification for categorical policy. For example, in *Yonas* a prison service's policy was challenged, which limited visitation rights for prisoners sentenced for security-related offences and members of terrorist organizations, to include only first-degree family members. The basis for the policy was that these prisoners' contact with the outside world posed a security threat. Alternatives such as having a security guard present or conducting the meeting behind a partition were held not equally effective. As for the possibility of individually assessing the level of risk per prisoner, the court accepted that individual evaluations were more limited in their accuracy, and upheld the policy.[239]

*Adalah (family unification I)* and *Galon* posed the question of whether the complete ban on naturalization of Palestinian spouses within a certain age limit could be replaced with an individual-based security evaluation. The security services claimed there were severe practical difficulties in conducting individual security evaluations, but moreover, in principle, they held that individual assessments were limited: Palestinians gaining permanent status in Israel only become valuable assets for terrorist recruitment after receiving the status, therefore by definition the threat could not be properly evaluated in advance. They presented data regarding the number of individuals that had passed the individual security evaluation and were subsequently involved in terrorist activity after naturalization.[240] The majority of justices in both rounds of judicial review, including those which failed the policy at the final stage, were of

exception, acknowledging the consideration of administrative burden in individual assessment, see *Peled* (n 105) [16] (Justice Beinisch).

239 *Yonas* (n 126) [74] (Justice Danziger) and [1] (Justice Amit). Since all those to whom the policy applied had been convicted of security-related offences, there was some individual indication of risk, and thus the generalization was found to be less offensive. There was also a possibility, after the passage of time, for a prisoner to prove disassociation from the hostile organization with which he had been associated and become eligible for individual assessment. See also HCJ 11120/05 *Hamdan v IDF Southern Commander* (7 August 2007, unpublished), which upheld the general prohibition on students from Gaza to enter the West Bank, based on statistics regarding the increased security threat at particular ages, declining the possibility of individual evaluation.

240 The number was 26 in the first round of judicial review and 54 in the second round, out of more than 100,000 permits granted over a period of more than 10 years.

the view that the complete ban passed the necessity test, based on the assertion that individual security evaluations, no matter how efficient, could not prevent terrorism at the same level as a complete prohibition.[241] Only one justice failed the policy at the necessity test, holding that individual evaluations could be designed in a way that would sufficiently minimize the security risk, such as by creating a presumption of dangerousness to be rebutted by the petitioner.[242]

### 2 Narrowing the Frequency of the Limitation: Approval Procedures

The right-limiting nature of the policy may also be narrowed by introducing approval procedures, including both judicial oversight and administrative approval processes. It is, however, important to distinguish between judicial oversight as a narrowing mechanism, that adds a layer of approval, and judicial oversight as part of the right to due process, without which there is an independent right limitation.[243]

This type of narrowing is generally not one that the court will impose, but rather it is predominantly brought by the state to support its claim that the policy is narrowly tailored and proportional. Although in some cases the court will mention approval mechanisms as an additional justification for finding the policy proportional,[244] no cases were found

[241] See the position as phrased by Justice Barak in *Adalah* (Family Unification) (n 44) [88]–[89]. The justices were then split on the question of whether the policy passed the final balancing stage or not. In the first round of judicial review four justices found the measure to pass proportionality and five found it failed (but one refrained from striking it down at the remedy stage, considering that is was due to expire shortly), and in the second round five found it passed proportionality and four found that it failed.

[242] Justice Levy in *Adalah* (Family Unification) (n 44) and *Galon* (n 39). In *Galon*, he failed the policy much earlier, finding it incompatible with the values of the state. However, he continued through to the necessity stage to demonstrate that the policy failed this stage as well.

Consideration of administrative resources may be mixed with considerations of policy effectiveness. In the *ACRI* (Profiling) case regarding ethnicity-based profiling at airports, the court pointed out that applying a uniform level of security for all passengers would place an extreme administrative burden on the management of the airport which would result in a lesser degree of security. *ACRI* (Profiling) (n 188) [13] (Justice Grunis).

[243] See, e.g., in the second and third infiltrator cases - *Eitan* (n 82) and *Dasta* (n 83) – the lack of judicial review of detention as a disciplinary measure was itself considered a limitation of the right to due process and was required by the court.

[244] Examples of cases where judicial oversight was viewed as a contribution to the narrowly tailored nature are *ACRI* (Data Communication) (n 129) [38] (Justice Beinisch) (regarding warrants for transfer of metadata from communication companies to

where the court's decision to strike down a measure was based on lack of sufficient approval mechanisms.

### 3 Narrowing the Limitation in Time

Another dimension for narrowing the scope of the policy is time. There are two types of temporary limitations: the first is when the the limitation applies to an individual for a certain amount of time. For example, in *Adalah (familiy unificaiton I)* Justice Naor pointed out that the fact that the naturalization ban was applied based on an age-based criteria made the prohibition temporary vis-à-vis every individual: naturalization was not permanantely prevented but rather postponed, which in her opinion was less severe.[245] At times the right limitation is by definition for a restricted period of time – such as a period of detention before being brought before a judge, or a temporary prevention of a suspect meeting with an attorney.[246]

The second type of temporal narrowing is when the provision contains a sunset clause.[247] Several right-limiting bills in Israel were passed in the format of temporary provisions, including anti-terrorism measures and

investigative authorities); HCJ 5304/15 *Israeli Medical Association v Knesset* (11 September 2016, unpublished) (regarding forced feedings of prisoners on hunger strikes which included judicial review), available in English at <http://versa.cardozo.yu.edu/opinions/israel-medical-association-v-knesset>.

Examples of cases where the administrative process through which the limitation was to be approved was cited as contributing to the narrowly tailored nature are *Avneri* (n 102) [44], [53] (Justice Melcer) and [16]–[17] (Justice Hendel) (which challenged administrative sanctions that could be used against individuals or companies that expressed support of a boycott against the state, such as limiting their ability to participate in public tenders or receive special tax exemptions. The process for imposing such sanctions included approval of the Ministers of Finance and Justice and the Constitutional Committee in parliament). See also *Nakba* case (n 98) [28]–[29] (Justice Naor); HCJ 5277/13 *Association for Civil Rights in Israel v Security Services* (7 February 2017, unpublished).

245 *Galon* (n 39) [11]–[14] (Justice Naor).

246 On analysing the proportionality of cases including a quantitative aspect see text accompanying n 332–45 below.

247 Narrowing a limitation in time can also be achieved by postponing the 'start date': when introducing a new regulation, allowing time for right-holders to adjust is a way of minimizing the right limitation. See HCJ 956/06 *Banks Association v Minister of Communications* (25 March 2007, unpublished) [9] (Justice Hayut); *Menachem* (n 113) (Justice Beinisch); *Cigarette vendors* (n 95) [12] (Justice Grunis). But see the *Hoff Azza* case, where a request to postpone disengagement to allow adequate time for preparation was rejected. *Hoff Azza* (n 41) [441]–[56], and [9] Justice Levy, in the minority on this point.

policy regarding African infiltration through Israel's Southern border.[248] In theory, a rights-restricting policy that is temporary should be treated by the court as more proportionate than a permanent policy. However, an interesting shift in the way temporariness was treated by the court can be found between *Adalah (Family Unification I)* and *Galon*, both reviewing the ban on naturalization of Palestinian spouses. In the first instance of review of the policy, in *Adalah,* some of the justices who held the law to be proportional listed the temporary nature of the legislation as cause for greater judicial restraint.[249] Justice Barak, however, claimed the temporary nature itself should not substantially affect the assessment of proporitonality.[250] Subsequently, the provision was extended more than thirteen times before being brought before the court again. In the second policy review, in *Galon*, the minority justices who supported striking down the legislation voiced very critical opinions against the prolonged use of the temporary provision machanism: the temporary nature itself attested to the fact that the legislature recognized how severe the limitation of rights was, but it did not effectively result in any restraint, since the legislation was serially renewed.[251] The majority justices, who upheld the law, no longer cited temporariness as a consideration in favor of its proportionality.[252]

[248] The temporary nature of the law is not necessarily analysed at the necessity stage: it can be cited as a preliminary reason for increased restraint, or at the balancing stage as basis for assigning lesser weight to the harm.

[249] *Adalah* (Family Unification) (n 44) [118] (Justice Cheshin); [1]–[6], [17] (Justice Rivlin); Justice Levy addressed the temporary nature only with reference to the remedy – despite failing the necessity test he refrained from striking down the legislation due to its sunset clause, which was scheduled to expire shortly.

[250] ibid [92] (Justice Barak).

[251] *Galon* (n 39) [24]–[27] (Justice Arbel); [33] (Justice Levy); [9] (Justice Beinisch).

[252] See Justice Rubinstein, who was part of the majority, who stated that the temporariness placed an extra responsibility on the security authorities to reasess the need for the measure and the possibility of developing alternatives. ibid [47]–[49]. It should be noted that the policy has continued to be renewed temporarily since the *Galon* decision and is currently still in place.

Perhaps due to the experience with the naturalization ban, the court has developed a more suspicious approach to temporary legislation. In the *Eitan* case (n 82), reviewing prolonged detention of illegal migrants, the provision was passed as a temporary measure. However, Justice Vogelman assumed that the measure would be renewed and therefore effectively analysed the legislation as though it were permanent. [188] (Justice Vogelman). Justice Grunis, in his minority opinion, at para. 33, accepted the temporary nature at face value and upheld the legislation, but explicitly emphasized that it would not be considered proportional to renew this provision beyond three years.

### B Are There Alternative, Less-Restricting Measures?

Besides the possibility of narrowly tailoring the existing policy design, the necessity test may also address alternative, less-restricting measures. Some believe the court should confine itself to evaluating the design of the chosen measure, and not consider alternative measures. This was the opinion of Justice Shamgar in the seminal *Mizrahi Bank* case: 'we are referring to a search for a less harmful measure within a range or zone of similar or close possibilities (. . .) in order to search for the measure that is least harmful, the court does not redraft the purpose and does not redraft the program. Facing it is a purpose and measures as formulated by the legislature, and it examines them in terms of their substance, consequences and ramifications.'[253] Although this approach has been subsequently mentioned, it is a marginal one.[254]

Despite the fact that the state bears the burden of proof at the necessity stage, the general consensus seems to be that it is not required to proactively present the court with possible alternatives. In *Mizrahi Bank*, Justice Shamgar stated that the state is to present the path chosen by it and the considerations supporting its choice, but not the full gamut of 'infinite alternate paths' that could have been chosen. In his opinion, the party claiming that an alternative route should have been taken is required to present proof to support its claim.[255] Justice Barak places the burden to raise a claim regarding the existence of a particular less-restricting alternative on the plaintiffs, but once such a claim has been made, the burden shifts to the state to persuade that the particular alternative raised is not feasible or would not adequately fulfil the goal.[256] It seems that the practice in the case law is generally compatible with this approach.

However, when the government undertook a substantial decision making process, particularly when it was led independently by professionals such as an independent commission, the state will tend to present the court, of its own initiative, with the alternatives that were considered

[253] *Mizrahi Bank* (n 1) [85] (Justice Shamgar).

[254] See *Adam* (n 80) [3] (Justice Grunis), leaving as an unresolved question whether as part of the necessity stage the court should only evaluate possible changes in the legislation challenged before the court, or whether it should also address 'physical' alternatives that originate with decisions of the executive branch, such as the physical barrier built along the southern border.

[255] *Mizrahi Bank* (n 1) [85] (Justice Shamgar). He was joined on this point by Justices Mazza, Tal, and Goldberg. See Barak (n 3) 447–48.

[256] Barak (n 3) 412–13, 449.

and the rationale which supported the ultimate choice.[257] Another context where the state tends to present the court with alternatives it considered is spatial planning, probably since consideration of alternatives is integral to the planning process.[258] The state may also present less-restricting measures when such measures were previously implemented, but proved unsuccessful.[259]

When the state does not present alternatives on its own accord, the plaintiffs or the court might point to hypothetical alternatives. Generally, these will be intuitive alternatives based on common sense. At times they will be drawn from comparative experience, either from other policy contexts in Israel or experience abroad.[260] One example of a common-sense alternative to detention often mentioned by plaintiffs or the court is house arrest or monetary guarantees.[261] Additional common-sense alternatives are improving enforcement of an existing policy instead of the addition of further right-restricting measures;[262] using only one measure instead of simultaneously applying more than one;[263] and

[257] Some examples include the *Adalah* (Child Immunization) (n 92) case, regarding incentives to child immunization which included data on methods used abroad; the *Cigarette vendors* (n 95) [12], regarding ban on cigarette dispensers; the *prison privatization* case (n 82); *Gavish* (n 141) [4]–[5] (Justice Naor), regarding mandatory retirement age; and *Menachem* (n 113), regarding regulation of the taxi market.

[258] See, e.g., *Alaksa Almubarak* (n 167); HCJ 52/06 *Alaksa Company for Developing Muslim Holy Properties in Israel Inc. v Simon Wiesenthal Center Museum* (29 October 2009, unpublished).

[259] see *Adalah* (Child Immunization) (n 92) (presenting the unsuccessful efforts to increase vaccination rates through merely increasing access to information); *Abu Madigam* (n 37) (presenting attempts to prevent unlawful agricultural use of state-owned land by Bedouin tribes though use of warning signs, legal charges, overturning the land and spraying it from the ground. The ineffectiveness of these measures led the state to resort to the drastic means of aerial spraying).

[260] See, e.g., in *Hassan* (n 78) [68] (Justice Beinisch) brings the German solution as a less-restricting alternative; *Adam* (n 80); *Eitan* (n 82).

[261] This is an accepted alternative in the criminal context, that is often mentioned in the context of detention of illegal migrants and foreign workers. See *Adam* (n 80), and *Kav Laoved* (Binding Workers) (n 81).

[262] See *Adam* (n 80); *Kav Laoved* (Binding Workers) (n 81); *Commitment to Peace and Social Justice Society* (n 96) [20] (Justice Levy).

[263] *Avneri* (n 102) Justices Melcer and Hendel (holding that the use of a civil suit and administrative sanctions were sufficient to deter against calls for boycott, and therefore there was no justification for punitive damages as well); *Adam* (n 80) (the barrier on the border may be sufficient to prevent infiltration without prolonged detention); *Investment consultants* (n 43) (claiming that either minimum capital or insurance were needed to insure stability of investment consultants, rather than requiring both).

subjecting an activity to regulation instead of completely prohibiting it.[264] In some cases the plaintiffs might choose to supply the court with expert opinions describing and supporting potentially less-restricting alternatives.[265]

## C Comparatively Assessing Alternatives

After identifying potential alternative measures, the main challenge is comparatively evaluating them to determine whether they can be considered a less-restricting alternative for the purpose of this test. The three aspects that are assessed comparatively are: the severity of the right limitation (the alternative must be less-restrictive), the relative costs of the alternatives, and the relative efficiency of the alternatives in promoting the policy goal.

Comparatively assessing the severity of right limitation is relatively straightforward, and is generally based on common sense: a partial restriction is less-limiting than a total prohibition; a temporary limitation is less-restricting than an indefinite limitation; a monetary fine is less restricting than imprisonment; etc.[266] When differences in right

[264] *Ibillin Breeders* (n 79); *Tishim Kadurim* (n 113).

[265] See in the security context of the security fence (*Beit Sourik* (n 49)); and in military closing of travel routes (*Abu Safiyeh* (n 81); *Dir Samet* (n 115)). The security fence litigation presents an interesting example of how evaluation of alternatives originating with experts for the plaintiffs ultimately led to a change in state practice. In *Beit Sourik*, the first security fence case, the military defended the route it had chosen by presenting the security rationale upon which it was based, but without presenting alternative routes. The plaintiffs provided the court with an expert opinion that pointed to a less-restricting alternative route. Although rejected by the court at the necessity stage, it served as the basis for the incremental balancing conducted at the final stage, which resulted in the military route being deemed disproportional. This precedential decision was followed by dozens of petitions against segments of the fence. In responding to these petitions the state reopened its planning process, and gradually internalized the court's expectation to base its analysis on alternatives. The state began to actively present the court with its comparative assessment of possible routes both in terms of security and effect on rights. See, e.g., *Marabe* (n 135); *El Khawaja* (n 77); *Yassin* (n 77).

[266] There are rare cases where determining which alternative is less right-limiting is more complex. See, e.g., in the *Abu Madigam* (n 37) [41] case, Justice Arbel struggles with the comparison between the risk of bodily harm caused by the aerial spray with the risk of bodily harm from the violent responses triggered by manual over-turning of land. The *Gavish* case (n 141) also presented difficulty in ascertaining which alternative (uniform retirement or individual evaluations of capability) was less restricting in terms of dignity of the elderly employees.

limitation between alternatives are not substantial, the court generally defers to the decision-maker's choice.[267]

The comparison between costs of alternatives is slightly more complex, and raises the question of whether the court should require a less-restricting alternative even when it would entail greater financial investment. Generally, the state can be required to invest additional funds to prevent unjustified limitation of rights. The leading case in this regard is *Tzemach*, which reviewed the 96-hour period a soldier could be detained before being brought before a military judge. At the necessity stage, the court considered the possibility of setting the standard closer to the civilian standard of 24 hours. At the court's request the army specified the resources and addition of manpower required to reach a 48-hour period, and the majority of the court held that the resources required, although not miniscule, were not unreasonable and therefore held the 96-hour arrest period to be disproportional. Justice Zamir concluded that 'the importance [provided to liberty] should express itself not only in lofty statements, not only in legislation, but in the budget. The protection of human rights often demands a price. Society must be willing to pay a reasonable price on behalf of the protection of human rights.'[268] In the context of narrow tailoring the court will not accept conservation of resources as a legitimate justification for choosing a categorical or generalized policy design over an individualized one.[269]

On the other hand, the court has acknowledged that policy-makers cannot be totally oblivious to considerations of cost. Justice Dorner has stated that 'public resources are naturally limited. Despite the undisputed importance of individual rights, it is not possible, nor is it warranted, to give absolute precedence to the realization of individual rights over all other public goals.'[270] Therefore, the court's approach is that additional resources should be invested on behalf of a less-restricting alternative up to a 'reasonable point'.[271] The amount that

[267] Barak (n 3) 328; *Adalah* (Child Immunization) (n 92); *Investment consultants* (n 43); *Shtanger* (Lawyers) (n 95).

[268] *Tzemach* (n 186) [32], [36], [38]–[39] (Justice Zamir) (my translation T. S.); but see minority [4c] Justice Kedmi objecting to less restricting policy being implemented at any price, providing considerations of resources substantial weight.

[269] *Hoff Azza* (n 41) [191]; *Hassan* (n 78) [69] (Justice Beinisch), where this point is expressed as part of the final stage.

[270] *Investment consultants* (n 43) [4] (Justice Dorner) (my translation T. S.).

[271] Barak's opinion is that the necessity test should only address alternatives that are similar in all characteristics except the level of right limitation, and alternatives that vary in price

will be considered 'reasonable' depends on the context – the overall budget framework of the policy, the severity of the limitation, and the degree to which the additional resources reduce or nullify the limitation.[272]

The most difficult challenge, which cuts to the core of the necessity test, is comparing effectiveness of alternatives in achieving the policy goal. Interestingly, the case law presents a wide variety of approaches to the standard of effectiveness required from a less-restricting alternative and the method for ascertaining effectiveness. Often, the choice of the standard used is directly correlated to the final outcome of the case.[273]

I will elaborate upon three formulations found in the case law: The first is what I call the classic formulation, requiring a less-restrictive means to be chosen if it can achieve the policy goal with equal effectiveness, although within this formulation different approaches exist as to how equal effectiveness should be ascertained. The second formulation is more demanding, giving preference to a less-restricting means even if it is less effective. The third formulation is more relaxed than the classic formulation, not requiring the state to choose a less-restricting means even when one exists, so long as the chosen means is reasonably located within the 'proportionality range'.

should be evaluated at the stage of proportionality in the strict sense. See Barak (n 3) 326. In practice, this does not seem to be the common practice. Justice Dorner has explicitly stated that the consideration of cost should be evaluated as part of the necessity test. See *Investment consultants* (n 43) [4]–[8] (Justice Dorner); Dorner (n 100) 289–90.

272 See HCJ 1676/09 *Ministry of Defence v Qalandia Village Council* (30 November 2011, unpublished), [22]–[25], Justice Beinisch holding that the fact that an alternative was more expensive did not automatically disqualify it, but that the additional cost had to be reasonable relative to the overall cost of the project. In that case, the cost of a less-restricting alternative to the reviewed segment of the security fence was estimated at 22 million NIS. Since the overall cost of the fence in the area was 35 million NIS, the additional cost was found unreasonable. Similarly, see *Alaksa Almubarak* (n 167) [12]–[14] (Justice Vogelman).

273 Thus, holding the state to its burden of proof regarding the effectiveness of alternatives at this stage, or requiring less-restrictive alternatives to only be adequately effective always leads to failing the necessity test, whereas locating the measure within the range of proportional alternatives at the necessity test *de facto* means that it will pass the final balancing test. Following this point see Bilchitz (n 75) 50–51, claiming that confusion regarding the exact standard required by the necessity test leads courts to vary the standard dependent upon whether the court wishes to save or strike down a government measure.

### 1 The Classic Formulation of the Necessity Test Standard: Equal Effectiveness

According to the classic formulation of the necessity test, the legislature must choose the least-restricting among equally effective measures.[274] However, there are different approaches to establishing equal effectiveness: the first approach treates this question as a matter of logic, the second treats it as a question of fact but accepts the state's assumptions without proof, and the third treats it as a question of fact which the state is actually required to prove.

According to the first approach, comparing effectiveness is a matter of logic. Therefore, a drastic alternative is, almost by definition, more effective than a less-drastic one, resulting in the drastic alternative passing the necessity test. This logical approach characterized the opinions of the majority of the justices in *Adalah (Family Unification I)* and *Galon*, in comparing the effectiveness of the complete ban to individual security evaluations: as phrased by Justice Barak, no matter how effective individual assessments may be, they cannot compete with the level of security provided by a complete ban.[275]Applying this approach to the necessity stage is not necessarily correlated to the final outcome, but rather has the effect of postponing the final decision to the last stage.

The second approach treats the question of comparative effectiveness as a factual issue to be proven, but in practice accepts the state's expert evaluation, and in cases of uncertainty gives the state the benefit of the doubt.[276] The burden of proof required from the plaintiffs to challenge the state's position is high, to the point where it is nearly impossible to fulfil.[277] This approach was applied in *Beit Sourik* evaluating the proportionality of the route of the security fence. The plaintiffs pointed to an alternative route which was undisputedly less-restrictive of the Palestinian residents' freedom of movement and access to agricultural land; the dispute was over whether this alternative route could provide the same level of security. The plaintiffs submitted an expert opinion by

[274] Barak (n 3) 320–23; *Investment consultants* (n 43) [18] (Justice Barak); *Prison Privatization* case (n 82) [49] (Justice Beinisch); *Adalah* (Family Unification) (n 44) [104] (Justice Barak).

[275] *Adalah* (Family Unification) (n 44) [89] (Justice Barak) and [8] (Justice Beinisch); *Galon* (n 39) [12] (Justice Joubran). See also *Yonas* (n 126) [74] (Justice Danziger); *Adam* (n 80) (Justice Vogelman); *Eitan* (n 82) (Justice Vogelman).

[276] See Barak (n 3) 408–11, where he states that uncertainty should be decided by deferring to the state.

[277] See also Cohen-Eliya (n 90) 491, in his critique of the *Beit Sourik* decision.

ex-military officials according to which not only did the alternative route provide an equal level of security but it was superior to the route designed by the military. However, the court sided with the military expertise, holding that the plaintiffs had not proven that the alternative was equally efficient.[278] This approach is also not necessarily correlated to the outcome, but postpones the determination of the case to the final stage.

The third approach treats effectiveness as a question of fact, but places the burden of proof on the state to persuade that the less-restrictive means is not equally efficient. If convincing evidence is not presented or the factual reality is uncertain, the court will decide in favour of the less-restricting means. This approach seems to be adopted primarily when there are signs that the state did not adequately evaluate the alternatives. In all cases identified implementing this approach, it led to failure at the necessity test.

An example is *Hassan*, which challenged an irrefutable presumption that ownership or use of a car disqualifies a person from receiving income support. The position of the National Insurance Institution was that it could not monitor and evaluate individual car use. The court held that the state had not presented convincing evidence that the less-restricting measures could not be sufficient.[279]

### 2 The Second Formulation of the Necessity Test Standard: Adequate Effectiveness

The second formulation of the necessity standard emphasizes *adequate*, rather than *equal* effectiveness of the less-restricting alternative. Under this formulation a less-restricting alternative can be required even if it is not equally effective, so long as it fulfils the goal at an adequate level, or if there is a reasonable probability that it will attain the goal. The result is that extremely right-restricting measures will be rejected regardless of their enhanced effectiveness. This approach seems to properly represent

278 *Beit Sourik* (n 49) [56], [58], [66]–[67] (Justice Barak); *Prison Privatization* case (n 82) [48]–[49] (Justice Beinisch). However, see Justice Naor in a minority opinion placing the burden of proof on the state and finding they did not provide adequate evidence, in accordance with the third approach.

279 *Hassan* (n 78) [67]. Also see *Dir Samet* and *Abu Safiyeh* cases, where the court held that the military had failed to convince that alternative security measures mentioned by the plaintiffs could not achieve the level of security required. The court also remarked that these possibilities did not seem to even have been sincerely considered. *Dir Samet* (n 115) [26]; *Abu Safiyeh* (n 81) [31]–[36] (Justice Vogelman).

the metaphor of the ladder often used to describe the necessity test: the state must begin at the lowest level of limitation and proceed until an adequate degree of attainment of the goal is achieved, rather than begin from the most limiting means and descend only so long as the effectiveness remains similar.[280] This formulation is primarily applied in contexts of severe limitations of liberty and dignity, and in all cases identified where this formulation was used it led to the failure of the measure at the necessity test.

For example, in *Adam*, Justice Arbel surveyed alternatives to three-year detention of illegal migrants that could fulfil the goal of preventing the 'setting down of roots' in a way that might hinder the ability to deport them in the future. She addressed alternatives such as limitations on areas of residence, periodical reports to police stations, cash deposits as guarantee for departure or open-residence centres, and referred to comparative law implementing such solutions to support the claim for their effectiveness. Her conclusion was that there was 'a reasonable probability' that these less-restricting means would fulfil the goal, and therefore the prolonged detention failed the necessity test.[281] In the subsequent *Eitan* case, reviewing a three-year detention period in a semi-open centre, Justice Joubran criticized the strictly logical interpretation that resulted in the most restricting version of the centre to be by definition the most effective, stating that this approach rendered the necessity test powerless.[282] He held that the accumulation of various measures could adequately prevent unlawful employment of migrants, hence failing the measure.[283]

The emphasis of this approach is not placed on the effectiveness of the alternative, but the extremity of the chosen measure, demonstrating its excessiveness despite it being more effective. This point can be demonstrated by *Kav Laoved (pregnant workers)*. As part of an overall effort to prevent foreign workers from remaining in the country illegally after the expiration of their work permit, a policy was put in place requiring female foreign workers to leave the country within three months of giving birth, and permitting them to re-enter the country for the

280 For the ladder metaphor see *Investment consultants* (n 43) [18]; Barak (n 3) 317.

281 This approach was not joined by the other justices in the case, who struck down the legislation at the final stage.

282 He was referring to a semi-open centre that mandated residents to sign-in on the premises three times a day.

283 *Eitan* (n 82) [9]–[10] (Justice Joubran). Similarly, see *El Khawaja* (n 77) [37]–[38] (Justice Beinisch); *Seif* (n 92).

remainder of their permit period without the infant, since raising a child in Israel was considered to make enforcing departure more difficult. At the necessity stage Justice Procaccia characterized the means chosen as the most infringing possible, 'ten times more severe' than the alternatives. She briefly described potential alternatives, such as requiring a deposit to ensure departure and better enforcement at the end of the period, but she did not delve into an in-depth evaluation of the relative effectiveness of the alternatives – her underlying assumption was that the extreme means could not pass the necessity test.[284] Similarly, Justice Levy's minority opinion in *Galon*, in the context of the naturalization ban, held the absolute ban to be the most infringing measure possible. He briefly pointed to possibilities by which the effectiveness of the individual assessment system could be increased, but did not treat the absolute ban as a legitimate point of reference, and therefore did not even attempt to claim that these were capable of attaining an equal level of effectiveness.[285]

As part of this approach to the necessity test, the court may expect the state to experiment with a less-restricting alternative to ascertain whether it is adequately effective, or actively invest in the development of less-restricting measures if such an alternative does not yet exist.[286]

### 3 The Third Formulation of the Necessity Test Standard: Within the Range of Proportional Alternatives

There are cases where the chosen measure is not required to be less-restrictive relative to equally effective alternatives, so long as it itself is deemed to be located within the 'proportionality range'. In such cases the focus is on the reasonableness of the chosen measure; there is no actual comparative evaluation of alternatives. This formulation is rooted in a

284 *Kav Laoved* (pregnant workers) (n 164) [61]–[63]; See also the *Avneri* (n 102) case, regarding the possibility of punitive damages, without proof of harm, against someone who calls for boycott against the state. Justice Melcer, at para. 43, categorized this as an extreme measure in civil law that cannot be justified; Justice Rubinstein, at paras. 15–16, sees the punitive damages sanction as 'one step too far' in terms of deterrence, beyond the adequate attainment of the goal achieved by other sections of the law. However, Justice Danziger, at para. 16, takes the logical approach, according to which punitive damages pass the necessity test because they are, by definition, more effective, subsequently failing them at the balancing stage.

285 *Galon* (n 39) [36]–[37] (Justice Levy).

286 See *Eitan* (n 82) [7]–[8] (Justice Arbel), regarding experimentation with a shorter period of detention; *Kirsch* (n 155) [7] (Justice Dorner).

position of deference to the discretion of the legislature or administrative body,[287] and all cases identified where the necessity test was formulated in this manner resulted in the reviewed measure being upheld. The term 'proportionality range' seems to have stemmed from the pre-existing term 'reasonableness range', which was developed in administrative law. The term 'reasonableness range' is typically invoked to express the idea that there are several reasonable outcomes from which the state is free to choose, and this same concept was borrowed into the context of proportionality.[288]

The formulation of the necessity test in terms of a range was first applied in *Tnufa Human Resources Company*, which dealt with a substantial cash deposit as a prerequisite for obtaining a human resources sub-contractor license. At the necessity stage Justice Dorner accepted that there were alternative ways to achieve the goal of ensuring employee salaries in case of bankruptcy. However, since the measure chosen by the legislature was located within the 'proportionality range', she found that it passed the necessity test.[289] Since then it has been applied in contexts of regulation of the taxi drivers market;[290] privatization of the postal services;[291] prohibition on gambling;[292] cuts in old-age benefits;[293] revocation of tax-benefits;[294] design of pension arrangements;[295] and design of tax regimes.[296]

[287] Barak, in his book, attempts to limit the use of this approach, claiming that it should be restricted to situations of inherent uncertainty regarding effectiveness, which justifies deference. Barak admits that he contributed to a 'misunderstanding', according to which there is an actual possibility of relaxing the standard and knowingly approving of a measure that is not the least restrictive in *Menachem* (n 113). Barak (n 3) 408–11, 415–17. See also Guy Davidov, 'Constitutional Review in Budgetary Matters' (2007) 49 Hapraklit 345 (in Hebrew).

[288] See, e.g., HCJ 389/80 *Yellow Pages v Broadcasting Authority* [1980], IsrSC 35(1) 421; Barak-Erez (n 2) 763.

[289] *Tnufa* (n 101) [4] (Justice Dorner); and [15] (Justice Barak).

[290] *Menachem* (n 113) [26] (Justice Beinsich).

[291] *Banks Association* (n 247) [9] (Justice Hayut).

[292] *Tishim Kadurim* (n 113) (Justice Grunis); *Cigarette vendors* (n 95).

[293] *Manor* (n 95) [15] (Justice Barak).

[294] *Beer Sheva Municipality* (Mosque) (n 130) [16] (Justice Naor).

[295] HCJ 6784/06 *Major Shlitner v The Director of Pension Payments* [2011], IsrSC 64(2) 581 (Justice Melcer).

[296] HCJ 6304/09 *Lahav – Israel Organization of the Self-Employed v Attorney General* (2 September 2010, unpublished) [113]; HCJ 6061/08 *Yisraeli v Ministry of Agriculture* (19 August 2009, unpublished), Justice Arbel.

Often the court will provide no insight into how it concluded that the means were located within the 'proportional range'.[297] However, in some cases the court provides some form of reasoning: one such reasoning involved the existence of similar or even more-restricting alternatives in comparative law;[298] the second was the fact that the challenged means was an improvement relative to the previous situation.[299]

This formulation of the necessity standard seems to be predominantly found in contexts of financial rights and regulation.[300] This can be attributed both to the fact that in these contexts the financial nature of the limited rights is considered less severe, and to the court's hesitance to intervene in financial policy, due to the complexity of the issue or the inherent uncertainty in such matters.[301] In all cases identified where this formulation was used it led to the reviewed measure passing the necessity test and ultimately being upheld.

## VIII Proportionality in the Strict Sense

### A *The Interplay between the Final Stage and the Previous Stages*

The final stage of proportionality in the strict sense holds a prominent role in Israeli case law. However, the quantitative analysis demonstrates that, counter to the common perception, the importance of this stage does not stem from it serving as the sole basis for striking down reviewed measures: only 15 per cent of the failure cases failed at the final test alone.

[297] See *Tishim Kadurim* (n 113); *Beer Sheva Municipality (tax benefits)* (n 185); *Manor* (n 95). Similar criticism has been voiced against the use of the term 'margin of appreciation' by the European Court of Human Rights. See Ronald St J Macdonald, 'The Margin of Appreciation' in Ronald St J Macdonald, Franz Matscher and Herbert Petzold (eds), *The European System for the Protection of Human Rights* (Martinus Nijhoff Publishers 1993) 85; George Letsas, 'Two Concepts of the Margin of Appreciation' (2006) 26 Oxford Journal of Legal Studies 705, 714.

[298] *Tnufa* (n 101); *Menachem* (n 113).

[299] ibid.

[300] As an exception to this rule, see the *Ploni* (Unlawful Combatants) (n 101) [38], [39], [41], [44], [46] (Justice Beinisch). Two possible explanations can be offered for the unique use of this standard in a case concerning security measures: first, the guiding assumption that within the constraints of international law the Israeli legislature enjoys freedom – in the case was hence, the 'proportional range'; second, the structure of the decision is PA with reference to the law as a whole, and then, within the necessity stage, the analysis is split up into mini-analyses of seven specific measures, each found to be in the 'proportional range', which may be a form of 'short hand' analysis considering the length and complexity of the decision.

[301] *Tnufa* (n 101) (Justice Dorner); *Beer Sheva Municipality (tax benefits)* (n 185).

Nevertheless, the centrality of this stage manifests itself in several other ways.

First, this stage is the final stage in all judicial decisions upholding measures under the proportionality framework. Deeming a measure proportional in the strict sense is the final stamp of approval necessary for the petition to be rejected and the measure to be upheld. Second, as was demonstrated earlier, there is a prevalent practice of continuing the analysis through to the last stage despite failure at an earlier stage: only 22 per cent of the cases in the database that ended in failure did not reference proportionality in the strict sense. This practice reinforces the status of the last test as an essential component of the analysis, where the judicial message is concluded. Inadvertently, this has a weakening effect on earlier stages, since it implies that failing in an earlier stage is not a strong enough basis to support the outcome. It entrenches the conception that ultimately, constitutionality is a function of striking the right balance between benefit and harm, as opposed to promoting strictly worthy goals or ensuring suitability and necessity of means.

As detailed earlier, the continuation of the analysis after a failure can be framed by the court in different ways. At times, subsequent stages are reasoned briefly; but in some cases, the court places the weight of the decision on the final stage despite the existence of a previous failure, going into the most elaborate and detailed reasoning and referring to the failure at the final stage as the most convincing.[302]

A third expression of the centrality of the last test is deferral of the decision to the final stage despite difficulties being discussed earlier. At times justices 'signal' the presence of a difficulty at one of the earlier stages but refrain from failing the measure at that point, instead deferring the failure to the final stage.[303] In five out of the six cases in the database that failed for the first time at the final stage, at least one of the justices on the panel pointed to a problem at a previous stage but left it unresolved.

A fourth and final expression of the last stage's centrality is in concurring or minority opinions, which are often shorter opinions that appear chronologically after the first, most detailed decision. These justices do not always feel obliged to carry out a full analysis, and therefore may

[302] See *Adam* (n 80) (Justice Arbel); *Abu Madigam* (n 37) (Justice Arbel); and see detail in Section III.C on the characteristics of continuation of the analysis after failure.

[303] See, e.g., see *Adam* (n 80) [19], [23] (Justice Vogelman), [10] (Justice Joubran); *Eitan* (n 82) [52], [59], [68]–[71], [111]–[13], [193] (Justice Vogelman); *Raai* (n 82) (Justice Vogelman); *Prison Privatization* case (n 82) [47] (Justice Beinisch).

present their opinion solely in terms of proportionality in the strict sense, thus perhaps demonstrating that it is the essence of the analysis.[304]

A rare position of explicit rejection of the centrality of the final stage was voiced by Justice Levy. In his view, the sub-tests are ordered from the most important to the least important, so that the farther a policy strays from the constitutional order, the earlier in the analysis it should be struck down, signalling the need for a more fundamental change to the policy. Less fundamental flaws will be struck down at later stages, where more limited alterations may be sufficient. Justice Levy warned against awarding the final stage too dominant a status, to the point where it becomes almost exclusive, overshadowing all other stages of the analysis. Due to its value-laden framing and ill-defined nature, he believed it should be avoided when possible.[305] In practice, he indeed refrained from continuing the analysis to the final stage after failing at a previous stage.[306]

### B *Formulations and Applications of Proportionality in the Strict Sense*

As noted previously, Barak has been extremely influential in developing the framework of constitutional review, and summarized his conception of this stage in his book, following his judicial decisions. Formally at least, his formulation is treated as the consensus in the case law. The essence of this stage according to Barak is investigating whether there is a proper relation between the benefit arising from the attainment of the policy goal and the harm caused to the constitutional right, so that the benefit is greater than the harm.[307] First, each is evaluated separately – the importance of the goal and the probability of its attainment on the one hand, and the importance of the right and the probability of its limitation on the other hand. Barak emphasizes that balancing is not to be conducted between the entire benefit and harm, but only the marginal benefit and harm caused by the means, relative to the preceding situation. When there is a clear alternative that limits the right to an acceptable degree, the incremental benefit and harm are weighed relative to that alternative.[308]

304 See, e.g., *Avneri* (n 102) [12] (Justice Danziger) and [11], [14] (Justice Hendel).

305 *Galon* (n 39) [19], [25]–[26] (Justice Levy).

306 See n 81.

307 Barak (n 3) 340, 343–44, and see his references to case law in (n 3–8, 24–28, 32).

308 ibid 350–57. Bendor has pointed out that this incremental formulation of the proportionality test had only become dominant in Justice Barak's case law towards the end of

After evaluating the benefit and the harm separately, the common denominator that enables the comparison between the two, in Barak's opinion, is the 'relative social importance', which is based on the values and norms of the particular society. In assessing the 'social importance' of the protection of the constitutional right, what is considered is the relative importance of the right and the extent, degree, and strength of the limitation. Barak summarizes the rule by stating that the more severe the limitation, the benefit to the public goal must be more important and necessary, and the probability of attaining the benefit must be higher.[309]

The main question that arises is to what extent this formulation is indeed applied in by the court. From my analysis, three main practices can actually be found at the final stage: balancing in absolute terms, balancing in marginal terms, and the location of the policy within the 'proportionality range'. I will elaborate on the characteristics of each of these practices.

### 1 Balancing in Absolute Terms

Balancing in absolute terms directly contrasts the importance of the policy benefit with the severity of the limitation. Typically, only two levels are used to categorize each side: high or low importance of the expected benefit, and severe or minimal harm to the right. This two-level categorization system can theoretically result in a 'mismatch' between the two sides of the scale (severe limitation and low benefit, or minor limitation and substantial benefit), or equality with both sides categorized as either high or low. In practice, weighing in absolute terms is most commonly used in a 'mismatch' setup, where one side is categorized as high and the other as low.

For example, in a case reviewing the constitutionality of a privatized prison, the ongoing limitation of prisoner dignity was categorized as a highly severe core infringement, whereas the financial benefit of the policy was not perceived to be of great importance.[310] More commonly in the mismatch structure, the substantial benefit of the policy will be contrasted with a minimal level of right limitation. For example, in

his term, despite it being the dominant formulation in his book. See Bendor and Sela (n 65) 1109–10.

309 Barak (n 3) 348–50, 362–65; *Investment consultants* (n 43) [18] (Justice Barak); *Adalah* (Family Unification) (n 44) [74] (Justice Barak); *Abu Madigam* (n 37) [43] (Justice Arbel); *Hamifkad Haleumi* (n 34) [12] (Justice Beinisch).

310 *Prison Privatization* case (n 82) [52]–[55] (Justice Beinisch); similarly, see *Raai* (n 82) [28]–[31] (Justice Vogelman); *Bakri* (n 130).

*Investment Consultants*, the benefit to consumer protection was considered substantial, whereas the limitation of freedom of occupation was marginal.[311] Similarly, in *Cigarette Vendors*, the benefit to public health from prohibiting automatic cigarette dispensers was categorized as high, as opposed to the marginal limitation on freedom of occupation, considering alternative venues for tobacco sale.[312] The main criteria used by the court to establish that the limitation is relatively marginal are when narrowly tailoring efforts were made[313] and when the limitation only affects a peripheral aspect of the right.[314]

Although the most common cases of absolute balancing are mismatch cases, at times both the harm to the right is classified as severe and the benefit to the goal is categorized as high. In some cases reviewing house demolitions the grave limitation of rights caused by the measure was acknowledged, alongside the substantial importance of deterring future terrorists and the potential of saving lives. Ultimately, in such cases the benefit was held to outweigh the harm.[315] A categorization of both the benefit and the limitation as low does not seem to occur.

A more nuanced reading of the absolute balancing cases reveals that the emphasis of the reasoning is placed primarily on the right limitation, whereas the actual evaluation of the policy benefit is often far less detailed. For example, in *ACRI (data communication)*, reviewing legislation regulating warrants for providing communication data for

[311] *Investment consultants* (n 43) [27], [38] (Justice Barak).

[312] *Cigarette vendors* (n 95) [9], [12] (Justice Grunis); See also *Shtanger* (Lawyers) (n 95) [15] (Justice Barak); *Alaksa Almubarak* (n 167) [16] (Justice Vogelman).

[313] See, e.g., in the *Adalah* (Child Immunization) case, as a basis for categorizing the limitation of parental autonomy as minimal, the court noted that the condition was limited to the four most important immunizations, the amount conditioned was limited and an appeal mechanism was created. *Adalah* (Child Immunization) (n 92) [63] (Justice Arbel) and [67] (Justice Barak-Erez). In *Shtanger* the court mentioned that the extension of periods between judicial reviews of detention during criminal proceedings was limited to severe criminal charges, complex cases, and required the approval of a higher instance as basis for the conclusion that the limitation of right to freedom was in proportion to the benefit. *Shtanger* (Suspects) (n 168) [41] (Justice Grunis).

[314] See *Peled* (n 105) [18] (Justice Beinsich) (locating prisoners' right to pornographic materials at the periphery of freedom of speech); *Abu Musaed* (n 112) [45] (Justice Procaccia) (categorizing the right to an individual connection to the water system in the unrecognized Bedouin settlements as a peripheral aspect of the right to accessibility to water).

[315] See, e.g., HCJ 6288/03 *Sa'ada v IDF Home Front Command* [2003] IsrSC 58(2) 289 (Justice Turkel). Recently, there have been more sceptical views voiced regarding this policy. See Section VI.C.2.

investigations, the balancing stage was devoted entirely to the ways in which the limitation of privacy had been narrowly tailored. The other side of the scale – the added value of obtaining the data for advancing investigations – was essentially taken for granted and therefore not elaborated upon in the judgment or explicitly weighed.[316] Similarly, in *Avneri*, reviewing the boycott law which created various sanctions against those calling for boycott against the state, Justice Melcer focused his analysis on the extent of the limitation caused to freedom of speech, deeming one aspect of the policy disproportionate and others proportionate, entirely based on the extent of the right limitation involved, with nearly no analysis of the actual benefit the elements were expected to have in preventing the harm of the boycott.[317]

In the opposite direction as well, the conclusion of disproportionality at the final stage often focuses entirely on the severity of the limitation, whereas the benefit to be gained by the policy is barely mentioned. For example, *Ploni* reviewed a provision enabling the extension of the detention of a suspect without his presence in court for the hearing, when security considerations required an uninterrupted interrogation. Justice Rivlin elaborated at length on the severity of the limitation of the right to due process, with nearly no mention of the contribution to the effectiveness of the interrogation and national security.[318] Justice Hendel, in the minority in *Avneri*, conducted his balancing analysis of the civil measures against boycotters entirely in terms of the severity of the harm to speech, without any reference to the expected benefit of the policy and its weight.[319] Justice Levy's opinion in *Kav Laoved (binding workers)*

316 *ACRI* (Data Communication) (n 129) [38]–[39 (Justice Beinisch). The need for the measure is described in para. 11 in the context of the worthy purpose, quoting from the state's claims before the court, and is essentially taken for granted for the remainder of the analysis.

317 *Avneri* (n 102) [42]–[43] (Justice Melcer) (regarding the element struck down – punitive damages); and para. 53 (regarding the other sanctions upheld). But see [18]–[21] Justice Amit, who, as part of the majority opinion, did frame the test in terms of assessing the weight of both sides, and included a slightly more detailed account of the benefits expected from the law. Interestingly though, his phrasing of the policy goal is entirely in terms of individual rights, namely protecting the dignity of those being boycotted; thus his analysis is still confined to weighing severity of right limitations.

318 Ploni (Due Process) (n 101) [28]–[31] (Justice Rivlin). Justice Naor, in the minority, was of the opinion that in extreme cases in which the interrogation could save lives, the importance of the goal could outweigh the severity of the limitation.

319 *Avneri* (n 102) [7]–[8] (Justice Hendel). On the other hand, [34]–[39] Justice Danziger, who was also part of the minority, addressed the potential benefit of the law, explicitly evaluating it as low.

exemplifies this phenomenon: the case reviewed a policy binding foreign workers' permits to one particular employer without any ability to transfer to another employer, and the data showed that the policy did not obtain the goal of decreasing the number of workers that remained in the country illegally after their permit expired. This lack of rational connection could have served as sufficient justification for striking down the policy, but Justice Levy went on to add that even if the policy had benefited the goal the limitation would have still outweighed the benefit, considering its severity. Meaning, it was important for him to frame the outcome of the case as one that was determined by the severity of the limitation, not merely the lack of public benefit.[320]

These examples demonstrate that when conducting absolute balancing, the court tends to primarily evaluate the severity of the right limitation. This may be due to the court's conception of its own expertise: it may feel more competent to base the decision primarily on whether the limitation of the right has gone beyond the justifiable limit, rather than an evaluation of the weight of the policy benefit.[321]

It should be pointed out that even when analysis is phrased in terms of absolute balancing, it may in essence be a reflection of incremental-balancing, relative to a narrowly tailored option. This can be demonstrated by Justice Grunis's opinions in the *Adam* and *Eitan* infiltrators cases. His conclusions at the final stage were phrased in absolute terms: the severity of the limitation of the migrants' liberty outweighed the benefits to the policy goals. However, in both cases he went on to describe the narrowly tailored formulation that would, in his opinion, survive the balancing test, arguably exposing the fact that this version of the policy was present in the background of his balancing analysis.[322]. Theoretically, his analysis could have been resolved at the necessity test by pointing to the need for narrow tailoring, or alternatively, his

[320] *Kav Laoved* (Binding Workers) (n 81) [55] (Justice Levy).

[321] See in the context of the critique voiced by Ailenkoff (n 156) 984–92 that judicial balancing is a replication of the legislature's task, and his suggestion that balancing by the Court should be conducted from a perspective grounded in the constitution.

[322] In *Adam* (n 80) [4], he added that detention for a shorter period of time would be deemed proportionate: meaning that essentially he found the incremetal benefits of the prolonged period to fail to outweigh the incremental limitation caused by the period of time. In the remedy stage in *Eitan* (n 82) [28], he struck down only the afternoon sign-in requirement, leaving the morning and night sign-ins in place: meaning, the incremental harm caused by the mid-day requirement was held by him to be greater than its incremental benefit.

balancing stage could have been phrased in incremental rather than absolute terms, by comparing the policy to the less-restricting alternative.

## 2 Balancing in Incremental Terms

As detailed previously, Barak's position, crystalized in his book, is that the balancing at the final stage should be conducted in incremental terms. Incremental balancing can be conducted relative to the situation preceding the adoption of the measure (either previous measures that were in place, or none at all), or relative to a hypothetical less-restricting alternative.[323] Barak himself applied incremental balancing in three seminal decisions handed down in his final years on the court: *Beit Sourik*, challenging the route of the security fence; *Adalah (Family Unification I)*, challenging an absolute ban on naturalization of Palestinian spouses to Israeli citizens; and another *Adalah* case, challenging an irrefutable presumption of state immunity from tort liability.[324] In all three cases he held the government policy to be disproportionate, with the incremental analysis serving as an 'antidote' to over-weighting the policy benefit: by weighing only the incremental value of the benefit, it was possible for it to be outweighed by the severity of the right limitation.[325]

Interestingly, Justice Naor has consistently used the method of incremental analysis in the opposite direction: to minimize the severity assigned to the limitation, allowing it to be outweighed by the benefit.[326]

323 Barak (n 3) 352–57.

324 *Beit Sourik* (n 49) [59]–[61] (Justice Barak); *Adalah* (Family Unification) (n 44) [90]–[93], [110] (Justice Barak); *Adalah* (Tort Liability) (n 132) [40]–[41] (Justice Barak). In the two *Adalah* cases, the analysis was conducted relative to the measures that had existed before the new legislation had been introduced. In *Beit Sourik*, the incremental analysis was conducted relative to a hypothetical less-infringing route. This is considered a relatively activist position since it can be seen as an endorsement of a particular alternative policy. See Rivka Weill, 'Did the Lawmaker Shoot a Cannon to Hit a Fly? On Proportionality in Law' (2012) 15 Mishpat Veasakim 337, 406–8 (in Hebrew).

325 In all three cases the goal was security related, which tends to be over-weighted when treated in the absolute. For similar incremental analyses in security-oriented cases, see *Abu Safiyeh* (n 81), and *Dir Samet* (n 115), where the justices addressed the benefit to security incrementally, relative to alternative security measures that could be adopted instead of a complete ban on Palestinian access to roads.

326 Justice Naor also relied on incremental analysis in the *Prison Privatization* case (n 82) [24]–[27], striking down the policy. In this case she applied it similarly to Barak, to emphasize the limited nature of the benefit. However, she was primarily emphasizing the lack of evidence to support the state's claim that partial privatization was not financially feasible – a conclusion she had already reached at the necessity stage.

For example, in *Rubinstein*, which challenged the exemption of ultra-orthodox high schools from teaching the mandatory core-curriculum subjects, Justice Naor approached the limitation of students' right to education incrementally, relative to the fact that the core-curriculum was taught in elementary school. She found the incremental level of right limitation to be proportional to the policy benefit of maintaining parental autonomy in shaping children's education.[327]

The fact that incremental balancing engages with less-restricting alternatives can lead it to take on a role that arguably should have been conducted at the necessity test. As described previously, some approaches to the necessity stage do not effectively engage with alternatives, but instead merely assert the chosen measure's superiority in terms of effectiveness. In such cases, incremental analysis at the balancing stage can be the first time alternatives are mentioned and discussed, leading to a blurring in the role played by the balancing stage relative to the necessity stage.

For example, in reviewing the prolonged detention period for illegal migrants in *Adam*, at the necessity test Justice Vogelman accepted the chosen measure as the most efficient, without analysing alternatives in detail. Only at the final stage did he point to the arsenal of potential alternatives that together could plausibly contribute in a less right-limiting manner to the policy goal of minimizing the ill-effects of illegal migration (including geographical limitations on migrants' living parameters, open or half-open living centres, controlled integration in specific branches of the labour market, etc.). Pointing to the complexity of evaluating these alternatives, however, he did not conduct a full incremental analysis. Instead, he concluded generally that the existence of potential alternatives deemed the chosen policy disproportionally right-limiting.[328] He did criticize the State's simplified presentation of reality,

[327] *Rubinstein* (Core Education) (n 40) [7] (Justice Naor). Similarly, in *Hamifkad Haleumi* (n 34), which challenged the prohibition of advertising controversial issues on public broadcasting, [56]–[59] Justice Naor, dissenting, assessed the limitation of speech incrementally, finding it to be minimal considering the existence of alternative methods of expression, including the written press and the internet. She found the minimal limitation to be outweighed by the substantial public benefit of upholding the fairness doctrine in public broadcast. Also see the *ACRI* (Passports) case (n 99), regarding an increase in passport renewal fee, where [23]–[29] Justice Naor held, in the minority as well, that relative to the previous fee the incremental limitation caused by the addition was outweighed by the benefits.

[328] *Adam* (n 80) [39]–[41] (Justice Vogelman). For an additional example of this kind of use of incremental balancing see *Prison Privatization* case (n 82) [23]–[27] (Justice Naor),

according to which there are only two options: prolonged detention of the migrants or presence of massive amounts of migrants in city centres without any possibility of oversight or treatment. The failure of the state to present an evaluation of such alternatives, instead choosing to directly proceed with an extreme measure, seems to be essential to his conclusion. However, rather than hold the state to its burden of proof at the necessity stage, his analysis was framed in terms of incremental balancing.

### 3 Locating the Policy within the 'Proportionality Range'

Rather than evaluate the relationship between benefit and harm in either absolute or incremental terms, the court may merely locate the means within the 'proportionality range'. As detailed previously, this concept can also be used at the necessity test, meaning that the court will refrain from comparing the policy to possible alternatives, instead holding the means to be generally reasonable. At the final stage the logic is similar: the court declares the policy proportional without actually conducting a detailed evaluation of the balance.[329]

Evoking the concept of 'proportionality range' at the final stage is most common in two contexts: the first is of complex regulation which involved multiple potential designs, leading the court to be hesitant in engaging in evaluation of the benefits and harms. The term 'proportionality range' in this context seems to express the position that other regulatory options could equally have been considered proportional.[330] For example, in *Gavish*, a reform setting a uniform retirement age was challenged. The court acknowledged there being advantages and disadvantages to different schemes, and then held the chosen model to be located within the range.[331]

who states explicitly that the state failed to fulfil its burden of proof at the necessity stage, but that rather than failing the legislation at the necessity stage based solely on the issue of burden of proof, she instead proceeds to conduct incremental balancing at the final stage.

329 Another use of the 'proportional range' is a way for the court to express the borderline nature of the policy: by stating that the balance struck by the policy is 'at the very edge of the proportional range', the policy-maker is encouraged to reconsider the policy, or refrain from executing the powers to the utmost extent. See *Shlitner* (n 295) [26] (Justice Melcer); *Shtanger* (Suspects) (n 168) (Justices Melcer and Rubinstein); *Ploni* (Unlawful Combatants) (n 101) (Justice Beinisch).

330 *Tishim Kadurim* (n 113) [26]–[29] (Justice Grunis).

331 *Gavish* (n 141) [48]–[56] (Justice Naor); Also see *Rubinstein* (Core Education) (n 40) [7]–[8] (Justice Naor).

The second context where use of the 'proportionality range' can be found is cases involving a quantitative characteristic, such as an amount of time or money.[332] In surveying such cases it seems that the court's willingness to intervene in the quantitative choice of the policy-maker depends primarily upon the nature of the right being limited and the severity of the limitation. Nearly all quantitative cases located by the court in the 'proportionality range' involved the limitation of financially oriented rights, such as property or freedom of occupation.[333] Some techniques used by the court to support the conclusion that the amount is within the proportional range include the involvement of an expert committee in setting the amount; sensitivity of the amount, to some degree, to circumstances;[334] comparison to relevant benchmarks in similar contexts;[335] and a previous decrease in the amount during the policy-making process or the parliamentary debate.[336]

In contrast, in cases of detention and limitations of liberty, despite the fact that the challenged policy has a quantitative characteristic the court has not necessarily been deferential and has held lengths of time to be disproportional. The reasoning of the court in such cases was often principled, critiquing the assumptions upon which the periods of time had been set. In one such decision the court emphasized that long periods of detainment could not be justified by lack of resources.[337] In another, the court emphasized the integral role that judicial oversight of

332 There are cases that involve both multiple regulative options and a quantitative aspect, and the 'proportional range' can be referenced twice: in the *Menachem* case (n 113), reviewing reform in taxi licensing, the chosen method of regulation – setting a high fee for obtaining a taxi driver's license – was recognized at the necessity test as neither the only system of regulation nor the optimal one, but it was deemed to be located in the 'proportional range'. At the final stage the particular amount set for the fee was held not to diverge from the range of proportionality. [26]–[27] (Justice Beinisch). For similar duplicity in using the 'range of proportionality' see *Investment consultants* (n 43) [32]–[34] (Justice Barak).

333 Three main examples are *Menachem* (n 113) (the set fee for a taxi-operating license); *Investment consultants* (n 43) (amount of minimal capital and insurance for obtaining a investment-consultant license); and *Tnufa* (n 101) (deposit amount required for a human resources sub-contracting license).

334 *Menachem* (n 113) [27] (Justice Beinisch); *Hoff Azza* (n 41) [143]–[150] (cut-off date for compensation for evacuated settlers).

335 *Investment consultants* (n 43) [33]–[34] (Justice Barak); *ACRI* (Passports) (n 99) [23]–[27] (Justice Naor).

336 *Tnufa* (n 101) [15] (Justice Barak); *ACRI* (Passports) (n 99) [23]–[27] (Justice Naor).

337 *Tzemach* (n 186) (96-hour period before an arrested soldier is brought before a judge) [36]–[39] (Justice Zamir), but see Justice Kedmi in the minority invoking the 'proportional range'.

detention is meant to play throughout the interrogation process, rather than it serving as a final destination to be reached after the interrogation process fully ripens.[338] In a third case, the court criticized a lengthy period of detention in which the suspect was not brought to court in person, emphasizing the importance of both sides being effectively heard in the judicial process for the procedure to be considered fair.[339] These cases demonstrate the court's willingness to scrutinize a quantitative characteristic of a policy, when the limited right is of great importance.[340]

The appropriate approach to evaluating proportionality in quantitative contexts was disputed in the series of cases dealing with the detention policy of illegal migrants originating from Africa. The justices of the majority struck down portions of the legislation in three consecutive cases, basing their decision, inter alia, on the disproportionality of the periods of the detention.[341] Two types of reasoning accompanied their decisions. The first was tied to the purpose of the detention: when the period of time could not be reasonably correlated to a legitimate purpose it was subsequently held disproportionate. Meaning, the quantitative element was treated as a reflection of the purpose, and finding the period to be disproportionate was an indirect critique of the motivation at the core of the policy.[342] The second type of reasoning tackled the quantitative element head-on, comparing the length of the period to comparable

[338] *Marab* (n 161) [31]–[34], [48]–[49] (Justice Barak).

[339] *Ploni* (Due Process) (n 101) [4]–[6] (Justice Grunis) (18-day period in which the extension of arrest of a suspect in security offences can be done without the suspect being present in the extension hearings).

[340] This does not mean that the court will always intervene in limitations of liberty with a quantitative nature. See *Ploni* (Unlawful Combatants) (n 101) [41] (Justice Beinisch) (reviewing detention of unlawful combatants for up to 14 days before being brought before a court); *Shtanger* (Suspects) (n 168) [2] (Justice Rubinstein); and [2] (Justice Melcer) (reviewing extensions of detention during trial by up to 150 days at a time). Interestingly, in both cases the court stated that the period of time was at the 'very edge' of the proportional range, and emphasized that efforts should be made to shorten the timeframes in practice.

[341] *Adam* (n 80); *Eitan* (n 82); *Dasta* (n 83). The periods struck down were: three years of full detention in the first round, one year of full detention and three years of mandatory living in a semi-open centre subject to sign-in three times a day in the second round, and a 20-month period in the semi-open centre in the third round.

[342] This was the reasoning for striking down 36 and 24 months of full detention in *Adam* and *Eitan*, respectively. The justices held that detention was justified only for the purpose of deportation, and when no effective deportation process was in place the detention was unjustified. A period of 90 days was upheld in *Dasta* (n 83) (Justice Naor); *Eitan* (n 82) [193] (Justice Vogelman); *Adam* ibid (Justice Naor).

lengths in comparative law, concluding that they significantly and unjustifiably diverge from the norm.[343]

Two of these three cases included minority opinions, which located the detention periods within the 'proportionality range', holding that the quantitative characteristic justified a higher level of deference. In the words of Justice Grunis, the category of 'constitutional questions of a quantitative nature' should, by definition, be afforded a particularly broad margin for legislative manoeuvre, since pinpointing where the amount turns disproportional is impossible. In his opinion, the court should limit itself to intervening only in substantial divergences from the 'proportionality range'.[344] To support this general position of deference on quantitative matters Justice Grunis referred to previous cases, all of which were in financial contexts.[345] Interestingly, he did not refer to cases reviewing quantitative periods of detention, where – as demonstrated earlier – the court tends to be less deferential.

### C *Probability and Risk in the Balancing Formula*

Questions of probability can arise at various stages of limitation analysis: at the initial stage of establishing that a right has been limited, if the limiting effect is not certain; at the suitability stage in evaluating the ability of the means to achieve the goal; and at the final stage of proportionality in the strict sense in establishing the weight of the policy benefit, which may be a matter of probability. This is primarily the case when the policy is aimed at preventing a potential threat to the public good; the benefit is dependant upon the level of probability that

343 This was the reasoning for striking down 36 months of full detention in *Adam*, and both 36 months and 20 months of detention in a semi-open facility in *Eitan* (n 82); and in *Dasta* (n 83) [102]–[106] (Justice Naor).

344 *Eitan* (n 82) [16]–[17] (Justice Grunis); *Dasta* (n 83), Justice Hendel, holding the difference between a 20-month period that the majority found disproportional and a 12-month period which he inferred that the majority would of upheld was arbitrary. Despite the first *Adam* (n 80) case being unanimous in its outcome of disproportionality, the majority of justices focused on flaws in the policy beginning with the goal, suitability, and possible less-restricting alternatives, whereas Justices Hendel and Grunis focused solely on the proportionality of the timeframe, holding three years to be excessive but essentially stating that shorter periods would be considered proportional.

345 *Menachem* (n 113), and Justice Naor's minority opinion in *ACRI* (Passports) (n 99). Interestingly, Grunis did not refer to his own opinion in the *Ploni* (Due Process) case (n 101), intervening in a quantitative period of time for detention, which is more similar to the case at hand.

the harm will occur if the means are *not* taken. The question of how probability is to be factored in is relevant to balancing both in absolute and incremental terms.

This question was at the core of the disagreement between the justices in the cases reviewing the ban on naturalization of Palestinian spouses, and three main positions were articulated:

The first rejected the idea of probability, and treated the potential harm as certain. The justices holding this position relied on the fact that out of the hundreds of thousands of naturalized citizens who passed individual security evaluations, there had been a few dozen involved in terror-related activity. They therefore concluded that without the complete ban it was certain that lives would be lost, and so proceeded to balance the benefit of saving lives against the harm to family life in absolute terms and concluded that the benefit outweighed the harm.[346]

The second position accepted the existence of a probability factor, but treated it as nearly irrelevant, considering the potential dimensions of harm to life and strategic state interests. Using the logic of the precautionary principle, grave potential harm of even low probability could justify drastic preventative measures, therefore proclaiming the ban proportionate.[347]

The third position emphasized the issue of probability, requiring the balancing formula to involve a level of risk-taking: the incremental level of risk was to be balanced relative to the incremental increase in right limitation. Since determining the optimal level of risk combines questions of fact and value, it can result in different outcomes: Justice Naor concluded that the complete ban's marginal addition to security outweighed the incremental harm caused to the right to family, as opposed to the justices led by Chief Justice Barak who found the harm to the right to outweigh the addition to security.[348] These justices were critical of the over-sensitivity to the harm prevented, as opposed to the

346 This position was held by Justices Cheshin, Rivlin, and Grunis in the first case, and Justices Rivlin, Grunis, and Hendel in the second case. see *Adalah* (Family Unification) (n 44) [109]–[22] (Justice Cheshin) and [16] (Justice Rivlin); *Galon* (n 39) [3] (Justice Grunis), and [5] (Justice Hendel). Similarly, see *Kirsch* (n 155) [10]–[13]. Justice Turkel rejected the use of probability with regard to the risk to life by treating the harm as certain, and categorically outweighing all other considerations.

347 *Galon* (n 39) [34]–[38] (Justice Melcer). Similarly see *Sa'ada* (n 315) [3] (Justice Turkel).

348 Justices Procaccia, Beinisch, Hayut, and Joubran. Similarly, see *Kirsch* (n 155) [8] (Justice Dorner); *Seif* (n 92) [7].

under-sensitivity to the harm caused, and emphasized that a democratic society could not legitimately aspire to nullify risk.

The *Eitan* case also dealt indirectly with the question of the optimal level of risk-taking – a rare example outside the national security context. The case dealt with prolonged detention of illegal migrants, aimed at preventing mass-infiltration to Israel from Africa through the Southern border. Following the legislation and the completion of a wall on the border, the number of migrants dropped dramatically, from over 1,000 entries a month to merely a handful, raising the question of whether this change in circumstances justified shortening the length of the detention period set by law. While Justice Hendel argued that the situation was still in flux and changing the balancing point should not yet be risked, the majority opinion maintained that the uncertainty regarding the ongoing need for the policy should be factored into the balancing formula, decreasing the weight ascribed to the benefit, thus leading it to be outweighed by the severe limitation of liberty. Justice Arbel also emphasized that the situation was reversible: if the number of migrants should suddenly rise, the detention could always be lengthened with relatively little damage done, a risk worth taking.[349]

Before the adoption of the proportionality framework, balancing formulas were commonly used, defining the conditions for limiting rights for the sake of a public interest, which were often based on notions of probability. For example, when limiting speech for the protection of national security, near-certainty for substantial damage had to be demonstrated.[350] Barak has expressed the opinion that under the proportionality framework these balancing formulas continue to exist, and should be incorporated into the final balancing stage.[351] Nevertheless, over time

349 *Eitan* (n 82) [11] (Justice Hendel); [8] (Justice Arbel); [4] (Justice Joubran); [68]–[70] (Justice Vogelman).

350 See, e.g., HCJ 680/88 *Schnitzer v Chief Military Censor* [1988] IsrSC 42(4) 617 (discussing the censoring of a newspaper article critical of the head of the Mossad), available in English at <http://versa.cardozo.yu.edu/opinions/schnitzer-v-chief-military-censor>.

351 Barak (n 3) 542–47. See also *Bakri* (n 130) [10] (Justice Dorner); *Kirsch* (n 155) [8] (Justice Dorner); PPA 4463/94 *Golan v Prisons Service* [1996] IsrSC 50(4) 136 [5], [10] (Justice Dorner) (discussing the right of a prisoner to publish an article in a newspaper), available in English at <https://supremedecisions.court.gov.il/Home/Download?path=EnglishVerdicts\94\630\044\Z01&fileName=94044630_z01.txt&type=4>. Other positions have held that these formulas should be incorporated at the worthy purpose test. See n 176. A rare case where the balancing formula of 'near certainty' of harm for

these balancing tests, and together with them the explicit consideration of questions of probability, have been side-lined.[352]

### D Additional Factors Taken into Account in the Balance

The court at times will emphasize the particular identity of the right-holders as an additional factor contributing to the severity of the harm. Some of the groups the court has highlighted as such whose rights should be particularly protected include people of the lowest level of income,[353] foreign workers,[354] migrants and asylum seekers,[355] and the Bedouin minority.[356] Interestingly, the court has not included criminal suspects and prisoners as a group deserving of particular protection: instead, in such contexts the court tends to focus on the importance of liberty and due process in the abstract.[357]

The court may also break down the abstract concept of the 'public interest' into the level of the individuals it protects. For example, some justices have translated the abstract and 'faceless' goal of national security into the protection of individual lives, boosting the weight provided to

restricting speech was integrated into the necessity test is Justice Melcer's opinion in the *Avneri* (n 102) case [46].

352 Stopler and Cohen-Eliya (n 17).

353 *Hassan* (n 78) [69] (Justice Beinisch) (emphasizing that the right-holders were of the most marginalized and struggling members of the lowest ranks of society). See also *Commitment to Peace and Social Justice Society* (n 96) [26] (Justice Levy), who in the minority struck down a cut in welfare benefits while pointing out that the effects of the constitutional revolution should not be limited to 'women who want to be pilots or investment consultants' (referring to central constitutional cases), but protection of the rights of the poor as well.

354 *Kav Laoved* (pregnant workers) (n 164) [9] (Justice Joubran) and [11]–[13] (Justice Rubinstein) (emphasizing that these workers were brought to the country by power of Israeli policy, and that they could not be treated merely as 'working hands' but people, often employed in terrible conditions and posed with impossible choices); see also *Kav Laoved* (Binding Workers) (n 81) [27], [38], [56] (Justice Levy).

355 *Adam* (n 80) [112], [114], [119] (Justice Arbel) including (citation from Jewish sources implying special duties and sensitivity to foreigners and historical references to the Jewish plight and the heightened moral duty to treat such refugees with empathy and support); *Eitan* (n 82) [187] (Justice Vogelman) (emphasizing the particular vulnerability of children, physically ill, and mentally traumatized within the population of migrants).

356 *Abu Madigam* (n 37) [49] (Justice Arbel) (emphasizing that the law-breaking behavior cannot be separated from the distress it stems from, considering that the Bedouins are the poorest population in Israeli society).

357 See, e.g., *Shtanger* (Suspects) (n 168); *Ploni* (Unlawful Combatants) (n 101); *Prison Privatization* case (n 82); *Marab* (n 161).

this consideration.[358] In the cases dealing with the prolonged detention of illegal migrants some justices have concretized the abstract goal of preventing the massive presence of migrants in city-centres as the protection of the safety of the residents of those areas, which are typically vulnerable populations themselves.[359]

In some cases the court will broaden the scope of the balancing to include long-term and indirect harm to the public interests underlying the individual rights. For example, in *Galon*, Justice Arbel emphasized that beyond the direct harm the ban on naturalization caused to the dignity, equality, and right to family of the citizens denied from uniting with their spouses, broader harm was caused to the Arab citizens' solidarity with Israeli society, deepening their feelings of alienation and exclusion, ultimately eroding social cohesion and weakening Israel's social and moral standing, which in the long term would affect the ability to deal with national challenges.[360] In *Ploni*, which reviewed a provision allowing the extension of a suspect's detention without his presence in court, beyond the obvious harm to the individual suspect's right to due process, the justices also addressed the long-term ramifications for public trust in the veracity of the judicial process.[361] In the *Prison Privatization* case, besides the effect on the prisoners' rights, some justices pointed to the symbolic damage privatization would cause to the legitimacy of the justice system.[362]

Comparative law is often referred to as a benchmark for assessing proportionality. There is not, however, uniformity in the integration of comparative law in the analysis. Comparative law can appear in the form of background before PA officially begins, or after it is completed, to support and strengthen its outcome. It may be referenced at the necessity test as a source for alternatives, or worked into the final balancing stage as a benchmark for over all evaluation of proportionality.

[358] *Adalah* (Family Unification) (n 44) [15]–[16] (Justice Rivlin); *Kirsch* (n 155) (Justice Turkel). For critique of this practice see Gazal-Ayal & Amnon Reichman (n 158).

[359] *Eitan* (n 82) [210] (Justice Vogelman); [1] (Justice Hendel); [1] (Justice Danziger); [44] (Justice Grunis); and [5] (Justice Naor). See also *Design 22* (n 40) [19]–[20] (Justice Barak) (recognizing that the public interest in a common day of rest included the individual interests of the employees); *Hamifkad Haleumi* (n 34) [43]–[48] (Justice Naor) (the objective of preserving the 'fairness doctrine' in public broadcasting as representing the interests of those who lack resources, against the monopolization of the 'market of ideas' by those who have unlimited access to resources).

[360] *Galon* (n 39) [29] (Justice Arbel).

[361] *Ploni* (Due Process) (n 101) [28]–[33] (Justice Rivlin) and (Justice Procaccia).

[362] *Prison Privatization* case (n 82) [42]–[50] (Justice Procaccia).

When the comparative law surveyed is more or equally restrictive as the policy under review, this will generally strengthen the conclusion that the policy is proportional.[363] However, there are cases where the court held the state to a higher standard than that found in comparative law, determining policy to be disproportional despite the existence of similar examples elsewhere.[364] When the comparative law is predominantly less-restricting than the policy under review, this will push the analysis in the direction of finding the policy disproportional, unless there is a convincing way to distinguish Israel from other countries.[365]

Often, the outcome of the survey of comparative law is that a clear standard cannot be found. In such cases, the Israeli policy will typically be held to be within the proportionality range.[366]

## IX Overview of the Means Struck Down

Taking an overview perspective of the cases struck down provides a rough typology of common constitutional flaws in policy. In a handful of cases the flaw is rooted in the motivation for the policy, including promotion of narrow sectorial interests at the expense of the general public,[367] intentional discrimination or complete disregard for discriminatory outcomes,[368] and – to a lesser degree – targeting particular speech based on content.[369]

363 For comparative law that is more restrictive, see *Tnufa* (n 101); *Adalah* (Child Immunization) (n 92); *ACRI* (Data Communication) (n 129) [38] (Justice Beinisch). For comparative law that is equally restricting see *Hamifkad Haleumi* (n 34); *Galon* (n 39) [3] (Justice Grunis); *Eitanit* (n 34) [40] (Justice Hendel).

364 *Tzemach* (n 186) [35] (Justice Zamir).

365 See, e.g., justices of the majority in *Adam* (n 80); *Eitan* (n 82); *Dasta* (n 83.) However, compare to minority Justices (Hendel, Grunis, and Amit) in *Eitan*; *Avneri* (n 102) [8] (Justice Hendel) (concluding that comparative law is less-restricting as support for striking down the civil sanction). However, Justice Melcer concludes that the comparative law supports the conclusion of proportionality, without addressing the distinction between civil and administrative sanctions.

366 See *Tishim Kadurim* (n 113) (prohibition on gambling); *Menachem* (n 113) (regulation of the taxi market); *Cohen* (n 192) (restrictions on class actions against the state); *Gavish* (n 141) [53]–[56] (Justice Naor) (mandatory retirement age).

367 *Oron* (n 93); *Ibillin Breeders* (n 79); *Nasser* (n 135).

368 Intentional discrimination is difficult to prove and therefore such explicit analysis is typically avoided by the court. See *Sabach* (n 98). For disregard for discriminatory outcomes see *Supreme Monitoring Committee for Arab Affairs* (n 178); *Abu Labda* (n 184).

369 This point is under-developed in Israeli case law. See *Bakri* (n 130); the *Nakba* case (n 98), that was left undecided. In the *Avneri* (n 102) case [40], Justice Danziger viewed

A small amount of cases involve means that are inherently problematic, despite their effectiveness in attaining a legitimate goal. For example, the use of aerial spray to prevent trespassing on publicly owned lands by Bedouin tribes was considered to inherently express indignity and insensitivity to rights.[370] In the view of some justices, home demolitions for the sake of deterrence of terrorists are inherently problematic because of the component of collective punishment, regardless of the question of its effectiveness.[371]

Policy may be fundamentally flawed since it is ineffective in attaining its goal. These cases are puzzling since although policymakers may not always be minded towards rights, they are expected to be minded towards achieving policy goals. Such cases of seeming disconnect between the measure and the goal may be a sign that the policy was actually motivated by goals other than those officially stated. In addition, lack of rational connection can also be a result of relying on flawed assumptions which were not verified or scrutinized,[372] or by a political dynamic resulting in the policy design being pushed off its original course due to pressure of interest groups.[373]

A frequent flaw is that of excessive means, resulting in limitations that go beyond what is necessary to achieve the policy goal. Excessiveness may present itself in various forms: at times it is the choice of extremely right-limiting means even though less-restrictive means could

the content-based, non-neutral regulation of political speech to be especially severe and problematic.

370 *Abu Madigam* (n 37) [38]–[48] (Justice Arbel). This case is especially puzzling since it is clear that the state must take measures against trespassing use of public land. Without saying so explicitly, it seems Justice Arbel was willing to accept potentially larger numbers of injuries caused by the ploughing of the land relative to use of aerial spray, due to an inherent wrong with this particular measure. Justice Naor joined Justice Arbel's opinion, instructing the state to find more proportional means, but did not detail what such alternative means might be, considering no real effective alternative had been presented.

371 See minority Justice Cheshin in HCJ 2722/92 *Alamarin v IDF Commander in the Gaza Strip* [1992] IsrSC 46(3) 693, available in English at <https://supremedecisions.court.gov.il/Home/Download?path=EnglishVerdicts\92\220\027\Z03&fileName=92027220_Z03.txt&type=4>, repeated in numerous following cases. More recently, see minority Justice Mazuz in *Aliwa* (n 181).

372 *Kav Laoved* (Pregnant workers) (n 164); *Kav Laoved* (Binding Workers) (n 81); *Stamka* (n 164); *Oren* (n 127); *Ben Atiya* (n 43).

373 *Ressler* (n 100); *Students Association of Israel* (n 191); *Yekutieli* (n 79).

have been sufficient.[374] Motivation for such excessive choices may be public demand for firm and uncompromising policy, and little support in public opinion for being cognizant of rights, especially when dealing with the rights of 'others' such as illegal migrants, criminal suspects, or Palestinians. Other manifestations of excessiveness include absolute bans, over-broad categories of application, and generalizations rather than individual assessments.[375] These may be motivated by conservation of resources, and will typically not be upheld by the court.[376] Generalizations may also, however, be used due to the implausibility or insufficient effectiveness of individual assessments, and in such circumstances they may at times be upheld.[377]

Finally, policy may be flawed by not providing sufficient weight to the right limitation, either due to over-weighting the benefit or under-evaluating the harm.[378] Financial benefits have often been found by the court to be over-weighted, causing right limitations that could have been prevented or significantly reduced by additional investment of funds.[379] Security is another goal which may be over-weighted, such as by setting the goal at zero-risk.[380] Rights may be underweighted due to policy-makers taking a narrow view rather than considering the full ramifications of the limitation, or treating it in technical rather than substantive terms.[381]

[374] Such as prolonged detention of migrants. See *Adam* (n 80); *Eitan* (n 82); *Dasta* (n 83); draconian restrictions on foreign workers – *Kav Laoved* (Pregnant workers) (n 164) and *Kav Laoved* (Binding Workers) (n 81); punitive damages without any proof of harm or causation, *Avneri* (n 102).

[375] See *Medical Association* (Testimonies) (n 193); *Investment consultants* (n 43).

[376] *Hoff Azza* (n 41); *Hassan* (n 78); *Raai* (n 82); *Mustaki* (n 238); *Adalah* (Tort Liability) (n 132).

[377] Struck down in *Seif* (n 92); *Abu Safiyeh* (n 81); *Yonas* (n 126); minority opinion in *Adalah (Family Unification)* (n 44) and *Galon* (n 39); but upheld by the majority in the two latter cases.

[378] *Beit Sourik* (n 49); *Abu Safiyeh* (n 81); *Dir Samet* (n 115); *Prison Privatization* case (n 82); *Ploni* (Due Process) (n 101).

[379] *Kav Laoved* (Pregnant workers) (n 164); *Prison Privatization* case (n 82); *Tzemach* (n 186); *Marab* (n 161).

[380] *Adalah* (Family Unification) (n 44) and *Galon* (n 39); *Abu Safiyeh* (n 81); *Dir Samet* (n 115).

[381] See, e.g., treating limitation of movement technically rather than fully considering its ramifications – *Abu Safiyeh* (n 81); *Dir Samet* (n 115); *Beit Sourik* (n 49); *Ploni* (Due Process) (n 101) – Treating extension of detention without the prisoner's presence in court as a technical matter; treating limitation of dignity in *Prison Privatization* case (n 82), solely from the perspective of potential abuse rather than a principled limitation inherent to privatization.

5

# Proportionality Analysis by the Polish Constitutional Tribunal

ANNA ŚLEDZIŃSKA-SIMON

## I Introduction*

In Poland, the principle of proportionality is the product of judicial law making. It was derived from the rule of law clause which was added to the 1952 Constitution in December 1989,[1] and remained the only legal basis for proportionality analysis (PA) until the adoption of the new Constitution in 1997. In this early period of democratic transition, the principle of proportionality was recognized as a constitutive element of the principle of rule of law and the principle of citizens' trust towards the state and state-made law.[2]

The Constitutional Tribunal constructed a multi-step proportionality test inspired by the German legal doctrine as well as the case-law of the Federal Constitutional Court and of the European Court of Human Rights.[3] The test is thus a legal construct and an example of judicial borrowing.[4] At the same time, the concept of proportionality understood as a prohibition of excessiveness, providing *inter alia* that the state shall

* I would like to thank Mordechai Kremnitzer, Andrej Lang, and Talya Steiner for their valuable comments on the earlier drafts of this chapter. I am also grateful to Ewa Łętowska, Lech Garlicki, Andrzej Wróbel, and Michał Ziółkowski for insightful conversations on the application of the proportionality test in Poland.

1 Decision of 11 February 1992, Case No. K 14/91 OTK 1992, Item 7; Decision of 26 January 1993, Case No. U 10/92 OTK 1993, Item 2.

2 Sławomira Wronkowska, 'Zarys koncepcji państwa prawnego w polskiej literaturze politycznej i prawnej' in Sławomira Wronkowska (ed), *Polskie dyskusje o państwie prawa* (Wydawnictwo Sejmowe 1995) 75.

3 Lech Garlicki, 'Komentarz do art. 31' in Lech Garlicki (ed), *Konstytucja Rzeczpospolitej Polskiej. Komentarz* (Vol. III, Wydawnictwo Sejmowe 2003) 14.

4 Allan Tatham, *Central European Constitutional Courts in the Face of EU Membership. The Influence of the German Model in Hungary and Poland* (Martinus Nijhoff Publishers 2013); Magdalena Krzyżanowska-Mierzewska, 'The Reception Process in Poland and Slovakia', in Helen Keller and Alec Stone Sweet (eds), *The Impact of the ECHR on National Legal System* (OUP 2008) 531–603.

not abuse its powers or impose overly restricted sanctions, was well-known in Polish public law (particularly in criminal and administrative law) long before the implementation of the constitutional proportionality test.[5] Therefore, the novelty of PA lies in the formulation and application of the proportionality criteria (suitability, necessity, and proportionality in the strict sense) in the constitutional review of rights limitations.[6]

In 1997, the new Constitution was adopted and accepted by a nation-wide referendum. It is a modern document incorporating the main tenets of a democratic constitution. The Constitution affirms its supreme normative value, specifies a hierarchy of sources of law, and includes a broad catalogue of fundamental rights and freedoms, deriving from the concept of human dignity. With its coming to force, the Constitutional Tribunal acquired a new legal basis for applying the proportionality test, as implied from the general limitation clause contained in Article 31(3) of the Constitution, which stipulates general conditions for limitations of constitutional rights and freedoms.[7]

This chapter analyses how the Polish Constitutional Tribunal applies the proportionality test in cases concerning limitations of constitutional rights and freedoms. The main focus of the chapter is the role of the different subtests within the framework of PA. It is based on both a qualitative and quantitative analysis of the Tribunal's case-law under the 1997 Constitution. While the qualitative study engages with main scholarly views and key judgments concerning limitations of constitutional rights and freedoms based on the proportionality test, the quantitative analysis is based on a database of 100 judgments which constitute all

[5] Andrej Stępkowski, 'Zasada proporcjonalności w Europejskiej kulturze prawnej. Sądowa kontrola władzy dyskrecjonalnej w nowoczesnej Europie' (Biuro Trybunału Konstytucyjnego 2010).

[6] In its early decisions the Tribunal used the proportionality test to review laws imposing limitations both on individuals and public law entities or units of local self-government. See Decision of 17 October 1995, Case No. K 10/95 OTK 1995, Item 30.

[7] After 1997 the Constitutional Tribunal developed two distinct ways of analysing proportionality. The first method encompasses cases which do not trigger the protection of constitutional rights or freedoms and is exclusively based on the rule of law clause (Article 2). These cases instead concern limitations affecting public law entities such as local self-government bodies that may not claim to be 'subjects' of constitutional rights or freedoms. The second type of PA is either based on the general limitation clause (Article 31(3)) or on specific limitation clauses attached to some guarantees of constitutional rights and freedoms. On the two distinctive applications of the proportionality principle, see: Judgment of 25 November 2003, Case No. K 37/02 OTK-A 2003, No. 9, Item 96. Also see: Piotr Tuleja, 'Komentarz do art. 2' in Marek Safjan, Leszek Bosek (eds), *Konstytucja RP, Komentarz do art. 1-86*, vol. I (Duże Komentarze Becka 2016) 15.

judgments in which the Constitutional Tribunal applied PA during the four-and-a-half-year period between 14 December 2010 and 17 November 2015.[8]

## II Legal and Institutional Context

### A *The Rise and Fall of the Constitutional Tribunal*

Constitutional review was established in Poland in 1985 during the wave of democratizing reforms at the end of the Communist era. Under the old 'Soviet-type' Constitution of the People's Republic of Poland of 1952 marked by the principle of unity of powers, the introduction of constitutional review brought a substantive change to the system of government and the protection of human rights. This change continued after the adoption of constitutional amendments of 1989, even though the Parliament retained its power to overrule decisions of the Constitutional Tribunal (by a two thirds majority vote). Consequently, among other

[8] The database was put together by searching through the Tribunal's docket backwards from 17 November 2015 until reaching 100 decisions. The selection of the proportionality cases in this period was not based on a search engine but on a case-by-case study of all judgments. In the analysed period the Tribunal passed a total of 329 substantive judgments, and therefore 100 judgments based on the proportionality review amount to 30 per cent of all judgments (the Tribunal also rendered 327 procedural decisions in this period, so overall there were 706 decisions in the analysed period). The criteria for inclusion in the database was that the Tribunal's decision was based on the application of the proportionality test (even if some stages were skipped or not addressed comprehensively). Therefore, all cases in which the principle was only mentioned in the pleadings of the subject initiating the review or positions of other participants in the proceedings, or mentioned but not actually applied by the Tribunal, were excluded. Eleven cases in which the Tribunal found that the challenged law did not amount to an infringement of constitutional rights or freedoms, thus bringing the analysis to an end, were not included in the database either.

The coding in the database reflects the opinion of the majority of judges in the adjudicating panels. Seventy-six decisions in the database were decided by unanimous vote and 24 by majority vote. Fourteen majority decisions ended with a finding of disproportionality. The database does not include cases in which only dissenting judges apply the proportionality test, if the majority makes the final decision using a different doctrine. See: Judgment of 28 October 2015, Case No. K 21/14 OTK-A 2015, No. 9, Item 152 (tax-free amount), in which the Tribunal decided the case on the basis of the rule of law concept and discontinued the proceedings with regard to the question of whether a limitation of constitutional rights meets the proportionality standard.

In cases in which a judgment included more than one application of the proportionality test, the applications were aggregated. The outcome of the proportionality review at a particular stage was coded as fail if at least one of the applications of the test ended in a negative finding.

factors leading to the establishment of a constitutional democracy in Poland, the Constitutional Tribunal played a very important role in the regime transition by developing and refining the principle of separation of powers and the concept of rule of law.[9]

In Polish constitutional adjudication, the period between 1989 and 1997 is often characterized as 'heroic', since the Constitutional Tribunal had to lay out entirely new standards of law making and human rights protection.[10] First, it introduced the principle of supremacy of the Constitution and asserted its normative value. On this basis, it established a hierarchical structure of legal sources and explained, amongst others, the relationship between international and domestic law and between statutory and delegated legislation. This early case-law also expounds the meaning of the rule of law clause, and specifies its core elements, such as the principle of citizens' trust towards the state and state-made law, the principle of legal certainty, the protection of acquired rights and legitimate expectations, the prohibition of retroactivity, the principle of adequate *vacatio legis*, as well as the principle of proportionality. All of these principles set clear limitations on legislative power.

Constitutional standards regarding government limitation of individual rights and freedoms developed gradually. First, the Tribunal required that any such limitation be provided for in a statute.[11] Later, it also drew a list of substantive requirements concerning justification of government limitation of individual rights.[12] Moreover, the Tribunal also derived several individual rights from the rule of law clause that were not explicitly guaranteed by the Constitution of 1952 (such as the protection of the right to life, privacy, and personal data).[13]

After a period of judicial activism in the early years of its existence the Tribunal tried to avoid charges of judicial law making. In some cases,

[9] Lech Garlicki, 'Pierwsze orzeczenie Trybunału Konstytucyjnego (refleksje w 15 lat później)' in Ferdynand Rymarz and Adam Jankiewicz (eds), *Trybunał Konstytucyjny: Księga XV-lecia* (Biuro Trybunału Konstytucyjnego 2001) 40–47.

[10] Marek Safjan, 'Trybunał Konstytucyjny po 1997 roku – przełom czy kontynuacja?' in Ferdynand Rymarz and Adam Jankiewicz (eds), *Trybunał Konstytucyjny: Księga XV-lecia* (Biuro Trybunału Konstytucyjnego 2001) 78–86.

[11] Decision of 3 March 1987, Case No. P 2/87 OTK 1987, Item 2; Decision of 12 February 1991, Case No. K 6/90 OTK 1991, Item 1.

[12] Case No. U 10/92 (n 1).

[13] Wojciech Sadurski, *Rights before Courts: A Study of Constitutional Courts in Postcommunist States of Central and Eastern Europe* (Springer 2005) 128.

it even adopted a state-oriented interpretation of the law,[14] protecting the government from negative political or financial consequences of its rulings. For example, the Tribunal upheld challenged laws because declaring them unconstitutional could have led to the obstruction of important governmental goals[15] or financial instability.[16] In addition, there are several decisions in which the Tribunal upheld laws compromising rights of minorities (in particular religious minorities[17]) or politically disempowered groups (such as women[18] or individuals with disabilities[19]) in order to steer clear of political backlashes.

Characteristically, in all decisions pertinent to freedom of conscience and religion, the Tribunal granted robust protection to the religious majority. It even went as far as recognizing that freedom of conscience is ranked higher than other constitutional rights and freedoms and may only be restricted to protect human life.[20] Approving laws that provide a special place to the Catholic religion in public life and the privileged position of the Catholic Church as compared with other churches and denominations, the Tribunal deferred to the legislative choice of the parliamentary majority.[21] It is thus evident that the Tribunal has not

[14] According to some authors, the statist tradition in Polish constitutionalism is stronger than the civic one. Bogusia Puchalska, *Limits to Democratic Constitutionalism in Central and Eastern Europe* (Routledge 2011) 126.

[15] Judgment of 16 October 2012, Case No. K 4/10 OTK-A 2012, No. 9, Item 106; Judgment of 9 February 2015, Case No. SK 50/13 OTK-A 2015, No. 2, Item 12.

[16] Judgment of 4 November 2015, Case No. K 1/14 OTK-A 2015, No. 10, Item 163; Judgment of 12 December 2012, Case No. K 1/12 OTK-A 2012, No. 11, Item 134; Judgment of 6 March 2013, Case No. Kp 1/12 OTK-A 2013, No. 3, Item 25.

[17] Decision of 30 January 1991, Case No. K 11/90 OTK 1991, Item 2; Decision of 20 April 1993, Case No. U 12/92 OTK 1993, Item 9; Judgment of 5 May 1998, Case No. K 35/97 OTK 1998, No. 3, Item 32; Judgment of 14 December 2009, Case No. K 55/07 OTK-A 2009, No. 11, Item 167; Judgment of 2 December 2009, Case No. U 10/07 OTK-A 2009, No. 9, Item 163.

[18] See, e.g., Decision of 28 May 1997, Case No. K 26/96 OTK 1997, No. 2, Item 19; Judgment of 7 October 2015, Case No. K 12/14 OTK-A 2015, No. 9, Item 143.

[19] See judgments that failed to recognize special needs of people with disabilities: Judgment of 23 January 2014, Case No. K 51/12 OTK-A 2014, No. 1, Item 4; Judgment of 22 November 2016, Case No. K 13/15 OTK-A 2016, Item 88.

[20] Case No. K 12/14 (n 18).

[21] Resolution of 2 March 1994, Case No. W 3/93 OTK 1994, Item 17; Decision of 7 June 1994, Case No. K 17/93 OTK 1994, Item 11; Decision of 6 February 2007, Case No. K 16/06 OTK-A 2007, No. 2, Item 13; Judgment of 8 June 2011, Case No. K 3/09 OTK-A 2011, No. 5, Item 39; Judgment of 6 October 2015, Case No. SK 54/13 OTK-A 2015, No. 9, Item 142.

emerged as a true defender of minority rights in this context,[22] but rather has often limited its role to correcting obvious flaws of the legislative process and protecting constitutional rights pertinent to the democratic majority. Notwithstanding this caveat, the Constitutional Tribunal is viewed as carrying a leading role in the protection of human rights in Poland.[23]

Over the years, the Constitutional Tribunal has gained widespread recognition, but remained rather detached from society. Its legitimacy has been primarily bestowed by academia rather than popular support.[24] In recent years, however, the staggering detachment of the Constitutional Tribunal from society was skilfully used in an open political attack on the institution amid the conflict over the selection of judges in 2015.[25] Remarkably, this conflict led to street protests in support of the Constitutional Tribunal.[26] That said, many people supported the populist rhetoric arguing that the Constitutional Tribunal is politicized and lacks democratic control. The political attack on the Constitutional Tribunal coincided with the anti-establishment attitude of the electorate. This strategy could not effectively be countered by the defenders of the Constitutional Tribunal given the general lack of education or interest of the citizenry in constitutional debates.

In 2015, the ruling majority of the Law and Justice party prompted amendments to the Act on the Constitutional Tribunal which weakened

[22] See Aleksandra Gliszczyńska-Grabias and Wojciech Sadurski, 'Freedom of Religion versus Humane Treatment of Animals: Polish Constitutional Tribunal's Judgment on Permissibility of Ritual Slaughter' (2015) 11 European Constitutional Law Review 596–608.

[23] See various milestone judgments in the area of human rights, such as Judgment of 27 June 2006, Case No. K 16/05 OTK-A 2006, No. 6, Item 69; Judgment of 18 January 2006, Case No. K 21/05 OTK-A 2006, No. 1, Item 4; Judgment of 7 March 2007, Case No. K 28/05 OTK-A 2007, No. 3, Item 24; Judgment of 30 September 2008, Case No. K 44/07 OTK-A 2008, No. 7, Item 126; Judgment of 19 July 2011, Case No. K 11/10 OTK-A 2011, No. 6, Item 60.

[24] Sadurski (n 13) chapter II (explaining that the uncritical approach to constitutional courts is a broader phenomenon in the post-communist world due to their ability to draw upon the appearance of neutrality).

[25] Anna Śledzińska-Simon, 'Midnight Judges: Poland's Constitutional Tribunal Caught between Political Fronts' *VerfBlog* (23 November 2015) available at <https://verfassungsblog.de/midnight-judges-polands-constitutional-tribunal-caught-between-political-fronts>.

[26] Marcin Sobczyk, 'Protest and Counter-Protest over Court Nominees Fill Streets in Poland' The Wall Street Journal (New York City, 13 December 2015) available at <www.wsj.com/articles/protest-and-counter-protest-over-court-nominees-fill-streets-in-poland-1450030070>.

the procedural safeguards of independence and effectiveness of constitutional review in Poland.[27] These amendments introduced changes in the procedure and organization of the Tribunal, including new rules on the appointment of judges, the terms of office of the Chief Justice, the disciplinary procedure, the composition of adjudicating panels, and voting. Not only were they met with criticism by the Venice Commission and European Union institutions, but further declared unconstitutional by the Constitutional Tribunal, which led to further escalation of the conflict.[28]

Although some institutional problems like the implementation of judgments by the legislature indeed called for urgent reforms,[29] the government plan to reform the procedure and organization of the Constitutional Tribunal as well as the appointment of the Chief Justice in violation of the procedure was aimed to dismantle the independent constitutional review in Poland.[30] Still, the need for a 'reform' turned out to be short-lived as the government withdrew from most of the amendments after it appointed a majority of judges who remain loyal to its political whim. In the current phase of constitutional affairs in Poland, the government uses the Tribunal to legitimize its political decisions, by sending requests for constitutional review of controversial laws such as the new law on public assemblies.[31] This practice marks a new era of constitutional adjudication in which the Tribunal transformed into a 'positive, active aide of the government and the parliamentary majority'[32].

[27] The most significant amendments were introduced by the Act of 22 July 2016 on the Constitutional Tribunal (Journal of Laws, item 1157), and later nullified by the Constitutional Tribunal.

[28] See, e.g., Judgment of 3 December 2015, Case No. K 34/15 OTK-A 2015, No. 11, Item 185; Judgment of 9 December 2015, Case No. K 35/15 OTK-A 2015, No. 11, Item 186; Decision of 9 March 2016, Case No. K 47/15 OTK-A 2018, Item 31; Decision of 11 August 2016, Case No. K 39/16 OTK-A 2018, Item 32.

[29] Sylwia Jarosz-Żukowska and Kazimierz Działocha (eds), *Wykonywanie wyroków Trybunału Konstytucyjnego w praktyce konstytucyjnej organów państwa* (Wydawnictwo Sejmowe 2013).

[30] Clearly, these laws were intended to (1) exempt the recent legislation from constitutional scrutiny; (2) paralyze decision-making by the Tribunal; (3) increase the political control over the Tribunal. See Wojciech Sadurski, 'How Democracy Dies (in Poland): A Case Study of Anti-constitutional Populist Backsliding' (2018) Sydney Law School Research Paper No. 18/01 <https://ssrn.com/abstract=3103491> accessed 21 June 2019.

[31] Judgment of 16 March 2017, Case No. 1/17 OTK-A 2017, Item 28.

[32] Sadurski, 'How Democracy Dies' 31.

### *B Powers of the Constitutional Tribunal Set Forth in the Constitution of 1997*

The Polish Constitution as adopted on 2 April 1997 recognized the Constitutional Tribunal as an independent judicial organ and organized it as a specialized constitutional court that is institutionally separated from ordinary courts.[33] The powers of the Constitutional Tribunal were thus limited to the constitutional review of normative acts. It was established as a 'court of law' rather than a 'court of facts'.[34] According to Article 188 (1)–(3) of the Constitution, the Constitutional Tribunal reviews the conformity with the Constitution of: (1) statutes and international agreements; (2) statutes ratifying international agreements before they come into force; and (3) legal provisions issued by central State organs. The Tribunal only adjudicates on the vertical conformity of normative acts with the Constitution and acts of higher rank rather than on the horizontal coherence of the legal system.[35]

Constitutional adjudication in Poland is based on a centralized model of constitutional review by which only the Constitutional Tribunal may declare the law unconstitutional, whereas other courts, including the Supreme Court, are required to refer questions of law to the Tribunal in case of doubts regarding the constitutionality of the law as applied in concrete cases. The process of establishing the Constitutional Tribunal as the final arbiter in constitutional matters and the interpreter of the Constitution led to a rivalry with the Supreme Court.[36] Although it was

[33] In the following part, a reference to the specific provisions of the statute regulating the procedure before the Constitutional Tribunal was intentionally avoided due to their constant change over the recent years. It is important to note, however, that the case-law analysed in this chapter was decided exclusively on the basis of the Act on the Constitutional Tribunal of 1 August 1997 (Journal of Laws, No. 102, Item 643). Later, this law was repealed by the Act of 25 June 2015 and radically amended in 2016. Currently, the procedure is laid down in the Act on the Organization of the Constitutional Tribunal and the Mode of Proceedings before the Constitutional Tribunal (Journal of Laws, Item 2072) (2016).

[34] The power of the Tribunal to declare aims and activities of political parties as contrary to the Constitution (Article 188(4)), as well as rule of temporary incapacity of the President of the Republic to discharge its official duties (Article 131(1) of the Constitution) are of lesser practical significance.

[35] However, several horizontal problems concerning conflicts between statutory norms or legislative omissions resulting in problems with the effective protection of constitutional rights or freedoms are addressed in signalizing decisions. See: Judgment of 4 November 2014, Case No. SK 55/13 OTK-A 2014, No. 10, Item 111.

[36] Lech Garlicki, 'Constitutional Courts Versus Supreme Courts' (2007) 5 International Journal of Constitutional Law 44.

generally accepted that the Constitutional Tribunal has the exclusive power to find a statute unconstitutional and that its decisions are binding on other courts and have *erga omnes* effect, the Supreme Court challenged the Tribunal's power to adopt interpretative decisions that eliminate the unconstitutional application of a law without declaring the law itself unconstitutional, as this power is not explicitly stated in the Constitution. Most recently, the political conflict over the Constitutional Tribunal strengthened the support for a dispersed, decentralized constitutional review as well as the direct application of the Constitution by courts.[37]

Constitutional adjudication in Poland is framed by the principle of presumption of constitutionality and the subsidiary role of constitutional review.[38] The principle of presumption of constitutionality implies that the challenged law is valid unless declared unconstitutional. It also requires a person initiating proceedings before the Constitutional Tribunal to establish that the law under review cannot be interpreted in conformity with the Constitution. The subsidiary role of constitutional review is rather a matter of practice than official doctrine. It was introduced as part of the Tribunal's institutional strategy aimed at limiting the consequences of its decisions that invalidate acts of the Parliament.[39] In order to avoid the guillotine effect of a negative judgment declaring the law unconstitutional, the Tribunal often uses interpretative[40]

[37] Tomasz T. Koncewicz calls for an emergency constitutional review by ordinary courts in order to shield the constitutional order from being further weakened and dissembled. Tomasz T Koncewicz, '"Emergency Constitutional Review": Thinking the Unthinkable? A Letter from America' (*VerfBlog*, 23 March 2016) <https://verfassungsblog.de/emergency-constitutional-review-thinking-the-unthinkable-a-letter-from-america/> accessed 20 June 2019.

[38] Piotr Radziewicz, 'Wzruszenie "domniemania konstytucyjności" aktu normatywnego przez Trybunał Konstytucyjny' (2008) 5 Przegląd Sejmowy 55. However, the political attack on the Tribunal prompted an exceptional approach to acts regulating the very procedure of the constitutional review. *See* Piotr Radziewicz, 'Refusal of the Constitutional Tribunal to Apply the Act Stipulating the Constitutional Review Procedure' (2017) 1 Review of Comparative Law 23.

[39] Zbigniew Czeszejko-Sochacki, 'Orzeczenie Trybunału Konstytucyjnego: pojęcie, klasyfikacja, skutki prawne' (2000) 12 Państwo i Prawo 20.

[40] For example, in the decision concerning the Lustration Act, the Tribunal held that the legal definition of collaboration is constitutional: 'provided that it is understood as the collaboration, for the confirmation of which the mere expression of a person's will to undertake one with security organs shall not suffice, and these shall be actual activities undertaken that materialize the collaboration'. Decision of 11 April 2007, Case No. K 2/07 OTK-A 2007, No. 4, Item 43.

and scope judgments,[41] or postpones the date by which the law loses legal force.[42]

### C *Bringing a Case before the Constitutional Tribunal*

There are three ways to bring a case before the Tribunal: a request for abstract review,[43] a constitutional complaint,[44] and a question of law.[45] Additionally, the President of the Republic may, before signing a bill, refer it to the Tribunal for preventive review.[46] Most frequently, cases reach the Tribunal through requests for abstract review or through constitutional complaints, whereas submissions of questions of law are less common.[47] The majority of requests for abstract review are submitted by the Ombudsman, who may also join proceedings initiated by a constitutional complaint.[48] In the database, 43 per cent of proceedings were initiated by constitutional complaints, 38 per cent by requests for

[41] Scope judgments restrict the decision on unconstitutionality to the narrowest scope possible. For example, in the decision concerning medical ethics, the Tribunal found that the law is unconstitutional due to its prohibition of the expression of public statements on professional activities of another physician, which are veracious and justified by the protection of the public interest. Judgment of 23 April 2008, Case No. SK 16/07 OTK-A 2008. No. 3, Item 45.

[42] Polish Constitution, Article 190(3).

[43] According to Article 191(1) of the Constitution, such a request can be made by the President of the Republic, the Marshal of the Sejm, the Marshal of the Senate, the Prime Minister, 50 deputies, 30 senators, the First President of the Supreme Court, the President of the Supreme Administrative Court, the Public Prosecutor-General, the President of the Supreme Chamber of Control, and the Ombudsman. Additionally, some subjects may initiate constitutional review in matters concerning their constitutional mandate – this category provided by Article 190(2) of the Constitution includes the National Council of the Judiciary, the constitutive organs of units of local government, the national organs of trade unions, the national authorities of employers' organizations and occupational organizations, as well as churches and religious organizations.

[44] Polish Constitution, Article 79(1): 'everyone whose constitutional freedoms or rights have been infringed, shall have the right to appeal to the Constitutional Tribunal for its judgment on the conformity to the Constitution of a statute or another normative act upon which basis a court or organ of public administration has made a final decision on his freedoms or rights or on his obligations specified in the Constitution'.

[45] Polish Constitution, Article 193.

[46] Polish Constitution, Article 122(3).

[47] For example, in 2015, there were 29 cases initiated by a request for abstract review, 21 by constitutional complaints, and 11 by questions of law.

[48] The Ombudsman is an independent constitutional organ in charge of the protection of rights and freedoms specified in the Constitution and other normative acts. See Polish Constitution, Articles 208–12.

abstract review, 15 per cent by questions of law, and 4 per cent by preventive review.

It is important to emphasize the relatively limited nature of constitutional complaints in Poland. While the right to lodge a constitutional complaint is a legal remedy guaranteed by the Constitution that is a significant element of the national system of rights protection,[49] its role is restricted by certain structural limitations. Most importantly, individuals may use this proceeding only to challenge the normative basis of a final decision affecting their constitutional rights or freedoms – meaning, a statue. Individuals may not contest the constitutionality of a decision issued by a court of law or an administrative organ, but only the statute upon which the decision was based. Moreover, if the Tribunal finds the law applied by a court or an administrative organ to be unconstitutional, it cannot directly change the outcome for the subject initiating the review. Therefore, the subject initiating the review, as well as all other persons concerned by the Tribunal's decision, may only request that the legal proceedings in their case be re-opened.[50] Due to these structural limitations, the effectiveness of constitutional complaints in Poland as a 'shield' against violations of individual rights is rather low.[51]

It should be further noted that proceedings before the Tribunal are not only burdened by the procedural requirements laid down by law. In addition, there is the internal practice of the Tribunal to strictly follow the concept of binding limits of the application, which implies that the subject initiating review needs to adequately identify a challenged norm

[49] Between 1997 and 2015, the number of constitutional complaints lodged every year has gradually increased from 27 to 408. See Trybunał Konstytucyjny, 'Informacja o istotnych problemach wynikających z działalności i orzecznictwa Trybunału Konstytucyjnego w 2015 roku' (Biuro Trybunału Konstytucyjnego 2016).

[50] Polish Constitution, Article 190(4): 'A judgment of the Constitutional Tribunal on the non-conformity to the Constitution, an international agreement or statute, of a normative act on the basis of which a legally effective judgment of a court, a final administrative decision or settlement of other matters was issued, shall be a basis for reopening proceedings, or for quashing the decision or other settlement in a manner and on principles specified in provisions applicable to the given proceedings.' The Tribunal emphasized that the re-opening of proceedings on the basis of a ruling on unconstitutionality does not have to lead to a diametrically opposite decision from the one made earlier or the one the applicant is seeking to ensure in the re-opened proceedings. Judgment of 27 October 2004, Case No. SK 1/04 OTK-A 2004, No. 9, Item 96.

[51] For the European Court of Human Rights, a constitutional complaint in Poland could only be considered as an effective remedy in exceptional circumstances. *See: Szott-Medyńska v Poland* App. no 47414/99 (ECtHR, 9 October 2003).

as the object of the review as well as a constitutional provision as the basis of the review.[52] The specific claim contained in the petition is decisive for the Tribunal as it does not modify claims *ex officio*.[53] In cases of a claim not adequately specifying the constitutional problem, the Tribunal terminates the proceedings.[54] It is only under exceptional circumstances that the Tribunal reformulates the petition.[55] Consequently, the principle of the binding limits of application poses a significant procedural obstacle to subjects initiating the proceedings before the Constitutional Tribunal as the indication of an inadequate ground of the review may lead to the termination of the proceedings in their entirety or in part.

The aforementioned practice may influence the number of cases decided using PA. In many cases, individuals lodging constitutional complaints (or their legal representatives) are not sufficiently experienced in identifying constitutional standards which should be used as the basis for their review. Nevertheless, a complaint alleging that there is a limitation of a constitutional right or freedom does not need to invoke the limitation clause. As long as the claim is substantiated with regard to limitation of a constitutional right or freedom, the Tribunal will consider the limitation clause regardless of whether it refers to it in the sentence of a judgment.[56]

[52] See Aleksandra Kustra, 'Zasada związania granicami wniosku w orzecznictwie Trybunału Konstytucyjnego' (2010) 3 Przegląd Sejmowy 41; Krzysztof Wojtyczek, 'Zasada skargowości w procedurze kontroli norm przed polskim Trybunałem Konstytucyjnym' (2003) 1 Przegląd Sejmowy 25.

[53] Judgment of 15 April 2014, Case No. SK 12/13 OTK-A 2014, No. 4, Item 41. In this case, the Tribunal complemented the basis of the review with Article 31(3) of the Constitution as a relative provision applicable to all limitations of constitutional rights or freedoms.

[54] Judgment of 31 July 2015, Case No. K 41/12 OTK-A 2015, No. 7, Item 102, dissent by Judge Zbigniew Cieślak.

[55] Case No. K 4/10 (n 15). In this case, the Ombudsman challenged the law on the basis of the right to a fair trial in conjunction with the right to protection of property. However, the majority reviewed the law with regard to the right to protection of property in conjunction with the right to a fair trial. As noted by the dissent, the Tribunal reconstructed the claim against the intentions of the Ombudsman because the alleged breach of property rights was only mentioned to show that there had been a 'case' (a legal dispute) that was to be solved by a court in an adequate procedure. Therefore, in the view of the dissent, the Tribunal failed to view the case as an infringement of the right to a fair trial.

[56] Ewa Łętowska and others, 'Zasada skargowości – wątpliwości i uwarunkowania na tle acquis constitutionnel' in Krzysztof Budziłło (ed), *Księga XXV-lecia Trybunału Konstytucyjnego* (Biuro Trybunału Konstytucyjnego 2010) 103.

## III Structure of Limitation Analysis

### *A The Limitation Clause*

The general limitation clause is contained in Article 31 (3) of the Constitution, and reads as follows:

'Any limitation upon the exercise of constitutional freedoms and rights may be imposed only by statute, and only when necessary in a democratic state for the protection of its security or public order, or to protect the natural environment, health or public morals, or the freedoms and rights of other persons. Such limitations shall not violate the essence of freedoms and rights.'

This provision is in the opening part of chapter II dedicated to constitutional rights, freedoms, and obligations of persons and citizens. It resembles limitation clauses incorporated in the European Convention of Human Rights, the International Covenant on Civil and Political Rights, as well as the German Basic Law.[57] The Tribunal has repeatedly confirmed that the general limitation clause has a systemic character and is inherently related to the concept of a democratic state ruled by law.[58]

Although the principle of proportionality is not explicitly stated in the limitation clause, it is encapsulated in the 'necessary in a democratic state' formula.[59] This formula is an adaptation of the 'necessary in a democratic society' clause used in international human rights treaties. The limitation clause applies to restrictions of all rights and freedoms guaranteed in the Constitution.[60] However, some of the specific rights also contain specific limitation clauses that vary in their structure and content.[61] Some of them do not, for example, contain the statutory reservation requirement or the prohibition of violation of the essential core. Others include a separate list of grounds justifying limitations of a specific right or freedom.

The relationship between Article 31(3) of the Constitution and the specific limitation clauses was not defined when the new Constitution came into force, which is why it was subject to competing interpretations.[62] Later, the Tribunal explained that guarantees of constitutional

[57] Garlicki (n 3).

[58] Judgment of 20 February 2008, Case No. K 30/07 OTK-A 2008, No. 1, Item 6.

[59] Garlicki (n 3).

[60] Judgment of 10 April 2002, Case No. K 26/00 OTK-A 2002, No. 2, Item 18.

[61] See Polish Constitution, Article 59(3) sentence 1 or Article 61(3).

[62] According to one view, Article 31(3) of the Constitution applies unless a limitation clause specifically excludes its application. See Krzysztof Wojtyczek, *Granice ingerencji*

rights and freedoms that are not followed by a specific limitation clause need to always be read in conjunction with the general limitation clause.[63] In practice, the general limitation clause is also used as a subsidiary basis in cases concerning rights that are subject to specific limitation clauses. More precisely, it complements requirements which are not entailed in specific limitation clauses, provided of course that they are not explicitly excluded by these clauses.[64]

### B *The Proportionality Test*

The proportionality test is an element of the multi-step analysis of laws entailing limitations of constitutional rights and freedoms. The standard approach to limitations of constitutional rights and freedoms is based on four questions:

(1) whether there has been a limitation of a constitutional right or freedom;
(2) whether the limitation was provided for by law;
(3) whether the limitation was justified by a constitutional value enumerated in the limitation clause;
(4) whether the limitation was necessary in a democratic state.[65]

In a recent restatement on the meaning of the general limitation clause, the Tribunal emphasized that the limitation of constitutional rights and freedoms must be introduced only by statutory law which meets both the substantive and procedural standards of a 'statute'.[66] Sub-statutory laws may only concretize limitations set out by statutory laws.[67]

*ustawodawczej w sferę praw człowieka w Konstytucji RP* (Zakamycze 1999) 92, 94. See also Mirosław Wyrzykowski, 'Granice praw i wolności – granice władzy' in Barbara Oliwa-Radzikowska (ed), *Obywatel – jego wolności i prawa* (Biuro Rzecznika Praw Obywatelskich 1998) 53.

63 Lech Garlicki, 'Przesłanki ograniczania konstytucyjnych praw i wolności (na tle orzecznictwa Trybunału Konstytucyjnego)' (2001) 10 Państwo i Prawo 5, 7–8.

64 Case No. K 26/00 (n 60).

65 Judgment of 25 July 2013, Case No. P 56/11 OTK-A 2013, No. 6, Item 85.

66 Michał Ziółkowski, 'Standard legalności ustawy w orzecznictwie konstytucyjnym' in Piotr Radziewicz (ed), *Kontrola legalności ustawy w Sejmie* (Wydawnictwo Sejmowe 2015) 258.

67 For example, the Tribunal held that in view of the constitutional requirement of statutory reservation, it is necessary to have a statutory law rather than a ministerial regulation determine the subject matter of medical records created by the minister and specify which data could be collected in those registers. Judgment of 18 December 2014, Case No. K 33/13 OTK-A 2014, No. 11, Item 112.

As for the final requirement, that the limitation be necessary in a democratic state, the Tribunal refers back to an early 1995 decision in which the three prongs of the analysis were specified:[68]

(1) whether the rights-restricting law is suitable for the realization of the intended results;
(2) whether it is necessary for the protection of the public interest it aims to promote; and
(3) whether the effects of the law are in an adequate proportion to the burdens imposed on individuals.

In cases in which the law entirely excludes the possibility for the realization of a constitutional right or freedom falling within the prescribed scope, the Tribunal may treat the law as a total ban on the right rather than merely a limitation.[69] As a consequence, the Tribunal may not apply the limitation clause, but rather hold the limitation itself to be contrary to constitutional principles.[70] This approach stems from the idea that ordinary legislation may not redefine the scope of protection of constitutional rights and freedoms set forth in the Constitution, but only impose certain limitations on their exercise.

Still, the proportionality doctrine has not gained considerable academic interest in Poland.[71] Generally speaking, there is consensus in

[68] Decision of 26 April 1995, Case No. K 11/94 OTK 1995, Item 12.

[69] For example, the Tribunal held that the law excluding the right of victims to effectively participate in a court trial does not constitute a limitation subject to PA. Judgment of 30 September 2014, Case No. SK 22/13 OTK-A 2014, No. 8, Item 96. Also see: Judgment of 2 June 2015, Case No. K 1/13 OTK-A 2015, No. 6, Item 80. In this case, the Tribunal reviewed the Trade Union Act which excluded an entire category of right holders (precarious workers) from the protection of the right to establish trade unions solely on the basis of a provision which guarantees freedom of association.

[70] A special category of this type concerns the denial of access to a court or the right to appeal. In case of such a denial, the Tribunal usually does not conduct PA but instead relies on the substantive norm stipulating the right to a fair trial or the right to appeal. In general, the law which precludes a particular category of subjects from lodging a claim in courts or an appeal is viewed as a total bar for the realization of the constitutional right. In such cases, Article 31(3) of the Constitution does not even have to be invoked. In contrast, excessive court fees are treated as a limitation of the right to a fair trial, which ultimately requires the application of PA.

[71] Wyrzykowski (n 62); Wojtyczek (n 62); Garlicki (n 63); Anna Łabno, 'Ograniczenie wolności i praw człowieka na podstawie art. 31 Konstytucji III RP' in Bogusław Banaszak and Artur Preisner (eds), *Prawa i wolności obywatelskie w Konstytucji RP* (Wydawnictwo CH BECK 2002) 664; Krzysztof Wojtyczek, 'Zasada proporcjonalności' in Bogusław Banaszak and Artur Preisner (eds), *Prawa i wolności obywatelskie w Konstytucji RP* (Wydawnictwo CH BECK 2002) 669; Krzysztof Wójtowicz, 'Zasada proporcjonalności

the Polish academia that proportionality is the appropriate standard for constitutional courts to deal with rights limitations, and this has been met with little deliberation or critique.[72]

### C The Contexts of Proportionality Analysis

The Constitutional Tribunal only applies the proportionality test with regard to normative acts adopted by Parliament (in the form of statutes or resolutions containing general and abstract norms) or regulations issued by executive organs following statutory authorization, since administrative actions and judicial decisions do not fall in the jurisdiction of the Constitutional Tribunal.

More than half of the cases in the database (52 per cent) are public law cases,[73] whereas 27 per cent concern civil law and procedure[74] and the remaining 21 per cent criminal law and procedure. Figure 5.1 presents the distribution of cases within the database by subject matters.[75]

The largest subject matter category to which PA was applied concerns criminal procedure (13 per cent), which involves many instances of

jako wyznacznik konstytucyjności norm' in Marek Zubik (ed), *Księga XX-lecia orzecznictwa Trybunału Konstytucyjnego* (Biuro Trybunału Konstytucyjnego 2006) 265–78; Joanna Zakolska, *Zasada proporcjonalności w orzecznictwie Trybunału Konstytucyjnego* (Wydawnictwo Sejmowe 2008); Garlicki (n 3).

[72] In Poland, the lack of democratic legitimacy of the constitutional adjudicator or the problem of judicial activism have not been frequently debated by academia. See Bogusław Banaszak and Michał Bernaczyk, *Aktywizm sędziowski we współczesnym państwie demokratycznym* (Warszawa 2012). The populist attack on the Constitutional Tribunal was officially driven by the need to establish democratic control over 'juristocracy'.

[73] The category of public law encompasses cases concerning administrative procedure and administrative court procedure, regulation of the courts and other state institutions, electoral law and political party financing, assembly law, regulation of the press, higher education, civil service and military, environmental protection, land and infrastructure, medical law, social protection, tax and transportation law, gambling law, hunting law, and possession of guns.

[74] Civil law cases concern cooperative law, copyright, competition law, family law, labour law, real estate, and state tort liability.

[75] The social law category includes eligibility for social benefits and the organization of pension funds. The land planning and development category includes real estate and mortgage, but excludes cases on housing cooperatives, which are considered to be civil law cases. The economic regulation category includes gambling, transportation, and or alcohol licensing. The electoral law category includes political party financing. The category referred to as 'other' includes cases that can be broadly defined as administrative law, including assembly law, allotment gardens, environmental law, hunting law, medical profession, ritual slaughter, and student fees.

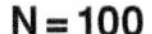


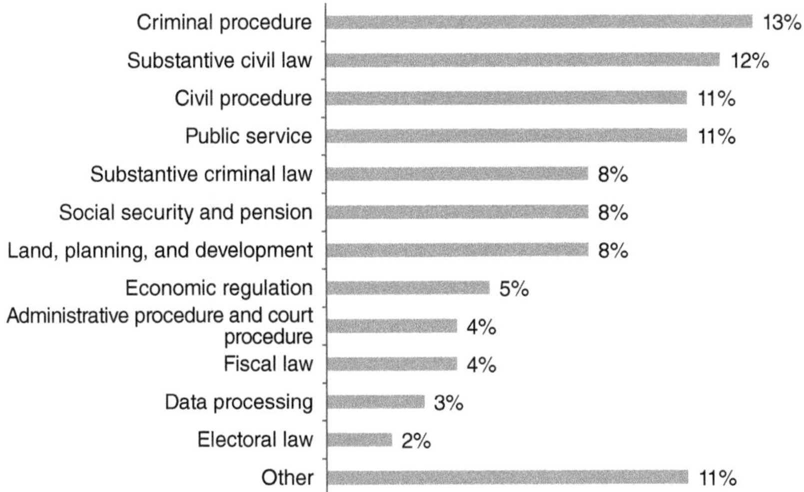


**Figure 5.1** Proportionality cases by subject matter

rights limitations, including temporary arrests, legal representation in a criminal trial, and the enforcement of criminal court orders. Further categories to which proportionality is frequently applied are civil law (12 per cent), most dominantly including housing cooperative cases, as well as civil procedure (11 per cent), dealing with access to courts, procedural guarantees, and enforcement of court decisions. A significant number of cases (11 per cent) concern matters related to public service, such as access to work in the public service and the status of public servants.[76] In substantive criminal law cases, constitutional problems largely arise due to excessive sanctions.[77]

## Categories of Rights

Figure 5.2 presents the categories of rights and freedoms that were subject to proportionality in the analysed period.[78] The rights to which

[76] Including court enforcement officers, firemen, judges, policemen, and soldiers.

[77] Additionally, some of the cases in the database concerned the criminalization or penalization of certain conducts. See Judgment of 12 February 2015, Case No. SK 70/13 OTK-A 2015, No. 2, Item 14; Case No. SK 55/13 (n 35); Case No. K 11/10 (n 23); Judgment of 21 September 2015, Case No. K 28/13 OTK-A 2015, No. 8, Item 120.

[78] The total number of rights is higher than the number of cases analysed since some decisions applied the proportionality framework to more than one right.

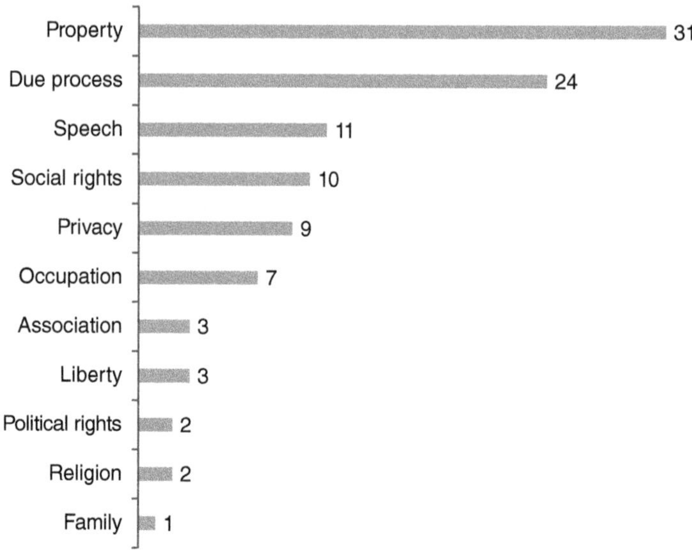


**Figure 5.2** Rights triggering proportionality analysis

PA was most frequently applied are property (31 cases) and due process (24 cases). The latter typically encompasses the right to a fair trial, the right to appeal, and the right to defence.[79] It should be noted that limitations of due process were discussed not only in the criminal context but also in administrative contexts. This finding is not surprising, and can be traced back to the changing legal framework affecting property protection and the administrative and court proceedings.[80] Some problems regarding property protection resulted from the rapid transformations of the property regime after the fall of Communism (see cases on co-operatives and housing co-operatives in particular, or rent control) and the intensive legislative changes concerning land, planning, and development (see cases on building permits, expropriation, local spatial planning, or road investments). Further recurring claims invoking property protection are brought by public officials (often by court enforcement officers or even judges), challenging the method of

[79] Conceptually, this category corresponds with the rights guaranteed in Article 6 of the European Convention of Human Rights.

[80] Similar conclusions could be made with regard to individual applications to the European Court of Human Rights. State-comparing statistics available at <www.echr.coe.int/Pages/home.aspx?p=reports&c>.

calculating their remuneration. In turn, due process rights are usually invoked in relation to procedural laws limiting access to a court, defence or legal aid, and imposing excessive formal requirements or foreclosing the right to appeal.[81]

The proportionality framework was also relatively frequently applied with regard to limitations on freedom of speech,[82] social rights,[83] privacy,[84] and freedom of occupation.[85] Among the least frequently invoked rights are freedom of association, political rights,[86] liberty, freedom of religion, and the right to protection of a family life. These rights tend to be limited not through legislation but rather through state action or court decisions, and therefore tend to come up less often in the case law of the Tribunal. Furthermore, the laws regulating the exercise of rights and freedoms in the latter category have not been extensively amended in recent years, and were thus less likely to be subject to a constitutional challenge in the analysed period.[87]

Interestingly, the database does not contain any cases dealing with limitation of equality, since the proportionality test is not directly applicable to limitations of the principle of equal treatment.[88] In addition,

81 In eight cases, due process was invoked because of barriers in access to a court.

82 Including access to information and freedom of assembly.

83 The social rights category includes the right to education, social insurance, health, and annual leave.

84 Including respect of private life and data protection.

85 The category of freedom of occupation encompasses both freedom of economic activity and freedom of choice and exercise of one's profession.

86 The category marked as 'political rights' refers exclusively to equal access to public service.

87 In general, it is a dominant feature of the laws subject to PA to be adding new criteria or conditions to existing legal rules, which the Tribunal considers as amendments of existing limitations of constitutional rights or freedoms.

88 If laws differentiate between two similarly situated categories of subjects, the Tribunal examines whether a derogation from the principle of equal treatment is acceptable. In such cases the Tribunal answers the following questions: (1) whether there is a rational link between the differentiating criterion and the goal and content of the law; (2) whether the gravity of the interest that the differentiation is supposed to serve remains in an adequate proportion to the gravity of interests which will be infringed in result of the differentiation; (3) whether the differentiating criterion is related to the protection of other constitutional values, principles, or norms to justify the differentiating treatment of similar subjects. Although some elements of this test correspond to the stages of the PA, they differ in their structure and order. While the first question resembles the suitability test, the second, the proportionality in the strict sense, and the third, the legitimate aim test, the constitutional review of derogations from the principle of equal treatment, does not include the necessity stage. Moreover, the Constitutional Tribunal does not refer to this process as proportionality review.

although the proportionality test can be applied to limitations affecting life and dignity, no such cases occurred in the analysed period. In general, the rights to life and human dignity appear very rarely in the Polish constitutional jurisprudence, due to the fact that constitutional review in Poland only concerns legislative measures, which seldom impose limitations on human life. Human dignity is often evoked as a subsidiary ground of review; during the analysed period, however, the Tribunal did not review the merits of such claims.

#### The Outcome of Proportionality Analysis

In all cases included in the database, the final outcome of the constitutional review was determined by the outcome of the PA. In other words, a failure of the proportionality test led to the decision of declaring the law unconstitutional. Overall, in cases in which the Tribunal applied PA in order to review the constitutionality of limitations imposed on constitutional rights or freedoms, the law was proportional in 41 out of all 100 cases in the database (41 per cent) and disproportionate in 59 of all cases (59 per cent). On average, the rate at which cases fail the PA appears to be slightly higher than the overall rate in which the Tribunal invalidates laws.[89]

In some proportionality cases, the outcome was predictable due to a similar, previously decided, case by the European Court of Human Rights. In those instances, the Tribunal usually invokesd and followed the standard established by the Strasbourg Court. Moreover, a significant number of cases in which a law was deemed disproportionate (15 out of 59 cases, or 25 per cent) concerned procedural issues such as the access to court, the right to a hearing, the right to appeal, or the right to defence. In addition, 7 out 59 cases that failed the proportionality test (12 per cent) concerned the deprivation of liberty or related to extremely deficient protection of rights, and were therefore decided unanimously.[90]

### *D Division of Labour between the Stages of the Proportionality Analysis*

The generally accepted scholarly view in Poland is that the legitimate aim requirement is a threshold stage, which does not pose a substantive

[89] During the analysed period the average rate at which legislation was struck down was 51.8 per cent.

[90] Except one case in which one judge dissented on formal grounds. See Case No. SK 12/13 (n 53).

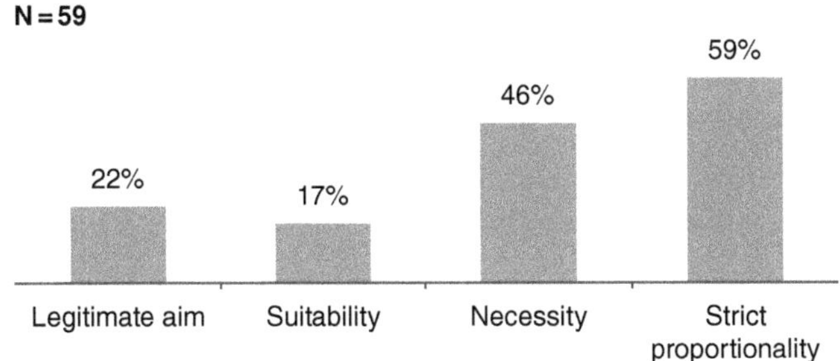


**Figure 5.3** Frequency of failure at each stage of proportionality analysis

hurdle to the legislator.[91] In addition, the presumption of a rational legislator suggests that the law passes the suitability stage easily, whereas the outcomes of the necessity and proportionality in the strict sense stages are much harder to predict.[92] In practice, the quantitative findings tend to slightly differ from these generally accepted views.

Figure 5.3 sets forth the frequency of failure at each subtest of PA for the 59 decisions in which the Tribunal found at least one provision of law to fail the proportionality test. Despite the widely held view that the legitimate aim requirement does not represent a significant challenge, a surprisingly high number of cases (13, or 22 per cent) failed at this stage.[93] The frequency of failure was the lowest at the suitability stage, but still proved to be significantly higher than expected, with a total of 10 cases (17 per cent) failing this stage.[94] A large number of cases failed the necessity test (27 cases, or 46 per cent),[95] while the highest failure rate occurred at the final stage of proportionality, the strict sense test (35 cases, or 59 per cent).

The picture arising from Figure 5.3 indicates that the majority of cases fail at the two final stages of the PA. However, contrary to the general conception, the first two stages also play a significant role in PA.

[91] Wojtyczek (n 62) 152.

[92] ibid.

[93] The outcome of the worthy purpose analysis was negative in 14 cases, 2 of which were marked as 'partial'. Therefore, taking into account the aggregated outcome, there were 13 failures.

[94] The outcome of the suitability analysis was negative in 11 cases, with 2 decisions being marked as 'partial'. Therefore, after the aggregation, there were 10 failures.

[95] The outcome of the necessity analysis was negative in 28 cases, but after the aggregation of decisions marked as 'partial' because of a different outcome regarding several norms under review, there were 27 failures.

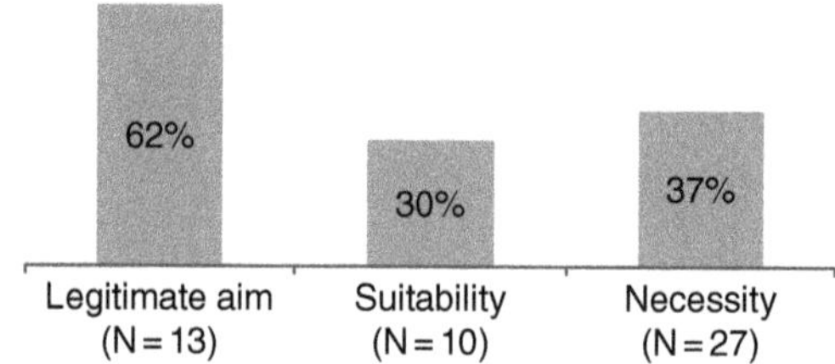


**Figure 5.4** Termination of proportionality analysis after failure

Although the final stage of PA displays the highest rate of failure , a law solely failed on these grounds in only 16 out of all 59 failure cases, or 27 per cent.

In the majority of cases, the Tribunal's analysis does not come to an end immediately after a failure, but tends to be continued. Overall, out of the 43 cases that failed at a stage prior to the final stage, 22 cases (51 per cent) were continued beyond the stage at which they failed. In these cases, the Tribunal carried on through the proportionality test until the final stage.

Figure 5.4 presents the termination rate for each stage of the analysis. The data show that failure at the worthy purpose stage was a sufficient ground to find the law disproportionate in 62 per cent of the failures at this stage (in 8 out of 13 cases). Hence, the Tribunal was willing to strike down the law exclusively on this ground in the majority of cases in which the law failed the legitimate aim test. The data indicate that the legitimate aim test constitutes a substantive obstacle in the Polish proportionality practice. The termination rates are significantly lower at the suitability and necessity stages, at which the analysis was terminated after a failure only 3 out of 10 times, or 30 per cent, and in 10 out of 27 cases, or 37 per cent, respectively. The data therefore show that the Tribunal tends to continue the PA after a failure at the suitability or the necessity stage. While the necessity stage has led to a failure in almost half of all failed cases, the Tribunal continued its analysis in the majority of those cases. As a result, only one quarter of all cases that failed the test of proportionality in the strict sense were to be seen as 'first failures'.

In the majority of cases, a measure that was deemed disproportionate failed more than one subtest. The combination of the data regarding the failure rates and termination rates point to the necessity test as an essential element of PA, mostly in combination with the final test of proportionality in the strict sense. In 18 out of all 59 failure cases, or 30.5

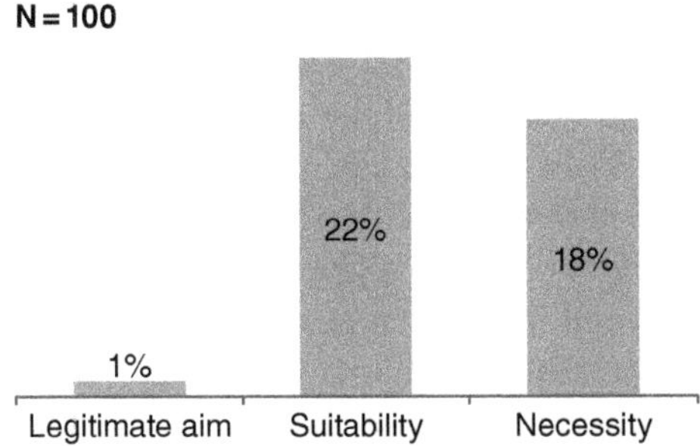


**Figure 5.5** Frequency of each stage being skipped in the analysis

per cent, the law failed both the necessity and the proportionality in the strict sense stage.

Figure 5.5 presents the percentage of cases in which the Tribunal skipped a stage of the proportionality test. The phenomenon of skipping a test occurred regardless of the final outcome of the PA.[96] In the analysed period, the Tribunal entirely skipped the legitimate aim stage in only one case, whereas the suitability stage was left out in 23 cases. In most of those suitability cases, the appropriateness of the means was either tacitly assumed or implicitly confirmed. This finding confirms the scholarly view according to which the examination of the suitability criterion is in some situations redundant.[97] The necessity test was skipped in 18 cases.

A practice that is related to, but to be distinguished from, skipping is that of addressing a stage without making a determination as to whether the means passes or fails the stage. While the practice of skipping a stage suggests that the Tribunal tacitly confirmed the law's passing the test, the practice of leaving a stage undecided suggests that the Tribunal was

[96] In the only decision in which the Tribunal skipped the legitimate aim stage, the law was later found disproportionate. In seven decisions in which the Tribunal skipped the suitability test, the law was upheld; in 16 cases, it was found disproportionate. In eight decisions in which the Tribunal skipped the necessity test, the law was upheld; in ten, the law was found disproportionate.

[97] Krzysztof Wojtyczek notes that in order to assess whether the means are suitable to achieve the intended objective, the legislative aims first need to be determined on the basis of the effects of the law. In consequence, a legislative aim determined in relation to the effects of the law is not necessarily identical with the actual legislative goal. Therefore, he proposes to skip this test and only examine the effects of the law. Likewise, he argues that the officially declared legislative purpose is almost never contrary to the Constitution. Thus, the examination of whether the declared aims are lawful is generally impractical. Wojtyczek (n 62) 153.

reluctant to fail the law on this particular ground. The Tribunal left the legitimate aim stage undecided in 2 out of all 100 cases in the database, the suitability stage in 8 cases, and the necessity stage in 6 cases. In most of those cases, the Tribunal ultimately struck down the law at a later stage; this occurred in both cases in which the legitimate aim stage was left undecided, in five out of the eight cases that were left undecided at the suitability stage, and in four out of the six cases at the necessity stage. The practice of addressing but ultimately leaving a stage undecided is closely related to the phenomenon of continuing the analysis after a failure at a previous stage, as pointed out previously; both reflect the Tribunal's reluctance to have an outcome of striking down a law that does not address the final stage of strict proportionality.

In general, the Tribunal only rarely strikes down a law without considering the test of proportionality in the strict sense. However, at the same time, the final stage of PA does not carry the burden of a failure alone in most cases. The Tribunal seems reluctant to rely on single test for failure. Instead, its decisions to fail laws are typically based on a failure in more than one subtest, particularly necessity and strict proportionality.[98] The tendency to have a justificatory basis as broad as possible for striking down a law is particularly encapsulated in four decisions in which the scrutinized law failed the suitability, the necessity, and the proportionality in the strict sense stages.[99]

## IV Limitation of a Constitutional Right or Freedom

### *A Constitutional Guarantees of Rights and Freedoms*

The Constitution of 1997 contains an extensive catalogue of constitutional rights and freedoms as specified in chapter II. This chapter follows the model of international human rights treaties and divides personal, political, as well as economic, social, and cultural rights and freedoms into three separate categories.[100] Some of the guarantees are very specific

[98] Precisely, in 22 cases (37 per cent of all failed cases), the Tribunal found that the law fails on more than one ground of the PA.

[99] Judgment of 5 June 2014, Case No. K 35/11 OTK-A 2014, No. 6, Item 61; Judgment of 10 December 2013, Case No. U 5/13 OTK-A 2013, No. 9, Item 136; Judgment of 25 June 2013, Case No. P 11/12 OTK-A 2013, No. 5, Item 62; Judgment of 23 October 2012, Case No. SK 11/12 OTK-A 2012, No. 9, Item 107.

[100] In contrast, literature draws a distinction between rights denoting freedoms, negative rights, entitlements, competences, institutions, and procedures. Wojtyczek (n 62) 24–40.

as they detail aspects of constitutional protection which fall into more general categories of fundamental rights or freedoms (like speech[101] or privacy[102]).

The Constitution does not make a clear distinction between absolute and relative rights. However, the widely shared view is that all rights and freedoms guaranteed in the Constitution are relative and may be subject to limitations, except for rights and freedoms that are considered absolute under international law. In contrast, it is understood that the prohibition of torture or cruel, inhuman, or degrading treatment or punishment is absolute and precludes any legislative interference.[103] Following this view, the Tribunal held that the use of torture or cruel, inhuman, or degrading treatment may not be subject to PA.[104] Further, for the Tribunal, it is also not conceivable to limit the presumption of innocence. As a consequence, the limitation clause and, by implication, the PA, do not apply to cases in which the principle of presumption of innocence is invoked.[105]

### B *The Hierarchy of Constitutional Rights and Freedoms*

The Tribunal's case-law confirms that there is an internal hierarchy of constitutional rights and freedoms enshrined in the Polish Constitution. Although the Constitution does not explicitly state so, the Tribunal inferred the rank of constitutional rights and freedoms from its structure and axiology.[106] The hierarchy of constitutional rights and freedoms does

101 In the Polish Constitution, freedom of speech, right to information as well as academic freedom are stipulated in separate provisions, all of which are located in different titles of chapter II. See Polish Constitution, Article 54(1), 61, 73.

102 In addition to the right to respect for private and family life, the Constitution also stipulates freedom and privacy of communication, inviolability of home as well as data protection and informational autonomy. See Polish Constitution, Articles 47, 49, 50, and 51.

103 Wyrzykowski (n 62) 58.

104 Judgment of 13 December 2004, Case No. K 20/04 OTK-A 2004, No. 11, Item 115; Judgment of 26 May 2008, Case No. SK 25/07 OTK-A 2008, No. 4, Item 62.

105 Judgment of 30 September 2015, Case No. K 3/13 OTK-A 2015, No. 8, Item 125.

106 Judgment of 10 June 2008, Case No. SK 17/07 OTK-A 2008, No. 5, Item 78; Judgment of 10 July 2007, Case No. SK 50/06 OTK-A 2007, No. 7, Item 75; Case No. K 21/05 (n 23); Judgment of 11 September 2005, Case No. Kp 1/05 OTK-A 2005, No. 8, Item 93; Judgment of 11 May 1999, Case No. K 13/98 OTK 1999, No. 4, Item 74; Judgment of 12 January 1999, Case No. P 2/98 OTK 1999, No. 1, Item 2; Judgment of 10 November 1998, Case No. K 39/97 OTK 1988, No. 6, Item 99; Decision of 31 January 1996, Case No. K 9/95 OTK 1996, Item 2; Case No. K 11/94 (n 68); Judgment of 30 October 2006, Case No. P 10/06 OTK-A 2006, No. 9, Item 128.

not directly indicate that a right that belongs to the highest hierarchical level automatically prevails on balance. However, their rank is relevant for determining the strength of arguments justifying their limitations. The Tribunal requires that limitations of personal rights and freedoms must come with a particularly strong and unambiguous justification.[107] Therefore, a more important right or freedom requires a more compelling justification for its limitation. Additionally, some constitutional provisions (like Article 51 regarding informational autonomy) entail other specific conditions for legislative limitation of their scope than those implicated in the general limitation clause.[108]

There is another particularity regarding the right to life. The Tribunal has held that limitations of the right to human life may not be justified by any other reason than the protection of life of others. It thus accepted that the right to life requires a strict symmetry of values: the sacrificed and the saved one.[109] In other words, the right to life can be limited only when such sacrifice is absolutely necessary to save the lives of other individuals. As a result, other constitutional values enumerated in Article 31(3) of the Constitution may not be used to justify a limitation of the right to life.[110]

### Dignity, Liberty, and Equality as the General Principles of Law

Human dignity, liberty, and equality have a special status of general principles.[111] Although the structure of the Constitution suggests their priority over other constitutionally protected rights and freedoms, their practical importance is rather limited. Human dignity stands at the top of the hierarchy of constitutional rights and freedoms, but its role in the Polish constitutional jurisprudence is secondary. It is a consequence of a procedural standard according to which subjects initiating the review need to invoke specific guarantees of constitutional rights and freedoms in their pleadings before appealing to more general ones.

In practice, the human dignity and liberty clauses are mostly used to support allegations regarding other more specific rights and freedoms.[112] The Tribunal usually refers to them as constitutional values that need to

[107] Judgment of 20 July 2011, Case No. K 9/11 OTK-A 2011, No. 6, Item 61.

[108] Judgment of 30 July 2014, Case No. K 23/11 OTK-A 2014, No. 7, Item 80.

[109] Some authors argue that the PA should not be applied to limitations of the right to life. See, e.g., Marek Piechowiak, 'Klauzula limitacyjna a nienaruszalność praw i wolności' (2009) 2 Przegląd Sejmowy 56.

[110] Case No. K 44/07 (n 23).

[111] See Polish Constitution, Articles 30,31(1), 32.

[112] Judgment of 15 October 2002, Case No. SK 6/02 OTK-A 2002, No. 5, Item 65.

be taken into account in the process of interpretation of constitutional guarantees of other rights and freedoms.[113] In contrast, the Tribunal has not yet developed an autonomous interpretation of the liberty clause moving beyond guarantees of specific freedoms contained in the Constitution. In sum, the application of both dignity and liberty as directly enforceable rights is still to be tested.[114]

### Economic and Social Rights

As previously noted, personal and political rights and freedoms enjoy a higher constitutional protection than social, economic, and cultural rights.[115] Therefore, the latter can be subject to more extensive statutory regulation.[116] However, the category of social, economic, and cultural rights is not homogenous, but comprises three different categories which essentially differ from one another. In the Tribunal's proportionality case-law the majority of cases concern limitations of economic rights. Their status is evidently weaker than that of personal and political rights or freedoms.

According to the Tribunal's case-law the Constitution protects ownership, but this right also entails certain obligations towards the general public.[117] Although freedom of economic activity is recognized both as a subjective right and a principle of the economic order established by the Constitution (Article 20 of the Constitution), it is followed by a specific limitation clause (Article 22 of the Constitution) that permits a broad intervention in its scope.[118] Consequently, subjects alleging a breach of economic freedom carry a much heavier burden in rebutting the presumption of constitutionality than they would in case of limitations of

[113] Judgment of 4 April 2001, Case No. K 11/00 OTK 2001, No. 3, Item 54. It should be noted, however, that human dignity denoting the prohibition of using humans as the means of government action was effectively used as a substantive right in a number of decisions. Case No. K 11/00 (n 114); Judgment of 8 November 2001, Case No. P 6/01 OTK 2001, No. 8, Item 248; Case No. K 44/07 (n 23).

[114] Marek Safjan, 'Prawo do ochrony życia prywatnego i autonomia jednostki w orzecznictwie Trybunału Konstytucyjnego' in Marek Zubik (ed) *Księga XX-lecia orzecznictwa Trybunału Konstytucyjnego* (Biuro Trybunału Konstytucyjnego 2006), 430.

[115] Case No. K 11/94 (n 68).

[116] Judgment of 8 April 1998, Case No. K 10/97 OTK 1998, No. 3, Item 29 ('economic activity, because of its nature, and especially the close relationship both with the interests of others and the public interest, may be subject to various types of limitations to a greater extent than personal or political rights and freedoms').

[117] Judgment of 5 November 1997, Case No. K 22/97 OTK 1997, No. 3/4, Item 41.

[118] Case No. K 41/12 (n 54); Decision of 13 October 2010, Case No. Kp 1/09 OTK-A No. 8, Item 74; Judgment of 10 April 2001, Case No. U 7/00 OTK 2001, No. 3, Item 56.

other constitutional rights or freedoms.[119] First, limitations imposed on freedom of economic activity may be introduced 'by means of statute' (rather than by statute itself) and for 'important public reasons' (Article 22). Therefore, government limitation of economic freedom does not need to be directly related to constitutional values enumerated in Article 31(3) of the Constitution.[120] As a result, the level of constitutional scrutiny in case of limitations imposed on freedom of economic activity is much lower than in case of other rights or freedoms.[121]

### C *Application of the Infringement Test*

The infringement test is the opening question in the review of limitations imposed on constitutional rights and freedoms. An infringement may come in various forms depending on the category of a right or freedom at stake[122] and the type of state action (legislative, administrative, or judicial).[123] For the purpose of constitutional review, the Tribunal examines only whether there has been a legislative limitation of the constitutionally guaranteed scope of protection of a right or freedom. This substantive test is intrinsically linked to the initial (procedural) question regarding the basis of the review.

As noted earlier, applicants requesting constitutional review need to indicate a relevant constitutional standard. More specifically, they need to identify provisions of the Constitution that will serve as the basis of the

[119] Judgment of 27 February 2014, Case No. P 31/13 OTK-A 2014, No. 2, Item 16.

[120] Judgment of 19 March 2001, Case No. K 32/00 OTK 2001, No. 3, Item 50.

[121] In Case No. P 31/13 (n 119), the Tribunal accepted that a limitation of economic freedom could be justified by the protection of stability of the financial market and security of savings, which is not a constitutional value. As noted in the dissent, in lowering the threshold for limitations of economic freedom, the Tribunal gave priority to indeterminate interests of the banks.

[122] It is noted in the literature that the type of possible interference depends on the type of the right at stake. In case of rights denoting freedoms, it may take the form of a prohibition of certain activities falling in the scope of the freedom, an imposition of duties on individuals who take advantage of their freedom, and the establishment of authorities supervising whether these prohibitions or duties are respected. A different type of interferences occurs in regard to negative rights derived from constitutional prohibitions of certain government actions (such as prohibition of torture or extradition), rights-entitlements (like the right to social insurance), rights-competences (voting rights), rights-institutions (protection of marriage or property), and procedural rights. Wojtyczek (n 62) 64–74.

[123] Marek Szydło, 'Komentarz do art. 31' in Lech Garlicki (ed), *Konstytucja Rzeczpospolitej Polskiej. Komentarz*, vol. III (Wydawnictwo Sejmowe 2003) 63.

review. It is quite frequent that the Tribunal discontinues the proceedings entirely or in part because the subject initiating the review invokes inadequate constitutional standards.[124] In practice, the Tribunal may exceptionally redefine the claim and decide such a case on the merits.

In order to establish that the challenged norm infringes a right, the imposed limitation needs to fall under the scope of constitutional protection, which is well-established in the existing scholarship and case-law.[125] Throughout the analysed period, most cases passed the infringement stage allowing the Tribunal to move to the question of whether it was provided by law. However, in 11 decisions rendered during this period, the Tribunal found that there was no infringement of a constitutional right, and upheld the law without proceeding to PA.[126] One of the reasons for this is that the Polish Constitution does not entail all-encompassing formula like the right to free development of one's personality and the protection of human dignity or liberty, meaning that some aspects of human activity will simply fall outside the scope of constitutional protection.[127]

In addition, some statutory restrictions affecting individual liberties are not conceived as infringements of constitutional rights, but as

[124] In Judgment of 25 March 2014, Case No. SK 25/13 OTK-A 2014, No. 3, Item 33, the Tribunal admitted that the impugned law raises a constitutional problem, although unrelated to the protection of constitutional rights or freedoms. See also Case No. K 23/11 (n 108).

[125] Judgment of 17 July 2014, Case No. SK 35/12 OTK-A 2014, No. 7, Item 74. In this case, criminalization of ineffective incitement to a criminal act did not infringe upon the personal liberty from 'criminal repression'. Although the Tribunal noticed other potential constitutional problems regarding the scope of criminalization, it did not address them, relying on the principle of binding limits of the application as they remained unchallenged in the constitutional complaint.

[126] For this reason, these cases are not included in the sample. Among these 'no infringement' decisions there are cases concerning members of the military, judiciary, or public servants. Their claims were unsuccessful as the Tribunal ruled that the law under review does not limit a constitutional right or freedom. Instead, it held that the law specifies conditions of public service. See Judgment of 12 July 2012, Case No. SK 31/10 OTK-A 2012, No. 7, Item 80.

[127] This problem can be illustrated with the example of the alimony debtors case. The law at issue in this case aimed to compel child alimony debtors to pay their dues by withholding their driving licence. The law could not be effectively challenged as an infringement of a constitutional right or freedom since the Constitution does not guarantee a right to drive a car. The Tribunal decided not to derive such a right from constitutional rights or freedoms (such as the right to protection of private life or freedom of economic activity). Instead, the law was challenged as a violation of the principle of proportionality derived from the rule of law clause. Judgment of 12 February 2014, Case No. K 23/10 OTK-A 2014, No. 2, Item 10.

regulations of constitutional obligations.[128] Furthermore, statutory laws 'forming' constitutional rights, that include regulations laws that make the realization of these rights effective, such as introducing institutional guarantees of their exercise, cannot themselves be considered as limitations.[129] Only prohibitions explicitly restricting the exercise of rights or freedoms are typically considered as infringements subject to PA.[130]

When addressing the question of whether a law imposes a limitation on a constitutional right or freedom, the Tribunal first reconstructs the scope of protection enshrined in the Constitution by referencing the legal doctrine, the existing case-law, and sometimes the case-law of the European Court of Human Rights or foreign courts. On this basis, the Tribunal determines to what extent the impugned legislation affects the enjoyment or exercise of the constitutional right or freedom at stake. In some cases, however, the infringement may result from a legislative gap resulting from a lack of statutory regulation of specific subject matters deemed as necessary for the constitutional protection of a particular right or freedom.

Although the scope of constitutional rights and freedoms usually remains undisputed, it can become a contested issue in ideologically divisive cases. For example, in the abortion case, the Tribunal found that the Constitution protects the negative aspect of privacy (freedom not to have children) only if a child has not yet been conceived.[131] Consequently, it held that after conception, the constitutional protection extended only to the right to bear children.[132]

## V Statutory Reservation Requirement

### *A The Statutory Form of Rights Limitations*

The requirement of statutory reservation is a distinctive criterion used by the Constitutional Tribunal in the examination of all cases concerning

[128] A poignant example concerns tax laws that specify tax obligations in pursuance to Article 84 and 217 of the Constitution that may only in exceptional circumstances be considered as a limitation of individual rights (e.g. when the imposed tax amounts to the confiscation of property). See Judgment of 19 June 2012, Case No. P 41/10 OTK-A 2012, No. 6, Item 65.

[129] Szydło (n 123) 67.

[130] ibid [67].

[131] Case No. K 26/96 (n 18).

[132] The Polish abortion case was called 'the most outrageous case of all constitutional courts [cases] in CEE, of judicial usurpation of the law-making power'. See Sadurski (n 13) 135.

constitutional rights and freedoms. The principle of statutory reservation was established by the Tribunal's early case-law.[133] It requires any limitation of fundamental rights and freedoms to be provided for in a statute. The requirement of statutory reservation establishes a connection between a limitation and the democratic majority. This linkage contributes to the protection of constitutional rights and freedoms for the following reasons: first, statutes are adopted in a procedure which is transparent to the public and enables interventions when legislative proposals go beyond what is necessary to attain the purpose of the law. Second, only statutory laws may be subject to constitutional (preventive) review before their promulgation.[134] The requirement of statutory reservation breaks away the legacy of the Communist era during which a limitation of individual rights or freedoms was often introduced as part of an executive act issued without statutory authorization or without official promulgation, as well as in internal guidelines or instructions (*prawo powielaczowe*).[135]

The Constitution of 1997 recognizes a special rank of statutory acts. In particular, only statutory acts may introduce limitations of constitutional rights or freedoms. In contrast, executive acts, internally binding acts as well as enactments of local government need to comply with statutory laws and may not autonomously impose limitations on individual rights and freedoms. As the Tribunal explained, sub-statutory acts may regulate only technical aspects of limitations related to the exercise of constitutional rights and freedoms. However, sub-statutory acts imposing limitations on constitutional rights and freedoms need to be based on explicit and specific statutory authorization (delegation) and serve the implementation of statutory aims.[136] The Constitution further provides that some limitations may be regulated exclusively in statutory acts.[137]

[133] Case No. P 2/87 (n 11); Decision of 22 September 1997, Case No. K 25/97 OTK 1997, No. 3/4, Item 35; Decision of 28 May 1986, Case No. U 1/86 OTK 1986, Item 2; Decision of 1 March 1994, Case No. U 7/93 OTK 1994, Item 5. See also: Judgment of 8 January 2008, Case No. P 35/06 OTK-A 2008, No. 1, Item 1; Judgment of 8 July 2003, Case No. P 10/02 OTK-A 2003, No. 6, Item 62; Judgment of 20 February 2001, Case No. P 2/00 OTK 2001, No. 2, Item 32.

[134] Wyrzykowski (n 62) 48–49.

[135] Case No. U 1/86 (n 133).

[136] Judgment of 27 November 2012, Case No. U 4/12 OTK-A 2012, No. 10, Item 124.

[137] See Polish Constitution, Article 51(5). See also Judgment of 14 July 2015, Case No. K 2/13 OTK-A 2015, No. 7, Item 100.

To date, the Polish Constitutional Tribunal continues to often render decisions of unconstitutionality on the basis of a lack of statutory form.[138] Characteristically, the failure to introduce limitations of constitutional rights or freedoms in a statutory form brings the Tribunal's analysis to an end, as this serves as a sufficient basis for declaring the impugned law unconstitutional.[139] Additionally, the Constitutional Tribunal may scrutinize the procedure in which the law was adopted, declaring the law unconstitutional for inconsistency with the constitutional standard of law-making.[140]

### *B The Requirement of Statutory Specificity*

The requirement of statutory reservation includes further substantive preconditions regarding legislative specificity[141] and quality (clarity, precision, and appropriateness).[142] The standard of statutory specificity

[138] Solely within the year of 2013, 9 out of 71 judgments (13 per cent) rendered by the Tribunal concerned normative acts issued by the executive without statutory authorization or in subject matters which may not be regulated in sub-statutory acts. Among these judgments, there were 7 decisions concerning limitations of constitutional rights (personal liberty, privacy, freedom to choose and exercise one's profession, property, equality, and the right to education). See Judgment of 8 January 2013, Case No. K 38/12 OTK-A 2013, No. 1, Item 1; Judgment of 5 March 2013, Case No. U 2/11 OTK-A 2013, No. 3, Item 24; Judgment of 26 March 2013, Case No. K 11/12 OTK-A 2013, No. 3, Item 28; Judgment of 16 July 2013, Case No. P 53/11 OTK-A 2013, No. 6, Item 78; Judgment of 30 July 2013, Case No. U 5/12 OTK-A 2013, No. 6, Item 88; Judgment of 24 September 2013, Case No. K 35/12 OTK-A 2013, No. 7, Item 94; Judgment of 29 October 2013, Case No. U 7/12 OTK-A 2013, No. 7, Item 102.

[139] See Judgment of 13 October 2015, Case No. P 3/14 OTK-A 2015, No. 9, Item 145 – regarding the lack of statutory determination of the execution fee applicable to a particular category of executions (and debtors); Judgment of 5 February 2015, Case No. K 60/13 OTK-A 2015, No. 2, Item 11 – regarding the lack of statutory protection of right of a former member of a housing cooperative; Judgment of 3 June 2014, Case No. K 19/11 OTK-A 2014, No. 6, Item 60 – regarding the lack of guarantees of the right to defence in the explanatory stage of the preparatory proceedings.

[140] Judgment of 19 September 2008, Case No. K 5/07 OTK-A 2008, No. 7, Item 124; Judgment of 19 June 2002, Case No. K 11/02 OTK-A 2002, No. 4, Item 43.

[141] Kazimierz Działocha and Tomasz Zalasiński, 'Określoność' przepisów prawa jako przedmiot kontroli konstytucyjności prawa w poglądach Trybunału Konstytucyjnego' in Stanisław Bożyk (ed), *Prawo, parlament i egzekutywa we współczesnych systemach rządów. Księga poświęcona pamięci Profesora Jerzego Stembrowicza* (Wydawnictwo Temida 2, Białystok 2009) 48.

[142] The latter requirements form the 'standards of appropriate law-making', known as the principles of the legislative technique. See Regulation of the President of the Council of Ministers on the Principles of the Legislative Technique (Journal of Laws, No. 100, Item 908) (2008).

requires a statute to determine all essential aspects of a limitation imposed on constitutional rights and freedoms in a definite and complete way, including its personal and material scope, the applicable procedures, and sanctions.[143] This standard serves the principle of legal certainty and aims to facilitate better comprehension of the law, so that the precise meaning and scope of the limitation can be identified solely by reading the statutory law.[144] The distinction between essential and non-essential elements of right limitations was a decisive factor in many cases in which the Tribunal found the law to be unconstitutional for failing to comply with the formal requirement of statutory specificity.[145]

The constitutional standard of statutory specificity is raised for limitations of personal liberty. The Tribunal explained that the 'provided by law' clause contained in Article 41(1) of the Constitution is not a mere repetition of Article 31(3) of the Constitution, but a special requirement addressed to the legislator. Therefore, the legislator needs to determine all rules and procedures applicable to deprivation or limitation of personal liberty in a statute.[146]

In the analysed period, the Tribunal applied the aforementioned standard of statutory specificity to ministerial regulations on the use of arms or other means of coercion by public officials, which triggered limitation of personal liberty.[147] It thereby found that the determination of circumstances in which public officials can lawfully use arms and other means of coercion, as well as the applicable procedure, constitute essential elements of a limitation. Consequently, these aspects necessitate specific statutory regulation adopted in pursuance of Article 41(1) of the Constitution. In contrast, technical specifications of arms used by a certain type of uniformed forces in the exercise of their duties could be provided for in a sub-statutory act (like a ministerial regulation).

[143] Garlicki (n 3) 20–21; Bogusław Banaszak, *Konstytucja Rzeczpospolitej Polskiej. Komentarz* (Wydawnictwo CH Beck 2012); Wojtyczek (n 62) 110. Case No. K 2/07 (n 40). In contrast, technical aspects of such limitation could be introduced in a ministerial regulation provided that they are based on an explicit statutory authorization. Case No. U 7/12 (n 138).

[144] Judgment of 21 April 2009, Case No. K 50/07 OTK-A 2009, No. 4, Item 51.

[145] It is legitimate to introduce non-essential limitations of constitutional rights or freedoms on the basis of sub-statutory laws. Garlicki (n 4) 20–21; Banaszak (n 143); Wojtyczek (n 62) 110.

[146] Judgment of 17 May 2012, Case No. K 10/11 OTK-A 2012, No. 5, Item 51; Judgment of 10 March 2010, Case No. U 5/07 OTK-A 2010, No. 3, Item 20.

[147] Case No. K 11/12 (n 138); Case No. U 5/07 (n 146).

The requirement of statutory specificity is notably weaker in the context of freedom of economic activity. While Article 31(3) of the Constitution provides that limitations are imposed 'only by statute', Article 22 of the Constitution stipulates that freedom of economic activity may be restricted 'by means of statutory law'. Due to this textual difference, the Tribunal has held that limitations affecting essential elements of freedom of economic activity may be provided in sub-statutory norms as long as they are based on the grant of a general statutory authorization.[148] In contrast, all essential aspects related to the exercise of other constitutional rights and freedoms need to be determined in a statute.[149]

### C *The Requirement of Legislative Clarity, Precision, and Appropriateness*

The principle of statutory specificity also includes the requirement of legislative clarity, precision, and appropriateness. Notably, these three criteria may be an independent ground of constitutional review based either on the rule of law clause (Article 2 of the Constitution) or the limitation clause (Article 31(3) of the Constitution). The requirement of legislative clarity, precision, and appropriateness serves not only a better understanding of the law but also provides for its uniform interpretation. It also limits the discretion of the organs applying the law.[150] The Tribunal has emphasized that statutes imposing limitations on the exercise of constitutional rights or freedoms should not be written in broad language, but should rather precisely stipulate premises upon which organs applying the law should base their acts and narrow the scope of their decisional discretion.[151]

The Tribunal may, however, only declare the law unconstitutional for a lack of sufficient clarity, precision, and appropriateness if this deficiency takes a qualified form. In other words, the Tribunal does not invalidate laws due to their unclear, imprecise, and inappropriate

[148] Judgment of 25 June 2013, Case No. K 30/12 OTK-A 2013, No. 5, Item 61; Case No. P 35/06 (n 133); Judgment of 9 November 1999, Case No. K 28/98 OTK 1999, No. 7, Item 156; Judgment of 24 March 1998, Case No. K 40/97 OTK 1998, No. 2, Item 12.

[149] Judgment of 26 April 2004, Case No. K 50/02 OTK-A 2004, No. 4, Item 32; Judgment of 19 February 2002, Case No. U 3/01 OTK-A 2002, No. 1, Item 3.

[150] Szydło (n 123) 86.

[151] Judgment of 24 July 2013, Case No. Kp 1/13 OTK-A 2013, No. 6, Item 83; Judgment of 20 November 2012, Case No. SK 3/12 OTK-A 2012, No. 10, Item 123; Judgment of 30 October 2001, Case No. K 33/00 OTK 2001, No. 7, Item 217.

formulation if it is possible to remove these legislative flaws in the process of legal interpretation.[152]

In the analysed period there were no cases of a law being declared unconstitutional solely on this ground.[153] However, the standard of legislative clarity, precision, and appropriateness was sometimes examined within the necessity and proportionality in the strict sense stages. The Tribunal has been reluctant to invalidate laws that used broad terms and general clauses exclusively on the formal ground of lacking statutory specificity. Instead, it relied on the proportionality test to require that limitations of constitutional rights or freedoms be narrow in scope and include procedural mechanisms in order to prevent arbitrariness and allow individualized decisions.[154]

The examination of legislative clarity and precision in the course of PA may also be viewed as part of a deliberate judicial strategy to avoid striking down laws purely on formal grounds. For example, in the case concerning the Aviation Act, the provision authorizing the Minister of National Defence to order shooting down a passenger aircraft hijacked by terrorists was challenged as vague in regard to the specification of conditions for this use of power and the applicable procedures. Nevertheless, the Tribunal rejected this claim and disqualified the law on substantive grounds for the breach of human dignity and the right to life.[155]

## VI Legitimate Aim

The question whether the challenged law has a legitimate aim is almost always addressed as part of proportionality review.[156] However, it does not

[152] Judgment of 28 October 2009, Case No. Kp 3/09 OTK-A 2009, No. 9, Item 138.

[153] See Case No. K 11/10 (n 23), where the Tribunal focussed on the lack of required clarity of criminal law, but included arguments pointing towards excessiveness of the analysed means.

[154] Judgment of 25 February 2014, Case No. SK 65/12 OTK-A 2014, No. 2, Item 13. In this case, the Tribunal examined the terms 'incite to hatred' and 'other totalitarian system' used in the Criminal Code, ultimately finding that the challenged law does not lead to an excessive penalization and thus passes the proportionality test.

[155] Case No. K 44/07 (n 23).

[156] The legitimate aims test was not solely addressed in 1 out of the 100 cases in the dataset. The case dealt with a fiscal law that entirely excluded the prescription for tax liability guaranteed with compulsory mortgage. Instead, the Tribunal held that the exclusion of a limitation period could not be considered as necessary to ensure the effectiveness of tax collection. See Judgment of 8 October 2013, Case No. SK 40/12 OTK-A 2013, No. 7, Item 97.

always appear as a separate stage in the Tribunal's analysis.[157] In some cases it was an opening part of the suitability analysis,[158] whereas in others, it was included in the necessity analysis restricted to the question of whether the limitation is necessary to the protection of constitutional values.[159]

In the analysed period, 13 cases (22 per cent of all failed cases) failed at the legitimate aim test. This surprisingly high failure rate was brought about by two types of flaws. In the first type, the challenged norm was not sufficiently related to the protection of constitutional values enumerated in a relevant limitation clause. The second flaw lay in the reviewed law's inability to provide necessary procedural guarantees of constitutional rights protection.

The majority of failures (eight cases) occurred due to the lack of a sufficient link between legislative purposes and values enshrined in the Constitution.[160] It needs to be highlighted at this point that in these cases the Tribunal adopted a restrictive interpretation of grounds entailed in the limitation clause such as 'public order' or 'rights of others'. In six cases failure at the legitimate aim test resulted from a failure to regulate certain elements of constitutional rights in statutory law. This legislative failure (omission) created a gap in statutory protection that could not be justified by any legitimate consideration.[161] Most of these cases

[157] Case No. K 12/14 (n 18) point 5.3.3.

[158] Case No. P 56/11 (n 65).

[159] Judgment of 10 July 2014, Case No. P 19/13 OTK-A 2014, No. 7, Item 71.

[160] Judgment of 14 October 2015, Case No. Kp 1/15 OTK-A 2015, No. 9, Item 147; Case No. K 12/14 (n 18); Judgment of 27 March 2003, Case No. K 50/13 OTK-A 2014, No. 11, Item 121; Judgment of 10 December 2014, Case No. K 52/13 OTK-A 2014, No. 11, Item 118; Judgment of 18 September 2014, Case No. K 44/12 OTK-A 2014, No. 8, Item 92; Judgment of 12 January 2012, Case No. Kp 10/09 OTK-A 2012, No. 1, Item 4; Judgment of 11 July 2012, Case No. K 8/10 OTK-A 2012, No. 7, Item 78; Case No. K 9/11 (n 107).

[161] Judgment of 26 November 2013, Case No. P 33/12 OTK-A 2013, No. 8, Item 123. In this case, the law excluded the possibility to deny paternity after the child's death. It also provided for the discontinuation of the denial proceedings after the child's death. In both regards, it was considered as a violation of the right to protection of family life (of the mother as well as the putative father in the positive aspect, and of the father denying paternity in the negative aspect). The Tribunal explained that the right of parents to establish their parenthood after the death of a child may not be justified by the protection of the child's best interest. Despite having said this, the Tribunal also stated that 'the pursuit of the statutory principle of not changing civil status after the death of a person due to the personal nature of civil status matters remains in gross incommensurability in relation to an interference with the right to protection of family life (referred to the mother and the actual and presumed father of the child), including the right of a man to protect his paternity (in particular with regard to the possibility of establishing it in accordance with the reality).'

concerned procedural guarantees as the laws under review did not contain provisions ensuring individuals the right to appeal certain decisions in courts.[162]

Notably, there was no single case in the database in which the Tribunal found the legislative purpose to be explicitly illegitimate. In case of doubts regarding the motives of the legislator, the Tribunal preferred to discern the goals of the law at a later stage of the proportionality framework by reassessing them in the light of the actual effects of the law.[163]

### *A The Catalogue of Constitutional Values Justifying Restrictions of Constitutional Rights or Freedoms*

The general limitation clause stipulated in Article 31(3) of the Constitution contains a closed list of constitutional values considered as legitimate grounds for limitations of constitutional rights or freedoms. The catalogue includes: (1) security of the state, (2) public order, (3) natural environment, (4) health, (5) public morals, and (6) constitutional rights and freedoms of other persons. In addition, there are separate grounds listed in specific limitation clauses.[164] Moreover, the legislator imposing restrictions on the exercise of a right or freedom subject to a specific limitation clause may not refer to grounds which are not enumerated therein.[165]

Although the enumeration of legitimate grounds does not reflect a hierarchical order of their importance,[166] state security is deemed to be the most important justification, whereas public morality is considered the weakest.[167] It can moreover be asserted that a threat to state security

[162] Judgment of 8 April 2014, Case No. SK 22/11 OTK-A 2014, No. 4, Item 37; Judgment of 10 December 2012, Case No. K 25/11 OTK-A 2012, No. 11, Item 132; Judgment of 6 November 2012, Case No. K 21/11 OTK-A 2012, No. 10, Item 119; Judgment of 30 October 2012, Case No. SK 20/11 OTK-A 2012, No. 9, Item 110.

[163] In two cases in which the answer to the legitimate aims test was unclear, the Tribunal held the law unconstitutional at the later stage. See Judgment of 9 April 2015, Case No. K 14/13 OTK-A 2015, No. 4, Item 45; Judgment of 18 November 2014, Case No. SK 7/11 OTK-A 2014, No. 10, Item 112.

[164] For example, Article 61(3) of the Constitution stipulates that limitations of the right to public information may be imposed by statute solely to protect freedoms and rights of other persons and economic subjects, public order, security, or important economic interests of the state.

[165] See Case No. K 52/13 (n 160).

[166] Garlicki (n 63) 13.

[167] Public morality may justify limitations that are not only considered as violating in the perception of the majority, but as generally harmful. See Case No. K 52/13 (n 160).

tends to be more serious than a threat to the public order.[168] Nevertheless, the hierarchy between the constitutional values enumerated in Article 31(3) of the Constitution is still flexible and relational, meaning that the weight given to a particular value depends on the case at hand.[169] Also noteworthy is that the Tribunal often accepts that laws imposing limitations on constitutional rights or freedoms have several legitimate grounds and considers their cumulative value to be a strong justification.

The most frequently invoked ground is public order, which denotes a broad concept engrained in the continental tradition of administrative law. It refers to the undisturbed functioning of state institutions providing for the realization of public and individual interests and relates to values such as public trust in state institutions, neutrality of public service, standards of good administration, etc. The public order clause also entails the notion of a harmonious social co-existence,[170] which often justifies limitations of property[171] and freedom of economic activity.[172] It also covers the prevention of crime, the introduction of transitory justice mechanisms such as lustration, the improvement of government efficiency, as well as the preclusion of frivolous litigation by means of court fees. The aforementioned examples demonstrate that the protection of public order could serve as a justification of virtually every potential limitation of constitutional rights and freedoms.[173]

Another frequently invoked ground is the protection of rights of others. It is a widely shared view that only the protection of constitutional rights and freedoms of others could counterbalance limitations of rights and freedoms guaranteed by the Constitution;[174] such

[168] Garlicki (n 3) 23.

[169] Szydło (n 123) 94.

[170] Wojtyczek (n 62) 188–90. Judgment of 26 September 2000, Case No. P 11/99 OTK 2000, No. 6, Item 187; Judgment of 7 February 2001 Case No. K 27/00 OTK 2001, No. 2, Item 29; Case No. P 2/98 (n 106).

[171] Case No. P 2/98 (n 106).

[172] Case No. K 27/00 (n 170). See also: Case No. K 41/12 (n 54). In this case, the Tribunal stated that public order includes the organization of a particular area of social life, in which private law entities (like credit and loan co-operatives) have the freedom to realize their aims and are relatively independent from state institutions, although subject to administrative supervision ensuring at least a minimum level of public interest and protection of common good.

[173] Wojtyczek (n 62) 201.

[174] In practice, the protection of rights of others is often combined with other public interests. For example, in the case concerning the Code of Medical Ethics prohibiting medical doctors from expressing public criticism about activity carried out by another doctor, the Tribunal found that this rule limiting freedom of speech is justified by the

limitations cannot be justified for the sake of protection of rights that lack constitutional status (such as the right to employment or a satisfactory level of income).[175] However, in a number of cases, the protection of rights of others was accepted as a justification of limitations imposed on individuals for purely paternalistic reasons. In these cases, the law was primarily intended to prevent self-inflicted harm rather than harm inflicted on others.[176]

The least frequently invoked ground is public morality. Neither the existing scholarly commentaries nor the Tribunal's case-law define which moral norms constitute the content of this clause. In this way, the Tribunal seems to distance itself from making philosophical or moral arguments. In the case concerning ritual slaughter, the Tribunal merely expressed that in a constitutional sense, public morals are informed by 'Judeo-Christian religion and tradition'.[177] However, it also pointed out that its role is not to assess the morality of ritual slaughter as such, but rather to examine whether the absolute prohibition of ritual slaughter is necessary to protect morals.[178] In the context of this case, the Tribunal stated that a general prohibition of ritual slaughter violates the moral norms of freedom of religion. It did not, however, accept public morality as a legitimate ground for the justification of such ban (as it would require a definition of the exact content of the public morality norms commanding prohibition of ritual slaughter).

protection of patients' confidence in health care, which is 'indispensable for the proper functioning of medical profession as a whole, specific relations between a physician and a patient, based on the trust the patient reposes in the physician, and, finally, the specific character of diagnostic and therapeutic decisions'. Case No. SK 16/07 (n 41), referring to *Stambuk v Germany* App. no 37928/97 (ECtHR, 17 October 2002) [41]. In this case, the legitimate aim was related to the medical profession as a whole rather than the individual dignity of an individual physician. Therefore, in the balancing stage, the Tribunal put the 'social image of the health service and its employees' in contrast with the freedom of speech of medical doctors, and the right of patients to appropriate health case as well as their right to information.

175 Judgment of 21 April 2004, Case No. K 33/03 OTK-A 2004, No. 4, Item 31.

176 Case No. SK 55/13 (n 35) citing Gerald Dworkin, 'Paternalism' in Rolf Sartorius (ed), *Paternalism* (University of Minnesota Press 1983) 20 and Wojciech Sadurski, *Racje Liberała. Eseje o państwie liberalno-demokratycznym* (Presspublica Warszawa 1992) 64.

177 Case No. K 52/13 (n 160).

178 In this case, the Tribunal's decision over the legitimate aims test was very controversial. The majority held that the law could not be justified by any of the constitutionally enlisted grounds except animal welfare. This finding did not terminate the PA. In contrast, five out of seven dissenting judges argued that the law could be justified by the protection of public morality.

In consequence, it found that the challenged law on animal protection could not be justified by any of the constitutional values enumerated in the specific limitation clause attached to the constitutional guarantee of freedom to practise religion.[179]

While the categories of legitimate grounds enumerated in Article 31(3) of the Constitution or in other limitation clauses are broad in scope and cover a wide spectrum of interests, it is hardly conceivable to develop a precise interpretation of these concepts.[180] Still, the Tribunal has repeatedly emphasized that they should be interpreted narrowly.[181] In practice, such narrow interpretation of constitutional values may lead the Tribunal to find that the law under review fails the legitimate aim test. Nevertheless, in many decisions, the Tribunal adhered to a broad interpretation of the enumerated categories of legitimate grounds, particularly when the interest of the state budget was at stake.[182] In addition, the Tribunal recognized that values expressed in other constitutional provisions than a relevant limitation clause may also serve as a legitimate justification of limitations imposed on constitutional rights or freedoms.[183]

An important example concerns the 'budgetary equilibrium', which was used to justify conditions for receiving student benefits[184] or

[179] It is important to note that the protection of the natural environment is not enumerated in the limitation clause attached to the freedom to publicly manifest religion provided in Article 53(5) of the Constitution.

[180] Bartosz Rakoczy, *Ograniczenie praw i wolności jednostki ze względu na ochronę środowiska w Konstytucji Polskiej* (TNOiK Toruń 2006) 111.

[181] Judgment of 25 February 1999, Case No. K 23/98 OTK 1999, No. 2, Item 25.

[182] For example, the Tribunal recognized the interest of the State Treasury to secure income, to limit financial liability of the state, or to execute public debts as legitimate. Judgment of 24 May 2012, Case No. P 11/10 OTK-A 2012, No. 5, Item 52; Case No. SK 11/12 (n 99); Judgment of 14 December 2010, Case No. K 20/08 OTK-A 2010, No. 10, Item 129.

[183] Judgment of 25 July 2012, Case No. K 14/10 OTK-A 2012, No. 7, Item 83. In this case, the purpose of the challenged provision was to ensure trust in professions of public trust. The Tribunal accepted it as a legitimate aim with reference to Article 17 of the Constitution. See also Judgment of 18 July 2012, Case No. K 14/12 OTK-A 2012, No. 7, Item 82 with the reference to Article 11 of the Constitution.

[184] Judgment of 5 November 2013, Case No. K 40/12 OTK-A 2013, No. 8, Item 120. In this case, the Tribunal emphasized that in conditions of economic recession, the state may need to adjust the scope of implementation of social rights to economic conditions. The Tribunal, however, stated in another decision : 'The constitutional value of budgetary equilibrium may not legitimize restrictions of rights and freedoms in situations where the threat to budgetary equilibrium lies not so much in the exercise of those rights and freedoms by individuals, but as a consequence of the legislative actions taken in violation of that equilibrium.' Case No. Kp 1/12 (n 16).

determining state liability for repressions against persons involved in the struggle for independence.[185] Other examples include 'stability of public finances' and 'stability of credit and deposit institutions' that are accepted as legitimate grounds for limitations imposed on the right to social insurance[186] and freedom of association.[187] In any case, all aforementioned interests could be linked with the public order or the protection of rights of others and thus pass the legitimate aim test on these grounds.

The Tribunal's practice of applying the legitimate aim test shows that there is correlation between a narrow interpretation of the categories of legitimate grounds and a failure at this stage. In all eight cases in which the failure at the legitimate aim test occurred due to their inability to meet a enumerated legitimate aim, the interpretation of legitimate aim test was executed very restrictively. In these cases, the Tribunal refused to consider some public interests as contingent to public order or rights of others.[188] There is also a pattern in the fact that in six out these eight cases, the law additionally failed on other grounds beside the legitimate aim test. This observation suggests that the Tribunal did not fully rely on the persuasiveness of the narrow approach to legitimate aims[189] and was particularly vigilant not to openly contest public reasons motivating the legislator.

### *B Establishing the Relationship between a Legislative Purpose and a Legitimate Aim*

#### (a) Legislative Purpose

Answering the question whether a limitation has a legitimate aim always requires the determination of the challenged law's legislative purpose. On this basis, the Tribunal may further examine the relationship between the legislative purpose and the catalogue of constitutional values justifying limitations of constitutional rights or freedoms. In practice, the determination of legislative purposes is central for the legitimate aim analysis.

[185] Judgment of 1 March 2011, Case No. P 21/09 OTK-A 2011, No. 2, Item 7.

[186] Judgment of 7 May 2014, Case No. K 43/12 OTK-A 2014, No. 5, Item 50.

[187] Case No. K 41/12 (n 54).

[188] For example, in the case concerning local spatial planning, the Tribunal did not declare that the equilibrium of local budgets (budgets of units of local self-government) falls into any of the categories justifying a limitation of property rights. Case No. K 50/13 (n 160).

[189] Case No. Kp 1/15 (n 160); Case No. K 12/14 (n 18); Case No. K 52/13 (n 160); Case No. K 44/12 (n 160); Case No. Kp 10/09 (n 160); Case No. K 8/10 (n 160).

It means that the outcome of the legitimate aim test depends on the specification of a purpose furthered by the challenged law.

The Tribunal uses two approaches to identify the purpose of the challenged law. According to the objective view, a legislative purpose is a purpose furthered by law which could be identified by an external observer as the real motive of a legislative action.[190] It can be derived from the content of the law and its actual or intended consequences. In contrast, the subjective view holds that the legislative purpose is provided by the legislator in the preparatory documents. The declared purpose of the law can primarily be found in a statement of purpose that needs to accompany any legislative draft.

According to the Rules of the Sejm, the statement of purpose is required to explain the need for a new regulation, its purpose, the actual state of law, the impact of the proposed legislation on the relevant field of law, as well as its anticipated social, economic, financial, and legal consequences.[191] The statement of purpose must additionally indicate whether or not the law requires funding from state or local budgets, provide guidelines for the delegated regulation, and explain whether or not the law is compatible with the European Union law. In the case of government bills, the statement of purpose must also present results of public consultations and inform about external opinions in the draft, particularly if the obligation to seek such opinions is explicitly specified in the law.

In case of doubts regarding the actual purpose of the law, the Tribunal determines the legislative aim according to the subjective test – on the basis of the preparatory documents, legislative history, and intentions of the legislator declared prior to the enactment of the law.[192] However, the Tribunal has not yet developed a consistent methodology for the examination of cases in which the specific legislative purpose of the challenged law is unknown or in which divergent legislative motives emerge from various sources.[193]

[190] Wojtyczek (n 62) 154.

[191] Rules of the Sejm, Article 34, Resolution of the Sejm of 22 July 1992 as amended, Official Journal of 2018, Item 729.

[192] Judgment of 23 November 2009, Case No. P 61/08 OTK-A 2009, No. 10, Item 150.

[193] On the motive-oriented judicial review see Wojciech Sadurski, 'Judicial Review and Public Reason' (2017) Sydney Law School Research Paper No. 17/38 <https://papers.ssrn.com/sol3/papers.cfm?abstract_id=2965225> accessed 21 June 2019.

In this context, it should be noted that the statement of purpose refers to the entire draft, which implies that the specific purpose of a challenged provision may actually remain unknown. For example, a provision introducing limitations of constitutional rights or freedoms may be added at a later stage of the legislative process (i.e. during the second reading or in the Senate). The reason for its proposal could differ from the overall purpose of the legislative draft. In such cases, the determination of a legislative purpose can follow throughout parliamentary debates. Still, it is quite frequent that the Tribunal remains in doubt when attempting to discern the specific purpose of the provision under review from all the preparatory documents, particularly when no specific reasons for the adoption of a particular provision (or its part) were reflected in the statement of purpose or discussed during the legislative process.[194]

In cases in which the law emerged from a complex parliamentary debate and political parties had conflicting views about its goals and content, the Tribunal is usually inclined to accept the purpose declared by the legislator.[195] Especially in divisive cases, the Tribunal avoids the examination of the actual purpose of the law or raising doubts in sincerity of the legislative intentions. In such cases, the Tribunal may, however, find the law unconstitutional on a different – formal or procedural – ground, in an attempt to escape the substantive review of proportionality criteria.

A case in point concerns the law prohibiting denigration of the Polish Nation, which was allegedly in breach of freedom of speech and academic research as well as the constitutional standards of law making.[196] The law under review was an amendment to the Criminal Code which was introduced in the context of a controversy related to the 'anti-Polish' publication of a book written by Jan T. Gross.[197] It was evident that criminal laws against authors revealing unpopular historical facts such as the involvement of Poles in the Holocaust would have a chilling effect. However, the Tribunal discontinued the proceedings with regard to the substantive grounds of the review and decided the case solely on procedural grounds. It found that a bill amending the Criminal Code should

[194] Judgment of 24 February 2010, Case No. K 6/09 OTK-A 2010, No. 2, Item 15.

[195] Judgment of 18 October 2010, Case No. K 1/09 OTK-A 2010, No. 8, Item 76.

[196] Case No. K 5/07 (n 140).

[197] The book described the massacre of the Jewish population of Jedwabne, a small town in Poland, by the Polish nationalist part of the population. Jan Tomasz Gross, *Sąsiedzi: Historia zagłady żydowskiego miasteczka* (Pogranicze 2000), translated as *Neighbors: The Destruction of the Jewish Community in Jedwabne, Poland* (PUP 2001).

have been adopted in a different legislative procedure, given the scope of legislative amendments introduced in the Senate. As a result, the Tribunal ruled that the challenged law violated constitutional provisions which set out the right to introduce a legislative draft and define the scope of competences of the Senate in the legislative procedure.[198] In this way, it avoided the assessment of the legislative purpose and the proportionality of the chosen means. Had the Tribunal decided the case on substantive grounds, it would have had to determine whether the legislator actually aimed to censor scientific works and target specific publications or authors. It would also have had to make a politically contentious decision as to whether or not the protection of 'historical truth' is a constitutional value that could justify restrictions of freedom of speech and academic freedoms.[199]

The Tribunal made use of a different strategy of avoidance in the totalitarian symbols ban case.[200] In this case, the Tribunal did not question the legislative purpose stated in the preparatory documents, and it thereby passed the legitimate aim test.[201] By advancing to the next stage of the analysis, the Tribunal implicitly accepted the position presented by the Speaker of the Sejm, who supported the law and argued that the impugned provisions were justified by the protection of a democratic legal order against the threat of Communism and Fascism as well as by the need to prevent the spread of racial hatred. The Tribunal refrained from deciding the case on the ground of the legitimate aim test but still declared the law unconstitutional for its lack of sufficient clarity required in criminal laws interfering with individual freedom. Again, in this case, the Tribunal avoided a head-on engagement with the politically controversial question of whether the abstract and general goals cited could be considered legitimate purposes for limiting freedom of speech.

### (b) Goals Unworthy of Constitutional Protection

It is striking that in the entire case-law of the Constitutional Tribunal, there is no definition or exemplary list of goals unworthy of constitutional

198 Polish Constitution, Article 118(1) and 122(2).

199 Aleksandra Gliszczyńska-Grabias and Anna Śledzińska-Simon, 'Victimhood of the Nation as a Legally Protected Value in Transitional States – Poland as a Case Study' (2016) 6 Wroclaw Review of Law, Administration, and Economics 45.

200 Case No. K 11/10 (n 23).

201 The Tribunal shortly referred to the statement of purpose included in the draft, recalling 'the painful memories of the Polish society of the Second World War, and the crimes of the Fascist and Communist regimes'.

protection. In fact, the Tribunal has never expounded the concept of illegitimate grounds or explicitly stated which legislative goals would be deemed illegitimate. It only repeatedly stated that any limitation of constitutional rights or freedom needs to be justified by a legitimate ground included in a relevant limitation clause. Consequently, legislative goals unrelated to the protection of constitutional values are generally not accepted as legitimate.[202]

In the Electoral Code case, for example, the Tribunal held that certain provisions regulating the size of electoral billboards and prohibiting broadcasting of paid electoral advertisements on television and radio interfere with freedom of political speech and are not justified by any legitimate grounds.[203] The challenged law was officially justified by the need to improve the quality of the political discourse and to rationalize spending of campaign money. The Tribunal, however, found these aims to not be sufficiently linked with any of the constitutionally protected values enumerated in the general limitation clause, including the broadest category of public order. The Tribunal considers such purposes as valid as long as they do not interfere in the scope of constitutional rights or freedoms. It accepted that they are legitimate, but required the legislator to choose different means to pursue them. Notably, in this case, a failure at the legitimate aim test was conclusive for the finding of unconstitutionality.

A failure at the legitimate aim test has the potential to be very controversial in ideologically divisive cases. There are at least two decisions (one of which was made before the Constitution of 1997 came into force) in which the Tribunal stated that the challenged law does not serve any legitimate ground, even though the legislator had explicitly defined the goal to be the protection of rights. The first example deals with the case of abortion on social (rather than medical) grounds, in which the majority rejected the argument that a limitation of the right to life of a foetus was justified by the protection of the private life of a pregnant woman.[204] The other case concerns the law prohibiting doctors from refusing medical treatment in 'other cases of urgency' beyond saving the life of a patient, thereby legally obliging doctors to perform an abortion.

[202] Judgment of 7 December 2010, Case No. P 11/09 OTK-S 2010, No. 10, Item 128; Judgment of 21 July 2009, Case No. K 7/09 OTK-A 2009, No. 7, Item 113; Case. Judgment of 9 July 2009, Case No. K 31/08 OTK-A 2009, No. 7, Item 107.

[203] Case No. K 9/11 (n 107).

[204] Case No. K 26/96 (n 18).

Again, the Tribunal rejected the argument of the law being justified as promoting the protection of health and privacy of women.[205]

In both cases, the Tribunal turned a blind eye to the evident conflict between constitutional rights and freedoms and completely disregarded the explicit purpose of the law at stake, which was to protect the health and private life of women. The Tribunal not only adopted its own subjective reading of the legislative purpose but also unduly limited the scope of constitutional protection of privacy. In the abortion case, the majority characteristically held that the law was not intended to protect the right to self-determination, but to preserve the social and material status of a pregnant woman.[206] By diminishing reasons for accepting abortion on social grounds, the Tribunal found that the protection of social and material well-being of pregnant women was not sufficiently important to justify a limitation of the right to life.[207]

These two decisions share a common characteristic: in both, the Tribunal pinpointed vague terms used by the legislator and held that the challenged provisions contravene constitutional standards due to lack of clarity. Referring to the principle of legislative specificity, the Tribunal ruled that the challenged provision, of carrying out abortion on 'social grounds' and denying medical treatment in 'cases of urgency' were characterized by a very high degree of generality. As a result, the Tribunal stated that it is impossible to 'determine the nature of the constitutionally protected values due to which the legislator decides to legalize a restriction of other constitutional values'.[208]

Ultimately, the Tribunal held that the use of such vague terms in provisions imposing limitations on constitutional rights and freedoms (the right to legal protection of the life of a foetus and the freedom of conscience of medical doctors) did not allow identifying the protected value justifying these limitations. Although the limitations imposed by the challenged provisions could be justified in some situations by the protection of constitutional rights of others, they could, due to their vagueness, also be applied in situations where rights or freedoms protected by the Constitution were not at stake.

[205] Case No. K 12/14 (n 18).

[206] According to the declared purpose, the aim of the law was to protect women's right to self-determination in reproduction matters. In contrast to the majority view, the dissenters argued that the Tribunal's interpretation of the legislative purpose distorted the purpose presented and discussed in the course of the legislative process.

[207] Case No. K 26/96 (n 18).

[208] Case No. Case K 12/14 (n 18).

### (c) Mixed Legislative Motives

In Poland, the problem of mixed legislative motives arose in cases concerning transitory measures adopted after the fall of the Communist regime in order to counteract its legacy and provide for transitional justice. In transitory democracies, it is typically acknowledged that punishing perpetrators of past atrocities may constitute a legitimate government aim.[209] However, this aspect of transition from a totalitarian past to democracy can pose a major challenge in the context of PA. Particularly, measures intended to serve the protection of the new constitutional order or rights of others can be motivated by political revenge and used to target political opponents.[210] In such cases the Tribunal had to determine whether the sole motivation of the law was political revenge or whether it was accompanied by additional valid objectives, such as the protection of state security and public order.[211]

Mindful of the political poignancy of such decisions, the Tribunal usually followed the tactic of judicial restraint and accepted officially declared purposes as legitimate grounds. This approach can be demonstrated in cases concerning the lustration law mandating disclosure of the Communist past in order to hold public offices. One should keep in mind that the lustration law in Poland did not punish Communist collaborators, but individuals holding public offices or seeking election or appointment to public offices who lied about their service in the Communist regime in a lustration declaration.[212]

209 Resolution 1096 (1996) on measures to dismantle the heritage of former communist totalitarian systems adopted by the Parliamentary Assembly of the Council of Europe on 27 June 1996 (23rd Sitting).

210 Case No. K 2/07 (n 40) point 1.

211 For example, the 2002 amendment to the Lustration Act was accompanied by a short statement of purpose, explaining that the stigmatization of collaborators is neither fair nor justified by the interest of the state. However, in the course of parliamentary work, deputies often invoked the interest of the state and the need to protect its security service from serious threats or even disorganization resulting from the disclosure of state secrets and the network of intelligence and counter-intelligence agents. The Speaker of the Sejm, participating in the proceedings before the Tribunal, admitted that the purpose of the law was to minimize the threat of blackmail against individuals running for or holding public offices. Judgment of 28 May 2003, Case No. K 44/02 OTK-A 2003, No. 5, Item 44.

212 See the Lustration Act of 11 April 1997 on the disclosure of work or service in state security authorities or the cooperation with them in the years 1944–90 of persons performing public functions, replaced by the Act of 18 October 2006 on the disclosure of information on the documents of state security authorities from the years 1944 to 1990 and the content of those documents, and the Act on the Institute of National Remembrance of 18 December 1998 in their amended versions.

In one of the lustration cases the Tribunal found that the penalization of the 'lustration lie' served the principle of transparency of public life and the right of others to obtain information on the activities of organs of public authority as well as persons discharging public functions.[213] The Tribunal acknowledged that a past collaboration with the Communist regime is morally neutral in a democratic regime, but there are valid reasons as to why public servants should reveal the fact of their collaboration with secret security organs as a condition for admission to public office. In this context, the Tribunal held that the aim (and effect) of the Polish lustration law was not to stigmatize Communist collaborators, but rather to provide transparency of public life.

In another case concerning old-age pension benefits for former security officers, the Tribunal found the reduction of their privileges to be legitimate. The challenged law reduced the level of benefits for former security officers to the average level in the universal social security system.[214] Referring to the official statement of purpose, the Tribunal found the acquisition of the old-age pension benefits of former security service officers to be unjustly acquired. Thus, according to the majority opinion, the goal of the challenged law was to restore lawfulness rather than to seek political revenge. The majority did not accept the argument of the applicants (a group of MPs), who suggested that the stigmatizing and retaliatory character of the law was evidently laid down in the legislative preamble. In consequence, the majority refused to review the legislative preamble of the challenged act and instead focused on its specific provisions.

For the dissenting judges, however, the review of the preamble was necessary in order to expose the illegitimate motives of the legislator and to further examine the relationship between the act and its goals. The preamble stated that officers of state security had profited from numerous legal and material benefits while simultaneously supporting an inhumane system of government. According to the applicants, the legislator falsely assumed that all former officers were involved in violations of human rights of the Communist regime, while in fact many had duly passed the verification procedure and were admitted to public service after 1989. One of the judges dissenting, Ewa Łętowska, argued that the genuine purpose of the law was to collectively punish former security officers because the scope of the law was broader than the aim of the law

[213] Judgment of 21 October 1998, Case No. K 24/98 OTK 1998, No. 6, Item 97.
[214] Case No. K 6/09 (n 194).

required.[215] In her view, the legislator unjustly assumed that serving the totalitarian regime could in and of itself be a legitimate reason for pension reduction, which serves as an explanation as to why the law was also applied to categories of former security officers who were not involved in any unlawful activities of the Communist regime. Nevertheless, the majority in this case was satisfied with the proportionality of the law, since pensions of former security service officers remained higher than pensions within the universal social security scheme.

### (d) Administrative Efficiency and Procedural Economy

Administrative efficiency and procedural economy are generally accepted as legitimate grounds justifying limitations of constitutional rights or freedoms. Nevertheless, in order to pass the legitimate aim test, the law may not exclusively serve the interest of state officials (reducing their organizational effort).[216] This view follows the scholarly opinion according to which limitations of constitutional rights and freedoms may only be introduced in the public interest, and not solely in the interest of the government or public administration.[217]

In the analysed case-law, administrative efficiency was accepted as a legitimate aim as long as the Tribunal could identify at least one other relevant legitimate ground, such as the protection of public order or rights of others.[218] In case of doubts as to whether the law should actually pass this stage, the Tribunal preferred to scrutinize legislative aims at the later stage of the PA. It thus sought 'stronger' reasons related to the means of declaring the law unconstitutional.

In several decisions which concerned laws that aimed to enhance effectiveness of the administration of justice by improving the procedural economy of court proceedings,[219] the Tribunal ruled that limitations of the right to access a court or the right to an adequate court procedure could be generally justified by the principle of procedural formalism.[220] In this context, the Tribunal explained that swift and efficient court proceedings are necessary to secure the effective protection of individual

[215] ibid, dissent by Judge Łętowska.

[216] Judgment of 20 November 2002, Case No. K 41/02 OTK-A 2001, No. 6, Item 83.

[217] Szydło (n 123) 22. See Constitutional Tribunal, K 44/12 (n 161) or P 11/12 (n 99).

[218] Judgment of 30 October 2012, Case No. SK 8/12 OTK-A 2012, No. 9, Item 111.

[219] See Judgment of 28 April 2009, Case No. P 22/07 OTK-S 2009, No. 4, Item 55; Judgment of 22 September 2009, Case No. P 46/07 OTK-A 2009, No. 8, Item 126; Case No. K 1/09 (n 195).

[220] Case No. SK 8/12 (n 218).

rights guaranteed by the Constitution.[221] However, it additionally emphasized that these aims should solely be achieved by means that do not excessively limit constitutional rights.[222] In other words, speedy proceedings can only be accepted as a legitimate reason if the means used to further such purpose are proportional.[223]

In contrast, speedy proceedings could not be used as a reason to entirely bar access to court. Moreover, the Tribunal has held that procedural formalism as a condition of effective and fair court proceedings needs to be interpreted in the light of the right to a fair trial. The effectiveness of court proceedings may thus not be achieved by means that deprive individuals of the right to a fair trial.[224] As the Tribunal explained, '[s]implification and acceleration can certainly relate to formal issues (i.e. the introduction of forms and shorter deadlines for appeals), but (. . .) cannot refer to the rights of the parties enabling the defense of their rights and interests'.[225]

## VII Suitability

The suitability test requires that the rights-restricting measure meets the standard of instrumental rationality. The Tribunal is required to determine at this stage whether, based on the available knowledge, the adopted law exhibits the ability to bring about the intended results.[226] The view laid down in scholarly literature is that the Tribunal uses the suitability test in a modest manner, limiting its intervention to rare cases of drastic violations of the rational legislator axiom.[227] That said, some scholars have vigorously encouraged the Tribunal to increase its use of the

221 Judgment of 22 October 2013, Case No. SK 14/11 OTK-A 2013, No. 7, Item 101.

222 See also Case No. K 4/10 (n 15). In this case, the Tribunal upheld a special regime for road investments which excluded the right to seek invalidity of a permit for the realization of road investment in courts.

223 Case No. SK 8/12 (n 218). The Tribunal held that provisions providing for the rejection of an appeal without requesting rectification of formal defects do not alone violate the principle of procedural justice, but should be considered as unconstitutional due to their excessiveness in the view of other rules disciplining the parties to the proceedings. In this context, the Tribunal pointed out that the establishment of such formal requirements for filing an appeal is an indirect violation of the right to a fair trial, making it excessively difficult to carry out.

224 Case No. SK 22/11 (n 162); Case No. SK 20/11 (n 162).

225 Judgment of 27 October 2015, Case No. K 5/14 OTK-A 2015, No. 9, Item 150.

226 Case No. P 61/08 (n 192).

227 Szydło (n 123); Marek Szydło, *Wolnosc dzialalnosci gospodarczej jako prawo podstawowe* (Branta 2011) 198–201.

suitability test since it includes considerations that seem more objective than those underlying the necessity and proportionality in the strict sense tests. By striking down the law at the suitability stage, the Tribunal could avoid an open contestation of value choices made by the legislator and ultimately enhance the legitimacy of its final decisions.[228]

Contrary to the assumption found in the scholarly literature, 17 per cent of all failed cases included failure at the suitability stage in the analysed period. However, in several of these decisions, the suitability examination leading to failure was based on reasons that extended beyond the narrow definition of the suitability test. Some cases included reasoning regarding the legitimate aim, while others focused on the problem of overbreadth of the means in relation to a specific, narrowly defined aim of the law. Moreover, a failure at the suitability stage was the sole ground for the final outcome of the Tribunal's analysis in only three of the examined cases.[229] In the remaining cases the analysis continued after this failure, with the law failing on additional grounds. This practice reveals that the Tribunal does not consider a failure at the suitability stage as sufficient on its own to declare the law unconstitutional.

Finally, the Tribunal often fails to even address the suitability stage. In 23 per cent of all cases in the analysed period the Tribunal skipped this stage. In these cases the Tribunal merely presumed that the means are suitable to the aims and continued its analysis.

### *A The Presumption of a Rational Legislator*

The presumption of legislative rationality is particularly important for the suitability analysis. The point of departure in the assessment of suitability is that the legislator does not act in an irrational manner. Building upon this presumption, the Tribunal has repeatedly stated that it does not consider itself sufficiently competent to review the desirability or relevance of legislative solutions unless they are contrary to the Constitution or contradict the rule of law.[230] Only means that thwart the realization of the legislative purpose or are not related thereto fail the

[228] Wojtyczek (n 62) 157.

[229] Judgment of 20 January 2015, Case No. K 39/12 OTK-A 2015, No. 1, Item 2; Judgment of 14 February 2012, Case No. P 17/10 OTK-A 2012, No. 2, Item 14; Judgment of 10 July 2012, Case No. P 15/12 OTK-A 2012, No. 7, Item 77.

[230] Judgment of 24 October 2000, Case No. K 12/00 OTK 2000, No. 7, Item 255; Judgment of 26 July 2012, Case No. P 13/11 OTK-A, No. 6, Item 67 referring to Judgment of 17 May 2005, Case No. P 6/04 OTK-A 2005, No. 5, Item 50; Case No. K 11/94 (n 68).

suitability test,[231] whereas the adopted means may pass the suitability test even if they serve the legislative purpose only partially.[232]

In practice, the presumption of a rational legislator is strengthened by certain procedural rules regarding the burden of proof that are applied in the constitutional review proceedings, adopting the adversarial model of civil procedure. In this model, the onus falls on the subject challenging the law to prove the law's unconstitutionality.[233] In order for the subject challenging the law to prove that the law fails the suitability test, it needs to refute the double negation implying that the Parliament has not acted irrationally.[234] Such allocation of the burden of proof acts in favour of the state, and in practice suitability of the means is not frequently challenged by petitioners. It is arguably more convenient for the subject initiating the review to focus on the issue of excessiveness.

### B Establishing Whether the Means Are Suitable

According to the scholarly literature, the assessment of suitability does not require the examination in practice of the actual effects of the law.[235] In fact, at the suitability stage, the Tribunal does not investigate whether the means actually achieved the legislative purpose. For the sake of the suitability analysis, the Tribunal instead chooses to presuppose an *ex-ante* perspective of the time of decision-making and asks whether it could have been reasonably presumed that the means could realize the legislative purpose at that point. Therefore, failures at the suitability stage are based on an underlying flaw in common sense leading to ineffectiveness

231 Case No. P 61/08 (n 192).

232 Szydło (n 123) point 113.

233 Some scholars and even dissenting judges argued, however, that in cases concerning limitations of constitutional rights and freedoms, the burden of proof should be shifted to the organ that promulgated the impugned law. Krzysztof Wojtyczek, 'Ciężar dowodu i argumentacji w procedurze kontroli norm przez Trybunał Konstytucyjny' (2004) 1 Przegląd Sejmowy 22; Kazimierz Działocha, 'Prawa i wolności jednostki i obywatela' in Artur Preisner and Tomasz Zalasiński (eds), *Podstawowe problemy stosowania Konstytucji RP* (University of Wroclaw 2005) 122–23. See the dissenting opinion of Judge Andrzej Mączyński, Judgment of 16 April 2002, Case No. 23/01 OTK-A 2002, No. 3, Item 26; of Judge Zdzisław Czeszejko-Sochacki, Case No. K 26/96 (n 18).

234 See the dissenting opinion of Judge Stanisław Rymar who claimed that the proceedings concerning the tax-free amount should be discontinued due to the inability of the review-initiating subject to prove that the means chosen by the legislator are irrational and thus in breach of the right to social minimum. Constitutional Tribunal, Case No. K 21/14 (n 8).

235 Wojtyczek (n 62) 154–56.

or counter-effectiveness rather than an empirical analysis of the law's actual effects.

In the analysed period, the Tribunal held that the law under review failed the suitability test in ten cases. In these cases, the Tribunal either found the means to not serve the aims of the law or to run counter to these aims.[236] In the case concerning forfeiture of assets that did not belong to the offender used to commit certain crimes, the Tribunal stated that the means served neither crime prevention nor punishment of the offender, instead punishing the owners of assets who could not have foreseen that they would be used to commit a crime.[237] Similarly, the Tribunal found that the introduction of student fees for admission to second-degree studies does not forward the goal of expanding the availability of full-time studies at public universities.[238]

At times the Tribunal has even gone so far as to find that the means actually thwarted the realization of the legislative aim. In the case concerning real estate and mortgage division, the Tribunal found that the adopted means did not improve the legal situation of creditors, but rather had the opposite effect: the real estate and mortgage division made the execution of debt more problematic and increased the financial burden. The Tribunal questioned the logic of a limitation imposed on property rights of debtors and furthermore found the means unsuitable to serve the protection of the property rights of creditors.[239]

In a number of cases, failure at the suitability stage is based on a finding of overbreadth, which implies that the overbroad segments of the provision are not rationally connected to the goal. One such example is the case concerning the power of the Supreme Chamber of Control to process sensitive data.[240] The Tribunal ruled that certain sensitive data (such as related to health, criminal convictions, judicial decisions, and fines or membership in various parties and organizations) are essential for the realization of the constitutional mandate of this body. However, other types of sensitive data (concerning political, religious or philosophical beliefs, genetic code, addictions, or sexual life) were found unrelated

[236] Judgment of 28 October 2015, Case No. SK 59/13 OTK-A 2015, No. 10, Item 162; Case No. U 5/13 (n 99); Case No. SK 11/12 (n 99); Case No. P 11/12 (n 99).

[237] Case No. SK 59/13 (n 236).

[238] Case No. K 35/11 (n 99).

[239] Case No. P 15/12 (n 229). The Tribunal also noted that during the suitability test, the horizontal conflict between the challenged law and other statutory provisions defining the mortgage needs to be taken into consideration.

[240] Case No. K 39/12 (n 229).

to the realization of the body's function and therefore failed to fulfil the suitability requirement.[241] Another example concerns the conscience clause case, in which the Tribunal found that the duty imposed on medical doctors to inform patients about the availability of 'sensitive' medical services (such as abortion) in other publicly funded health care institutions was 'inadequate' to achieve the law's aim, namely to ensure the timely provision of medical care to patients.[242] The Tribunal argued that it could not be rationally presumed that individual doctors would have such sensitive information at hand at all times and that consequently, the challenged provision did not facilitate the timely delivery of medical services.

### C *The Role of Evidence in the Suitability Stage*

In practice, the Tribunal assesses the suitability of the means on the basis of a common sense standard, rather than on the basis of an empirical evaluation of the policy's effectiveness. This common sense standard was applied with regard to such means as temporary arrest, expropriation, court fees, or criminal sanctions; all of which are legal means. Therefore, the Tribunal could rely on its own legal expertise to assess their suitability.[243] Clearly, the Tribunal did not need to examine scientific evidence to find that court fees can be rationally used to improve efficiency of the administration of justice.[244]

Sometimes, however, the Tribunal does need to rely on other sources of knowledge than its own expertise. When confronted with such cases, the Tribunal has requested additional information from respective authorities or admitted evidence presented by parties in the proceedings.

[241] For an additional example, see Judgment of 22 October 2013, Case No. SK 14/13 OTK-A 2013, No. 7, Item 100.

[242] Case No. K 12/14 (n 18).

[243] For example, the Tribunal accepted that criminal sanctions are suitable to prevent construction works without a building permit or prior notification despite the lack of further proof that such sanctions would be effective. Judgment of 9 October 2012, Case No. P 27/11 OTK-A 2012, No. 9, Item 104.

[244] Case No. P 11/10 (n 182). In this case, the Tribunal found that the law foreclosing exemptions from court fees in bankruptcy proceedings was reasonable in the light of the duty of care, which requires that a motion for the declaration of bankruptcy is filed when the company still avails of sufficient funds to cover court fees. In another case, however, the Tribunal stated that court fees are suitable to prevent manifestly ill-founded claims, but deemed them unconstitutional only because of alleged excessiveness. Case No. SK 12/13 (n 53).

These included generally available data, statistics, reports, or expert opinions.[245] One example is the Aviation Act decision that concerned the permissibility of shooting down a passenger aircraft in the event of danger and threat to state security.[246] A central point in the case was whether the legal regime laid out in the Aviation Act would actually enable the protection of state security against threats posed by a hijacked civilian aircraft. In particular, it was disputed whether there would be sufficient time to meet the procedural requirement set forth in the Aviation Act and shoot down the aircraft in a timely manner. The Minister of Defence presented a hypothetical calculation of the flight duration of a civilian aircraft over the territory of Poland and the response time of the Polish air defence forces before the Tribunal. Although the Minister did not agree on the law being unconstitutional, he conceded that in some situations, it would practically be impossible to take timely action. In addition, the President of the Civil Aviation Office noted that due to the lack of experience in this area and the complexity of accessing information about the situation of the hijacked aircraft, it would not be possible to assess the time constraints of a decision to destroy it. Based on this information, the Tribunal found that a decision to shoot down a civilian aircraft hijacked by terrorists was unsuitable to attain the legislative aim, since due to time constraints it would not be effective in most Polish airports. In particular, the Tribunal established that there would be no time to initiate the required procedure if a hijacked aircraft took off from one of the Polish airports and the intention of terrorists was to hit objects in its close proximity.[247]

## VIII Necessity

It is imperative to distinguish the necessity test as an element of the PA from the necessity criterion that is explicitly mentioned in the limitation clause. The general limitation clause stipulates that the legislator may only establish restrictions of constitutional rights and freedoms that are necessary in a democratic state for the protection of specific constitutional values enumerated therein. The Tribunal refers to the

[245] See, e.g., Judgment of 9 July 2009, Case No. SK 48/05 OTK-A 2009, No. 7, Item 108; Judgment of 16 October 2014, Case No. SK 20/12 OTK-A 2014, No. 9, Item 102; Case No. SK 55/13 (n 35).

[246] Case No. K 44/07 (n 23).

[247] However, the Tribunal did not terminate its analysis after a failure at the suitability stage, but went on to find that the law was also necessary and disproportionate in the strict sense.

broad concept of necessity entailed in the limitation clause as a proxy of the PA.[248]

The broad criterion of necessity entailed in the limitation clause includes the more narrow criterion of necessity (in addition to suitability and proportionality in the strict sense).[249] The narrow criterion of necessity is used to determine whether a specific legislative goal could be achieved through the use of alternative, less restrictive means than the means initially chosen by the legislator.[250] There is thus broad agreement that the Tribunal should consider whether goals pursued by the legislator can be achieved by equally effective but less burdensome means from the perspective of the individual.[251]

In the light of the quantitative data, the necessity stage appears to be a significant hurdle for laws scrutinized using the proportionality test. In the analysed period, 46 per cent of all failed cases, or 27 cases, failed the necessity test. At the same time, the necessity test was most commonly relied upon jointly with the strict proportionality test to justify outcomes of failure, with such joint failures appearing in 18 cases, which make up 30 per cent of all failure cases. In these instances, the Tribunal carried through the analysis to the last stage, notwithstanding a failure at the necessity test. Overall, it was extremely rare that the Tribunal relied solely on the necessity stage in order to justify striking down a law. In 25 cases, which make up 93 per cent of all cases that failed to pass the necessity test, the scrutinized law failed to pass at least one further proportionality subtest in addition to the necessity test.

Another phenomenon putting the role of the necessity test into perspective is the act of skipping the necessity stage. Throughout the analysed period, the Tribunal skipped this test in 18 cases, suggesting that it did not expect the necessity test to make a relevant contribution to almost one fifth of all cases in the database. Overall, it seems that the necessity test is rarely applied as a sole basis for the justification of failure, but rather as a supporting stage; either by elaborating on the topic of overbreadth to strengthen failures resulting from the suitability stage[252]

[248] Szydło (n 123) 109.

[249] Case No. Kp 1/05 (n 106) or Case No. P 46/07 (n 219). It is sometimes even referred to as 'necessity in the strict sense'. Szydło, 'Komentarz do art. 31' (n 123) 109.

[250] Case No. P 56/11 (n 65).

[251] Judgment of 11 April 2000, Case No. K 15/98 OTK 2000, No. 3, Item 86.

[252] Case No. Kp 1/15 (n 160); Case No. K 50/13 (n 160); Case No. K 44/12 (n 160); Case No. Kp 10/09 (n 160); Case No. K 12/14 (n 18); Case No. K 8/10 (n 160); Case No. SK 14/13 (n 241).

or by introducing a failure which is then finalized at the final proportionality review.

### A *The Formulation of the Necessity Test*

In the very first decision that introduced the concept of the PA, the Tribunal framed the necessity test in relation to the question of whether the impugned law is indispensable for the protection of the public interest it aims to pursue.[253] The Tribunal explained that the necessity stage entails the least restrictive means test, contemplating whether there are any less restrictive means that could serve the legislative purpose equally well. Since then, in its practice, the Tribunal seems to have developed two different approaches to the necessity stage. According to the standard interpretation approach, the Tribunal starts by asking whether a limitation is necessary to attain a legislative aim before it moves to the least restrictive means test. In those cases, the process at the necessity stage includes an examination of alternative solutions serving the same legislative goal and an investigation as to whether there are equally effective, but less restrictive means.[254]

In the second approach, however, the Tribunal only asks whether the means are necessary to protect a specific constitutional value to which the legislative aim is related.[255] This version of the necessity test does not add any substantive requirements to the legitimate aim test. In fact, it equates the necessity test with the broad criterion of necessity entailed in the limitation clause and avoids the comparison to alternative means.[256] This

[253] Case No. K 11/94 (n 68). See also: Case No. P 2/98 (n 106).

[254] See, e.g., Decision of 30 October 1996, Case No. K 3/96 OTK 1996, No. 5, Item 41; Judgment of 12 January 2000, Case No. P 11/98 OTK 2000, No. 1, Item 3; Case SK 52/05, 29 September 2008; Case No. K 30/07 (n 58); Decision of 5 February 2008, Case No. K 34/06 OTK-B 2008, No. 6, Item 265; Judgment of 26 March 2007, Case No. K 29/06 OTK-A 2007, No. 3, Item 30; Judgment of 20 February 2007, sygn. P 1/06 OTK-A 2007, No. 2, Item 11; Case No. P 10/06 (n 106); Judgment of 19 April 2005, Case No. K 4/05 OTK-A 2005, No. 4, Item 37; Case No. K 37/02 (n 7); Judgment of 29 June 2001, Case No. K 23/00 OTK 2001, No. 5, Item 124; Judgment of 3 October 2000, Case No. K 33/99 OTK 2000, No. 6, Item 188; Case No. K 13/98 (n 106).

[255] Case No. P 19/13 (n 159).

[256] A similar practice could be observed in the case-law of the European Court of Human Rights, which the Polish Constitutional Tribunal often follows. In the framework of the limitation analysis regarding Articles 8–11 of the European Convention of Human Rights, the ECtHR usually examines only two questions – whether an inference is justified by a 'pressing social need' and whether the national authorities struck a fair balance between the realization of public interest and the protection of individual rights

second approach can be found in cases in which a law is upheld as well as in cases in which it is struck down.[257] The existing case-law lacks clear criteria to determine which approach to the necessity test the Tribunal will take in a particular case. Consequently, the necessity test constitutes the least predictable stage in the proportionality framework.

### *B Comparison to Alternative Measures*

According to a common formulation of the least restrictive means test, a law will pass the test if there are no less restrictive means that could serve the legislative purpose equally well.[258] However, the Tribunal has not yet developed a consistent method of comparing alternative legislative solutions. Although the Tribunal has repeatedly instructed the legislator not to choose the most restrictive means available to serve the legislative goal,[259] it does not actually conduct an analysis of different potential means that serve the same legislative aim in order to determine the least restrictive option.

A recurring practice of the Tribunal that restricts the role of the necessity test is the strong emphasis it places on the determination of a specific aim of the challenged law. If the chosen measure and its alternative do not pursue identical legislative purposes, the Tribunal does not deem the measures to be comparable and therefore holds the adopted means as necessary. In one case, for example, the Tribunal's arguments highlighted a specific, narrowly defined legislative purpose of the challenged law, thus leading to the conclusion that such purpose could be furthered only by the means chosen by the legislator.[260] By focusing on a

or freedoms. In consequence, its analysis focuses on balancing rather than comparing alternative solutions.

[257] For examples of the outcome being intended to uphold the legislation, see Judgment of 25 October 2012, Case No. SK 27/12 OTK-A 2012, No. 9, Item 109; Case No. SK 31/10 (n 127); Case No. K 8/10 (n 160); Case No. K 6/09 (n 194). For examples of negative outcomes, see Case No. Kp 1/15 (n 160) or Case No. K 52/13 (n 160).

[258] In some cases, however, the Tribunal asked whether less restrictive solutions would be similarly effective for the realization of the legislative purpose. Case No. P 56/11 (n 65).

[259] Case No. K 29/06 (n 254).

[260] Case No. K 14/10 (n 183). In this case, the law under review provided for suspension of court enforcement officers in the case of their indictment for committing a criminal offence, even if unrelated to official duties. The Tribunal found that there are no alternative means that could effectively protect public confidence in persons who pursue professions of public trust. In this way, it assumed that public trust can be damaged not only by committing crimes related to official duties (suggested as less restrictive means) but also by crimes unrelated to official duties (means adopted by the legislator).

specific legislative purpose, the Tribunal actually limits the pool of measures that could be taken into account at the necessity stage.

In cases in which the Tribunal carried out a thorough analysis of alternative solutions, the law under review was compared to previously binding laws or draft laws pending in the legislative process. In such cases the Tribunal could also rely on scholarly opinions addressing the need for change in the regulatory regime or expressing criticism about the pending changes.[261] Less frequently, the Tribunal took foreign sources or divergent regulatory models used abroad into consideration. For example, in the case concerning the ministerial regulation deeming all HIV-positive persons ineligible for police service,[262] the Tribunal referred to the ILO Code of Practice on HIV/AIDS[263] to state that other means than a total employment ban (like transfers or reassignment to different positions) could be effectively used in order to prevent HIV/AIDS at the workplace.[264] In some other cases, however, the Tribunal rejected foreign solutions as unattainable[265] or too costly.[266]

Overall, the Tribunal usually does not comprehensively compare alternative legislative solutions to assess their restrictiveness.[267] Instead, such comparison is usually presented in the opening part of the Tribunal's

[261] Case No. K 44/12 (n 160) or Judgment of 25 November 2014, Case No. K 54/13 OTK-A 2014, No. 10, Item 114.

[262] Case No. U 5/13 (n 99).

[263] International Labour Organization, *An ILO Code of Practice on HIV/AIDS and the World of Work* (Geneva 2011) <www.ilo.org/wcmsp5/groups/public/—ed_protect/—protrav/—ilo_aids/documents/publication/wcms_113783.pdf> accessed 21 June 2019.

[264] In this case, the Tribunal also referred to decisions of international and foreign courts in employment cases where a dismissal from work solely on the basis of one's HIV-positive status was found an infringement of the right to protect private life.

[265] Judgment of 22 July 2014, Case No. K 25/13 OTK-A 2014, No. 7, Item 76 – arguments that were used in relation to the pseudonymization procedure.

[266] Case No. SK 55/13 (n 35). In this case, the Tribunal compared the Polish law to the Dutch and German models. It also compared the effectiveness of three consecutive regulatory regimes in Poland which were changed due to the increase in drug abuse and the ratification of international treaties. Finally, it compared criminal sanctions with a regime of administrative sanctions, finding that the latter could not be regarded as an alternative because it is based on the assertion of objective guilt. Nevertheless, the Tribunal used this argument in its signalizing decision calling for legalization of the medical use of marijuana. See Signalling Decision of 17 March 2015 relating to Case No. SK 55/13 of 4 November 2014, Case No. S 3/15 OTK-A 2015, No. 3, Item 39.

[267] It is rare that the Tribunal compares the adopted means to several alternative and less restrictive solutions. In the case concerning student fees, however, the Tribunal elaborated at length three alternatives that permit elimination of potential abuses inherent in the law under review. See Case No. K 35/11 (n 99).

analysis describing the challenged law in the broader legislative context and the history of its adoption. If the law under review is more restrictive than the previously binding law and if there were no significant reasons for change besides the convenience of public authorities, the Tribunal is easily persuaded that the new law is unnecessary.[268] In other cases, the consideration of less restrictive alternatives was conducted by comparing other statutory laws serving the same purpose.[269]

At times, the fact that the legislator did not even consider less restrictive means in the parliamentary work or debated them but rejected without a proper justification was used as an argument to deem the law unnecessary.[270] In the case concerning the rigorous demand for domicile on the territories left behind the Polish borders after the invasion on 1 September 1939 as a condition to receive compensation for lost property (the Bug River case), the Tribunal agreed that the legislative work on the challenged law provided additional arguments undermining the necessity of this premise. As revealed during the hearing of the Sejm's representative before the Tribunal, the adoption of the law had not been preceded by an analysis of the interwar provisions regarding the possibility of having several places of residence, and whether and how the differences between the past and current legal status would be reflected in the draft legislation was not considered. Moreover, the legislator did not adequately consider alternative ways of regulating the eligibility criteria and calculate their financial consequences for the state budget. The Tribunal noted that the assessment of the challenged law's impact was very brief – in fact, it made up less than three pages of the parliamentary print. On the basis of this, the Tribunal did not consider the adopted means to be the best suitable and thus found it unnecessary.

### C *Means Found Unnecessary*

Typically, the Tribunal finds means that could potentially be applied in an overbroad manner, and that cannot be justified by any constitutionally

[268] Case No. K 44/12 (n 160).

[269] Case No. Judgment of 11 December 2012, Case No. K 37/11 OTK-A 2012, No. 11, Item 133. In this case, the purpose of the law was to prevent obstructions of a criminal trial in case of a detained person. The challenged law that mandated the presence of a police officer during conversations of a detained person with the defence lawyer was compared to the law applicable to persons in temporary arrest where the presence of a police officer could be introduced only as an exception to the no-presence rule. Additionally, the Tribunal found that the challenged law violated international standards.

[270] Case No. K 35/11 (n 99); Case No. SK 11/12 (n 99).

protected values, as unnecessary.[271] A case in point concerned the absolute prohibition of telephone communication between a person detained pending trial and his or her defence lawyer.[272] While the prohibition served the purpose of preventing the obstruction of criminal proceedings, e.g., through encouraging the accused to give false testimony, the Tribunal stated that this prohibition was overbroad because in many cases, communication between a person detained and the defence lawyer was simply conducted to properly prepare the accused to participate in the upcoming proceedings. It went on to argue that it is thus not necessary for the protection of constitutional values enumerated in Article 31(3) of the Constitution. For this reason, the Tribunal found that such blanket prohibition could only be accepted as an exception to the rule, but not as a general rule applied to every case. The Tribunal went so far as to say that a law permitting individuals in temporary arrest to have access to their lawyer via telephone would, under certain conditions, most likely pass the necessity standard if the conditions were provided explicitly within the law.[273]

Another poignant example is the previously mentioned aviation case. In this case, the impugned law was held unnecessary because of the procedure to shoot down a plane hijacked by terrorists also being applicable to situations in which the attack only threatened material goods or the infrastructure. In such situations, taking the life of passengers would not be adequate to the claim of protecting the civilian population.[274] After determining failure at the necessity stage, the Tribunal continued its analysis and held the law to also be disproportionate when the procedure would be used to save human lives.

## IX Proportionality in the Strict Sense

### *A The Relationship between Strict Proportionality and the Previous Tests*

According to the quantitative analysis, the final stage of proportionality in the strict sense test is the most common ground for a means failure.

[271] Judgment of 28 July 2014, Case No. K 16/12 OTK-A 2014, No. 7, Case No. 78; Case No. K 19/11 (n 139); Judgment of 15 April 2014, Case No. SK 48/13 OTK-A 2014, No. 4, Item 40; Case No. K 25/13 (n 265).

[272] Case No. K 54/13 (n 261).

[273] In this case, the Tribunal also considered the challenged law in comparison with the legislative draft that permitted telephone communication of individuals in temporary arrest with the external world (not only with their defence lawyers) under certain conditions.

[274] Case No. K 44/07 (n 23).

Laws failed this stage in 35 out of all 59 failure cases, amounting to 59 per cent. The cases in which a law failed the proportionality in the strict sense stage can be divided into two categories. On the one hand, there are cases in which the judgment of disproportionality is exclusively based on a failure at the final stage. Out of all 35 cases that failed the proportionality in the strict sense stage, this was the case in 16 cases, or 46 per cent. On the other hand, 19 out of those 35 cases, or 54 per cent did not only fail the proportionality in the strict sense test, but also failed at another, earlier stage. In 14 out of those 19 cases, the Tribunal found that the law failed at both the necessity and proportionality in the strict sense stage. In four other cases, the law failed the suitability, the necessity, as well as the proportionality in the strict sense test.[275]

In the majority of cases in which the law failed at both the necessity and the strict proportionality stages, the arguments concerning the necessity test were not explicit or directly expressed. In such cases, the Tribunal usually did not carry out the least restrictive means test but noted either that another, less restrictive measure would pass the constitutional standard or that the prohibition provided in the law is not consistently used in the legal system. At times, the Tribunal implied the existence of a less restrictive means when it suggested a more adequate solution in the last stage of PA. In some of such cases, the law under review was introducing more restrictive rules to an existing legal framework, to which the Tribunal responded by implicitly referring to less restrictive means that were in place before the new rules became binding.[276] In cases in which the law failed at both of the final tests, the Tribunal generally tended to place a greater emphasis on arguments suggesting that the burden imposed on individuals is excessive in relation to the effects of the law at the strict proportionality test.

There were, however, a number of cases in which the law failed to meet both the necessity and the proportionality in the strict sense standards, with the Tribunal justifying its answers to each test meaningfully and to a similar extent.[277] The least frequent approach in the Tribunal's analysis was to conduct a thorough, well-reasoned examination of the necessity

[275] There was also a case in which the Tribunal held the law unsuitable and disproportionate in the strict sense. In these instances, the proportionality test was regarded as a sum of the proportionality criteria rather than their logical junction.

[276] Case No. K 52/13 (n 160).

[277] See Case No. K 1/14 (n 16) or Case No. SK 11/12 (n 99).

test resulting in a failure, followed by a shorter note on an inadequate balance between the competing interests.[278]

A characteristic feature of some of the cases failing at both the necessity and the strict proportionality stage is that on multiple occasions, the scrutinized law was struck down for overbreadth at the necessity stage and followed by a failure at the strict proportionality stage on the ground of excessiveness. In those cases, the law introduced automatically applicable limitations that did not leave room for exceptions or individualized decisions. The joint failure at the necessity and strict proportionality tests based on excessiveness appeared, for instance, in the case concerning penalization of stowaways. In this case, the law under review allowed carriers and controllers to order passengers travelling without a valid ticket to remain in a particular place and wait for the police regardless of whether they intended to run away, and to punish them if they disrespected this order. The Tribunal found that the challenged law was overbroad because it covered situations in which there was no evident risk for the transportation carriers to not be able to collect the due travel fee. On this ground, the Tribunal found that the law distorted the balance between the personal freedom of passengers and the property rights of carriers as it granted greater protections to the property interests of carriers than to the personal freedom of passengers. It also notably argued that the means it employed opened up the possibilities for abuse of powers.[279]

Another example is provided by the case concerning unconditional payment of court fees in the bankruptcy proceedings.[280] In this decision, the Tribunal emphasized that it is the legislator's role to specify premises upon which the debtor could be exempted from court fees. It noted that each situation of bankruptcy is different and therefore the legislator should not treat all debtors uniformly. On this basis, the Tribunal found that the law failed the necessity test. In the final step, it emphasized the excessiveness of the means, pointing to a more suitable solution, in which courts would be enabled to assess each situation individually whether a legal entity initiating the bankruptcy proceedings deserves to be exempted from court fees, according to clear and objective criteria set by the law. Such a solution would pass the strict proportionality test because it would allow courts to consider the individual situation of a

[278] Case No. K 35/11 (n 99).
[279] Case No. K 16/12 (n 271).
[280] Case No. P 11/10 (n 182).

debtor in each case, taking into account not only the fundamental value of the right to court in a democratic society but also economic risks which are inherently related to the economic activity it pursued.

In the four cases in which the law successfully passed the legitimate aims test but failed suitability, necessity, and proportionality in the strict sense, the Tribunal approached the proportionality test as a sum of these three criteria.[281] In these decisions, each stage of the proportionality test was specifically addressed. Remarkably, three out these four cases concerned statutory laws specifying the scope of social rights, falling within a category in which PA is not frequently applied. In the decision concerning social pension, the Tribunal declared that the measure under review is 'entirely irrational' since it contravenes the aim for which the law was adopted.[282] Its further analysis of the necessity and proportionality in the strict sense tests was significantly more concise. In the decision concerning a ban on accepting persons who carry infectious diseases or viruses (like hepatitis C, AIDS, or HIV) to serve in the police and fire service, the Tribunal first carried out a very detailed examination of the suitability test and then succinctly concluded that the arguments used to examine the suitability test also make the law fail on necessity and proportionality in the strict sense grounds.[283] In the decision on compensation for the property left behind the pre-WWII borders of Poland, the Tribunal focused its analysis on the necessity and proportionality in the strict sense tests but also meaningfully addressed the previous stages of PA.[284]

In the cases in which a failure occurred exclusively at the proportionality in the strict sense stage, the Tribunal predominantly struck down the law based on a critical assessment of the actual effects of the law. Notably, the arguments used at this stage are often related to problems with the legislative aim. For example, in one of such cases the last stage of the proportionality review revealed that the law was justified by a hypothetic reason of protecting the state budget instead of providing concrete financial calculations justifying the need to restrict constitutional rights.[285]

[281] Case No. K 35/11 (n 99); Case No. U 5/13 (n 99); Case No. P 11/12 (n 99); Case No. SK 11/12 (n 99).

[282] Case No. P 11/12 (n 99).

[283] Case No. U 5/13 (n 99).

[284] Case No. SK 11/12 (n 99).

[285] Case No. SK 21/09 (n 185). In this case, the Tribunal stated that a mere invocation of the threat to the budgetary balance of the state does not serve as a sufficient justification of a

Finally, it is interesting to remark upon the relationship between the strict proportionality test and the essential core clause. It is evident that the Tribunal's approach to the essential core clause differs from case to case. In five cases, the Tribunal addressed both grounds, finding the law proportionate as well as not infringing of the essential core. It is notable that all of these five cases concerned limitations of the right to property.[286] In other cases the encroachment upon the essential core of the right was sufficient to find the law unconstitutional. In such cases the Tribunal followed an absolute and abstract concept of the core.[287] Throughout the analysed period, there were three cases in which the Tribunal's decision to strike down a law was exclusively based on a violation of the essential core clause.[288] In these cases, the Tribunal abstractly defined which constitutionally protected elements made up the essential core. As a result, it found that the law was unconstitutional without conducting PA. In other cases, however, the Tribunal approached the essential core question only after the PA was completed. In these cases the Tribunal determined the essential elements of the right's core in relation to the circumstances of the concrete case.[289] Only in one case did the Tribunal find that the infringement was not only disproportionate but also an encroachment of the essential core of the right at stake.[290] In this case, the concept of the essential core served as a proxy of a very serious interference into the scope of rights, strengthening the argument for its disproportionality. However, there was another case in the analysed period in which the Tribunal held the means to be disproportionate, but later found it to not violate the

limitation of constitutional rights or freedoms. It is thus required that a reference to a precise calculation confirming the real threat to the state budget be made instead of generally revoking the right to compensation for unlawful deprivation of liberty. See also Judgment of 28 February 2012, Case No. K 5/11 OTK-A 2012, No. 2, Item 16.

[286] Judgment of 10 January 2012, Case No. SK 25/09 OTK-A 2012, No. 1, Item 1; Judgment of 6 December 2011, Case No. SK 3/11 OTK-A 2011, No. 10, Item 113; Judgment of 18 October 2011, Case No. SK 24/09 OTK-A 2011, No. 8, Item 82; Judgment of 19 May 2011, Case No. K 20/09 OTK-A 2011, No. 4, Item 35; Judgment of 5 May 2011, Case No. P 110/08 OTK-A 2011, No. 4, Item 31.

[287] According to the absolute concept of the core, there is an abstract definition, which is absolutely protected regardless of the circumstances. This approach allows judges to disqualify laws or policies under review without interfering with the PA.

[288] Case No. SK 20/11 (n 162); Judgment of 5 October 2015, Case No. SK 39/14 OTK-A 2015, No. 9, Item 140; Judgment of 31 July 2014, Case No. SK 28/13 OTK-A 2014, No. 7, Item 81.

[289] Case No. P 11/12 (n 99).

[290] Case No. SK 59/13 (n 236).

essential core of a constitutional freedom subject to a limitation.[291] This approach contradicts the Tribunal's official position considering that an analysis of such kind is superfluous if the law was already deemed disproportionate.[292]

### *B The Application of the Strict Proportionality Test*

The legal doctrine in Poland uses various formulations of what is implied by the strict proportionality test, at times referring to the proportionality of aims and means but occasionally also to the proportionality of limitation and its justification, or balancing between advantages and disadvantages, between costs and benefits, or more precisely between the impact of the challenged means on individuals and the society at large.[293]

In the Tribunal's case-law, the proportionality in the strict sense test is presented as a question of whether the effects of the challenged law remain in an adequate proportion to the burdens it imposes on individuals.[294] It requires the legislator to strike a fair balance between the sacrificed value (right or freedom) and the value it aims to protect. In order to satisfy this requirement, the legislator needs to optimize each of the colliding values to the highest degree possible. It is further acknowledged that the optimization exercise should not be based on abstract values, but take into account the concrete factual situations that fall into the scope of the law.[295]

A fitting example of this approach being applied is the case concerning the disqualification of individuals diagnosed as HIV-positive from police service.[296] While proportionality requires the optimization of both conflicting values, the legislator maximized public health, to the point where it had completely overridden the right to equal access to public service. The Tribunal concluded that the benefit to public health resulting from such a provision was statistically of insufficient significance and therefore could not outweigh the right to continue service in the police of a person subclinically carrying HIV.[297]

[291] Judgment of 14 December 2011, Case No. SK 42/09 OTK-A 2011, No. 10, Item 118.

[292] This position was affirmed in Case No. P 19/13 (n 159).

[293] Ewa Łętowska, 'Wprowadzenie do problematyki proporcjonalności' in Piotr Szymaniec (ed), *Zasada proporcjonalności a ochrona praw podstawowych w państwach Europy* (Wydawnictwo Państwowej Wyższej Szkoły Zawodowej 2015) 18.

[294] Case No. P 61/08 (n 192).

[295] Szydło (n 123) 122–35.

[296] Case No. U 5/13 (n 99).

[297] It is important to note, however, that the classic demonstration of weighing exhibited in this case is actually quite rare in the Tribunal's case-law.

In cases concerning conflicts between two rights the Tribunal typically assesses the importance of the one right and the extent of its limitation in relation to the importance of the other protected right and the extent of its restriction, all in the context of the concrete situation.[298] An example is provided by the case concerning the establishment of the central registry of bone marrow donors that caused a collision between the right to privacy of stem cell donors and the protection of life and health of persons in need of a bone marrow transplant.[299] The Tribunal found that the limitations on the rights to privacy and informational autonomy were limited, since registration as a bone marrow donor is both voluntary and revocable, and in addition the processing of personal data for the purpose of creating a central registry of donors was secure and confidential. Considering that the creation of a central register of bone marrow increased the possibility of finding suitable donors and significantly improved the chances of saving human life and health, the Tribunal found the establishment of a central registry of bone marrow donors to be proportionate.

When weighing the cost to the rights against the benefit, the Tribunal usually takes a broad perspective that looks beyond the specific provision under review. It therefore takes mitigating factors related to other legal provisions into account to determine the actual impact of the challenged law on individuals. It could, for example, be counted as a mitigating factor that individuals have the right to present their views regarding a limitation of constitutional rights or freedoms in courts. Thus, the existence of the possibility to pursue the protection of property rights in court favours the recognition that measures restricting the use of property are proportionate in the strict sense.[300] Similarly, in criminal law cases, the Tribunal found that rights limitations introduced by provisions criminalizing certain behaviours are mitigated by general provisions in the criminal code that, under certain circumstances, allow courts to renounce inflicting a punishment, discontinue criminal proceedings, or suspend the penalty execution. This was the Tribunal's approach in the case regarding the criminalization of cultivation and possession of cannabis,

[298] In cases concerning conflicts between rights, the last stage of the proportionality test is often the central focus of the Tribunal's analysis, a failure at this stage usually making up the sole ground of the Tribunal's decision.

[299] Case No. K 25/13 (n 265). Also see Judgment of 23 June 2015, Case No. SK 32/14 OTK-A 2015, No. 6, Item 84.

[300] Case No. SK 25/09 (n 286).

as well as in the case regarding the creation of a criminal offence of presidential insult, in response to arguments raised in both cases fearing that the provisions would also be applied in cases of very non-severe and insignificant behaviour.[301] It should be noted, however, that this approach did not always lead the Tribunal to uphold the law under review: at times, the Tribunal found that the negative potential effects of the law could be outweighed by procedural guarantees provided in other laws. For instance, the Tribunal did rule that the burden imposed by high statutory fees blocking access to courts in certain cases is not mitigated by the possibility of legal aid afforded to the needy.[302]

### C *The Prohibition of Excessiveness*

One of the central ideas in the application of proportionality in the strict sense is the prohibition of excessiveness. Some flaws that are characteristic in this context include the lack of availability of basic procedural guarantees, an insufficient number of safeguards against administrative abuse, as well as the inability to limit the application of a measure to exceptional situations.

One specific type of flaw that can lead the Tribunal to concluding that the law under review violates the prohibition of excessiveness, often in the context of property rights, is the lack of basic procedural guarantees allowing individuals to challenge the scope of the imposed limitations. In a case concerning hunting districts, for example, the Tribunal struck down the scrutinized law because the hunting district regime had overly restricted the rights of property owners. In particular, the Tribunal criticized that property owners were not sufficiently involved in the decision-making process, that they could not exclude their property from the hunting district regime under any circumstances, and that the law did not provide any exemptions from restrictions imposed by the hunting law. As a result, the Tribunal ruled that the legislator did not adequately balance environment and property protection concerns and thus found the burden imposed on citizens to be excessive.[303]

A second typical flaw leading to a finding of excessiveness is the lack of sufficient safeguards to prevent administrative abuse. The law is usually

[301] Case No. SK 55/13 (n 35); Judgment of 6 July 2011, Case No. P 12/09 OTK-A 2011, No. 6, Item 51.

[302] Case No. SK 12/13 (n 53).

[303] Case No. P 19/13 (n 159). Also see Case No. P 11/98 (n 254).

required to provide institutional and procedural safeguards that prevent arbitrary application, especially if the interference concerns personal liberty or privacy.[304] In exceptional cases, public authorities may be granted the very broad and nonspecific power to impose limitations on constitutional rights for the sake of law enforcement, but in such cases the legislator must establish an independent review process of the decisions made in pursuance of such law, as a control mechanism.[305]

The Tribunal's findings on procedural safeguards are often supported by references to the case-law of the European Court of Human Rights. A prominent example of this kind is the decision regarding data retention.[306] The Tribunal reviewed several provisions that enabled surveillance of telecommunication data in light of the standard established by the European Court of Human Rights, as well as the Court of Justice of the European Union and several European constitutional courts. It ruled that the Polish law under review did not comply with the given standard and found it disproportionate for failing to provide adequate safeguards against the potential abuse of power. The Tribunal pointed to some of the necessary requirements for the regulation of surveillance operations by law, including the establishment of an independent authority to review the legality of surveillance in individual cases, mechanisms to delete unlawful interception of data, and the destruction of data that had become irrelevant for the purpose of law enforcement.

Another example is the case concerning a five-year limitation period for re-opening civil proceedings.[307] The Tribunal held that such a limitation period violated the right to a fair trial as interpreted by the European Court of Human Rights. In particular, the Tribunal argued that this restriction was overly burdensome for individuals that had won their case in Strasbourg after the limitation period had expired. Additionally, it found the limitation to unduly obstruct the enforcement of judgments of the European Court of Human Rights.

[304] Judgment of 9 July 2012, Case No. P 8/10 OTK-A 2012, No. 7, Item 75, where the majority held that the adopted means were not excessive due to the courts' ability to reduce the amount of statutory sanctions, postpone their payment, or order exemptions, while the dissenting opinion argued that these procedural guarantees did not diminish the excessiveness of the law.

[305] Judgment of 20 April 2004, Case No. K 45/02 OTK-A 2004, No. 4, Item 30; Judgment of 12 December 2005, Case No. K 32/04 OTK-A 2005, No. 11, Item 132.

[306] Case No. K 23/11 (n 108).

[307] Judgment of 22 September 2015, Case No. SK 21/14 OTK-A 2015, No. 8, Item 122.

A third type of flaw that can potentially lead to a finding of excessiveness is when the application of the measure is not limited to exceptional situations.[308] For example, in the credit and loan cooperatives case, the Tribunal struck down a law that had not exempted small financial institutions from state supervision.[309] The Tribunal found that supervision over credit and loan cooperatives was only adequate when applied to big institutions, but excessive in regard to small ones. At the same time, the Tribunal upheld laws when evidence was brought to demonstrate that in practice, the law under review was applied only to exceptional cases. Proving this may lead the Tribunal to conclude that the means are not excessive. In the case concerning criminalization of Presidential insult, for example, the Tribunal relied on the fact that charges have only rarely been brought under the law and that the sanctions subjected by the law were relatively modest. Therefore, it held the law to be proportionate.[310]

However, in some cases, the Tribunal used a strategy of aggregating several constitutional values for justifying the limitation of a right, thus bolstering their importance. This can be problematic in cases concerning the most important constitutional rights or freedoms, such as freedom of speech. In these cases, the Tribunal first accepted that the law serves the protection of several constitutional values in the legitimate aim stage, and later found that their aggregated value prevails over the value of a constitutional right subject to limitation in the final stage of PA.[311] In the Presidential insult case, the Tribunal reviewed criminal provisions which penalized insulting of the President, and thus could have a chilling effect. Nevertheless, the Tribunal decided that the law is proportionate, since it was justified by important reasons. By stating so, it considered the aggregated value of the legitimate aims it found, including rather abstract ideas such as the dignity of the Presidential office.

Similarly, in a case concerning criminal sanctions in the Press Law for journalists who did not receive authorization for an interview or a press article with directly cited statements,[312] the Tribunal conceded that the duty to receive authorization not only protects rights of others (referring to the interviewee) but also the public in general (in reference to the

[308] Case No. SK 3/12 (n 152); Case No. P 21/09 (n 185).
[309] Case No. K 41/12 (n 54).
[310] Case No. P 12/09 (n 301). Also see Case No. SK 70/13 (n 77).
[311] Case No. SK 65/12 (n 154); Case No. P 12/09 (n 301).
[312] Judgment of 29 September 2008, Case No. SK 52/05 OTK-A 2008, No. 7, Item 125.

readership). In this context, the Tribunal explained that authorization of directly cited statements is essential to guarantee others the right to reliable, truthful, fair, clear, non-deceiving, and accurate information. It further agreed that the duty to obtain authorization increases the authenticity of public debate. Moreover, the Tribunal noted that the scope of legislative interference in freedom of speech was relatively narrow because journalists could freely paraphrase what interviewees said without the need to obtain authorization. In contrast, according to the dissenting judges in this case, the impugned provision was not sufficiently justified by reasons of importance.[313] Arguing that the legislator wrongly assumed that all directly cited statements are libellous and may fall in conflict with rights of others, the dissent found the law to be overbroad as it required authorization of all interviews, regardless of their content.

## X Overview of the Means Struck Down

This section provides a general overview of the measures that were struck down by the Polish Constitutional Tribunal as a result of its PA. The Tribunal has struck down laws that imposed limitations on constitutional rights or freedoms but could not be justified by the protection of any constitutionally endorsed values.[314] Typically, a law, or at least part thereof, failed the legitimate aim test if its purpose could not be tied to any narrowly interpreted value enumerated in a relevant limitation clause.[315] Although the Tribunal has generally accepted administrative efficiency and procedural economy as legitimate aims, it has flatly rejected these aims as a justification for barring all access to courts.[316] The Tribunal has also struck down laws introducing means that, as it concluded, did not serve the legislative purpose, thwarted the realization of the legislative purpose or could not be rationally used to attain it.[317]

Furthermore, the Tribunal has struck down laws that introduced strict rules such as total bans on certain protected activities,[318] as well

313 Notably, the Tribunal did not conduct the least restrictive test in this case. It was the dissent suggesting that the protection of rights of others could be effectively achieved by less restrictive means, such as civil action for the protection of personal rights or the action for rectification of a publication.

314 Case No. K 50/13 (n 160); Case No. K 9/11 (n 108).

315 Case No. K 25/11 (n 162); Case No. K 39/12 (n 229); Case No. K 16/12 (n 271).

316 Case No. SK 20/11 (n 162).

317 Case No. U 5/13 (n 99).

318 Case No. K 52/13 (n 160).

as limitations on the compensation for unlawful deprivations of liberty.[319] Statutory fees[320] or sanctions for unlawful activities fall into the same category of excessive means[321] if the law did not permit exceptions or individualized decisions.[322]

The Tribunal has struck down laws that used both overbroad language and vague terms, since they provide the body applying the law with discretion that is too broad when interpreting the situations to which the rights restricting means should be used.[323] While recognizing that flexibility is essential for the effective operation of the state, it emphasized the importance of having the application of discretionary powers limited and subject to supervision.[324]

In some cases, the Tribunal found that the lack of detail in a statute regulating how public authorities can apply means restricting constitutional rights or freedoms could cause disproportionate outcomes, and on this ground deemed the law unconstitutional.[325] In this type of cases, the legislator's failure to provide specific criteria, conditions, or premises for the application of the challenged law in individual cases led to finding the means to be excessive.[326] In other cases, however, lack of sufficient clarity of the terms used in the challenged legislation led to a failure at the legitimate aim stage, since the Tribunal could not ascertain whether the means would indeed be applied only to cases justified by the necessity to protect constitutional values.[327]

The Tribunal has also struck down down laws that introduced overly restrictive limitations on individuals.[328] There are four scenarios of over-restrictiveness to be distinguished: first, the law stipulated that individuals may exercise their constitutional rights or freedoms on conditions

[319] Case No. P 21/09 (n 185).

[320] Case No. P 3/14 (n 139); Case No. P 11/10 (n 182).

[321] Case No. SK 32/14 (n 299). In this case, the law stipulated that compensation for violating economic copyrights equals triple royalty for using the work.

[322] Judgment of 1 July 2014, Case No. SK 6/12 OTK-A 2014, No. 7, Item 68; Judgment of 19 April 2011, Case No. K 19/08 OTK-A 2011, No. 3, Item 24.

[323] Case No. K 11/10 (n 23); Case No. K 37/11 (n 269).

[324] Case No. K 23/11 (n 108).

[325] Judgment of 20 May 2014, Case No. SK 13/13 OTK-A 2014, No. 5, Item 54. See also Case No. K 5/14 (n 225).

[326] Case No. K 25/13 (n 265). In this case, however, the Tribunal found that the law fails both the 'provided for by law' and the proportionality test.

[327] Case No. K 12/14 (n 18).

[328] Case No. SK 21/14 (n 307).

that are unfair or impossible to fulfil.[329] Second, the law introduced automatic limitations, leaving no room for exceptions.[330] The third scenario concerned laws of evident unfairness, either because they treat identical subjects differently[331] or because they treat differing subjects as the same[332] without creating customized rules to account for the differences.[333] Fourth, laws that failed to provide procedural guarantees enabling individuals to appeal against decisions restricting their constitutional rights or freedoms or to defend their position in courts.[334]

329 Judgment of 12 February 2015, Case No. SK 14/12 OTK-A 2015, No. 2, Item 15. In this case, the Tribunal found that preferential tariffs or exemption from excise tax should not depend on unfulfillable conditions. See also: Judgment of 14 July 2015, Case No. SK 26/14 OTK-A 2015, No. 7, Item 101. In this case, the law was excessively burdensome only with regard to previous co-owners of expropriated property as it made their claim inevitably dependent on co-operation of all previous co-owners or their legal successors.

330 Case No. P 11/10 (n 182).

331 Case No. SK 26/14 (n 329).

332 Case No. SK 8/12 (n 218). See also Case No. P 3/14 (n 319). In this case, the Tribunal held that a statutory fee for activities of court enforcement officers applying to all situations, and thus not treating debtors who voluntarily comply with the notice of eviction differently, was excessive.

333 Case No. K 41/12 (n 54).

334 Case No. P 19/13 (n 159).

# 6

# Limitation Analysis by the Indian Supreme Court

APARNA CHANDRA

## I Introduction

India shares many of the same normative commitments as other countries that use proportionality analysis (PA).[1] It also has a well-established practice of seeking justification for limitations of fundamental rights, with the judiciary routinely reviewing rights-limiting measures – both legislative and administrative. However, the Supreme Court's approach to evaluating justifications for rights limitations remains open to debate. Traditionally, common law has followed *Wednesbury* unreasonableness as the standard of judicial review, which permits the judiciary to strike down state action only on the ground of illegality, irrationality, and procedural impropriety.[2] Irrationality for the purposes of this standard implies that impugned action is so 'outrageous in its defiance of logic or of accepted moral standards that no sensible person who had applied his mind to the question to be decided could have arrived at it'.[3]

However, from the mid-1980s onwards, the UK House of Lords, under the influence of other European jurisdictions, started signalling that the *Wednesbury* standard might give way to the doctrine of proportionality.[4] Borrowing from these cases, arguments were raised in Indian courts about moving away from *Wednesbury* to the proportionality rule. It is in this context that Indian courts began engaging with the applicability of the doctrine of proportionality in India. In some cases, the Court has

[1] See Constitution of India 1950, Preamble resolving to constitute India into a 'Sovereign Socialist Secular Democratic Republic and to secure to all its citizens: Justice, social, economic and political; Liberty of thought, expression, belief, faith and worship; Equality of status and of opportunity; and to promote among them all Fraternity assuring the Dignity of the individual and the Unity and Integrity of the Nation'.

[2] *Associated Provincial Picture Houses Ltd v Wednesbury Corporation* [1948] 1 KB 223. The traditional *Wednesbury* review was confined to judicial review of administrative action.

[3] *Council of Civil Service Unions v Minister for the Civil Service* [1984] UKHL 9.

[4] ibid; *Regina v Secretary of State for the Home Department ex parte Brind* [1991] UKHL 4.

mentioned that its approach to fundamental rights analysis mirrors the PA.[5] In a few cases the Court's dicta also appears to traverse the same terrain of justification for rights limitations as proportionality.[6] In other cases, however, the Court has found this proposition debatable.[7] Scholars have also cautioned that the Court's invocation of proportionality to characterize its own approach is not only inconsistent but is also misplaced, at least in the sense that the term 'proportionality analysis' is invoked in other jurisdictions.[8]

In a recent series of cases such as *Modern Dental College and Research Centre v State of Madhya Pradesh*,[9] *Puttaswamy v Union of India (Right to Privacy)*,[10] and *Puttaswamy v Union of India (Aadhaar)*,[11] Constitution Benches of the Supreme Court have stated that a rights-limiting measure has to satisfy a structured proportionality test in order to be constitutionally valid. However, despite these pronouncements, the status of the proportionality test in Indian rights jurisprudence remains in doubt. This is because in subsequent judgments, the Supreme Court has failed to apply a structured proportionality test.[12] Further, the exact

[5] See, e.g., *Om Kumar v Union of India* (2001) 2 SCC 386; *Indian Airlines Ltd v Prabha D. Kanan* (2006) 11 SCC 67; *Teri Oat Estates (P) Ltd v UT, Chandigarh* (2004) 2 SCC 130; *Sahara India Real Estate Corporation Ltd v SEBI* (2012) 10 SCC 603; *MP Housing and Infrastructure Development Board v B S S Parihar* (2015) 14 SCC 130; *Modern Dental College and Research Centre v State of Madhya Pradesh* (2016) 7 SCC 353.

[6] See, e.g., *Chintaman Rao v State of MP* AIR 1951 SC 118; *V. G. Row v State of Madras* AIR 1952 SC 196; *Anuj Garg v Hotels Association of India* (2008) 3 SCC 1. See generally, Vivek Krishnamurthy, 'Proportionality in Indian Constitutional Law' March 2008 (unpublished manuscript, on file with the author).

[7] See e.g., *Tata Cellular v Union of India* (1994) 6 SCC 651; *State of Andhra Pradesh v McDowell & Co* (1996) 3 SCC 709; *Union of India v G. Ganayutham* (1997) 7 SCC 463 (leaving open the question of the applicability of proportionality to rights-limiting administrative action); *Chairman, All India Railway Recruitment Board v K. Shyam Kumar* (2010) 6 SCC 614.

[8] Abhinav Chandrachud, 'Wednesbury Reformulated: Proportionality and the Supreme Court of India' (2013) 13 Oxford University Commonwealth Law Journal 191; Prateek Jalan and Ritin Rai, 'Review of Administrative Action' in Sujit Choudhry, Madhav Khosla, and Pratap Bhanu Mehta (eds), *Oxford Handbook of the Indian Constitution* (OUP, 2016); Ashish Chugh, 'Is the Supreme Court Disproportionately Applying the Proportionality Principle?' (2004) 8 SCC (J) 33.

[9] *Modern Dental College* (n 5).

[10] (2017) 10 SCC 1.

[11] (2018) SCC Online SC 1642.

[12] See, e.g., *Navtej Johar v Union of India*, Writ Petition (Criminal) No. 76 of 2016 decided on 6 September 2018; *Joseph Shine v Union of India*, Writ Petition (Criminal) No. 194 of 2017 decided on 27 September 2018.

test to be followed is also a matter of doubt, with different judgments having laid down differing tests.[13] And finally, the judgments that do expressly recognize a structured proportionality test themselves do not adequately apply the test to the impugned state action in those very judgments.[14] These judgments have therefore added to the conceptual confusion around the nature of limitations analyses under the Indian Constitution.

[13] For example, in *Modern Dental* (n 5), a five-judge bench of the Court stated that 'a limitation of a constitutional right will be constitutionally permissible if: (i) it is designated for a proper purpose; (ii) the measures undertaken to effectuate such a limitation are rationally connected to the fulfilment of that purpose; (iii) the measures undertaken are necessary in that there are no alternative measures that may similarly achieve that same purpose with a lesser degree of limitation; and finally (iv) there needs to be a proper relation ('proportionality stricto sensu' or 'balancing') between the importance of achieving the proper purpose and the social importance of preventing the limitation on the constitutional right.'

Contrast this with the Right to Privacy case (n 10), decided by a bench of nine judges, where the plurality opinion prescribed a proportionality framework for limitations review of measures that infringe the right to privacy. It stated that any limitation on the right to privacy must meet the criteria of being authorized by law, pursuing a legitimate aim, and through a means that is proportional to the ends sought to be achieved by the law. However, in its conclusion, the opinion appears to revert to a more traditional reasonableness review, prescribing the three-fold criteria of legality ('existence of a law'), need ('a legitimate state aim'), and what the opinion calls proportionality, but describes as 'a rational nexus between the objects and the means adopted to achieve them'.

And finally, in the Aadhaar case (n 11), a five-judge bench of the Court stated that the proportionality test to be followed should require that '[f]irst, a range of possible alternatives to the measure employed by the Government must be identified. Secondly, the effectiveness of these measures must be determined individually; the test here is not whether each respective measure realises the governmental objective to the same extent, but rather whether it realises it in a "real and substantial manner". Thirdly, the impact of the respective measures on the right at stake must be determined. Finally, an overall judgment must be made as to whether in light of the findings of the previous steps, there exists an alternative which is preferable . . . '

[14] While the *Right to Privacy* case (n 10) did not require the Court to apply a limitation test to a specific measure, both *Modern Dental* (n 5) and the Aadhaar (n 11) cases did. In *Modern Dental*, after propounding the test, the Court did not apply the test to the facts of the case at all. In *Aadhaar*, though the Court did apply the test, the majority opinion, running into 567 pages, dealt with the necessity limb of the test in one short paragraph, and stated, in effect, that the necessity of the measure was satisfied because the components of legitimate aim and rational nexus between means and ends was satisfied and 'there is no alternative measure with lesser degree of limitation which can achieve the same purpose'. The Court did not engage with alternatives suggested by the Petitioners, as mentioned in other parts of the judgment. It is therefore unclear from the judgment how exactly this crucial limb of the test should be conducted.

So, what exactly is the Indian Supreme Court's approach to limitations analysis? Only by evaluating the Court's approach on its own terms, rather than through the lens of the practices of other countries, can one determine whether the practice is the same as, similar to, or different from that of countries that expressly follow the PA. To enable this comparison, in this chapter, I evaluate the Indian Supreme Court's practice of conducting limitations analyses. Based on quantitative and qualitative analyses of fundamental rights decisions, I argue that although the text of the Constitution and the Court in its interpretation have not formally established a single limitations structure for the various fundamental rights, the Court's practice does reveal a common structure of limitations analysis across rights.

In what follows, I first explain the legal and institutional context in which rights review takes place in India. Following that, in Part III I describe the Court's stated position on limitations analyses. Part IV then deconstructs the Court's approach to identify the distinct elements of the limitation analysis. I argue that this approach generally comprises three elements after limitation of the right is established: worthy purpose analysis, rational nexus analysis (which, at times, includes an element of narrow tailoring), and a general balancing between various interests at stake. I provide examples of what each stage of analysis can entail. Following on from this analysis, I discuss the relationship between the limitations analysis and the remedial strategies followed by the Court once it disapproves of a state action or omission. The final and concluding part provides an overview of the measures struck down.

A few methodological points are in order before I begin. My argument that the Court follows a common limitation analysis is based on deconstructing the Court's dicta and parsing through its doctrine. Therefore, this chapter goes beyond the Court's stated doctrine and objectives. Based on a qualitative and quantitative analysis of case-law, the chapter seeks to understand how in practice the Court evaluates state actions and omissions for compliance with rights.

Second, this limitation analysis does not follow a step wise analytical structure. Rather, I use the term to refer in a shorthand manner to the common elements that the court examines in its limitations analyses. The Court's analysis proceeds in a holistic manner, where the discussion and analysis of the various elements are blended together. For example, the Court might discuss the purpose of a law and the need for a particular measure in some detail, and on that basis come to a conclusion about whether or not the law is following a worthy purpose, the rational nexus between means and ends, as well as a general balance between the various interests at stake in adjudicating the constitutionality of the measure. The Court may not discuss all the elements in a given case, or discuss them in any particular order.

As I describe later, the Court is often criticised for inconsistencies and the lack of certainty in its dicta, its multiple approaches to standards of review, and the decisional flexibility retained by the Court in its decisions.[15] As such, it is important to note that the attempt here is not to impose uniformity on a discordant reality. This chapter should not be understood as saying that all the elements of the limitation analysis are present in all cases, or that there are no counterfactuals available. This chapter attempts to draw together the recurring themes in the Court's analysis and comes to the conclusion that despite textual and doctrinal differences, the practice of the court reveals a common approach to understanding limitations upon rights.

The analysis in this chapter is based on a combination of quantitative and qualitative analyses. The quantitative analysis is based on a database of 98 Supreme Court cases dealing with the question of limitation of the rights to equality (Article 14), fundamental freedoms (Article 19), and life and personal liberty (Article 21), from the years 2004–16. I focus on these rights since the Supreme Court has considered these to be the most important fundamental rights, has named them the 'Golden Triangle', and has stated that these rights 'stand above the rest'.[16] Since my main research objective is to understand how the Supreme Court conducts rights analysis, I have included in this database all cases where the Supreme Court analysed whether an Article 14, 19, or 21 right was limited or not, and if found to be limited, whether the limitation was valid. Therefore, the database includes cases where the court held, after analysis, that an Article 14, 19, or 21 right was not limited, as well as cases where the court found a right to be limited and analysed whether this limitation was valid.[17] It excludes cases where parties claimed the

[15] Pratap Bhanu Mehta, 'The Rise of Judicial Sovereignty' (2007) 18 Journal of Democracy 70; Nicholas Robinson, 'Structure Matters: The Impact of Court Structures on the Indian and US Supreme Courts' (2013) 61(1) American Journal of Comparative Law 101.

[16] *Ashoka Kumar Thakur v Union of India* (2008) 6 SCC 1.

[17] The Supreme Court found a right to be limited and engaged in a limitations analysis in 68 cases.

limitation of an Article 14, 19, or 21 right but this claim was not addressed by the court.

The 98 cases were selected using a combination of two complementary selection methods, meant to create an overall representative portrait of Indian Supreme Court limitation analysis. The database includes all Constitution Bench[18] decisions regarding these rights from the years 2004–13. In addition, the database also includes all decisions regarding these rights, regardless of bench size, from the years 2014–16. I employed this twin method because while Constitution Bench decisions hold the highest precedential value as to the constitutional requirements of a rights analysis, the smaller bench decisions represent the more 'run of the mill' fundamental rights cases, and therefore showcase how the court conducts rights analysis more generally. Twenty-one Constitution Bench cases from the 2004–13 period were found to be relevant for the purposes of this study out of a total of 89 Constitutional Bench decisions delivered during this period. Seventy-seven cases from the 2014–16 period were found to be relevant, out of a total of 506 cases tagged as relating to these rights in the case reporter Supreme Court Cases ('SCC').[19] To put these numbers in context, other research has shown that the Supreme Court delivers

[18] A Constitution Bench has a bench size of five or more judges and is constituted to decide 'any case involving a substantial question of law as to the interpretation of the Constitution'. Article 145 (3), Constitution of India.

[19] In order to identify the decisions that meet my parameters, I relied on SCC Online, a private reporter. Within the set of Constitution Bench decisions for the period 2004–13 and the set of decisions in 2014–16, I searched for all cases that mentioned Articles 14, 19, or 21. From this set, I discarded the following types of cases: (1) where the Reporter had tagged the case as dealing with one of these articles, but the Court itself did not mention any of the three articles; (2) where the Articles were mentioned in passing but were not actually discussed in the judgment; (3) where one of the Articles was mentioned in the arguments advanced by the parties, but the Court did not engage with the article at all; (4) where the only reference to the Article was in a case cited by the Court and the Court did not independently analyse the facts in relation to that Article; (5) where, because of precedent, the Court proceeds on the basis that a particular fundamental right is in play, but does not discuss the nature, scope, extent of, or limitation on that right, either explicitly or implicitly.

A limitation of the study is that the database is limited to cases where the Court expressly invokes Articles 14, 19, or 21. Cases which are decided on the principles in these sections, but where the Court has not invoked the Articles themselves, as for example, decisions regarding arbitrariness of an executive action which do not expressly mention Article 14, have not been captured within the study.

around 1,000 judgments per year, out of which 4 per cent deal with constitutional challenges.[20]

I analysed these cases on a range of parameters to understand the factors that the court considers in its limitations analysis. Since the court does not have a structured test, I have attempted to tease out the various elements of analysis through a close reading of the judgments in the database. The court's discursive style often involves discussing many elements together or engaging in a common discussion and on that basis coming to a conclusion on more than one element. In such cases, I have coded each element of the analysis separately, even though the court discusses these elements together.

The quantitative analysis was enriched by qualitative examination and reference to approximately 130 other landmark cases on these rights and on rights adjudication more generally, chosen based on references in secondary literature.

## II Legal and Institutional Context

### A *Institutional Structure*

The Indian Constitution was framed in the immediate aftermath of World War II, contemporaneously with India's independence from British rule in 1947. Influenced both by the constitutional traditions of Western liberal democracies and the distinct challenges and experiences of India's freedom struggle, the Constitution framers sought to create a liberal democratic order while at the same time empowering and guiding the State to address rampant social and economic inequality. Therefore, while the Constitution contains an elaborate bill of civil and political rights, it also provides a set of Directive Principles of State Policy – binding but not judicially enforceable mandates for securing socio-economic justice for all.[21] Judicial review is expressly entrenched in

[20] Aparna Chandra, Sital Kalantry, and William Hubbard, 'The Supreme Court of India: A People's Court?' (2017) 1 Indian Law Review 145. The bulk of the judgments relate to appeals to the Supreme Court from decisions of lower courts and tribunals in non-constitutional matters. In constitutional matters, apart from those cases that deal with the rights under study, matters may involve other rights, as well as constitutional challenges not involving fundamental rights claims, such as federalism-related claims.

[21] Constitution, part IV.

Article 32 of the Constitution, which guarantees the right to directly move the Supreme Court of India against violations of fundamental rights.[22]

India has a three-tier judicial system which can be broadly characterized as follows: civil and criminal trial courts at the district level; High Courts at the State level;[23] and one national Supreme Court. The Constitution empowers the High Courts and the Supreme Court to exercise constitutional review, including striking down legislative and executive state action for violation of fundamental rights.[24] The Supreme Court is both the final court of appeal from decisions of all courts and tribunals in the country[25] and a court of first instance for violations of fundamental rights.[26] Fundamental rights cases can therefore come before the Supreme Court on appeal from decisions of High Courts, or can be filed directly before the Court under its original jurisdiction. In the database of my study, for example, 59 per cent of cases came to the Supreme Court by way of appeal; 40 per cent were filed directly before the Court in exercise of its original jurisdiction; and in one single case, the president sought the opinion of the Court under its (non-binding) advisory jurisdiction.[27] Regardless of the avenue through which a fundamental rights case reaches the Supreme Court, once the Court admits a matter, it exercises similar scrutiny on the impugned action.[28] Decisions of the Supreme Court have the force of law, and constitute binding precedent for all lower courts.[29]

Thirty-one judges can serve on the Indian Supreme Court.[30] The court does not sit en banc but typically in benches of two or three judges. For cases that raise 'substantial questions as to the interpretation of the

[22] Constitution, art. 32.

[23] Some High Courts exercise jurisdiction over more than one State. Thus, India has 24 High Courts for a total of 29 States and 7 Union Territories.

[24] Constitution, arts. 32 and 226, respectively.

[25] Constitution, arts. 132, 133, 134, and 136.

[26] Constitution, art. 32.

[27] Constitution, art. 143.

[28] The Court has not articulated distinct standards of review for cases admitted under the appellate jurisdiction and under the original jurisdiction.

[29] Article 141 of the Constitution provides that 'The law declared by the Supreme Court shall be binding on all courts within the territory of India.'

[30] Constitution, art. 124 (1).

Constitution', judges sit on 'Constitution Benches' of five or more judges.[31] Decisions of a larger bench are binding on a smaller bench.[32]

The Supreme Court of India enjoys a very high degree of legitimacy within the Indian polity,[33] and has often been referred to as the 'most powerful court in the world' because of its wide jurisdiction, the nature of orders it passes, and the 1.3 billion people under its authority.[34] After battles with the Executive and Legislature for control over the Constitution in the 1970s, the Supreme Court's authority to review the actions and omissions of the other branches of government has not been seriously challenged either in the political sphere or in academic literature.[35] The court has in this time appropriated through judicial construction the power to strike down constitutional amendments in order to protect a judicially determined basic structure of the Constitution;[36] the power to self-appoint judges to the higher judiciary;[37] the

[31] Constitution, art. 145.

[32] Decisions of a previous co-ordinate bench is also normally binding on a subsequent bench, except that, if the latter disagrees with the ratio of a previous bench, it can refer the matter for decision to a larger bench. See *Central Board of Dawoodi Bohra v State of Maharashtra* (2005) 2 SCC 673.

[33] A survey conducted by Gallup in 2013 found that 71 per cent of Indians had faith and confidence in the court system. The poll attributed this to 'visible efforts to strengthen rule of law such as high-profile cases in which the judiciary ruled against corrupt politicians, businessmen and celebrities and held them accountable. This, in addition to improvements in the Right to Information Act and fast-track courts, may have bolstered confidence in the judicial system and courts.' Shawnette Rochelle and Jay Loschky, 'Confidence in Judicial Systems Varies Worldwide' (*Gallup News*, 22 October 2014) <http://news.gallup.com/poll/178757/confidence-judicial-systems-varies-worldwide.aspx> (accessed 6 January 2018). See also, Nicholas Robinson, 'India and the Rise of the Good Governance Court' (2009) 8 Washington University Global Studies Law Review 1.

[34] See George Gadbois, 'Supreme Court Decisionmaking' (1974) 10 Banaras Law Journal 1; V R Krishna Iyer, *Our Courts on Trial* (B. R. Publishing Corporation 1987) 18; Shylashri Shankar, 'India's Judiciary: Imperium in Imperio?' in Paul Brass (ed), *Routledge Handbook of South Asian Politics* (Routledge, 2010) 165; Alexander Fischer, 'Higher Lawmaking as a Political Resource' in Miodrag Jovanović and Kristin Henrard (eds), *Sovereignty and Diversity* (Eleven International Publishing, 2008) 186.

[35] For a history of the Court's struggle with the Executive, see Granville Austin, 'The Supreme Court and Struggle for the Custody of the Constitution' in B N Kirpal and others (eds), *Supreme but Not Infallible: Essays in Honour of the Supreme Court of India* (OUP 2000).

[36] *Keshavananda Bharati v State of Kerala* (1973) 4 SCC 225.

[37] See, e.g., *Supreme Court Advocates on Record Association v Union of India* (1993) 4 SCC 441; *In Re Special Reference 1 of 1998* (1998) 7 SCC 739; *Supreme Court Advocates on Record Association v Union of India* (2015) 6 SCC 408.

power to issue detailed guidelines virtually amounting to legislation in order to fill any gaps in the law;[38] the power to hold the government accountable for its failure to provide socio-economic justice to citizens and to issue detailed directions to the government to remedy such omissions;[39] the power to monitor the implementation of its orders and directions through the use of continuing mandamus;[40] and, the power to take suo moto cognizance of a rights violation, based for example on newspaper reports, and pass appropriate orders accordingly, etc.[41]

Thus, the power of judicial review is not only explicitly stated in the Constitution, its invocation is both routine, and widely accepted as legitimate within political and legal discourse. The court receives approximately 68,000 petitions every year, including both appeals and direct petitions. The bulk of these cases are denied admission in limne. Data suggests that overall the court has about a 14 per cent admission rate.[42]

Taken together, judges of the Supreme Court deliver around 1,000–1,200 judgments a year.[43] The Supreme Court has been repeatedly criticized for speaking in multiple and very discordant voices because it is in effect not just one Supreme Court, but as many Supreme Courts as there are benches.[44] As a result, as I demonstrate later, the court's own jurisprudence has become increasingly disparate such that various parallel meanings, interpretations, approaches, and analyses exist on a single point of law. Subsequent benches and policymakers can therefore pick and choose their law.[45] Consequently, how

[38] See, e.g., *Vishaka v State of Rajasthan* (1997) 6 SCC 241.

[39] See, e.g., the series of orders in *PUCL v Union of India* (Right to Food case), arising out of Writ Petition (Civil) No. 196/2001.

[40] ibid. See also, *Vineet Narain v Union of India* (1996) 2 SCC 199.

[41] See Marc Galanter, 'Snakes and Ladders: Suo Moto Intervention and the Indian Judiciary' (2014) 10 FIU Law Review 69.

[42] For details regarding the Court's petition and admissions procedure, including an analysis of data on the number of petitions received and admitted, see Chandra, Kalantry, and Hubbard (n 20).

[43] Data collated from www.judis.nic.in.

[44] See, e.g., Robinson (n 15) (calling the Supreme Court 'poly-vocal').

[45] The clearest example of this discordant approach is in death penalty analysis. The ruling precedent on this point is the 1980 Supreme Court decision (delivered by a five-judge bench) in *Bachan Singh v State of Punjab* (1980) 2 SCC 684. In this case the Supreme Court held that the death penalty could be awarded only in rarest of rare cases, where the alternative punishment of life imprisonment was unquestionably foreclosed. The interpretation of this 'rarest of rare' standard has fallen upon various subsequent benches of

the Supreme Court will decide a case, what type of limitation analysis it will use, which aspect of the analysis it will focus on, etc., differs from bench to bench, and leads to a situation where one may have no clear direction ex-ante as to what standard the court is likely to adhere to.

### B *Normative Structure*

Article 13 (2) of the Constitution prohibits the State from making any law which takes away or abridges fundamental rights; and declares that any such law will be void.[46] Article 32 guarantees that any person can directly move the Supreme Court for enforcement of fundamental rights. The court has the power to strike down any state action that violates fundamental rights and provide other appropriate remedies for the enforcement of fundamental rights.[47]

The fundamental rights guaranteed by the Constitution can broadly be classified as including the right to equality;[48] the right to life and liberty,[49] and to fundamental freedoms;[50] rights against exploitation;[51] cultural, religious, and linguistic rights;[52] and the right to

two and three judges. As scholars have pointed out (and recently the Court itself has admitted) a review of the case-law reveals that various benches have created multiple parallel and inconsistent interpretations of this standard, such that the award of the death penalty has become a 'lethal lottery'. For a detailed discussion, see Law Commission of India, *The Death Penalty* (Law Com No. 272 2015) ch. 5.

46 Constitution, art. 13. 'Law' in Article 13 includes any ordinance, order, bye-law, rule, regulation, notification, custom, or usage having the force of law.

47 Constitution, art. 13 read with art. 32.

48 Constitution, arts. 14–18. These include the right to equality before the law, the equal protection of laws, prohibition on discrimination, the abolition of certain caste-related practices, as well as the express recognition of affirmative action for certain vulnerable groups, as an aspect of equality.

49 Constitution, art. 21 (a broad due process guarantee for the protection of life and liberty) and Constitution, arts. 20 and 22 (specific criminal process rights, and rights of persons detained preventively).

50 Constitution, art. 19 (freedom of speech and expression, movement, assembly and association, and trade and occupation. Each fundamental freedom has a corresponding limitations clause which specifies the conditions under which the right may be justifiably limited).

51 Constitution, arts. 23 and 24 (rights against exploitative labour practices, child labour, slavery, etc.)

52 Constitution, arts. 25–30 (including the freedom of religion and specific guarantees for the protection of minority cultural, educational, and associational rights).

constitutional remedies for the violation of fundamental rights, i.e. the right to approach the Supreme Court for remedies against the violation of fundamental rights.[53] The Constitution also guarantees a very diluted right to property, which consists of the right to adequate compensation in case of acquisition by the State of certain types of property.[54]

The Supreme Court has considered Articles 14, 19, and 21 to be part of a 'Golden Triangle' of rights, situated above the rest of the fundamental rights.[55] However, inter se, neither Constitutional text nor the court places these rights in any form of hierarchy. In practice too, the court does not rely on any hierarchy between rights for its decision-making.[56]

In addition to Fundamental Rights, the Constitution also enumerates Directive Principles of State Policy (DPSP).[57] As per Article 37, DPSPs are not 'enforceable by any court, but the principles therein laid down are nevertheless fundamental in the governance of the country and it shall be the duty of the State to apply these principles in making laws'. These principles reflect norms of socio-economic justice and include exhortations to the State to ensure equitable distribution of resources, a living wage for labour, a clean and healthy environment, respect for the principles of international law, etc.

DPSPs have come to play an important role in rights adjudication. In the initial years, the court was of the view that fundamental rights would prevail over directive principles in the event of any clash between the two.[58] Since then, it has come to accept the view that 'harmony and balance between fundamental rights and directive principles is an essential feature of the basic structure of the Constitution'.[59] The court has read DPSPs into fundamental rights, and has used these principles to

[53] Constitution, art. 32.

[54] Constitution, art. 31A.

[55] *Minerva Mills v Union of India* AIR 1980 SC 1789; *I. R. Coehlo v Union of India* (2007) 2 SCC 1; *Ashoka Kumar Thakur* (n 16).

[56] The only exception to this general principle is adjudication on the death penalty, where the Court has held that the right to life is of supreme importance, and since the death penalty irreversibly extinguishes this right, there should be stringent procedural safeguards for cases involving the capital punishment. *Mohd. Arif v Registrar, Supreme Court of India* (2014) 9 SCC 737; *Shatrughan Chauhan v Union of India* (2014) 3 SCC 1.

[57] Constitution, part IV.

[58] *State of Madras v Champakam Dorairajan* AIR 1951 SC 226.

[59] *Minerva Mills* (n 55).

enlarge the scope of fundamental rights. Since Directive Principles have been read into fundamental rights, any question of a clash between directive principles and fundamental rights gets translated into questions of clashes between rights themselves, or questions as to the scope of the fundamental right.[60]

Another implication of reading DPSPs into Fundamental Rights has been that the court views fundamental rights not only as limits on state power but also as imposing positive and judicially enforceable socio-economic mandates upon the State. A significant portion of the court's most high-profile work involves the court examining whether state inaction or failure violates fundamental rights as read with DPSPs.[61]

In addition, seeking to further DPSPs is considered a legitimate object of state action, and counts towards the legitimacy of the object and reasonableness of the action.[62] So also, an action that is inconsistent with DPSPs is generally considered unreasonable.[63]

Reading DPSPs into Fundamental Rights fits in well with the court's general approach towards the interpretation of rights. The court interprets the scope of constitutional provisions, especially fundamental rights, in a broad, liberal, and purposive manner,[64] so as to 'expand the reach and ambit of Fundamental Rights rather than to attenuate their meaning and content by a process of judicial construction'.[65] Apart from

[60] On reading Fundamental Rights in light of Directive Principles of State Policy see *Bandhua Mukti Morcha v Union of India* (1984) 3 SCC 161. On using Directive Principles to limit the scope of the right to personal liberty see, *Javed v State of Haryana* (2003) 8 SCC 369 (Elections Disqualification I case).

[61] See n 163–65 and accompanying text.

[62] *Kasturi Lal Lakshmi Reddy v State of Jammu and Kashmir* AIR 1980 SC 1992.

[63] ibid.

[64] *S.P. Gupta v Union of India* AIR 1982 SC 149 ('A Constitution of a country is a living document and cannot, therefore, be interpreted in a narrow pedantic sense. A broad and liberal spirit should inspire those who are called upon to interpret the Constitution.'); *M. Nagaraj v Union of India* (2006) 8 SCC 212 ('[A] purposive rather than a strict literal approach to the interpretation should be adopted [in interpreting the Constitution]. A Constitutional provision must be construed not in a narrow and constricted sense but in a wide and liberal manner so as to anticipate and take account of changing conditions and purposes so that a constitutional provision does not get fossilised but remains flexible enough to meet the newly emerging problems and challenges'); *Francis Coralie Mullin v Administrator, Union Territory of Delhi* (1981) 1 SCC 608 ('the principle of [liberal interpretation [of Constitutional provisions] ... applies with greater force in relation to a fundamental right enacted by the Constitution'.)

[65] *Meneka Gandhi v Union of India* AIR 1978 SC 597. See also, *I. R. Coehlo v Union of India* (n 55); Right to Privacy case (n 10).

DPSPs, the court has relied on international law norms,[66] fundamental duties contained in the Constitution,[67] and foreign law in defining the scope of fundamental rights.[68]

## III Limitations Analyses in Theory

The Constitution does not provide any common structure of limitations analysis for all rights in the Fundamental Rights chapter. Some rights, for example, the fundamental freedoms enumerated in Article 19, have express limitation clauses. Others, like the right to equality in Article 14, do not. However, through judicial interpretation limitations have been read into the right. Below, I map the court's dicta on the limitations analyses to be followed in reviewing state action for compliance with Articles 14, 19, and 21. In subsequent segments, I argue that though the court sets up distinct structures of limitations analyses for the various rights, its practice reveals that regardless of the right in question, it analyses a common set of elements in determining the validity of limitations on rights.

### *A Article 14: Right to Equality*

Article 14 provides that 'the State shall not deny to any person equality before the law or the equal protection of the laws within the territory of India'.[69] The Constitution itself does not provide any limitations on the Right to Equality under Article 14. Through judicial construction, two distinct tests have emerged in evaluating state action for compliance with this right: the classification test and the arbitrariness test. The classification test strikes at discriminatory state action, and requires that

[66] See, e.g., *Vishaka* (n 38).

[67] See, e.g., *Charu Khurana v Union of India*, (2015) 1 SCC 192.

[68] See, e.g., *Shreya Singhal v Union of India* (2015) 5 SCC 1.

[69] Other articles of the 'Equality Code' in the Indian Constitution include Article 15(1) which prohibits discrimination against any citizen 'on grounds only of religion, race, caste, sex, place of birth or any of them'. Articles 15 (3) (4) and (5), however, empower the State to make special provisions for women, children, socially and educationally backward classes, and for certain historically discriminated against castes and tribes (called Scheduled Castes and Scheduled Tribes). Article 16 prohibits like discrimination in matters of public employment, but saves affirmative action in relation to backward classes, Scheduled Castes and Scheduled Tribes. Article 17 abolishes the practice of 'untouchability', and Article 18 prohibits the State from conferring non-military and non-academic titles upon persons.

persons similarly situated with respect to a law should be treated alike.[70] To determine whether state action is discriminatory, the court examines whether the impugned action makes an unreasonable classification, by following a two-step analysis:[71] first, whether the classification provides for an 'intelligible differentia' between the two classes. The differentia, i.e., the 'basis of the classification' or the line of demarcation between the included and excluded groups, should be clear and determinable, as opposed to vague and illusory. Thus, the classification must be 'based on some qualities or characteristics which are to be found in all the persons grouped together and not in others who are left out'.[72]

Second, the court asks whether there is a 'rational nexus' between the classification and the object of the state action in question. This limb works to ensure that 'equal laws [are] applied to all in the same situation, and there [is] no discrimination between one person and another if as regards the subject-matter of the legislation their position is substantially the same'.[73] The rational nexus test thus asks and answers the question of whether the classification advances the goals of the state action.[74]

In a parallel line of cases, the court has developed an alternative test to the classification standard – the arbitrariness test. In these cases, the court has held that the guarantee of equal protection of laws is a guarantee of the Rule of Law. Any action that is arbitrary or unreasonable strikes against the Rule of Law and is therefore against the guarantee of equality. The right to equality has therefore been read as a right against arbitrary and unreasonable state action.[75] In an arbitrariness analysis, there is no requirement to show that similarly placed classes were treated differently. In other words, unlike the classification test, under arbitrariness analysis there is no requirement of a comparator.

The arbitrariness test examines whether the impugned law was a principled action based on 'legitimate and relevant considerations' as opposed to those that are 'extraneous and outside the area of permissible

70 *In re: Special Courts Bill* 1978 AIR 1978 SC 478.

71 See generally, *State of West Bengal v Anwar Ali Sarkar* AIR 1952 SC 75.

72 N 70.

73 *In re: Special Courts Bill* (n 70).

74 See Tarunabh Khaitan, 'Beyond Reasonableness – A Rigorous Standard of Review for Article 15 Infringement' (2008) 50 Journal of Indian Law Institute 177. In some cases, the Court additionally asks whether the object of the law is itself valid. However, this is not a consistent practice, and examining the legitimacy of the object is not part of the doctrinal framing of the reasonable classification test. See *infra* n 203–204 and accompanying text.

75 *E. P. Royappa v State of Tamil Nadu* (1974) 4 SCC 3; *Meneka Gandhi* (n 65).

considerations'.[76] However, the court has not laid down any specific test or standard to determine what types of considerations are legitimate and relevant.[77] Instead, it has held that the arbitrariness analysis depends on the facts of a given case, as does the determination of whether the State's reasons were legitimate.[78]

Arbitrariness Review has been the subject of much controversy in Indian constitutional scholarship, inter alia, on the ground that the court has not formulated any 'objective' criteria by reference to which the terms 'reasonable' and 'arbitrary' can be defined. In the absence of any objective criteria, the arbitrariness doctrine gives judges 'untrammeled power' to strike down any law that they do not like.[79] There is little clarity on the standard of review under the arbitrariness doctrine. In one line of cases, the court appears to consider arbitrariness review to be the same as *Wednesbury* review.[80] In another line of cases, mostly dealing with the exercise of administrative discretion (particularly in the context of imposing penalties), the court has stated that a disproportionate state action will fall foul of the test of arbitrariness and will therefore violate the equality guarantee.[81] While the court has termed this the proportionality test, it generally does not adopt any stage-wise analysis of proportionality.[82] Instead, the court has converted the PA into a *Wednesbury* analysis by stating that the court will interfere only when the state action is 'shockingly' and 'grossly' disproportionate.[83] In a third set of cases,

[76] *E. P. Royappa* (n 75).

[77] With the exception, of course, of the general proposition that Directive Principles of State Policy are considered legitimate reasons for state action.

[78] See, e.g., *Union of India v International Trading Co* (2003) 5 SCC 437.

[79] HM Seervai, *Constitutional Law of India* (3rd ed, N. M. Tripathi 1983) vol. 1, 277; B N Srikrishna, 'Skinning a Cat' (2005) 8 SCC (J) 3. See also *Natural Resource Allocation, in re: Special Reference No. 1 of 2012* (2012) 10 SCC 1 (the Court itself criticizing the 'arbitrary use of the "arbitrariness doctrine"'.).

[80] *Wednesbury* (n 2) (Lord Greene M. R.) ('a person entrusted with a discretion must, so to speak, direct himself properly in law. He must call his own attention to the matters which he is bound to consider. He must exclude from his consideration matters which are irrelevant to what he has to consider. If he does not obey those rules, he may truly be said, and often is said, to be acting "unreasonably." Similarly, there may be something so absurd that no sensible person could ever dream that it lay within the powers of the authority.') See, e.g., *McDowell* (n 7) (holding that even when administrative action is examined on the touchstone of Article 14, 'the scope of judicial review is limited to three grounds, viz., (i) unreasonableness, which can more appropriately be called irrationality, (ii) illegality and (iii) procedural impropriety'). See also, *Tata Cellular* (n 7).

[81] *Om Kumar* (n 5).

[82] Ibid.

[83] For a detailed discussion on this point, see Chandrachud (n 8); Jalan and Rai (n 8).

concerning the appropriate method for allocating natural resources, the court has held that to comply with the Article 14 non-arbitrariness standard, state action 'has to be fair, reasonable, non-discriminatory, transparent, non-capricious, unbiased, without favouritism or nepotism, in pursuit of promotion of healthy competition and equitable treatment. It should conform to the norms which are rational, informed with reasons and guided by public interest, etc.'[84]

Apart from the fact that the standard of reasonableness in the arbitrariness doctrine is not clear (*Wednesbury*, proportionality, or something else); and the informational focus of the doctrine (the types of factors or details that the court examines to determine whether the impugned state action is reasonable) varies from case to case, the confused conceptual realm of operation of the arbitrariness principle is most evident in the divergence of views about whether a legislative provision can be struck down on the ground of arbitrariness alone. This issue remains unresolved in doctrine.[85]

Both the formulations under Article 14 – classification and arbitrariness – exist in parallel.[86]

84 *Natural Resource Allocation* (n 79).

85 In one line of cases, e.g., *Mardia Chemicals Ltd v Union of India* (2004) 4 SCC 311, the Court has used arbitrariness alone, without the violation of any other fundamental right, as enough reason for striking down a legislative provision. In other cases, however, the Supreme Court has stated that arbitrariness alone cannot be a reason to strike down legislative actions, though it is sufficient to strike down executive actions. See *McDowell* (n 7); *Natural Resource Allocation* (n 79); *Rajbala v State of Haryana* (2016) 2 SCC 445. This issue was referred to a Constitution Bench for resolution. However, the Constitution Bench in *Subramanian Swamy v CBI* (2014) 8 SCC 682 did not answer the question, and chose to examine the case at hand from the perspective of the classification doctrine. In August 2017, in *Shayara Bano v Union of India* (2017) SCC Online SC 963, a five-judge bench decision invalidated the practice of instantaneous unilateral divorce by Muslim men. A plurality opinion on behalf of two judges stated that arbitrariness is indeed a ground for invalidating legislations. Nariman and Lalit JJ., ibid. One other judge agreed with this proposition, but invalidated the practice on other grounds. Joseph J., ibid. It is therefore unclear whether his opinion would form part of the ratio for the case. The interpretation of this judgment in subsequent decisions is likely to decide the future fate of the arbitrariness doctrine as it applies to legislations.

86 It should be noted that the question of adopting the American doctrine of strict scrutiny for suspect classifications has come up before the Court in cases involving Articles 15 and 16 (which prohibit classification on certain grounds, but permit affirmative action for specified vulnerable groups). In some cases, the Court has held strict scrutiny to be applicable to review under these articles. See *Anuj Garg* (n 6) ; *Saurabh Chaudri v Union of India* (2003) 11 SCC 146. However, in other, larger, bench decisions, the test has been expressly rejected. *Ashoka Kumar Thakur* (n 16). Some authors have attempted to reconcile these lines of cases. See example, Raag Yadava, 'Taking Rights Seriously: The Supreme Court on Strict Scrutiny' (2010) 22 National Law School of India Review 147. However, since the tests are not used regularly, and in any case are not part of the Article

## B Article 19: Fundamental Freedoms

Art. 19[87] of the Constitution enumerates rights of citizens[88] to six fundamental freedoms and permissible limitations thereon viz., the rights

14 review, though they are referenced in the context of equality review under Article 15 and 16, studying the elements of this test is beyond the scope of this paper.

[87] 19. Protection of certain rights regarding freedom of speech, etc.

(1) All citizens shall have the right
  (a) to freedom of speech and expression;
  (b) to assemble peaceably and without arms;
  (c) to form associations or unions;
  (d) to move freely throughout the territory of India;
  (e) to reside and settle in any part of the territory of India; and
  (f) [REPEALED]
  (g) to practise any profession, or to carry on any occupation, trade, or business.

(2) Nothing in sub-clause (a) of clause (1) shall affect the operation of any existing law, or prevent the State from making any law, in so far as such law imposes reasonable restrictions on the exercise of the right conferred by the said sub-clause in the interests of the sovereignty and integrity of India, the security of the State, friendly relations with foreign States, public order, decency or morality, or in relation to contempt of court, defamation, or incitement to an offence.

(3) Nothing in sub-clause (b) of the said clause shall affect the operation of any existing law in so far as it imposes, or prevents the State from making any law imposing, in the interests of the sovereignty and integrity of India or public order, reasonable restrictions on the exercise of the right conferred by the said sub-clause.

(4) Nothing in sub-clause (c) of the said clause shall affect the operation of any existing law in so far as it imposes, or prevent the State from making any law imposing, in the interests of the sovereignty and integrity of India or public order or morality, reasonable restrictions on the exercise of the right conferred by the said sub-clause.

(5) Nothing in sub-clauses (d) and (e) of the said clause shall affect the operation of any existing law in so far as it imposes, or prevent the State from making any law imposing, reasonable restrictions on the exercise of any of the rights conferred by the said sub-clauses either in the interests of the general public or for the protection of the interests of any Scheduled Tribe.

(6) Nothing in sub-clause (g) of the said clause shall affect the operation of any existing law in so far as it imposes, or prevent the State from making any law imposing, in the interests of the general public, reasonable restrictions on the exercise of the right conferred by the said sub-clause, and, in particular, nothing in the said sub-clause shall affect the operation of any existing law in so far as it relates to, or prevent the State from making any law relating to
  (i) the professional or technical qualifications necessary for practising any profession or carrying on any occupation, trade or business, or
  (ii) the carrying on by the State, or by a corporation owned or controlled by the State, of any trade, business, industry or service, whether to the exclusion, complete or partial, of citizens or otherwise.

[88] Two, Article 19 protects the rights of *citizens* and not of all persons. Therefore, individuals who are not citizens of India cannot invoke this article. See *Anwar v State* (1971) 3 SCC 104. So also, juristic persons such as companies cannot, in their own name, invoke

to free speech and expression, peaceful assembly, association, movement, residence, and to carry on one's profession, business, trade, and occupation.[89]

Each of these rights has its own specific limitation provision.[90] While the grounds of limitation vary for each right, the structure of each limitation clause is similar and provides that the State can impose 'reasonable restrictions' on the right in order to meet specifically listed goals, e.g., public order, national security, etc. Each freedom has its own corresponding list of goals for which reasonable restrictions may be imposed. Therefore, the court asks three questions in analysing rights limitation under Article 19.[91] First, the court examines whether the impugned state action limits a right specified in Article 19. If yes, then the court investigates whether the state action furthers a specified goal in the relevant limitation clause associated with that right. If no, then the limitation is not justified. If yes, then the third stage studies whether the limitation is a reasonable restriction on the right for the purposes of advancing the specified goal.

A few features of Article 19 review bear emphasis. One, the court has not created any hierarchy between the rights guaranteed under Article 19. The court has also not articulated any distinction between the various rights in terms of the scrutiny to which a law will be subjected. Nor is any such distinction apparent from the practice of the court.

Two, the court has held that any restriction on an Article 19 right has to be authorized by the legislature, either directly or through delegation. The executive cannot, by its fiat alone, restrict an Article 19 right.[92]

the guarantee of this article, since they are not citizens. See *R. C. Cooper v Union of India* (1970) 1 SCC 248; *Bennett Coleman v Union of India* (1972) 2 SCC 788. However, the Court has held that if the State action impairs the rights of shareholders who are citizens, then Article 19 can be invoked, even if the state action in question refers to the company and not to the shareholders directly. Through this route, the Court has extended Article 19 protections to corporations, albeit indirectly.

89 Initially, article 19(1)(f) of the Constitution provided a fundamental right to acquire, hold, and dispose of property. However, this clause was deleted by the 44th Constitutional Amendment, 1978.

90 Constitution of India, art. 19(2)–19(6).

91 *Dharam Dutt v Union of India* (2004) 1 SCC 712.

92 See, e.g., *U.P. Co-operative Cane Unions Federations v West U.P. Sugar Mills Association and Ors* (2004) 5 SCC 430 where the question before the Court was whether the State Government was competent to fix a 'State Advised Price' for the purchase of sugar cane over and above the minimum price fixed by the central government. In a concurring opinion, the judge held that a compulsorily payable higher price is a restriction on the fundamental right guaranteed under Article 19(1)(g), which 'cannot be legally done

Finally, under Article 19, once a rights-limiting measure is found to satisfy a stated goal in the limitation clause, the court is required to determine whether the restriction imposed on the right is reasonable. The court has not articulated any right-specific approach to determining reasonableness. For that matter, it has not propounded any specific test of reasonableness of restrictions on Article 19 rights at all. It has repeatedly held that no common test or abstract standard of reasonableness can be articulated for determining the reasonableness of restrictions. Rather, the very essence of reasonableness is that the court should look at a case by case analysis and determine whether the measure is reasonable in the facts and circumstances of a specific case.[93]

Instead of a common standard or approach to determining the reasonableness of restrictions on Article 19 rights, the court has often propounded *factors* that it should normally consider while determining reasonableness of restrictions. Two early cases of the Supreme Court specify these factors. These cases are cited repeatedly in court decisions, and bear repetition in full. In 1950, in *Chintaman Rao v State of M.P.*,[94] the Supreme Court discussed the meaning of 'reasonable restrictions' and held that

> [T]he limitation imposed on a person in enjoyment of the right should not be arbitrary or of an excessive nature, beyond what is required in the interests of the public. The word "reasonable" implies intelligent care and deliberation, that is, the choice of a course which reason dictates. Legislation which arbitrarily or excessively invades the right cannot be said to contain the quality of reasonableness and **unless it strikes a proper balance between the freedom guaranteed in article 19 (1) (g) and the social control permitted by clause (6) of article 19**, it must be held to be wanting in that quality.[95]

except under a law'. In the facts of the case, the opinion held that no law authorized the State government to fix such a price, and this was, inter alia, a ground for striking down the executive notification on the issue. See also, *Kharak Singh v State of UP* AIR 1963 SC 1295; *Union of India v Naveen Jindal* (2004) 2 SCC 510.

93 See, e.g., *I. C. Golaknath v State of Punjab* AIR 1967 SC 1643 ('The standard is an elastic one; it varies with time, space and condition. What is reasonable under certain circumstances may not be so under different circumstances'); *Pathumma v State of Kerala* (1978) 2 SCC 1 ('No abstract or general pattern or fixed principle can be laid down so as to be of universal application. It will have to vary from case to case and having regard to the changing conditions, the values of human life, social philosophy of the Constitution, prevailing conditions and the surrounding circumstances all of which must enter into the judicial verdict').

94 *Chintaman Rao* (n 6).

95 ibid.

Soon after, in *V. G. Row v State of Madras*,[96] the court held that:

> In considering the reasonableness of laws imposing restrictions on fundamental right . . . no abstract standard or general pattern of reasonableness can be laid down as applicable to all cases. **The nature of the right alleged to have been infringed, the underlying purpose of the restrictions imposed, the extent and urgency of the evil sought to be remedied thereby, the disproportion of the imposition, the prevailing conditions at the time should all enter into the judicial verdict.**

Some commentators have argued that the Article 19 rights analysis structure describes the 'proportionality' test as prevalent in other countries.[97] The Supreme Court itself, in *Sahara v SEBI*,[98] stated that the definition of reasonable restrictions in *Chintaman Rao* is similar to the test of proportionality used by the European Court of Human Rights. While it is true that taken cumulatively, the dicta traverses the same terrain as the factors in the European Court's proportionality test, it has to be remembered that the Indian Supreme Court has not regarded the limitations analysis in Article 19 as a formulaic approach requiring a step-by-step analysis. In *V. G. Row* itself, the court cautioned that it was not laying down any 'abstract standard or general pattern of reasonableness'" As I describe in the next segment, the court treats these factors as relevant considerations, and not as stages of a limitations analysis or even as a check list for determining the reasonableness of restrictions. The practice of the court indicates that different judges pick and choose, and focus on different aspects of the limitations analysis. While some go through the entire set of factors, others can find a measure valid the moment it is found to be a pursuing a legitimate social goal. Therefore, I argue, to say that the Indian Supreme Court follows the PA in its Article 19 jurisprudence would be incorrect.

### C *Article 21: Right to Life and Personal Liberty*

Article 21 mandates that 'no person shall be deprived of his life or personal liberty except according to procedure established by law'. The Supreme Court has read these rights very expansively and has understood the guarantee of right to life as creating both negative and positive obligations upon the State. In this expanded form, Article 21 is

[96] *V. G. Row* (n 6).
[97] See, e.g., Krishnamurthy (n 6).
[98] *Sahara India* (n 5).

characterized as guaranteeing the right to human dignity as well as various socio-economic rights derived principally from the Directive Principles of State Policy. Through this device, the court has converted the formally non-justiciable Directive Principles of State Policy into judicially enforceable fundamental rights guarantees.[99]

The right under Article 21 can only be limited by 'procedure established by law'. In *Maneka Gandhi v Union of India*,[100] the Supreme Court held that rights-limiting procedure has to be 'just, fair and reasonable' for it to pass constitutional muster. *Maneka Gandhi* overturned a nearly 30-year-old precedent which had held that any procedure, as long as it is established by law, would suffice to validly limit the right to life and liberty. In rejecting this precedent, *Maneka Gandhi* drew from the 'brooding omnipresence' of reasonableness of state action in Articles 14 and 19 to hold that procedure to limit Article 21 must be '"right and just and fair" and not arbitrary, fanciful or oppressive ...'[101]

However, the court has not articulated, in *Maneka Gandhi* or beyond, any principle or method to determine what amounts to 'fair, just and reasonable' or on the other hand 'fanciful, oppressive or arbitrary'. As with arbitrariness under Article 14, the court has held that '[t]here is no static measure of reasonableness which can be applied to all situations alike'.[102]

*Maneka Gandhi* made the move from 'procedure established by law' to 'due process of law' by invoking the common thread or 'brooding omnipresence' of reasonableness, which runs through Articles 14, 19, and 21. Similarly, in other cases the Supreme Court has held that 'the concept of reasonableness and non- arbitrariness pervades the entire constitutional scheme and is a golden thread which runs through the whole of the fabric of the Constitution'.[103]

Although the court has articulated a common requirement of reasonable state action running through the entire fundamental rights chapter, it has not defined the scope, limit, and test for a common reasonableness standard. The court generally conducts an article by article analysis to determine whether an impugned measure complies

[99] For a discussion on the Supreme Court's approach to the right to life and liberty see MP Singh, *V. N. Shukla's Constitution of India* (12th edn, Eastern Book Company 2013).

[100] *Meneka Gandhi* (n 65).

[101] ibid.

[102] *Olga Tellis v Bombay Municipal Corporation* AIR 1986 SC 180.

[103] *Ajay Hasia v Khalid Mujib* AIR 1981 SC 487. See also Elections Disqualification I (n 60).

with the requirements of each article. There is, of course, significant overlap between Articles 14 and 21, such that a measure that is not just, fair, or reasonable under Article 21 will naturally fall foul of Article 14 arbitrariness review, though the opposite may not be true in case the measure in question does not deal with the right to life or personal liberty. Despite this, the court has not expressly understood there to be a common framework of analysis running through the three articles.

## IV Limitations Analyses in Practice: Overview

Despite the multiple frames of limitations analysis under the various articles, I argue that in practice there is in effect a common framework of analysis running through rights review under Articles 14, 19, and 21. I argue that the court focuses on the worthiness of the purpose (Worthy Purpose Analysis), the suitability of the means in achieving the purpose of the law (Rational Nexus Analysis), and overall, given the values and interests at stake in the matter, whether the State is justified in limiting the right (General Balancing). If the court finds that the measure is otherwise justified, but needs to be narrowly tailored or needs modification to better balance the various interests and stake, the court will generally remedy the measure itself. The elements of limitation analysis in India are not structured in a step wise form. Rather, these are factors that the court considers as part of a holistic analysis of the reasonableness of the rights-limiting measure.

### *A Overview of Rights Adjudication*

Since the purpose of my study was to understand how the Indian Supreme Court addresses rights limitations, and whether its practice is similar to or distinct from the PA, my database covered all cases where the court addressed a rights limitation. Of the 98 cases in the database, the court found, after scrutiny, that in six cases (6 per cent) no rights limitation had been made out, and ended the analysis at this point.

Of the remaining (n = 92), in nine cases (10 per cent) the court found the measure to be unreasonable simply by virtue of it infringing a right. In these cases, after infringement was established the court shifted its focus to remedies for the violation, without discussing whether there are any valid reasons for the rights limitation. These cases mostly involved state omission to secure rights, for example, inadequate provisioning of aid in drought hit areas leading to a limitation of the right to life,[104] or mismanagement of prisons leading to limitation of the right to liberty.[105] Eight of these nine cases dealt with the infringement of Article 21 rights, and the last case involved the infringement of all three rights.

In one additional case, the Court found that the right to occupation had been limited, and that the limitation was without the backing of law. As such, the measure was struck down for not meeting the basic threshold of legality, and the Court did not conduct any further limitations analysis.[106]

In the remaining 82 cases in the database, a right had been limited, and some justification was sought by the court. In 14 of these cases, the court's analysis focused on whether a right was limited without due process. In these cases, the chief concern was that the procedure adopted for implementing an otherwise reasonable rights-limiting measure should itself be fair and non-discriminatory. This concern about procedural fairness is not necessarily linked to the means-ends analysis. That is, the concern is not primarily that an unfair process will distort the link between means and ends, or that the unfair process masks an illegitimate purpose. Rather, limiting a right without following certain fair process norms, as, for example, depriving someone of their means of livelihood without giving them the opportunity to be heard, is itself seen as an unjustified limitation on the right. Fair process is seen as serving substantive values of equality, non-discrimination, participation, and accountability, which are important to preserve regardless of whether they impact the means-ends analysis. The principles of natural justice, in particular, the right to be heard by an impartial decision maker before an adverse order is passed against a person and the right to a reasoned order, are at the core of procedural fairness guarantees that the court looks for.[107] If there are any procedural infirmities, the court often interprets the law in a manner so as to rectify the infirmity.[108] By and

[104] *Swaraj Abhiyan v Union of India* (2016) 7 SCC 498.

[105] *In re Inhuman Conditions in 1382 Prisons* (2016) 3 SCC 700.

[106] *U.P. Co-operative Cane Unions Federations* (n 92).

[107] Not following principles of natural justice, including giving of reasoned orders renders a procedure arbitrary and unreasonable. See *Meneka Gandhi* (n 65); *Union of India v Tulsiram Patel* (1985) 3 SCC 398; *Central Inland Water Transport Corporation v Brojo Nath Ganguly* (1986) 3 SCC 156; *DTC v Mazdoor Congress* AIR 1991 SC 101; *Shrilekha Vidyarthi v State of UP* (1991) 1 SCC 212; *Tata Cellular* (n 7).

[108] For example, in *Meneka Gandhi* (n 65) as well as in *Olga Tellis* (n 102), the Court read in the requirement of *audi alterem partem* into the impugned law.

large, though not exclusively, these issues regarding fair process norms come up before the court in the context of Article 14 arbitrariness analysis, since arbitrariness review has virtually subsumed the entirety of judicial review of administrative action,[109] which would otherwise be the domain for questioning procedural impropriety.[110]

In the remaining 68 cases, constituting 74 per cent of all cases where the court found a right limitation (n = 92), the Supreme Court found a right to be limited, and engaged in limitations analysis to determine whether the limitation was justified.[111] In reading these decisions, I found common themes in the court's limitations analysis across rights: the worthiness of purpose of the rights-limiting measure; its suitability to further those purposes; and a general balance between various interests at stake to determine whether all things considered, the rights limitation is justified. In determining the worthiness of purpose, the court asks what purpose the rights-limiting measure is pursuing, why, and whether such purpose is legitimate. Suitability of the measure to achieve its purpose is generally tested through a rational nexus analysis – a mostly abstract, common-sensical evaluation of whether the measure can indeed advance the goal in question. In a few instances, the court might ask, as part of the suitability analysis, whether the measure is narrowly tailored to achieve the objective; if not, the measure is deemed unsuitable to advance the objective. The court can also be found engaging in a general balancing exercise, where it evaluates the various interests at stake in the matter, to determine which amongst the various interests should trump the other, all things considered.

The remainder of this analysis will be based on this dataset of 68 cases ('dataset') where the court engaged in a limitations analysis after

[109] Tarunabh Khaitan, 'Equality: Legislative Review under Article 14' in Action' in Sujit Choudhry, Madhav Khosla and Pratap Bhanu Mehta (eds), *Oxford Handbook of the Indian Constitution* (OUP, 2016); Jalan and Rai (n 8).

[110] Of the 98 cases, the Court found upheld the impugned state action in toto in 44 cases and struck down or otherwise modified the measure in 54 cases. In the 14 cases where the measure was impugned for limiting a right without following due process, the Court upheld the measure in one case, and struck down or otherwise modified the measure in 13.

[111] Note that in cases alleging the denial of the right to equality under Article 14, there is no requirement of establishing the infringement of the right. The Court has to determine whether the classification made by the state is unreasonable, or whether the impugned state action is arbitrary. For this reason, all equality cases where the Court examined whether the impugned measure was a reasonable classification or action have been included in the dataset of 68 cases.

determining that the impugned state action or omission resulted in a rights limitation.[112]

## *B Contexts of Limitation Analysis*

The cases in the dataset can be divided based on the types of measures they review: legislation, administrative acts, and judicial decisions. Challenges to legislation (57 per cent) and challenges to administrative measures (38 per cent) make up the majority of the dataset, with challenges to judicial measures comprising only 4 per cent of such cases.[113] The majority of the cases are public law cases (88 per cent), encompassing a broad spectrum of policy areas. The remaining 12 per cent relate to criminal law. Traditional private law areas such as family law or laws relating to private contracts, though not specifically excluded from constitutional scrutiny by constitutional text or doctrine, are not represented in the dataset. While the Constitution includes some fundamental rights that are applied horizontally, the dataset does not contain any case involving such horizontal application of rights against non-state actors.[114]

[112] The dataset includes cases where the Court considers whether a particular remedy sought by a party, or proposed by the Court itself, or granted by the Court in a previous case would violate fundamental rights. For example, in *Sahara India* (n 5), the Court considered whether and in what circumstances it has the power to grant 'postponement orders' directing media outlets to not publish details of a sub-judice matter. Or, in *Natural Resource Allocation* (n 79), the President sought the advice of the Court on whether its decision in a previous case, which seemed to suggest that the only constitutional method of allocating natural resources was through an auction method, was indeed the holding of the Court. In such cases, the Court has subjected the proposed/ impugned action to a limitations analysis, and for this reason such cases are included in the dataset.

[113] I count all challenges to the constitutionality of enactments passed by the Parliament or State Legislatures, as well as delegated legislation made under a legislative enactment, as challenges to legislation. I count challenges to decisions given by lower courts on the ground that such interpretation or decision violates fundamental rights as judicial challenges. For example, this includes cases where the imposition of the death penalty by a lower court is challenged on the ground that it is an unjustified limitation of the petitioner's right to life. Further, cases involving challenges to procedures in the judicial process (where such procedures are not derived from legislative enactments) have also been coded as a challenge to a judicial measure.

[114] Articles 15 (2), 17, 23, and 24 allow for horizontal application of rights against non-state actors. The Supreme Court has understood Article 21 as also regulating the actions of non-state actors. See, e.g., *Bodhisattwa Gautam v Subhra Chakraborty* AIR 1996 SC 922.

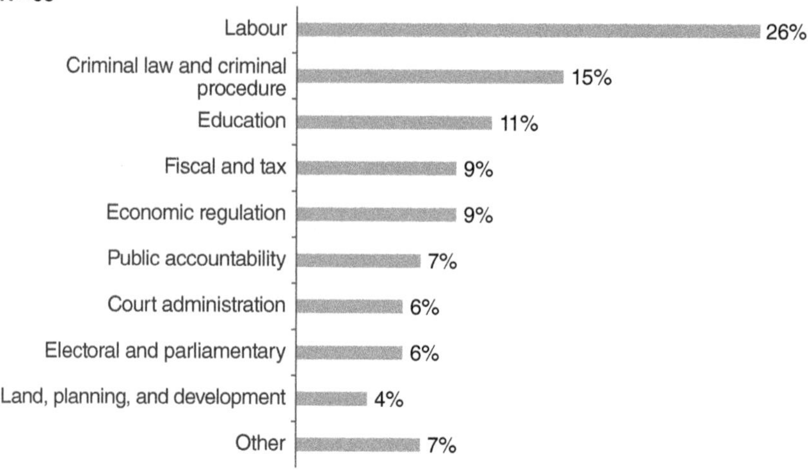


**Figure 6.1** Limitation analysis cases by subject matter

Figure 6.1 details the subject matters covered by cases in the dataset.[115] Labour was the most dominant subject matter to which limitation analysis was applied. The bulk of these cases come under Article 14 (right to equality) review, and involve public employment. These cases are about the rights and entitlements of public employees and the corresponding duties of the State as an employer, and are all regulated by statute. Many such cases involve questions that would typically be part of an administrative law review under common law, such as the quantum of penalty imposed against a public employee in a disciplinary proceeding. However, these issues become of constitutional concern because of the wide ambit of the arbitrariness doctrine under Article 14.

Criminal law cases appear in significant numbers because criminal law cases ipso facto involve the deprivation of liberty (and possibly life). So

[115] One case in the dataset, *E.V. Chinnaiah v State of Andhra Pradesh*, (2005) 1 SCC 394, dealt with affirmative action in both education and employment, and is therefore counted as half under both categories. Cases under the heading Court Administration include challenges to setting up new courts and tribunals, challenges to high court rules relating to practising before the court; and a case on the Court's own power to order postponement of any media coverage of an ongoing matter, to ensure fair administration of justice. The 'Others' category comprises a challenge to the constitutionality of a legislation on civil remedies for domestic violence; challenges to government contracting; and cases dealing with health, nutrition, and environment.

also, criminal penalties are often used to prohibit or regulate activities that might fall within the ambit of a right, such as criminal laws prohibiting certain forms of speech.[116] Education forms a large subset of cases for a few reasons. Aspects of education have been interpreted to be part of the right to free speech and expression. Further, the Constitution empowers the state to take affirmative action measures in educational institutions, as part of the equality guarantee. Disputes around these issues, which have been very contentious in India's socio-political history, come up before courts as disputes on equality.

As might be expected, cases relating to commercial and economic regulation or those relating to fiscal and tax matters are also present in significant numbers. Given barriers to access to courts, and particularly to the highest court in the country,[117] it is not surprising that a significant proportion of cases before the Supreme Court involve substantial business interests. Cases relating to public accountability, for example in the allocation of state resources, also form a distinct subset of issues before the court. While these cases could be addressed through administrative law, such cases have become a focal point of the court's constitutional docket because of pervasive corruption and associated scandals, including allegations of involvement of the highest offices of State in such practices. The court has understood the diversion of resources through corruption as a major challenge for an otherwise poor country, which requires these resources for much needed socio-economic interventions, poverty alleviation, and the like. The welfare goals of the State, as enshrined in DPSPs, are threatened because of leakage of funds through corruption.[118] For this reason, the court has repeatedly examined issues of accountability for allocation of public resources as part of fundamental rights analysis under Article 14. These cases form part of the court's most high profile work, and provide the court with immense legitimacy as the last bulwark against corruption.[119]

Figure 6.2 represents the rights involved in the cases in the dataset. Since one case can involve multiple rights, the number of rights is higher

[116] See, e.g., *Shreya Singhal* (n 68).

[117] On barriers to access to the Indian Supreme Court, see Nicholas Robinson, 'A Quantitative Analysis of the Indian Supreme Court's Workload' (2013) 10 Journal of Empirical Legal Studies 570.

[118] See *Natural Resource Allocation* (n 79).

[119] Rochelle and Loschky (n 33).

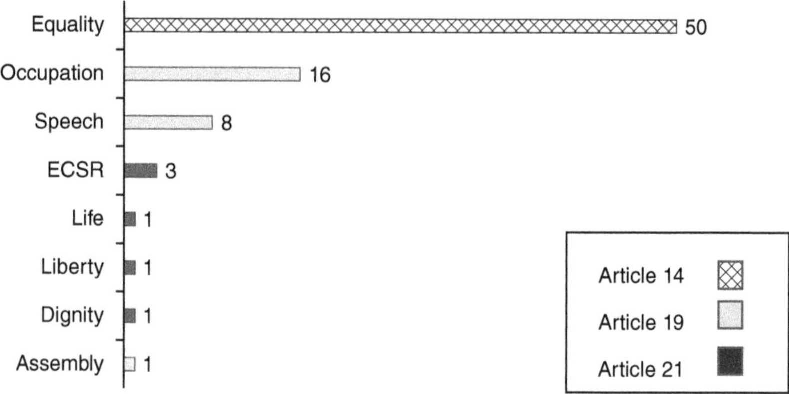


**Figure 6.2** Rights triggering limitation analysis

than the number of cases in the dataset.[120] The three rights included within the scope of this study but not found in this dataset relate to the right of association, the right to move freely throughout the territory of India, and the right to reside and settle in any part of the territory of India. These rights have not been the subject matter of many cases over the years, and hence it is unsurprising that they do not find mention in the dataset.

The right to equality is the most prominent in the dataset, appearing in 50 of the 68 cases (73.5 per cent). As mentioned previously, this has to do with the fact that the Supreme Court has read the guarantee of equality as protecting against any arbitrary state action, both procedural and substantive. As a result, challenges to administrative decisions, on grounds such as violation of principles of natural justice, are treated as violation of fundamental rights in India.

The right to practise any profession or to carry on any occupation, trade, or business forms a significant subset of the rights involved in the dataset of cases. Since the limitation of this right directly hampers business interests, it is unsurprising that it gets litigated so often, both

[120] Rights relating to ECSR (Economic, Cultural, and Social Rights), Dignity, Liberty, and Life are guaranteed by Article 21 of the Constitution. Cases tagged as dealing with the right to life directly implicate the state actions that take away life – for example, the death penalty. Cases tagged as dealing with liberty cover criminal process-related issues where the physical liberty of persons is implicated. Speech, Assembly, Association, and Occupation are covered by Articles 19 (1) (a), (b), (c), and (g), respectively.

because potentially any commercial regulation might impact this right, and because those impacted by limitations on this right are likely to have the resources to litigate these issues right up to the Supreme Court. Overall, Article 19 freedoms find mention in 37 per cent of the cases.

On first blush, it is surprising to see that Article 21 (life and personal liberty) rights form such a small subset of the dataset (9 per cent). As discussed previously, the Supreme Court has read this right very expansively, and has understood it as imposing both positive and negative obligations upon the State. Through a wide reading of the right to life, the court has created a wide domain of justiciable socio-economic rights, far beyond what was originally envisaged in the Constitution.[121] Indian constitutional law canon is replete with examples of the types of rights that the Supreme Court has read into Article 21, and these cases are held in very high regard in Indian legal discourse.[122] Many such cases deal with state failure to secure socio-economic justice. In these cases, once the court finds a rights limitation through state omission, it often moves directly to determining remedies for the violation. As such, these cases though present in the database of 98 cases, do not form part of the more limited dataset of 68 cases where the court engaged in a limitations analysis. Likewise, Article 21 provides a due process guarantee for the violation of the right to life and liberty. Many cases that invoke Article 21 do so on grounds of procedural irregularity in depriving a person of the life or liberty. As such, the question before the court in these cases is whether fair process norms were followed in the impugned action. These cases too are part of the larger database of 98 cases but are excluded from the dataset of 68 cases because they do not trigger a limitations analysis.[123]

### C *Division of Labour between the Elements of Limitation Analysis*

Out of the 68 cases in which the court engaged in limitation analysis, it found the impugned measure reasonable in 37 cases (54 per cent) and

121 See Anup Surendranath, 'Life and Personal Liberty,' in Sujit Choudhry, Madhav Khosla and Pratap Bhanu Mehta (eds), *Oxford Handbook of the Indian Constitution* (OUP 2016) 756.

122 ibid. See also, Singh (n 99).

123 Of the nine cases that directly moved from a finding of infringement of rights to remedies, eight cases involved an Article 21 claim, and the remaining case involved claims relating to Articles 14, 19, and 21.

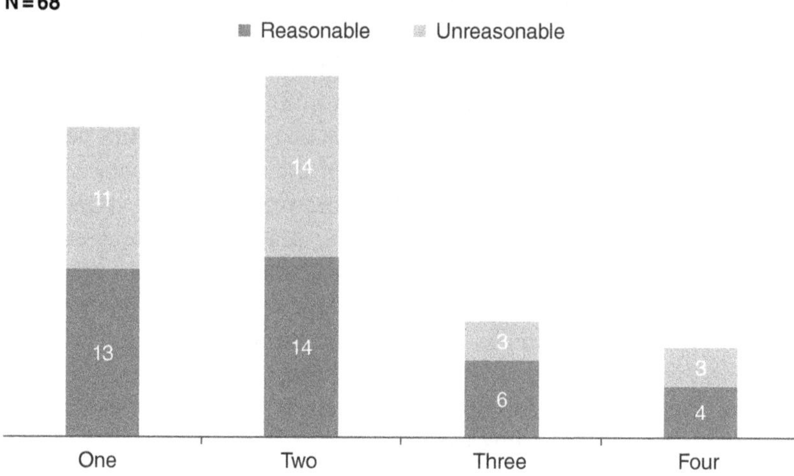


**Figure 6.3** Number of elements addressed in limitations analysis

unreasonable in 31 cases (46 per cent).[124] Figure 6.3 shows the number of cases, disaggregated by whether the measure was found reasonable or not, where the court addressed one, two, three, or all four of the elements – worthy purpose, rational nexus, narrow tailoring, and general balancing. The findings indicate the degree to which limitation analysis in Indian case-law follows a 'pick and choose' model. Alongside elements that are always discussed, others are addressed selectively. Interestingly, the patterns are similar across cases which found the impugned measure to be unreasonable and those that did not. It is striking that all elements of analysis were present in only seven cases (10 per cent of the dataset). In close to half the cases the analysis comprised two elements alone, most often the purpose of the measure and the rational nexus between means and ends. The single-element cases all focused either on the worthiness of the law's purpose, or on the suitability of the law to achieve its stated purpose.

One might assume that in a robust limitations analysis, once a rights infringement has been established, the court will go through each

[124] Any case where, after rights review, at least one element of the reviewed measure (in cases of state action) or status quo (in cases of state omission) was struck down, read down, or otherwise modified, has been coded as a finding of unjustified rights limitation. Where the measure or status quo was approved in full, this was coded as a finding of upholding the measure.

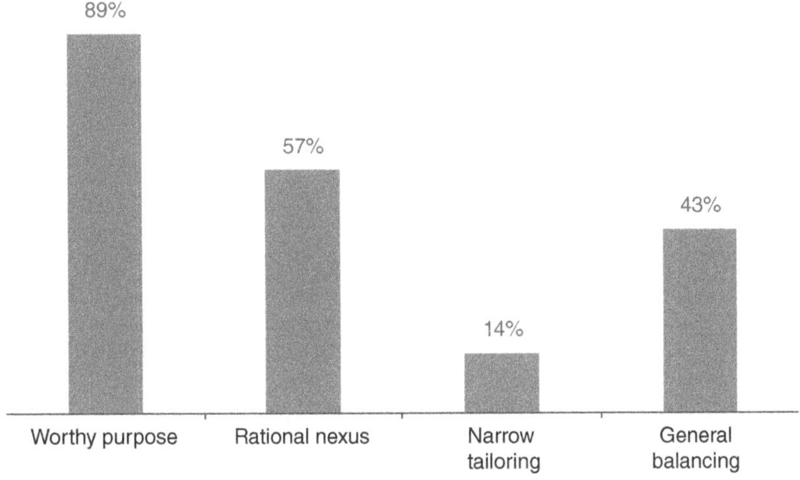


**Figure 6.4** Frequency of the elements in cases found reasonable

element to check whether the measure passes muster on all counts, before holding that a measure is constitutional. However, Figure 6.4 indicates otherwise. This figure presents the frequency with which each element appeared in cases where the measure was found to be reasonable, and Figure 6.5 does the same for cases where the measure was found to be unreasonable. Both figures broadly show similar patterns of engagement with different elements (with the exception of the rational nexus analysis).

The worthy purpose analysis appears to be the only essential element, which is almost always present in the limitations analysis.[125] The single element analysis cases in Figure 6.3 most frequently involve only a worthy purpose analysis.[126] This presents a surprising result: in 9 of the 37 cases (25 per cent) where the court finds a measure reasonable, it does

[125] In one case, *A N Sachdeva v MD University, Rohtak* (2015) 10 SCC 117, involving the reasonable classification test under Article 14, the Court did not expressly discuss what the purpose of the law was, and went straight to the question of whether the two classified groups were similarly situated in relation to the law (as opposed to the object of the law). This case has been coded as one where the Court did not discuss purpose at all. In all other cases, the Court discussed what the purpose of the law was; but in seven of them, does not discuss whether the purpose is worthy. Instead it moves on to discussing whether the measure was suitable for achieving the stated purpose of the law.

[126] See ibid.

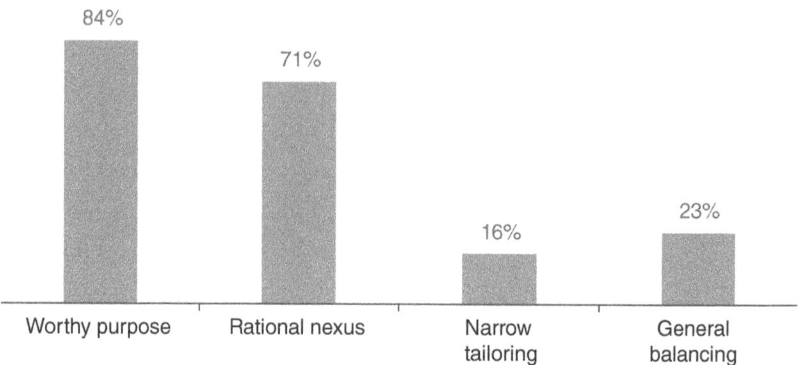


**Figure 6.5** Frequency of the elements in cases found unreasonable

so solely on the finding that the measure was pursuing a worthy purpose, without engaging in any further analysis of whether the measure was justified.

Next in frequency is the rational nexus analysis, in which the court in 57 per cent, or roughly half the cases, found the measure reasonable, but in 71 per cent of the cases the measure is held to be unreasonable. As I will discuss later, the rational nexus analysis is generally based on abstract, common-sensical reasoning, rather than through evidence of its suitability to achieve the ends in question. This is why, in very few cases does the court ask the additional question of whether the rights-limiting measure was narrowly tailored to serve its purposes (14 per cent and 16 per cent of cases where the measure was held to be reasonable and unreasonable, respectively).

The court may also engage in a broad, 'all things considered' analysis of whether the measure is justified, given all the interests at stake, through a balancing of these interests. This balancing analysis, found in 43 per cent and 23 per cent of cases where the measure was found reasonable and unreasonable, respectively, is generally folded into the legitimate aim analysis.

Taken together, these data indicate that the locus of inquiry for the court in conducting its limitations analysis is whether the rights-limiting measure advances a legitimate state goal through means that will plausibly advance those ends.

Figure 6.6 represents the frequency with which measures fail each element of the analysis, in cases where the measure is found to be

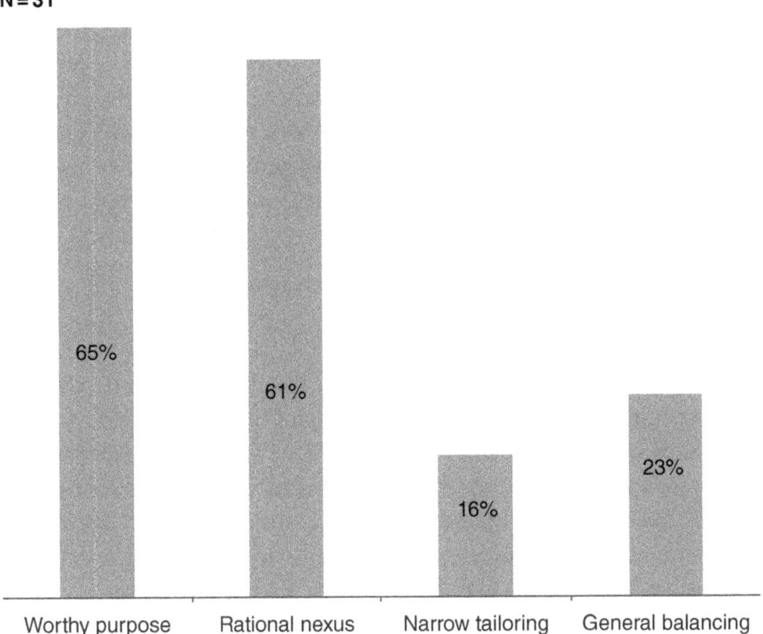


**Figure 6.6** Frequency of failure for each element of the analysis

unreasonable. Measures are most likely to fail at the worthy purpose and rational nexus elements. Only in 16 per cent of the cases did the measure fail for being overbroad, and not narrowly tailored to the purposes of the measure. And while, as Figures 6.4 and 6.5 indicate, the court conducts general balancing in a significant number of cases, measures are found to fail this ground in only 23 per cent of the cases. In no case in the dataset did a case fail solely based on this element, though such instances are present for other elements: of the 31 cases that contained a finding of failure, 16 cases failed a single element of analysis. Of these, seven were failures at the worthy purpose stage and nine at the rational nexus stage.

These findings indicate that the bar for finding a right limitation to be unjustified is relatively high: the court usually finds limitations to be unjustified only if the State failed to demonstrate that the measure was following a legitimate aim or that even the low threshold for rational nexus analysis was not met. The court is primarily concerned with determining whether the impugned measure follows a worthy purpose, generally through a means rationally connected with such purposes, and less often whether the measure is overall justified, on a balance between all the interests at stake in the matter. It is not concerned with how well the measure fits its purpose, or whether it is the best, most efficient, or least rights-restricting means to achieve such a purpose. Sometimes, though not very often, the court will consider whether the measure is narrowly tailored to the purposes it seeks to serve, and where a measure is found wanting on this score, the court generally rectifies the defect itself by reading down the scope of the measure.

## V Limitation of a Constitutional Right

### *A Establishing the Limitation of a Right*

**Presumption of Constitutionality and Burden of Proof:** the court presumes state action to be constitutional and that the burden of proving otherwise is on the party challenging the law.[127] The rationale for such a presumption is deference to legislative wisdom regarding the problem at hand, the needs of the people, and the solutions required.[128] Recently, the court has held that the presumption of constitutionality also extends to pre-constitutional laws like the Indian Penal Code since, by not amending the law, the legislature has implicitly supported the law.[129]

In some cases, the court has discussed the scope of the presumption of constitutionality and the burden of proof. Specifically, an issue before the court has been whether the burden shifts to the State once the petitioner shows that the right is limited. In a few cases, it has held that the burden does shift to the State once the petitioner has demonstrated a limitation of a fundamental right,[130] while in others it has held that once the State has proved that the measure served a legitimate aim, the burden shifts back to the petitioner.[131]

A classic example of the impact of the presumption of constitutionality on the court's decision arises from the case concerning the constitutionality of the death penalty. In *Bachan Singh v State of Punjab*,[132] the majority opinion held that given the presumption of constitutionality, it was on those challenging the death penalty to show that it serves no valid

[127] *Ram Krishna Dalmia v Justice S. R. Tendolkar* AIR 1958 SC 538.
[128] *Pathumma* (n 93); *Mohd. Hanif Quareshi v State of Bihar* AIR 1958 SC 731.
[129] *Koushal v Naz Foundation* (2014) 1 SCC 1.
[130] *Saghir Ahmad v State of UP* AIR 1954 SC 728; *Mohd. Faruk v State of Madhya Pradesh* (1969) 1 SCC 853.
[131] *Dharam Dutt* (n 91).
[132] *Bachan Singh* (n 45).

penological purpose and is therefore unreasonable. Since empirical evidence as well as theoretical opinion is divided on the question of whether the death penalty serves the function of deterrence, the court held that the burden had not been discharged by the petitioners and, therefore, the death penalty was constitutional.

The dissenting opinion in the case, however, took a different view of the presumption of constitutionality. Opining that while as a general matter state action should be presumed constitutional, in exceptional cases 'having regard to the nature and character of the legislation, the importance of the right affected and the gravity the injury caused by it and the moral and social issues involved in the determination',[133] the court may set aside its usual deference to legislative judgment and seek justification from the State for the exercise of state power. For the dissenting judge, the uncertainty in the empirical evidence on the link between death penalty and deterrence therefore indicated its unconstitutionality.[134]

However, *Bachan Singh* is an exceptional case in that as a general matter the presumption of constitutionality and burden of proof are not substantial hurdles in rights review. In practice, very rarely, if at all, does the court make any distinctions between the submissions of parties on the basis of onus of proof. The question of whose burden it is to prove a particular point in a specific case is not addressed frequently. In the entire dataset the court mentioned the presumption of constitutionality and burden of proof in 10 per cent of the cases. In 80 per cent of these, the court mentioned the presumption and burden to underscore the point that the court would not lightly interfere with legislative and policy decisions. However, these points were not determinative of the court's final ruling, and in all these cases it went on to discuss all the rival merits of both parties for each step of the rights analysis.[135] In all these cases, the court upheld the impugned measure.

[133] ibid (Bhagwati J dissenting).

[134] ibid.

[135] *Subramanian Swamy v CBI* (n 85); *Amarendra Kumar Mohapatra v State of Orissa* (2014) 4 SCC 583; *Hindustan Zinc Ltd v Rajasthan Electricity Regulatory Commission* (2015) 12 SCC 611; *Vikram Singh v Union of India* (2015) 9 SCC 502; *Essar Steel Ltd v Union of India* (2016) 11 SCC 1; *State of Punjab v Jagjit Singh* (2017) 1 SCC 148. In *State of Gujarat v Mirzapur Moti Kureshi Kassab Jamat* (2005) 8 SCC 534 (Cow Slaughter case) and in *State of Himachal Pradesh v Rajesh Chander Sood* (2016) 10 SCC 77 the Court held that the petitioners had failed to discharge the burden.

In another two cases the court did discuss whether the petitioner had discharged the burden and found in both that it had not. These cases pertained to reasonable classifications, and the court held that the petitioners had failed to show that they were,[136] or were not,[137] similarly situated to the comparator group.

In a few recent cases, the Supreme Court has required the state to demonstrate 'intelligent care and deliberation' in designing the rights-infringing measure.[138] For example, in *Cellular Operators Association v Telecom Regulatory Authority of India*,[139] the court struck down regulations that imposed a penalty upon telecom companies for call drops, on the ground that the regulations in question must be based on 'intelligent care and deliberation' to pass constitutional muster, and that this standard had not been met. This is because the materials relied upon by the State to justify the measure contained inconsistencies, lack of logical clarity, and elements of guess-work, and thus demonstrated arbitrariness. While not framed as a burden of proof issue, the requirement upon the state to demonstrate 'intelligent care and deliberation' in the policy-making process implies that it is upon the state to show that its decision-making process complied with the Constitution.

**Intent of the Lawmaker vs. Impact of the Law:** in rights review, the focus of the court's scrutiny is on the impact of the law on a person's fundamental rights, and not on the intent or stated purpose of the impugned measure. That is, just because the State was pursuing a laudable objective, or was not intending to limit fundamental rights, does not immunize the action from scrutiny. A person challenging a state action does not have to show that the state action was 'actuated by a hostile or inimical intention against a particular person or class'.[140]

The court has stated that it will examine the direct consequence of a law, rather than its object or purpose, to determine whether a right has been limited or not. The court approved this proposition in *Bennett*

However, the Court examined the State's deliberative process in detail in both cases to make the affirmative point that the state action was substantively justified.

136 *Amin Merchant v Chairman, Central Board of Excise and Customs* (2016) 9 SCC 191.

137 *V. Lavanya v State of Tamil Nadu* (2017) 1 SCC 372.

138 *M.P. Oil Extraction v State of M.P.* (1997) 7 SCC 592 (stating that policy that is not informed by any reason whatsoever and is 'founded on mere ipse dixit of the executive functionaries' offends Article 14).

139 (2016) 7 SCC 703.

140 *Anwar Ali Sarkar* (n 71). See also, *State of M.P. v Bhopal Sugar Industries Ltd* AIR 1964 SC 1179.

*Coleman v Union of India.*[141] This case involved a challenge to various laws which placed restrictions on the import and usage of newsprint by media houses. Petitioners challenged this law on the ground that the restriction curtailed the freedom of the press by limiting the volume of newsprint. On the other hand, the State contended that the direct object of the impugned law or action and not its effect should determine whether the right in question is attracted. The object of the impugned policy was the rationing of an imported commodity and the equitable distribution of newsprint, in order to effectively deal with the scarcity of newsprint. Since the law's impugned policy did not 'directly and immediately' deal with the freedom of the press, the right to free speech would not be attracted just because as a consequence of the law, the right is incidentally abridged. The court rejected this argument. It held that to determine whether a fundamental right has been limited or not, the court would examine whether the law has the consequence of directly affecting a fundamental right, and not whether the subject matter or object of the law directly affected the right in question. In the specific case, the court found that regardless of the object of the law, the direct effect of the policy was that freedom of speech and expression was limited.

That the impact of a given law and not the intention behind the law will determine whether a law violates fundamental rights is now so well settled that arguments such as these are not raised in recent case-law. No case in the dataset contained argumentation on this point.

**Scope of the Right:** as a first step, the court has to decide whether the petitioner's claim falls within the scope of the right, and if so, whether the right has actually been limited. Upon finding that the right has been limited, the court will move to the next step and evaluate whether the limitation was justified.

Article 14, the right to equality, only prohibits the State from acting in a discriminatory or arbitrary manner. It does not affirmatively guarantee a right, and then permit the State to limit that right. In that sense, Article 14 analysis does not proceed along a two-step analysis of whether there was a limitation of a right, and whether the limitation was justified. As a basic requirement for the classification test to be triggered, the State has to classify between persons or things, which is a very low threshold – almost every law will meet this condition. The classification should be clear; that is, it should be possible to distinguish who falls within the

141 *Bennett Coleman* (n 88).

purview of the law and who does not. If it is not possible to determine whom the law targets, then the law is likely to suffer from vagueness, and will fall foul of Article 14.[142] If the classification is clear, the court moves to its analysis of the rational nexus between the classification and the object of the law.

Under Articles 19 and 21, the first step in the rights review process is determining whether a right is engaged because of the impugned measure. The court generally interprets rights broadly to include within its ambit every right that 'is an integral part of a named fundamental right or partakes of the same basic nature and character as that fundamental right'.[143]

The court has held that the scope of a right encompasses everything necessary for the *effective exercise* of that right. To illustrate the court's approach, in *Sakal Newspapers v Union of India*,[144] petitioners challenged the constitutionality of a law that empowered the government to regulate the price of newspapers and the allocation of space for advertisements. The government fixed the maximum number of pages that must be published by a newspaper according to a price-schedule, and prescribed limits on the number of supplements that could be issued by newspapers. These laws were challenged on the ground that they violated the freedom of speech. The government contended, inter alia, that these laws had been promulgated for curbing monopolistic practices in the print media and were intended to enhance free speech and expression and therefore serve the 'interests of the general public' by curbing unfair practices. The court held that the practices sought to be restricted fell within the scope of freedom of speech, because that right not only guarantees the right to propagate one's ideas, but also publish, disseminate, and circulate those ideas for purposes of propagation. Therefore, the freedom of speech extends 'not merely to the matter which he is entitled to circulate, but also to the volume of circulation'. The government could restrict this right only on the constitutionally specified grounds for limiting freedom of speech. Since 'interests of the general public' was not such a ground, the law was declared invalid.

Following a similar approach, the Court has held that the right to free speech includes the right to education because free speech as well as other fundamental rights 'cannot be appreciated and fully enjoyed unless a

[142] See n 272–75 and accompanying text for a discussion on vague laws.
[143] *Meneka Gandhi* (n 65).
[144] AIR 1962 SC 305.

citizen is educated and is conscious of his individualistic dignity'.[145] Moreover, the right to education has itself been held to include the right to receive education in a medium of one's choosing.[146]

The court approaches the right to life and personal liberty in a similar manner and includes within the scope of the right all that is required to make the right effective. The court has interpreted 'right to life' to include not only physical well-being but also those components of social and economic well-being that influence the quality of a person's life.[147] The right to life with dignity,[148] as well as the 'right to food, the right to clothing, the right to decent environment and a reasonable accommodation to live

[145] *Mohini Jain v State of Karnataka* (1992) 3 SCC 666. In this case, petitioners challenged a government order permitting private medical colleges to charge capitation fees from out of State students. The Court held that since the right to education was guaranteed by part III of the Constitution, the State had an obligation to provide educational opportunities to all citizens through State-run or State-recognized institutions. 'Opportunity to acquire education cannot be confined to the richer section of the society . . . Every citizen has a `right to education' under the Constitution . . . Charging capitation fee in consideration of admission to educational institutions, is a patent denial of a citizen's right to education under the Constitution. Capitation fee is nothing but a price for selling education.'

[146] *State of Karnataka v Associated Management of (Government Recognised-Unaided-English Medium) Primary and Secondary Schools* (2014) 9 SCC 485 (English Medium case). Using a similar approach, the Court has held that the right to free speech and expression includes the right to know the antecedents of a candidate for elections because '[p]ublic education is essential for functioning of the process of popular government and to assist the discovery of truth and strengthening the capacity of an individual in participating in decision making process. The decision making process of a voter would include his right to know about public functionaries who are required to be elected by him.' *Union of India v Association for Democratic Reforms* (2002) 5 SCC 294.

[147] *Francis Coralie Mullin* (n 64) ('[T]the right to life enshrined in Article 21 cannot be restricted to mere animal existence . . . [T]he right to life includes the right to live with human dignity and all that goes along with it, namely, the bare necessaries of life such as adequate nutrition, clothing and shelter and facilities for reading, writing and expressing one-self in diverse forms, freely moving about and mixing and commingling with fellow human beings. Of course, the magnitude and content of the components of this right would depend upon the extent of the economic development of the country, but it must, in any view of the matter, include the right to the basic necessities of life and also the right to carry on such functions and activities as constitute the bare minimum expression of the human-self. Every act which offends against or impairs human dignity would constitute deprivation protanto of this right to live and it would have to be in accordance with reasonable, fair and just procedure established by law which stands the test of other fundamental rights.'); *Confederation of Ex-Servicemen Associations v Union of India* 2006 (8) SCC 399 ('It cannot be gainsaid that right to life guaranteed under Article 21 of the Constitution embraces within its sweep not only physical existence but the quality of life'). See also, *P. Rathinam v Union of India* AIR 1994 SC 1844; *Peerless General Finance and Investment Co. Ltd. v Reserve Bank of India* (1992) 2 SCC 343.

[148] *Francis Coralie Mullin* (n 64).

in',[149] have all been included within the scope of the right to life. So, also, the right to livelihood,[150] the right to a clean environment,[151] the right to reputation,[152] the right to health,[153] the right to education,[154] and even the right to sleep,[155] have been held to be part of the right to life.

In deciding what rights comprise the right to life, the court again follows a very functional analysis. If a particular human need or interest is essential for securing the physical, mental, or social well-being of a person, such need or interest is captured within the right to life guaranteed by Article 21. An example of such reasoning is *Olga Tellis v Bombay Municipal Corporation*,[156] where the court held that the right to life includes the 'right to livelihood' because a person cannot live without having the means to live, which is derived from livelihood. Depriving a person of their livelihood 'would not only denude the life of its effective content and meaningfulness but it would make life impossible to live'.[157] Extending this analysis further, in another case, the court has held that a worker has a right to health as part of the right to life, since '[l]ack of health deprives him of his livelihood'.[158] On this basis the court held that workers had a right under Article 21 to be provided with medical facilities to protect their health.[159]

149 *M/s. Shantistar Builders v Narayan Khimalal Totame* AIR 1990 SC 630.

150 See *Olga Tellis* (n 102).

151 See, e.g., *Vellore Citizens Welfare Forum v Union of India* AIR 1996 SC 2715.

152 *State of Maharashtra v Public Concern for Governance Trust* (2007) 3 SCC 587; *Board of Trustees of the Port of Bombay v Dilip Kumar Raghavendranath Natkarni* 1983 (1) SCC 124.

153 *Parmanand Katara v Union of India* AIR 1989 SC 2039.

154 *Unni Krishnan v State of AP* AIR 1993 SC 2178.

155 *In re: Ram Lila Maidan Incident* (2012) 5 SCC 1.

156 *Olga Tellis* (n 102). In this case, the Court had to decide whether the eviction of pavement and slum dwellers from the city of Bombay, and their removal to their places of origin or to places outside the city, would violate their right to livelihood and therefore their right to life under Article 21. The Court agreed that the livelihood of the pavement dwellers and street hawkers would be infringed by the measure because their livelihood depended upon jobs in the city. The proposed removal would therefore render them jobless and impact their livelihood.

157 The Court held that the limitation of the right would be valid if just, fair, and reasonable procedure was followed by the State. This requirement would be satisfied if the State gave those affected a reasonable opportunity to be heard before evicting them, or provided them with alternative accommodation within the city.

158 *Consumer Education & Research Centre v Union of India* (2000) (2) SCC 599.

159 But see, *Meneka Gandhi* (n 65), where the Court has held that a right under Article 19 (1) does not encompass within its scope every activity which is necessary for, or facilitates, the exercise of that fundamental right. The Court held that '[i]t is not enough that a right claimed by the petitioner flows or emanates from a named fundamental right or that its existence is necessary in order to make the exercise of the named fundamental

The right to personal liberty under Article 21 has also been broadly construed.[160] The court has included within it various autonomy interests, such as the right to privacy,[161] the right to travel abroad,[162] and rights against arbitrary arrest and detention. All matters involving the criminal sanction, or otherwise the loss of physical liberty, are considered limitations of the right to personal liberty. In such cases, the court often does not analyse whether the right was implicated or not. It directly engages with the limitations analysis.

The court has not formulated any clear principle or method for determining whether a particular interest is essential for the effective exercise of a right. Instead, the court has relied on textual guides such as the Directive Principles of State Policy,[163] the Preamble to the Constitution, and the Chapter on Fundamental Duties (of Citizens);[164] on precedents,[165] comparative insights,[166] and international law;[167] or on a functional analysis of the value and purpose of the right, to determine the

right meaningful and effective. Every activity which facilitates the exercise of a named fundamental right is not necessarily comprehended in that fundamental right nor can it be regarded as such merely because it may not be possible otherwise to effectively exercise that fundamental right. What is necessary to be seen is, and that is the test which must be applied is, whether the right claimed by the petitioner is an integral part of a named fundamental right or partakes of the same basic nature and character as the named fundamental right so that the exercise of such right is in reality and substance nothing but an instance of the exercise of the named fundamental right. If this be the correct test, the right to go abroad cannot in all circumstances be regarded as included in freedom of speech and expression.' See also, *All India Bank Employees' Association v National Industrial Tribunal* [1962] 3 SCR 269. However, very few cases, if any, appear to follow this dicta.

160 *Meneka Gandhi* (n 65).

161 Right to Privacy case (n 10); *Gobind v State of MP* AIR 1975 SC 1378; *PUCL v Union of India* (1997) 1 SCC 301.

162 *Meneka Gandhi* (n 65).

163 See, e.g., *Bandhua Mukti Morcha* (n 60), where the Court stated that 'the right to live with human dignity . . . derives its life breath from the Directive Principles of State Policy and particularly clauses (e) and (f) of Article 39 and Article 41 and 42 . . . These are the minimum requirements which must exist in order to enable a person to live with human dignity . . . '

164 Elections Disqualification I (n 60).

165 Every case in the 2004–13 dataset which discussed the scope of Article 19 (1) rights, first looked to precedents on the point.

166 See example, *Secretary, Ministry of Information and Broadcasting, Govt. of India v Cricket Association of Bengal* (1995) 2 SCC 161, where the Court referred to Article 10, European Convention on Human Rights and decisions of the European Court of Human Rights under that provision, to read in 'broadcasting freedom' into Article 19 (1) (a).

167 For example, *Union of India v Association for Democratic Reforms* (n 146), citing Article 19, ICCPR for reading in a 'right to information' into Article 19 (1) (a). See also, *People's*

scope of the right.[168] This latter approach is most evident in right to free speech cases, where the court has generally linked the protection of free speech to the importance of free speech for a well-functioning democracy,[169] or to its importance for individual well-being,[170] to determine the scope of the right.[171]

Apart from expansively interpreting rights, the court has also understood rights, especially the right to life, as imposing negative as well as positive obligations upon the State.[172] Therefore, the State not only has an obligation to ensure that it does not violate the expanded right to life but also to ensure through its actions that these rights are secured.[173] The court has not established any minimum core content of rights which cannot be limited. The court also makes no distinctions between core and peripheral or 'derivative' rights. In *PUCL v Union of India*,[174] the court specifically rejected the contention that certain rights (in this case, the right to know the antecedents of candidates for elections) were 'derivative rights' and therefore stood on a different footing from core fundamental rights. The court rejected this contention on the basis that rights have no fixed content and what the court does in interpreting the right is to give it content. It does not thereby *create* a new or derivative right.

*Union for Civil Liberties v Union of India* (2004) 2 SCC 476; *C.E.S.C. Ltd. v Subhash Chandra Bose* (1992) 1 SCC 441; *PUCL v Union of India* (n 162).

[168] See *Kuldip Nayar v Union of India* AIR 2006 SC 3127, as an example of a case employing all sources.

[169] See *Sahara India* (n 5). Here the question before the Court was whether a court could issue orders directing newspapers to postpone the publication of information relating to subjudice matters. In describing the importance and scope of Article 19 (1) (a), the Court held that 'Freedom of expression is one of the most cherished values of a free democratic society. It is indispensable to the operation of a democratic society whose basic postulate is that the government shall be based on the consent of the governed. But, such a consent implies not only that the consent shall be free but also that it shall be grounded on adequate information, discussion and aided by the widest possible dissemination of information and opinions from diverse and antagonistic sources. Freedom of expression which includes freedom of the press has a capacious content . . . '

[170] See *English Medium* case (n 146) (citing John Stuart Mill and Harold Laski, to emphasize the importance of free speech for individual growth and development).

[171] *Shreya Singhal* (n 68).

[172] *P. Rathinam* (n 147).

[173] It is pertinent to note that the right to livelihood is an exception to this norm. The Court has clearly stated that the right to livelihood does not obligate the State to provide livelihood to individuals. However, a person's existing livelihood cannot be deprived without just, fair, and reasonable process. See *Olga Tellis* (n 102).

[174] (2003) 4 SCC 399.

Since rights are generally interpreted liberally, most cases clear this part of the test (the court found a rights limitation in 94 per cent of the database of 98 cases), and the court moves to examine whether the limitation was justified. However, two exceptions exist to the general practice. First, very infrequently, the right articulated is considered so important that the court finds that no limitation of the right can be justified as reasonable.[175] The right against torture is a classic example of a right that can have no justified limitation, on the reasoning that torture violates the right to life with dignity.[176] The court has also used language indicative of a non-derogable right in discussing the right to medical assistance in cases of serious injuries as part of the right to health.[177] It is unclear, however, whether the court's expression was just overbroad, or whether the court was actually articulating a principle that allowed for no limitation. While the case has been cited frequently, the court has not engaged with the implications of framing the right as non-derogable in subsequent cases.

Second, while the court generally begins its discussion on the right by reiterating the broad parameters as developed in landmark cases, in most cases, the court moves very quickly past the scope of the right stage to focus on the limitations stage. It examines – as opposed to merely stating – the scope of the right only when it is advancing the right in new directions, or when the State challenges the petitioner's claim that in the case at hand the right is limited. Examples of the former include cases where the court read in, for the first time, the right to self-identification of gender identity as protected by Articles 19 and 21;[178] the right to

[175] In no case in the database did the Court take this position.

[176] *Francis Coralie Mullin* (n 64) ('Now obviously, any form of torture or cruel, inhuman or degrading treatment would be offensive to human dignity and constitute an inroad into this right to live and it would, on this view, be prohibited by Article 21 unless it is in accordance with procedure prescribed by law, but no law which authorises and no procedure which leads to such torture or cruel, inhuman or degrading treatment can ever stand the test of reasonableness and non-arbitrariness: it would plainly be unconstitutional and void as being violative of Articles 14 and 21').

[177] See, e.g., *Parmanand Katara* (n 153). This case dealt with a then prevalent practice in medico-legal cases, where doctors would refuse to provide treatment to a seriously injured patient till the police were notified. The Court held that this practice violated the right to life, and that the obligation of doctors to provide treatment to seriously injured persons 'being total, absolute and paramount, laws of procedure whether in statutes or otherwise which would interfere with the discharge of this obligation cannot be sustained and must, therefore, give way'.

[178] *NALSA v Union of India* (2014) 5 SCC 438.

reputation as protected by the right to life with dignity;[179] and the right to safe working conditions for workers as part of the right to life.[180] Cases involving significant opposition to the petitioner's understanding of the right include *Shabnam Hashmi v Union of India*,[181] where the court refused to read the right to adopt as part of the right to life in Article 21 based on strong opposition to such an interpretation by the Muslim Personal Law Board, which produced various religious scriptures to show that under Islamic law, adoption is not permitted.[182] Similarly, in the *English Medium* case,[183] where the court had to decide whether the right to free speech includes the right to be instructed in a language of one's choice, the State argued that it did not. The court examined the scope of the right to free speech, and held that the right to free speech did include the right to be instructed in a language of one's choice.[184]

Sometimes, though not often, the court balances the right against the countervailing state interest and limits the scope of the right so that no limitation is found. That is, the court engages in a balancing exercise within the scope of the right itself. The countervailing interest is presented either as public interest traceable to a directive principle of state policy, or as countervailing fundamental rights of other individuals or group. The court engaged in this form of analysis in only one case in the database of 98 cases. In *State of Karnataka v Umadevi*,[185] the court held

[179] *Om Prakash Chautala v Kanwar Bhan* (2014) 5 SCC 417.

[180] *Occupational Health and Safety Association v Union of India* (2014) 3 SCC 547.

[181] (2014) 4 SCC 1.

[182] This case, where the petitioner argued that the right to life with dignity under Article 21 should include the right to adopt for all persons (regardless of their religion), has to be understood in the context of a long drawn political and legal battle over whether the family laws of particular communities should be governed by religious laws (as is currently the case) to which fundamental rights should not apply; or by a uniform civil code. The Court has generally been wary of treading on the domain of religious scriptures and has said time and again that it is for the legislature to decide this issue.

[183] English Medium case (n 146).

[184] The only case in the dataset where the Court examined the scope of an Article 19 right in detail without either extending the right in new directions, and without the Petitioner's claim of limitation being challenged, was in *Shreya Singhal* (n 68). In this case, petitioners challenged Section 66A of the Information Technology Act, 2000, which made it an offence to send over the computer or other communication devices information that is grossly offensive, menacing, or for the purpose of causing annoyance, inconvenience, etc. Though it was patently clear that the provision limited the right to freedom of speech, and no one argued otherwise, the Court went into a detailed discussion of the scope of the right, its importance, and what exactly the right seeks to protect.

[185] (2006) 4 SCC 1.

that temporary public employees do not have a 'right to employment' as part of their right to livelihood, which is itself protected by the right to life. As such, they cannot claim a right to be made permanent. This analysis was based on the consideration that recognizing such a right might deny opportunities to others who might be desirous of seeking public employment, but who lose out because of the purported 'right to employment' in these offices of the temporary employees. The court held that such a scenario would go against the DPSP mandate to secure livelihood for all, and therefore, the right to life cannot extend to covering a right to employment.

Additional examples, not included in the scope of the database, can be brought to demonstrate this phenomenon. In *Harish Uppal v Union of India*,[186] the question before the court was whether lawyers had a right to strike work as part of their right to free speech and expression under Article 19 (1) (a). The court rejected this contention. Holding that the right to speedy trial is part of the guarantee of right to life and liberty under Article 21, the court opined that a strike by lawyers will infringe this right, and therefore the right to strike was not available to lawyers under Article 19 (1) (a).[187]

The court has also limited the scope of rights in order to advance other public interests. Take for example, Article 19 (1) (g), which guarantees the freedom to practice any profession or to carry on any occupation, trade, or business. In a series of cases the court has held that certain trades and activities can be excluded from the scope of Article 19 (1) (g) on the ground of their adverse and reprehensible moral and social effects. Such activities are deemed to be 'res extra commercium', i.e., these activities are outside the limits of permissible trade and commerce, and therefore no one has a right to engage in them. On this basis the court has held that trade in liquor,[188] gambling

[186] (2003) 2 SCC 45.

[187] See also, *Communist Party of India (M) v Bharat Kumar* (1998) 1 SCC 201 (holding that there is no right to call a *bandh*, that is, a cessation of all work and a complete shut down across a city or a State, because 'the fundamental rights of the people as a whole cannot be subservient to the claim of fundamental right of an individual or only a section of the people . . . [T]here cannot be any right to call or enforce a "Bandh" which interferes with the exercise of the fundamental freedoms of other citizens, in addition to causing national loss in many ways.'). On the point of conflicts between fundamental rights being resolved as a matter of the scope of a right, see also, *Union of India v Motion Pictures Association* (1999) 6 SCC 150.

[188] *Narishwar v State of MP* (1975) 1 SCC 29.

activities,[189] and 'unscrupulous money-lending'[190] are not protected by Article 19 (1) (g).[191]

In other cases, the court frames the countervailing interest as a right itself and therefore as a legitimate restriction on the scope of the right. An example is *G. Sundarajjan v Union of India*,[192] where the setting up of a Nuclear Power Plant was challenged, inter alia on the ground that the potential ecological and health impact of nuclear radiation would violate the right to life of those living in the vicinity of the power plant. In deciding this question, the court framed the issue as one of balancing the right to life of those residing near the power plant and the right to life of the larger community, which would benefit from the nuclear energy through economic growth, poverty alleviation, and employment generation. Balancing between the public interest and the right to life of the individuals affected, the court held that the nuclear power plant would protect the right to life in the 'larger sense' and as such would not 'negate right to life but to protect the right to life guaranteed under Article 21 of the Constitution'. As such, the establishment of the nuclear power plant was held to not limit the right to life.

Logically, once the court finds that the right in question is engaged, it has to determine whether the right has been limited on the facts of the case. Questions like the severity of limitation, whether the limitation meets some minimum threshold so as to warrant interference by the court, and whether the petitioner has discharged the evidentiary burden required to prove that the right was actually limited, etc., would arise at

[189] *State of Bombay v R M D Chamarbaugwala* AIR 1957 SC 699 ('We find it difficult to accept the contention that those activities which encourage a spirit of reckless , propensity for making easy gain by lot or chance, which lead to the loss of the hard earned money of the undiscerning and improvident common man and thereby lower his standard of living and drive him into a chronic state of indebtedness and eventually disrupt the peace and happiness of his humble home could possibly have been intended by our Constitution makers to be raised to the status of trade, commerce or intercourse and to be made the subject-matter of a fundamental right guaranteed by Art. 19(1) (g)').

[190] *Fatehchand Himmatlal v State of Maharashtra* (1977) 2 SCC 670.

[191] In 2015, in *Kerala Bar Hotels Association v State of Kerala* (2015) 16 SCC 421, the Court had to determine the constitutionality of a provision that limited the sale of liquor in the State of Kerala to only five-star hotels. In doing so, the Court revisited the issue of whether Article 19 (1) (g) protects the right to trade in liquor. It held that while trade in liquor is 'res extra commercium' and therefore generally not protected by Article 19 (1) (g), once the State itself permits trade in liquor, the right to such trade does become protected, and can be validly limited only within the parameters permitted by Article 19 (6).

[192] (2013) 6 SCC 620.

this stage. However, this stage of the analysis is generally absent from the court's framework of review. As soon as the court finds that the petitioner's claim falls within the scope of the right, the court moves onto the limitations analysis.

## VI Worthy Purpose

### *A The Role of Worthy Purpose in Limitation Analysis*

Once the court finds that a right has been limited, its limitations analysis first turns to the purpose for which the State has limited the right. This element is central to the limitations inquiry and in nearly every case in the database where limitation analysis was triggered the court engaged in an analysis of purpose. The purpose analysis sets the stage for the subsequent analysis, if any, of rational nexus and general balancing between means and ends. The general balancing stage in particular draws heavily on the purpose inquiry, since the purpose inquiry clarifies the interests that the State is pursuing. The court almost never skips this element, and if the State fails to demonstrate that it was following a worthy purpose, the measure will fail.[193] Sixty-five per cent of the cases where a measure was found unreasonable failed at this stage, which is a high number since, as discussed later, the court is generally very deferential to the State's articulation of purpose. Administrative and legislative measures failed this element in almost equal numbers.[194]

### *B Establishing a Worthy Purpose*

In examining this element of the State's justification for limiting the right, the court asks three distinct questions: what is the purpose, why is the State pursuing that purpose (the 'needs' analysis), and whether it is a legitimate purpose for the State to pursue. As article 19 (fundamental freedoms) lists the purposes for which rights guaranteed by that provision can be limited, these questions are asked with reference to the listed purposes. Despite the fact that articles 14 (equality) and 21 (life and personal liberty) do not provide an explicit list of legitimate purposes, all

193 See, e.g., *Virendra Krishna Mishra v Union of India* (2015) 2 SCC 712; *Vikram Cement v State of Madhya Pradesh* (2015) 11 SCC 708; *Union of India v N S Rathnam* (2015) 10 SCC 681 (where the State failed to show what purpose it was following, and the measure was held to be unreasonable on that count).

194 11 (out of 17) and 9 (out of 14), respectively.

three questions also appear in analysing limitations of Article 21, as well as Article 14 in arbitrariness review. Per doctrine, in Article 14 classification analysis, only the first question has to be asked. However, the court generally goes into the second question and often the third as well.

An example will help explain the aspects of the worthy purpose analysis. In *Subramanian Swamy v Raju (Juvenile Justice Case)*,[195] petitioners challenged the interpretation of the Juvenile Justice Act, which treated all offenders below the age of 18 as juveniles and diverted them to a distinct adjudicative set up, instead of the regular criminal justice system. The law also provided reduced sentences for offences committed by such persons. In the case at hand (which followed in the wake of a high profile and horrific gang rape in Delhi where one of the accused persons was a juvenile), the petitioners argued that the Juvenile Justice Act should be understood as prescribing a mental age of 18 years as opposed to a chronological age. According to them, different persons grow in mental and emotional maturity at different speeds, and to put all persons under the age of 18 in a separate class, without any individualized determination of their mental capacities, violates Article 14.

In defending the law, the State argued (and the court accepted) that the law was enacted to fulfil India's international commitments, as well as in light of scientific evidence regarding the age of maturity. The court further held that enacting legislation to further India's international commitments, with the objective of rehabilitating young offenders so that they can become useful members of society, was a legitimate reason for enacting the law.[196] Note that the court goes beyond just stating what the object of the law is. It also examines the need for pursuing the object and its legitimacy.

In an Article 19 inquiry, the need to analyse legitimacy of purpose is explicit since the structure of the Article 19 limitations clauses itself requires the court to evaluate whether the impugned measure serves one or more of the enumerated purposes.[197] Take for example, *Romesh Thapar v State of Madras*,[198] where a law regulating the circulation, sale, and distribution of documents was sought to be justified on the ground

[195] (2014) 8 SCC 390.

[196] The Court held that the lack of individualized determination of mental maturity, was for the Court, not reason enough to strike down the law since 'the broad features of the categorization are identifiable and distinguishable and the categorization made is reasonably connected with the object targeted'. Therefore, the law complies with Article 14.

[197] See Constitution, art. 19 (n 87).

[198] AIR 1950 SC 124.

of securing 'public safety' or maintaining 'public order'. Since neither were expressly stated grounds for limiting the freedom of speech, the court found the impugned measure invalid.

A recent case along similar lines is the *English Medium* case,[199] where the question before the court was whether the State could by law mandate that a child will be educated only in her mother tongue in primary and early secondary schooling. Petitioners challenged this law on the ground that the freedom of speech encompasses a child's (and her parents') right to choose the medium of education. On behalf of the State it was argued that the law was enacted because educationists agreed that a child learns better when she is taught in her mother tongue. Further, the law was also aimed at protecting local languages and cultures. As such, the law was 'in the larger interest of the nation'. The court held that the measure, however necessary or important, did not relate to any of the specified grounds for limiting freedom of speech, and was therefore invalid.[200]

While the legitimacy analysis is integral to the Article 19 review, in Article 14 and 21 analyses, the court has tended to state that it will not question the wisdom of the State's purpose, i.e., the court will not examine whether the State should be pursuing that purpose in the first place. However, in practice it appears that the court does evaluate the legitimacy of objectives. So, for example, in the *Juvenile Justice* case,[201] discussed earlier, while on the one hand the court refused to look at data on the rates of violent crimes by juveniles and held that it would not examine the wisdom of the law, on the other hand, it did validate the rehabilitative goal behind the Juvenile Justice Act.

Similarly, in Article 14 arbitrariness analysis relating to the distribution of public resources, the court examines whether the distribution was in the public interest or for private benefit – the latter being illegitimate.[202] In classification analysis too, the court has increasingly tended to examine the legitimacy of the object itself, exemplified in the dataset by *Subramanian Swamy v Director, CBI*,[203] where the court struck down a provision requiring the authorities investigating corruption cases against senior Central Government bureaucrats to seek prior approval of the Central Government. The court held that the avowed objective of this

199 *English Medium* case (n 146).
200 Along similar lines, see *Mohd. Faruk* (n 130).
201 *Subramanian Swamy v Raju* (n 195).
202 *Natural Resource Allocation* (n 79).
203 *Subramanian Swamy v CBI* (n 85).

law, to protect senior policy-making bureaucrats from harassment, was illegitimate since the provision 'thwarts an independent, unhampered, unbiased, efficient and fearless inquiry/investigation to track down the corrupt public servants'. Further, the stated objective of the law was found to subvert the more fundamental objective of the system as a whole, to 'deal with corruption and act against senior public servants'. The court therefore found the objective of the measure illegitimate.[204]

Similarly, in Article 21 analysis, the court has held that if the objective of the State is geared towards a DPSP, it is presumptively legitimate.[205] *Chameli Singh v State of UP*[206] is an example of this approach. Here, the state compulsorily acquired the petitioners' agricultural land to provide housing for marginalized communities. Petitioners claimed that since they depended upon the acquired land for their livelihood, their right to livelihood, as part of their right to life, had been unjustifiably infringed by the acquisition. The court held that, in light of DPSP which enjoin the State to ensure socio-economic justice, the guarantee of the right to life has to be read to include a right to shelter. The Government therefore has a positive obligation to provide shelter to those who do not have shelter. Since the exercise of the power of acquisition fulfilled a social need and was for a legitimate purpose, the exercise was valid.

Taken together, the inquiry into purpose serves three goals. One is to clarify what the object of the law is, so as to determine whether there is a nexus between means and ends. Two, this stage sets up the stakes in the matter, by clarifying the importance of the objective. In this, the discussion on purpose feeds into the general balancing aspects of the limitations analysis. Third, the purpose inquiry serves to identify measures that are pursuing illegitimate objectives, and to weed out irrational decisions made without 'intelligent care and deliberation'.[207] Of the measures that

[204] See also, *Air India v Nargesh Mirza* AIR 1981 SC 1829, where the Court had to determine the constitutionality of a rule that required the termination of services of an air-hostess if she became pregnant. The State contended that the object of the law was to prevent the difficulties for the pregnant woman if she were to continue in service. The Court held this to be an illegitimate purpose for the State to pursue because whether or not she finds it difficult 'is her personal matter' and not for the State to interfere with. In this case therefore, the Court was evaluating the object itself, instead of merely stating it.

[205] See, e.g., *Cow Slaughter* case (n 135).

[206] (1996) 2 SCC 549.

[207] *M.P. Oil Extraction* (n 138) (stating that policy that is not informed by any reason whatsoever and is 'founded on mere ipse dixit of the executive functionaries' offends Article 14).

are found unreasonable, 65 per cent fail this stage, indicating that this stage is not a formality.

An illustrative example of the first two goals of the purpose inquiry is *Rajbala v State of Haryana* (*Election Disqualification II*),[208] where petitioners challenged the constitutionality of a law which disqualified persons who had not attained certain minimum educational qualifications from being elected to offices of local self-government. The purpose of the law according to the State was that the work of a local government official was such that it required literacy. The court found the measure to be related to this object. It went further and also examined need for and legitimacy of the purpose, and held that education was important not only for a person to understand her work but also to discern between right and wrong, good and bad. Therefore, the goal itself fulfilled a social need since it enabled better administration of local governments. As such, it was reasonable and rational. Additionally, since this was a legitimate goal for the State to pursue, the fact that a large number of people would be rendered ineligible to contest (which the petitioners were able to demonstrate through data) was not sufficient to render the measure unconstitutional. Therefore, balanced against the goal, the severity of the limitation did not render the measure unconstitutional. The worthy purpose analysis enabled the court to not only state what the purpose was but also determine the need and importance of the purpose, which fed into the balancing stage of the limitations analysis.

*John Vallamattom v Union of India*,[209] is an example of the use of the purpose analysis to identify measures that do not demonstrate intelligent care and deliberation. In this case, petitioners challenged a provision of law which disallowed bequests made within a year of death by Christian men having a nephew or niece or any nearer relative. This colonial era legislation had the stated purpose of preventing ill-considered death-bed bequests under religious influence. The section was challenged, inter alia, for violation of Article 14. The court held that the object of the Act was satisfied by another provision which made void any will obtained by fraud, coercion, or importunity. Beyond that, it was not clear what specific object the impugned provision sought to achieve. The section did not prevent other bequests on the death bed under influence. It did not prohibit religious and charitable bequests under religious influence at other times and did not prohibit gifts *intervivos* for religious and

[208] *Rajbala* (n 85).
[209] (2003) 6 SCC 611.

charitable purposes. Further, by virtue of definitions in the Act, a wife did not count as a 'near relative'. Therefore, if a person with a wife but no nieces, nephews, or nearer relations were to make such a will, the will would not be void. For these reasons the court found that the reasonable classification test was not satisfied.

Similarly, in a case where the State engaged in en masse termination of appointment of government counsel without any individualized consideration, the action was struck down as being arbitrary because the government could not show any rational principle or purpose on the basis of which this decision was taken.[210]

### C *What Are Worthy Purposes?*

Since Article 19 enumerates the purposes for which fundamental freedoms can be validly limited, the analysis of worthy purpose under Article 19 follows a distinct trajectory from that of other rights. Any impugned measure that is challenged for violating Article 19 has to be relatable to one of these enumerated purposes. Two lines of cases have emerged on the question of whether rights can be restricted for goals other than those mentioned in the Article 19 limitations clauses. On the one hand, are the cases that require strict compliance with the enumerated purposes mentioned. For example, in *Shreya Singhal v Union of India*,[211] the court required the State to demonstrate that it was pursuing one of the goals listed in the limitations clause of Article 19. Here, the court struck down Section 66A, Information Technology Act, 2000, for limiting the freedom of speech and expression without advancing any of the enumerated grounds for limiting the right.

On the other hand are cases where the court has held that rights can be restricted for other reasons as well, including the general public interest, other constitutional rights, and Directive Principles of State Policy. An example of an open-ended approach to purposes is *Sahara v SEBI*,[212] where the Supreme Court held that courts can pass orders directing that the publication of information regarding a *subjudice* matter be postponed, because such a postponement order will serve 'societal interest' in the administration of justice. Though such 'societal interest' is not a

[210] *Shrilekha Vidyarthi* (n 107).

[211] *Shreya Singhal* (n 68).

[212] *Sahara India* (n 5). The Court did not attempt to read such 'societal interest' into any existing ground mentioned in the relevant limitations clause.

ground mentioned in the relevant limitations clause, the court held that serving societal interest is a legitimate reason to restrict the freedom of speech.[213]

Similarly, in *Subramanian Swamy v Union of India*,[214] (*Criminal Defamation* case) the court repelled a challenge to the constitutionality of provisions that made defamation a criminal offence, inter alia on the ground that the protection of the 'right to reputation' is part of the right to life with dignity, and that the criminal defamation provision furthers this right to reputation, and therefore was valid limitation upon the freedom of speech and expression.[215]

Finally, *Security Association of India v Union of India*[216] exemplifies Article 19 rights being limited to give effect to DPSP.[217] This case was on the constitutionality of regulation of the employment conditions of private security guards. Certain provisions were challenged for violating the freedom to carry on business of private security agencies. The court held that these provisions were in furtherance of the welfare of private security guards, as envisaged under DPSP, and were for that reason pursuing a legitimate purpose.[218]

Pursuing DPSP is also a legitimate reason for limiting Article 14 and 21 rights. *Javed v State of Haryana* (*Election Disqualification I*),[219] exemplifies this point. Here, petitioners challenged a law that prohibited persons with more than two children from being eligible for, or continuing in, local government posts. The stated object of the provision was to limit population growth, and the provision attempted to do so by providing disincentives for having more than two children. Though, as per the classification test on which this law was challenged, the court was not required to go into the legitimacy of the object itself, the court validated the need to limit population growth, particularly so as to be able to direct

213 In this case, the Court was following its dicta in *Cricket Association of Bengal* (n 166), where it had held that the Article 19 (2) grounds 'are all conceived in the national interest as well as in the interest of society . . . It is true that Article 19(2) does not use the words "national interest," "interest of society" or "public interest" but . . . the several grounds mentioned in clause (2) are ultimately referable to the interests of the nation and of the society.'

214 (2016) 7 SCC 221.

215 See also, *Sahara India* (n 5); *Pramati Educational and Cultural Trust v Union of India* (2014) 8 SCC 1.

216 (2014) 12 SCC 65.

217 *Indian Handicrafts Emporium v Union of India* (2003) 7 SCC 589.

218 See also, *Hindustan Zinc Ltd* (n 136).

219 *Elections Disqualification I* case (n 60).

state resources towards achieving the ideals of socio-economic justice enshrined in DPSPs. For this reason, the object of the law was legitimate, and the measure was held to not infringe fundamental rights.

### *D What Are Unworthy Purposes?*

Typically, the court does not enumerate specific purposes that are per se illegitimate. Rather, a review of the cases in the dataset indicates that the court has developed certain tools to determine whether the purpose of the law is legitimate. If the objective of an impugned law goes against DPSP, that counts against the legitimacy of such an objective.[220] In cases involving the distribution of public resources, a significant part of the court's inquiry is directed towards evaluating whether the distribution was for a public purpose or for private benefit, the latter being unreasonable. This proposition is based on the understanding that DPSPs require the state to works towards ensuring 'that the ownership and control of the material resources of the community are so distributed as best to subserve the common good'. Distribution of public resources for private benefit therefore goes against Directive Principles and hence is illegitimate.[221]

Another factor that the court looks at to determine whether the purpose of an impugned provision is legitimate is whether that purpose is in consonance with the larger objective of the law. For example, in *Subramanian Swamy v Director, CBI*,[222] the court held that the purpose of a provision which sought to shield senior bureaucrats from vexatious litigation by putting in a requirement to seek sanction for investigation of cases went against the larger purpose of combatting corruption.[223]

Further, a purpose that was once legitimate can become illegitimate over time, if the rationale for the law is no longer applicable. Take, for instance, *Malpe Vishwanath Acharya v State of Maharashtra*.[224] In this case, petitioners challenged provisions of the Bombay Rents, Hotel and Lodging House Rates Control Act, 1947, which had placed a ceiling on rents that could be collected by landlords. The ceiling was calculated as the rent on 1 September 1940 or on the date of the first letting. This

220 *Senior Divisional Commercial Manager, South Central Railways v SCR Caterers, Dry Fruits, Fruit Juice Stalls Welfare Association* (2016) 3 SCC 582; *Kasturi Lal Lakshmi Reddy* (n 62).

221 *Natural Resource Allocation* (n 79).

222 *Subramanian Swamy v CBI* (n 85).

223 See also *Wipro Ltd v Assistant Collector of Customs* (2015) 14 SCC 161.

224 (1998) 2 SCC 1.

measure was to be temporary in nature. However, through various amendments the measure was extended from time to time. In 1997, the Supreme Court held the impugned measure to be arbitrary and unreasonable since the necessity and expediency of the law, which justified the law when it was enacted, were no longer present; hence, the law was no longer serving a worthy purpose in 1997, though it might have done so in 1938 when the law was originally enacted. In coming to this conclusion, the court held that 'a statute which when enacted was justified may, with the passage of time, become arbitrary and unreasonable', if the rationale behind the law is no longer present.[225]

There are two exceptions to the general proposition stated earlier that the court typically does not enumerate specific purposes that are per se illegitimate. First is the recurring issue of whether financial incapacity to fulfil a rights obligation is a legitimate reason for limiting the right. Take for example, *Khatri v State of Bihar*,[226] where the court held that criminal prosecution without legal representation was a violation of personal liberty, and that access to free legal services is part of a reasonable, fair, and just procedure. Therefore, the court required the State to provide free legal aid to an indigent accused person, and the State's plea of financial or administrative inability was rejected as an illegitimate ground to limit this right.

Similarly, in *Paschim Banga Khet Mazdoor Samity v State of West Bengal*,[227] the court dealt with the failure of Government hospitals to provide timely emergency medical treatment to patients in serious conditions. Stating that the denial of prompt medical attention had resulted in a limitation of the petitioner's right to health which was part of his right to life, the court held that such limitation could not be justified on the ground of the State's financial inability to provide emergency medical assistance.

Likewise, the court held in *All India Imam Organisation v Union of India*,[228] that the right to life with dignity cannot be curtailed by the State

225 See also, *Bhopal Sugar Industries* (n 140); *Narottam Kishore Dev Varma v Union of India* (1964) 7 SCR 55; *H.H. Shri Swamiji of Shri Admar Mutt v The Commissioner, Hindu Religious & Charitable Endowments Department* (1980) 1 SCR 368; *Motor General Traders v State of Andhra Pradesh* [1984] 1 SCR 594; *Rattan Arya v State of Tamil Nadu* (1986) 3 SCC 385; *Synthetics and Chemicals Ltd. v State of U.P.* (1990) 1 SCC 109.

226 (1981) 1 SCC 627.

227 (1996) 4 SCC 37.

228 AIR 1993 SC 2086. In this case, Imams who performed Islamic religious service petitioned the Court stating that they were entitled to emoluments commensurate with the service they provided. This was challenged by the State primarily on the ground that the nature of work was voluntary. However, an argument was also made that the Wakf Boards – the institutions that were responsible for the administration and oversight of

by pleading financial inability, since '[f]inancial difficulties of the institution cannot be above fundamental right of a citizen'.

It another series of cases, however, the court has evaluated the legitimacy of claims of financial incapacity differently. For example, in *State of Punjab v Ram Lubhaya Bagga,*[229] the court has held that since the State does not have unlimited resources to spend on any of its projects, any provisions relating to supply of medical facilities to its citizens must necessarily be limited by the State's financial capacity. Therefore, limitations on the right to medical aid are permitted, keeping in mind the State's financial inability. Similarly, in *Confederation of Ex-Servicemen Associations,*[230] the court held that while the right to health was protected under Article 21, the limits on the State's financial capacity justified seeking financial contribution from a patient for his treatment.

The distinction between the cases where the court rejects the financial capacity of the State as a legitimate reason for limiting a right and those cases where it accepts such reasoning appears to be the extent of deprivation of rights resulting from state inaction. *Khatri*[231] dealt with denial of legal representation in criminal matters, and thus involved potential denial of liberty. *Paschim Banga Khet Mazdoor Samity*[232] concerned the complete denial of emergency medical assistance. *All India Imam Organisation*[233] involved the complete denial of livelihood due to non-payment of any wages to Imams. On the other hand, in *Ram Lubhaya Bagga,*[234] the issue was whether the reimbursement of medical expenses of civil servants only up to government hospital rates, regardless of where medical facilities were availed, was in violation of the State's obligation to secure the right to health of its citizens. *Confederation of Ex-Servicemen*[235] similarly involved the question of whether the State could require retired army personnel to pay a contribution towards their health coverage. These were not cases of complete deprivation of a right, which

mosques where the Imams worked – did not have the financial ability to pay Imams. The Court rejected this contention on the ground that the Imams had a right to livelihood as part of their right to life with dignity under Article 21 of the Constitution, and this right could not be defeated by pleading financial inability.

229 (1998) 4 SCC 117.

230 *Confederation of Ex-Servicemen Associations* (n 147).

231 *Khatri* (n 226).

232 *Paschim Banga Khet Mazdoor Samity* (n 227).

233 *All India Imam Organisation* (n 228).

234 *Ram Lubhaya Bagga* (n 229).

235 *Confederation of Ex-Servicemen Associations* (n 147).

appears to be the distinguishing factor between the cases where the court has rejected the State's financial capacity as a valid ground for rights limitation, and those where it has accepted such a contention.

A second set of cases where the court deals with the per se illegitimacy of certain purposes involves the distribution of public resources. In these cases, the court has repeatedly emphasized that the only legitimate object for the State to pursue is the common good and public interest. Any allocation of state resources for private benefit at the cost of public interest is completely illegitimate.[236] In such cases the question presented to the court is whether the distribution was in the public interest or for private benefit (the latter being an impermissible objective).[237] Questions of *mala fide* often play an important role in such inquiries. In such cases, the court evaluates the nature of resource being distributed, the existence of publicly available, objective, and transparent criteria for distribution, the method of evaluation of competing bids for the resource, and the overall method of allocation, to determine whether the government was indeed pursuing its declared objective.[238] In sum, the court looks at the method of distribution of state resources as an indicator of whether the State was pursuing a public interest or another, ulterior and illegitimate objective.

For example, in a case concerning the appropriate method for allocating telecommunication spectrum amongst various applicants, the court held that the purpose or object of allocation of natural resources has to be guided by the DPSP, which states that the State should ensure that 'that the ownership and control of the material resources of the community are so distributed as best to subserve the common good'.[239] Any method or purpose of allocation of natural resources that did not serve this purpose would be arbitrary, and thus in violation of Article 14. In a series of cases thereafter, the court has examined whether the distribution of public resources meets this purpose or not.[240] In a case relating to the allocation of the right to mine coal, the court held that the State adopted a process that was not fair or transparent or based on objective criteria,

236 *Natural Resource Allocation* (n 79).

237 *Common Cause v Union of India* (2014) 6 SCC 552; *Manohar Lal Sharma v Principal Secretary* (2014) 9 SCC 516; *Institute of Law, Chandigarh v Neeraj Sharma* (2015) 1 SCC 720.

238 See, e.g., *Neeraj Sharma* ibid.

239 *Natural Resource Allocation* (n 79).

240 *Common Cause* (2014) (n 237); *Manohar Lal Sharma* (n 237); *Institute of Law, Chandigarh* (n 237); *Common Cause v Union of India* (2015) 7 SCC 1.

did not demonstrate proper application of mind, and was based on irrelevant considerations. As such, the allocation was opposed to public interest and the common good.[241]

Apart from cases involving the distribution of public resources, the court places a very heavy burden on the person impugning a state action to show that the State was motivated by *mala fides*. In *E. P. Royappa v State of Tamil Nadu*,[242] for example, where the court made the arbitrariness doctrine explicit, it held that to impugn any action on *mala fides*, the petitioner has to show that the action was 'so irrational or unjust that it could not have been made by any reasonable administration except for collateral reasons'. Here, the petitioner, who was the Chief Secretary of his State, alleged that his transfer from his post to another had been made in pursuance of *mala fide* intentions because he had refused to follow illegal orders of the Chief Minister. In this context the court held that 'the burden of establishing mala fides in very heavy on the person who alleges it. The allegations of mala fides are often more easily made than proved, and the very seriousness of such allegations demands proof of a high order of credibility.' On facts, the court found that apart from allegations and insinuations, the petitioner had not produced any proof that the impugned action was based on mala fides.[243]

The worthiness of the purpose is not generally linked to the severity of the limitation, except in cases where the State pleads financial incapacity, as discussed previously. Generally, the inquiry into purpose is for evaluating whether, independent of the rights limitation in question, the State is pursuing a legitimate goal.

### E *Proof of Purpose*

We have seen that as part of its inquiry into purpose, the court examines what the purpose was, its need, and its legitimacy. How does the court determine what purpose the State is pursuing?

A legislative enactment is generally accompanied by a Statement of Objects and Reasons, which explains what the legislature is trying to achieve through the legislation, and why.[244] The court tends to rely on

241 *Manohar Lal Sharma* (n 237).

242 *E. P. Royappa* (n 75).

243 See also, *Ram Krishna Dalmia* (n 127).

244 A statement of objects and reasons is a document appended to a Bill by the sponsoring ministry when it is presented in the Legislature. The Statement explains why the law is

this statement for understanding the legislative objective and intent behind the statute. Similarly, statements made by government representatives during legislative debates on the law, and committee and commission reports on the basis of which the law was brought about, are some other sources used by the court to determine the object behind the legislation.[245] These are the most common sources used by the court to determine purpose.

The court also often accepts the State's *ipse dixit* on the importance of the aim on the presumption that the executive and the legislature 'understand and correctly appreciate the needs of their own people and that laws are directed to problems made manifest by experience'.[246] In many cases, the court relies on affidavits by the State on the circumstances that necessitated the passing of that law.[247] However, where the importance or legitimacy of the objective is challenged, the court determines the importance of the object by relying on facts and figures, recommendations of expert committees, reports of the government or UN, and international bodies.[248] The *Cow Slaughter* case[249] is an example of the court's approach in this regard. In this case, the petitioners had challenged a law that prohibited the slaughter of cows, inter alia, on the ground that such a law did not serve the 'general interests of the public, which was the relevant enumerated ground of limitation. Here, in deciding the object of the law, the court examined the Preamble and the Statement of Objects and Reasons appended to the legislation. Stating that these sources 'indicate the thought process of the elected representatives of the people and their cognizance of the prevalent state of affairs, impelling them to enact the law', the court conclude that the object of the law was to protect cows and calves because of their utility to various facets of social life, such as agriculture, as a source of organic fuel and milk, etc. In coming to this conclusion, the court relied on studies and reports conducted by various governmental bodies which highlighted the importance of cows for the agriculture and energy sectors. On this basis,

being brought about, what problem/issue it seeks to tackle, what purpose/aim it seeks to achieve, and what are significant provisions of the law. While the Statement does not form part of the Legislation it is often used by Court to determine legislative intent.

245 See generally, *Sashikant Laxman Kale v Union of India* (1990) 4 SCC 366.

246 *Ram Krishna Dalmia* (n 127).

247 *Thangal Kunju Musaliar v M. Venkitachalam Potti* [1955] 2 SCR 1196; *Pannalal Binjraj v Union of India,* [1957] SCR 233.

248 As, for example, in the *Elections Disqualification I* case (n 60).

249 *Cow Slaughter* case (n 135).

the court was satisfied that the ban on slaughter of cow progeny as imposed by the impugned enactment was in the interests of the general public within the meaning of clause (6) of Article 19 of the Constitution. Interestingly, though public discourse around cow slaughter bans revolves primarily around the religious motivation behind such bans, the judicial narrative was silent on this aspect of the case.[250]

Other statements made by government representatives in connection with the law are also referred to in understanding the objective of the law. For example, in *Subramanian Swamy v Director, CBI*,[251] discussed earlier, the court looked at statements made by the Minister concerned on the floor of the house, as well as Parliamentary Committee Reports on the issue, to determine the object behind the provision which shielded senior bureaucrats from prosecution without previous sanction by the State.

## VII Suitability or Rational Nexus

### *A The Role of Rational Nexus in Limitation Analysis*

An additional element of the limitation analysis is an evaluation of whether the impugned measure serves its purpose. Framed as the 'rational nexus' analysis, the court generally asks whether the measure advances the object of the law. The rational nexus test is therefore analogous to the suitability test under the proportionality doctrine.[252] The purpose of the test is to determine whether the measure in question is a suitable means to achieve the purpose of that measure. If not, the measure is unreasonable and therefore invalid. In some cases, the court asks an additional question – is the measure narrowly tailored to achieve the ends in question, and nothing more? If the measure is overbroad and includes within its ambit aspects which are not relatable to the object of the law, then the measure is not a suitable means to achieve the objective.

After the purpose test, the rational nexus test is the most common element of analysis in limitations review. The nexus analysis is generally

[250] See generally Anup Surendranath, 'A Constitutional Misadventure' *Indian Express* (Mumbai, 30 May 2017) ('While political discussion on the issue [of cow slaughter] is driven by religious considerations, the judicial journey pretends very hard to be about considerations other than religion. The long line of Supreme Court decisions goes to absurd lengths to justify anti-cow slaughter legislations on grounds of agriculture').

[251] *Subramanian Swamy v CBI* (n 85).

[252] See Khaitan, 'Beyond Reasonableness' (n 74).

based on common-sense, abstract, and logical reasoning rather than empirically grounded claims. Apart from requiring a direct and proximate rather than a far-fetched nexus, the court has not explained the level of probability at which the analysis is to be pegged. The role of this stage appears to be to test the general plausibility of the State's claim that the measure advances the object in question, rather than any specific level of probability, supported by empirical claims.

However, the nexus analysis is significant in cases where the court finds the limitation unjustified. The court conducted a rational nexus analysis in 71 per cent of such cases, as opposed to only 57 per cent in cases where it found the measure to be justified. In 61 per cent of the cases that result in a failure, the case fails at the rational nexus stage. In 32 per cent of *these* cases (n = 19), the court finds the measure to have failed the purpose inquiry, and therefore also finds that there is no rational nexus between the impugned measure and any legitimate objective.[253] In such cases, the lack of rational nexus is a mere formality. In a few other cases, mainly concerning the constitutionality of legislative enactments, the court finds the purpose of the law to be different from that which is argued by the state, though still legitimate. However, once the purpose is stated differently, the impugned provision is found to not have any nexus with the purpose of the law.[254] In an additional 47 per cent of cases, some of which are discussed later, the court finds that the measure fails the rational nexus element alone. The bulk of these cases deals with Article 14 claims. Since, by and large, the court deals with this stage in a very abstract common-sensical manner, a high failure rate at this stage indicates that the State is not even able to show a plausible link between the classification and the object of the law.

[253] See, e.g., *State of Punjab v Jagjit Singh* (n 136), where the question before the Court was whether temporary public employees were entitled to the same wages as those in regular employment who were performing similar services. The Court held that paying less wages to temporary employees performing similar work as those in regular employment served no legitimate purpose as it violated the principles of 'equal pay for equal work', and of human dignity. As such there was no nexus between the classification between temporary and regular employees and any legitimate purpose of the law.

[254] See, e.g., *Harsora v Harsora* (2016) 10 SCC 165, where the Court looked at the Statement of Objects and Reasons of the Protection of Women from Domestic Violence Act, 2005 to hold that the purpose of the law was to protect women from 'any kind' of domestic violence. Therefore, a provision which permitted women to file cases under this provision only against adult male members of her natal family was held to have no nexus with the purpose of the law.

Often the court's inquiry stops at this stage. If there is a rational nexus between the measure and the aim of the law, that is enough to find the law reasonable. As Figure 6.3 indicates, the largest proportion of cases where the court conducts a limitations analysis involves only a two-element inquiry. Sixty-eight per cent cases of all such cases involve inquiry into the purpose and nexus.

### B *Establishing Rational Nexus*

According to the jurisprudence of the court, rational nexus has to be direct and proximate, not remote or illusory. This is especially true of restrictions on Article 19 rights. Such restrictions have to be 'in the interests of' certain specified goals. The court has interpreted the phrase 'in the interests of' as requiring a direct and proximate link between the restriction and the goal. For example, the court held in *Superintendent, Central Prison v Ram Manohar Lohia*,[255] that a reasonable restriction in the interests of public order 'should be one which has a proximate connection or nexus with public order, but not one far-fetched, hypothetical or problematical or too remote in the chain of its relation with the public order'. In this case, the impugned provision penalized instigating any person to not pay or defer the payment of government dues like taxes. The State justified this law on the ground that this restriction on the right to free speech was in the interests of public order, which was a permissible ground of restriction. It drew a link between the measure and public order by arguing that instigation of a single individual to not pay tax or dues 'is a spark which may in the long run ignite a revolutionary movement destroying public order'. Rejecting this argument, the court held that 'fundamental rights cannot be controlled on such hypothetical and imaginary considerations'.[256]

[255] AIR 1960 SC 633.

[256] See also, *O K Ghosh v E X Joseph* AIR 1963 SC 812 (reiterating the requirement of a direct and proximate link between the restriction and the goal, and stating that '[a] restriction can be said to be in the interests of public order only if the connection between the restriction and the public order is proximate and direct. Indirect or far-fetched or unreal connection between the restriction and public order would not fall within the purview of the expression "in the interests of public order."'). In *Meneka Gandhi* (n 65), the Court adopted a similar view and held that restrictions on the right to go abroad did not violate Article 19(1)(a) or (g), because the direct and inevitable impact of such law was only on the right to go abroad and not on the right of free speech and expression or the right to carry on any trade, business, profession, or calling.

While this is the standard laid down by the court, questions about the proximity of the linkage between the measure and the goal are not raised very often. In the dataset, the court mentioned the need for a direct and proximate connection between the measure and the goal in only two cases, upholding the measure in one and striking it down in the other.[257] In neither of those was the court's final decision based on the quality of nexus between the measure and the object of the law.

The nexus analysis is largely implicit or based on an abstract, logical connection and common-sensical reasoning rather than on concrete evidence. Even in cases where the link is found to not be made, this is generally on abstract reasoning and connections rather than empirical evidence. A typical case of how the nexus analysis is carried out is the *Election Disqualification I* case.[258] Here, on the issue of testing whether the law, which prohibited persons with more than two children from occupying posts in village councils, unjustifiably limits the right to equality, the court found that since village councils are empowered to deal with issues of family planning, having leaders who can act as role models will enable the local body to discharge its duties more effectively. Therefore, there was nexus between the rights-limiting measure and a legitimate purpose. This nexus analysis between the measure and its ends was not backed by any evidence.[259]

Similarly, in *Election Disqualifications II*,[260] in dealing with disqualifications on the basis of minimum educational requirements, the court stated that education is required for a person to discriminate between right and wrong and therefore minimum educational requirements will further the goal of efficient administration of local government. This abstract (and questionable) reasoning was backed by no evidence whatsoever.

*M. J. Sivani v State of Karnataka (Video Games Parlour* case)[261] exemplifies one of the few instances where the court did consider the evidence presented by the State in determining whether the nexus between means and ends was made out. This case concerned the constitutionality of regulations that imposed restrictions and requirements on video game parlours which the petitioners challenged for violating their

[257] *Shreya Singhal* (n 68); *Modern Dental College* (n 5).

[258] *Elections Disqualification I* (n 60).

[259] See also, *Prakash Kumar Prakash Bhutto v State of Gujarat* (2005) 2 SCC 409.

[260] *Rajbala* (n 85).

[261] AIR 1995 SC 1770.

right to trade and business as well as their right to livelihood. The State countered that the rights limitation was 'in the interests of the general public', which is a permissible ground for limiting the right. In order to determine whether the 'interests of the general public' were served by the impugned measure, the court relied on a report of a committee of police officers that had found that video game parlours frequently manipulate machines so that customers rarely win. Further, the games themselves are often based on chance or require a level of skill that ordinary customers generally cannot attain. As such, these games are likely to impact young and impressionable minds who may squander their money on such games. For these reasons, the court found that the impugned measures serve a public interest.

Importantly, in the *Video Games Parlour* case, the court made no distinction between different types of video games which may have varying impact on consumers. It makes a broad sweep generalization that playing video games is against the public interest and that therefore the nexus between the measure and its purpose is made out. This is true of most rational nexus analyses, where the court stops at determining whether the measure advances a legitimate law. The court followed this broad brush approach in all the three cases discussed earlier in this section.

These are all examples of cases where the court found that the link had been made out. Likewise, even where the court finds that a measure fails at the nexus stage, the court's analysis is generally based on abstract, logical reasoning, rather than on concrete evidence. A bulk of the cases where the measure failed only on nexus analysis dealt with Article 14 claims. Typically, in these cases, after establishing the purpose of the law, the court moves to examining whether an impugned classification bears a nexus to the purpose. The cases that fail this test are generally those where the court finds that the distinction between the two classified groups as argued by the state bears no nexus to the object of the law as determined by the court. An example is *S. T. Sadiq v State of Kerala.*[262] Here the state acquired certain cashew plantations out of a larger group of cashew plantations, and sought to repel an Article 14 challenge to the measure on the ground that the two groups of plantations (those that were acquired, and those that were not) were distinct because they were regulated by different state agencies, and were therefore not comparable

[262] (2015) 4 SCC 400.

in the first place. The court held that the object of the legislation that authorized such acquisition was to protect the interests of workers in these plantations and to protect the financial interests of the State. With reference to these objectives, the two sets of plantations were not situated differently. There was, therefore, no nexus between the object of the law and the classification.[263]

Another example is *Harsora v Harsora*, where the court invalidated a provision of the Protection of Women from Domestic Violence Act, 2005, on the ground that the classification contained in the provision bore no nexus to the object of the law. In this case, the court held that the object of the law was to provide the broadest protection possible to women from domestic violence. If this were the objective of the law, then a provision that allowed women to only file cases under that law against 'adult male' members of her family (except the female relatives of her husband) bore no nexus to the object of the law. The court did not discuss, even to dismiss, possible reasons that the legislature might have had for limiting the potential group of respondents to male members of the family.[264]

Likewise, in some cases, the court finds that failure to make a distinction between differently situated groups breaks the nexus between the object and the classification.[265] In all these cases, the court's findings on nexus are based on abstract, common-sensical reasoning, rather than on the basis of proof or evidence. That so many cases fail even such a low threshold suggests that the law making/ administrative decision-making

[263] See also *State of MP v Mala Banerjee* (2015) 7 SCC 698 where the Court considered whether Article 14 would be violated if a salary incentive scheme that was made available to all government employees was not extended to government teachers. The state argued that government teachers were differently situated from other employees because they had a distinct salary structure in place. The Court, however, held that the purpose of the incentive scheme was to prevent stagnation of employees in a particular salary bracket. In relation to this object, the Court held that the two groups – teachers and other employees – were similarly situated and therefore there was no rational nexus between the object of the law and the classification.

[264] The state did not defend the provision in this case. On why the legislature was justified, at least in part, in making the classification that it did in this provision, see Aparna Chandra, 'Women as Respondents under the Domestic Violence Act: Critiquing the SC Decision in Harsora v Harsora' *Live Law* (14 October 2016) <www.livelaw.in/women-respondents-domestic-violence-act-critiquing-sc-decision-harsora-v-harsora/> accessed 26 June 2019.

[265] See, e.g., *Shree Bhagwati Steel Rolling Mills v Commission of Central Excise* (2016) 3 SCC 643; *Ashoka Kumar Thakur* (n 16).

processes do not adequately pay attention to potential constitutional concerns that may arise, should the matter be taken to court.

In very few cases in the dataset did the court look for evidence of nexus.[266] A characteristic of the cases where the court did examine evidence on the point was that the link was specifically challenged by the petitioners. So, for example, when the state claimed that differential retirement ages for persons serving at a particular post in the Air Force, based on the avenue of promotion by which the person reached that post, was justified since it sought to incentivize meritorious work, the court rejected this claim on the ground that the state had led no evidence to suggest that the measure would achieve the purpose.[267] In this case, the link between the stated purpose and the classification was specifically challenged by the petitioners. It appears therefore, that the court normally looks for a common-sense standard of plausibility in making the link between the means and the ends. Only when the link is challenged, either by arguments or evidence, does it look for concrete evidence.

### C *Narrow Tailoring*

Sometimes, though not often, the court also engages in a narrow tailoring analysis as part of the nexus analysis. This element is folded into the nexus analysis and appears very infrequently, in 14 per cent and 16 per cent of cases where the impugned measures are found to be justified and unjustified, respectively. Significantly, though measures fail this analysis in 16 per cent of the cases where the measure is found unreasonable, in no case does the measure fail only because of narrow tailoring. This is because, where conducted, narrow tailoring is part of the nexus analysis, and a failure in the narrow tailoring analysis is seen as failure to prove that the measure is suitable to achieve the aims that it is pursuing.

In this analysis, the Court asks: is the measure narrowly tailored to achieve the ends in question, and nothing more? If the measure is overbroad and includes within its ambit aspects which are not relatable to the object of the law, then the measure is not a suitable means to achieve the objective.

Inquiry into the narrow tailoring is found in limitations analysis under all three rights, although the Court does not use the phrase 'narrowly

[266] See, e.g., *Union of India v Atul Shukla* (2014) 10 SCC 432; *Cellular Operators Association* (n 139); *Anita Thakur v State of J&K* (2016) 15 SCC 525.

[267] *Atul Shukla* (n 266).

tailored' or any other specific term for such an analysis. This stage is generally folded into the rational nexus analysis such that all narrow tailoring failures are also failure to prove nexus. A law may fail this analysis not only when it goes beyond the object of the law but also when the law is vague or does not provide adequate guidance on how to apply the law, leaving open the possibility of overbroad application.

*Shreya Singhal v Union of India*[268] is an example of a case where the Court conducted a narrow tailoring evaluation as part of its nexus analysis. Here the Court was reviewing a provision that penalized the use of a computer or a communication device to send any information that is 'grossly offensive' or of a 'menacing character', any information known to be false, sent for the purpose of causing annoyance, inconvenience, danger, obstruction, insult, injury, criminal intimidation, enmity, hatred or ill will, or any email or message for the purpose of causing annoyance or inconvenience or to deceive or to mislead the addressee or recipient about the origin of such messages. The State claimed that this law was a valid limitation on the freedom of speech since it served the specified goals of public order, defamation, incitement to commit offences, and preserving decency and morality. The Court disagreed and held that the law captured within its fold conduct that did not offend any of the goals mentioned in Article 19 (2). An annoying message, for example, need not disturb public order (understood as disturbing the life of the community as a whole, as opposed to one or some individuals), nor need it be defamatory, or incite a person to commit offences, or meet the test for obscenity. On the public order ground specifically, the Court held that the section, by not making any distinction between mass dissemination of information and dissemination to one person, and by not confining the operation of the section to those messages which have a clear tendency to disrupt public order, fails to demonstrate a nexus with public order. Therefore, in being overbroad, the law was not a justified limitation on the right to free speech.

Similarly, in *State of Maharashtra v Indian Hotels and Restaurants Association* (*Bar Dancers* case),[269] dealing with a prohibition on professional dancing in bars, the Court held that if the purpose of the law was to end practices derogatory to the dignity of women, the law was over-inclusive since it prohibited all forms of dancing in certain establishments regardless of the nature of such dancing. Therefore, in not being

[268] *Shreya Singhal* (n 68).
[269] (2013) 8 SCC 519.

narrowly targeted only at obscene or sexually suggestive dancing, the law placed a blanket prohibition on all dancing, thus impacting activities beyond what was required to achieve the object of the law.[270]

Similarly, in *Mithu v State of Punjab*,[271] where petitioners challenged, on the grounds of arbitrariness, the constitutionality of a mandatory death sentence for murders committed by persons serving life imprisonment, the Court held that if – as argued by the State – the purpose of the law was to protect jail officials from hardened recidivist murderers, then the law was overbroad, because it did not capture only those who murdered jail officials but also those who committed other murders. The law was also not limited to those who were initially serving their life imprisonment for murder but also extended to those who were serving life imprisonment for other crimes such as economic offences. Further, by not allowing the judge to make an individualized determination of the sentence, the law did not allow the Court to take into account mitigating circumstances, such as if the murder was motivated by torture or continuous harassment by the said jail official. Therefore, the law was overbroad in relation to the object it sought to achieve, and had to be struck down.

The Court also engages in a narrow tailoring analysis when confronted with vague laws. Vague laws raise two concerns regarding the suitability of means to ends. The first concern is that such laws do not provide adequate guidance for applying the law, increasing the chances of overbroad application.[272] Where an impugned law empowers an official to exercise her discretion in classifying between persons or things, the Court examines if the enabling law has provided any guidance by reference to which the decision-maker can exercise her discretion. If the discretion is completely unguided, such that the law does not provide the decision-maker with any clear basis for classification in order to achieve the object of the law, it will be struck down as a violation of equality, since by being unguided, the power of classification may be used in ways that go beyond the object of the law. *State of West Bengal v Anwar Ali Sarkar*[273] exemplifies this point. Here, the impugned law empowered

[270] See also, *Chintaman Rao* (n 6) (finding a law unreasonable because it was 'so drastic in scope that it goes much in excess of that object'.); *R M Seshadri v District Magistrate, Tanjore* AIR 1954 SC 747.

[271] AIR 1983 SC 473.

[272] *Kartar Singh v State of Punjab* (1994) 3 SCC 569. See also, *K.A. Abbas v Union of India* [1971] 2 SCR 446.

[273] *Anwar Ali Sarkar* (n 71).

the government to refer certain types of cases or offences for trial before a special court which followed attenuated procedures. The Act did not prescribe any policy or guideline by reference to which the Executive would exercise this power. It merely stated that the purpose of the Act was to provide for 'speedier trial of offences'. The Court found that this purpose was too vague to be useful in determining a rational basis for classification.

By contrast, in *Kathi Raning Rawat v State of Saurashtra*,[274] a similar provision was upheld when the preamble to the impugned law stated that the purpose of the law was to provide for public safety, maintenance of public order, and the preservation of peace and tranquillity in the State. The Court found that the preamble afforded sufficient guidance to the executive in exercising its discretion.[275]

The second concern is that vague laws do not clarify their restrictions and prohibitions clearly and therefore do not provide fair notice to a person to modify her behaviour accordingly. In effect, citizens are forced to steer away from the zone of operation of the law. Therefore, the law has a chilling effect beyond its intended object.[276] For this reason, the Court in *Shreya Singhal v Union of India*[277] found the vagueness of the terms used in the impugned provision of the Information Technology Act as offending its constitutionality on the ground of overbreadth.

Apart from a lack of guidance on how to apply the law in a way that limits its application only to the object of the law, a law may be open to overbroad application by reason of other procedural norms. In such cases, the court either corrects the procedural infirmities that create the possibility of abuse of the power, or strikes down such a law. The court's inquiry in such cases is directed towards ensuring that the procedure permits safeguards against abuse of state power, such as requiring a decision-making authority to provide reasons for her decision; providing a right to be heard before being deprived of a right; providing for review of the action by an impartial body such as the court; or placing the decision-making power in the hands of a high-ranking official who, the court assumes, exercises greater care in the discharge of the power. These

274 AIR 1952 SC 123.

275 See also, *Kedar Nath Bajoria v State of West Bengal* AIR 1954 SC 660; *Jyoti Pershad v Administrator, Union Territory of Delhi* [1962] 2 SCR 125; *Maganlal Chaganlal v Municipal Corporation of Greater Bombay* AIR 1975 SC 648; *Special Courts Bill* (n 70).

276 *Kartar Singh* (n 272).

277 *Shreya Singhal* (n 68).

procedural safeguards are seen as ways to ensure that the law is applied in relation to its object alone.[278] *Virendra v State of Punjab*[279] illustrates the point well. In this case, in the wake of severe communal tensions in a State over issues of language and identity, an order passed under the impugned law prohibited the printing or publication of any article, news report or other item relating to the 'Save Hindi Agitation' and imposed a ban on the entry and circulation of newspapers carrying such reports from other States. The law was assailed as enabling unjustifiable right limitations, since it gave unfettered and uncontrolled discretion to the State Government without providing any safeguard against an abuse of the power.

The court rejected the contention and held that the law did provide sufficient guidance on the nature of circumstances when the restriction should be imposed, since the law required the decision-making authority to be satisfied that the action was necessary for 'preventing or combating any activity prejudicial to the maintenance of communal harmony affecting or likely to affect the public order'. In addition, the court took into consideration that an order passed under the law would remain in force for a limited duration of two months and an aggrieved person could seek modification or cancelling of the order.

However, the power to ban the entry and circulation of papers from outside the State was held to be an unjustified limitation because the safeguards contained in the first provision, which limited its application to the object of the law, were not present in the second provision: the restriction was not limited by time and no provisions were made for making representations against the exercise of power.[280]

It is important to note that a total prohibition on a particular activity does not necessarily violate a narrow-tailoring requirement. Take, for example, *Sushila Saw Mills v State of Orissa*.[281] Petitioners in this case were owners of a saw mill operating in an area declared as a reserved forest. The legislature completely prohibited the operation of saw mills within reserved forest areas, limiting the petitioner's freedom of occupation. The court held that while the impugned law did amount to a total

[278] See, Mrinal Satish and Aparna Chandra, 'Of Maternal State and Minimalist Judiciary: The Indian Supreme Court's Approach to Terror Related Adjudication' (2009) 21 National Law School of India Review 51 (for application of this approach in terrorism-related cases).

[279] AIR 1957 SC 896.

[280] ibid.

[281] AIR 1995 SC 2484.

prohibition, in rare cases this could be justified. Protecting reserved forest areas was held to be one such rare case which can trigger a total prohibition.[282]

In summation, narrow tailoring techniques preferred by the court are those of clearly defined laws and nuanced categories rather than broad, general, or vague prohibitions; the possibility of individualized assessment by giving the affected party a hearing; and procedural norms to ensure that the law is not applied beyond its bounds.

### *D The (Non) Consideration of Alternative Means*

The court generally does not consider whether there are better alternatives for advancing the aims of the law, and does not examine less-restricting or more efficacious ways of achieving the aim. The court has said repeatedly that it will not examine whether a better policy could be made, or a better law designed,[283] but rather determines the constitutionality of the law presented before it. Even in the case of distribution of state resources, where the court puts the method to scrutiny to ensure that it operates in a fair and non-discriminatory manner and is directed towards serving the public good, the court has refused to analyse whether, in a given case, another method of distribution would better achieve the aims of the law.[284]

The only exception to this general rule is the case of total prohibitions, where the court has held that although it is permissible to place a total ban amounting to prohibition on any profession, occupation, trade, or business, such cases attract an additional element in the limitations analysis, that a total prohibition must also satisfy the test that a less-restricting alternative would be inadequate.[285] In the *Bar Dancers* case,[286] for example, the court held that the prohibition on dancing in establishments of a certain type amounted to total prohibition because the business of such establishments depended primarily on such dance performances. The court examined and concluded that alternative mechanisms to achieve the law's objectives, like licencing norms, periodic

[282] The court did not provide any guidance on how to determine which cases would fall into this rare category.

[283] See, e.g., *Natural Resource Allocation* (n 79); *Manohar Lal Sharma* (n 237), *Shrilekha Vidyarthi* (n 107), *Premium Granites v State of Tamil Nadu* AIR 1994 SC 2233.

[284] *Manohar Lal Sharma* (n 237).

[285] *Cow Slaughter* case (n 135).

[286] *Bar Dancers* case (n 269).

inspections, and the power to suspend or cancel a licence for any breach of the license conditions, already existed in the law. Further, police officers were empowered to stop any performance that violated the law or the licensing norms. The court held that these powers vested with the licensing authority were enough to safeguard any violation of the dignity of women through obscene dances. Since the less-restrictive alternative could achieve the purpose, the total prohibition was unjustified. Interestingly, the court did not discuss whether the less-restrictive alternative was an equally efficient means for achieving the ends in question.

Engaging in analysis of alternatives is extremely rare. In the entire dataset the court engaged with analysis of alternatives only once. In this case, the impugned law provided for a 100 per cent penalty for defaulting by even a single day in the payment of excise. The court found this provision to be unduly harsh and oppressive, and stated that the goal of deterrence, which this provision was pursuing, could be achieved by a less harsh law as well.[287]

## VIII General Balancing

A final element of the limitations analysis is a general 'all things considered' balancing exercise between various interests, rights, and duties at stake in the matter at hand. The general balancing element of the analysis focuses on which amongst the various interests is weightier in the specific context of the case regardless of whether the interests in question are connected to each other in a means-ends relation. Stephan Gardbaum gives the following instructive example of such a conflict of duties and how balancing them may proceed in such a case:

> A paradigmatic case of this sort is Sartre's example of a son's duty to leave home to join the French Resistance and the duty to stay behind to look after an ill mother. Another, more prosaic, example is the person who has promised to meet a friend for coffee but shortly before the appointed time learns that his wife has just been admitted to an emergency room. Here, balancing is not used to evaluate the proportionality of the means employed as the two duties are independent values: there is no means-end relationship between them to assess the proportionality of. One of the values is simply weightier in the context . . . [W]eighing or balancing two independent or unrelated values does not involve a judgment about proportionality. To fulfill the promise to meet for coffee because it is

[287] *Shree Bhagwati* (n 265).

> deemed weightier than the duty to rush to the emergency room is to be guilty of moral error but it isn't to act disproportionately.[288]

This is the sort of balancing that can appear in limitation analysis in rights review in India: all things considered, given the various interests at stake, should the measure outweigh the right in the context at hand. The question is not whether a hammer should be used to kill an ant, but (to take the analogy further) whether killing the ant is justified, all things considered. The court's focus is not on proportion but on priority. That is, the focus of the analysis is on which interest trumps the other, not on whether the measure is a proportional response to the interest being pursued. In this sense, in balancing, the court assumes that the various interests at stake are incommensurable with each other, and the balancing exercise itself is a zero-sum game of one interest winning over the other.

Balancing is not an independent stage but a distinct element that draws heavily from the other elements of analysis. In the cases where it is found, elements of balancing permeate the entire discussion from limitation through justification to remedies. The court engages in a balancing exercise somewhat frequently – in 43 per cent of cases where the measure is found justified and in 23 per cent of cases where it is not. The impugned action failed this stage in 23 per cent of the cases that resulted in a failure, and in no instance did a measure fail only because it fails this analysis. That is, in no case did the court hold that though the impugned measure was pursuing a legitimate aim, through a suitable means, the measure was not justified on a balance of the various interests at stake, all things considered. This indicates that the court engages in this analysis as additional grounds to support a rights-limiting measure, rather than to strike it down.

In some cases, balancing completely overlaps with the discussion on the scope of the right, as for example where the court rejects the petitioner's claim regarding the scope of the right because of countervailing public interest.[289] In such cases this element is not distinguishable from the analysis of the scope of the right.

Similarly, elements of the balancing analysis are often drawn from the court's discussion on the importance and legitimacy of purpose, as for

[288] Stephen Gardbaum, 'Positive and Horizontal Rights: Proportionality's Next Frontier or a Bridge Too Far? in Vicki C Jackson and Mark Tushnet (eds), *Proportionality: New Frontiers, New Challenges* (CUP 2017).

[289] See n 185–191 and accompanying text.

example in the *Video Games Parlour* case,[290] where, in upholding the prohibition on video game parlours, the court set up the stakes involved in the case as the right of trade and commerce on the one hand, and the protection of vulnerable and impressionable people, especially students, on the other.

An example will illustrate how balancing generally takes place. *Sahara v SEBI*[291] involved the publication of reports regarding confidential proposals for a judicially ordered settlement in a *subjudice* matter. The petitioners contended that the disclosure prejudicially affected their interests in the case. They sought appropriate orders to the media regarding reporting of details of on-going cases. This case therefore involved a conflict between the right to free speech and expression of the press, as well as the people's 'right to know', and the interests of protecting the integrity of the judicial process and the fair administration of justice. The court, in the very first sentence of the judgment framed the issue as one of '[f]inding an acceptable constitutional balance between free press and administration of justice'. Discussing the stakes at hand, the court recognized that both sets of interests were important within the constitutional scheme. To resolve the conflict, it crafted a remedy of postponement orders rather than complete prohibitions on publishing details of the *subjudice* matter. It directed judges to determine, on a case by case basis, whether the publication of case details would create a 'real and substantial risk of prejudice to the proper administration of justice or to the fairness of trial'. Where such a risk of prejudice exists, judges should grant postponement orders; otherwise not.

The analysis in this case centred on how the court should balance the two conflicting interests, and the court's decision was geared towards evaluating in what situations one interest should win out, and in which circumstances should the other dominate.

Similarly, in the *Election Disqualifications* case,[292] an element of the analysis revolved around the importance of family planning to national welfare, and the importance of limiting population growth so that the State has enough resources for meeting the socio-economic and welfare goals enshrined in the DPSPs. Balanced against the right to personal liberty, the court held that the national interest outweighed the right in question. The court's focus was on whether the measure was justified,

[290] *Video Games Parlour* case (n 262).
[291] *Sahara India* (n 5).
[292] *Elections Disqualification I* case (n 60).

given the competing values of personal liberty on the one hand, and the interest in securing socio-economic justice for the citizenry on the other. It did not go into questions such as the severity of limitation, the degree of benefit to the national interest, or whether the measure itself was an excessive response to the purpose it was pursuing.

*The Election Disqualifications* case also exemplifies the court's oft-repeated dicta that not only does it have to strike a balance between individual rights and public interest but also that such a balance should generally be struck in favour of the public interest. The following passage demonstrates the court's approach:

> This court while acting as a sentinel on the qui vive to protect fundamental rights guaranteed to the citizens of the country must try to strike a just balance between the fundamental rights and the larger and broader interests of society, so that when such right clashes with the larger interest of the country it must yield to the latter.[293]

Thus, in balancing between fundamental rights and public interest, the court will generally lean in favour of the public interest. Often therefore, where the court upholds a fundamental right, it does so in the name of the larger public interest involved in protecting the fundamental right, such as cases invaliding restrictions on free speech which stress the importance of free speech to a well-functioning democracy.[294] Similarly, in the *Bar Dancers* case,[295] while the court stated in detail the importance of the object of the law – protecting women from exploitative conditions – it also emphasized that as a result of the prohibition around 75,000 women had become unemployed and many had had to take up sex work in order to sustain themselves. This fact, according to the court added weight in favour of the right and against the limitation.

Sometimes in the balancing analysis, the court does not perform the balance itself, but issues guidelines to future decision makers on how to decide in a way that appropriately balances the interests at stake, and gives effect to as many interests as possible. The case of postponement orders, discussed earlier, is an example.[296]

[293] *Pathumma* (n 93).

[294] See, e.g., *Shreya Singhal* (n 68), citing a series of cases where the importance of free speech to a well-functioning democracy was stressed. See discussion on the scope of right in this chapter.

[295] *Bar Dancers* case (n 269).

[296] *Sahara India* (n 5).

*PUCL v State of Maharashtra*[297] also illustrates this point. In this case, petitioners approached the court seeking directions for proper and independent investigation into instances of 'extra-judicial executions', that is, deaths caused by police personnel on duty, for example, in the process of arresting a person. Petitioners argued and the court accepted that extra-judicial killings limit the right to life, and as such require that due process is followed in such cases. Due process would require having an independent inquiry into such instances. Therefore, there was a positive obligation to impartially investigate instances of extra-judicial executions. Further, the court held that apart from the importance of the right to life itself, killings of this sort affect the credibility of the rule of law and the administration of justice. On the other hand, the court also took cognizance of the 'difficult and delicate task' that police officers have to perform in dealing with hardened criminals, terrorists, and the like. However, it held that upholding the rule of law trumped this consideration. The court then proceeded to frame detailed guidelines for independent investigation into such deaths.[298] Here, the issue was framed as one of competing interests of upholding the sanctity of the rule of law on the one hand and protecting police officers who operate in dangerous situations on the other. The solution offered was a series of guidelines to enable impartial and speedy investigation into such offences to address both concerns.

*Lalita Kumari v Govt of UP*[299] is another example of such balancing. This case concerned the interpretation of a provision that requires the police to register a report (called First Information Report or FIR) upon information being provided by any person about the commission of certain offences, in order for an investigation to begin. The question before the court was whether it was mandatory for the police to register an FIR immediately upon receiving the information, or whether they could first conduct a preliminary inquiry into the matter and register an FIR only if they were convinced that the allegation had some merit. The argument advanced in favour of non-mandatory registration of FIRs was

[297] (2014) 10 SCC 635.

[298] These guidelines include procedures for ensuring that a prompt and independent police investigation into the death is opened; guidelines for securing the crime scene and preserving/ dealing with evidence; mandatorily conducting a magisterial inquiry into the death; sending information to the National or State Human Rights Commission; the conduct of trials in such cases; guidelines on the payment of compensation to the next of kin; and redressal mechanisms if these guidelines are ignored, etc.

[299] (2014) 2 SCC 1.

that an FIR affects the reputation of an individual, causes her mental stress, and can lead to arbitrary arrest. As such, the requirement of mandatory registration without inquiry is arbitrary and unreasonable and therefore an unjustified limitation of Article 21. The court held that 'a delicate balance has to be maintained between the interest of the society and protecting the liberty of an individual'. It found that the requirement of mandatory registration of FIRs was important for protecting the interests of victims and the society, because non-registration of an FIR by the police would prevent an investigation into the crime. At the same time, there were various instances where persons had been unnecessarily harassed and investigated on false charges. In balancing between these two interests, the court reviewed the Criminal Procedure Code and found various safeguards against arbitrary deprivation of liberty of an individual in case of registration of a false FIR. Therefore, the court held that the law did protect the rights of an individual named in an FIR. Therefore, the mandatory registration of FIRs was held to be a valid limitation on Article 21. At the same time, however, the court issued various directions to the police regarding precautions that they should take, as well as some very limited exceptions where the police could conduct a preliminary inquiry in order to provide additional safeguards to accused persons, and hence better balance these interests in individual cases.

There is one set of cases – those involving the imposition of criminal and administrative penalties – where the court's analysis does not focus on which amongst the various interests should prevail, but on whether the rights-limiting measure is a proportionate or an excessive response to the ends in question. In these cases, the court often examines whether the penalty is disproportionate to the wrong-doing for which it was imposed. The threshold of inquiry is very high in such cases. The court essentially examines whether the penalty imposed was so disproportionate to the alleged wrong-doing that no reasonable person would have imposed such a penalty.[300] *Ebrahim Vazir Mavat v State of Bombay*[301] is a case in point. Here the petitioner challenged the constitutionality of a law which empowered the Central Government to remove from India any person, including an Indian citizen, who entered India from Pakistan without a permit. The petitioner in this case was an Indian citizen who violated this law. He was arrested and ordered to be deported to Pakistan. The court

300 See Chandrachud (n 8).

301 AIR 1954 SC 229.

held that the law which imposed such an 'extreme penalty of a virtual forfeiture of his citizenship' for a mere breach of permit regulations is 'utterly disproportionate to the gravity of the offence' and is therefore unreasonable.

Similarly, where the penalty in question places a disproportionately heavy burden on the person subject to the penalty, the measure is found to be unreasonable. For example, in *Shatrughan Chauhan v Union of India*,[302] the court held that any undue delay in deciding the mercy petition violates just, fair, reasonable procedure under Article 21 since it amounts to a double sentence – the death penalty itself plus the extended time on death row. The burden imposed on the person is therefore disproportionate to the offence. Such cases merit commutation of the death sentence. So also, in *Vikram Singh v Union of India*,[303] the court examined whether the provision of the death penalty as a possible sentence for kidnapping for ransom involving threat to the life of the kidnaped person was so grossly disproportionate to the crime so as to render the sentence arbitrary, but concluded it was not.

## IX Relationship between Limitation Analysis and Remedies

When the court finds that the state action is an unjustified limitation on a right it can provide a wide variety of remedies. Primarily, it can of course strike down the offending state action, which has immediate effect, as the court does not give the State time to rectify the shortcoming after striking down the law.[304]

Alternatively, the court often uses its remedial power to correct limitation errors. For example, it may read down the law in order to narrowly tailor the provision to its purpose. An example of this approach is *Kedar Nath Singh v State of Bihar*.[305] Here, the court held that a sedition law which made it an offence to spread disaffection against the government

[302] *Shatrughan Chauhan* (n 56).

[303] *Vikram Singh* (n 135).

[304] In some cases, the Court does keep final decision pending while the State corrects the impugned state action or omission. In such cases, the Court indicates to the State during arguments that it is inclined to hold against the State, and gives the State the time to correct its limitation error. One such example is a case seeking prohibition on surrogacy, where the Court has kept the case pending for years on repeated assurances being given to the Court that the State is working on enacting legislation that addresses this issue. *Jayashree Wad v Union of India* W.P. (Civil) No. 95 of 2015.

[305] AIR 1962 SC 955.

would be in compliance with the permissible limitations on freedom of speech only if it is limited to those instances where the speech has a tendency to disrupt public order by inciting violence. Instead of striking down the law for being overbroad, the court read it down to limit the meaning of the provision to that which was constitutionally permissible.[306]

Similarly, the court may uphold an impugned law, but issue guidelines to direct future decision-makers on how to implement the law in a way that does not unjustifiably limit a fundamental right. For example, in *PUCL v Union of India*,[307] the petitioner impugned the constitutionality of a law that permitted phone tapping as a violation of the right to privacy. They contended that the legislature had not laid down any procedure for the exercise of this power, and as such power could be used in constitutionally impermissible ways. The court agreed and held that in the absence of just and fair procedure for regulating the power to intercept phone calls, citizens' right to privacy would be unreasonably limited. The court then laid down procedural safeguards to ensure that the law is applied in a fair manner, narrowly tailored to the object of the law.[308]

So also, in *Bachan Singh v State of Punjab*,[309] the court laid down norms to guide decision-makers in determining when to award the death penalty, to ensure that such decisions were not arbitrary and therefore in violation of Article 21 (right to life). The court mandated that the death penalty should only be awarded 'in the rarest of rare cases' when the alternative of life was unquestionably foreclosed, because there was no possibility of reform. Similarly, in cases like *D. K. Basu v State of West Bengal*[310] and *Kartar Singh v State of Punjab*,[311] the court provided

306 See generally, *Shreya Singhal* (n 68), on reading down.

307 *PUCL*(1997) (n 167).

308 In this case, the Court rejected the petitioner's contention that a just, fair, and reasonable procedure would necessarily involve prior judicial scrutiny of a phone-tapping order (because, according to the Court, no provision was made in the law for such scrutiny). The Court held, inter alia, that all such orders should only be issued by the Home Secretary of the concerned government; such an order should only be issued after taking into account whether the information sought to be intercepted could be acquired by other means; the order shall, unless renewed, be operational for a period of two months, and shall not exceed a period of six months in total.

309 *Bachan Singh* (n 45).

310 AIR 1997 SC 610.

311 *Kartar Singh* (n 272).

extensive guidelines to protect the rights of arrested and accused persons in the criminal process against executive abuse.[312]

Through these guidelines, the court sometimes performs narrow tailoring, as in *Bachan Singh*, and sometimes it modifies the application of the law to protect against its use for illegitimate purposes, as in *D. K. Basu* and *Kartar Singh*. This later use of remedies is also illustrated in *Shatrughan Chauhan v Union of India*,[313] where after commuting the death sentence of many of the petitioners for violation of due process requirements in hearing their mercy petitions, the court issued detailed guidelines for observing due process standards with respect to death row prisoners, to ensure that their right to life was not limited in an unjustified manner. Similarly, in *Common Cause v Union of India*,[314] the court, after constituting and consulting an expert committee on this matter, issued extensive guidelines on when, in what manner, and for what purposes the government can issue advertisements using public funds. These guidelines were aimed at ensuring that public resources are not spent in a manner that does not serve the common good.[315]

## X Overview of the Means Struck Down

As presented in detail previously, the court's framework for justification of rights limitation does not strictly follow a structured analytical

[312] The *D. K. Basu* guidelines include obligation on arresting police officers, inter alia, to wear accurate, visible, and clear identification and name tags; prepare a memo of arrest at the time of arrest, and such memo shall be attested by at least one witness; inform, as soon as practicable, a relative or friend of the arrested person about their arrest and location; provide periodic medical examination of the arrested person during police custody; send all documents relating to the arrest to the Magistrate; and permit the arrested person to meet his lawyer. In *Kartar Singh*, the Court issued 'guidelines so as to ensure that the confession obtained in the pre-indictment interrogation by a police officer not lower in rank than a Superintendent of Police is not tainted with any vice but is in strict conformity with the well-recognised and accepted aesthetic principles and fundamental fairness'.

[313] *Shatrughan Chauhan* (n 56).

[314] *Common Cause* (2014) (n 237); *Common Cause* (2015) (n 240).

[315] Similarly, in *Centre for Public Interest Litigation v Union of India*, 1995 Supp. (3) SCC 382, the Court found that the allotments of petrol pumps had been made out of discretionary quotas of government ministers on arbitrary grounds and extraneous considerations. Holding such allotment to be arbitrary and in violation of Article 14, the Court went on to issue detailed guidelines to be followed by the government in allotting petrol pumps through the discretionary quota. Guidelines included such matters as the eligibility criteria and the procedure to be followed for purposes of allotment, to ensure that the allotment was not made for illegitimate purposes.

framework. Rather, the court engages in a more holistic analysis of the State's justification, where worthiness of purpose, rational nexus, sometimes narrow tailoring, and an 'all things considered' balancing between the various interests at stake form the distinct elements of analysis but are generally discussed together. The court picks and chooses amongst these elements and rarely analyses all of them.

The court's limitation analysis is structured as a framework for judicial *review*, not a framework for *primary* decision-making. The clearest proof of this is the court's oft-repeated statement that it will defer to the policy-maker regarding the wisdom of the law, the existence of better alternatives, etc.[316] Limitations analysis is primarily targeted at ascertaining not whether the primary decision-maker made the best decision amongst available choices, but whether the decision was an available choice at all within the framework of fundamental rights. This is why, often, the court's limitation analysis devolves into a *Wednesbury* style review, where the sole focus of the analysis is whether the decision is such that a reasonable decision-maker could have made. If no reasonable decision-maker could make that choice, then the limitation is not justified. Questions of necessity, probability, uncertainty, risk, etc., or empirical and data-driven analysis of issues play little role in how the court approaches rights review. The court is concerned not so much with the proportionality between the right and the rights-limiting measure as with a broad policing of boundaries of reasonable state action.

Therefore, normatively, the constitutional flaws that are present in invalidated limitations do not address the entirety of possible constitutional concerns with state action. The constitutional flaws discussed in this section are in the nature of the outer bounds of constitutionality; a policy that does not contain these flaws may pass judicial review but that does not imply it is the most constitutionally just policy to follow.

With this caveat, the case-law does reveal common constitutional flaws in state action that may render them unjustified limitations on rights. These are:

(a) The purpose of the measure is core to its constitutional scrutiny. If the policy-maker is not able to state a purpose,[317] or the purpose is based

[316] See, e.g., *Subramanian Swamy v Raju* (n 195) (making a distinction between the necessity for or wisdom of the law and its constitutionality).

[317] Most often in cases involving unreasonable classification claims where the State is not able to justify why a policy that provides benefits to one class of persons has not been

on outdated norms and customs,[318] or the purpose goes against a constitutional norm, such as those embodied in the Directive Principles of State Policy,[319] then the rights limitation will be found invalid. Purposes of specific provisions that go against objectives of the broader law or legal regime of which the provision is a part will also render the measure unjustified.[320]

(b) The measure should prima facie advance the objectives for which it has been enacted. Most constitutional flaws are found at this stage, which might appear surprising at first glance because this test is generally performed in a very abstract common-sensical manner, and one would assume that most policies would pass this test. Measures fail this test, however, because the court might understand the purpose of the law differently from the state, which might make it difficult for the state to justify the link between the measure and the purpose. Measures also fail this test because they are vague and do not provide guidance to a decision-maker on when and how to apply the law. Such laws are likely to fail since they are open to misuse, overbroad application, and tend to create a chilling effect, thus having a greater impact on the exercise of the right than is required to achieve the purposes of the law. Similarly, laws that are overbroad, instead of being narrowly tailored to the law's purposes, cover more than is required to achieve the law's purposes, and are hence deemed unjustified. Laws that do not provide for an individualized assessment, especially when imposing a financial,[321] penal,[322] or other onerous burden[323] upon rights bearers, also often fail the nexus test.

(c) When procedural norms put in place to carry out the purpose do not in fact align with the purpose, this is an indication that the measure

extended to another similarly situated class. See, e.g. *P Ramakrishna Raju v Union of India* (2014) 12 SCC 1 (where the state was not able to explain the purpose behind not extending retirement benefits available to judges of higher courts promoted from the lower judiciary to judges who were directly appointed from the Bar); *Vikram Cement* (n 193) (where the impugned law reduced entry tax on certain goods with retrospective effect, but stated that those who had already paid the tax would not be refunded. The State failed to explain the purpose behind treating differently those who had already paid a withdrawn tax and those who had not).

318 *John Vallamattom* (n 209); *Anuj Garg* (n 6).

319 *Kasturi Lal Lakshmi Reddy* (n 62).

320 *Subramanian Swamy v CBI* (n 85); *Wipro* (n 223).

321 *Wipro* (n 223); *Cellular Operators Association* (n 139).

322 *Mithu* (n 271).

323 *Shree Bhagwati* (n 265).

does not advance the purposes of the law.[324] Even when the object of the law and its scope of application are reasonable, the procedure for implementing the law should follow norms of procedural justice and should contain safeguards to protect an individual against arbitrary, excessive, or *mala fide* application of the law. Failing this, the rights-limiting measure is deemed unreasonable.

(d) In recent times, the court has also been asking the state to demonstrate that it exercised 'intelligent care and deliberation' in enacting the law.[325] That is, the law should address a social need and should not be whimsical, based on individual preferences alone rather than principles which apply equally to all. The policy-maker should be able to state what the principle behind the measure is, the aim it is pursuing, and how the measure advances the aim. To demonstrate 'intelligent care and deliberation' the court puts to scrutiny the enactment process to examine whether the decision was principled and reasoned.[326]

The discussion in this chapter reveals that though the Supreme Court has been increasingly describing India's rights limitation analysis as following the doctrine of proportionality, in practice, the court is generally still adhering to *Wednesbury* standards of review. The court reviews state action to determine whether the State is pursuing a legitimate aim through suitable means, and that such action is justified, given the various interests at stake in the matter. The nature of the court's inquiry into reasonableness flows not only from what elements the court analyses but also how it analyses them: generally, on broad claims and abstract common-sensical reasoning, rather than insisting on strong empirical proof. Overall, the court's practice suggests that its analysis focuses on ensuring that state action is within the realm of reasonable action rather than on ensuring that it is the most suited or least rights-restricting measure for achieving the state's aims.

[324] See examples of cases involving the distribution of state resources, discussed above in text accompanying n 236–38–42.

[325] *Chintaman Rao* (n 6); *Cellular Operators Association* (n 139).

[326] *Cellular Operators Association* (n 139).

7

# Comparative and Empirical Insights into Judicial Practice

## Towards an Integrative Model of Proportionality

TALYA STEINER, ANDREJ LANG, AND MORDECHAI KREMNITZER

## I Introduction

Proportionality is one of the most important global constitutional principles of our time, but despite the vast normative literature on the doctrine, there has been nearly no systematic research on the actual application of the doctrine in judicial practice.[1] This book constitutes one of the first in-depth empirical and comparative analyses of the application of the proportionality doctrine in practice across a considerable number of jurisdictions, based on case-law in six apex courts in six jurisdictions: Germany, Canada, South Africa, Israel, Poland, and India.

Methodologically, the country chapters in this book employ a combination of qualitative and quantitative analysis, based on a large sample of case-law, to allow for both meaningful engagement with the substance of the decisions and the benefits of quantifiable, comparable measures. The individual chapters are rich with findings, and the comparative analysis of them could go in many directions; we cannot comprehensively explore all of these directions here. This chapter focuses primarily on the structure of the doctrine, specifically the relationship and division of labour among the subtests and the function of the multi-stage doctrine as a whole.[2]

[1] See more detail on this point in the Introduction to this book.

[2] Some additional aspects that are explored in the country chapters and were not followed up on from an integrative perspective, together with additional potential directions for comparative research that we believe could be developed based on the preliminary findings in the country chapters, are detailed in Section VI of this chapter.

As specified in detail in the Introduction and in each of the country chapters, the quantitative findings are based on the systematic coding, conducted at the country level, of all cases applying the proportionality doctrine in a pre-defined time period tailored per country. The cases were coded according to the subject matter and rights invoked, as well as the outcome of each stage of the proportionality analysis (PA) and the final outcome.[3] This integrative chapter draws upon the coding conducted in each jurisdiction, involving 745 decisions overall, ranging from 98 to 161 cases per jurisdiction. More specifically, the quantitative analysis presented in this chapter focuses primarily on the data regarding cases that apply the proportionality doctrine and conclude that the reviewed measure is at least partially disproportionate. We term these 'failure cases', and the data presented in this chapter are based on these 377 cases, ranging from 31 to 84 per jurisdiction.[4]

The analysis in this chapter focuses on two levels of comparison: The main emphasis is on proportionality in practice compared to the theoretical approach to proportionality. This comparison focuses on the extent to which the application of proportionality follows or deviates from abstract accounts, as found in academic literature as well as in the court's explanations of its reasoning method. This juxtaposition should enable us to evaluate the extent to which the normative debate over proportionality is aligned with or disconnected from the actual practice of proportionality and to provide empirical grounding for the abundant normative literature on proportionality. A second level of comparison concerns the practice of proportionality between jurisdictions as seen in the empirical analysis. Finding and characterizing similarities and variations uncovers some of the forces affecting the application of the proportionality doctrine that are not accounted for in the literature. In addition, the comparative perspective reveals some of the strengths and weaknesses of the different applications of the doctrine, shows what specific jurisdictions have to offer in terms of effective engagement with the doctrine, and shines a light on shortcomings.[5]

[3] The coding was based on the majority of justices on the panel.

[4] For elaboration on the comparative failure rate per jurisdiction, see Section VI.

[5] A note is due regarding the reference to India within this comparative perspective. As discussed in the Introduction, India is an intriguing jurisdiction in terms of limitation analysis, as a country that appears to be in the process of adopting a more explicit proportionality framework. Chapter 6 generally demonstrates that India is located on the spectrum between proportionality and reasonableness. Since limitation analysis in India is conducted based on such an interim model, we will not be addressing it in the

The main argument put forth in this chapter is that, from a descriptive standpoint, a majority of the courts analysed demonstrate a tendency towards what we term an integrative approach to proportionality, in contrast to the traditional, strictly sequential approach typically referred to in theoretical writing and abstract descriptions of the doctrine by judges themselves. The integrative approach diverges from the sequential model in several ways, including flexibility in whether to end each stage of analysis with a clear positive or negative outcome, a tendency not to terminate the analysis after failure, and a greater sharing of responsibility among the stages of the analysis rather than having a single dominant stage. From a normative standpoint, we argue that the integrative approach has several advantages over the strictly sequential approach, and therefore we encourage more intentional and consistent implementation of this method of analysis.

This chapter is structured as follows: Section II opens with a presentation of the theoretical conception of the proportionality doctrine as a sequential doctrine that relies on a single dominant element – either the necessity test or the strict proportionality test.[6] This portrayal will then be contrasted with an overview of our findings, which demonstrates several types of deviations from this theoretical conception. This will set the scene for our claim that several of the courts analysed tend towards an integrative approach to PA. Sections III and IV detail our two main findings that support this claim: Section III addresses judicial practice concerning the first two stages of PA – the worthy purpose and suitability tests – and contrast the theory attributing a very limited role to these stages with our empirical findings pointing to a more significant role in the case-law. It also sets forth ways in which we believe these tests can be further invigorated. Section IV addresses the relationship between the last two elements of PA – necessity and strict proportionality – in the analysed case-law, again contrasting the theory, which generally chooses one dominant element, with our finding that some courts tend to rely on a combination of the two. It then presents our conception of a more

sections of this chapter devoted to evaluating the gaps between proportionality in theory and practice. The Indian application of the doctrine will serve us primarily as a comparative contrast when analysing the function served by the threshold stages – worthy purpose and suitability.

[6] When referring to the theoretical conception of the doctrine, we refer not only to the conception presented by scholars in academic literature but also to abstract opinions set forth by justices regarding the structure of the doctrine and how it is to be applied.

commensurate relationship between these two tests. Next, Section V discusses two questions that arise from our finding of a tendency towards an integrative, 'responsibility-sharing' application of proportionality: first, on an explanatory level, why courts may gravitate towards this model, and second, on the normative level, what the advantages and disadvantages of such a model are. We argue that this model should be embraced and applied deliberately and consistently. Section VI concludes the chapter by setting out specific points of interest from the country-based chapters as a foundation for further empirical and comparative analyses of proportionality in action.

## II The Structure of Proportionality Analysis in Theory and in Practice

The focal point of our comparative perspective is the structure of the doctrine, especially the division of labour between the stages of the analysis. By contrasting conventional conceptions and judicial practice, we demonstrate that the reality of proportionality deviates from common conceptions of the doctrine, and uncover previously unrecognized variations between jurisdictions.

Since our findings and our argument have to do with the relationship and interplay between the proportionality subtests, a preliminary point should be made regarding two possible perspectives on the role played by the subtests. The first concerns the judicial decision-making process. From this perspective, the subtests serve as steps that help judges evaluate the policy under review and reach their conclusion on the proportionality of the measure. The second perspective relates to the presentation and reasoning of the judicial decision in the written judgment. From this perspective, the subtests provide structure to the written decision and help to rationalize the outcome and persuade the different audiences of its justifiability.[7]

Our arguments in this chapter target both roles and both perspectives. While it is an open question whether and to what extent legal doctrine constrains judicial decisions – i.e., whether judges in their internal decision-making process indeed follow and rely upon the stages and questions set out by the doctrine[8] – we believe that it is reasonable to

[7] We thank Barak Medina for this point.

[8] See Raanan Sulitzeanu-Kenan, Mordechai Kremnitzer, and Sharon Alon, 'Facts, Preferences and Doctrine: An Empirical Analysis of Proportionality Judgement' (2016) 50 Law and Society Review 348.

assume that at least in some cases the proportionality framework guides judicial decision-making to some extent. Therefore, the way in which the doctrine is approached at the decision-making stage may somewhat affect judicial decision-making. In addition, judicial reasoning in the constitutional realm is central to judicial legitimacy and acceptance,[9] and therefore the way in which decisions are written represents a choice made by judges regarding how they wish to publicly justify their rulings. Given the centrality of courts in the public arena, judicial constitutional reasoning also tends to penetrate political and administrative decision-making, serve as a day-to-day tool for legal advisors, and affect public discourse and rhetoric.[10] How proportionality and its subtests are applied in a written decision has ramifications for the legitimacy and acceptance of the particular decision as well as the judiciary more broadly, and also affects the application of PA by different players in the policy-making process. It is against this background that we argue that an integrative approach to proportionality results in better-reasoned judgments, offers better guidance to policy-makers, and contributes to better protection of rights.[11]

9 John M Schebs and William Lyons, 'The Myth of Legality and Public Evaluation of the Supreme Court' (2000) 81 Social Science Quarterly 928; John Ferejohn and Pasquale Pasquino, 'Constitutional Courts as Deliberative Institutions: Towards an Institutional Theory of Constitutional Justice' in Wojciech Sadurski (ed), *Constitutional Justice, East and West* (Springer 2002) 21, 24–26; Barry Friedman, 'Taking Law Seriously' (2006) 4 Perspectives on Politics 261, 265–67; Michael L Wells, '"Sociological Legitimacy" in Supreme Court Decisions' (2007) 64 Washington and Lee Law Review 1011; Robert J Hume, 'Courting Multiple Audiences: The Strategic Selection of Legal Grounding by Judges in the US Court of Appeals' (2009) 30 The Justice System Journal 14; Dion Farganis, 'Do Reasons Matter? The Impact of Opinion Content on Supreme Court Legitimacy' (2012) 65 Political Research Quarterly 206; Chris W Bonneau and others, 'Evaluating the Effects of Multiple Opinion Rationales on Supreme Court Legitimacy' (2016) 45 American Politics Research 335; Ryan C Black and others, *US Supreme Court Opinions and Their Audiences* (CUP 2016).

10 Alec Stone Sweet, *Governing with Judges: Constitutional Politics in Europe* (OUP 2000); Janet L Heibert, *Charter Conflicts: What Is Parliament's Role?* (McGill-Queen's University Press 2002). Also see: Lila Margalit, Proportionality and Consideration of Rights in the Policy Process: The Case of the Israeli Counter Terrorism Act; Andrej Lang, Non-Judicial Constitutional Review of Counter-Terrorism Policies: The Role of Fundamental Rights in the Making of the Anti-Terror Database and Data Retention Legislation in Germany; Fiona de Londras, Proportionality and Rights in the Making of the EU Directive on Combating Terrorism (unpublished, all on file with the authors).

11 We develop this argument in detail in Section V.B.

### A Setting the Stage: Deviations from the Conventional Sequential Structure

Proportionality is conventionally portrayed as a structured, sequential doctrine. It comprises a number of different stages, each posing a specific, defined question, that together amount to all the required conditions for justifying a limitation of rights. A court conducting PA proceeds, in order, from one question to the next, and ends the analysis of each stage with a binary outcome: the measure either passes or fails the test. The analysis continues to the next test only if the previous step has been successfully passed. As a consequence, the final stage of strict proportionality – the apex of the analysis – is reached only once a measure has successfully passed all previous stages; a measure that has failed any of the previous tests is by definition unconstitutional and therefore no further discussion is needed.[12]

This structured and sequential characteristic is viewed by several supporters of the doctrine as one of its cardinal virtues: proportionality provides the judicial decision with structure, guiding judges through the decision-making process and ensuring that all relevant elements are considered in the appropriate order and context. Thus, proportionality allows 'judges to be analytical, by breaking one complex question into several sub questions that can be analyzed separately'.[13]

Interestingly, the South African Constitutional Court, following the language of the Constitution, has explicitly rejected this traditional

[12] Alec Stone Sweet and Jud Matthews, 'Proportionality, Balancing and Global Constitutionalism' (2008) 47 Columbia Journal of Transnational Law 72, 76: 'if the government's measure fails on suitability or necessity the act is *per se disproportionate*; it is outweighed by the pleaded right and therefore unconstitutional . . . If the measure under review passes the first three tests, the judge proceeds to balancing *stricto senso*.' See also Dieter Grimm, 'Proportionality in Canadian and German Constitutional Jurisprudence' (2007) 57 University of Toronto Law Journal 383, 397; Aharon Barak, *Proportionality: Constitutional Rights and their Limitations* (Hebrew edition, CUP 2012) 460–65.

[13] Kai Möller, 'Proportionality: Challenging the Critics' (2012) 10 International Journal of Constitutional Law 709, 727. See also: Mattias Kumm, 'Constitutional Rights as Principles: On the Structure and Domain of Constitutional Justice' (2004) 2 International Journal of Constitutional Law 574, 579; David M Beatty, *The Ultimate Rule of Law* (OUP 2004) 169–200; Charles-Maxime Panaccio, 'In Defence of the Two-Step Balancing and Proportionality in Rights Adjudication' (2011) 1 Canadian Journal of Law and Jurisprudence 109, 118, referring to proportionality as a 'heuristic tool for practical-moral reasoning'; Aharon Barak, 'Proportionality', in Michel Rosenfeld and Andras Sajo (eds), *The Oxford Handbook of Comparative Constitutional Law* (OUP 2012) 738; Barak (n 12) 558–61.

sequential approach as rigid and formalistic. Instead, it has developed a 'holistic' or global approach to PA, in which all elements must be taken into consideration in reaching the outcome.[14] According to Section 36(1) of the Constitution, the worthy purpose, suitability and necessity tests are all among the factors that must be considered in a global judgment on proportionality. Given that each subtest is only one of five factors listed in Section 36 that the Court must take into account, the analysis should not end after a single test, even if the finding is negative. This South African model of the application of proportionality is generally treated as a unique outlier approach,[15] and has typically either been ignored or explicitly rejected in the theoretical literature.[16]

Based on the traditional theoretical account of the internal structure and operation of proportionality, our expectation from the empirical data, from all countries other than South Africa, would be that the analysis should proceed through the stages, concluding each stage with a binary finding of either pass or fail, and that failure at any stage, by definition, would bring the analysis to an end.[17] Thus, every measure ultimately struck down is expected to fail as the result of a failure at a single, specific stage. However, our research revealed certain features in the application of PA across jurisdictions that substantially deviate from this theoretical conception of sequential analysis. They include leaving stages undecided, passing stages while making use of negative signalling, and continuing the analysis despite previous failures. These features have not received attention previously in the academic literature, and we see

[14] See *S v Manamela & Another* 2000 (3) SA 1 (CC) [32]; *S v Bhulwana; S v Gwadiso* 1996 (1) SA 388 (CC) [18]. According to Justice Ngcobo, '[n]one of these factors are individually decisive. Nor are they exhaustive of the relevant factors to be considered. These factors together with other relevant factors are to be considered in the overall enquiry. The limitation analysis thus involves the weighing up of competing values and ultimately an assessment based on proportionality' *Prince v The President of the Law and Society of the Cape of Good Hope* 2001 (2) SA 388 (CC). Stu Woolman and Henk Botha, 'Limitations' in Stu Woolman and Michael Bishop (eds), *Constitutional Law of South Africa* (2nd edn, Juta 2005) 94.

[15] Stone Sweet and Matthews (n 12) 72, 125–32.

[16] Barak (n 12) 132.

[17] On the sequential approach in Germany, see Chapter 1, Section III.E. For Israel, see Barak (n 12) 460–62; for Canada, see Vicki C Jackson, 'Pockets of Proportionality: Choice and Necessity, Doctrine and Principle' in Erin F Delaney and Rosalind Dixon (eds), *Comparative Judicial Review* (Edward Elgar 2018) 357, 368; and Richard Stacey, 'The Magnetism of Moral Reasoning and the Principle of Proportionality in Comparative Constitutional Adjudication' (2019) 67 The American Journal of Comparative Law 435, 450.

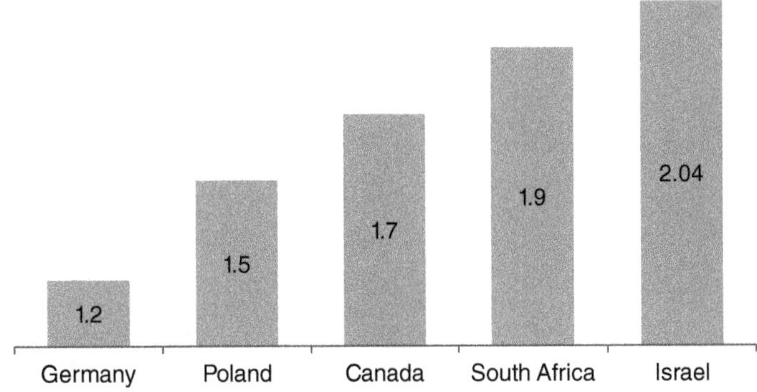


**Figure 7.1** Average number of failures per failure case

them as challenging the traditional conception of proportionality as a sequential doctrine.

If proportionality were truly applied in a strictly sequential fashion in judicial practice, we would expect to have an average of one failure per failure decision because the analysis is meant to terminate immediately after the failure at one stage. However, the data presented in Figure 7.1 show deviations from this theoretical account in varying degrees.

In Germany 65 failures occurred in 58 failure decisions, for an average of 1.2 failures per decision, only slightly higher than the sequential conception. As we will show, the single failure in Germany is typically on the final strict proportionality test. In all other jurisdictions the average number of failures per failure decision is substantially higher. In Poland 91 failures were found in 60 failure decisions, for an average of 1.5 failures per decision. In Canada 144 failures were found in 84 decisions, for an average of 1.7 failures per decision. The finding of 156 failures in 82 decisions in South Africa, for an average of 1.9 failures per decision, is to be expected considering the explicit rejection of the sequential model there. Surprisingly, Israel leads with the highest average: 2.04 failures per decision, based on 84 failures in 41 decisions.

The reason these average numbers of failures per decision are higher than one is that these courts regularly continue their analysis past the first stage of failure. This approach is further demonstrated by the rate of termination of the analysis after a failure. The termination rate measures whether failure at a particular stage is in itself sufficient to justify the final outcome, or whether the measure needs to fail an additional subtest before the final result is reached. The termination rates reflect the

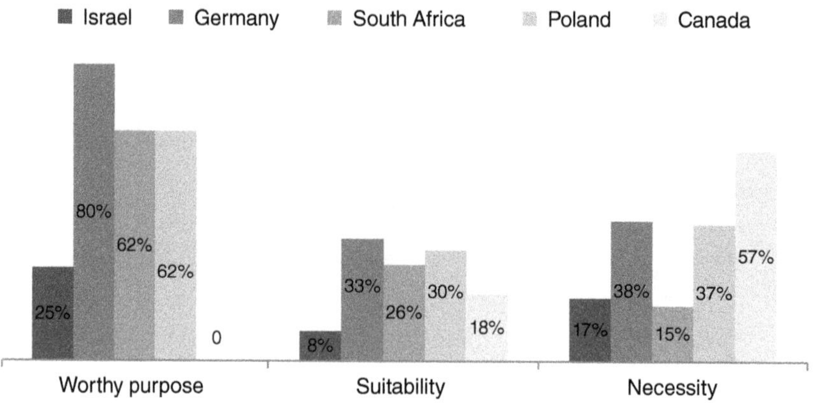


**Figure 7.2** Termination rates after failure at each stage

internal dynamic between the subtests and the way in which the sequential structure actually functions, and provide insights into the relative strength of individual stages. In theory, the termination rate after a failure at any stage should be 100 per cent. As we can see in Figure 7.2, which presents the termination rates per stage for each country, the termination rates never reach 100 per cent at any stage or in any country. Instead, they range from zero to 80 per cent, and are most commonly between 30 and 50 per cent.

In subsequent sections of this chapter we will discuss specific termination rates per stage and per country.[18] For now, however, it suffices to say that the termination rates demonstrate overall that in no country does the analysis consistently come to an end after failure. Rather – to differing degrees – the analysis continues, often until the last stage. Thus, in a portion of cases – and in Israel, South Africa, and Poland in a majority of cases – the final outcome is not based on a single failure but rather on a combination of at least two failures. Considering South Africa's explicit rejection of the sequential model, the findings on South Africa are not surprising. However, these findings demonstrate substantial deviation of practice from the traditional theoretical conception of the sequential structure of the doctrine in countries that supposedly do operate within this theoretical framework.

[18] See Sections III.B, III.D and IV.B.

An additional finding concerns deviation from the binary pass/fail outcome of each stage of the analysis. While the theoretical model requires the outcome of each stage to be either pass or fail, in practice in all the countries analysed a broader spectrum of possibilities exists. At times courts may engage in forms of negative signalling, raising difficulties with the measure under review at a particular stage, but still refrain from failing the measure at that point, and instead defer the failure to the final stage. For example, courts may discuss a stage, raise a problem, and then refrain from coming to a conclusive decision on it, leaving the stage undecided. Alternatively, courts may raise difficulties with regard to a specific test in the analysis but still go on to 'barely pass' it through this stage. Finally, the judges may state that they are 'willing to assume', for the sake of the analysis, that it passes the particular stage. These are often ways for the court to signal the existence of a problem with the policy, without explicitly failing it.[19] In most cases, if not all, these negative signals will ultimately lead to a failure at a later stage. These practices strain the traditional conception of the sequential analysis, in which each stage of analysis carries its own weight and is meant to be decided independently, and the analysis in subsequent stages is based on the assumption that the previous stages have been passed and therefore those issues are closed.

### *B A Single Dominant Element or Shared Responsibility between Tests?*

Given the multi-test structure of the proportionality doctrine, one important issue is the relationship and division of labour between the different subtests. A significant portion of the theoretical literature on proportionality either explicitly or implicitly portrays it as relying primarily on a

[19] The practice of signalling occurs most commonly in Germany and Israel. In Germany the Federal Constitutional Court pointed out a problem with a measure at the worthy purpose stage and/or the necessity stage but left the issue unresolved and ultimately struck that measure down with the strict proportionality test in 13 out of 58, or 22.4 per cent, of the 'fail' cases. In Israel at least one of the justices had pointed to a problem at a previous stage in five out of six, or 83 per cent, of the few cases in the database that failed for the first time at the final stage. While the Israeli Supreme Court is much more willing to fail a measure at one of the earlier stages – in addition to the strict proportionality test – the Federal Constitutional Court seems to prefer to reserve the determination of failure for the final test. Leaving stages undecided is also quite common in Poland; see Chapter 5, Section III.D.

single dominant element. While some point this out merely as a descriptive feature, others support it from a normative standpoint as well.

In the traditional portrayal, the two opening tests – worthy purpose and suitability – are easily passed threshold stages that do not contribute significantly to determining the outcome of the analysis.[20] With regard to the other two elements – necessity and strict proportionality – theorists are roughly divided on the question of which should fill the role of the dominant component of the analysis.[21] Thus, except with respect to the South African Constitutional Court, the majority of the theoretical literature reflects the conception that the different stages do not share equally in the weight of the decision and do not contribute evenly to the final outcome, but rather that a single dominant test – typically the last or the penultimate – bears the brunt of the analysis.[22]

This conception raises the question of the feasibility of maintaining a system of structured analysis that is made up of several independent tests but also includes a single dominant stage. In our view, there is reason to question the stability of the doctrine when structured in this way and the ability to sustain it in practice. Expecting courts to adhere strictly to a multi-stage doctrine and proceed through several stages even though they rarely make a significant contribution to the final outcome seems unrealistic. In practice we may expect deviation in one of two directions: First, these threshold stages may be skipped so as to not 'waste judicial energy' on stages that are by definition easily passed, in order to reach the essence of the analysis, making the final stage an all-encompassing one in which the major portion of the analysis is conducted. Alternatively, the

[20] Julian Rivers, 'Proportionality and Variable Intensity of Review' (2006) 65 Cambridge Law Journal 174, 195–98; Denise G Reaume, 'Limitation on Constitutional Rights: The Logic of Proportionality' (2009) 26 Oxford Legal Studies Research Paper 1, 9–11; Stavros Tsakyrakis, 'Proportionality: An Assault on Human Rights? A Rejoinder to Madhav Khosla' (2010) 8 International Journal of Constitutional Law 307, 308; Paul Yowell, 'Proportionality in US Constitutional Law' in Liora Lazarus, Christopher McCrudden, and Niels Bowels (eds), *Reasoning Rights: Comparative Judicial Engagement* (Hart Publishing 2014) 87, 88; Stone Sweet and Matthews (n 12) 72, 76; Barak (n 12) 246–49, 315–16.

[21] Stone Sweet and Matthews (n 12) 72. For a proponent of necessity serving as the dominant element see Jochen von Bernstorff, 'Proportionality without Balancing: why Judicial Ad Hoc Balancing in Unnecessary and Potentially Detrimental to the Realization of Individual and Collective Self Determination' in Liora Lazarus, Christopher McCrudden, and Niels Bowels (eds), *Reasoning Rights: Comparative Judicial Engagement* (Hart Publishing 2014) 63. For a proponent of balancing serving as the dominant element, see Barak (n 12) 340, 344.

[22] Reaume (n 20). She calls this structure 'heavy on the bottom' (as opposed to 'heavy on the top' or 'heavy on the middle').

narrow interpretation of the preliminary stages may be rejected and they may instead be infused with more significant value, somewhat diminishing the dominance of the final test.

In our empirical and comparative analysis of the application of the proportionality doctrine, we find evidence of both of these deviations. To a more limited extent, primarily in Germany and to some extent in Poland, we find stages – specifically, suitability, and necessity – being skipped to reach what is considered central: proportionality in the strict sense. In the German case-law the court skipped either the suitability or the necessity stage in 25 per cent of the cases in the dataset. In addition, in 28 per cent of the cases the court glanced at the suitability stage extremely briefly, and in 25 per cent it only briefly addressed the necessity stage. Putting skipping and brief analysis together, the result is that the suitability stage was either entirely skipped or merely glanced over in 50 per cent of the cases, and the necessity stage in 44 per cent. In Poland the court skipped the suitability stage in 23 per cent of the cases in the dataset, and the necessity stage in 18 per cent.[23] Stages of the analysis that are skipped entirely or only very briefly addressed pose a challenge for the conception of proportionality as a practice different from, and superior to, merely balancing, and can significantly erode the status and contribution of the separate stages. These findings correspond to a critique that has been raised in the literature, according to which regardless of the official multi-stage structure, in practice proportionality is essentially balancing.[24]

However, there is also significant evidence of evolution in the opposite direction: In several countries, primarily Israel, South Africa, and Poland but to some extent Canada as well, we find cases in which the application of proportionality relies on significant contributions by the earlier stages, resulting in a sharing of responsibility for the final outcome rather than a single dominant stage. As will be detailed in Section III of this chapter, we find surprising evidence of the significance of the opening (worthy purpose and suitability) tests. In several jurisdictions these stages play a more meaningful role than previously considered, both in terms of actual failures at these stages (particularly the suitability test) and in terms of the contribution of the analysis at these stages to the final outcome even

[23] To a lesser degree, skipping – primarily of the suitability test – and extremely brief analyses can be found in other countries as well.

[24] Tsakyrakis (n 20) 468; Ernst-Wolfgang Böckenförde, 'Schutzbereich, Eingriff, Verfassungsimmanente Schranken: Zur Kritik gegenwärtiger Grundrechtsdogmatik' (2003) 42 Der Staat 165, 190.

if not by way of explicit failure. In addition, as will be detailed in Section IV of this chapter, we identify a prominent and previously unrecognized model of basing the final outcome on a combination of failures at both the necessity and the strict proportionality stages, rather than at one or the other.

In our view, the accumulation of these findings – deviation from a strictly sequential structure that mandates a positive or negative outcome at each stage and termination of the analysis after one failure, as well as a greater sharing of responsibility among the stages of the analysis – points to a tendency towards an integrative approach to PA, rather than the traditional sequential and single dominant stage approach.

Two interesting questions arise in light of these findings. At the descriptive level, what might explain the draw of such a model for courts in practice, leading them to apply the doctrine contrary to the theoretical portrayal? No less importantly, at the normative level, what are the advantages and disadvantages of this model of application? Descriptively, we tie the gravitation of courts towards such an integrative model to the complex and debatable nature of proportionality decisions and the institutional sensitivities courts face when conducting constitutional review. Specifically, courts may be understandably drawn towards the final balancing stage due to the decisional flexibility and engagement with constitutional values it allows. Nevertheless, we also recognize the apprehension courts may have regarding this stage, considering its explicit political nature. We argue that the integrative practice of proportionality allows courts to incorporate the balancing test without making it the sole basis for the decision. By bolstering the final stage with additional failures, courts are able to make use of the advantages of the final stage while protecting themselves from some of its downsides. This practice recognizes the relative weaknesses of each stage of the analysis, and by integrating them gives the outcome a stronger foundation.

In our opinion, an integrative application of PA is also desirable from a normative perspective if, and to the extent that, it meaningfully addresses each and every stage of the analysis. We believe that recognizing the connections between the stages and allowing feedback between them, rather than isolating each test as a separate inquiry, can improve the quality of judicial practice and more fully exploit the analytical potential inherent in PA. We also believe that this type of PA best reflects the role of the court in ensuring that rights are limited only when the limitation is justified, and provides the most meaningful guidance to policy-makers in terms of what is expected of them when they design policy that restricts rights. Specifically, the inquiry at each stage should not be limited to whether the reviewed measure meets the threshold for failing or passing the test. Of course, where a measure clearly does not meet the requirement of one of the stages, this should be stated. However, courts should also focus on asking questions at each stage that will generate information that can contribute to the analysis at subsequent stages and to the overall outcome, regardless of whether this will serve as a basis for failure at the particular stage.

These points will be further developed in Section V, after we present a fuller description of two of our findings: the significance of the threshold stages (Section III) and the relationship between necessity and strict proportionality (Section IV). In each of these sections, after presenting our findings and how they diverge from the theory, we will also briefly suggest possibilities for invigorating each individual test, in order to better fulfil its potential within the overall framework of PA in line with an integrative approach.

## III The Significance of the Threshold Stages

### *A The Threshold Stages in Theory*

The worthy purpose test permits infringement of a constitutional right only in pursuit of a proper purpose. The suitability test demands that the rights-infringing measure be suitable for achieving the purpose. Both subtests can be designed to set a more demanding or more permissive standard. With regard to the worthy purpose test, either any public interest as defined by the legislature could suffice to meet the requirement so long as it is not constitutionally proscribed,[25] or more demandingly, the purpose could have to be 'related to concerns which are pressing and substantial in a free and democratic society'.[26] Moreover, the analysis could be restricted to an objective evaluation of the policy goals as ascertained from the policy itself or official statements, or go further to address the subjective intentions of the legislators, including unofficial statements made throughout the policy-making process. Similarly, the suitability test could be conceptualized as only sanctioning

[25] This is essentially the standard for determining the worthiness of a purpose set forth by the German Federal Constitutional Court. Chapter 1, Section V.B.1. See, e.g., BVerfGE 116, 202 [224], noting that 'it is primarily a matter of the legislator to decide on the basis of its political ideas and objectives which measure it intends to take in the public interest'.

[26] *R v Oakes* [1986] 1 SCR 103.

instances of manifest arbitrariness in which the measure is not at all suitable for achieving the purpose and therefore infringes a constitutional right without contributing to solving a social problem.[27] Alternatively, the measure could be required to achieve the purpose more demonstrably and substantially.

The defining question in constitutional practice regarding the role of the threshold stages is therefore what specific requirements must be met with regard to each subtest. For the worthy purpose test, key factors are how abstractly or concretely the legislative purpose is formulated, and how carefully courts distinguish multiple purposes and examine evidence of the subjective intentions. For the suitability test, it matters how fully – partially, substantially, or entirely – the measure has to achieve the purpose of the law and what degree of likelihood is required. Other variables are whether this contribution to the goal is determined merely based on common-sense or whether evidence is required, who bears the burden of proof, and whether the perspective for evaluating effectiveness is the time of legislation or the time of evaluation.

In the literature on proportionality, the two opening stages of the analysis are overwhelmingly perceived as threshold tests for weeding out extreme outlier cases, and they only rarely result in failure. Although legal scholars agree that limitation analysis should not be conducted in cases in which the goal of the limitation obviously cannot justify limitation,[28] it seems to be almost taken for granted that such cases rarely occur, perhaps based on the assumption that policy-makers generally promote legitimate public interests. As for the suitability requirement, the general understanding in the literature is that the bar to be met at this stage tends to be very low, requiring merely a theoretical demonstration that the measure is capable of promoting the goal to some degree, and therefore it is assumed that measures would rarely fail such a basic

[27] Under this conception, a court that disqualifies such a measure with the suitability test can be compared to a 'lunacy commission sitting in judgement upon the mental capacity of legislators'. Panaccio (n 13) 109, 112; citing Lucy Kramer Cohen (ed), *The Legal Conscience: Selected Papers of Felix S Cohen* (Yale University Press 1960) 44.

[28] These are often termed 'exclusionary reasons'. See Iddo Porat, 'The Dual Model of Balancing: A Model for the Proper scope of Balancing in Constitutional Law' (2006) 27 Cardozo Law Review 1393, 1403–06; Mattias Kumm, 'Political Liberalism and the Structure of Rights: On the Place and Limits of the Proportionality Requirement' in George Paulsen (ed), *Law, Rights, Discourse. Themes from the Legal Philosophy of Robert Alexy* (Hart Publishing 2007) 131, 142–48; Matthias Klatt and Moritz Meister, 'Proportionality: A Benefit to Human Rights? Remarks on the ICON Controversy' (2012) 10 International Journal of Constitutional Law 687, 690.

requirement.[29] All in all, the two threshold stages are viewed as primarily setting the stage for the later tests, in which the 'real' analysis takes place.[30]

### B *Judicial Practice Concerning the Worthy Purpose Test*

Given the overall consensus on the ease of passing the opening stage, we would expect this stage to exhibit very low failure rates across all jurisdictions. We use the failure rate at each stage (the number of failures at that stage as a percentage of total cases in which the analysis resulted in the court striking down a measure) as a quantitative indicator of the centrality of a particular test. Figure 7.3 shows both the frequency of failure of measures at the worthy purpose stage for each country and the

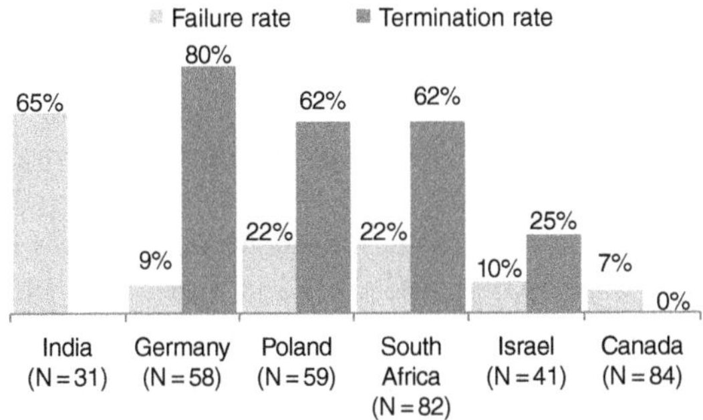


**Figure 7.3** Failure and termination rates at the worthy purpose stage[31]

[29] Two examples: Dieter Grimm describes the function of the suitability test as eliminating a 'small number of runaway cases'. Grimm (n 12) 383, 389. Aharon Barak notes that the purpose of suitability is weeding out a small number of irrational means. Barak, *Proportionality* (n 12) 315–16.

[30] For example: Yowell (n 20): 'the tests of legitimacy and suitability are – to the extent that they are separately addressed in a case – usually treated in a cursory fashion. It is very rare for a court to hold that the means are unsuitable for reaching that aim.'; *Tsakyrakis (n 20) 307, 308:* 'although judges . . . pay lip service to the first two subtests, they really don't attribute much significance to them'; Stone Sweet and Matthews (n 12) 72, 76 (when surveying the structure of the doctrine present worthy purpose and suitability, and then when arriving upon the necessity test state that it 'has more bite', meaning that the previous two tests do not). Also see: Rivers (n 20) 195–98; Barak (n 12) 246–47, 315–17; Reaume (n 20).

[31] The failure rate is the number of cases that failed the worthy purpose stage as a percentage of all failure cases. The N appearing under the name of each country represents the overall number of failure cases in that country's database.

The termination rate is the number of cases in which the analysis came to an end after failure at the worthy purpose stage as a percentage of all failures at that stage. The number

termination rate after failure at the worthy purpose stage. While the failure rates express the extent to which the worthy purpose test is used, at least in part, to justify the failure of the measure, the termination rates show whether failure at this stage is itself sufficient to justify the final outcome, or whether the measure needs to fail an additional subtest to support such a finding.

The data shown in Figure 7.3 affirm that in several of the jurisdictions the failure rate at the worthy purpose stage is low (although not miniscule). In Canada and Israel this is the stage with the lowest failure rate (7 and 10 per cent, respectively), and in Germany the rate is similarly low (9 per cent). In South Africa and Poland, however, the failure rate at the worthy purpose stage is surprisingly significant, amounting in both countries to 22 per cent, over a fifth of all failure cases. India stands out as a distinct outlier, with 65 per cent of failure cases failing at the worthy purpose stage, emphasizing a clear difference between analysis that is strongly rooted in a tradition of reasonableness review and analysis that has transitioned to the proportionality standard, as will be demonstrated later.[32]

Figure 7.3 also shows relatively high termination rates at the worthy purpose test in South Africa, Poland, and Germany. In other words, failing the worthy purpose test is considered a blow significant enough for the analysis to come to an end. Although the termination rate is not 100 per cent, these findings support the conclusion that this stage is viewed as a significant component in South African and Polish jurisprudence. This constitutes an exception to the South African approach, as in principle the analysis there is not meant to rely on a single element, and it demonstrates the particular strength a failure at the worthy purpose test can have. Germany is unique in the sense that failures at the worthy purpose stage are extremely rare, but when they occur they are considered sufficient. Because it is final, it is a good reason to be careful in finding unworthiness. In Israel and Canada, in contrast, the termination rate at the worthy purpose test is surprisingly low, demonstrating that this stage does not have independent standing in these countries and

of failures at the worthy purpose stage in each country are: Germany, N = 5; Poland, N = 13; South Africa, N = 18.5; Israel, N = 4; Canada, N = 6.

Considering that limitation analysis in India does not currently follow the structured proportionality framework, the analysis in India is not expected to adhere to a specific order and terminate after a failure, and therefore India is not included in the termination rate measure.

32 See Section III.F.

must be combined with at least one additional failure. There is most often a certain degree of inherent uncertainty when the purpose seems to be unworthy; this may explain the reluctance to make a final finding at this stage. There is also heightened political sensitivity to this test, since it essentially accuses the decision-makers of malice.

The qualitative analysis sheds some light on the unexpected finding of significant failure rates at the worthy purpose stage in South Africa and Poland. Despite the similar quantitative failure rates, the two courts actually demonstrate very different approaches to this stage: whereas in South Africa this stage is often explicitly value-oriented and is used to denounce illegitimate goals at the very opening of the analysis, in Poland a combination of more formalistic requirements have been introduced into this stage, which emphasize its function as a means of striking down measures at the start because they are not connected to the enumerated purposes. Thus the court can avoid explicit evaluation of the policy content itself.

A unique factor found to contribute to the significant failure rate in South Africa is the review of apartheid-era legislation. A majority of the cases in which a South African measure failed at the worthy purpose stage (12 of the 18.5) were reviews of pre-1994 legislation. In such cases, the judicial review explicitly delegitimizes the premises underlying legislation from the previous regime, and the court emphasizes in its decision that apartheid-era commitments to social segregation and differentiation can never justify rights limitations.[33] In this unique situation, part of the court's core mandate is to critique legislative goals of a former unjust regime, and it enjoys the utmost legitimacy in doing so. The South African court is uniquely positioned – specifically with regard to legislation from a particular pre-constitutional era – to apply a consensus benchmark for evaluating the legitimacy or illegitimacy of policy goals and to send the kind of unequivocal message that is conveyed by failure in the worthy purpose test.

Although much rarer, similar situations can occasionally be found in other jurisdictions. When reviewing very old legislation or when society has undergone a significant change, courts seem to enjoy greater backing

[33] See, e.g., *National Coalition for Gay and Lesbian Equality & Another v Minister of Justice and Others* 1999 (1) SA 6 (CC); *Moseneke & Others v The Master & Another* 2001 (2) SA 18 (CC); *Bhe & Others v Khayelitsha Magistrate & Others* 2005 (1) SA 580 (CC).

if they rule that the goals and values reflected by a law are no longer considered legitimate.[34]

Although the Polish Constitutional Tribunal could be viewed as being in a similar position to that of the South African Constitutional Court in the sense of practising constitutional review following a regime change, and although it indeed regularly reviews Communist-era policy, its approach differs from that of the South African court. A significant feature of the Communist era was the limitation of individual rights in executive acts, internal circulars, or instructions, often issued without statutory authorization and without official publication. One of the central tools with which the Tribunal deals with this Communist legacy is through the principle of the 'rule of law', which requires that limitations of fundamental rights be explicitly enshrined in statute.[35] Such cases most often do not even reach the worthy purpose stage, since they fail to meet this preliminary formal requirement.[36]

Several other factors, then, contribute to the significant failure rate at the worthy purpose stage in Poland. One such factor is the text of the

[34] In Canada this can be found in the review of very old criminal offences, as well as in the context of sexual orientation, in which social change made the court able to affirm the lack of any worthy purpose. *R v Zundel* [1992] 2 SCR 713; *Vriend v Alberta*, [1998] 1 SCR 493. In Germany such cases can be found in the areas of family law and professional conduct, with regard to legislation seeking to protect antiquated moral standards or outdated professional rules. See: BVerfGE 7, 377 [410]–[12]; BVerfGE 25, 1 [12]; BVerfGE 39, 210 [225]; BVerfGE 36, 146. In India this can be found with regard to colonial-era or other very old legislation. See: *John Vallamattom v Union of India* (2003) 6 SCC 611; *Malpe Vishwanath Acharya v State of Maharashtra* (1998) 2 SCC 1. It should be pointed out in this context that in Israel, laws from before 1992 – the year when Basic Law Human Dignity and Freedom was passed – are immune from constitutional review, and therefore it is rare to find cases of judicial review of antiquated laws.

[35] Decision of 28 May 1986, Case No. U 1/86 OTK 1986, Item 2; Judgment of 3 March 1987, Case No. P 2/87 OTK 1987, Item 2; Decision of 22 September 1997, Case No. K 25/97 OTK 1997, No. 3/4, Item 35.

[36] Such cases were not included in the Polish database, since its focus was on the Tribunal's engagement with proportionality. However, in the process of establishing the database, such data were collected, pointing to the existence of nine cases in 2013 alone (13 per cent of all judgments handed down that year) in which the Tribunal reviewed normative acts issued by the executive without the required statutory authorization; seven of them concerned limitations of constitutional rights. See Judgment of 8 January 2013, Case No. K 38/12 OTK-A 2013, No. 1, Item 1; Judgment of 5 March 2013, Case No. U 2/11 OTK-A 2013, No. 3, Item 24; Judgment of 26 March 2013, Case No. K 11/12 OTK-A 2013, No. 3, Item 28; Judgment of 16 July 2013, Case No. P 53/11 OTK-A 2013, No. 6, Item 78; Judgment of 30 July 2013, Case No. U 5/12 OTK-A 2013, No. 6, Item 88; Judgment of 24 September 2013, Case No. K 35/12 OTK-A 2013, No. 7, Item 94; Judgment of 29 October 2013, Case No. U 7/12 OTK-A 2013, No. 7, Item 102.

limitation clause in the Polish Constitution. Article 31(3) of the Polish Constitution contains a fixed list of constitutional values that can be considered legitimate grounds for limitations of constitutional rights or freedoms. The list includes state security, public order, the natural environment, health, public morals, and constitutional rights and freedoms of other persons.[37] Whereas in other jurisdictions the text of the constitution does not specify which goals or concerns may justify limitation of a right, thus giving courts broad freedom of interpretation to determine, in light of constitutional values, which policy goals are considered worthy,[38] the Polish Constitutional Tribunal conducts a more formal process of reviewing at the worthy purpose stage whether the goal pursued by the legislature fits into one of the general goals enumerated in Article 31(3), regardless of whether it might be a legitimate goal in and of itself. Some of these goals are quite vague and in most cases the Tribunal interprets the listed goals broadly, thereby managing to include most public interests under them. Nevertheless, this structure of the limitation clause does lead the Tribunal at times to fail a measure at the worthy purpose test, based on the finding that it fails to meet any of the enumerated goals, without making a confrontational statement that the legislature's goals are illegitimate, unworthy, or abhorrent per se. Because this type of outcome is more formalistically anchored in the text of the Constitution, its rhetoric is much less explicitly value-based.[39]

Additional failures at the worthy purpose stage in Poland concern situations in which rights-restricting legislation has completely failed to provide any legal outlet or remedy for the individuals to whom the law applied. The court held that such complete denial of rights without any

[37] Similarly, Article 19 of the Constitution of India lists – for each of the six rights guaranteed by this provision – the various purposes for which the guaranteed rights can be limited, including 'the sovereignty and integrity of India', 'the security of the State', and 'public order or morality'. In contrast, Articles 14 and 21 do not provide an explicit list of legitimate purposes. In Germany, the expropriation clause of Article 14(3) of the Basic Law and Article 13(7) BL concerning the right of inviolability of the home contain, amongst others, qualified limitation clauses that limit the discretion of the legislator in determining the worthiness of a purpose in the context of specific fundamental rights. In judicial practice, however, these qualifications typically only constitute minor differences in comparison to the general public interest requirement set forth at the worthy purpose stage. For more detail, see Chapter 1, Section V.B.1.

[38] The constitutions of Canada, South Africa, and Israel do not contain lists of enumerated goals that may justify a limitation of a right.

[39] See, e.g., Judgment of 20 July 2011, Case No. K 9/11 OTK-A 2011, No. 6, Item 61; Decision of 28 May 1997, Case No. K 26/96 OTK 1997, No. 2, Item 19; Judgment of 18 July 2012, Case No. K 14/12 OTK-A 2012, No. 7, Item 82.

procedural opening – something that is not infrequent in Polish legislation – could not be justified by any worthy purpose.[40] This kind of reasoning might be considered under the necessity heading in other countries, but it is incorporated into the worthy purpose requirement in Poland. Finally, the Tribunal has at times introduced the principle of specificity in legislative language as a requirement at the worthy purpose stage. Thus, the Tribunal has held that vagueness in the wording of a law makes it impossible to precisely ascertain the legislative goal, thus preventing it from evaluating whether the law meets one of the enumerated goals.[41] These two additional practices of the Polish Tribunal similarly reflect a relatively formalistic, or rule-like, approach to the worthy purpose test, pointing out flaws in legislation that make it unworthy from the outset.

The low (although not negligible) failure rates at the worthy purpose stage in Israel, Germany, and Canada generally correspond to the expectation in the literature. Still, we believe it may be superficial to conclude from these low failure rates that these courts are only rarely faced with problematic goals. At least partially, the low failure rates at the worthy purpose stage reflect choices made by these courts not to engage directly with the question of legitimate purpose. In some cases the court may fail the measure later on for a different reason, whereas in others the court may ultimately uphold the measure under review without engaging with the legitimacy of the goal, ignoring issues that arguably are worthy of debate.[42]

The qualitative analysis does reveal that in a large portion of cases in these countries the scrutinized policy unquestionably promotes a

[40] Judgment of 3 June 2014, Case No. K 19/11 OTK-A 2014, No. 6, Item 60; Judgment of 26 November 2013, Case No. P 33/12 OTK-A 2013, No. 8, Item 123; Judgment of 8 April 2014, Case No. SK 22/11 OTK-A 2014, No. 4, Item 37; Judgment of 10 December 2012, Case No. K 25/11 OTK-A 2012, No. 11, Item 132; Judgment of 6 November 2012, Case No. K 21/11 OTK-A 2012, No. 10, Item 119; Judgment of 30 October 2012, Case No. SK 20/11 OTK-A 2012, No. 9, Item 110.

[41] See, e.g., Decision of 28 May 1997, Case No. K 26/96 OTK 1997, No. 2, Item 19 and Judgment of 18 July 2012, Case No. K 14/12 OTK-A 2012, No. 7, Item 82.

[42] In Germany, see BVerfGE 135, 126. In Israel, see HCJ 7052/03 *Adalah Legal Centre for Arab Minority Rights v Minister of Interior* [2006], IsrSC 61(2) 202, available in English at <https://supremedecisions.court.gov.il/Home/Download?path=EnglishVerdicts\03\520\070\a47&fileName=03070520_a47.txt&type=4> accessed 16 December 2019; HCJ 1213/10 *Eyal Nir v Knesset Chairman* (23 February 2012, unpublished); HCJ 2311/11 *Sabach v Knesset* (17 September 2014, unpublished); HCJ 3166/14 *Guttman v Attorney General* (12 March 2015, unpublished).

legitimate purpose and the judicial analysis at this stage is therefore justifiably brief. Nevertheless, in a subset of cases the policy goal could potentially raise significant questions and be worthy of in-depth discussion – regarding the sincerity of the goal, the existence of additional, less legitimate goals and the possibility that the importance of the policy is being exaggerated – and yet such meaningful debate does not often occur.

One possible reason why the worthy purpose stage is so rarely emphasized in such cases may be the sensitivity of these questions; the judges may choose to avoid such analysis because they prefer to defer to the legislature in the matter of the policy goal. The court may decide to refrain from delving into problematic inquiries at this opening stage, knowing that this is only the first of several stages and it will be able to raise problems with the policy later on. It should be mentioned that avoidance of sensitive questions at the worthy purpose stage is seen to occur in South Africa and Poland as well, despite the significant failure rates there.[43]

Deflecting significant analysis from the worthy purpose stage can be easily achieved by using a high level of abstraction when defining the policy goal – such as maintaining public order or promoting national security. The court may also address the goal of a policy 'writ large' as opposed to breaking down the specific goal promoted by the challenged section.[44] Alternatively, the court can state that it is categorically

[43] In Africa, such avoidance occurs with regard to legislation introduced by the current government rather than the previous regime whose motives are easier to critique. See: *United Democratic Movement v President of the Republic of South Africa and Others* (No 2) 2003 (1) SA 495 (CC), 2002 (11) BCLR 1179 (CC); *Glenister v President of the Republic of South Africa & Others* 2009 (1) SA 287 (CC); 2009 (2) BCLR 136 (CC). In Poland avoidance at the worthy purpose test can be found in cases raising sensitive political issues, such as a ban on Communist symbols and the treatment of those involved in the Communist regime, and the differentiation between political revenge and necessary protection of the new constitutional order. In Judgment of 19 July 2011, Case No. K 11/10 OTK-A 2011, No. 6, Item 60, the measure was struck down at the balancing stage, where the focus was on lack of legal certainty regarding how specific elements would be interpreted. The court did not deal with what the actual goal was and whether it was a worthy limitation of speech. Judgment of 6 July 2011, Case No. P 12/09 OTK-A 2011, No. 6, Item 51 also does not discuss whether there was a goal that could limit speech. See also Judgment of 24 February 2010, Case No. K 6/09 OTK-A 2010, No. 2, Item 15; Judgment of 21 October 1998, Case No. K 24/98 OTK 1998, No. 6, Item 97.

[44] In the *Adalah* case in Israel, the Supreme Court accepted the general goal of a series of amendments as legitimate, not addressing the specific goal of the final amendment under review, and only later reaching the conclusion that the goal had already been achieved by

refraining from addressing evidence pertaining to the subjective motivations of policy-makers promoting the policy, instead basing the analysis strictly on the officially declared purpose.[45]

Interestingly, however, we find that even in courts with low failure rates at the worthy purpose stage, the analysis at this stage sometimes contains more than is generally recognized, making it significant for later stages. In Germany, for example, the Federal Constitutional Court will at times use this stage to weed out particular purposes as unworthy, while still passing the measure at this stage because it may be based on a different, worthy purpose. Thus, although failing in only 9 per cent of failure cases (5 of 58), the court has pointed out a specific unworthy purpose among several purposes in 21 per cent of all cases in the German database (24 out of 114), a practice which almost always leads to striking down the measure later on.[46] In Israel, difficulties or questions regarding the policy goal will at times be raised at the worthy purpose stage, but the stage will nevertheless be passed or left undecided until a later stage. Thus, although only 10 per cent of failure cases failed the worthy purpose stage in Israel, in an additional 12 per cent of failure cases negative signalling was used at the worthy purpose stage, and the cases subsequently ended in failure.[47]

### C *Invigorating the Worthy Purpose Test*

Our findings show that in the majority of jurisdictions, the worthy purpose stage explicitly or implicitly plays a more substantial role than

a prior amendment, leaving no additional need for the final amendment. See HCJ 8276/05 *Adalah Legal Centre for Arab Minority Rights v Minister of Defence* [2006], IsrSC 62(1) 1, available in English at <https://supremedecisions.court.gov.il/Home/Download?path=EnglishVerdicts\05\760\082\a13&fileName=05082760_a13.txt&type=4> accessed 16 December 2019. Regarding Poland, see Constitutional Tribunal, Judgment of 24 February 2010, Case No. K 6/09 OTK-A 2010, No. 2, Item 15.

45 See for this phenomenon in Israel: HCJ 246/81 *Agudat Derekh Eretz v Broadcasting Authority* [1981], IsrSC 35(4) 2001, Justice Barak, at para. 12; *Sabach* (n 42) [5] (Justice Melcer).

46 See Chapter 1, Section V.C. In 84 per cent of the cases in Germany (16 of 19) in which a single goal was struck down and upheld on another goal, the policy was ultimately struck down.

47 See, e.g., HCJ 7146/12 *Neget Adam v Knesset* (16 September 2013, unpublished); HCJ 7385/13 *Eitan Israel Migration Policy v Government of Israel* (22 September 2014, unpublished); HCJ 616/11 *Students Association of Israel v Government of Israel* (25 May 2014, unpublished).

generally perceived, and yet it could still be more consistently used in a significant manner. In line with our normative argument as set out at length in Section V of this chapter, that each stage of the analysis should be maximally utilized to contribute significantly to the overall investigation of the justification of the rights-restricting measure, we briefly demonstrate how the worthy purpose test can be invigorated so that its potential is more fully realized.

It is important to distinguish between two different functions of the worthy purpose test, both of which should be strengthened in the analysis. The first and more traditionally emphasized function is that of a gatekeeper. In this capacity, a court determines whether the policy goal can establish a prima facie case for a rights limitation and weeds out illegitimate goals.[48] Identifying and striking down rights-restricting policies that promote unworthy goals is of utmost importance, especially in light of recent trends of democratic backsliding and rising populism, because fundamental rights constitute central constitutional values that should only be limited for sincerely legitimate purposes.

By enacting rights-restricting measures that fail to meet the minimum threshold of pursuing a legitimate public interest, policy-makers violate their constitutional duty as public trustees. These measures should therefore be struck down for lacking a worthy purpose. Of course, detecting an unworthy purpose is a difficult undertaking as policy-makers will likely seek to conceal the unworthy purpose, and instead claim that they were trying to accomplish a different purpose that is recognized as worthy. It is therefore important to be aware that it may be impossible to determine the worthiness of the policy goal solely based on the worthy purpose stage; this determination may require subsequent support from later stages. Instead, particularly suitability and necessity. In an integrative approach to proportionality the court is not pressured to conclude the stage with a binary pass/fail finding. When doubts exist, the court is encouraged to 'air out' the questions and flag problematic aspects even if these cannot serve as sufficient independent basis for failing the measure at the worthy purpose stage.[49] In cases in which sufficiently unequivocal evidence of an unworthy purpose is lacking, courts should err on the side of caution and leave the issue of worthiness undecided, while pointing out their concerns about the purpose of the measure. In other words,

[48] Kumm (n 28) 131; Porat (n 28); Barak (n 12) 245-02.

[49] This judicial practice is common in Germany. See Chapter 1, Sections V.A.3. and VIII.A.1.

evidence pointing to the possibility of unworthy purposes should be presented and analysed at the worthy purpose stage and, when inconclusive, trigger heightened scrutiny in the subsequent suitability and necessity stages to adequately rule out the possibility that unworthy motivations guided the making of the policy at issue.

When faced with antiquated legislation that is no longer considered to serve a worthy purpose due to societal changes, the old, unworthy purpose is sometimes replaced with a new, worthy purpose that is retrospectively brought up by the state during litigation or supplied by the court itself.[50] We believe, however, that courts should not 'save' these laws by reading a worthy purpose into them post hoc for several reasons. First, inventing a new goal for an old law that serves an unworthy purpose risks creating a mismatch between the design of the old law and the newly declared goal, inevitably changing 'the coordinates of proportionality, its contours and contents'.[51] Second, identifying and discarding outdated legislation sends an important normative message to legislators and to society at large about the unworthiness of a certain purpose and the value of constitutional rights. Third, striking down outdating legislation reminds legislators of their responsibility to continuously replace old-fashioned laws serving outdated purposes with new legislation reflecting contemporary values. Finally, substituting the improper, subjective purpose with a proper, objective purpose plainly contradicts values of honesty and transparency.

Alongside the important function of identifying possibly unworthy goals motivating policy and striking down such policies either at the

[50] An example from German constitutional adjudication is the *Sibling Incest* case, BVerfGE 120, 224, in which the Constitutional Court upheld the criminalization of sexual intercourse between natural relatives – whose officially stated purpose was to protect the family order from the damaging effects of incest and to avoid serious genetic diseases in children of incestuous relationships – by supplying the legitimate purpose of protecting the sexual self-determination of the inferior or weaker partner in an incestuous relationship. For more detail, see Chapter 1, Section V.A.2. Similarly, in *S v Jordan*, some justices of the South African Constitutional Court demonstrated willingness to reinterpret an old and obsolete purpose of legislation over time. See *S v Jordan and Others (Sex Workers Education and Advocacy Task Force and Others as Amici Curiae)* 2002 (6) SA 642, 2002 (11) BCLR 1117 (CC), [104]–[14]. For more detail, see Chapter 3, Section V.A.1. By contrast, the Supreme Court of Canada in *Zundel* (n 34) rejected the government's attempt to save the old, unworthy purpose of preventing 'slanderous statements against nobles' by replacing it with the new, worthy purpose of protection against hate speech, arguing that that the new objective was too far from the initial objective that had motivated the legislation. For more detail, see Chapter 2, Section V.A.

[51] See BVerfGE 120, 224 [255]–[273] (dissenting opinion Hassemer).

worthy purpose stage or with the assistance of subsequent stages, we believe that the worthy purpose test fulfils a second, less recognized but critical function of clarifying the concrete goal or goals of the policy and evaluating their relative importance as a crucial basis for the subsequent stages of analysis. The worthy purpose stage serves as a critical point of reference for the subsequent proportionality tests. It is analytically difficult, if not impossible, to analyse whether a measure is suitable, necessary, and proportional if its objective has not been previously well defined. As the stage that opens and grounds the analysis, it should be given adequate attention rather than brushed over, as often happens. The worthy purpose stage should therefore be devoted to clarifying and refining the definition of the goal as well as establishing its practical importance, with special sensitivity to the tendency towards hyperbole that can typify policy-making.[52] Even if these are not requirements for passing this stage or grounds for failing the measure at this point, they set the tone for the analysis conducted at subsequent stages and thus contribute to the final outcome.

In order for its importance to be determined, the policy goal must be concretized, beyond the generalizations commonly found in case-law such as national security or public order. Inquiring after the specific problem the policy is meant to address can help clarify the importance of the specific measure and allow the court to critically evaluate the severity of the problem and the extent to which other measures are already dealing with it, thereby shedding light on the importance of the measure being reviewed. The consistency with which the government deals with this problem relative to similar policy problems can also serve as an indication of the sincerity of the purpose and the possibility of ulterior motives. This type of concrete discussion about policy goals provides a more significant basis for the subsequent analysis at the suitability stage.

If a policy is meant to promote multiple goals, the court should refrain from focusing its analysis on a single, dominant goal. It is important that the court clearly distinguish the different goals, separate worthy from unworthy ones, the important from the less important and the central from the peripheral. Another important distinction is between the overarching goal of a statute and the goal of the specific rights-restricting

[52] Mattias Kumm, 'The Idea of Socratic Contestation and the Right to Justification' (2010) 4 Law and Ethics of Human Rights 142.

measure under review. Such distinctions are often not sufficiently drawn in the policy-making process itself, and drawing them as early in the analysis as possible will increase the nuance with which the subsequent analysis can be conducted, making the discussion at the suitability and necessity stages significantly more refined and meaningful.

### D *Judicial Practice Concerning the Suitability Test*

Figure 7.4 shows the frequency of failure of measures at the suitability stage for each country analysed, as well as the termination rate after a failure at the suitability stage. The significant failure rates at the suitability stage are highly surprising. In all countries except for Germany this stage plays a significant role in justifying the failure of measures: 17 per cent of failure cases in Poland include a failure at the suitability stage, as do 30 per cent in South Africa and 32 per cent in both Israel and Canada. Again India is an outlier, with the rational nexus (suitability) test playing the most dominant role in justifying failures: 61 per cent of all failure cases fail this stage.

However, Figure 7.4 also demonstrates that across jurisdictions courts overwhelmingly tend to continue their analyses after failure at the suitability stage. The numbers are especially telling with regard to Israel and Canada: While roughly one-third of the cases that fail the proportionality test include a failure at the suitability stage, the Israeli and Canadian supreme courts virtually never rely exclusively on the suitability test to strike down a law. Hence, the quantitative analysis shows that failures at the suitability stage are not considered sufficient to justify a judgment of disproportionality, and are hardly ever dispositive of a case on their own.

The quantitative data presented in Figure 7.4 with regard to failure rates on the suitability test contradicts the common conception of this stage in legal scholarship as a threshold stage. It also seems to be inconsistent with the relatively lax requirements of most apex courts in the jurisdictions analysed at this stage. The qualitative analysis of the case-law shows that it is common in Germany, Israel, Poland, and Canada to sum up the suitability stage in one or two sentences by finding that a measure is suitable or rationally connected to the goal, without further analysis. Furthermore, many courts seem not to insist on evidence to support the claim that the policy can effectively promote the goal, instead accepting statements made by policy-makers, even when the issue cannot necessarily be determined merely by common-sense and

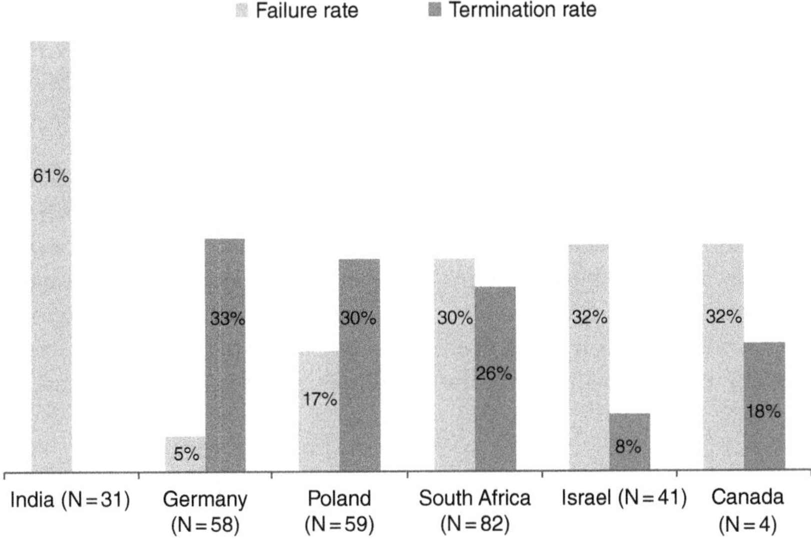


**Figure 7.4** Failure and termination rates at the suitability stage[53]

their reasoning could perhaps be challenged.[54] The South African case-law presents a partial exception in its relatively heightened tendency to require actual evidence of effectiveness, particularly in reviews of policy in place for a significant amount of time, where evidence of effectiveness might be expected to be available. In those instances, the court considers evidence to assess whether the law 'does in fact achieve its purpose' and

[53] The failure rate is the number of cases that failed at the suitability stage as a percentage of all failure cases. The N appearing under the name of each country represents the overall number of failure cases in that country's database.

The termination rate is the number of cases in which the analysis came to an end after failure at the suitability stage as a percentage of all failures at that stage. The number of failures at the suitability stage in each country are: Germany, N = 3; Poland, N = 10; South Africa, N = 25; Israel, N = 13; Canada, N = 27.

Considering that limitation analysis in India does not currently follow the structured proportionality framework, the analysis in India is not expected to adhere to a specific order and terminate after a failure, and therefore India is not included in the termination rate measure.

[54] This approach has been summarized with respect to the Supreme Court of Canada by Justice *Iacobucci* in *RJR-MacDonald Inc. v Canada*: 'Rational connection is to be established, upon a civil standard, through reason, logic or simply common sense.' [1995] 3 SCR 199 [364]. See also *R v Bryan* [2007] SCC 12.

has struck down legislation that has been shown to be ineffective or cannot be proven effective.[55] A number of similar examples can be found in Israeli jurisprudence as well, in which evidence regarding effectiveness was addressed at the suitability stage,[56] although this standard is not uniformly applied in all cases.[57]

Moreover, several of the courts analysed tend to impose the burden of proof at the suitability stage on the plaintiff. In Poland and India there is a presumption of constitutionality at this stage, thus explicitly imposing the burden on the plaintiff to prove the means unsuitable.[58] In Germany the Constitutional Court tends to grant the legislature a broad margin of appreciation when making predictions and assessing legislative facts,[59] thereby effectively imposing the burden of proof on the individual to

[55] See, e.g. *S v Makwanyane & Another* 1995 (3) SA 391 (CC); *De Lange v Smuts NO* 1998 (3) SA 785 (CC), 1998 (7) BCLR 779 (CC); *Sandu – South African National Defence Union* 1999 (4) SA 469 (CC); *Teddy Bear Clinic for Abused Children and Another v Minister of Justice and Constitutional Development & Another* 2014 (2) SA 168 (CC).

[56] See, e.g. HCJ 4542/02 *Kav Laoved v Government of Israel* [2006], IsrSC 61(1) 346; HCJ 6298/07 *Ressler v Knesset* (21 February 2012, unpublished); HCJ 1877/14 *The Movement for Quality Government v Knesset* (12 September 2017, unpublished); *Neget Adam* (n 47).

[57] Examples in Israel in which this is not the case include: HCJ 2605/05 *Academic Center of Law and Business v Minister of Finance* [2009], IsrSC 63(2) 545, available in English at <http://versa.cardozo.yu.edu/opinions/academic-center-law-and-business-v-minister-finance> accessed 16 December 2019; HCJ 2150/07 *Abu Safiyeh v Minister of Defense* [2009], IsrSC 63(3) 331; HCJ 3969/06 *Dir Samet Village Council v Commander of IDF in the West Bank* (22 October 2009, unpublished). In addition, the Supreme Court displays reluctance to require evidence on the effectiveness of house demolitions for deterrence of terrorism, CJ 2006/97 *Ghanimat v IDF Central Command* [1997], IsrSC 51(2) 651. See also HCJ 7040/15 *Hamad v Commander of IDF in the West Bank* (12 November 2015, unpublished) [1] (Justice Solberg). But see a recent statement that evidence will be required in the future: HCJ 8091/14 *Centre for the Defence of the Individual v Minister of Defence* (31 December 2014, unpublished).

[58] A classic example of the impact of the presumption of constitutionality in India is a case concerning the constitutionality of the death penalty. In *Bachan Singh v State of Punjab* (1980) 2 SCC 684, the majority held that given the presumption of constitutionality, those challenging the death penalty bore the burden of showing that it serves no valid penal purpose and is therefore unreasonable. Since empirical evidence as well as theoretical opinion is divided on the question of whether the death penalty serves the function of deterrence, the court held that the burden had not been discharged by the petitioners and therefore the death penalty was constitutional.

[59] For example, in the context of the freedom of occupation, the court held that 'the FCC is not entitled to challenge the value judgements of the legislator so long as it is not evident that those are based upon incorrect factual premises or that they contradict the constitution'. BVerfGE 13, 97 [113].

show that the factual premises of the legislature are not evidently or clearly false. Furthermore, in Poland and Germany, by definition, the perspective of this test is *ex ante* – testing whether at the time of the creation of the policy a reasonable legislature could have found a rational connection; in other words, the actual effects of the law in practice are beyond the scope of the test.[60]

Our findings therefore seem to reveal a paradox: on the one hand, most of the courts examined set low thresholds for the suitability test and constitutional scholarship in those countries contends that this test does not pose a substantial hurdle to rights-infringing policies. On the other hand, the empirical analysis shows – except in Germany – substantial failure rates at the suitability stage. How can the discrepancy between low standards and high failure rates be reconciled, and what does this practice say about the role of the suitability test in the proportionality framework?

Our substantive comparative analysis of the case-law reveals that there are generally three types of situations in which measures fail the suitability test. First, there are indeed cases in which the reviewed policy fails the test of rationality at the most basic level – using a common-sense approach the court concludes that the means do not promote the goal, and are perhaps even counterproductive.[61] Second, several of the failures at the suitability stage can be categorized as 'spillovers' from the worthy purpose stage, reflecting the unwillingness of the court to tackle an unworthy purpose head on. Instead, the court may claim lack of

[60] The German Federal Constitutional Court maintains that for a policy to pass the suitability test, 'a means is suitable if it is capable of attaining the desired purpose'. BVerfGE 30, 250 [263]; BVerfGE 39, 210 [230]; BVerfGE 30, 250 [263]; BVerfGE 118, 1 [24]; BVerfGE 67, 157 [175]; BVerfGE 25, 1 [13]; BVerfGE 30, 250 [263]. See also BVerfGE 50, 290 [331]–[32]; BVerfGE 113, 167 [234]; BVerfGE 123, 186 [242]. Similarly, the Polish Constitutional Tribunal asks 'whether it could have been reasonably presumed that the means could realize the legislative purpose at that point'. See Chapter 5, Section VII.B. The formulation that the measure only needs to be 'capable of' achieving the goal indicates that there is no requirement that the measure adopted actually promotes the purpose.

[61] In Israel see: HCJ 2355/98 *Stamka v Minister of Interior* [1999], IsrSC 53(2) 728; AAA 4614/05 *State of Israel v Oren* [2006], 61(1) 211. In Poland, see Judgment of 7 October 2015, Case No. K 12/14 OTK-A 2015, No. 9, Item 143; Judgment of 22 October 2013, Case No. SK 14/13 OTK-A 2013, No. 7, Item 100; Judgment of 10 July 2012, Case No. P 15/12 OTK-A 2012, No. 7, Item 77. In South Africa, see *Lawyers for Human Rights v Minister of Home Affairs and Others*, 2017 (5) SA 480 (CC).

suitability as a way of indirectly exposing the insincerity of the goal presented or proving its illegitimacy.[62] Finally, in practice the suitability stage has often been interpreted to include the idea of extreme overbreadth. Overbroad policies could be conceptualized as failing the necessity test since they could attain their goal in a less restrictive manner. Incorporating the idea of overbreadth in the suitability stage stresses that part of the policy is not rationally connected to the policy goal and therefore the policy fails to meet the basic standard of rationality.[63]

These qualitative insights into the nature of failures on the suitability test help clarify the function of this stage in practice. They establish the suitability stage as an intermediate stage between worthy purpose and necessity that catches cases that 'fell through' the worthy purpose test, as well as cases that are so grossly overbroad that they fail even before reaching the more refined less-restrictive-means (necessity) test. The low

[62] In Israel, see, e.g., HCJ 1030/99 *MK Haim Oron v Knesset Chairman* [2002], IsrSC 56(3) 640; HCJ 4264/02 *Ibillin Breeders Partnership v Ibillin Local Council* (12 December 2006, unpublished); *Students Association of Israel* (n 47). In Germany, see BVerfGE 17, 306. In Poland see Judgment of 9 April 2015, Case No. K 14/13 OTK-A 2015, No. 4, Item 45; Judgment of 18 November 2014, Case No. SK 7/11 OTK-A 2014, No. 10, Item 112. In South Africa, see *Larbi-Odam and Others v MEC for Education (North-West Province) and Others,* 1998 (1) SA 745 (CC); *Minister of Home Affairs & Another v Fourie & Another,* 2006 (1) SA 524 (CC). In India, see: *Harsora v Harsora* (2016) 10 SCC 165.

More broadly, on rationality as a technique for smoking out illegitimate motives, see Elana Kagan, 'Private Speech, Public Purpose: The Role of Governmental Motive in First Amendment Doctrine' (1996) 63 University of Chicago Law Review 413, 453–54; Wojciech Sadurski, 'Searching for Illicit Motives: Constitutional Theory of Freedom of Speech, Equal Protection, and Separation of State and Religion' (2014) Sydney Law School Research Paper 14/61; David Kenny, 'Proportionality and the Inevitability of the Local: A Comparative Localist Analysis of Canada and Ireland' (2018) 66 American Journal of Comparative Law 537, 547.

[63] An overbroad or over-inclusive policy goes beyond what is required to achieve its purpose. It is a suitability issue if the analysis is focused on the overbroad portion of the policy. However, overbreadth can also be conceptualized as a necessity issue if the analysis concentrates on a policy in its entirety that partially furthers the goal but is not sufficiently narrowly tailored. Examples of cases in which a measure failed the suitability stage due to overbreadth: in South Africa, see, e.g. *Ex Parte Minister of Safety and Security and Others: In Re S v Walters and Another,* 2002 (4) SA 613 (CC); *Twee Jonge Gezellen (Pty) Ltd & Another v Land and Agricultural Development Bank of South Africa t/a The Land Bank & Another,* 2011 (3) SA 1 (CC); in Poland, see Judgment of 20 January 2015, Case No. K 39/12 OTK-A 2015, No. 1, Item 2; in Germany, see BVerfGE 17, 306; BVerfGE 55, 159; BVerfGE 100, 59; BVerfGE 79, 256; in India, see *Shree Bhagwati Steel Rolling Mills v Commission of Central Excise* (2016) 3 SCC 643; *Ashoka Kumar Thakur v Union of India* (2008) 6 SCC 1.

termination rates at the suitability stage as shown in Figure 7.4 reinforce the observations made regarding the nature of failures at the suitability stage. For one, they support the existence of some blurring between the suitability and necessity stages, as overbreadth applies to both. This will often lead to a continuation of the analysis past the suitability stage, to make the point of overbreadth at the necessity stage as well, thus concluding that the overbreadth not only undermines the connection of the means to the end but also does not constitute a less restrictive means. Of course, this finding also implies that at the suitability stage, courts, in practice, rarely meaningfully address the question of whether the rights-restricting means can indeed significantly promote the goal.

### E *Invigorating the Suitability Test*

Aharon Barak once suggested that the suitability stage may be superfluous,[64] and our comparative analysis of judicial practice has indeed shown that many laws that failed the suitability test could also have been challenged with the worthy purpose or necessity test. However, rather than marginalizing the suitability test due to its interrelatedness to the worthy purpose and necessity tests, we suggest strengthening its unique contribution.

In our view, in almost none of the jurisdictions examined does judicial practice take the suitability test sufficiently seriously, despite significant failure rates. In line with our general approach, we believe that the suitability test should be invigorated as a significant component in PA. Before we elaborate on how we propose this be done, it is important to clarify that our argument in favour of paying serious attention to all stages of PA, including the suitability stage, is aimed primarily at cases that have been determined to involve significant limitations of important rights.[65] The opening stage of the judicial analysis – establishing a limitation of a right – sets the tone for the rest of the analysis. The trigger for demanding that the state justify its chosen policy is a limitation on a constitutionally protected right. However, due to the 'rights inflation' that has been intricately linked with the development of the

[64] Barak (n 12) 315–16.

[65] See Barak (n 12) 539–40. For a critical discussion of the nature of the evidentiary requirements placed on the state as part of proportionality analysis, see Sujit Choudhry, 'So What Is the Real Legacy of Oakes? Two Decades of Proportionality Analysis under the Canadian Charter's Section 1' (2006) 34 Supreme Court Law 501.

proportionality framework as a trademark of contemporary rights adjudication,[66] even trivial limitations of a peripheral interest can trigger PA. Application of proportionality must be sensitive to this fact, and cannot require a uniform level of state justification or lead to the same degree of judicial engagement in all cases of rights limitation. Courts should invest effort at the opening stage of the analysis in characterizing the precise nature and scope of the rights limitation and determining the relative importance of the right involved and the severity of the limitation. These preliminary findings should then determine the level of scrutiny with which the court should apply the subsequent analysis.

Under this premise, the suitability stage should not merely be conceptualized as a threshold stage establishing the existence of a commonsense relationship between the means and the end. In keeping with our position regarding the worthy purpose stage, according to which the policy goal should be concretized and defined precisely for the sake of the subsequent analysis, the suitability stage should inquire into the extent to which the measure is capable of promoting the specific concrete goal or goals, and the factors upon which this is dependent. Even if the findings that emerge from these inquiries are not themselves a basis for independent failure at the suitability stage, they contribute significantly to the subsequent analysis, including the evaluation of alternative measures and the weighing of the actual benefit of the policy relative to the harm. Importantly, we believe that the burden of proof should be placed on the government to establish its expectations of effectiveness.

Courts should consider the effects of a law over time and not limit themselves to an *ex ante* perspective that is based only on the information available to the legislator when the law was enacted, especially when a statute has been in force for several years. The court should use the available knowledge about the suitability of the measure at the time of its review, at the very least since this can shed light on the basis for a rational connection in the first place. Such a practice would also constitute valuable guidance for policy-makers, who should continuously assess the proportionality of rights-restricting policies.[67]

[66] Kai Möller, 'Proportionality and Rights Inflation' in Grant Huscroft, Bradley Miller and Grégoire Webber (eds), Proportionality and the Rule of Law (Cambridge University Press 2014) 155; Mattias Kumm, 'Is the Structure of Human Rights Defensible? Three Puzzles and Their Resolution' in Vicki C Jackson and Mark Tushnet (eds), *Proportionality: New Frontiers, New Challenges* (CUP 2017) 30.

[67] Barak (n 12) 312–16.

Moreover, courts should not limit themselves to assessing the effectiveness of a rights-infringing measure but should also take into account its counter-productiveness. In other words, they should not only look at the ability of the means to achieve the goal but should also examine whether it might at the same time have effects that hinder the achievement of the goal.[68]

To clarify, we are not saying that every suitability analysis needs to be detailed or that common-sense has no place in assessing whether a policy is suited to achieving its objective; we are not trying to overburden courts with high evidentiary standards for proving generally accepted facts or causalities. However, we regard the suitability test as an important element of the proportionality framework that bolsters its factual basis and enhances its reasoning. As a general rule, therefore, a more demanding standard is warranted, as has sporadically surfaced in the case-law of the Supreme courts of Israel and India, requiring that the rational connection or nexus be not 'slim and strictly theoretical'[69] but 'real and significant',[70] or 'direct and proximate, not remote or illusory'.[71]

[68] Courts sporadically consider the counter-effectiveness of a measure at the suitability stage but they should do so more regularly and more systematically. For example, in Israel, the Supreme Court has pointed out in its *Centre for the Defence of the Individual* (n 57) decision that destroying the houses of innocent family members of terrorists may not only have a deterring effect on committing terrorist acts but may also increase the motivation to carry out acts of terror, to abet them and to identify with them and thereby to frustrate the very purpose for which they were employed. The Indian Supreme Court struck down a law prohibiting professional dancing in bars with the rational nexus test in *State of Maharashtra v Indian Hotels and Restaurants Association* (2013) 8 SCC 519 (The *Bar Dancers* Case). Although the purpose of the law was to protect women from exploitative conditions, it had actually resulted in the unemployment of around 75,000 women, many of whom had had to take up sex work in order to sustain themselves. The German Federal Constitutional Court found that a statutory provision that legally entitled children to contact with their parents and, correspondingly, obligated the parents to engage in such contact against their will was 'not suitable for achieving the sought purpose' to protect children's welfare, for '[i]f coercive measures are necessary to force an unwilling parent to have contact with a child, this contact is not usually in the best interests of the child'. BVerfGE 121, 69 [98].

[69] *Neget Adam* (n 47) [101] (Justice Arbel), and [21] (Justice Vogelman).

[70] HCJ 6427/02 *The Movement for Quality Government v Knesset* [2006], IsrSC 61(1) 610 [75] (Justice Naor); *Ressler* (n 56) [65]–[66] (Justice Beinisch).

[71] Chapter 6, Section VII.B. Specifically, the Indian Supreme Court held in *Superintendent, Central Prison v Ram Manohar Lohia* AIR 1960 SC 633 that a reasonable restriction in the interests of public order 'should be one which has a proximate connection or nexus with public order, but not one far-fetched, hypothetical or problematical or too remote in the chain of its relation with the public order'. See also *Canada (Attorney General) v PHS*

South African practice may provide some useful guidance on how the suitability test can be turned into a test with meaningful requirements. The South African court generally imposes the burden of proof on the government to show that a measure can actually achieve its purpose and regularly requires at least some evidence to establish a causal linkage.[72] In addition, the South African Constitutional Court enquires into how probable it is that the measure will actually achieve its purpose and requires a certain level of effectiveness to be demonstrated.[73] Perhaps because the South African court consciously applies proportionality in an integrative manner and internalizes the fact that the suitability test will not be the sole basis for failure, it allows itself to conduct a more thorough analysis that can support other stages, as well as being supported by them.

### *F The Threshold Stages as the Gravitational Centre of Limitation Analysis: Judicial Practice in India*

In evaluating the role played by the worthy purpose and suitability stages within the proportionality framework, the contrast to India is illuminating. India, as explained earlier, has not comprehensively adopted the proportionality framework, although it has stated that its analyses mirror PA.[74] The quantitative data demonstrate that justifications of failures in India are dominated by the worthy purpose and rational nexus (suitability) elements, with failure rates of 65 and 61 per cent, respectively, while

*Community Services Society* [2011] 3 SCR 134 , which sets out that the court must 'closely examine' the relationship between a law's ends and its means.

72 Chapter 3, Section VI.C. Justice Levy of the Supreme Court of Israel used a similar approach in his minority opinion in HCJ 366/03 *Commitment to Peace and Social Justice Society v Minister of Finance* [2005], IsrSC 60(3) 464, available in English at <https://supremedecisions.court.gov.il/Home/Download?path=EnglishVerdicts\03\660\003\a39&fileName=03003660_a39.txt&type=4> accessed 16 December 2019, concluding that the state had failed to establish the rational connection that a significant cut in social benefit rates would minimize the number of benefit recipients who were unjustifiably supported because it had neither presented data regarding the estimated scope of the phenomenon of 'wilfully unemployed', nor regarding the projected decrease in the phenomenon following the cut in benefits.

73 Chapter 3, Section VI.C.

74 See, e.g., *Om Kumar v Union of India* (2001) 2 SCC 386; *Teri Oat Estates (P) Ltd v UT, Chandigarh* (2004) 2 SCC 130; *Indian Airlines Ltd v Prabha D. Kanan* (2006) 11 SCC 67; *Sahara India Real Estate Corporation Ltd v SEBI* (2012) 10 SCC 603; *MP Housing and Infrastructure Development Board v B S S Parihar* (2015) 14 SCC 130; *Modern Dental College and Research Centre v State of Madhya Pradesh* (2016) 7 SCC 353.

narrow tailoring and balancing (strict proportionality) considerations serve strictly as additional justifications in a smaller portion of cases, and never as independent bases for failure. These findings are not surprising considering that the official standard applied for decades by the Indian Supreme Court, based on the UK-based tradition of *Wednesbury*, is reasonableness, with scrutiny of purpose and rationality of the means constituting its core features.[75]

From a comparative perspective, the judicial practice of the Supreme Court of India with respect to the worthy purpose and rational nexus tests is at times more demanding than that of the other apex courts examined. For example, the Indian court strikes down laws with the worthy purpose test even though they do not pursue an illegitimate or unworthy goal per se, because they do not match any of the expressly enumerated grounds for limiting a right (as is done in Poland). Article 19 of the Indian Constitution includes six fundamental freedoms: the rights to free speech and expression, peaceful assembly, association, movement, residence, and professional occupation. Each of these rights has its own specific limitation provision, according to which the state can impose 'reasonable restrictions' on the right in order to achieve specifically listed goals that differ from right to right.[76] When analysing a rights limitation under Article 19, the court begins by investigating whether the state action furthers a goal specified in the limitation clause associated with that right. In several cases the court has held that the purpose of a rights limitation, while not necessarily an illegitimate or unworthy goal per se, did not match any of the expressly stated grounds for limiting the particular right.[77] At the rational nexus stage, in some cases the court has

[75] In this context it is also important to consider the centrality of the right to equality in limitation analysis in India. The Supreme Court of India has read the guarantee of equality very broadly as protecting against any arbitrary state action, whether procedural or substantive. It has, in other words, transformed the constitutional equality guarantee into a comprehensive protection against arbitrariness that seems hermeneutically amenable to a reasonableness standard of review.

[76] Constitution of India, art. 19(2)–19(6).

[77] See, e.g. *Ramesh Thapar v State of Madras* AIR 1950 SC 124. An attempt was made to justify a law regulating the circulation, sale, and distribution of documents on the grounds of securing 'public safety' or maintaining 'public order'. Since neither was expressly stated grounds for limiting freedom of speech, the court found the impugned measure invalid. Another example is *State of Karnataka v Associated Management of (Government Recognised-Unaided-English Medium) Primary and Secondary Schools* (2014) 9 SCC 485, involving the state mandating primary and early secondary schooling only in a child's mother tongue, for the sake of protecting local languages and cultures, 'in the larger interest of the nation'. The court held that the measure, however necessary or

expressed a higher standard, requiring that the rational connection between means and ends be 'direct and proximate, not remote or illusory'.[78] It also seems to include questions of narrow tailoring in the suitability test.

The limitation analysis of the Indian Supreme Court hence illustrates that the so-called threshold tests have the capacity to do much of the work of PA if applied rigorously. If we expect all proportionality stages to contribute meaningfully and seriously to the analysis rather than being relegated to the status of mere threshold stages, the apex courts in Germany or Canada – which tend to neglect these stages to rush to the supposedly 'real' tests – can learn some lessons from the Indian Supreme Court's use of the worthy purpose and rational nexus stages.

For the future, it is of the utmost interest to follow the development of case-law in India and assess the ramifications of the adoption of a more formalized structure of PA. Will this shift decisions that might previously have been framed in terms of failure at the worthy purpose and rational nexus stages towards necessity- and balancing-based reasoning? Or will the adoption of the proportionality standard broaden the scope of review to strike down measures that would previously have been upheld? In our view, it appears unlikely that increased use of the structured PA will lead to a marginalization of the first two stages, considering how firmly they are anchored in Indian limitation analysis. It is therefore in the realm of possibility that, in the future, the Supreme Court of India will turn into one of the few apex courts that assigns a substantial role to all subtests of proportionality.

## IV Necessity and Strict Proportionality

### A *The Relationship between the Two Elements in Theory*

The necessity test proclaims that a measure should not limit a right more than is necessary to achieve its purpose, so if there is an alternative method of attaining the policy goal that is less restrictive of rights, it should be preferred. The necessity test includes two distinct comparisons of the chosen and alternative means: a comparison of the effectiveness of the measures for achieving the purpose and a comparison of the degree

important, did not relate to any of the specified grounds for limiting freedom of speech, and was therefore invalid. Also see *Shreya Singhal v Union of India* (2015) 5 SCC 1.

[78] Chapter 6, Section VII.B.

of infringement of a fundamental right by the measures. The strict proportionality (balancing) test, simply put, states that the potential benefit of the policy for promoting the public interest must outweigh the harm caused by the limitation of the right.

A central theme in the literature on the proportionality doctrine is the relationship between the necessity test and strict proportionality. Most disagreements over the proper application of the doctrine concern the relationship between these two components. This is also one of the main points where the literature acknowledges variation between jurisdictions in terms of which of the two is the dominant element, carrying the main burden in justifying the outcome. It has been pointed out that in the UK as well as in the case-law of the European Court of Justice and the European Court of Human Rights, proportionality is typically applied without a distinct balancing stage, instead culminating with the necessity test. Similarly, in Canada the less-restrictive-means (necessity) test is the dominant component, leaving the final stage almost meaningless. In contrast, in German jurisprudence most of the significant judicial deliberation is conducted at the balancing stage.[79]

Conceptually, there are two possible constructions of the necessity test that dramatically affect the centrality of this test and, as a result, the division of labour between it and the final stage of strict proportionality: under one interpretation the necessity test could, given the importance of fundamental rights, generally require adoption of a less restrictive alternative if one of similar (albeit not identical) effectiveness exists, even if it is somewhat more costly in terms of resources. This interpretation turns the necessity test into a significant hurdle for rights-restricting policy. Under the other interpretation the necessity test could only require adopting a less restrictive alternative if it achieves the purpose with identical effectiveness and using the same resources; this has the effect of deferring decisions concerning measures with slightly different degrees of effectiveness – i.e., the majority of cases – to the strict proportionality stage.[80]

Different positions can be found in the literature regarding the desirability of each of the approaches. Those who support the centrality of the necessity test generally favour avoiding the strict proportionality stage

[79] Rivers (n 21) 174, 177–79; Grimm (n 12) 383; Stone Sweet and Matthews (n 12).

[80] David Bilchitz, 'Necessity and Proportionality: Towards a Balanced Approach' in Liora Lazarus, Christopher McCrudden and Niels Bowels (eds), *Reasoning Rights: Comparative Judicial Engagement* (Hart Publishing 2014).

when possible, due to its open-ended and openly value-laden nature, instead preferring the more constrained boundaries of the necessity inquiry.[81] On the other hand, those who support minimizing the necessity stage in favour of the strict proportionality stage tend to base themselves on a demand for judicial honesty and transparency: comparing alternatives that are not identical in terms of effectiveness requires a trade-off of rights-restrictiveness versus effectiveness. This is essentially balancing, which should be left for the final stage for the sake of analytical clarity (maintaining the separate function of each stage) and honesty (so that it is clear that the court is balancing).[82]

What is common to both sides in the debate is that they conceptualize the doctrine as relying upon a single dominant component, leading to a dichotomous choice: either the necessity test 'swallows' the strict proportionality test and leaves it with little added value, or the necessity test is effectively emptied, collapsed into the strict proportionality test.[83]

### B *Judicial Practice*

Our findings regarding Canada and Germany support the existence of two distinct models discussed in the literature. However, they also identify a third, previously unrecognized model that includes significant use of both the necessity test and the strict proportionality test. Figure 7.5 shows the failure rates at the necessity and strict proportionality stages for each of the six countries analysed.

#### 1 The German vs. the Canadian Model

The German data demonstrate that, as expected, the majority (84 per cent) of failure decisions include failure at the strict proportionality stage, and in 65.5 per cent of failure cases this is the sole basis for failure. The necessity stage does not play a significant role in these decisions, with only 14 per cent of the failure cases including a failure at that stage. In contrast, in Canada minimal impairment is the central test of PA. Overall, the vast majority (92 per cent) of failure decisions include a

[81] von Bernstorff (n 21); Bernhard Schlink, 'Proportionality' in Michel Rosenfeld and Andras Sajo (eds), *The Oxford Handbook of Comparative Constitutional Law* (OUP 2012) 718.

[82] Guy Davidov, 'Separating Minimal Impairment from Balancing: A Comment on R. v Sharpe' (2000) 5 Review of Constitutional Studies 195; Grimm (n 12) 383, 395–97; Barak (n 12) 323–27.

[83] See Bilchitz (n 80) 41.

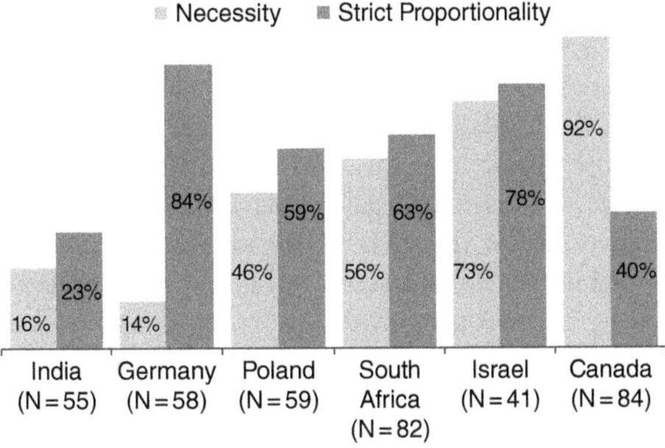


**Figure 7.5** Failure rates at the necessity and strict proportionality stages

failure at the less-restrictive-means test, whereas the strict proportionality stage plays a significantly lesser role, with only 40 per cent of failure cases including a failure at this stage. It seems fair to say that the Supreme Court of Canada has effectively relegated the strict proportionality test to a residual stage that is not determinative of the outcome of the PA.

In the German and Canadian cases, the dominance of one of the elements – necessity or strict proportionality – comes at the expense of the other. Thus, in Canada the centrality of the less-restrictive-means test causes the discussion at the stage of strict proportionality to be either non-existent (this stage is not discussed in 60 per cent of the failure cases) or extremely brief and redundant, serving primarily as a conclusion of the Court's argument. On the other hand, in the German case-law the necessity stage is skipped entirely in 20 per cent of all cases and merely brushed over in 25 per cent, suggesting that the Court does not deem this stage to contribute meaningfully to solving these cases. Even when it is analysed to a significant degree, it is narrowly interpreted, thus essentially deflecting the discussion to the final stage of strict proportionality. Interestingly, in the relatively rare cases in which a measure fails the necessity test in German case-law, the Constitutional Court seems to consider an alternative equally effective even though it is actually slightly less effective than the adopted measure, clandestinely deviating from the official standard of necessity.[84]

[84] Examples are the decisions in *Chocolate Candy Bunny*, BVerfGE 53, 135, and in testamentary dispositions, BVerfGE 99, 341. In the former case, the court used the necessity

These different priorities of the German and Canadian courts are manifested doctrinally in several ways. While the German Federal Constitutional Court is determined to keep value-laden elements out of the necessity stage, the Canadian approach is characterized by the inclusion of precisely those elements in the minimal impairment test. In fact, the prevailing belief in Canadian legal scholarship is that 'it is artificial in practice to divorce the question of overall proportionality from the potential availability of less-intrusive means'.[85] The limited role of the necessity test in German proportionality practice is caused by a narrow conception of this test. In particular, the court strictly conceptualizes necessity as a less-restrictive-means test and insists, at least formally, on the (illusory) identical effectiveness of the alternative means, defining a measure as necessary for the achievement of its purpose if 'the legislator could not have chosen a different means which would have been equally effective but which would have infringed on fundamental rights to a lesser extent or not at all'.[86] When comparing the effectiveness of the chosen and alternative measures, the German court amplifies the legislative margin of discretion in determining equal effectiveness,[87] and 'is reluctant to assume that an alternative is as effective as the means chosen

test to strike down an excessive consumer protection regulation that prohibited the marketing of Easter bunnies primarily made of puffed rice but covered with chocolate icing creations, stating that the regulatory purpose could still be achieved with a much less intrusive policy than a total ban. Strictly understood, however, a labelling requirement is never as effective as a total marketing prohibition because some consumers will only give the label a cursory look and not read it carefully. In the latter case, testamentary dispositions had to be accomplished either by the testator declaring his last will to the notary or by the testator handing the notary a self-written last will. Mute and illiterate persons were incapable of doing either. These strict requirements had the purpose of ensuring legal certainty with regard to last wills, in particular in order to reliably ascertain the content of a deceased person's will, and to protect persons who lack the ability to decide for themselves. The court concluded that less intrusive but equally effective means for reliably ascertaining one's last will were available, such as a procedure that would include a special confidant and a second notary. As these examples show, the FCC interprets the necessity test as requiring policy-makers to choose slightly less effective alternatives that do not ensure in all cases that the regulatory purpose will be achieved, as some hasty consumers will inadvertently purchase puffed rice instead of chocolate and some mute and illiterate persons will leave wills even though they lack the ability to decide for themselves. Put differently, the court implicitly balances the public benefits of a total ban with the costs incurred by the fundamental rights infringement.

[85] Tim Hickman, 'Proportionality: Comparative Law Lessons' (2007) 12 Judicial Review 31.

[86] BVerfGE 90, 145 [172]; BVerfGE 30, 292 [316]; BVerfGE 113, 167 [252]; BVerfGE 117, 163 [189]; BVerfGE 120, 224 [240]; BVerfGE 126, 112 [144]–[45].

[87] Grimm (n 12) 383, 390.

by the policy-maker'.[88] Moreover, the court strictly excludes measures from the necessity test that require additional financial resources, noting that a measure is only less restrictive if it is 'as cost-effective for the public purse'. Of course, the exclusion of measures that require additional financial resources significantly limits the scope of the necessity test.

In contrast to Germany, the lack of equal effectiveness of an alternative measure is not 'likely to decide the outcome of cases' in Canada. In *Alberta v. Hutterian Brethren of Wilson Colony*, Chief Justice McLachlin held that 'the court need not be satisfied that the alternative would satisfy the objective to *exactly* the same extent or degree as the impugned measure'.[89] The relevant question is 'whether there is an alternative, less drastic means of achieving the objective in a real and substantial manner'.[90] Moreover, the Canadian Supreme Court at times includes more expensive alternative means in the necessity test and 'generally seems to have little concern with finding that the government could have adopted a more expensive and less impairing alternative'.[91]

### 2 An Integrated Model of Proportionality

An unexpected finding is the existence of an integrative model that does not correspond to the two traditionally recognized models. In this third model, both the necessity stage and the stage of strict proportionality play significant roles in supporting failure decisions.

In the countries that follow this model, the failure rate at the necessity stage is significant, ranging from 46 per cent in Poland to 56 per cent in South Africa and 73 per cent in Israel. However, this significance does not translate, as it does in Canada, into a marginalization of the stage of strict proportionality. On the contrary, the necessity stage, with all its significance, often still plays a supporting role vis-à-vis the strict proportionality test.[92] This strict proportionality stage constitutes the last word in all pass decisions and the final stage in the majority of failure decisions, showing the highest failure rates among all subtests: 59 per cent in Poland, 63 per cent in South Africa, and 78 per cent in Israel. Last but not

[88] Chapter 1, Section VII.B.1.
[89] [2009] 2 SCC 567.
[90] ibid.
[91] Chapter 2, Section VII.C.
[92] The final test is referred to as the 'lodestar of the court's limitations jurisprudence' in South Africa (see Chapter 3, Section VIII.A); a stage that plays a 'prominent role' in Israel (see Chapter 4, Section VIII.A) and a stage which the court rarely strikes down a measure without considering in Poland (see Chapter 5, Section III.D).

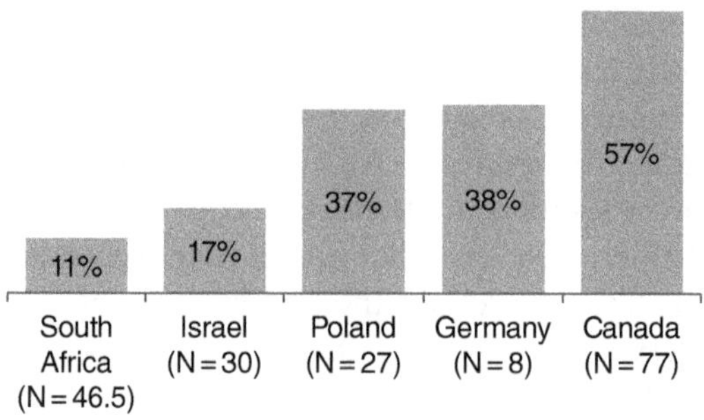


**Figure 7.6** Termination of the analysis after failure at the necessity stage[93]

least, significant work in terms of reasoning seems to be done at the last stage, indicating that this stage arguably bears most of the justificatory burden for deeming a law disproportionate in a sizeable portion of decisions.

The termination rates further clarify the relationship between the two elements of the analysis. Figure 7.6 measures whether the constitutional and supreme courts in the countries analysed terminate their proportionality analyses after a failure at the necessity stage. It indicates the relative strength of the necessity test by showing to what extent courts are willing to exclusively base their overall judgement of disproportionality on a failure on the necessity test without continuing their analysis to the strict proportionality stage. The data in Figure 7.6 show that the Israeli Supreme Court, the South African Constitutional Court, and the Polish Constitutional Tribunal tend not to terminate their proportionality analyses after failing a measure on the necessity test (South Africa: 11 per cent; Israel: 17 per cent; Poland: 37 per cent). Instead, they typically continue on to the strict proportionality test. In contrast, in the Canadian Supreme Court the necessity test is generally dispositive of the overall proportionality judgement and the PA ends after a failure on the necessity test in half of the cases.

At first glance, the data in Figures 7.5 and 7.6 might seem paradoxical: On the one hand, the necessity test is an important component of the proportionality practice of the courts in Israel, Poland, and South Africa.

93 Considering that limitation analysis in India does not currently follow the structured proportionality framework, the analysis in India is not expected to adhere to a specific order and terminate after a failure, and therefore India is not included in the termination rate measure.

Findings of disproportionality are based, at least in part, on the necessity test in approximately every other case (Poland: 46 per cent; South Africa: 56 per cent), or in almost three out of four cases (Israel: 73 per cent). On the other hand, a failure at the necessity stage is rarely dispositive of an overall judgement of disproportionality (South Africa: 11 per cent; Israel: 17 per cent; Poland 37 per cent). In other words, the conclusion that a measure is disproportionate will typically be based jointly on the necessity test *and* the strict proportionality test (and to some extent on the suitability test as well).

This finding is important considering that in the literature, significant failure at the necessity stage has been viewed as an attempt by the court to avoid explicit value-based balancing for legitimacy reasons.[94] We find that in Israel, South Africa, and Poland significant use is made of the necessity stage, and this cannot be explained as attempting to avoid balancing, since these courts choose to address balancing voluntarily, even though doctrinally speaking they are not required to. On the contrary, the apex courts in those countries seem to continue their PA until the final stage notwithstanding failures at the necessity stage or at another earlier stage, because it enables them to consider broader normative and societal implications and to weigh numerous factors that are relevant to the particular case at hand. At the same time, the fact that these courts typically rely on both the necessity and the strict proportionality tests to strike down a measure shows that they do not base their judgements of disproportionality exclusively on value balancing.

The qualitative analysis of the dynamic between stages in these countries demonstrates that this finding may not have the same meaning in Israel and South Africa as it does in Poland. In South Africa and Israel the dual use of necessity and strict proportionality in justifying failures is generally based on meaningful engagement with both stages, thus creating a foundation of two separate rationales for these failures. The necessity stage demonstrates either that the chosen policy is excessive and can be narrow-tailored; that a review of other areas of law or comparative law indicates that less-restrictive but similarly effective alternatives exist; or that the existing policy can be left in place, with no need for amendment. Nonetheless, the additional attention to the balancing stage allows the court to go beyond a relatively factual

[94] Grimm (n 12) 383.

evaluation of policy design and policy alternatives, sharing the value-based underpinnings of its decision.[95]

In contrast, in Poland failure at both the necessity and strict proportionality stages seems to reflect a different dynamic: a substantial degree of blurring between these two tests. In a significant number of cases, the court seems to interpret the two stages quite similarly. The overall emphasis in Polish PA is often on the prohibition of excessiveness. Following this general idea, the most common type of reasoning pattern includes the court briefly stating at the necessity stage that the law under review goes beyond what is necessary to secure the policy goal, and then going on to justify this conclusion using language of the strict proportionality stage, namely, that the burden imposed on the individual is excessive relative to the benefit of the law. Such cases tend to deal primarily with the absence of procedural guarantees or safeguards against administrative abuse. The result seems to be that the court does not engage in significant analysis of alternatives at the necessity stage, and limits its focus to excessiveness at the strict proportionality stage as well.[96]

These differences between what can roughly be considered the Israeli and South African approaches on the one hand and the Polish approach on the other are based on variations in the doctrinal construction of the necessity test. The practices of the three courts grouped within the integrative model are not identical and can actually be placed along a continuum between two poles: the narrow 'less restrictive but equally effective means' conception of necessity of the German court and the broad 'minimal impairment' conception of the Canadian court. While the South African Constitutional Court and the Israeli Supreme Court have incorporated doctrinal elements into their necessity analysis that resemble the Canadian approach, the case-law of the Polish Constitutional Tribunal is more closely aligned with the German approach. For

[95] In Israel see, e.g., HCJ 2887/04 *Abu Madigam v Israel Land Administration* [2007] available in English at <https://supremedecisions.court.gov.il/Home/Download?path=EnglishVerdicts\04\870\028\h05&fileName=04028870_h05.txt&type=4> accessed 16 December 2019, IsrSC 62(2) 57; HCJ 2577/04 *El Khawaja v Prime Minister* (19 July 2007, unpublished); HCJ 4124/00 *Yekutieli v Minister of Religious Affairs* [2010], IsrSC 64 (1) 142; *Adalah Legal Centre for Arab Minority Rights* (n 44); *Neget Adam* (n 47).

[96] Chapter 5, Section IX.A. Blurring and repetitiveness between the necessity and strict proportionality stages can also be found in some cases in Israel. See Chapter 4, note 230.

example, the Israeli and South African courts do at times, like the Canadian court, expect the legislature to choose less effective means in order to attenuate the rights infringement[97] and require that 'additional resources should be invested on behalf of a less-restricting alternative up to a "reasonable point"'.[98] The Polish court, in contrast, is generally less demanding of the legislature at the necessity stage.[99]

Overall, the findings display a significant degree of variance between countries with regard to the application of the last two stages of the doctrine: relying primarily on one or the other to justify failures (e.g., Germany and Canada), using both in a way that is essentially identical or very similar and therefore limits the full potential of each (Poland), or using two types of reasoning to ultimately justify the result (Israel and South Africa). However, the countries do converge in the sense that it is rare for a policy to be struck down solely on the basis of a failure at the strict proportionality stage; Germany emerges as an outlier rather than the rule it is often perceived to be.

### *C Towards a More Commensurate Relationship between Necessity and Strict Proportionality*

The different conceptions of the relationship between necessity and strict proportionality in the case-law of the courts analysed raise the normative question of how this relationship *should* be constructed. As recognized earlier, the key factor determining the significance of the necessity stage is the standard against which alternative, less restrictive measures are evaluated. An approach that requires that less restrictive alternatives meet a standard of identical effectiveness relative to the measure under review

[97] The South African Constitutional Court clarified in *De Reuck v Director of Public Prosecutions (Witwatersrand Local Division) and Others,* 2004 (1) SA 406 (CC) that 'less restrictive alternatives need not be equally effective in achieving the stated purpose as the impugned measure'. It suffices that the less restrictive alternative is 'sufficiently effective'.

[98] The rationale behind this approach was set forth forcefully by Justice Zamir in the Tzemach case, which reviewed whether the government was required to decrease the 96-hour period after which a detained soldier must be brought before a military judge. The government had argued that reducing the waiting period to 48 hours would require additional resources. Justice Zamir countered that 'the importance [provided to liberty] should express itself not only in lofty statements, not only in legislation, but in the budget. The protection of human rights often demands a price. Society must be willing to pay a reasonable price on behalf of the protection of human rights'. See HCJ 6055/95 *Tzemach v Minister of Defence* [1999] IsrSC 53(5) 241 [32], [36], [38]–[39] (Justice Zamir).

[99] Chapter 5, Section VIII.B.

(as most often occurs in the German court[100] and as has been expressed at times by the Israeli court[101]) renders it extremely difficult if not impossible to come up with satisfactory alternatives.[102] Barak took an even stronger stance: he stated that for the sake of the necessity test, all relevant factors (e.g., resources required to implement the policy) should be identical to those in the proposed measure, except for the degree of rights restrictiveness.[103] This interpretation of the necessity stage ends up leaving it with little practical significance, turning it into a conceptual rather than a real test.[104] Such an interpretation is in line with a conception that views the early stages as threshold stages that primarily establish the need for balancing.

Once a court internalizes that the standard required at the necessity test is one of equal effectiveness – which essentially cannot be met – this stage becomes more of a ritual than an actual analysis. The court may then develop a tendency to quickly dispense with the analysis at this stage, leading to what we find most distinctly in Germany: most often, the court either briefly states that there are no alternatives that achieve the policy goal equally, or it skips this stage entirely.

In keeping with our general normative approach that the analytic potential of each subtest should be fully realized for it to contribute maximally to the overall analysis, we are sceptical of a practice in which one subtest largely supersedes or marginalizes all others. In our opinion, the necessity stage should be constructed in a way that maximizes its unique contribution to the overall analysis. This stage should be devoted to understanding the scope of the policy alternatives and reaching the best possible understanding of their levels of rights-restrictiveness and effectiveness compared to the measure under review, in order to conclude whether the rights limitation could be reasonably avoided or minimized. We support adopting a more realistic standard of feasible, less restrictive alternatives that are similarly – even if slightly less – effective than the measure adopted.[105] As will be elaborated in the next

[100] BVerfGE 90, 145 [172]; BVerfGE 30, 292 [316]; BVerfGE 113, 167 [252]; BVerfGE 117, 163 [189]; BVerfGE 120, 224 [240]; BVerfGE 126, 112 [144]–[45].

[101] Chapter 4, Section VII.C.

[102] Bilchitz (n 80).

[103] Barak (n 12) 323–26.

[104] Bilchitz (n 80); Mordechai Kremnitzer, 'Constitutional Proportionality: (Appropriate) Guidelines?' in Gideon Sapir, Daphne Barak-Erez and Aharon Barak (eds), *Israeli Constitutional Law in the Making* (Hart Publishing 2013) 225.

[105] Bilchitz (n 80). See Chief Justice McLachlin in *Alberta v Hutterian Brethren of Wilson Colony* (n 89): 'the *court need not be satisfied that the alternative would satisfy the*

section, this is especially important for the court's role in guiding policy-making behaviour, since seeking less restrictive alternatives is one of the most significant tools policy-makers can use when designing rights-restricting policy. The strict formula of necessity exempts decision-makers from truly making an effort to come up with and analyse alternatives, when judicial review should be incentivizing just that.

Moreover, it is important in our view to impose the burden of proof at the necessity stage on the state to justify the infringement of a fundamental right. This does not mean that the state must proactively present all types of potential alternatives to the chosen policy. However, the state should be required to show that it seriously considered alternatives in the decision-making process, and that there is a real basis for believing that the alternatives presented by the complainant are significantly less effective. As a corollary, the necessity test should not be limited to asking whether the chosen policy is sufficiently narrowly tailored or whether it could possibly be narrowed even more, as is often found in practice. Instead, courts should also ask whether the state considered alternative policy approaches, and the state should be expected to show that it did.

Finally, at the necessity stage courts should engage more often in comparative analysis of alternative means used in other jurisdictions – whether other countries or, in federal systems such as Germany and Canada, different states or provinces – in order to assess whether less restrictive means are reasonably available.[106] Although assessing the

*objective to exactly the same extent or degree* as the impugned measure. In other words, the court should not accept an unrealistically exacting or precise formulation of the government's objective which *would effectively immunize the law from scrutiny* at the minimal impairment stage. The requirement for an "equally effective" alternative measure ... should not be taken to an impractical extreme. It includes alternative measures that give sufficient protection, in all the circumstances, to the government's goal .... While the government is entitled to deference in formulating its objective, that *deference is not blind or absolute*. The test at the minimum impairment stage is *whether there is an alternative, less drastic means of achieving the objective in a real and substantial manner*.'

[106] Rosalind Dixon, 'Proportionality & Comparative Constitutional Law versus Studies' (2018) 12 Law and Ethics of Human Rights 203–24. For examples of this practice, see Germany: BVerfGE 7, 377; BVerfGE 9, 39. For Israeli examples, see: HCJ 450/97 *Tnufa Human Resources v Minister of Labour and Welfare* [1998], IsrSC 52(2) 433; HCJ 4769/95 *Menachem v Minister of Transportation* [2002], IsrSC 57(1) 235; Justice Arbel in *Neget Adam* (n 47). For South African examples, see: *Ferreira v Levin NO & Others; Vryenhoek & Others v Powell NO & Others*, 1996 (1) SA 984 (CC); *S v Dlamini; S v Dladla and Others; S v Joubert; S v Schietekat*, 1999 (4) SA 623 (CC). For Canadian examples, see: *Adler v Ontario* [1996] 3 SCR. 609; *Professional Institute of the Public*

comparability and effectiveness of regulatory policies across jurisdictions and varying legal and societal contexts is a complex undertaking, this practice can aid courts in coping with factual uncertainty and increase the legitimacy of an outcome of unconstitutionality. In any case, the existence of sufficiently effective, less restrictive laws in other jurisdictions should increase the justificatory burden for infringing a fundamental right.

Operationalizing the necessity enquiry as a real stage that contributes substantially to PA does not in our view require dispensing with the strict proportionality test or marginalizing its role, as seems to be the prevailing practice of the Supreme Court of Canada. We understand the strict proportionality stage as optimally fulfilling two main functions. The first is as the point of final determination in cases in which a decision could not be reached at the earlier stages. This is particularly true of cases in which less restrictive alternatives are not similar in effectiveness or cost but rather would significantly reduce attainment of the policy goal. These types of cases require a bolder type of balancing, which should be done solely at the final strict proportionality stage. While the judicial analysis at the necessity stage should focus primarily on the substantially factual undertaking of comparing the effectiveness and rights-restrictiveness of different policy alternatives even if this involves balancing considerations (which should not be hidden or denied), the strict proportionality stage allows more open value-oriented reasoning, still grounded in the factual context amply established in the previous stages.

The second function of the strict proportionality stage, for which it is particularly well suited, should be tying together the analyses conducted in the previous subtests, while clearly expressing the constitutional values that guide the decision and the balancing considerations that lie at its foundation.[107] Balancing conducted in this manner is not done independently after preliminary questions have been cleared away,[108] but

*Service of Canada v Northwest Territories (Commissioner)* [1990] 2 S.C.R. 367; *Quebec (Attorney General) v A* [2013] 1 SCR 61 [440]. For Polish examples see: Judgment of 22 July 2014, Case No. K 25/13 OTK-A 2014, No. 7, Item 76; Judgment of 4 November 2014, Case No. SK 55/13 OTK-A 2014, No. 10, Item 111; Judgment of 23 November 2009, Case No. P 61/08 OTK-A 2009, No. 10, Item 150.

107 See also Stacey (n 17).

108 This, however, appears to be the common conception of balancing. See: Stone Sweet and Matthews (n 12) 72, 76; Reaume (n 20).

rather serves as a concluding exercise, drawing on the findings and flaws raised throughout the stages of the analysis.[109]

Overall, we believe that a combination of the necessity and strict proportionality stages rather than a power struggle between them optimally realizes the analytical potential of each mode of reasoning and fulfils the overarching goal of an integrative approach to PA: reaching a well-reasoned, persuasive judgement that gives adequate weight to rights and insists on justification for limitations, while guiding policy-makers regarding best practices for rights-restricting policy-making.

## V Proportionality as an Integrative Method of Analysis: Explanatory and Normative Perspectives

Our findings show that the practice of proportionality in several of the jurisdictions analysed deviates – at times significantly – from the strictly sequential model.[110] We documented several unrecognized practices, such as leaving stages undecided, using negative signalling while passing a measure on a test and continuing the analysis to subsequent stages despite a previous failure. In addition, we found that reliance on a single dominant element does not, in fact, characterize the practice in the majority of jurisdictions analysed, and that an outcome of unconstitutionality is most often based on failure at both the necessity and strict proportionality stages. It appears that several apex courts use the final stage as a 'synthesizing finale' of PA, drawing on flaws identified in the previous stages. These findings demonstrate that an approach to proportionality that applies the different stages in an integrative manner to reach an overall judgement, as is done in the South African court, is more widespread than previously recognized, even if not always deliberate or consistent. In this section we will offer possible explanations for why courts tend to adopt an integrative mode of analysis, as well as why, in contrast, we do not find this tendency to the same extent in the German and Canadian courts. We will then proceed to make a case for why an integrative approach to PA, if properly applied, may also be desirable from a normative point of view.

[109] See also Kumm, 'The Idea of Socratic Contestation and the Right to Justification' (n 52) 142.

[110] For more detail on the sequential model of proportionality, see Section II.a.

### A *The Appeal of Integrative Proportionality Analysis from the Judicial Perspective*

Why do apex courts seem to gravitate towards an integrative application of the doctrine, rather than the strictly sequential model set out in theory? As we have seen, the South African Constitutional Court, the Israeli Supreme Court, and the Polish Constitutional Tribunal can be grouped into an integrative model of proportionality based on their tendency to support failure decisions using both the necessity and strict proportionality tests, together with significant failure rates at the suitability stage,[111] and tendency to leave stages undecided or use negative signalling. The case-law of the Canadian Supreme Court and the German Federal Constitutional Court, albeit largely following distinct models of proportionality in terms of relying on a single dominant stage, still display at least some elements of an integrative model, such as the common practice of using multiple failures to justify a judgement of disproportionality in Canada,[112] and the extensive use of negative signalling in Germany.[113] We believe that the appeal of integrative PA from the judicial perspective is tied to the disputable nature of proportionality decisions and the institutional sensitivities courts face when conducting a rights-based review. Proportionality serves courts as a framework for justifying the outcome of the decision; clearly the court invests in structuring the decision in a way that will be perceived as most persuasive and legitimate.[114] It is therefore to be expected that the implementation of the doctrine will be shaped by courts' aspiration to reach the most persuasive and legitimate decision possible.

111 And to some extent significant failure rates at the worthy purpose stage.

112 See Section II.A.

113 See Chapter 1, Section VIII.A. In addition, there are seven cases in the German case-law sample in which the Constitutional Court continued the analysis after a failure at either the suitability or the necessity stage, clearly demonstrating that even a court that formally subscribes to a sequential model of proportionality can see the need to deviate from this model.

114 Stone Sweet and Matthews (n 12) 72, 77 ('PA is an analytical procedure – it does not, in itself, produce substantive outcomes . . . judges use proportionality as a foundation on which to build doctrine, the 'argumentation framework' that governs right litigation'). Niels Petersen, *Proportionality and Judicial Activism: Fundamental Rights Adjudication in Canada, Germany and South Africa* (CUP 2017) 67–68; Wojciech Sadurski, 'Reasonableness and Value Pluralism in Law and Politics' in Giorgio Bongiovanni, Sartor Giovanni, and Chiara Valentini (eds), *Reasonableness and Law* (Springer 2009) 129, 139.

A good place to begin understanding the logic behind such an integrative approach to proportionality is with South Africa, where both the constitutional language and the Costitutional Court have consciously and explicitly rejected the sequential doctrine. The Court has stated that it views the sequential structure as technical, and rejects the idea that any one single element should be the sole basis for the decision.[115] It is important to point out, however, that the South African Court has essentially never upheld a policy that failed even one of the tests.[116] Therefore, the South African approach to proportionality is not that a failure on one test can be overridden by others, but rather that a failure in a single element most often can and should be supported by others, rather than serving as the sole basis for the outcome. Furthermore, the South African practice is not one of 'picking and choosing' elements for consideration from the list; rather, the analysis conducted by the South African court is structured similarly to that of other courts analysed, and the court does not skip or refrain from addressing stages any more often than the German court does.[117] Thus, the South African approach seems to differ specifically in its explicit embrace of applying several tests in tandem to support the final outcome.

It seems intuitive that additional failures make striking down a measure seem more justifiable by demonstrating that the measure is so significantly flawed that it failed several tests. In addition, courts may opt for multiple failures rather than terminating their analysis after the first failure due to the realization that PA as a whole, and each stage individually, rarely lead to clear-cut, undisputed outcomes. There are generally factual uncertainties regarding a measure's effectiveness and difficulties in assessing the feasibility of alternatives and comparing their effectiveness with that of the chosen measure. Furthermore, the balance between benefit and harm may vary depending on the weight assigned to

[115] *Manamela* (n 14) [32]: 'It should be noted that the five factors expressly itemized in section 36 are not presented as an exhaustive list. They are included in the section as key factors that have to be considered in an overall assessment as to whether or not the limitation is reasonable and justifiable in an open and democratic society. In essence, the Court must engage in a balancing exercise and arrive at a global judgement on proportionality and not adhere mechanically to a sequential check-list.' See also constitutional justice Albie Sachs in *Coetzee v Government of the Republic of South Africa, Matiso & Others v Commanding Officer Port Elizabeth Prison & Others*, 1995 (4) SA 631 (CC) [46]: 'In my view, faithfulness to the Constitution is best achieved by locating the two-stage balancing process within a holistic, value-based and case-oriented framework.'

[116] *Schietekat* (n 106).

[117] See Chapter 1, Section III; Chapter 3, Section III.D.

the right and the importance attached to the benefit, leaving room for subjective value decisions. Since each individual test suffers from particular weaknesses that can undermine the defensibility of the outcome at that stage, structuring the justification so that it aggregates several failures allows the weak points of each individual stage to be offset by the strengths of the others. A decision based on a strong combination of factual and value-based considerations results in a sounder and more defensible outcome, fully utilizing the potential of proportionality to achieve a value judgement firmly based on fact.

The practice of failing measures at early stages but not terminating the analysis after these failures also reflects the courts' ambivalence towards the strict proportionality stage: there is a clear judicial attraction towards it but also some hesitance and reluctance. It has been recognized that the strict proportionality stage gives courts decisional flexibility and an opportunity to address constitutional values, reasoning methods with which judges may feel most comfortable.[118] Nevertheless, courts may be apprehensive about basing their decision on this stage given its apparent political dimension, which leaves them exposed to criticism on the grounds of making value judgements, and therefore potentially subjecting themselves to the allegation that they are ideological and political actors.[119] These two contradictory sentiments concerning the final stage could lead to opposite results – either placing the entire weight of the decision on the final stage of strict proportionality, as we observe in the practice of the German Constitutional Court,[120] or generally avoiding this stage – at least in substance – altogether, as is the case in the Supreme Court of Canada.[121]

The integrative approach that we have seen does not fit into either of these binary conceptions. Although the majority of courts do often rely heavily on the strict proportionality stage rather than avoiding it, they tend to refrain from making it the sole basis for the decision, instead

[118] Stone Sweet and Matthews (n 12) 72, 76; Barak (n 12) 349–57, 414–15.

[119] Stone Sweet and Matthews (n 12) 72, 78: 'PA mitigates certain legitimacy problems, but creates another – does not camouflage judicial law making, but rather requires courts to defend honestly and openly the policy choices they make, exposes rights adjudication for what it is – constitutionally based law making. However, given strategic considerations, provides courts with a tool for rationalizing and defending rights review.' See also Petersen (n 114).

[120] Chapter 1, Section VIII.

[121] Chapter 2, Section VIII.

bolstering it with additional failures and input from previous stages.[122] This integrative tendency may be how courts can rely significantly on the advantages provided by the balancing test, while dealing somewhat with the difficulties it raises.

An additional characteristic that we connect to the integrative approach to proportionality is that courts do not necessarily give a binary pass/fail answer for each stage of the analysis, instead tying the outcome of one stage to previous stages, or having the analysis of one stage run into the next. Refraining from ending a particular subtest with a clear outcome allows the court to air its considerations without committing to a bottom line yet. It may reflect genuine indecisiveness as to whether the measure should pass or fail a subtest, or it may be a strategy used to cope with disagreement between the judges about the correct outcome at a certain stage. An additional draw of such a practice for courts is that it can make the decision harder to criticize, since the court does not commit to strong propositions. In cases where proclaiming a failure at the worthy purpose or suitability stage, for instance, would touch on particular political sensitivities, courts might understandably prefer leaving these stages officially undecided instead of blaming the legislature for pursuing an illegitimate purpose or adopting an irrational means, perhaps using negative signalling while postponing the official failure to a later, less sensitive stage.[123]

Do certain political and institutional factors promote a judicial preference for an integrative approach to proportionality? Without delving into an in-depth analysis of the social and political conditions of each of the courts analysed, the three apex courts that seem to subscribe at least partially to this integrative model (those in Israel, Poland, and South Africa) seem to face a common struggle: on the one hand, constitutional review is comparatively young in these countries, and as a result these courts have a significant constitutional role that requires them to make value-laden decisions with relation to fundamental values. On the other hand, they must steer through problematic waters in terms of their institutional legitimacy and their often strained relations with the other branches of government.[124] In Israel, for example, the lack of a full

[122] See Section IV.B.

[123] See. e.g., in Israel, *Neget Adam* (n 47); *Eitan Israel Migration Policy* (n 47); *Students Association of Israel* (n 47). In Canada, see *Eldridge v British Columbia (Attorney General)* [1997] 3 SCR 624 [84].

[124] All three courts have faced threats – more or less realized to date – of restructuring the judiciary and limiting the reach of the court. In the case of Poland, the risks were indeed realized. See Chapter 5, Section II.A, and see: Wojciech Sadurski, 'How Democracy Dies

formal constitution and the highly contested status of judicial review constitute the political context of the Supreme Court's decisions. Such tensions may support these courts' tendency towards an integrative application of proportionality that bases findings of disproportionality on multiple failures in order to emphasize the supposed inevitability of the outcome and avoid relying solely on the balancing stage due to the criticism this stage tends to draw.

In contrast, the practice of the German Constitutional Court is characterized by significantly less involvement of the earlier stages in supporting the outcome, relative to the other jurisdictions analysed. Outcomes tend to rely most often on a sole failure at the final stage. A possible explanation for these findings is that the court has gradually established itself as the ultimate authority for expounding and protecting constitutional values and does not shy away from making value-balancing explicit.[125] Furthermore, the traditional sequential conception of proportionality is firmly entrenched in German legal scholarship and seems to strongly influence the court's practice. As a result, the court puts a premium on analytical clarity and clear separation between the stages, resulting in regularly ending the analysis after a failure. But because the court prefers to ultimately decide proportionality cases with the final test, it is reluctant to fail measures at a previous stage; as it does not see a need to base a judgement of disproportionality on several failures, this is not a problem. Moreover, the German court is a specialized constitutional court that relies to a significant extent on the factual findings of ordinary courts.[126] When reviewing legislation, it emphasizes legislative prerogative and defers to the democratic legislator at the suitability and necessity

(in Poland): A Case Study of Anti-Constitutional Populist Backsliding' (2018) Revista Forumul Judecatorilor 104, 135–36. In the case of Israel, the threats to the independence and powers of the Supreme Court have escalated over the past decade, and following the 2019 elections may finally be realized. See: Nadiv Mordechai and Yaniv Roznai, 'A Jewish and (Declining) Democratic State: Constitutional Retrogression in Israel' (2017) 77 Maryland Law Review 244. In the case of South Africa, threats during the years 2009–13 were largely unrealized. See Chapter 3, Section II.E, and see: Catherine Albertyn, 'Judicial Independence and the Constitution Fourteenth Amendment Bill' (2006) 22 South African Journal on Human Rights 126.

[125] Moshe Cohen-Eliya and Iddo Porat, *Proportionality and Constitutional Culture* (CUP 2013) 52.

[126] Oliver Lepsius, 'Die maßstabsetzende Gewalt' in Matthias Jestaedt, Oliver Lepsius and others (eds), *Das entgrenzte Gericht* (Suhrkamp 2011) 159. For more detail on this point, see Chapter 1, Section II.C.

stages, preferring to ground its decisions on normative rather than factual considerations.[127]

The Canadian case-law exhibits some of the elements of the integrative approach (significant failure rates at the suitability and necessity stages) but without the substantial role of the final stage that we see in the other courts. The traditional explanation for the approach of the Canadian Supreme Court is that it intentionally avoids the strict proportionality stage in order to avoid explicit value-based framing of its decisions.[128] The fact that the court is a popular public institution in Canadian society that is much less controversial politically than the apex courts in Israel, Poland, and South Africa raises the question of why it so fervently avoids a more substantial and more explicitly value-oriented inquiry at the final stage. We tentatively suggest two potential factors that might contribute to the court's distinct approach to proportionality. First, the Canadian court originates and is embedded in the Anglo-American legal tradition, which is arguably more deferential to Parliament and less prone to value-balancing than the German Constitutional Court. Second, the central role of the concepts of federalism, pluralism, respect, and tolerance in Canadian constitutionalism seems to nudge the court towards a more deferential approach to the value-based decisions of other branches of government or the different Canadian provinces;[129] PA is then focused on minimizing infringement of fundamental rights, rather than challenging the underlying value choices of the legislators.

### *B The Virtues of an Integrative Approach to Proportionality Analysis*

We recognize that any normative evaluation of a specific approach to applying proportionality is inevitably set against the background of the extensive normative debate surrounding rights-based judicial review in general, and the proportionality framework in particular. As set out in the introduction to this book, our goal is not to engage directly in the normative debate on proportionality or propose a general case for the proportionality framework as a basis for rights adjudication. Instead,

[127] See Chapter 1, Sections VII and VIII.A.2

[128] Grimm (n 12) 383; Davidov (n 82) 195.

[129] Richard Albert, 'The Values of Canadian Constitutionalism' in Richard Albert and David R Cameron (eds), *Canada in the World: Comparative Perspectives on the Canadian Constitution* (CUP 2017), 1, 2–3.

from a pragmatic standpoint, we take proportionality-based judicial review as a given and present an argument for integrative application of PA as an optimal operationalization of the doctrine. In our opinion, this approach not only reflects (to some degree) an existing tendency of several courts; it is also desirable from a normative point of view, relative to alternative approaches to proportionality – provided, and to the extent, that every stage of the analysis is meaningfully addressed.

Optimal operationalization of proportionality is ultimately tied to an underlying conception of the function of proportionality-based judicial review. Two main conceptualizations of proportionality have been proposed in the literature: the first sees proportionality as essentially a practice of optimizing the balance between rights and conflicting interests, while the second conceptualizes it as a tool for assessing the soundness of government justifications for rights limitations.[130] Our case for an integrative approach to proportionality is aligned with this second conception of proportionality, described by Kumm as a form of 'Socratic contestation' meant to elicit a process of public reasoning.[131] Undoubtedly rights do conflict with other interests and in such cases balancing is required. However, we view the unique function fulfilled by courts when conducting proportionality-based rights adjudication not as autonomously taking on an optimizing exercise, but primarily as scrutinizing the design of the rights-restricting measure in light of several types of flaws that can occur in the policy-making process and can lead to unjustified rights limitations.[132]

We identify three main elements in the integrative approach to proportionality, inspired by practices we have seen in the jurisdictions analysed in the book, but we present them in idealized form. The first element is an absence of hierarchy between threshold stages and core stages of the analysis; all stages are to be interpreted in a way that maximizes their contribution to the shared function of critically evaluating the justification of the rights limitation. The second element is a nonbinary approach to the outcome of each subtest. The different stages

[130] For a characterization of two conceptions of proportionality, see Rivers (n 21) 174, 195–98. Similarly, see Francisco J Urbina, *A Critique of Proportionality and Balancing* (CUP 2017), 9–12.

[131] Kumm, 'The Idea of Socratic Contestation and the Right to Justification' (n 52) 142.

[132] ibid. As framed by Kumm elsewhere, the court is 'policing the boundaries of the reasonable, not the boundaries of justice'. Kumm (n 66) 30. See also Moshe Cohen-Eliya and Iddo Porat, 'Proportionality and the Culture of Justification' (2011) 59 The American Journal of Comparative Law 463.

serve as tools, questions meant to help the court reach a well-reasoned outcome. Therefore, while each test can lead to a clear pass/fail result, there are also intermediate options, such as barely passing or leaving a stage undecided. The third and final element in an integrative approach to proportionality is that the analysis does not necessarily have to be terminated after the first failure; rather, the court should evaluate whether aggregating failures would strengthen the final outcome. In contrast, a sequential approach concludes the analysis of each stage with a binary pass/fail outcome and only continues to the next stage if the measure has passed the previous one.[133] It is important to clarify, however, that the integrative approach to proportionality is still a structured mode of analysis that addresses all subtests of the doctrine, and that a measure must pass all subtests to be upheld.

Returning to the two functions of the subtests – guiding judges in arriving at a decision, and structuring the justificatory reasoning provided for the decision[134] – some of the main parameters for evaluating an approach to the proportionality doctrine from a normative point of view include supporting a well-reasoned judgment; providing a basis for adequate protection for rights; sincerely reflecting the actual judicial decision-making process, thus promoting judicial honesty; and offering guidance to policy-makers in creating policy that is sufficiently protective of rights. We believe that an integrative approach to PA accomplishes these functions better than a sequential approach.

In our view, an integrative approach to proportionality generally results in better-reasoned judgments, equipping the judiciary with more effective tools for evaluating the persuasiveness (or lack thereof) of a justification of a rights limitation and thereby contributing to better protecting rights, which we view as the ultimate function of proportionality. Considering that various kinds of flaws can present themselves in the policy-making process, in turn leading to unjustified rights limitations,[135] one of the advantages of an integrative approach is that it utilizes all stages of the doctrine in a joint effort to scrutinize the rights-restricting measure and its justification from all possible angles, maximizing the unique perspective that each stage contributes to the analysis.

In contrast, the traditional sequential approach attributes great importance to the analytical clarity of each stage individually and

[133] See Section II.A.
[134] See Section II.
[135] Kumm (n 52) 141.

therefore polices the boundaries between them to prevent blurring or overlap.[136] Accordingly, Dieter Grimm has described the considerations behind a sequential model as follows:

> What I can conclude is that the disciplining and rationalizing effect, which is a significant advantage of the proportionality test over a mere test of reasonableness or a more or less free balancing, as in many US cases, is reduced when the four stages are not clearly separated. Each step requires a certain assessment. The next step can be taken only if the law that is challenged has not failed on the previous step. A confusion of the steps creates the danger that elements enter the operation in an uncontrolled manner and render the result more arbitrary and less predictable.[137]

In our view, maintaining strict separation between the stages and providing clear-cut intermediate conclusions for each individual test are not themselves important goals, and are in many cases somewhat artificial. More importantly, this approach has negative side effects.

Central to the idea of analytic separation between the stages is that value balancing is undertaken only in the final stage, and is strictly excluded from the previous tests. As a result, the predominant judicial strategy for separating the stages seems to consist of an overly narrow construction of the stages before the strict proportionality test, exemplified by such doctrinal practices as minimally establishing that the purpose promoted is worthy, considering it sufficient that a measure is, based on common-sense, capable of partially promoting its purpose, and insisting that less rights-restrictive alternatives are as effective as the chosen measure. The effect of this narrow interpretation is that the early stages only tackle outlying cases, they do not consistently play a substantial role in the analysis, and judges rush towards the last test. The deliberative quality inherent in the structure of the multi-prong proportionality test is thus lost. Under the sequential model, the strict proportionality (balancing) stage stands out as the centrepiece of proportionality and constitutes, in Aharon Barak's words, 'the most important of proportionality's tests'.[138] Due to the narrow interpretation of the previous tests as threshold tests, only at the final test is the severity of the rights restriction established and the weight of the public interest ascertained through assessment of the importance of the public goal.

[136] Barak (n 12) 460–67.

[137] Grimm (n 12) 383, 397. Similarly, see Barak, *Proportionality* (n 12) 344–45, 460–65.

[138] Barak (n 12) 340.

Moreover, only at the final stage are the actual effectiveness of the means and the probability of their achieving the goal determined, and only at this point are less effective or more costly alternatives evaluated. Finally, all these considerations are then balanced.

In our opinion, there are significant downsides to a multi-stage justification doctrine that relies primarily on a single stage. Assigning too many functions to a single test may lead it to 'collapse' under the burden and fail to fulfil all of its functions adequately, ultimately reducing the rationalizing effect of the multi-stage doctrine so enthusiastically hailed by Grimm and others. In contrast, an integrative approach to proportionality that substantially addresses all the different stages utilizes a more refined toolbox for exposing the flaws of rights-restrictive laws, compared to resolving issues with the single tool of balancing. Borrowing from Kumm's metaphor of PA as 'Socratic contestation',[139] under an integrated approach each stage functions not merely as a requirement to be met and then removed from consideration, but as a question provoking a need for justification. The rigour and depth of PA are prioritized over reaching a clear-cut determination at each individual stage.

Recognizing the connections between the stages and allowing feedback to flow between them can improve the quality of judicial practice and fully exploit the analytical potential inherent in PA. This is because the rationality and analytical virtue of PA lie precisely in the fact that it consists of interconnected tests that require asking different questions, all of which are relevant in determining whether a rights infringement is justified or not.

For example, concretizing and inquiring after the precise goals of the policy and their importance will, by clearing away possible exaggerations or hype concerning the public interest at stake, make it possible for the analyses at all the subsequent stages to be more detailed and precise. Allowing the suitability stage to serve as a supporting test for worthy purpose can significantly bolster the court's ability to 'smoke out' illegitimate motives. An in-depth evaluation of a reviewed measure's ability to significantly promote the policy goal in its current design is a more solid basis for evaluating the comparative effectiveness of alternative, less restrictive measures at the necessity test. Finally, a finding at the necessity stage that less restrictive but slightly less effective alternatives are available may be productively supplemented by the strict proportionality

[139] Kumm (n 52) 141.

stage, in which additional normative considerations concerning the intensity of the infringement and the possibly vulnerable position of the rights bearer under the chosen policy can be incorporated, leading to a more well-rounded proportionality judgement. An integrative approach fully expresses the existing linkages between the different tests instead of artificially isolating them; thus they can contribute jointly to the power of the analysis.

Under the sequential model, courts may be reluctant to fail a law on the worthy purpose or suitability test because they would be required to end their analysis at that point, based on the single failure, and they might not be certain enough that a finding of unworthy purpose or unsuitability is sufficiently well founded to carry the burden of justification alone. As a result, they may prefer to allow the measure to pass these early stages – ignoring the problems they noted – in order to continue their analysis, and base the outcome on a later stage. This avoidance technique becomes unnecessary under an integrative approach because there is no insistence on ending the analysis after the first failure. In addition, an integrative model offers courts the possibility of leaving an individual stage undecided, thereby encouraging them to point out problematic aspects as they arise at earlier stages, without necessarily requiring that they serve as sufficient bases for failing the measure at that point. Each inquiry contributes to the analysis as a whole, and raising issues at a specific stage can contribute to the final, integrated evaluation, even if the measure does not fail at that stage. Thus, feedback can flow between the stages. An integrative approach also makes it possible to identify additional shortcomings at later stages as the analysis continues after a first failure, thus strengthening the justification for striking down the law, while a sequential structure requires ending the analysis after one failure even if the impugned law suffers from further flaws.[140] Finally, this integrative model may have an advantage over the sequential model

[140] We agree with Justice Levy of the Supreme Court of Israel that the strict proportionality test should not overshadow the previous subtests; see HCJ 466/07 *MK Zehava Galon v Attorney General* [2012], IsrSC 65(2) 44 [9] (Justice Levy available in English at <http://versa.cardozo.yu.edu/opinions/gal-v-attorney-general-summary> accessed 16 December 2019. We disagree, however, that the practice of continuation until the final stage is better avoided. In our opinion, it is defensible, if not good practice for courts to continue their analysis to the final stage to explicitly include in their finding of unconstitutionality the normative considerations that are best addressed at this stage, so long as they engage in a substantial and meaningful analysis of the worthy purpose, suitability, and necessity tests.

in the context of growing populism and democratic backsliding: basing a decision to strike down a law on multiple failures and combining factual and normative elements to a greater extent in proportionality reasoning gives the courts' conclusions additional strength and persuasiveness, which is important at a time when judicial review is being increasingly challenged.

In our view, the integrative approach also better reflects the judicial decision-making process, thus promoting judicial honesty. Judges are undoubtedly aware that any one individual stage of the analysis often does not result in a clear-cut or indisputable outcome, and therefore a finding at one stage can be bolstered or reinforced by others. In many cases, the individual stages of the analysis raise questions or problematic aspects that cannot result in a clear-cut outcome. These findings can, however, be of importance when combined with findings from subsequent stages. The intermediate findings at the individual stages serve as decisional aids for courts, providing structure and rules of thumb, but the final decision is often based on an integrated evaluation of a combination of factors. We believe that the analysis should not attempt to create artificial clarity or an illusion of a clear-cut finding. An integrative approach better reflects the reasoning process followed by judges, allowing them to express with nuance the different degrees of certainty on the level of the individual stage, and to make explicit the ways in which findings in one stage affected or reinforced conclusions at a subsequent stage. The result is greater transparency in judicial reasoning.

Interestingly, judicial honesty is often cited as a reason for placing the weight of the decision solely on the strict proportionality stage; otherwise balancing considerations are supposedly hidden in other stages.[141] An integrative approach, however, makes balancing considerations explicit throughout all stages, although still most dominant at the final stage. Since PA is viewed as being geared towards verifying the justification of the rights limitation, the entirety of the analysis is infused with value considerations. No stage is purely factual; they all refer back to the opening stages that set the tone for the entire analysis: the characterization of the rights limitation, complemented by the worthy purpose stage, which defined and characterized the policy goal. The inquiry at all stages is conducted against the backdrop of the conflict between the right and the public interest, and therefore takes them into consideration, albeit to

[141] Grimm (n 12) 383; Barak (n 12) 464.

varying degrees. Importantly, in an integrative approach, just as the different stages are not purely factual, the final balancing test is not purely value-based; it is also a combined exercise of empirical and value-laden considerations.

Finally, we believe that an integrative approach to proportionality provides better guidance for policy-makers by communicating what is expected of them when shaping rights-restricting policy.[142] By rigorously engaging with all the tests while providing them with significant content, the court sets an example to be followed by decision-makers when designing policy and creates incentives for them to address the questions posed by the different stages seriously. In contrast, placing the full weight of the decision on the strict proportionality test and treating the previous stages as threshold stages does not provide useful guidance for policy-makers. If evaluations of proportionality by policy-makers are reduced, in essence, to balancing the seriousness of the rights infringement against the importance of the public interest at stake due to a belief that the other requirements are easily met, they are likely to overestimate the importance of the public interest and overstate the effectiveness of the policy, a tendency that is often already heightened among policy-makers.[143] Basing a decision to strike down a policy solely on failure at the final stage may mislead policy-makers into thinking that the policy is generally sound as designed and that the court's intervention is solely based on a different balance of values. Furthermore, focusing the policy-maker on the final stage does not sufficiently capitalize on the institutional advantages of the policy-making process vis-à-vis the judicial process: the policy-making process is much more flexible, particularly in identifying and generating feasible alternatives. The goal of preventing unnecessary

[142] On the internalization of the judicial standard by policy-makers see: Alec Stone Sweet, *Governing with Judges: Constitutional Politics in Europe* (OUP 2000) 102–114; Janet L Heibert, *Charter Conflicts: What Is Parliament's Role?* (McGill-Queen's University Press 2002) 8–19; Lila Margalit, Proportionality and Consideration of Rights in the Policy Process: The Case of the Israeli Counter Terrorism Act; Andrej Lang, Non-Judicial Constitutional Review of Counter-Terrorism Policies: The Role of Fundamental Rights in the Making of the Anti-Terror Database and Data Retention Legislation in Germany; Fiona de Londras, Proportionality and Rights in the Making of the EU Directive on Combating Terrorism (unpublished, all on file with the authors).

[143] Social science research has demonstrated the existence of overconfidence among bureaucrats and experts, which has been found to influence risk assessment and alternative evaluation, and has been tied to risk-taking behaviour. See: Xinsheng Liu, James Stoutenborough, and Arnold Vedlitz, 'Bureaucratic Expertise, Overconfidence and Policy Choice' (2017) 30 Governance 705.

rights restrictions would be much better served if policy-makers rigorously assessed whether policy proposals are fully suitable and necessary for achieving their concretely defined worthy purposes, rather than merely balancing rights against public interests. We believe that courts can and should guide policy-makers in this direction.

Although an integrative approach to proportionality leads courts to better fulfil the function of demanding to know the reasoning behind rights-restricting measures and scrutinizing the justification to prevent unnecessary and unjustified rights limitations, we do also recognize potential downsides to this approach. An integrative application of proportionality may blur the judicial message regarding the nature of the policy flaw causing the measure to be struck down. In a sequential application, when a measure fails a specific stage, leading to termination of the analysis, a clear message is sent regarding the flaw that led the measure to be struck down. Since under an integrative application stages may be left undecided or there may be several failures, the basis for the failure may not be as clear. In addition, the practice of continuing the analysis to the final test regardless of failures at earlier stages tends to weaken the perceived importance of those stages because it sends the message that failing at an earlier stage does not suffice to support a finding of disproportionality.

While it may be true in theory that a sequential application sends a clearer message regarding the nature of the flaw, a strictly applied sequential approach will, in practice, only rarely result in failures prior to the strict proportionality stage, due to the narrow interpretation of these stages. Since decisions are usually deferred to the final test and outcomes are framed solely in terms of balancing, it is actually rare for more specific judicial messages regarding the nature of the flaw to be conveyed in a sequential approach.

Nonetheless, it is important that efforts be made when applying proportionality in an integrative approach to clarify rather than obscure the basis for the outcome. For example, when the suitability and necessity stages are used to amplify doubts raised regarding the policy goal at the worthy purpose stage, this connection should be made explicit, so that it is clear that the policy was struck down due to a problem with the policy goal, rather than merely unsuitability or a lack of necessity. In the rare clear-cut cases of policies that promote unworthy and illegitimate purposes, we support ending the analysis at the worthy purpose stage and refraining from addressing additional subtests. Continuing the analysis in such circumstances is not expected to strengthen the justification but will instead weaken it, because balancing an unworthy purpose against a rights limitation gives the scrutinized measure a level of legitimacy that it does not deserve. Support for this position can be found in the South African practice: despite the general principle the South African court holds by, that the analysis should not be determined by a single test but rather all elements should be evaluated, the court does often terminate its analysis after failure at the worthy purpose test.[144] Nevertheless, since most cases are not clear-cut, we believe that continuing the analysis can better clarify the grounds for the result and strengthen support for the final outcome.

In conclusion, while the sequential approach to proportionality may have analytical advantages in theory, in practice these do not increase the persuasiveness of the judicial reasoning or clarify expectations of decision-makers. In fact, although the integrative approach may seem to produce less straightforward outcomes, increasing judicial engagement with the tests prior to strict proportionality can sharpen the reasoning and strengthen the soundness of the final outcome of the analysis. In light of what we see as the advantages of the integrative approach to PA – including producing a more persuasive and well-reasoned outcome, better equipping courts to evaluate the justification of the rights limitation, promoting the transparency of the judicial decision-making process, and providing better guidance for policy-makers – we encourage courts to apply proportionality more deliberately and more consistently in keeping with this approach.

## VI Future Possibilities for Empirically Grounded Comparative Research on Proportionality

We hope this book has demonstrated the potential of comparative research on proportionality that is informed by an empirical foundation. Clearly, however, much remains to be explored. As explained in the introduction to this book, we chose an exploratory research design that broadly investigated the characteristics of the application of proportionality rather than focusing on a particular research question with a clear hypothesis. This design was selected due to the limited nature of systematic research in the field. We hope this book lays the groundwork for future research by offering a basic level of knowledge from which

144 See Section III.B.

additional research questions and hypotheses can be generated. We would like to point out some possible directions for future research that build upon this initial undertaking.

One direction would be extending our basic methodology to the application of proportionality in the case-law of additional apex courts. Our analysis has identified aspects common to the case-law in five jurisdictions, as well as three main models of proportionality: emphasizing the less-restrictive-means test (Canada), emphasizing strict proportionality (Germany), and an integrative model (South Africa, Israel, and Poland). It would be most interesting to place more countries, as well as supranational and international courts that apply the proportionality doctrine, on this emerging spectrum. By enlarging the sample of courts, additional patterns may emerge that make it possible to deepen the analysis of causes and explanations.[145]

Another direction for future research would be focusing on developments in the application of the doctrine over time. As explained in the introduction to this book, our comparative analysis is limited by differences in the time span of the case-law analysed in the different jurisdictions.[146] Our analysis looks at the application of the doctrine without delving into changes over time in each jurisdiction. Future research might put such changes at the centre of its research design.

A different type of extension that seems promising is analysis of the application of the doctrine relative to the context of application, in terms of both specific rights and specific subjects. The quantitative analysis set forth in the country chapters in this book concerning the various contexts in which proportionality is applied can serve as a starting point for such an inquiry. The findings of the country analyses on this point raise

[145] As mentioned in the Introduction, it would be particularly interesting to empirically document the application of proportionality in South American countries. On proportionality in Brazil, see: João Andrade Neto, *Borrowing Justification for Proportionality: On the Influence of the Principles Theory in Brazil* (Springer 2018); on Mexico and Colombia, see: Luisa Conesa, 'The Tropicalization of Proportionality Balancing: The Colombian and Mexican Examples' (Cornell Law School Inter-University Graduate Student Conference Papers. 13, 2008) <https://scholarship.law.cornell.edu/lps_clacp/13> accessed 16 December 2019; on Peru, see: Marcial Antonio Rubio Correa, *El Test de Proporcionalidad en la Jurisprudencia del Tribunal Constitucional Peruano* (Fondo Editorial de la Pontificia Universidad Católica del Perú 2011); on Chile, see: Dante Figueroa, 'Constitutional Review in Chile Revisited: A Revolution in the Making' (2013) 51 Duquesne Law Review 411–13.

[146] Introduction, Section III.

interesting questions concerning local contexts that we have not been able to address in this chapter.

For example, proportionality in Israel is largely confined to the traditional domain of public law, with 89.5 per cent of proportionality cases dealing with public law. In Germany and Poland, public law also accounts for the majority of proportionality cases, with 58 and 52 per cent, respectively. In South Africa, however, the branch of law that draws most proportionality cases is private law (43 per cent), and Canadian proportionality practice boasts a strikingly large share of criminal law cases (43 per cent).[147] This raises the unexplored question of a possible correlation between specific applications of proportionality and a field of law. Other contextual factors that may affect and shape the application of the proportionality framework and merit further investigation are socio-economic conditions (e.g., crime rates or levels of terrorism) and political structures such as a supranational structure.[148]

In addition, the quantitative data in the different country chapters reveals a stark contrast between the jurisdictions analysed in terms of the rights triggering PA. While the rights to occupation and property assume a prominent place in proportionality practice in Israel (property 46 per cent; occupation 19 per cent), Germany (property 11 per cent; occupation 35 per cent), and Poland (property 31 per cent; occupation 7 per cent), they are negligible in South Africa (property 5 per cent; occupation 0 per cent) and entirely absent in Canada. In contrast, the right to equality is one of the most frequent rights triggering PA in Israel (26 per cent), South Africa (21 per cent), and Canada (20 per cent), but it has only a minor share in proportionality cases of the German Constitutional Court (6 per cent) and by definition it is not adjudicated by means of proportionality in Poland (0 per cent).[149]

Moreover, the data in the country chapters concerning the various constitutional rights analysed within the proportionality framework reveals that, although proportionality or limitation analysis is applied to most constitutional rights in all six jurisdictions analysed, for each apex court there are certain kinds of rights that are not adjudicated with

[147] Criminal law makes up 35 per cent of proportionality cases in South Africa, 21 per cent in Poland, 13 per cent in Germany, and only 4 per cent in Israel.

[148] We thank Liora Lazarus for this point.

[149] On the relationship between PA and the right to equality, see Vicki C Jackson, 'Proportionality and Equality' in Vicki C Jackson and Mark Tushnet (eds), *Proportionality: New Frontiers, New Challenges* (CUP 2017) 171; Guy Lurie, 'Proportionality and the Right to Equality' (Forthcoming) German Law Journal.

PA. Interestingly, the rights that one court treats as not subject to the proportionality framework are regularly adjudicated on the basis of proportionality in other courts. This raises the question of why apex courts prefer not to apply proportionality to some rights even though proportionality is the preeminent constitutional principle in cases concerning most rights.[150]

One limitation of our comparative analysis is the fact that we analysed the application of proportionality in the case-law without regard to the specific fundamental rights. Differentiating between specific rights could provide more detailed insights into the similarities and differences in different jurisdictions. Comparative research conducted by Goold, Lazarus, and Swiney in the national security context found variations in the application of proportionality depending on which right was being limited.[151] This may indeed be a promising direction for future comparative analysis.

An intriguing factor in comparative assessment of judicial practice that could serve as a basis for further inquiry is the failure rate in proportionality cases. The quantitative data in the country chapters shows that the failure rates in South Africa and Canada (82 and 70 per cent, respectively) on the one side and Israel (27 per cent) on the other side diverge substantially from those in Poland and Germany, which are both close to the 50 per cent mark (59 and 51 per cent, respectively).[152] Various factors may help explain these stark differences, beginning with whether or not there is a selection process for cases brought before the court. Considering that the Supreme Court of Israel acts as a court of first instance in its capacity as High Court of Justice, it may deal with a larger proportion of manifestly unfounded rights claims than last-instance apex courts. Alternatively, the low failure rate in Israel may be tied to a high success rate for petitioners in out-of-court settlements, which would remove prima facie successful petitions from the court's docket.[153] The high South African failure rate may have to do with apartheid regime laws, many of them

[150] Relatedly, see: Stephan Gardbaum, 'Positive and Horizontal Rights: Proportionality's next Frontier or a Bridge to Far?' in Vicki C Jackson and Mark Tushnet (eds), *Proportionality: New Frontiers, New Challenges* (CUP 2017) 221.

[151] Benjamin Goold, Liora Lazarus and Gabriel Swiney, 'Public Protection, Proportionality and the Search for Balance' (September 2017). Ministry of Justice Research Series 10/07 <https://papers.ssrn.com/sol3/papers.cfm?abstract_id=2022365> accessed 16 December 2019.

[152] The failure rate in the Indian database was similarly 45.6 per cent.

[153] Chapter 5, Section II.D.

blatantly racist, discriminatory, or unjust, that remained in force to ensure legal continuity and were later struck down by the South African Constitutional Court.

An additional factor that may affect the failure rate in proportionality cases is the approach taken at the preliminary stage of establishing a limitation of a constitutional right. Applying a broad interpretation to what constitutes a right limitation results in PA being utilized more often, including a larger proportion of non-severe limitations. In contrast, courts that are more stringent towards recognizing a limitation of a constitutional right will tend to apply PA less often but to more substantial right limitations. Our analysis demonstrates that it is quite common for the Canadian court to conclude that a violation of a Charter right was not established, thus bringing the decision to an end.[154] It may therefore be the case that the threshold for establishing a Charter limitation in Canada is higher than, for example, Germany or Israel, where it is exceedingly rare for a petitioner to fail to establish a right limitation.[155] The result may be that the proportionality cases of the Canadian court tend to be characterized by a more significant right limitation, since cases of less-significant limitation are weeded out more frequently at the preliminary stage. Subsequently, the prospects of measures scrutinized with PA being upheld are lower, which may partially explain why proportionality cases in Canada have a comparatively high failure rate. Beyond such factors, it would be illuminating to explore whether different courts systematically apply the proportionality tests more stringently or leniently, and whether this can be tied to different levels of judicial legitimacy.

In conclusion, we would like to mention some topics addressed in the chapters of this book that could not be picked up on from an integrative, comparative perspective. Hopefully, by so doing we might trigger future comparative research, building on the findings presented in this book.

[154] In the time period analysed in Canada 134 cases were located in which the majority of the court concluded that a right had not been violated and terminated the analysis, relative to only 120 proportionality cases. See Chapter 2, Section IV.A.

[155] In the time period analysed in Israel only nine cases were identified in which the court concluded that no right had been limited and the analysis terminated, relative to 161 proportionality cases. See Chapter 4, Section IV.A. In the time period analysed in Germany only one case was identified in which the court concluded that the activity was not protected by the scope of a fundamental right and two cases in which the court concluded that the measure did not constitute an infringement. See Chapter 1, Sections IV.A and IV.B.

These topics include the existence and nature of formal conditions to be met by rights-restricting legislation prior to PA; the goals of financial savings and administrative efficiency as bases for rights-restricting measures; the interplay between the concept of the essential core of a right and PA; and deference and the burden of proof within the proportionality framework. In addition, each chapter of the book concludes with an overview of measures struck down using PA in each jurisdiction. An integrative perspective on these overviews could allow for comparative generalization regarding the nature of disproportional rights restrictions.

# INDEX

Lightning Source UK Ltd.
Milton Keynes UK
UKHW022150020822
406768UK00020B/428